The Victor Book of the Opera

STORIES OF THE OPERAS WITH ILLUSTRATIONS AND DESCRIPTIONS OF VICTOR OPERA RECORDS

NINTH EDITION

*Revised by Charles O'Connell, Author of
The Victor Book of the Symphony*

NOTE—Acknowledgment is gratefully made to
Oliver Ditson Co., G. Schirmer, Inc., and
Fred Rullman, Inc., for kind permission to
quote from their copyrighted publications.
These firms have set new standards with
their operatic publications—Schirmer with
superbly printed opera scores and collections
of opera arias entitled "Operatic Anthology";
Ditson with the Musician's Library; and
Rullman with a comprehensive edition of
the librettos of the operas in the repertoire
of the Metropolitan and Chicago Grand
Opera Companies.

Form 1356

INDEX

INDEX

(Continued)

METROPOLITAN OPERA HOUSE, NEW YORK

Ralph Young

SAN FRANCISCO OPERA HOUSE

Kaufmann & Fabry

CHICAGO OPERA HOUSE

German Tourist Information Office

BÜHNENFESTSPIELHAUS, BAYREUTH

THE GRAND OPERA HOUSE, PARIS

Bruni Foto

LA SCALA, MILAN

THE ROYAL OPERA HOUSE, BERLIN

Keyser

ACADEMY OF MUSIC, PHILADELPHIA

VISITORS INSPECT A STAGE SETTING RECENTLY DESIGNED FOR
THE FESTSPIELHAUS, BAYREUTH

SOME OF THE GREAT ARTISTS OF THE WORLD

WHO HAVE MADE RECORDS FOR VICTOR

BAMPTON   BORI   CARUSO   CHALIAPIN

CROOKS   DeGOGORZA   DeLUCA   EDDY

FLAGSTAD   GALLI-CURCI   GIANNINI   GIGLI

JEPSON   JERITZA   LEHMANN   LEJDER

MARTINELLI   McCORMACK   MELCHIOR   PINZA

PONS   PONSELLE   RETHBERG   SCHIPA

SCHORR   SWARTHOUT   THOMAS   TIBBETT

PREFACE

THE ninth edition of The Victor Book of the Opera, like all previous editions, has been prepared for the purpose of telling the stories of the operas and of showing the wealth of operatic music which is available on Victor records for study and for entertainment. No effort has been spared to make the book as complete, and as up-to-date, as possible. To add to the understanding and enjoyment of the records, they are listed at the points where they occur in the narratives.

Since the first edition of The Victrola Book of the Opera was issued in 1912, more than four hundred thousand copies have been sold—a sale, we believe, in excess of that of any other book devoted to Grand Opera, and an eloquent tribute to the public's appreciation of Victor's service in this field. During the twenty-four years that have elapsed since the first edition was printed, the science of recording music has undergone a profound revolution. The new Higher Fidelity Victor records are a remarkable advance over all earlier recordings and when played on modern RCA Victor instruments attain a realism hitherto unapproached. During those years a number of the great singers have disappeared from the operatic stage, yet through Victor records their voices may still be heard in all their unforgettable loveliness. Meanwhile a new generation of singers has arisen, artists worthy of carrying on the great traditions of their predecessors. Their work, too, is given a deserved recognition on these pages. Moreover, during these years, operatic performances have multiplied throughout the country, and the repertoire has been broadened and enlarged. It has been our aim to make the present edition of The Victor Book of the Opera as representative as possible by including all the standard operas regularly in the repertoire and the newer operas that seem to be of permanent interest.

Numbers marked with an asterisk "*" are of acoustical recordings, all others are of modern records. For the sake of completeness a number of records have been listed on these pages which for reasons of expediency it has been necessary to omit from the current Victor catalogs. All such records will be carried in stock by the RCA Mfg. Co., Inc., and may be ordered through Victor dealers. New Victor records are issued every month so that at any given time the most recent issues of operatic records will be found in the supplements to the Victor catalogs.

WHAT IS AN OPERA?

W HAT is an opera? That question may very well be uppermost in every-one's mind the first time he attends the opera. And even the seasoned opera-goer may have difficulty in trying to give a sentence definition in reply to that apparently simple question. An easy answer is the mere statement, "An opera is a play set to music." But that is only part of the truth, for an opera requires a special kind of plot—one that is adaptable to musical accom-paniment. Music being, as it is often called, the language of the emotions, then it is to a drama which permits or requires an added emotional appeal that music can be of value. But like every good thing won in life, this gain involves a sacrifice.

For instance, it no doubt seems strange, or even unnatural, the first time we go to the opera, to find all the characters singing their parts instead of speaking them as in a play—or real life. But that is just one of the necessary customs or conventions of opera. At a play we see people living in rooms that have only three walls, the fourth being open so that we can look in and see what is going on. Yet we accept this revelatory architecture as quite natural because it represents a convention to which we are accustomed. And at the movies we are transported instantly from place to place in a most miraculous manner, yet we believe the movies realistic. There again a con-vention has become such a habit that we forget that it is untrue to life. In the same way, then, if we are to add the emotional and aesthetic appeal of music to drama, we have to accept the convention of people singing their thoughts instead of speaking them. And it doesn't take long to become accustomed to it!

In order better to see what an opera is like, let's look at a well-known example, "Rigoletto," which has been completely recorded by Victor, being Album M-32 in the Musical Masterpiece Series. It begins with a gloomy or-chestral prelude that portends tragedy, sets us wondering what is to happen. Then the curtain rises on a brilliant festival scene and the music we hear is just as scintillating as the magnificent palace and the gorgeously dressed ladies and courtiers that we see *(Record 1)*. The festival music in the orches-tra actually becomes for us a part of the scene, and also starts us thinking in a musical way, so that when the Duke and Borsa enter it is not surprising that they begin to sing rather than speak their words. The stranger to opera, however, will be struck by the fact that they don't seem to be singing any tune. But if we notice the words, a series of rapid-fire questions and answers in which the Duke tells Borsa about the unknown beauty he has been fol-lowing from church, we will readily understand that here regular tunes would be out of place. Of course, it might be much simpler, if, instead of using this semi-musical speech, called in technical language recitative, they would merely talk in an ordinary manner. But then it would be rather star-tling for them suddenly to begin to sing at some more emotional place where music is needed. In a comic opera such changes are not objectionable, but a serious play is better all spoken or all sung. This is one of the sacrifices necessary in opera, but it's worth making!

The Duke now steps out and sings a gay song *(Record 2)*. But this song does something more than entertain us; its lilting swing gives us an idea of the Duke's character, while the words show him definitely to be a super-sheik, a profligate of the most extreme kind. After this, the courtiers, who are in the background heedless of the Duke's self-revelation, dance a Minuet, the dance of that age, even as the Fox-trot is the dance of ours. Naturally, the orchestra accompanies with Minuet music, tuneful, graceful, and charming like the dance itself. Meanwhile the Duke flirts with the Countess of Ceprano, "What, going? Cruel one!" Soon she tells him in most modern fashion, "Calm yourself . . . *please!*" And this suave frivolity is in the music, too.

In the next scene we come to another feature of operatic music *(Record 12)*. Gilda has been left alone, and having just learned the supposed name of her lover, sings a song expressing her feelings regarding that affair of the heart. But this aria (as such operatic songs are called), with its attractive melody, serves also as a bright contrast to the dramatic music with which it is surrounded. Also it is a means of displaying the vocal skill of the singer who takes the part of Gilda; display, unfortunate though it may be, still being one of the great attractions of opera. Modern opera composers have largely done away with show pieces like this, but as the older Italian operas containing many such arias are still popular, let's enjoy them, even though dramatic and musical purists decry their value.

Another feature that is sometimes confusing is the frequency of concerted numbers—portions in which the persons of the drama sing together. In life people are seldom so rude as to speak while another is talking; then why do they do it in that most polite of entertainments, opera? Again there is a sacrifice for the sake of the music! No group of instruments playing has quite the appeal of a group of voices singing together, and nothing else in all music is quite so luscious as two voices singing together in thirds or sixths—as a soprano and tenor in a duet. These are musical effects too valuable to be lost, and a skilful composer like Verdi can turn them to advantageous use. Thus in the last act of "Rigoletto" *(Records 23 and 24)* we see the Duke in the Tavern, making love ardently to the coquettish Maddalena, while outside Rigoletto, thirsting for vengeance, points out her unfaithful lover to the heartbroken Gilda. The music expresses simultaneously the emotions of these four people, yet it is most melodious and rises to a fine climax. It is true that the presence of a number such as this, the famous "Quartet," does tend to delay the action, and for those of us who are used to fast-moving mystery plays, this is a defect. But is not the gain in emotional understanding of the characters—not to mention the musical enjoyment—worth the sacrifice? It is in moments such as these, when the music is allowed room to expand, so to speak, that it can rise to its greatest heights.

When the action moves along rapidly the music is compelled to become more of a background. This accounts for many of the passages which may seem barren of melody. The subsequent scenes of "Rigoletto" are splendid examples of just such accompanying dramatic music *(Records 26, 27, 28)*. The rising storm, the despair of Gilda, torn between love of her father and her resolve to sacrifice herself to save her lover, the murderous determination of Sparafucile, the pleading of Maddalena, and finally the actual murder of Gilda, are all depicted by the orchestra in most telling fashion. This is no place for the tunes you can hum, for here the mood of tense dramatic suspense is maintained during a long period of time largely by means of the music. It is in such scenes as these in the last act of Rigoletto, where through its expressive power it can make the hearer feel the most varied emotions, that music justifies its being joined to poetry and action on the stage.

So much emphasis having been placed on the words that are sung, one well may ask, "Why not opera in English?" From one point of view, the question is pertinent. The Italians, French, and Germans always have their opera in the vernacular, even though that often requires singing in translation. But America is a very young country, operatically speaking, and up to the present we have produced few opera singers. Therefore, we have been compelled to import artists from Europe. While these singers might relearn their parts in English, almost inevitably the resulting foreign accent would produce laughable results where tragedy is intended. Also, unlike Europe, where everybody goes to the opera, in the United States opera has been largely supported by wealthy patrons who keep up at least a smattering acquaintance with the principal operatic languages. Thus the Metropolitan Opera Company of New York maintains the policy of producing nearly all operas (except the Russian) in the original language. But we can hardly demand that the entire population of the United States should learn French, German and Italian, for the sake of the exotic pleasure of appreciating opera. Even though more difficult to sing than Italian, English is no more impossible than French or German, and eventually we will find a way of making operatic texts in the language of Shakespeare, Shelley and Keats, worthy of, and intelligible on, the operatic stage. A beginning has been made in this direction by the successful performance of Deems Taylor's "The King's Henchman," the text of which is by a poet of recognized standing, Edna St. Vincent Millay. Victor is also doing its share towards creating opera in English by having the performances of the Victor Opera Company recorded in English. In regard to other recordings by the great artists, Victor's experience has been that Americans prefer to have the artists make the best possible recording regardless of the language. Naturally an artist can give the best rendition of an aria in the language in which he has already learned the rôle. This accounts for the great number of operatic recordings in foreign languages.

We have noticed that opera, even as good an example of opera as "Rigoletto," contains passages for vocal display, and there are others that go further

15

in this respect than "Rigoletto." Naturally such a state of things would move serious-minded composers to revolt. Such a musical-dramatic revolutionist was Richard Wagner, one of whose most beautiful works, "Die Walküre," has been recorded by Victor, being Albums M-26 and M-27 in the Musical Masterpiece Series. This music-drama (as Wagner believed his later works should be called) is one of a group, "The Ring of the Nibelungs," but it is so beautiful that it is well worth knowing, even as a separate work. As we become better acquainted with it we have an increasing appreciation of the advances which Wagner made over the older Italian opera.

First of all we will be struck by the fact that Wagner's music is a continuous symphonic web, from the beginning to the end of each act, there being no set numbers with pauses for applause. Moreover there are no chances for vocal display as in earlier opera—no cadenzas or long high notes to exploit the artist's ability. These features make for greater naturalness of action as well as a general tone of dramatic earnestness.

Also we will notice that Wagner's music has at times a most remarkable power of painting pictures through tones. The wonderfully graphic "Ride of the Valkyries" at the beginning of Act III (*Records 9172-B and 8542-B*), the equally notable "Magic Fire Music" at the end of the same act (*Record 9177-A, B*), and the foreboding storm music at the beginning of Act I (*Record 9164-A*) are only a few examples. Likewise the music is occasionally descriptive of the action of individual characters as well as of the general scene. Thus, near the beginning of the first act (*same record*) when Siegmund staggers into the room and sinks exhausted at the fireside, his actions are clearly portrayed by the orchestra. Moreover, the orchestra sometimes serves to characterize the persons of the drama. Note, for instance, the gentle melody that is heard at the entrance of Sieglinde in Act I and the pompous, majestic chords that often accompany the appearances and words of Wotan. In addition, it is the orchestra which frequently interprets the speeches of the characters, as in Sieglinde's narrative of the stranger who appeared at her wedding feast (*Record 9165-A*) the presence in the orchestra of one of the solemn motives that is associated with Wotan indicates to us that the unknown stranger was the god himself.

These motives, or Leading-Motives, as they are often called, are brief musical themes, short bits of melody, associated with characters or events in the drama. They are used by the composer in such a way as to give the entire music-drama a most remarkable feeling of musical unity. More important dramatically, they serve a valuable psychological purpose in calling to mind elements of the drama not directly narrated or enacted on the stage.

Important though any of these features may be, undoubtedly the outstanding characteristic of any one of Wagner's greater works is the expressiveness that pervades the music throughout the entire composition. It is the music which not only makes us feel the emotion of any certain individual, but also arouses within us a sentiment appropriate to the scene or action that it accompanies. It is the music which stirs us with the tenderness and exhilaration of the love of Sieglinde and Siegmund *(Records 9165-6)*, just as it is the music which impresses on us the awesomeness of Brünnhilde's appearance to Siegmund *(Record 9170-A)* in Act II. Also it is the music which makes it possible for us to share with Wotan his inexpressible grief as he bids farewell to Brünnhilde *(Record 9176-A)* as well as filling us with genuine excitement at the combat of Siegmund and Hunding *(Records 9171-B, 9172-A)*. Likewise the beginning of the third act (when played at concerts known as the Ride of the Valkyries), besides being a most realistic piece of tone-painting, actually makes us feel as well as visualize the wild abandon and reckless speed of the Valkyries as they come galloping up to the mountain-top with their savage war cry and their barbaric laughter. Finally, towards the end of the last act we have the music which pictures the magic fire encircling Brünnhilde's rock, music which is poignant with Wotan's sorrow, and music which clothes the scene with a sense of poetic finality, that feeling of an inevitable and universal justice, even in tragedy, which is attained only by the greatest of dramatists, and only at their supreme moments.

*   *   *   *   *

If we stop to note the points touched on in this brief sketch, a few general principles will become apparent. We will, indeed, remember that in order to have the pleasure of music combined with drama, several sacrifices are necessary: the loss of naturalness due to the actors' singing instead of speaking their parts, and a slowing up of the action because of the necessary length of time required to develop a climax musically. But we will recall with delight that in recompense for these sacrifices we will receive several distinct rewards: the purely sensuous pleasure of listening to voices and orchestra, and the esthetically higher enjoyment of feeling and understanding the emotions, actions and characters of a drama as interpreted in music —interpreted with that intensity of expression which words alone cannot achieve.

AN OUTLINE HISTORY OF OPERA

ITALY

ABOUT the year 1580 a group of Florentine scholars and musical amateurs began discussing the possibility of adapting music to the drama. They believed that the ancient Athenians had performed their tragedies in a sort of musical declamation. This the Florentines endeavored to revive. Therefore, avoiding the complex polyphony that was characteristic of the music of the period, they sought a style of solo music that would permit the words to be distinct—emotionalized speech rather than sustained song. The instrumental accompaniment was to be merely a support and background. The first application of this style of recitative to an entire play was made by Peri and Caccini, who collaborated in setting Rinuccini's "Dafne" (1597). In 1600 "Eurydice" was produced by the same poet, set to music by Peri, and also by Caccini. Portions of these settings have been recorded and afford a splendid illustration of operatic music at its earliest period *(Victor Record 21752).*

The next step in the development of the new art was made by Claudio Monteverde, whose "Orfeo" was produced at Mantua in 1607. He also sought for dramatic expression but employed more elaborate musical means. His search led him to become one of the boldest of innovators in musical history. He required a larger orchestra than had been previously demanded and made skilful use of it to intensify the mood of dramatic situations. From this opera there has been recorded *(Victor Record 21747)* the lament of Orfeo when that hero realizes that Eurydice has been forever lost to him. The music, dignified and subservient to the expression of the words, shows a greater feeling for melody than that of earlier writers.

The most important opera composer next after Monteverde was Alessandro Scarlatti (1659-1725). He emphasized the musical element of his works, sometimes at the expense of the dramatic, and was the first to make considerable use of the so-called Da Capo aria (he is often held to have been its inventor). In this form the first portion of an aria is repeated after a second has intervened, hence the Italian name, *Da Capo,* which means "from the beginning." Although satisfying musically, this form is not suitable to all dramatic situations. Yet so great was its musical appeal that it came to be used more and more. In his arias Scarlatti often attained a melodic beauty and poignancy of expression that were new to the art of music. (For example, *Victor Record 21747.*) Opera as he wrote it came to be known as Opera Seria and was the prevailing fashion during the following century. His successors being for the most part men of less genius, degeneration set in, and during the eighteenth century Opera Seria became stereotyped in form. The plots were generally based on legends of classical antiquity, the libretti the shallowest of verse, the music a string of arias. The form and character of these arias were determined by fixed rules and everything was arranged as a means of displaying the technical skill of the singers—during this epoch the art of singing attained its greatest perfection. Although the innumerable operas written along these conventional lines seem to have forever disappeared from the stage, many individual arias from these early operas have come to be highly treasured because of the unsurpassed beauty of their melodies. Handel, though German by birth and long resident in England, wrote operas in this Italian style, and although it is not generally known as such, the so-called "Largo" (originally Larghetto) is just such an aria. It occurs at the beginning of his opera "Xerxes" *(Serse,* London, April 15, 1738) where the hero (soprano or mezzo-soprano) seeks the shade of a plane tree. A brief recitative *(included on Victor Record 7115)* serves as introduction to the aria, the text of which is simply: *Ombra mai fù di vegetabile cara ed amabile soave più.*

Side by side with the Italian Opera Seria there developed its humorous counterpart, Opera Buffa. Its closeness to real life prevented its ever degenerating into the formalism of Opera Seria. During earlier times the dialogue was spoken, later it was set to what was called "secco recitative" a lightly accompanied form of recitative particularly adapted to rapid or humorous dialogue.

Italian opera was infused with a new breath of life at the beginning of the nineteenth century through the work of Gioacchino Rossini (1792-1868) who wrote both serious and comic operas. He was a genius at the invention of brilliant vocal melody but gave more prominence to the orchestra than had been previously the case. His school was continued by Gaetaneo Donizetti (1797-1848) and Vincenzo Bellini (1801-1835) . Both were gifted at composing fascinating melody, of a beauty that still wins the admiration of serious musicians.

Their successor, Giuseppe Verdi (1813-1901) was one of the world's greatest dramatic composers. He began his career with such works as "Oberto" (1839) and "Ernani" (1844), written in a style akin to that of Bellini and Donizetti, but already displaying greater vigor and dramatic force. Throughout his long career he showed a constant development of skill without any marked diminution of musical inspiration, and with an increasing seriousness of purpose. His final works are remarkable for their depth of expression, clearness of characterization, freedom of form and richness of harmony and orchestration.

The end of the nineteenth century was marked by the appearance of a new school of operatic composition, the *verismo*. This first appeared in Mascagni's "Cavalleria Rusticana" (1890) and Leoncavallo's "Pagliacci" (1892). The aim was to present dramas of real life—the most sordid of plots, set to music in a realistic fashion.

The greatest genius in Italian Opera since Verdi, and one of the most popular of opera composers, is Giacomo Puccini (1858-1924). A gifted melodist and endowed with an uncanny skill for what is dramatically effective, he is noteworthy among Italian composers for his interest in exotic color.

More recent Italian opera composers such as Giordano, Alfano and Montemezzi, have been influenced by the melodic style of Puccini and the methods of *verismo*; nor have they been blind to musical movements in France and Germany.

FRANCE

In France, opera had its rise in the ballet—the elaborate spectacles performed for the entertainment of the court. This may account for the interest in scenic effect that has characterized French opera. When in 1645 an Italian opera troupe appeared in Paris for the first time, it gave an impetus to the musical side of performances. Lully (1633-1687) was the first important composer of French opera. Although he reflects the conventional life of the court for which he wrote, yet in his effort to make the words distinct and in the prominence he gives to the visual elements of staging and pantomime, he reflects the permanent characteristics of French opera. His successor, Jean Phillipe Rameau (1683-1764), without altering the style, enriched it with a larger variety of harmony and an increased prominence given to the orchestra.

Meanwhile the opéra-comique was being gradually developed from the crude plays with interspersed songs which long had been popular. Among the early writers of opéras-comiques André Grétry (1741-1813) is important. His works are notable for the vivacity which enlivens his formal eighteenth century style. The aria "La Fauvette" from "Zemire et Azor" may be regarded as typical of his lighter vein.

Italian Opera Seria grew in favor in France during the eighteenth century so that in the course of time two schools of thought arose—one advocating the importance of the dramatic and poetic side of opera; the other maintaining the superiority of Opera Seria. The proponents of the former school found the ideal man to exemplify their belief in Christoph Willibald Gluck (1714-1787). He had written many operas after the prevailing style, but conscious of its inadequacy, had attempted something of a reform in several of his works. In this he had met with little success, for Vienna, the city where he labored, was given wholly to the Italian fashion. He therefore moved to Paris as a more likely field.

Gluck's thesis was, briefly stated, that the music should always perfectly express the drama it accompanies; nothing extraneous should be introduced for mere display, either in voice or orchestra. In his greater works he attains an unprecedented dramatic force.

Gluck's success, however, did not go unchallenged. His opponents brought to Paris the Italian, Piccinni, a composer of stereotyped Opera Seria. A strenuous rivalry grew up; in fact, so bitter was the "War of the Gluckists and Piccinnists" that it threatened to become more than merely verbal. The principles of Gluck finally triumphed, Piccinni even adopting his rival's manner.

With the triumph of Gluck, Paris became for a time the center of European opera, and during the next century was the scene of activity of a number of great operatic composers. Many of them were of foreign birth, but thoroughly blended their native characteristics to conform with the French language, taste, and spirit. Gasparo Spontini (1774-1851), whose "La Vestale" was a great triumph and still holds the stage, created a fashion for subjects of an heroic nature set in scenic and orchestral splendor. In this he was followed by Halévy (1799-1862) and Meyerbeer (1791-1864). The latter ranks among the great operatic composers—his best works, because of their gorgeousness of setting, largeness of dramatic conception, intensity at tragic moments, and demands for brilliant singing and acting, truly deserve the appellation *Grand Opera*. They are marred, however, by trivialities, pompousness, and the composer's inability to expand his musical ideas.

The heroic grand opera style was in time replaced by one of a more direct human appeal, as exemplified in Gounod's "Faust" (1859) and Bizet's "Carmen" (1875), two of the most popular operas on the modern stage. In both, the dramatic use made of accompanied recitative between the more formal vocal numbers is indicative of the French insistence on the importance of the text. One of the most famous and prolific of later French composers is Jules Massenet (1842-1912). His style is marked by a suave melodiousness and refinement rather than by dramatic vigor. Charpentier, in his "Louise" (1900), presents a study of modern sociological problems and a picture of contemporary life. Claude Debussy in "Pélléas et Mélisande" (1902), by the manner in which he makes the music subservient to the text, reverts to the principle of the original Florentine founders of opera.

GERMANY

In Germany we find the beginnings of opera under Italian influence. During the seventeenth and eighteenth centuries the court of every kingdom or principality maintained its own Italian or Italianized opera troupe. But during this same period there grew up in the folk theatres the Singspiel (song play), light, often comic, farcical or burlesque plays in which spoken dialogue was interspersed with songs—the characters were from humble and native sources.

The first of the great German composers to write operas was Wolfgang Amadeus Mozart (1756-1791). Important though his work in the realm of the symphony and string quartet may be, his greatest and most significant contribution to the art of music was undoubtedly in the realm of opera. Two of his greatest works "Le Nozze di Figaro" (1786) and "Don Giovanni" (1787) are written to Italian texts, with secco recitatives, and in fact, are offshoots of the Italian opera buffa. On the other hand, "Die Zauberflöte (1791) and "Die Entführung aus dem Serail" (1782) are set to German texts with spoken dialogue—and show the influence of the national style in their music and their origin in the Singspiel in the nature of their plots. Mozart ranks among the very greatest of opera composers because of his unerring skill at characterization and his ability to express every shade of emotion.

Mozart had learned much from his Italian and French predecessors. In turn Beethoven (1770-1827) learned much from Mozart, yet in his one opera, "Fidelio," there is a great deal that is of most striking and profound originality. The use of the orchestra to paint situations and to express the emotions of the characters is one important feature. As in the Singspiel, spoken dialogue is used between the musical numbers.

The Romantic movement, presaged in the work of Mozart and Beethoven, reached its culmination in the operas of Carl Maria von Weber (1786-1826). The interest in the beauties of the natural world and the terrors of the supernatural, love of the exotic, whether medieval, Spanish or oriental, and

21

the enthusiasm for national folk lore characteristic of the Romantic movement in general, all found expression in some one of Weber's operas. "Der Freischütz" is notable for its use of a typically German folk story, characteristically national melodies, and tone painting in harmony and orchestration.

The work of Beethoven and Weber was the starting point for Richard Wagner (1813-1883), one of the world's greatest combined musical and dramatic geniuses. During his lifetime of most bitter struggle he accomplished a veritable revolution in the realm of opera. His own ability and style as a composer also underwent a profound change beginning with the imitative "Rienzi" (1842) and never ceasing until his final work, "Parsifal" (1882). Since the music took its form and character from the drama, he held that his mature works should be called not "operas" but "music-dramas."

Among the later German composers who have attained distinction should be mentioned Humperdinck (1854-1921) and Richard Strauss (1864-   ).

ENGLAND

In England, opera has largely been dominated by foreign influences. The native born Purcell (1658-1695) showed the most remarkable ability in his incidental music to various masques and plays, and especially in his one real opera, "Dido and Aeneas." Had he not died prematurely he might have become one of the world's great operatic composers and the history of opera in England might have been different. At the beginning of the eighteenth century Handel made London the scene of his operatic activities. As a reaction from the Italian form made popular by him there appeared the distinctive English type, the ballad-opera, first made popular in Gay's "Beggar's Opera" (1728). Of much less virility are the nineteenth century contributions to this form such as Balfe's "The Bohemian Girl." But in keeping with the best of English traditions for literary worth and musical solidity are the works of Gilbert and Sullivan.

RUSSIA

In Russia the first definite move by a native composer to break away from the dominant Italian tradition was by M. Glinka (1803-1857). In his patriotic "A Life for the Czar" and the legendary "Russlan and Ludmilla" he opened up the path of Russian nationalism in music. His style was lyric, influenced by Italian forms, but the Russian flavor of his melodies and harmonies is unmistakable. His successor, Dargomyzsky (1813-1869), is notable for his use of a declamatory style of writing. The famous nationalist group of five, while disclaiming adherence to Wagner's theories, seem to show something of the influence of his work. Yet their major operas are of great originality—distinctly Russian in style. Certainly in Moussorgsky's "Boris Godounow" and "Khowantchina," Borodin's "Prince Igor," and in Rimsky-Korsakow's "Coq d'Or" and "Sadko" we have some of the most significant contributions to the modern operatic stage. The first named composer adopts the declamatory style; the second, the lyrical; the last unites both.

UNITED STATES

In North America operatic performances have been given with more or less regularity since the eighteenth century—antedating the formation of the Union. During the nineteenth century the popularity of opera was greatly increased by the establishment of permanent opera houses: New Orleans (1813); New York, Academy of Music (1854); and Metropolitan (1883); Chicago, Auditorium (1889). Of the many operas by native composers it is impossible to speak in a limited space. Mention should be made, however, of Deems Taylor's "The King's Henchman," Gruenberg's "The Emperor Jones," and Hanson's "Merrymount." Innumerable local and traveling companies are contributing greatly to the growing appreciation of opera in the United States, and the future is promising for all who hold the esthetic advancement of this country at heart.

NOTE ON PRONUNCIATION

LIKE all systems of pronunciation involving foreign languages, the system of pronunciation followed in The Victor Book of the Opera cannot hope to reproduce every sound exactly. It certainly is no grievous error frankly to anglicize those sounds which have no equivalents in English. The following suggestions are offered, however, as an aid in attaining an exact pronunciation:

A: in French, generally as *a* in *bat*; in German and Italian, like *a* in *father* (indicated *ah*).

A: German ä (ae): like *ay* in *day*.

C: in Italian, when before *e* or *i*, pronounced like *ch* in cheese; before other vowels, like *k*.

CH: in Italian is hard like *k*. In German it is very difficult to reproduce without an audible example and probably is best imitated by *k*.

G: in Italian, before *e* or *i*, soft, as in *gem*: before other vowels, hard, as in *gate*.

J: in French like *s* in pleasure.

N: in French *n* and *m* when followed by another consonant or when the last letter of a word, are not pronounced. They merely indicate that the vowel which precedes them is nasalized, that is, spoken through the nose. Thus to obtain the sound of *on*, pronounce very quickly and forcibly, rather snort, the word *song* without producing the final g; this gives the French nasal *on* (often rather inaccurately reproduced in English as *ong*). Similarly *thank* forcibly sounded without the *k* will give nasal *in* or *ain*; and *spunk* will give the nasal *un*. The French nasal sound *en* can likewise be reproduced in the word *fond*. *n* and *m* lose their nasal force and are pronounced as in English when doubled or followed by a vowel.

German ö (oe): make the lips tense and round as if to say *o* in *note*, then holding the lips in this position, pronounce *a* as in *say*.

U: in German and Italian as in *rule*. In French: holding the lips closely rounded as if to say *oo* as in *moon*, pronounce *ee* as in *bee*. German ü (ue) is pronounced like French *u*.

Gerardi

DON PEDRO'S VESSEL—ACT III
(SETTING FOR THE VERONA FESTIVAL)

L'AFRICANA

(The African)

OPERA in five acts; music by Giacomo Meyerbeer; words by Scribe. First produced at the Grand Opera, Paris, April 28, 1865. First performance in the United States, December 1, 1865, at the Academy of Music, New York.

Although *Les Huguenots* is now generally regarded as Meyerbeer's masterpiece, the composer himself assigned that position to *L'Africaine*. He labored over this opera many years, and, tragically enough, died the day after the score was finished. During the course of composition, the plot was frequently altered; in fact, the present rather vacillating hero, di Gama, was added to the characters as an afterthought! Though originally a French opera, it is now often played in Italian, and therefore we follow the Metropolitan Opera Company in using Italian titles throughout. (The French title, "L'Africaine," is pronounced *Laf-ree-cane'*, the Italian, "L'Africana," *Laf-ree-kah'-nah*.)

The action occurs during the early sixteenth century in Lisbon, Portugal, on Don Pedro's Ship at Sea, and in India.

ACT I

SCENE—*The Council Chamber of the King of Portugal*

AT A meeting of the Royal Council the great explorer, Diaz, is reported lost with all his company, including Vasco di Gama. The latter had been engaged to Inez, daughter of Don Diego, an important member of the

24

Council who is now anxious for her to marry Don Pedro, president of that assembly. Word is brought of the arrival of an officer and two captives, the sole survivors from the wreck. All are amazed that the surviving officer is Vasco, who, undaunted by the perils he has just passed, comes before the Council asking that he be made leader of an expedition to discover a new land that, he believes, lies beyond Africa. As proof of his theory, he has brought in the two captives, Selika and Nelusko. Though to the Portuguese they are mere "natives" of this strange country, Selika, unknown to di Gama, is in fact queen, and the two reply to their captors in a cold, haughty manner.

Vasco having retired so that the Council may consider this plan, the ambitious Don Pedro, who wishes Inez for himself, contrives to obtain a valuable chart from among Vasco's papers, and persuades the assembly to reject Vasco's plans as futile. When Vasco is informed of the Council's decision, he insults that august body by charging it with gross ignorance and prejudice. This is Don Pedro's opportunity: he has Vasco seized and thrown into prison.

ACT II

Scene—*The Prison of the Inquisition*

Vasco, asleep in prison, is watched over by the captive Selika, and protected by her from the dagger of the jealous Nelusko. When he awakens, she declares her love for him and reveals a safe route to the land he wishes to discover. Filled with joy at the prospect of finding his longed-for land, and overcome by the seductive, sensuous charm of the beautiful captive at his side, he embraces her passionately. The ecstasy of the new-found lovers is cut short by the sudden entry of Don Pedro and Inez. It had been whispered to Inez that Vasco loved the captive woman; this sight convinces her that the gossip is true. Vasco is filled with remorse at the sight of his former beloved, who, handing him a document granting him his liberty, starts to go away. Vasco calls to her, saying that her suspicions are groundless, and as proof he gives her these two slaves that he "bought in Africa." But his protestations are needless, for Inez has purchased Vasco's freedom by marrying Don Pedro. Moreover, that crafty Portuguese has had himself appointed leader of an expedition to seek the land described by Vasco.

Selika laments her mistreatment and Nelusko gloatingly plots revenge, while Vasco, thwarted in love and ambition, falls half faintly.

GIGLI AS VASCO

ACT III

SCENE—*Aboard Don Pedro's Ship at Sea*

NELUSKO, chosen to act as pilot for Don Pedro, directs the vessel out of her course towards a reef. A storm is lowering and Nelusko sings an impressive invocation to Adamastor, king of the ocean.

Adamastor, re dell'acque (*Adamastor, Ruler of Ocean*) **Titta Ruffo 7153-2.00**

Vasco, suspecting treachery and wishing to save Inez, who is on board, has followed in another ship and comes to warn Don Pedro. The latter distrusts Vasco and orders him shot. Before the order can be executed, the ship strikes the reef and is boarded by a tribe of natives that have been summoned by Nelusko. Only a few of the Portuguese survive the massacre that follows.

ACT IV

SCENE—*A Temple of Brahma on One Hand, a Palace at the Other*

SELIKA is placed on her throne as queen of the land amid a scene of the greatest luxury and semi-barbaric display.

Vasco, who has escaped the shipwreck and massacre, surveys this brilliant tropical paradise—the land which he had dreamed of discovering, and voices his joy and amazement in the aria "*O Paradiso!*" To a shimmering accompaniment high in the woodwind, di Gama sings a broad sustained melody expressive of his almost religious exaltation; then the music takes a more martial turn as he is thrilled with patriotic fervor by the thought that he will give this land he has discovered to his native country.

O Paradiso! (*Oh, Paradise!*) **Beniamino Gigli 7109-2.00**

He is captured, and in order to save his life, Selika declares that he is her husband. Nelusko, willing to make Selika happy, even at the cost of the bitterest pain to himself, affirms that he himself saw the wedding ceremony when a captive in Europe. At the priest's demand, Selika and Vasco are now married according to native ceremony. Then, in the distance is heard the voice of Inez, also escaped from the wreck. . . . Vasco is startled by the realization that he still loves her.

ACT V

SCENE I—*The Queen's Garden (Often omitted in performance)*

THE noble-minded Selika realizes after meeting Inez that this Spanish woman's love is true and worthy of Vasco, and thus she orders Vasco and Inez to be allowed to escape on a ship sailing for Spain.

SCENE II—*A Promontory by the Sea*

On a promontory overlooking the sea stands a mancinilla tree. From beneath it Selika gazes at the receding sail of the ship bearing Vasco and Inez; as it disappears in the distance she seizes some of the flowers of the tree and inhales their deadly perfume. The faithful Nelusko finds her just as she dies; he, too, drinks of the poisoned air of the flowers and falls beside his beloved.

ACT II, SCENE 2—THE TEMPLE OF VULCAN
(DESIGNED BY A. PASQUALI)

AÏDA

OPERA in four acts; music by Giuseppe Verdi; libretto the joint work of Bey, du Locle, and Ghislanzoni. First produced, December 24, 1871, at Cairo, Egypt. First performance in the United States, November 26, 1873, at the Academy of Music, New York.

Ismail Pasha, Khedive of Egypt, was to open a new Grand Opera House in Cairo, at the time of the dedication of the Suez Canal. Naturally he wanted a new opera for the occasion, and Verdi being one of the greatest masters of the art then living, he requested him to compose a work, something dealing with the past grandeurs of Egypt. After conferring with a friend who was more experienced in such matters than himself, Verdi named the fee of $20,000, a great sum for that time. His demand was, nevertheless, promptly granted.

The subject of Aïda had been proposed to the Khedive by the famous French Egyptologist, Mariette Bey, who evidently had come upon the idea during his Egyptian excavations. From the mere suggestion of the burial of living persons in ancient Egypt a plot was built up. So severe a punishment could only be deserved because of some great crime, such as treason, but treason could only win our deepest sympathy when brought about in a genuinely exalted and patriotic leader through that power which knows no nationality— Love. In this manner, piece by piece, grew the story of the Egyptian hero who spurns the hand of a princess for love of a slave—the captive daughter of a hostile sovereign. Thus jealousy and patriotism unite to bring destruction to the lovers. From the rough draft of this plot, Camille du Locle, a former director of the Opéra Comique in Paris, who happened to be visiting Verdi at Busseto, Italy, wrote a libretto in French prose. This was made into Italian verse by Antonio Ghislanzoni. Verdi himself grew to take a great interest in the work and suggested valuable features in the development of the story, among them the double scene in the last act. Mariette Bey contributed from

MARTINELLI AS RHADAMES

his great knowledge of ancient Egypt, designed costumes and scenery, and restored to life, as it were, the city of Thebes and the temple of Phtha.

Fate, that, through the operation of national or international affairs and politics, so often interfered with or delayed the first performance of Verdi's works, again took a hand. Verdi's score was ready and the Khedive's theatre was opened (November, 1869) but not with "Aïda." Before the scenery and costumes were shipped, the Franco-Prussian war broke out; those important accessories were compelled to remain in beleagured Paris till the close of the war. During this forced delay, Verdi had an opportunity to revise and improve his score; "Aïda" then was given its premier performance at Cairo, Egypt, December 24, 1871, with unprecedented success. At its first performance at La Scala, Milan, February 7, 1872, its reception was equally enthusiastic. The performance was under the direction of Verdi himself, who was recalled thirty-two times and, amid a tumult of applause, was presented with an ivory baton and a diamond star with the name "Aïda" in rubies and "Verdi" in other precious stones. "Aïda" was first performed in the United States at the Academy of Music, New York, November 26, 1873.

Musically, "Aïda" is of interest in that it is the first work in Verdi's "mature" style. At first unjustly accused of being Wagnerian, it is in reality anything but that. Verdi was too wise not to profit by the advances made by Wagner, but he did so while still remaining true to Italian tradition. He did away with numbers written to exhibit the technical skill of singers in florid runs and trills, and instead substituted music that is always appropriate to the action of the drama, yet music that is always melodious and beautifully written for the voice. The orchestra is not treated in the complex symphonic style of Wagner, yet it is richer and more colorful than the orchestra had heretofore been in Italian opera, still without ever overshadowing the singers. In keeping with the subject, Verdi skilfully introduced charming effects of the Oriental both in his melodies and in the orchestration; moreover, realizing that in presenting the life of ancient Egypt much pageantry was needed, he wrote rousing choruses for crowds of people and also exotic dances to enhance the oriental effect. Yet there is well drawn characterization; Rhadames, bold and romantic; Amneris, in varying moods, haughty, angry, jealous, or in terror; Aïda, simple and loving; Amonasro, crafty; Ramfis, stern and pompous; characters that are revealed in music as well as words. All these features combine to make of "Aïda" a landmark in the history of opera.

AÏDA COMPLETE ON VICTOR RECORDS

A delightful series of excerpts from "Aïda," by notable singers and orchestras, is included in Album M-303, recently released and listing at $10.00. The artists featured in this album include Caruso, Ponselle, Martinelli, Rethberg, Pertile, Giannini and La Scala Orchestra (Records 1744, 1745, 8993, 8994, 11897, 11898).

Opera lovers will also be happy to know that "Aïda" has been completely recorded for Victor by artists and members of the chorus and orchestra of the famous La Scala Opera House, of Milan, home of much that is great in Italian Opera. Among the artists are Aureliano Pertile, popularly known tenor, Irene Minghini-Cattaneo, leading mezzo-soprano at La Scala, and the beloved American soprano, Dusolina Giannini. The entire performance, directed by Maestro Cav. C. Sabajno, is recorded on nineteen double-faced records and issued in two volumes as Album M-54 (and in automatic sequence, as AM-54) in the Musical Masterpiece Series, List Price, $28.50. In the accompanying description, the numbers of the records in this remarkable presentation of "Aïda" are given in parentheses as they occur in the action. The distribution of rôles is indicated in the following list of—

CHARACTERS

Aïda *(Ah-ee'-dah), an Ethiopian slave*	Dusolina Giannini, *Soprano*
The King of Egypt	G. Masini, *Bass*
Amneris *(Am-nay'-riss), his daughter*	Irene Minghini-Cattaneo, *Mezzo-Soprano*
Rhadames *(Rahd'-ah-maze), Captain of the Guard*	Aureliano Pertile, *Tenor*
Amonasro *(Ah-moh-nahz'-roh), King of Ethiopia*	Giovanni Inghilleri, *Baritone*
Ramfis *(Rahm'-fiss), High Priest*	L. Manfrini, *Bass*
A Messenger	G. Nessi, *Tenor*

Priests, Priestesses, Ministers, Captains, Soldiers, Officials, Ethiopian Slaves and Prisoners, Egyptians, etc.

The action takes place at Memphis and Thebes during the epoch of the Pharaohs.

ACT I

Scene I—*A Hall in the Palace. Through the Great Gate at the Rear May Be Seen the Pyramids and the Temples of Memphis*

AFTER a beautiful, calm prelude *(Record 1)* based on a brief theme that recurs several times during the opera and seems to typify the gentle Aïda, the curtain rises revealing a hall in the palace of the King of Mem-

Photo by Crimelli

THE GREAT TRIUMPHAL SCENE
(SETTING BY A. PASQUALI)

phis. Ramfis, High Priest of Isis *(Record 2)*, is telling Rhadames that the Ethiopians are again advancing against Egypt. In reply to Rhadames' questions he adds, significantly, that the goddess Isis has appointed a certain brave young warrior leader of the army that is about to be sent against the invaders. Left alone, Rhadames ponders over this news *(Record 3)*, occasional fanfares of trumpets in the orchestra adding to the warlike atmosphere:

> If I were that warrior! if my dream
> Should become true! An army of brave men
> Led by me—victory—the applause
> Of all Memphis! And to thee, my sweet Aïda,
> To return, crowned with laurels!
> To say to thee—for thee I have fought, and for thee conquered!

This change of warlike sentiment of war to that of ardent love is clearly reflected in the music. Then as the young soldier continues meditating on his loved one, he sings a beautiful melody, expressive of the warmth of his love while the orchestral strings provide a shimmering accompaniment which would seem to picture for us the "celestial" vision of Aïda in Rhadames' mind.

> Heav'nly Aïda, beauty resplendent,
>   Radiant flower, blooming and bright.
> Queenly thou reignest o'er me transcendent,
>   Bathing my spirit in beauty's light.
> I would give back to thee thy beautiful heaven,
>   The sweet breezes of thy native land;
> A regal chaplet on thy tresses I would place,
>   And a throne by the sun to stand.

Céleste Aïda *(Heavenly Aïda!)* **Giovanni Martinelli 6595-2.00, Enrico Caruso *6000-7770-8993-2.00 each**

This popular aria dramatically serves a valuable purpose in convincing us of the genuineness of Rhadames' passion for Aïda, thus making logical his subsequent sacrifice on her behalf.

His musings are interrupted by the arrival of Amneris *(Record 4)*, the daughter of the King, and herself very much in love with Rhadames. By the expression on Rhadames' face she divines that he is in love and, wondering who the woman can be, wishes that she might be the chosen one. Rhadames tries to conceal his real emotion by saying that he was merely hoping that he might be the leader in the coming campaign. At this moment the slave, Aïda, enters, and instantly, by Rhadames' glance, Amneris knows that he loves Aïda. Aïda tries to conceal her real feelings from the jealous Amneris, who has assumed a friendly manner and asked her the reason of her anxious appearance *(Record 5)*, by answering that she is unhappy because she has just heard that her country, Ethiopia, is again at war. Rhadames, watching Amneris, is fearful that she suspects his love affair with

Aïda. The emotions of these three characters are expressed in the dramatic trio which they now sing.

The orchestra plays a brief martial phrase; the King enters and summons a messenger whose arrival has just been announced. This messenger comes with the expected though unwelcome news that the Ethiopian invasion is now a reality, for the enemy is approaching the city under Amonasro. "My father!" (*Mio padre*) exclaims Aïda, aside. The King appoints Rhadames leader of the army (*Record 6*), and Amneris, enjoying a moment of regal pride, presents him with the banner beneath which he is to go forth. Then, having been charged by their ruler to guard the Sacred Nile with their lives, the Egyptians depart, exclaiming, "To War! Death to the invader! Lead on, Rhadames, return victorious!"

de Gueldve

RETHBERG AS AÏDA

Aïda has so far forgotten her native country, that under the spell of her love, she has joined with the multitude in crying to Rhadames, "Return victorious," but now, left alone, she realizes the full significance of the words. In a remarkable aria (*Records 7 and 8*), she expresses her dismay that she has wished him to be victor over her father. She is appalled that

Ritorna vincitor (*Return Victorious!*) **Rosa Ponselle 8993-7438-2.00 each, Elisabeth Rethberg 7106-2.00**

the unavoidable workings of circumstances should have brought her to be so torn between love of homeland and such an overpowering love for Rhadames. Her conflicting emotions are admirably expressed in the varied melody and the harmonic changes. In her distress she implores:

> Love, fatal pow'r mystic and dread,
> Break thou my heart,
> Now let me die!
> Oh, hear, ye gods on high!

Scene II—*The Temple of Vulcan*

The gorgeous music of this scene is included in its entirety (except for the sacred dance) on the record:

Temple Scene—Parts I and II *Giovanni Martinelli, Ezio Pinza and the Metropolitan Opera Chorus 8111-2.00*

Through the long rows of massive Egyptian pillars in the dim temple of Vulcan, we see in the distance a great altar, illuminated by a mysterious light from above. There are heavy statues of many deities, and from golden tripods rises the smoke of incense. The High Priest, Ramfis, stands

31

before the altar, while outside, Priestesses sing a weird oriental chant *(Record 9)*:

> Almighty, almighty Phtha,
> Who makest life in all!
> Almighty Phtha! Almighty Phtha!

In contrast with this are heard the voices of Priests, also outside the temple, singing in solemn harmony their prayers to the same great god whom they hail as "the animating spirit . . . eternal fire . . . creator of all . . . Life of the Universe!"

Then Ramfis, joined by other Priests, invokes the blessing of the god on the expedition. Priestesses perform a stately sacred dance while Rhadames enters and receives the consecrated veil *(Record 10)*. Now Ramfis presents to Rhadames *(Record 11)* a consecrated sword . . . may it be to the enemy a death-bringing thunderbolt. Then *(beginning of Part II of Record 8111)* turning towards the altar, Ramfis prays:

> God, guardian and avenger
> Of this sacred land,
> Spread thy hand
> Over the Egyptian soil.

Rhadames prays similarly; then, while he is being invested with the sacred armor, the Priests and Priestesses resume the mystic hymn and dance. The music grows to a tremendous climax, as all turn towards the altar fervently praying "Protect Thou and defend the sacred soil of Egypt."

Copy't Mishkin

CARUSO AS RHADAMES

ACT II

Scene I—*A Hall in Amneris' Apartment*

AMNERIS is reclining languorously on a couch in her room surrounded by slave girls singing an oriental song in praise of her loved one *(Record 12)*. Even Amneris is moved to join in their song, exclaiming:

> O come love,
> O love with rapture cheer me,
> To joy my heart restore!

Then as she falls back indolently on her couch Moorish slave boys dance.

Introduction and Moorish Ballet *Creatore's Band* **35780-1.25**

Seeing Aïda approach, Amneris bids her slaves depart *(Record 13)*, and prepares herself for revenge. She achieves it cleverly, rather craftily. Pretending friendship, she wins Aïda's confidence, and then *(Record*

32

14), by telling her that Rhadames has been slain in battle, brings the poor slave to tears; thus her love for the Egyptian leader is revealed. This is further confirmed by Aïda's evident joy when Amneris admits her ruse and says that Rhadames lives. Then, impassionedly, Amneris declares that she herself loves him. Pharaoh's daughter is her slave's rival!

Aïda is helpless. She can only implore mercy—from a viper. She makes no attempt to conceal her love, only pleads, in vain, for pity *(Record 15)*. Amneris immediately pronounces death as her reward for having ever dared be her rival, but the sound of festival music outside announcing the return of the victorious Rhadames, suggests more cruel revenge to the princess. She demands that Aïda shall first witness Rhadames' triumphant procession and his obeisances to herself as she sits beside her father the King.

Scene II—*Without the City Walls*

The King and his court are assembled around a great throne erected at the city gates to welcome the conquering army. The people and priests unite in a majestic hymn, "Glory to Egypt, and to Isis who protects our sacred land!" *(Record 16.)* The Egyptian troops enter, preceded by musicians playing long, brazen trumpets. Then follow dancing girls who execute their curious Egyptian steps before the King, while the orchestra supplies ballet music of exotic hues *(Record 17)*.

Aïda-Ballet Suite *Boston "Pops" Orchestra, Arthur Fiedler, conductor* 11985-1.50
Aïda-Grand March *Boston "Pops" Orchestra, Arthur Fiedler, conductor* 11885-1.50

The song of praise is resumed *(Record 18)* and other troops enter, following war-chariots, banners, sacred vessels, and images of the gods, all borne aloft in triumph. Finally, as the music swells to a stupendous climax, Rhadames appears, under a canopy carried by officers.

The King descends from the throne to embrace Rhadames, as the saviour of his country *(Record 19)*. At his command, Amneris crowns the victor, the King promising to grant any boon that he may desire to ask. Rhadames suggests that first the prisoners should be brought in.

Thereupon the captives enter. Among them is the Ethiopian King, dressed as a plain soldier.

Quest'assisi ch'io vesto *(This My Habit Has Told You)* **La Scala Soloists and Orchestra** 8994-2.00

Aïda impetuously rushes to him, exclaiming, "My father!" Under cover of the resulting general excitement, Amonasro whispers to her not to betray his rank. Summoned by the King, Amonasro acknowledges his daughter, admits defeat, and describes *(Record 20)* how the "King of the Ethiopians" (himself), pierced by countless wounds, died at his feet. "If love of country is a crime," he adds, "we are all criminals—all ready to die." Then, addressing the King as "Powerful Ruler," he begs him to have mercy on his captured soldiers. "Today we are stricken by Fate," he says, "tomorrow Fate may strike you."

Amonasro's bluff, soldierly manner commends itself to the King. The populace and prisoners beg his release; the Priests demand his death, and that of the other captives. Rhadames pleads for mercy, and recalling the King's promise *(Record 21)*, demands the life and liberty of the Ethiopians. The King yields, stipulating, at the insistence of the Priests, that Aïda and Amonasro remain as hostages. Then, unknowingly enough, he blights Rhadames' joy by announcing that the hero shall have as his great and due reward, the hand of Amneris.

Then follows a magnificent finale *(Record 22)*. Amonasro swears vengeance upon his enemies; Amneris, having won her revenge against Aïda, exults in the thought of her own marriage to Rhadames, while Aïda and Rhadames gaze at one another in hopeless despair. The voices of their divers emotions are joined with the triumphal hymn of the people, Priests, and King, all uniting to form one of the most overwhelmingly impressive scenes of combined music and pageantry in the whole realm of opera.

Grand March and Finale—Act II   *Creatore's Band* 35780-1.25

ACT III—THE NILE SCENE
(SETTING BY GRIGIONI AND PANNI)

ACT III

SCENE—*The Banks of the Nile; Moonlight. The Temple of Isis Can Be Seen Behind Palm Trees*

A LONG sustained tone high in the strings as background for a tender melody played by the oboe gives us the atmosphere of the weird, exotic mystery of the banks of the Nile bathed in soft moonlight *(Record 23)*.

34

From within the temple floats the sound of voices, softly chanting their hymn of praise and intercession. Meanwhile, Amneris and the High Priest, having come up to the shore in a boat, go into the temple to pray that the approaching union of Amneris and Rhadames may be indeed happy. Scarcely have they disappeared when Aïda comes on the scene (Record 24), led thither by a vague hope that she may there meet Rhadames. If he bids her an eternal farewell she will find peace and oblivion in the dark waters of the Nile! These somber thoughts lead her to think of the happy land of her childhood and she sings the tender and despairing song, "O patria mia," one of the loveliest arias in the opera. Blending with it is a weird, wandering strain for the oboe, faint and mysterious (Record 25).

O patria mia *(My Native Land)* **Elisabeth Rethberg 8994-7106-2.00 each**

Aïda is startled by unexpectedly discovering her father at this place *(Record 26).* Amonasro has found in Aïda's passion for Rhadames a means of escape and even victory; and, a skilled strategist, he plays on the emotions of the innocent girl in the same manner Amneris had done. Almost cruelly, he tells her that because of the love between herself and Rhadames, she is no longer an Ethiopian nor fit to be called his daughter *(Record 27),* she is merely a bondmaid of the Egyptians. They can escape and their army can conquer if she will gain the secret from Rhadames of his plan of march. Aïda recoils horror-stricken at the thought; Amonasro denounces her and places all the blame of her people's misery on her shoulders, she alone can save them. Not able to resist the call of patriotism she at length yields; and Amonasro, seeing Rhadames approach, conceals himself among the palms. The hero seeks to embrace his beloved, exclaiming, "Again I see thee my own Aïda!" *(Record 28.)* But urged by the terror of her father's injunctions to exercise womanish ingenuity, Aïda bids him prove his affection by fleeing with her. The scene *(Record 29)* is a remarkable dialogue in music, the pleading accents of the girl and the agitation of the hero being in sharp contrast. For a time he resists, but the enchantment of the oriental night, the warmth of his passion for Aïda, the allurement of her presence and the desperate prospect of his forced marriage to Amneris, all weaken his resolve.

Fuggiam gli ardori *(Ah! Fly With Me)* **Pertile, Giannini, La Scala Orch. *(in Album M-303)* 11898-1.50**

Then *(Record 30),* when he yields to the spell of Aïda's enticement, he is in turn caught up by his own emotions and paints a rosy picture of an easy and happy life with his loved one in the blissful land of Ethiopia, far away from the cares of Egypt. They are about to flee, when in telling Aïda, in reply to her cleverly timed question, the road they can take, he lets slip the information of the planned route of the Egyptian army.

Rhadames, commander of the Egyptians, has disclosed his military secrets! Amonasro runs out from his hiding place and *(beginning of Record 31)* reveals himself as leader of the enemy. It is too late for Rhadames to repent;

35

it is pointed out to him, with subtle casuistry, by Amonasro, that he is guiltless, it is Fate that has betrayed him. He is assured that happiness awaits them all in Ethiopia. Moreover he dare not stay, but must make good his escape with Aïda, and, of course, her father.

Amneris, coming from the temple, has overheard. Mad with jealousy she rushes out and denounces the three, her wrath blazing forth with especial virulence against Rhadames, the betrayer of his country, his gods, and herself. Amonasro and Aïda escape, but Rhadames, filled with remorse, remains behind to yield himself to the High Priest.

ACT IV

Scene I—*A Room in the Palace. One Side, a Door Leading to Rhadames' Prison Cell*

Amneris is desperate *(Record 32)*; her rival has escaped and the one object of her passion is about to be tried as a traitor.

L'aborrita rivale **Pertile, Minghini-Cattaneo, La Scala Orch.** 11898-1.50

"Could he only love me!" she exclaims, "I would save him!" She decides to try, and the accused man is brought in. Exerting all the allurement of her beauty and the influence of any fear Rhadames might have of her power, she tries to persuade him to promise never to see Aïda again *(Record 33)*. He refuses. The music reaches a climax of great and passionate beauty as he declares that death is a blessing if it is for Aïda's sake. The love and pity of Amneris are transformed into hate and she calls on the gods for revenge.

Guards conduct Rhadames to the Judgment Room, while Amneris is left to suffer alone as she hears the punishment she has herself brought about pronounced on the man she loves. "Death approaches" *(Ohime, Morir mi sento!)* sings the unfortunate princess *(Record 34)*. As she turns she sees Ramfis and the Priests entering, solemnly, the Judgment Hall, and she cries, "Behold the fatal ministers of death—do not let me behold those white-robed phantoms!" But the law is stronger than the will of Amneris. Her lamentation, the stern voices of Ramfis and his Priests conducting the trial in the adjoining room, combine to produce a doubly tragic sense of foreboding *(Record 35)*. Amneris, in torture, covers her face with her hands; but she cannot shut out the terrible voices of Rhadames' accusers. Through it all, he remains silent. Finally the voice of Ramfis pronounces the sentence—

PERTILE AS RHADAMES

36

AÏDA: "CLASPED IN THY ARMS, LOVE, I RESOLVED TO PERISH!"

death by burial alive beneath the temple of the gods whose nobler attributes—faith and justice—Rhadames has offended. The Priests re-enter *(Record 36)* and again file impassively across the room, before the despairing eyes of Amneris. In a paroxysm of mingled wrath and anguish she denounces them, saying, " 'Tis they who offend Heaven with their cruelty," but the Priests sternly answer: "He is a traitor, he shall die!"

SCENE II

The scene shows the interior of the Temple of Vulcan, above the temple proper, where the chanting Priests intone their endless litanies; below, under the very statue of Osiris, the deity of the nether world, is the tomb where Rhadames has been condemned to die.

The hero believes himself alone, and his reflections are embodied in the incomparable music of the aria, "The fatal stone upon me now is closing."

La fatal pietra *(The Fatal Stone)* **Ponselle, Martinelli** 1744-1.50

His thoughts soon turn from his own unhappy fate to Aïda and he prays that happiness may be hers. He is startled by the thought that in the shadow of the tomb he sees Aïda. He is not mistaken, it is she! She says *(Record 37)* that she has come to partake of death beside him. Her father slain, his troops scattered, she has crept to earth like a stricken animal, her heart foreseeing the sentence to be passed upon Rhadames. Overwhelmed by the

37

thought of her meeting this untimely death Rhadames tries in vain to move away the heavy stone sealing the tomb. He sings, "To die! So pure and lovely," and Aïda repeats the melody, singing of the "Ecstasy of an immortal love."

Morir! si pura e bella! *(To Die! So Pure and Lovely!)* **Ponselle, Martinelli 1744-1.50**

Meanwhile the Priests above in the temple are going through their mysterious rites, solemnly chanting, "Oh mighty Phtha."

Together the lovers resign all hopes on earth and unite in a great duet, singing *(Record 38)*:

> Farewell, oh earth,
> Farewell, thou vale of sorrow,
> Brief dream of joy condemn'd to end in woe;
> To us now opens the sky,
> An endless morrow,
> Unshadow'd there eternally shall glow,
> Now opens the sky!

O terra addio *(Farewell, Oh Earth)* **Ponselle, Martinelli 1745-1.50**

The melody is in broad, calm phrases, suggestive of the limitless sweep of infinity, and peaceful as eternity. It is sung in unison—even the close identity of the voices being a symbol of the absorption of the lovers into an unending union free from all things earthly. Amneris, repentant and disconsolate, enters the temple above to weep and pray over the tomb of her beloved. Below, in the oppressive darkness of the tomb the lovers, clasped in one final, passionate embrace, sing their farewell to earth and its sorrows and together await Eternity.

Lande

THE GREAT CONSECRATION SCENE

ANDREA CHENIER

OPERA in four acts by Umberto Giordano; libretto by Lugia Illica. First produced at La Scala, Milan, March 28, 1896, and in the United States, at the Academy of Music, New York, November 13, 1896. Giordano, born in 1867, is among the more prominent modern Italian opera composers. *Andrea Chenier,* usually considered his best work, contains passages of lyric beauty and moments of dramatic force; not the old-fashioned type of opera with set "numbers," it follows rather the style of Verdi's later works. Illica's libretto gives us a picture of life in France just before and then during the Revolution, using as a basis for his fiction a historical character, the poet-patriot, Andrea Chenier (pronounced in French, *Ang-dreh-a' Shen-yea'*).

ACT I

As THE curtain rises, the servants of the Countess of Goigny are preparing for a ball. Among them is Gerard, afterward to become a revolutionary leader; he is filled with indignation at the sight of his aged father bent from years of servile labor for the aristocrats.

Mishkin

MARTINELLI AS ANDREA CHENIER

When the guests have arrived, a typical eighteenth century court pastoral is performed for their entertainment: while the chorus, dressed as shepherds and shepherdesses, sing idealized rustic music, the ballet mimic a rural love story in stately court fashion.

Among the guests is the poet, Andrea Chenier, whose work is growing popular just at this time. When the Countess asks him to improvise he refuses, but when her beautiful daughter, Madeleine, pleads with him he consents. She has rather coquettishly suggested the subject "Love," but he soon forgets this, and singing of the misery and suffering of the poor, he launches into a tirade against those in power in church and state.

Un di all'azzurro spazio *(Once O'er the Azure Fields)* **Giovanni Martinelli 6707-2.00**

All but Madeleine are outraged by the idealistic social and human creed shown in this dramatic song; and when a crowd of ragged men and women appear headed by Gerard, only to be ordered from the castle, Chenier follows them.

ACT II

CHENIER, now a revolutionary, is advised to flee by his friend, Roucher, who has managed to bring a passport for him. Chenier refuses to leave without Madeleine. Strangely enough, she arrives, incognito, and begs Chenier to save her from Gerard, now a revolutionary power and at-

39

tracted to her. They linger for a brief love scene, and are about to go, when they are caught by Gerard. While the rivals take to their swords, Madeleine is spirited away. Gerard, wounded, he believes mortally, magnanimously warns Chenier to flee from the wrath of his revolutionary enemies, and asks him to save Madeleine also. When the mob arrives on the scene a few minutes later, he tells them that his assailant is unknown to him.

ACT III

GERARD has recovered and is presiding over a revolutionary tribunal. A spy announces Chenier's arrest for having dared criticize Robespierre's cruelty. This is too good an opportunity to make away with a rival, and as he is about to put his signature to the fatal document, he laughingly asks himself, "An enemy of his country?" . . . he knows well that is the standard charge against one's personal enemies. Yet he hesitates for a moment recalling that it was Chenier's inspired verse that first awakened his own patriotism . . . now to satisfy his passions he sacrifices a friend. The struggle of honor and desire is beautifully expressed in the music . . . a bit of the *Marseillaise* is suggestively quoted by the orchestra. Finally desire triumphs and Gerard signs in a mood of cynicism.

Nemico della patria? *(An Enemy of His Country?)* **Titta Ruffo** 7153-2.00

Hurried before the tribunal, Chenier pleads for himself vehemently, saying that he, a soldier, fought for his country; if he must die, let him die fighting for it, not shamefully executed.

Madeleine also appears, and offers to give herself to Gerard to save Chenier's life. Gerard then pleads for the poet, but it is now too late, the mob thirsts for blood.

ACT IV

CONFINED in the gloomy St. Lazare prison, Chenier awaits execution while writing his last verses, "Come un bel di di Maggio" expressing his belief in truth and beauty.

Come un bel di di Maggio *(As Some Soft Day in May)* **Giovanni Martinelli** 6707-2.00

Madeleine having bribed her way, is ushered in by Gerard, who then goes for a last vain appeal to Robespierre himself. At dawn, the death tumbril comes for the prisoners. Madeleine, when the name of some condemned woman is called, rushes out beside Chenier and dies with her lover.

Landesman

A SCENE FROM "THE BARBER," AS PRESENTED BY THE CLEVELAND SYMPHONY ORCHESTRA

BARBER OF SEVILLE

(Il Barbiere di Siviglia)

COMIC opera in two acts by Gioacchino Antonio Rossini; text by Cesare Sterbini, based on the comedy by Beaumarchais. Produced, February 5, 1816, at the Argentina Theatre, Rome; New York, May 3, 1819, at the Park Theatre, in English.

Like many another opera that has come to be regarded as a masterpiece, "The Barber" was a total failure when first produced; urged by a variety of causes, the audience drowned out most of the opera in a storm of hisses, shouts, and catcalls. Rossini was present; in fact, sat in the front row. Calm soul that he was, he did not let this failure worry him; for the story goes that after the opera, the singers wished to console him and hurried to his house; there they found him, safely tucked in bed, fast asleep! The "Barber" soon became a success, however, and has deservedly held the stage to this day, for it is rich in melody, abounding in good spirits, and brilliant in its climaxes. Moreover, Rossini's melodies are so bubblingly spontaneous that the great skill with which they have been contrived to display the human voice is appreciated only by connoisseurs.

Many are the great artists who have distinguished themselves in this opera. For instance there was a performance at the Park Theatre, New York, November 29, 1825, in which three of the Garcias took part: Manuel (the elder) as Almaviva; Manuel (the younger) as Figaro; Signorina (afterwards the famous Malibran) as Rosina. Among the many prima donnas who have sung this latter rôle are Patti, Melba, Sembrich, Tetrazzini, and Galli-Curci, who appeared in "The Barber," January 1, 1917, at Chicago. Among the famous Figaros are Sammarco and Ruffo, and one of the most distinguished of Don Basilios is Chaliapin, who sang the rôle at the Metropolitan Opera House, in 1907, during his first visit to the United States.

CHARACTERS

COUNT ALMAVIVA *(Ahl-mah-vee'-vah)*	*Tenor*
BARTOLO *(Bahr'-toh-loh)*, physician	*Bass*
ROSINA *(Ro-zee'-nah)*, his ward	*Soprano*
BASILIO *(Bah-seel'-yoh)*, music master	*Bass*
FIGARO *(Fee'-gah-roh)*	*Baritone*

The action takes place at Seville, during the Seventeenth Century.

(The original Italian name of the opera, "Il Barbiere di Siviglia" is pronounced, *Eel Bahr-be-ay'reh dee See-veel'-yah.*)

The opera is preceded by a gay overture, quite in keeping with the action to follow, though, strangely enough, merely a revision of the overture to Rossini's earlier opera, "Elisabetta, Regina d'Inghilterra."

Overture *Toscanini, Philharmonic-Symphony Orchestra of New York* 7255-2.00

ACT I

SCENE I—*A Street in Seville*

THE handsome Count Almaviva is deeply in love with Rosina, the ward of the mean and suspicious old Doctor Bartolo. In the grey light of dawn, he comes with a band of musicians to serenade his beloved. The musicians play a ditty for her; then the Count himself sings to the accompaniment of their mandolins, "Ecco ridente in cielo."

Ecco ridente in cielo *(Dawn with Her Rosy Mantle)* **Tito Schipa** 1180-1.50

Then he pays his musicians, evidently generously, for they are moved to

Copy't Mishkin
THE BARBER

express their gratitude with such enthusiasm that surely they waken the sleeping Rosina if the Count's very lovely serenade has failed to do so. He seems inclined to linger near his loved one's house, even though she does not come out to thank him for the charming song, and as some one else seems to be coming down the street towards the house, making a great deal of noise for such an early hour, he conceals himself to see who this might be. The newcomer is none other than Figaro, the gay Barber of Seville. Besides being a barber, he is a sort of jack-of-all-trades, a so-called factotum. His profession gives him entry to the homes of people of all stations, and thus he is a convenient instrument for the execution of the intrigues of young lovers as well as of old rogues. He displays his loquacious character and the very gay life he leads in the brilliant and amazing rapid aria, "Largo al factotum."

Largo al factotum *(Room for the Factotum)* **Lawrence Tibbett** 7353-2.00

Room for the city's factotum here,
La, la la, la la, la.
I must be off to my shop, for the dawn is near,
La, la la, la, la.
What a merry life, what pleasure gay,
Awaits a barber of quality.
Ah, brave Figaro; bravo, bravissimo, bravo!
Of men, the happiest, sure, art thou, bravo.
La, la, la, la, la, la.

Oh! what a happy life, ready all hours of the night, and, by day, perpetually in bustle and motion. Razors, combs, lancets, scissors—behold them, at my command! All call me! all want me!—dames and maidens—old and young. My wig! cries one—my beard! shouts another—tend me! cries this—a love letter! whispers that. Figaro, Figaro! Heavens, what a crowd! Figaro, Figaro! Heavens, what a rush! One at a time, for mercy's sake! Figaro here, Figaro there: Figaro above: Figaro below. Always in a hurry—quick as lightning—the factotum of the town. Oh, what a life! A little work, but lots of fun, and a pocket always full of coin—what I get for my reputation. It's like this: without Figaro there's not a girl in Seville will marry; to me the little widows have recourse for a husband; I, under excuse for my comb by day, and under favor of my guitar by night, endeavor to please all in an honest way. Oh, what a life! What a life!

The Count now accosts Figaro and asks him to arrange a meeting with the fair Rosina, adding that his rank must not be known for he does not wish the girl to be influenced by the glamour of it. He has assumed the name of Lindor. Again, he serenades the favored one, this time with a tender, haunting strain, a tune of lovelorn youth, "Se il mio nome."

Se il mio nome (*If My Name You Would Know*) *Tito Schipa* 1180-1.50

The two plotters hide for a moment as Doctor Bartolo comes from his house. He gives strict orders to the servant that no one is to be admitted except the music master, Basilio. The Doctor hopes, with Basilio's aid, to arrange to marry Rosina this day; he likes the girl's dowry as much as herself. After he disappears down the street the Count and Figaro finish their plan. Troops are coming to the city, and Almaviva, disguised as a dragoon, may easily be billeted on the unwilling Bartolo!

SCENE II—*A Room in Bartolo's House*

Rosina, reading a note from her Lindor, is naturally enough rather agitated, and gives expression to her feelings in the delightfully brilliant coloratura aria, "Una voce poco fa."

Una voce poco fa (*A Little Voice I Hear*) *Amelita Galli-Curci* 7110-2.00 *Marion Talley* 6580-2.00 *Luisa Tetrazzini* 7883-2.00 *Lily Pons* 8870-2.00

Almost every resource known to the coloratura singer's art is employed in this glittering number. Rapid scales and arpeggios united with contrasts of soft and loud express with their bubbling gaiety the charm of the equally gay words.

A little voice I heard just now:
    Oh, it has thrill'd my very heart!
I feel that I am wounded sore;
    And Lindor 'twas who hurl'd the dart.
Yes, Lindor, dearest, shall be mine!
    I've sworn it, and we'll never part.
My guardian sure will ne'er consent;
    But I must sharpen all my wit:
Content at last, he will relent,
    And we, oh joy, be wedded yet.

From an Old Print

THE DISGUISED COUNT AND BARTOLO
IN SCENE II

When the highly spirited **Rosina** has run from the room, the guardian, Bartolo, enters with Basilio, the music master and master of intrigue. Bartolo is telling the music master—and acting matrimonial agent—that he wishes to marry Rosina himself—news doubtless already well known to Basilio. Her hand is also sought by one Count Almaviva, Basilio says, not suspecting that the Count and the serenader of the night before are one and the same. Basilio suggests that they start—a calumny—some disgraceful rumor that will make Rosina reject the Count. A calumny, says the bombastic Basilio, begins like a tempest howling through dreary forest caverns, until its full fury gathered, it falls, a terrific lightning-flash, on its helpless victim.

Thus calumny, a simple breath,
Engenders ruin, wreck and death,
And sinks the wretched man forlorn,
Beneath the lash of slander torn,
The victim of the public scorn.

This description of the devastating effect of gossip is set to music that grows, in an amazing crescendo, to a climax of fury; yet the music contains an element of humor suggesting that, in the mouth of Basilio, these words are rather a travesty.

La calunnia *(Slander's Whisper)* **Feodor Chaliapin 6783-2.00**

Rosina returns accompanied by Figaro, who tells her that her guardian plans to marry her himself. Laughing at the idea, she asks, significantly, who the young man is she has seen from the balcony. Figaro admits he is an excellent youth, but has one failing. "A failing?" cries the girl. "Yes, a great one," answers the factotum blandly, "he is dying of love." The girl, greatly interested, plies him with other questions. Figaro finally slyly admits that

44

the youth's adored one is named Rosina. "You are mocking," she cries, and the two make merry in a rollicking duet.

Rosina is impatient to see him, and Figaro assures her that her lover awaits only a line from her, then he will come. "I blush to do it," says the coy maiden. "Hurry up," answers Figaro, "write him a little note, hurry, hurry!" "Oh, here's one," she confesses, "I had already written it—how stupid!"

When Figaro has left with the letter, Bartolo enters in hopes of finding out about the serenader of that morning. He suspects that Figaro may be carrying messages between his ward and this stranger. The girl's blushes and the ink marks on her fingers betray her; she answers that she has used the ink as a salve

PONS AS ROSINA

for a small cut. He calls attention to a freshly trimmed quill pen and a missing sheet of paper: she replies that she used the paper to wrap up some sweets for a girl friend and the pen to design a flower for her embroidery. The old man's natural rage and the girl's impertinent answers are admirably characterized in the music of this scene.

A loud knocking is heard at the door—the Count, in his soldier's guise, pretending to be drunk. The old Doctor, penetrating the disguise, indignantly resists the order for the quartering of soldiers and pretends to go off to hunt for a license he has that grants him exemption from such imposition. This gives the lovers a brief moment to exchange words, but soon soldiers summoned by the sly Bartolo arrive. They arrest this peace-disturbing intruder, but immediately release him when he secretly reveals his identity to the astonished officer.

ACT II

SCENE—*A Room in Bartolo's House*

THOUGH the soldier scheme has fallen through, Figaro soon invents another by which the Count may obtain entry to Bartolo's dwelling. As the curtain rises, we find the old Doctor wondering if the drunken soldier may not be an emissary of Count Almaviva. He is interrupted by a stranger, none other than the Count himself, but this time disguised as a music master. He explains that Don Basilio is ill, and that he has come in his place to give Rosina her music lesson. He makes himself known in a melodious greeting, "Pace e gioia"—"Heaven Send You Peace and Joy." Neither is at hand.

To allay the suspicions that begin to arise in Bartolo's mind, the Count, in a bold stroke of daring, produces the note written by Rosina to her

ACT II—THE BARBER OF SEVILLE
(CLEVELAND SYMPHONY ORCHESTRA PRODUCTION)

charming Lindor. Asserting that he found it at the inn where Count Almaviva is staying, he offers to make Rosina believe she is the Count's dupe. The idea pleases Bartolo; in producing such a bit of slander, this strange music-master has proved himself a worthy pupil of Don Basilio! Rosina enters for her lesson. Rossini wrote a special trio for this scene, but unfortunately the manuscript is lost. Therefore, the artist singing the rôle of Rosina usually interpolates an air of her own choosing, thereby producing, often enough, the strangest effects of anachronism.

SCHIPA AS ALMAVIVA

Figaro arrives, declaring, in spite of Bartolo's remonstrance, that this is his day for a shave. When Bartolo gives him his keys to go fetch some linen, Figaro contrives to steal the key to the balcony and save it for future use. Don Basilio, the real music teacher, appears. The Count is resourceful, however, and reminding Bartolo of their scheme to deceive Rosina, he points out that the matrimonial agent-music teacher must be disposed of. Doctor Bartolo immediately asks the startled Basilio how he comes to be walking abroad in a fever! When the Count slips a purse in his hand, the wondering Basilio is convinced that he is really ill, at least that they want him to be so, and diplomatically takes hasty leave. The lovers plot their elopement while Figaro detains Bartolo at shaving with generous splashes of soap in his eyes. Finally the suspicious Bartolo approaches the preoccupied lovers and discovers that he is again being duped. The three conspirators laugh at him and run out, followed by the Doctor, purple with rage.

Lumière
GALLI CURCI AS ROSINA

Bartolo, driven to play his last card, shows Rosina the note, saying that her supposedly devoted Lindor is conspiring to give her up to Count Almaviva. Justly infuriated, Rosina offers to marry Bartolo at once, reveals the plan to elope and bids him have Lindor and Figaro arrested when they arrive. As soon as he has gone to bring the police and the marriage broker, the Count and Figaro enter by means of the stolen key. Rosina greets them with a storm of reproaches, accusing Lindor of pretending to love her in order to sacrifice her to the vile Count Almaviva. . . . The Count, delighted that Rosina would prefer a true though poor lover to an exalted though false husband, now reveals his real identity and the lovers are soon embracing amid a shower of blessings from Figaro.

They are interrupted by Don Basilio, who has returned in the office of notary and marriage broker, to unite Rosina and Bartolo, but with the aid of a pistol he is persuaded to marry Rosina to the Count instead. When Doctor Bartolo arrives a few minutes later with the police, it is too late, for the marriage contract has been signed, and Rosina is the wife of the distinguished Count Almaviva. The Doctor decides to accept his hard luck philosophically while the irrepressible Figaro showers on all present his garrulous good wishes.

47

AN OPEN-AIR PERFORMANCE OF THE BARTERED BRIDE AT ZOPPSOT

THE BARTERED BRIDE

COMIC opera in three acts; music by Friedrich Smetana; libretto by R. Sabina. First produced, May 30, 1866, in Prague; first performance in the United States, February 19, 1909, at the Metropolitan Opera House, New York. In the original Czech the opera is named "Prodaná Nevésta"; it is frequently called by the German title "Die Verkaufte Braut."

The Bartered Bride is one of the most delightful of comic operas, full of vivacious melody and abounding in local color. Moreover, it has an historic interest as it is one of the great works by the founder of the Bohemian nationalist school. It has been recorded in its entirety by the National Opera Company of Prague, under the direction of Prof. Otakar Ostrčil, in Masterpiece Album M-193. A complete English libretto, indicating also the occurrence of each record, accompanies the album. The Overture, with its merry folk tunes and sprightly fugato, deserves its great popularity as a concert number.

THE PLOT

MARIE, daughter of the rich farmer, Kruschina, is most unhappy, for today, the anniversary of the consecration of the village church, she must accept a suitor of her parents' choice. She loves only Hans, but as his ancestry is unknown her parents refuse to consider him. Marie's parents arrive with the marriage broker, Kezal, who wishes to unite Marie to Wenzel, the son of the rich peasant Micha. This pleases Marie's parents and they joyfully consent in spite of the girl's protests.

Wenzel comes in person to the village to propose to Marie, whom he has never seen. Thus when he happens to meet her and, as an entire stranger, starts to flirt with her, the quick-witted girl, disgusted with this stammering coxcomb, whom she recognizes as her chosen husband, tells him that Kruschina's Marie is in love with some one else and that he should not allow himself to marry her. The marriage broker, Kezal, tries to persuade Hans to give up his love affair with Marie; he offers him one hundred, then three hundred, florins to do so. Hans accepts this offer on condition that Marie shall marry none other than the son of Micha's wife. This is agreeable to Kezal as he understands it. The bystanders are justly disgusted at the light heart with which Hans has sold his bride.

Wenzel has fallen in love with a Spanish dancer, the danseuse of a troupe of acrobats, and when his parents demand that he marry Marie he refuses. When Hans appears and is upbraided by Marie for his faithlessness, he summons the villagers and declares to all present that it is his wish that Marie should be the wife of Micha's son. In despair, the girl says she will marry Wenzel as her parents desire. All are astonished until Micha appears and recognizes in Hans a long lost son by his first marriage. As Marie now can very properly belong to Hans by the terms of the contract with Kezal, who is out his three hundred florins, the lovers are happily united.

Furiant *Eugene Ormandy-Minneapolis Symphony Orchestra* 1761-1.50
Overture *Stock-Chicago Symphony Orchestra* 1555-1.50
Dance of the Comedians *Ormandy-Minneapolis Symphony Orch.* 8694-2.00
Polka *Ormandy-Minneapolis Symphony Orch.* 8694-2.00
Prodaná Nevěsta (Smetana) Complete *National Opera Company of Prague, cond. by Otakar Ostrčil Album M-193* (11617-11631) *2 Volumes AM-193* (11632-11646) *Price $22.50*

Bain
RETHBERG AS MARIE

Kaufmann & Fabry Co.—Chicago

THE ATTIC

LA BOHÊME

OPERA in four acts; music by Giacomo Puccini; text by Giuseppe Giacosa and Luigi Illica, founded on Henri Murger's book, *La Vie de Bohême*. Produced at the Teatro Reggio, Turin, Italy, February 1, 1896. First performed in the Western Hemisphere, at Buenos Aires, 1896. First played in the United States, at San Francisco, March, 1898, by the Royal Italian Opera Company.

To many people this is the most attractive of all of Puccini's many excellent works; one can well understand its being such a well-loved opera, for it combines the gay and the pathetic into a most fascinating picture of student life in the Latin Quarter of Paris during the early part of the nineteenth century.

LA BOHÊME COMPLETE ON VICTOR RECORDS

MUSIC lovers can now hear this delightful masterpiece at their leisure and in the quiet and comfort of their own homes, for it has been recorded for Victor by artists, chorus, and members of the orchestra of the world-famous La Scala Opera House, in Milan, Italy. The performance, conducted by Maestro Carlo Sabajno, and complete save for conventional cuts, has been recorded on thirteen Victor Records and is issued as album M-35 (and in automatic sequence, AM-35) in the Musical Masterpiece

50

Series, priced at $19.50. The accompanying description of the opera is keyed to these records, and the distribution of rôles is given in the following cast of

CHARACTERS

RUDOLPH, *a poet*	Sr. Giorgini, *Tenor*
MARCEL, *a painter*	Sr. Badini, *Baritone*
COLLINE, *a philosopher*	Sr. Manfrini, *Bass*
SCHAUNARD, *a musician*	Sr. Baracchi, *Baritone*
BENOIT, *an importunate landlord*	Sr. Baccaloni, *Bass*
PARPIGNOL, *a vendor of toys*	Sr. Nessi, *Tenor*
ALCINDORO, *a state councilor and follower of Musetta*	Sr. Baccaloni, *Bass*
MUSETTA, *a grisette*	Sra. Vitulli, *Soprano*
MIMI, *a maker of artificial flowers*	Sra. Torri, *Soprano*

Students, Workgirls, Vendors, Soldiers, Waiters, Children, etc.

The action takes place in Paris, about the year 1830.

ACT I

SCENE—*In the Attic*

THE garret home of the inseparable quartet—Rudolph, poet; Marcel, painter; Colline, philosopher; Schaunard, musician—is certainly large enough for such a family, and it is so sparsely furnished that it seems doubly large. Its fireplace, devoid of fire, a few chairs, a table, a small cupboard, a few books, many packs of cards and an artist's easel, seem quite swallowed up in the wide, empty space of this immense attic. While Marcel, busily painting at his never-finished canvas, "The Passage of the Red Sea," stops to blow on his hands from time to time to warm them, Rudolph, the poet, gazes through the window over the snow-capped roofs of Paris *(Record 2)*. Marcel breaks the silence by saying that he feels as though the Red Sea were flowing down his back; Rudolph replies with another jest, and when Marcel seizes a chair to break it up for firewood, the poet offers instead the manuscript of one of his own plays. They burn it one act at a time, feasting their eyes on the flames, but gaining scant warmth. The acts burn quickly, and Colline, who enters stamping with cold, declares that since brevity is the soul of wit, this drama is indeed sparkling. Soon Schaunard arrives *(Record 2)* with errand boys bringing wood for the fire, food for the table, wine and money—all in great plenty. He explains to his enraptured companions that he has been giving music lessons to a rich English amateur—this was before the days of the American tourist invasion of Paris. The festivities are cut short *(Record 3)* by the entry of the landlord who, after the manner of his kind, is after rent, long overdue. Reassured at the sight of money on the table, he joins the comrades in a friendly drink; they refill his glass several times, and as he becomes jovial and talkative, he boasts of his affairs with women in disreputable resorts. At this the young men feign great horror *(Record 4)* . . . the honor of their house is polluted by such talk . . . he a married man, too . . .

51

they seize the landlord, and push him out of the room. "I have paid the last quarter's rent," remarks Marcel as he locks the door.

When his companions go off to the Café Momus to celebrate, Rudolph stays behind to work, promising to join them in five minutes. His struggles at getting himself settled at his writing are interrupted by a timid knock at the door *(Record 5)*. It is a young girl, a neighbor, who has come seeking a light for her candle. As she enters the room she is seized with a fit of coughing and swoons. Rudolph supports her, and with the aid of a little water and a sip from a small glass of wine revives her. Rudolph lights her candle. She thanks him, and bidding him a good evening, leaves. Suddenly she remembers that when she fainted she dropped her key. As she returns for it she pauses at the threshold and the wind blows out her candle. Rudolph hurries to her with his candle, and it also goes out in the draught. Left in the dark they grope along the floor seeking the key. Rudolph finds it and quietly drops it in his pocket, then, pretending still to be searching but really guided by her voice, he approaches her. Their hands meet, "Ah,"

Che gelida manina *(Your Tiny Hand Is Frozen)* **Alessandro Ziliani 8872-2.00 Enrico Caruso *6003-2.00 Giovanni Martinelli 6595-2.00**

cries the surprised girl, rising to her feet. "Your hand is frozen," says Rudolph tenderly *(Record 6)*.

Then, after adding that it is useless to hunt for the key now in the darkness, he starts to tell her about himself.

Racconto di Rodolfo *(Rudolph's Narrative)*

"I am . . . I am a poet!" he boldly declares, and adds that though poor his dreams and castles in the air make him in spirit the owner of millions. Then in a melody hauntingly romantic and passionate he tells her that since she has appeared, his dreams and visions have all vanished, but he regrets not their loss, for hope has taken their place. And now that he has kept no secrets from her, he asks, at the very end of this appealing aria, "Who are you? Won't you tell?"

"They call me Mimi," she replies naïvely. Continuing her simple but very charming aria, she tells him how she makes artificial flowers for a living, though meanwhile she yearns for the blossoms of springtime and the green meadows of the country *(Record 7)*.

Mi chiamano Mimi *(My Name is Mimi)* **Lucrezia Bori 6790-2.00**

Rudolph is entranced by the charm of her frail beauty and sympathizes with her desire for a fuller, richer life. The voices of Marcel, Colline and Schaunard are heard calling to Rudolph from the street below *(Record 8)*. Rudolph and Mimi, as they stand by the window watching them go away merrily to the Café Momus, are suddenly enveloped in a flood of moonlight. Gazing at this fragile beauty before him, Rudolph is filled by a new emotion; "O enchanting vision!" he sings. Then, overpowered by the ecstasy of their mutual new-found love, the two unite in impassioned song.

O soave fanciulla *(Oh Lovely Maiden)* **Alessandro Ziliani, Mafalda Favero, La Scala Orch. Milan 8872-2.00**

Mimi shyly begs Rudolph to take her with him to the Café Momus, where he is to rejoin his friends, and as the lovers go out the door and down the stairs we hear them continuing to sing the melody of their love duet.

ACT II

Scene—*A Students' Café in Paris*

THIS being Christmas Eve, the street before the Café Momus, a typical students' restaurant in the Latin Quarter, is filled with a busy crowd. There are street-vendors, crying their goods; students, working girls and citizens passing across the scene and calling to one another; people at the café giving their orders to the bustling waiters . . . a joyful, continuous activity, pictured in the music by bits of chorus, snatches of recitative, and an orchestral accompaniment that runs through the varied patterns of the scene, and like a golden thread binds them together *(Record 9)*. Rudolph walks to and fro among the crowd with Mimi, and takes her to a milliner, where he buys her a new hat. Then the lovers go to the table which the three comrades, Colline, Marcel, and Schaunard, have had set outside of the café.

Parpignol, a vendor of toys, is heard approaching in the distance. Soon

53

SCENE FROM ACT II

(Record 10) he bursts onto the stage with his pushcart decorated with lanterns. He is followed by a troop of children, laughing, shouting and singing. A moment later he disappears down the street amid the cries and calls of mothers trying in vain to keep their children from following him.

No sooner has he disappeared than the shopwomen along the street begin to cry out at some new excitement *(Record 11)*. "It is Musetta," they say. "Some stammering old dotard is with her." Musetta and Marcel have loved, quarreled and parted; now she has put up with the aged but wealthy Alcindoro. This incongruous pair take a table near by. Musetta and Marcel attempt to appear indifferent to one another, with little success. In a bold stroke of daring Musetta sings a waltz song, sings it deliberately at Marcel, to make him aware, without arousing the suspicions of her aged escort, that she is still in love with him *(Record 12)*.

Valse di Musetta *(Musetta's Waltz)* **Lucrezia Bori** 1333-1.50

The melody floats lightly and airily along, a perfect expression of Musetta's gay, light-hearted nature. The voices of the other characters—Alcindoro trying to interfere, Mimi and Rudolph continuing to avow their love to one another, Marcel agitated at feeling his former love for Musetta reviving, and Colline and Schaunard wondering what will happen next—the voices of all these characters expressing their varied feelings unite with the fascinating melody of Musetta's waltz to form a climax of the most enchanting beauty. Musetta cleverly pretends that her shoe has hurt her foot, and that she can no longer stand; Alcindoro has to hurry away to the nearest shoemaker to have the shoe repaired. As soon as he has gone *(Record 13)*, she

54

runs to Marcel, the reunited lovers kiss, then she joins the five friends at their table and the elaborate supper ordered by Alcindoro is served to them with their own.

The distant sound of a band is heard and the townspeople run excitedly across the square trying to discover by which street the band is approaching. Amid the confusion the waiter brings the bill to the Bohemians. They are staggered by the amount. Schaunard searches in vain for his purse. Meanwhile the band is coming nearer and nearer, and the people along the street grow more and more excited. Musetta boldly comes to the rescue of her friends . . . she tells the waiter to add the two bills together, her escort, the old Alcindoro, will pay them both when he returns.

The patrol, headed by a drum-major, marches on the scene, and a great crowd of people rush in to watch. Musetta, without one shoe, cannot walk, so Marcel and Colline lift her to their shoulders, and carry her off triumphantly down the street. The crowd, seeing her borne thus, give her a regular ovation. The senile old Alcindoro comes running in with a pair of new shoes for Musetta. His bird has flown with her gay companions; but the bill is there for him to pay.

ACT III

SCENE—*A Gate to the City of Paris*

A COLD, dreary winter's dawn at one of the toll gates to the city *(Record 14)*. At one side of the snow-blanketed square is a tavern. In front of it hangs Marcel's picture of the "Red Sea" as a signboard. From within come sounds of revelry. Outside the gate is a motley crowd of scavengers, milk women, truckmen and farmers with their produce, demanding to be admitted. One of the group of customs officers seated warming themselves at a brazier, finally saunters over to the gate and lets them in. Musetta's voice is heard from the tavern. A crowd of peasant women enter declaring their butter, cheese, eggs and chickens to the officials. From a little side street that leads from the Latin Quarter comes Mimi, shivering with cold and shaken with frequent fits of coughing. She asks one of the officers where Marcel may be found. He directs her to the tavern.

Marcel comes to her immediately, greets her, exclaiming, "Mimi!" *(Record 15)*. "It is I," she replies. Marcel says that now he and Musetta live at this tavern, for he has found it more profitable painting signs than pictures, and Musetta gives music lessons. Mimi has come to him for help. She can no longer endure living with Rudolph, his jealousy and the resulting constant quarrels make life unbearable. In a lovely duet with her, Marcel

"FAREWELL SWEET LOVE"

55

shows his sympathy for her distress and his concern for the illness revealed by her frequent fits of coughing. When Rudolph, who has been in the tavern, comes out to hunt for Marcel, Mimi hides to avoid seeing him *(Record 16)*. She hears him telling Marcel that he wishes to give her up because of their frequent quarrels *(Record 17)*. Then another fit of coughing reveals her presence; Rudolph rushes to embrace her, for his love is partially aroused at the sight of her pale beauty. She breaks away from his embrace, however, and sings him a sad but beautiful farewell *(Record 18)*.

Addio! *(Farewell)* *Lucrezia Bori* 6561-2.00

In the meantime, Marcel has entered the tavern and caught Musetta flirting. This starts a quarrel that brings the couple to the street. "Farewell, sweet love" *(Addio, dolce svegliare)*, sing Rudolph and Mimi, while Musetta and Marcel continue their quarrel that threatens to become more than merely verbal *(Record 19)*. The difference in temperament of the two women—Mimi, sad, gentle and weak, Musetta bold and disputatious—and the difference in effect on the men, are clearly portrayed in the music. "Viper!" "Toad!" Marcel and Musetta call to each other as they part; while the delicate Mimi laments, "Ah! that our winter night might last forever," and she and Rudolph unite in singing, "Our time for parting is when the roses blow." Thus is the youthful romance of Mimi and Rudolph sadly, pathetically, broken.

ACT IV

Scene—*The Attic of the Bohemians as in Act I*

Back at their former home, Rudolph and Marcel are leading a "melancholy existence." Rudolph is at the table pretending to write, Marcel at his easel pretending to paint. Neither can work for thinking of his beloved.

Peyton

BORI AS MIMI

Rudolph tells Marcel that he passed Musetta on the street; she was well dressed and seemed happy *(Record 20)*. Marcel tries to act indifferent. But he has seen Mimi. She was riding in grand state in a carriage, like a duchess. Rudolph likewise attempts unsuccessfully to conceal his emotion. A renewed attempt to work proves useless. When Rudolph is not looking, Marcel takes from his pocket a bunch of ribbons that belonged to Musetta and kisses it. Meanwhile, Rudolph, soliloquizing, sings, "Ah! Mimi, false one! Ah! wonderful days forever passed!"

Ah, Mimi, tu più *(Ah, Mimi, False One!)* *Gigli, de Luca* 8069-2.00 *Caruso and Scotti* *8000-2.00

56

Marcel, likewise soliloquizing, wonders why his brush will not paint what it is supposed to, but instead, against his will, makes the dark eyes and red lips of Musetta. As Rudolph takes out Mimi's little bonnet and gazes regretfully at it, the voices of the two men join in a duet, melodious but filled with deep emotion.

They pretend to brighten up as Colline and Schaunard enter with some rather scanty provisions *(Record 21)*. The very poverty of the meal is made light of by the men in the mock solemnity of a great banquet with which they eat. Then a dance is suggested; Rudolph and Marcel entertain with a quadrille, but this is cut short by a fierce duel that develops between Colline and Schaunard, firetongs and poker being their weapons. Just as this develops into a riot as the two dancers encircle the duelists, Musetta bursts in. . . . She brings bad news . . . Mimi, who is with her, is very ill *(Record 22)*.

They help Mimi into the room and place her tenderly on Rudolph's bed. Past quarrels are now forgotten by Rudolph and Mimi: they are in each other's arms. Musetta suggests to the others that they give Mimi some food; they are forced to confess there is none in their house, not even coffee. Mimi asks for a muff, her hands are so cold; Rudolph attempts to warm them in his. Musetta gives her earrings to Marcel and tells him to sell them to buy medicine and summon a doctor *(Record 23)*; then, stirred by a sudden recollection, Musetta goes to get her own muff for Mimi.

Deeply touched by Musetta's sacrifice, Colline decides to sell his own much-loved overcoat so as to provide a few delicacies for Mimi. He bids farewell to the coat in a song of great pathos yet with a touch of whimsical humor that is a relief from the prevailing gloom.

> Faded friend, so tried and trusty,
> We must part, you and I:
> For never yet your back did you bow
> To rich man or mighty!

He kisses the coat, then steals softly away with Schaunard to sell it. "Have they gone?" asks Mimi faintly *(Record 24)*.

Death Scene—Part I—*Sono andati (Have they gone?)* Part II—*Oh Dio Mimi (Oh God! Mimi!)* **Bori, Schipa 8068-2.00**

Then she continues, "I only pretended to be asleep, for I wanted to be alone with you, beloved." The lovers unite in a beautiful duet, recalling other days spent together *(Record 25)*, while melodies of their first meeting are heard, poignantly suggestive. . . . Suddenly, half suffocated with another fit of coughing, Mimi sinks back fainting, and Rudolph cries out in great alarm, "Oh God! Mimi!" At this moment Schaunard returns and excitedly asks what the trouble is. Mimi revives, and smiling faintly says that it is nothing, she is better.

Musetta and Marcel enter cautiously, bringing a muff and medicine *(Record 26)*. Mimi eagerly seizes the muff and Musetta quickly assures her that Rudolph bought it for her. Mimi becomes very faint and seems to fall asleep. Marcel heats the medicine; the other men whisper together; Musetta prays. Rudolph is reassured as Mimi seems to sleep so peacefully. Schaunard tiptoes over to her; he sees that Mimi is dead. Terrifically shocked, he whispers the terrible news to Marcel. The music of this scene is of the most touching simplicity. Then, as Rudolph, who has been talking to Musetta, notices the actions of his friends, and suddenly realizes what has happened, chords of the most poignantly tragic force are heard. Musetta kneels at the foot of the bed, while Schaunard, overwhelmed, sinks into a chair. Colline stands dazed . . . Marcel turns away to hide his grief. . . . Rudolph rushes to the bed, throws himself despairingly across it and sobs, "Mimi! Mimi!"

Fantasia—Parts I and II *Victor Symphony Orchestra* 35871-1.25

HELEN JEPSON AS MIMI

THE CARNIVAL AT PRESBURG—ACT II

THE BOHEMIAN GIRL

OPERA in three acts; music by Michael William Balfe; text by Bunn. First produced at Drury Lane, London, November 27, 1843. First performance in the United States, November 25, 1844.

The never-failing melodic charm of "The Bohemian Girl" is not Bohemian but Celtic in origin, at least when geographically considered. The composer, Michael William Balfe, was born in Dublin in 1808, the son of a dancing master. Early proficiency as a violinist ripened into the greater gifts of musical composition, with a special faculty for writing simple but effective tunes. Of Balfe's many operatic works, "The Bohemian Girl" is by far the most famous; its popularity is justified by its melodious character. The composer's fame extended all over Europe. "The Bohemian Girl" won him the French decoration of "Chevalier of the Legion of Honor" as well as other honors from their governments. He lived chiefly in England, where he died in 1870.

The action is supposed to take place at Presburg, Hungary, during the early Nineteenth Century.

ACT I

THADDEUS, an exile from Poland, is pursued by Austrian troops, and to prevent his capture joins a band of gypsies, headed by Devilshoof. While the tribe is crossing the estate of the governor of Presburg, Count Arnheim, a wild stag happens to attack the Governor's little daughter, Arline. Thaddeus rescues her. In gratitude, the Count invites the gypsies to his hunting dinner. During the festivities Thaddeus refuses to drink the health of the Emperor and is about to be attacked by the Count's infuriated friends when Devilshoof intervenes. Thus Thaddeus is able to get away while the gypsy chief is himself imprisoned in the castle. As soon as the feast is resumed, however, Devilshoof escapes and also manages to steal the infant Arline. He is pursued but makes good his escape by pushing away a tree trunk that is the only bridge across a ravine.

ACT II

T WELVE years have passed and the Gypsies have again returned to Presburg. Some of them rob Florestine, the drunken nephew of the Count, of his watch and a valuable medallion. Arline has now grown to be a beautiful young woman and Thaddeus has fallen in love with her. Arline tells him of a dream she has had in the song, "I Dreamt I Dwelt in Marble Halls."

> I dreamt that I dwelt in marble halls,
>   With vassals and serfs at my side,
> And of all who assembled within those walls,
>   That I was the hope and the pride,
> I had riches too great to count,
>   Could boast of a high ancestral name;
> But I also dreamt, which pleas'd me most,
>   That you lov'd me still the same.

The Gypsy queen, who is in love with Thaddeus, tries to separate the lovers, but as Queen of the Gypsies is obliged to unite them in a Gypsy marriage ceremony. Seeking revenge, in the next scene, the Carnival at Presburg, she contrives to have Arline arrested for having stolen the medallion from Florestine. Arline is taken before the Count for trial. Just preceding her appearance the Count has been thinking of his lost daughter while singing "The Heart Bow'd Down."

> The heart bow'd down by weight of woe,
>   To weakest hopes will cling,
> To thought and impulse while they flow,
>   That can no comfort bring;
> With those exciting scenes will blend,
>   O'er pleasure's pathway thrown;
> But mem'ry is the only friend
>   That grief can call its own.

Arline is brought in, and during the course of the examination the Count recognizes her as his daughter when he notices the scar on her arm resulting from the wound made by the stag.

ACT III

A RLINE, restored, nevertheless pines for her Gypsy lover and is overjoyed when Devilshoof contrives to bring him to her chamber. Thaddeus recalls their former happiness with the song, "Then You'll Remember Me."

When other lips and other hearts
 Their tales of love shall tell
In language whose excess imparts
 The pow'r they feel so well;
There may perhaps in such a scene
 Some recollection be
Of days that have as happy been,
 Then you'll remember me.

The lovers are interrupted by the Count's approach, and Thaddeus hides in a closet as guests arrive for a reception in honor of the newly-found heiress. The Queen, still bent on revenge, now enters, closely veiled, and in a dramatic denunciation reveals the hiding place of Thaddeus. Arline pleads earnestly for her lover, but the enraged Count bids him depart. Before leaving, Thaddeus shows that he is of noble blood, and Arline reminds her father that Thaddeus once saved her life. The Count relents and all would end happily but for the vengeful Gypsy Queen, who secretly directs one of her followers to shoot Arline. Again Devilshoof intervenes, just in time to turn the rifle towards the Queen, who falls as the shot is fired. The safety and happiness of Arline and Thaddeus being assured, the opera closes with a scene of rejoicing.

Gems from The Bohemian Girl *Victor Light Opera Company* 35819-1.25

"GLORY TO CZAR BORIS!"

BORIS GODOUNOW

OPERA in three (or four) acts; music by Modeste Moussorgsky; libretto after Pushkin and Karamzin, by the composer. First produced (in its entirety) January 24, 1874, at the Maryinsky Theatre (Imperial Opera House), St. Petersburg. First performance in the United States, November 19, 1913, at the Metropolitan Opera House, New York.

"Boris Godounow" has long been regarded as the masterpiece of that strange, erratic genius, Moussorgsky, who lived a life of poverty and died before achieving all that his talents promised or his own enthusiasm desired. One of the most gifted of Russian composers, he was exceedingly sincere in his ideals of what should constitute an operatic work. Ardently patriotic, he wished above all to write a truly national opera, carried out along the lines first indicated by Glinka. Moussorgsky was, moreover, a musical realist; he cared little for beauty for beauty's sake, he wanted above all else, truth. In addition, Moussorgsky was democratic in his political views—the people should be the hero.

In Pushkin's play, to a large extent historically true, Moussorgsky found a perfect subject for the expression of his ideal, and undaunted by the vast scale on which the drama was built, or by his own slight training in the technique of musical composition, he set to work. Many of greater experience would have failed: he succeeded through enthusiasm, inspiration, and native ability.

On first acquaintance, "Boris" appears to be built upon a series of historical scenes, rather than upon a unified plot. More intimate knowledge, however, reveals a most remarkable fundamental unity underlying all its wealth of scattered though not irrelevant detail—the dual tragedy of a man and of a nation. In accordance with Moussorgsky's ideal of realism, there are no set arias, nothing for vocal display; there are some songs, introduced for atmosphere as are songs in a Shakespearian drama, for instance. Thus the vocal parts consist largely of a remarkably expressive recitative—expressive to a degree seldom attained except by Moussorgsky. The people being the hero are given great prominence by means of individualized choruses. Orchestral introductions are reduced to a minimum; the orchestra, important as a background for the voices, remains a background. And the opera being national, the music is distinctly Russian in character. All this is cleverly achieved by the ever-national Moussorgsky. He uses Russian folk tunes (only a few, however), melodies in the style of Russian folk song, and characteristically Russian harmonies, such as had been developed in the modal music sung in the Russian Church liturgy. In this connection it is interesting to compare Moussorgsky's treatment of a Russian folk song in the Coronation scene, with Beethoven's splendid, though thoroughly "European" development of the same melody in the finale of his great Quartet in E Minor, Opus 59, No. 2. During the scenes in Poland, however, Moussorgsky intentionally introduces for the sake of local color typical Polish dance rhythms, and in the Polonaise, a bit of melody in the Lydian mode—a characteristic feature of Polish folk-music. Leading motives, too, are used with profound psychological effect, although not in the complex manner of Wagner.

As Moussorgsky first wrote the opera, the committee of the Imperial Opera House refused it, and acting upon their advice, the composer set to work, added a "prima donna" part, enlarged the rôle of Gregory, and wrote the "Revolutionary Scene." To compensate for this, much was omitted, even from the first edition of the printed score. In this revised form the opera was produced (January 24, 1874) by the Imperial Opera with great success—three acts had been given at a benefit performance there in February, 1873. The great length of the opera, together with other real or imagined defects, led to a revision by Rimsky-Korsakow after Moussorgsky's death. This was a labor of love for Rimsky-Korsakow, who was an intimate friend of Moussorgsky. He smoothed out what he believed to be undue harshness in the orchestration, developed in a more orderly, musicianly manner some of the composer's ideas, as, for instance, the introduction to the "Coronation Scene." He omitted scenes, and changed the sequence of others. In his second revision, published a few years later, Rimsky-Korsakow restored much that he had previously omitted. Recently the complete opera as Moussorgsky wrote it has been published. It reveals a wealth of beautiful and effective detail, and elements of musical structure lending unity to the work—features unfortunately lost in the revised versions. Rimsky-Korsakow's revision has been the cause of much criticism. There are scholars who believe that on the whole his version is a vast improvement over the original: others maintain that Rimsky-Korsakow's is a much emasculated score: that the original is not only more daring in harmony and orchestration, but also more effective dramatically. The public has had little opportunity to judge, for up to the present, Rimsky-Korsakow's version has been generally used in performances. Moreover, frequently the "Prologue" of the score is named Scene I of Act I in performance; sometimes the order of scenes is changed from that which Moussorgsky or Rimsky-Korsakow assigned them; these customs do not facilitate the telling of the story in a manner adapted to all productions. Therefore in the following description

Mishkin

CHALIAPIN AS BORIS

63

of the opera we are adhering to the arrangement of scenes adopted by the Metropolitan Opera Company of New York.

As though all the splendor of Moussorgsky's masterpiece were not enough, a star has arisen in the musical firmament who has made of the rôle of Boris one of the most remarkable characterizations on the modern stage, either in drama or opera. To those who have witnessed Feodor Chaliapin portray this character, Boris and Chaliapin are nearly synonymous. Fortunate it is that his poignant and amazingly realistic interpretation of the great death scene has been recorded by Victor and thus preserved for music lovers of all times.

CHARACTERS

Boris Godounow *(Boh'-reess Goh'-doo-noff)*	*Bass*
Xenia, *his daughter*	*Soprano*
Theodore, *his son*	*Mezzo-Soprano*
Marina, *daughter of the Voyevode of Sandomir*	*Mezzo-Soprano*
Prince Shouisky *(Shoois'-ky)*	*Tenor*
Gregory, *a novice, afterwards the Pretender Dimitri*	*Tenor*
Varlaam and Missail, *vagabond monks*	*Bass and Tenor*
Pimenn *(Pee'-men), a monk and chronicler*	*Bass*
Tchelkalov, *secretary of the Duma*	*Baritone*

A Nurse, a Simpleton, Two Jesuits, Chorus of Boyards and People, etc.

The action takes place in Russia and Poland, 1598-1605.

ACT I

SCENE I

BORIS, a privy councilor of the Czar Feodor, has caused to be assassinated the Czar's younger brother and only heir, Dimitri. At the death of the Czar he pretends not to desire the throne and takes residence in the Novo-dievitch Convent at Moscow. At his secret order, however, officers have summoned the populace to the square before the convent and with threats and blows compel them to beg Boris to accept the crown.

After a brief orchestral prelude the curtain rises. At the stern command of an officer, the people, kneeling before the convent, sing their supplication: "Why hast thou abandoned us? Mercy, oh, father!"

> **Ma perchè tu ci abbandoni?** *(Opening Chorus)* **Royal Opera Chorus and Covent Garden Orchestra** 9399-1.50

Then Tchelkalov, the secretary of the Duma, comes before the people, saying that Boris is inflexible.

> **Moscoviti! Boris è inflessibil!** *(Pilgrims' Chorus)* **Royal Opera Chorus and Covent Garden Orchestra** 9399-1.50

Therefore Tchelkalov counsels them to pray that God may move the spirit of Boris to come to the rescue of Russia. Now, as the light of the setting sun falls across the square, the chant of a band of pilgrims is heard approaching. As the pilgrims pass on their way into the convent, they distribute amulets to the kneeling people . . . their song dies away . . . "Great is Thy glory, Lord!"

Scene II

The scene changes to a cell in the Convent of Miracles. Pimenn, an old monk and chronicler, reveals to Gregory, a novice, the story of Dimitri's death. Gregory, learning that the murdered youth was of his own age, resolves to spread the report that Dimitri still lives, and thus to usurp the Russian throne.

Scene III

DIMITRI

Again the scene changes and we behold the great square between the two Cathedrals of the Assumption and the Archangels. Gay banners, the vivid colored garments of the people, the gleaming domes of the cathedrals, the pealing of the great bells, form a brilliant background for the stately procession of Boyards, who go slowly towards the Cathedral of the Assumption, Boris himself, in their midst. From the portico of the cathedral Prince Shouisky cries, "Long live Czar Boris!"

The people reply with shouts of rejoicing, and sing "Glory to Czar Boris!"

Coronation Scene—Part 1 *Albert Coates-Symphony Orchestra* 11485-1.50 Coronation Scene—Part 2 *Feodor Chaliapin-Symphony Orchestra* 11485-1.50
Salve a te, Zar Boris Teodorovic! *(Coronation Scene)* *Royal Opera Chorus and Covent Garden Orchestra* 9400-1.50

ACT II

Scene I

GREGORY has escaped from the convent and come with two companions to an inn at the Lithuanian border. One of his companions, Varlaam, holding bottle in hand, sings a rollicking drinking song filled with a verve and grim humor that are characteristically Russian. The words tell with a fiendish glee how the terrible Czar Ivan, when he learned of the threatened rebellion of the Tartars in the town of Kazàn, scattered the rebels to pieces by exploding mines in their midst.

In the Town of Kazàn *Feodor Chaliapin* 1237-1.50

Gregory hopes to cross the frontier and raise an army. A government order has warned the guards at the border of his escape, yet when soldiers come to the inn searching for him he manages to make his get-away.

Scene II

Boris' son and daughter, Feodor and Xenia, are with their old nurse in the Czar's apartments in the Kremlin. Xenia is unhappy because of the loss of her affianced lover, and the nurse attempts to distract her with a song. Boris enters, consoles Xenia and sends her to seek comradeship among her young companions. He is happy at finding that Feodor has been studying a map, for the boy may need that knowledge some day: this train of thought leads him into a magnificent monologue in which he declares that even though he has obtained the highest power, he still searches vainly for peace of mind. Prince Shouisky appears, bringing the news that the people are in revolt under the belief that Dimitri lives. This pretended Dimitri is at the Russian border; if he enters the country with his followers, Boris' throne will surely fall. Boris orders military precautions be taken at once, then, terror-stricken, asks if murdered boys rise from their graves . . . or is Dimitri really dead? Shouisky reassures him; he describes the scene at which he saw the body of the murdered boy. As soon as he is left alone, Boris falls back in his chair, a prey to agonizing remorse. A steady, ominous pulsation is heard in the orchestra, like the relentless flight of time marked by the great clock that stands against the wall facing the Czar. His overwrought nerves conjure up before him an apparition of the boy whom he has murdered; Boris shrinks back in the utmost terror. At length, exhausted by the agony of his own conscience, he falls on his knees, praying, "Lord, have mercy on the guilty soul of Boris."

Scene III

Gregory is waiting for the lovely Marina, a Polish lady who serves the interests of her own country by helping him play the part of Dimitri. He lurks in the deep shadows of her garden while a banquet is being held within the palace. Suddenly dance music is heard; Gregory conceals himself, and the guests, coming into the garden, begin the Polish court dance, the Polonaise; it is music at once vivacious but dignified, marked by a rhythm peculiar to that dance. While executing the intricate, stately figures of the Polonaise, the guests sing: "Forward against Moscow . . . to victory!" The dance ended, the music dies away and the guests return to the palace.

Polonaise *Royal Opera Chorus and Covent Garden Orchestra* 9400-1.50

Soon Marina comes to Gregory and they unite in a beautiful duet. By playing first on his passion, then professing scorn for his lack of ambition, she spurs him on to swear that he will lead the attack against Moscow and seize the throne. Marina shall be queen! The music of this remarkable duet, with its seductive Polish mazurka rhythm, uniquely combines local color with romantic love song.

66

THE GARDEN SCENE

ACT III

Scene I

In the forest of Kromy peasants are taunting a nobleman who has fallen into their hands, singing at him in mock praise, "Glory to this great boyard and to his Czar Boris!" A village fool approaches followed by a crowd of jeering children. He seats himself on a rock, and swaying back and forth sings a plaintive song which the children soon drown out, however, with their mocking "Hail to our great Fool!" The two friars, Missail and Varlaam, are heard approaching in the distance, singing their chant-like denunciation of the cruel Czar Boris. The people, wrought to great excitement at this, sing a remarkably thrilling chorus proclaiming their loyalty to Dimitri and their desire for vengeance, "Death to the regicide!" Two Jesuits likewise approach, singing the praises of Dimitri in Latin, "Domine salvum fac Regem Demetrium Moscoviae" *(Part III);* but neither the people nor the friars desiring interference from Rome, they are bound and led off to be hanged. Martial music is heard and a procession of troops passes by, followed by Dimitri himself, i.e., Gregory pretending to be Dimitri. He is welcomed by the populace—"Glory unto our lawful Czar!" As he rides by he promises them "protection from oppression" *(Part IV),* and the people follow him, shouting joyfully, "Hail to thee, Czar Dimitri!" Snow has begun to fall, and the village fool, left alone in the gathering darkness, sees in the distance the red glow of a fire already kindled by the revolutionists, and sings a heart-rending ditty:

> The foe will come and blood will flow;
> Let thy tears flow, poor, starving people!

Scene II

The Duma has gathered at the Imperial Palace to plan measures against this uprising and the usurper. Shouisky tells the assembled nobles that he has witnessed the secret agony of Boris . . . he seemed to be addressing the ghost of Dimitri. The nobles are disturbed at this insinuation but their remarks are cut short by the entry of Boris, who at first seems much distracted, then, as he assumes the Czar's seat, regains his usual calm and poise. Shouisky begs that Boris will first grant audience to an aged monk who waits outside. In a vain hope that this holy man may bring peace to his distressed spirit, Boris assents. The venerable Pimenn enters, and tells how in the dead of night an old shepherd had come to the convent saying that in a dream a childish voice had counseled him to pray at the tomb of Dimitri. He did so and a miracle happened . . . he was cured of his blindness. Boris listens with a concern that grows into horror, and finally cries out, then falls fainting. When he revives he asks to be left alone with his son. He turns to the child and with the deepest pathos sings, "Farewell, my son." He tells him not to try to learn how he gained the throne, but to rule carefully and justly, and to defend their holy religion; then he tenderly asks him to shield well the beloved Xenia. He lays his hands in blessing on the child's head, and prays for Heaven's protection.

Farewell of Boris (*Farewell, My Son, I Am Dying*) **Death of Boris** (*Hark 'Tis the Passing Bell!*) **Feodor Chaliapin 6724-2.00**

The solemn tolling of bells is heard while outside the voices of the people rise in prayer for the soul of their sovereign. The music of this final scene, combining Russian choral song of the greatest beauty with a portrayal of the terror and agony of Boris, grows by degrees to a climax of stupendous power and realism, but a realism that is truly exalted. Boris, becoming ever weaker, cries out, "Lord, grant Thy mercy . . . forgive this my deed . . . O death!" A lugubrious procession of priests enters together with the nobles. . . . Boris stands up, exclaiming, "Hold! I still am Czar!" Then clutching at his heart he sinks into a chair . . . writhing in a struggle with death . . . the words "God . . . have mercy" on his lips. Pointing to his son he says, "Behold your Czar!" One last wrenching of physical and mental agony, a cry of "Mercy!" and death at last brings him peace. The nobles stand murmuring, heads bowed as if in prayer. . . .

GUIDO, POMPILIA AND CAPONSACCHI

CAPONSACCHI

OPERA in three acts, with a prologue and epilogue. Music by Richard Hageman; libretto by William Goodrich, after the poem "The Ring and the Book," by Robert Browning. As this edition of the Book of the Opera goes to press, the first American performance of this opera by an American, is scheduled for January, 1937, with Helen Jepson starring as the unhappy Pompilia. Some months in advance of the performance, it became possible to make permanent on Victor records two of the most dramatic, and at the same time, most melodious and moving moments of the opera, with Miss Jepson and a full orchestra under the direction of the distinguished operatic conductor Alexander Smallens.

VERY briefly condensed (the complete story may be found in Browning's poem, and, somewhat modified, in the play "Caponsacchi" made famous by Walter Hampden) the opera traces a series of events in the tangled lives of Caponsacchi, a priest of noble birth and singularly human yet saintly character; Guido, a swashbuckling, dissolute and greedy, cowardly man, and his wife Pompilia, little more than a child in years, beautiful, virtuous and meek.

Guido hates and abuses his wife, first because of her calm devotion to virtue, second for her parents' wealth which he is not able to get for himself. He plots to ruin her, and sees his opportunity when, on a night of festival, in which the disguised Caponsacchi and a priestly friend join as spectators, he observes a simple and harmless contact between his wife and the priest. He makes life miserable for Pompilia; so much so that she decides to flee to her parents in Rome. She asks Caponsacchi to protect her on her secret journey, telling him that she is pregnant, and that if her hate-

This Very Vivid Morn. *Helen Jepson, and orchestra under the direction of Alexander Smallens* 14183-2.00

ful husband knew this, her life would be in imminent peril. She is not deeply concerned for her own life, but is passionately determined to protect the little life within her; as she says, "When I was alone, it mattered not"; but now she has another to care for. Caponsacchi agrees to guard her on the journey.

Guido is fully cognizant of their plans, and plots to undo them with trumped up evidence of his wife's infidelity though he knows her virtue only too well. He, with a group of ruffians, goes before his wife and Caponsacchi, and conceals himself at an inn near Rome, where he rightly guesses Pompilia and her escort will be forced by exhaustion to stop. He bribes the landlord to have but one room ready for occupancy, no change of horses, and also to secrete incriminating letters in the bedroom. Pompilia and Caponsacchi arrive. The lady, filled with thoughts of what is in store for her and her child, asks to hold in her arms the infant child of a woman standing near, and sings to it a tender lullaby. She grows faint, and retires

Lullaby. *Helen Jepson, with orchestra under the direction of Alexander Smallens* 14183-2.00

alone. Guido appears, is vanquished by Caponsacchi and disarmed in a duel; he calls his ruffians who seize the priest, but in fear of the church later release him when he reveals his ecclesiastical standing.

Act III is laid at Rome, at the home of Pompilia's parents. Her baby is two weeks old, and for safety has been sent away to the care of nuns. Caponsacchi has been mildly punished by temporary banishment for the affair at the inn, but Pompilia receives a message that he will presently come to see her, and she is happy. There is a knock at the door, and a voice, which Pompilia in terror recognizes, cries that it is Caponsacchi. It is, instead, Guido who bursts in. To torture Pompilia into revealing the whereabouts of the child, Guido murders her father and her mother before her eyes. She, knowing her child is safe and caring nothing for life, still defies the bloodthirsty husband, and he orders his henchmen to kill her. They fall upon her with daggers; she dies, but in the arms of Caponsacchi, who at the last moment bursts in. He is about to kill Guido when the police arrive, and the priest regretfully cries, "Too soon!"

Both the prologue and the epilogue reveal the trial of Guido and Caponsacchi. The prologue takes place at the beginning of the trial, when the judges seem to incline toward Guido, and the mob howls for his freedom. The epilogue comes at the end of the trial, when Caponsacchi, bitter because his evidence, unsupported by any other testimony, is not believed, cries out in desperation at the cowardice of the judges, and begs not for his own life but for vindication of the dead Pompilia. At the climax a curtain, upstage, falls open, revealing the venerable presence of the Pope, who having heard the trial and weighed the evidence psychologically rather than factually, vindicates Pompilia, condemns Guido and his minions to death, and sets Caponsacchi free with his blessing.

THE PUBLIC SQUARE—ACT I

CARMEN

OPERA in four acts; music by Georges Bizet; words by Henri Meilhac and Ludovic Halévy, founded on the novel by Prosper Merimée. Produced at the Opéra Comique, Paris, March 3, 1875. First performance in the United States, October 23, 1878, at the Academy of Music, New York. Revived at the Metropolitan Opera House (1927-28) with Johnson and Jeritza and later with Ponselle as Carmen.

Three months after "Carmen" was first produced, Bizet died, depressed and discouraged by the failure of his work, and without any idea of the world-wide success it was to achieve. In view of its surpassingly fine qualities and later popularity, this failure of "Carmen" at its first performance has become historic. And through this one opera Bizet has come to be ranked among the greatest of operatic composers. Though successful in winning the famous *Prix de Rome* at the Paris Conservatoire where he studied, his subsequent career was troubed by poverty; like Wagner he was once compelled to waste valuable time in making cornet arrangements of popular tunes. Nevertheless his talent won recognition among fellow musicians, including Liszt, who, it seems, was always able to recognize genius.

In "Carmen" Bizet found a perfect subject for displaying his masterly ability in portraying musically "local color"—an ability that he had also revealed in "Les Pécheurs de Perles," and the glowing incidental music to Daudet's drama, "L'Arlésienne." Yet in "Carmen," despite his talent for local color, he never pauses to paint pretty though unessential tone pictures. Through all the lively scenes and the gay, reckless melodies that constitute a suitable and well-nigh indispensable background for the plot, one feels a sense of foreboding, of impending disaster, that grows in intensity until the final curtain.

Only a master of musical dramatics would be able to create with his sure, deft touches, this steady crescendo of emotion.

"Carmen" is, moreover, one of the few operas that win nearly universal approval. The man in the street whistles and loves its melodies; the opera-goer is thrilled by its swiftly moving scenes and tensely emotional music; the opera star is enthusiastic over its possibilities for singing and acting; the dramatic critic commends its carefully delineated characterizations; the musician admires its well conceived and masterfully handled musical numbers, its thorough musicianship and excellently wrought orchestration. Even so great a conductor as Leopold Stokowski thinks so highly of this music, that he has recorded an entire suite from "Carmen." And, by the way, when played by the Philadelphia Symphony Orchestra under the inspired hand of Stokowski, the Carmen music glows with a fire and beauty that is seldom given it in the opera house. Perhaps the very greatness of "Carmen" spelled failure for it on that memorable first night; many another fine opera has had a like fate.

On a canvas crowded with movement and colorful personalities, Carmen is the dominating figure. She does not live according to the conventions of the village-bred Micaela; a life of that sort is entirely unknown to her. Her *milieu* has always been that of smugglers, bandits, and outlaws, with whom wildness and audacity are the true "conventions." They are gamblers who play with life and liberty, who stake a fat purse against a bloody death, who know no greater disgrace than to fail to pay their own strange debts of honor. If these are conventions, then Carmen is the most conventional of all. She, too, is a gambler, taking gamblers' chances with what cards are dealt her. Her cards are her own audacious beauty, her wild coquetry, the dangerous fires of human passion; against the prize she plays for the hearts of men, she can stake only herself. If we do not accept this as the basic psychology of Carmen's nature, the last act of the opera becomes meaningless. Why should she face Don José alone when she might have gone into the bull ring, or commanded a body-guard of her own friends? She knows that Don José, a ruined man, is desperate and fearless when aroused. Yet she chooses to stay deliberately. According to gypsy law, she is his until the union is broken by mutual consent. Her "gamble" has been that he will weary of her when she wearies of him; and she has lost. Well, she will pay. None can accuse her of fear or falsehood. Thus conforming to gypsy convention she stands alone and "faces her man."

This ardent drama, skilfully evolved from Prosper Merimée's story, is portrayed with felicity and distinction in Bizet's music—music in which every scene, every character, is clearly reflected. The "Fate" motive which sounds so ominously just before the brilliant scene of the first act, is echoed again and again through the score, changing its form in a dozen ways. In the card scene it flickers through and through, like an angry tongue of flame in a bank of smoke. At the end, when the tragedy is done, it blazes forth luridly. Of this so-called "Fate" motive a story of supposed Oriental origin is told: when, according to Mohammedan tradition, Satan was cast from Paradise, he remembered only one strain of the music he had heard there. This, known as "Asbein," or the "Devil's Strain," Bizet used with fine symbolic as well as perfect musical fitness.

CARMEN ON VICTOR RECORDS

It is eminently just that the recording of "Carmen" should be made by artists and members of the chorus of the La Scala Orchestra, who have recorded so many other operatic works for Victor, and who constitute one of the foremost musical groups in Europe. The performance, accompanied by an orchestra of seventy musicians and conducted by M. Sabajno, is recorded on nineteen Victor records and is issued in two volumes as Album M-128 (11839-11857) in the Musical Masterpiece Series (also in automatic sequence, AM-128), List Price, $28.50. The following description of the opera is keyed to these records, and the names of the soloists are indicated in the accompanying cast of—

TIBBETT
AS THE TOREADOR

CHARACTERS

DON JOSÉ *(Don Ho-zay')*, *a Brigadier*   Piero Pauli, *Tenor*
ESCAMILLO *(Es-ca-mee'-yoh)*, *a Toreador*   Ernesto Besanzoni, *Baritone*
ZUNIGA *(Tsoo-nee'-gah)*, *a Captain*   Enrico Spada, *Bass*
MORALES *(Moh-rah'-layz)*, *a Brigadier*   Attilio Bordonali, *Baritone*
LE DANCAIRE   Neelo Palai, *Tenor*
LE REMENDADO   Amelio Venturini, *Tenor*
    Smugglers
MICAELA *(Mih-kah-ay'-la)*, *a Peasant Girl*   Maria Carbone, *Soprano*
FRASQUITA *(Frass-kee'-ta)*   Nerina Ferrari, *Soprano*
MERCEDES *(Mer-chay'-dayz)*   Tamara Beltacchi, *Soprano*
    Gypsies, friends of Carmen
CARMEN *(Kar-men)*, *a Cigarette Girl, and a Gypsy*   Gabriella Besanzoni, *Mezzo-Soprano*
An Innkeeper, Guide, Officer, Dragoons, Lads, Cigarette Girls, Gypsies, Smugglers.

Scene and period: Seville, Spain; about 1820.

The Prelude (M 128-1) brings before us, with a sudden stir of gay commotion, a vivid picture of the colorful crowd that we will see pouring into the bull ring at Seville. Magnificent, dark Spanish beauties with their lace mantillas and heavily embroidered silken garments . . . their escorts in gala attire, even more brilliant . . . the excitement of the bull fight that is about to take place. This high-spirited music is interrupted for a time by the proud, steady step of the world-famous "Toreador Song," gorgeous in its orchestral version.

Prelude to Act I   *Leopold Stokowski-Philadelphia Symphony Orchestra* 1356-1.50

For a moment the orchestra sounds the "Fate" motive, sinuously, ominously—then the curtain rises on

ACT I

SCENE—*A Square in Seville*

IT is the noon hour and the square is filled with townspeople, girls who work in the adjoining cigarette factory, and soldiers from the nearby guard-house. Through this scene of activity comes a simple peasant girl *(M 128-2)*. She tells the soldiers she is hunting for a corporal named José. He will not be there till the time the guard changes, they say; then, beginning to flirt, they ask her to remain till José comes *(M 128-3)*. She runs away like a timid animal that has been frightened.

An intriguing little march tune is heard, played by fifes and trumpets, at first distant then growing nearer *(M 128-4)*.

Soldiers Changing the Guard   *Stokowski-Philadelphia Orchestra* 6874-2.00

It is the change of guard that arrives, preceded by a troop of street urchins imitating the step of the dragoons who follow armed with their lances. Captain Zuniga and Corporal José are among them. The urchins and grown-ups watch with excited admiration the military ceremony of changing guard.

The ceremony over, some of the soldiers gather around Corporal José and jokingly tell him of the fair-haired girl who asked for him. "Micaela,"

JERITZA AS CARMEN

he explains, then adds, "I love her." Indeed, there are some magnificent dark beauties among the girls who have been watching the guard change, José has not given them one glance. Now he sits astride a chair, preoccupied in trying to join the links of a small chain that has broken.

The bell of the cigarette factory strikes the hour for work, and the cigarette girls wedge their way through the crowd towards the factory gates, loitering on the way to make eyes at the soldiers and young men who lounge around the square (M 128-5). The languorous calm of the noon hour and the coquettish charm of these Spanish girls are beautifully pictured in the music (M 128-6).

Suddenly there is a stir among the people, the "Fate" motive is heard in the orchestra, and a shout goes up, "Carmen!" A girl darts through the way that the crowd makes for her. "Love you?" she calls insolently to the men who swarm around her with their attention. "Perhaps tomorrow, but not now!" Then, to the swaying, insinuating rhythm of a Habanera, she begins to sing, an enticing gleam in her eyes (M 128-7).

> Ah! love is like a wilful wood bird,
> And none may hope his wings to tame,
> If it please thee to be a rebel,
> Say, who can try and thee reclaim?
> Threats and prayers alike unheeding;
> Oft ardent homage thou'lt refuse,
> Whilst he who doth coldly slight thee,
> Thou for thy master oft thou'lt choose.
> Ah, love!
> For love he is the lord of all,
> And ne'er law's icy fetters will he wear;
> If thou me lovest not, I love thee,
> And if I love thee, now beware!
> If thou me lovest not, beware!
> But if I love you, if I love you, beware! beware!

Habanera *(Love is Like a Wood-Bird)* **Maria Jeritza-Metropolitan Opera Chorus**
8091-2.00 *Marguerite d'Alvarez* 1145-1.50

While singing she glances often at José, and many times dances so near that she almost touches him; moreover, by insinuating inflections of her voice she seeks to win his attention. Apparently unaware of her presence, perhaps fortified against her attractions by thoughts of Micaela, the handsome soldier is occupied busily, almost obstinately, with the broken chain.

"But if I love you, beware!" she sings, and tearing a blood-red flower from her bodice, she throws it boldly at him (M 128-8). He springs to his feet, perhaps to rush madly at her. Instead he meets the look in her eyes and stands petrified on the spot. Carmen, with a cold, jeering laugh and a toss of the head, runs into the factory, followed by the other cigarette girls; the crowd, having had its amusement, saunters away.

José stoops hesitatingly, as if against his will, and picks up the flower lying at his feet. He presses it to his nostrils, inhaling its mysterious perfume in a long, enchanted breath. Then, as if unconscious, moved by some magic force, he thrusts the flower under his blouse, over his heart.

At this very instant, Micaela returns (M 128-9 and 10) and runs to José with exclamations of joy. She brings news from home, and money from his mother's savings with which to help eke out his small soldier's salary. His mother has also sent him a kiss. This, too, Micaela delivers, but most shyly and modestly. She cannot remain long, but her coming brings a welcome change of thought. José exclaims to himself, "Who knows of what a demon I was nearly a prey!" Alarmed at hearing this, Micaela asks what the peril may be. He replies that it is nothing, sings of his old home, and bids her return with a message of love to his mother.

When Micaela has gone, he takes Carmen's flower from under his blouse and is about to throw it away. Just then there are screams of terror in the cigarette factory, and a minute later the square is crowded with frightened

CARMEN SINGING THE "HABANERA"—ACT I

girls, soldiers and townspeople. From the agitated exclamations of the cigarette girls it is learned that Carmen has quarreled with another girl and stabbed her with a knife *(M 128-11)*. The soldiers drive away the crowd and Carmen is brought out and questioned. She answers insolently with a gay "Tra la la la," that makes even more alluring her dark beauty.

The officer loses patience at her conduct, orders her hands tied behind her back, and enters the guard-house to write a warrant.

José is left alone to guard Carmen. Pacing back and forth across the square he seems to be avoiding her. "Where is the flower I threw at you?" she coquettishly asks. Then she begins softly to sing another thoroughly Spanish dance rhythm, a "Seguidilla."

> Near by the wall of Seville,
> At the inn of my friend, Lillas Pastia;
> There I'll dance the light Seguidilla,
> And I'll drink Manzanilla,
> I'll go seek out my friend Lillas Pastia.
> *(Plaintively, casting glances at José):*
> Yes, but alone one's joys are few,
> Our pleasures double, shared by two!
> So just to keep me company
> My beau I'll take along with me!
> A handsome lad—deuce take it all!
> Three days ago I sent him off.
> But this new love, he loves me well;
> And him to choose my mind is bent.

Seguidilla *(Near the Walls of Seville)* **Marguerite d'Alvarez** 1145-1.50

"Keep still!" interrupts José, but Carmen continues unabashed:

> My officer is not a captain yet—
> Less than lieutenant—only a corporal . . .

The tormented dragoon knows that she is making the vulgarest of love to him, for purposes of her own; yet he cannot resist her beauty and her song *(M 128-12)*. "Near the walls of Seville . . . we'll dance the Seguidilla," she murmurs to him insinuatingly, and turns holding towards him her bound wrists. He loosens the knot quickly, but leaves the rope so that it still appears to be tied.

A minute later the captain comes from the guard-house with a warrant for Carmen; following him are the soldiers; and the crowd, drawn by curiosity, fills the square. The captain orders *(M 128-13)* José to take Carmen to prison. She is placed between two dragoons, and under the command of José the party starts. As they reach some steps at the back of the square, Carmen quickly frees her hands, pushes aside the soldiers, and, before they realize what has happened, dashes away.

ACT II—THE INN OF LILLAS PASTIA

ACT II

THE second act is preceded by a brief orchestral introduction, the steady-rhythmed music of the Dragoons of Alcala *(last half of M 128-13)*; it is recorded on the final portion of the following:

Les Dragons d'Alcala *Leopold Stokowski-Philadelphia Orchestra* 6873-2.00

At the inn of Lillas Pastia, gypsy smugglers from the mountains, joined by some officers and soldiers, have been having a dinner; now, the table in confusion, some of them sit back to smoke, others play the guitar while a few begin to dance. Carmen sits watching the dancers, heedless of the attentions of Zuniga; then, suddenly she rises and begins a song of gypsy life *(M 128-14)*:

> Ah! when of gay guitars the sound
> On the air in cadence ringing,
> Quickly forth the gypsies springing,
> To dance a merry, mazy round.
> While tambourines the clang prolong,
> In rhythm with the music beating,
> And ev'ry voice is heard repeating
> The merry burthen of our glad song.
> Tra la la la.
>
> Cheeks now flush and jewels shine,
> Scarfs are floating to the wind;

79

Round and round in merry maze
The sun-kissed gypsies dance entwined.
So the dance and song unite,
From measure slow to fastest strain;
Voices sounding, steps rebounding—
On they whirl again, again.

Chanson Bohême—Les tringles de sistres (*Gypsy Song*) *Maria Jeritza* 8091-2.00

Also played in an orchestral version as:

Gypsy Dance *Stokowski-Philadelphia Symphony Orchestra* 6873-2.00

The energetic, forward-moving rhythm, the piquant lilt of the melody, the surprising colors of the harmony, and the delicacy of the orchestration are made more vivid by the impetuous clashing of the gypsies' tambourines. Carmen clicks her castanets and joins the dance, which grows faster and more impulsive. At its close she drops to a seat, exhausted.

It is about time for the inn to close, and while all are hurriedly preparing to leave, one of the officers conveys to Carmen the valuable information that the handsome young corporal, who has been under arrest since the time he allowed her to escape, has just been released from prison (*M 128-15*).

Suddenly, from outside come shouts, "Long live the Toreador! Hail Escamillo!" The famous bull-fighter, victor of the ring at Granada, enters, and joining in their toast, sings a fiery tale of the bull fight, a glowing description of quick action, reckless daring, bloodshed, shouts of a great crowd . . . and love. The melody, a thrilling delineation of all this, also reveals to us more forcibly than words, Escamillo's character, brave to the point of recklessness, self-confident, and boastful (*M 128-16*).

Toreador Song (*Chanson du Toreador*) *Lawrence Tibbett-Metropolitan Opera Chorus*
8124-2.00

With you to drink will be a pleasure.
With soldiers
Should Toreadors go side by side;
For both delight in combats.
Crowded the Circus on a festival day,
Crowded the Circus from floor to roof,
Wild with excitement the populace are.
Each one among them of you is speaking—
Clamoring all—questions asking;
All are shouting till the combat is over,
Because 'tis a festival rare of its kind
Come!—on your guard!—attend!

Toreador, e'er watchful be:
Toreador, Toreador,
Do not forget the brightest of eyes
Now fondly thee await;
And love is the prize,
Yes, love's the prize awaits thee, oh, Toreador.

Escamillo's gay, care-free manner, his fame, his flashing uniform, all impress Carmen greatly. And she, too, seems to strike his fancy. But her heart is still set on José.

The Toreador departs, followed by the excited, cheering crowd. The officer tries to induce Carmen to go with him, but she refuses. He says he'll come back later (M 128-17). It is growing late, and the innkeeper again begins to close up. Carmen remains with two of her gypsy girl friends, Frasquita and Mercedes. Two of the smugglers approach them. They need the help of the girls in "vamping" the coast guard into forgetting duty (M 128-18). In a rollicking quinte they spontaneously express their amusement at the idea:

> When it comes to matters of cheating
> By deception or thieving,
> To succeed as one ought
> He should have women in on the deal.

The men are anxious for the girls to start at once, but Carmen wishes to wait; she confesses she expects José (M 128-19), and, as luck would have it, his voice is heard in the distance singing a military air, the theme of the interlude before this act. The gypsies peer through the shutter and admire his appearance and suggest that Carmen persuade him to join their band. Enthusiastic over this idea, she hurries them from the room just before José enters.

She welcomes him with joy, then at once makes him jealous by telling him that Morales and the officers made her dance for them. But now she will dance for José alone (M 128-20).

She begins to dance, to an odd little tune of her own composing and the clicking of her own castanets. José is absorbed in her motions. From the distance a bugle call is heard . . . "retreat," summoning all soldiers back to quarters. José stops the dance; he must go. Carmen laughs at the idea and resumes her dance. The sound of the bugle call draws nearer, passes by and fades away in the distance, mingling with the melody of Carmen's song. Again, with an effort, José tears himself away from the fascination of her actions. "You haven't understood," he cries, "I have to go back to quarters."

"What a dunce I am!" exclaims Carmen sarcastically. "I wear myself all out trying to entertain this gentleman . . . I thought he loved me . . . the bugle calls, and he runs off!" Then in a sudden fury she hurls his cap and sabre at him and shouts, "There! go, my boy, directly to the barracks!"

Mishkin

JOHNSON AS DON JOSÉ

Greatly hurt and humiliated, José seizes her by the arm declaring, "You *must* hear me, Carmen!" He takes from his uniform the flower she gave him that fateful day in the square at Seville. To a hauntingly lovely melody that grows by degrees to an impassioned climax, he tells her how he kept this flower with him during his dreary life in prison *(M 128-21)*.

> This flower you gave to me, degraded
> 'Mid prison walls, I've kept, tho' faded;
> Tho' withered quite, the tender bloom
> Doth retain its sweet perfume.
> Night and day in darkness abiding,
> I the truth, Carmen, am confiding,
> Its loved odor did I inhale,
> And wildly called thee without avail.
> My love itself I cursed and hated,
>
> .   .   .   .
>
> Then alone myself I detested,
> And naught else this heart interested,
> Naught else it felt but one desire,
> One sole desire did it retain,
> Carmen, beloved, to see thee once again!
> O, Carmen, mine! here as thy slave, love binds me fast,
> Carmen, I love thee!
> —*From Schirmer score. Copy't B. Schirmer.*

Air de la Fleur *(Flower Song)* **Edward Johnson** 9293-1.50 **Giacomo Lauri-Volpi** 7389-2.00 **Beniamino Gigli** 14030-2.00

Carmen seems to be touched *(M 128-22)*, but is more determined than ever that José shall go off with her to the freedom of the gypsies' life . . . the adventures, dangers and escapes, the long nights under the free winds and the stars . . . José is nearly won as he murmurs to her tenderly, "Carmen!" Then he starts up with a sudden realization, "A deserter of my flag . . . be shamed, dishonored!" He rushes towards the door and answers her "Good-bye" with "Farewell forever!"

At this very instant there is a knocking at the door, and a second later Zuniga, the officer who had been so struck on Carmen, bursts in *(M 128-23)*. He stops suddenly as he sees José, and says coldly to Carmen, "Your choice isn't so good . . . you don't do yourself justice to take a mere soldier when you might have his officer!" He insultingly orders José to go. The soldier naturally refuses; the officer strikes him, and José, mad with rage, draws his sabre. Carmen, to prevent bloodshed, screams to her companions for help. Officer and man are overpowered and separated. Some of the gypsies lead Zuniga away under close guard. For José the life of a law-abiding subject and loyal soldier is done. Guilty of insubordination and of an attempt upon the life of a superior, the only thing left for him to do is to join the gypsies, become a deserter and an outcast . . . and the lover of Carmen.

Castagneri   ACT III—THE SMUGGLERS' MEETING PLACE

ACT III

A N INTERLUDE of great beauty precedes the third act *(M 128-24)*. A pastoral melody, simple, but most exquisitely graceful, is first heard in the liquid tones of the flute and then taken up in imitation by other instruments; meanwhile the harp adds color and motion to the background. The tranquil purity of this interlude is a relief from the emotional strain of the preceding act. It is beautifully recorded on the first half of the following:

Intermezzo   *Leopold Stokowski-Philadelphia Symphony Orchestra* 6873-2.00

The smugglers are gathering at their meeting place, a wild desolate spot in the heart of the mountains. First one smuggler appears on a lofty pinnacle of rock in the distance, then several, finally the entire band, scrambling down over the barren rocks towards their camp. Their gradual arrival and stealthy movements are vividly pictured in music *(M 128-25)*.

March of the Smugglers   *Leopold Stokowski-Philadelphia Orchestra* 6874-2.00

Carmen and José are among them. José is not happy in this mode of life. Just now he is obsessed by thoughts of his mother . . . she still believes he is an honest man.

"If you don't like our way of living here, why don't you go?" Carmen asks sarcastically.

"And leave you! Carmen! . . . if you say that again . . ." he mutters and places his hand menacingly on his dagger.

Carmen merely shrugs her shoulders and calmly replies, "You may kill me, what does it matter?—I will die as fate dictates." José sulks away and Carmen watches Frasquita and Mercedes, who are telling their fortunes by playing cards (M 128-26). These girls are having a gay time for the cards predict love, wealth and happiness. She seizes a pack of cards and coolly begins to tell her own fortune (M 128-27 and 28). In silence she shuffles and draws; "Spades!—a grave!" she exclaims darkly, under her breath. She recoils as from some unseen hand that threatens her. From the orchestra is heard the terrifying "Fate" theme. "First I, then he!" she adds, indicating José, then continues to shuffle the cards while she sings:

> In vain! to shun the answer
> In vain I sort the cards.
> 'Twill nothing aid, the truth they declare,
> They deceive not.
> If in fate's book the page is clear,
> Fear not; throw, and play.
> The cards in thy hand will, if sorted rightly,
> Pleasure to thee foretell;
> But if thou must die, if the word so dread
> Already in heaven is decreed,
> The cards, to whose will thou art forced to yield,
> Will again repeat thy doom.

Only for a moment does her spirit of bravado desert her, and when the leader of the band of smugglers announces that it is a favorable time (M 128-29) to attempt the mountain pass with their contraband goods, she is all activity in helping prepare for the departure. After José has been stationed behind some rocks to watch for any surprise attack, the smugglers set out through the pass, singing joyfully of their anticipated conquest of the guard.

Unseen by José a guide comes from behind a cliff towards the camp, then quickly withdraws. It is Micaela whom he has directed to this haunt of desperate characters. She comes seeking José (M 128-30). She sings a beautiful air, praying for Heaven's protection. Then thinking of Carmen, she exclaims:

> I shall see the guilty one,
>   Who by infernal arts doth sever
> From his country, from his duty,
>   Him I loved—and shall love ever!
> I may tremble at her beauty,
>   But her power affrights me not.
> Strong, in my just cause confiding,
>   Heaven, I trust myself to thee!

A sudden shot rings out, and in terror she hides among the rocks (M 128-31). José has fired at a stranger coming up the pass. He might indeed have fired again, but the care-free manner in which the man waves his hat and exclaims, "An inch lower and it would have been all over with me!" causes

José to put down his gun and go to meet him. It is Escamillo. In a moment the men recognize each other as rivals. Daggers flash, soldier and bull-fighter struggle together. Escamillo falls, José's dagger at his throat. But the smugglers have returned (M 128-32), attracted by the sound of the shot. Like a flash, Carmen is at the two men and seizes José's arm. Escamillo rises, gallantly thanks Carmen for having saved his life, then with his usual bravado invites them all to the bullfight at Seville, and calmly takes his leave. José again rushes after the Toreador, and again is restrained by the gypsies. Just then Micaela is discovered and brought in. She begs José to return to his mother. Carmen interrupts (M 128-33), and tauntingly says that he should go, this life is not for him. He turns to her excitedly, replying:

> You command me to depart
> So that you may follow
> Another lover—the Toreador!
> No, Carmen, I will not go!

Copy't Mishkin

CARUSO AS DON JOSÉ

The gypsies also advise him to leave, but he is firm. Then Micaela pleads: "One last word, José, your mother is dying!" Now repentant and alarmed, José will go. He turns back for a moment, however, and calls darkly to Carmen, "Be happy . . . I'm going . . . but we'll meet again!"

As José leaves with Micaela, the Toreador is heard in the distance singing his boastful song. Carmen listens, as if enchanted and would run after him; José menacingly bars the way.

ACT IV

A THIRD intermezzo (M 128-34) indicates the changed scenes of the opera . . . a rapid, impetuous dance . . . tones of plaintive longing mingled with impassioned gypsy-like phrases . . . grow to a tumultuous climax, then die away with a pleading phrase in the oboe and a few runs and chords by other wood-wind instruments . . . a mood of vague foreboding.

Aragonaise Leopold Stokowski-Philadelphia Orchestra 1356-1.50

A brilliantly dressed crowd is waiting in the square before the bull ring in Seville for the procession into the arena. Street hawkers with oranges, fans, cigarettes, and wines are vigorously shouting their wares. Soldiers, citizens, peasants, aristocrats, bull-ring loafers, black-haired, black-eyed women, Spanish beauties with towering combs, floating mantillas, and embroidered silken shawls; all these, a many-colored throng, move excitedly about the scene (M 128-35). From the orchestra rings out the bright, vivacious theme of the Prelude to the opera. The procession is approaching, and the crowd cheers and applauds the divisions of the parade that go by and enter the arena. "The Alguacil . . . the Chulos . . . the Bandilleros, all in green and spangles, waving their crimson cloths . . . the Picadors with their lances . . . Now, Escamillo! Hail! Bravo! Escamillo!"

A thunderous shout goes up as the Toreador enters, Carmen on his arm. She is stunningly brilliant in her Spanish dress, and appears to be radiantly happy. Escamillo, gallant that he is, now takes leave of her, saying that if she loves *(M 128-36)* him she soon will have reason to be proud. Completely won, Carmen vows that her heart could hold no other love.

A blare of trumpets and a march in the orchestra announce the entry of the Alcade. During this, two of Carmen's gypsy friends approach. They warn her to leave the place . . . José is hiding among the crowd . . . he appears to be desperate . . . Carmen calmly replies that she is not afraid; she will stay, wait for him . . . talk to him.

When the Alcade has entered the arena the entire crowd follows, the brilliant music of the procession dies out in the distance, and Carmen is left face to face with Don José *(M 128-37)*. She looks at him fearlessly and says, "I was told that you were here . . . warned . . . but if the hours has come, live or die, I will never be yours again." José is haggard and wan, from his sunken eyes glow a dangerous light. "Carmen," he begs hoarsely, "come, let's go far from here, begin life again. I adore you!" "It's useless for you to keep repeating that you love me," she answers impatiently, "I don't love you any longer." "But I, I love you, I worship you!" he pleads and threatens at the same time. "What's the use, superfluous words!" is her indifferent answer. "Well," he urges, "if I can win your love, I'll be a smuggler, anything you wish, all—but don't leave me, don't forget our past, how we loved each other!"

THE DEATH OF CARMEN

Her freezing answer: "Carmen never will yield, free was she born, free shall she die!"

A sudden fanfare is heard from the arena, there are loud shouts of "Hurrah! Hail to the Toreador!" At the shout of victory Carmen lets escape a little cry of pride and joy. During this Don José has had his eyes glued on her. She starts to run towards the entrance; driven insane with jealousy, he bars her way.

In a sinister tone he mutters, "This man they are shouting for, he's your new lover!"

She defies him with, "Let me pass."

"On my soul! you'll never pass! Carmen, come with me!"

"Leave me, Don José."

"You're going to meet him . . . you love him?"

"Yes, I love him! even before death, I'd repeat, I love him."

Again there is a fanfare of trumpets and a shout of "Viva, Toreador!" Carmen again tries to enter the arena. José stops her violently. His voice hoarse with despair and jealousy, he again threatens: "And so I've sold my soul so that you can go to his arms and laugh at me!" The "Fate" theme sounds turbulently in the orchestra. From the arena is heard another fanfare and the song of the crowd acclaiming Escamillo victor. With a defiant cry, Carmen throws away José's ring and darts towards the entrance of the amphitheatre; there José overtakes her. A dagger flashes . . . Carmen falls. The crowd comes pouring from the arena singing praises of the Toreador. Leading the crowd is Escamillo, flushed with the victory he has won for his beloved. And he stops suddenly . . . she is lying at the gate . . . dead. There also stands Don José . . . he declares himself the guilty one, and bending over the lifeless form, cries out, "Carmen . . . Carmen . . . I loved you!" (M 128-38)

MISCELLANEOUS CARMEN RECORDS

Variations on Themes from Carmen *Vladimir Horowitz* 1327-1.50
Ballet Music *Banda di Chieti* 24822-.75
Selection *Creatore's Band* 35841-35842-1.25

THE METROPOLITAN OPERA HOUSE SETTING

CAVALLERIA RUSTICANA

OPERA in one act; music by Pietro Mascagni; libretto by G. Targioni-Tozzetti and G. Menasci, adapted from a story by G. Verga. First produced May 17, 1890, at Rome; in the United States, September 9, 1891, at the Grand Opera House, Philadelphia.

"Cavalleria Rusticana" brought its composer fame and fortune almost over night; before it was performed Pietro Mascagni was a struggling music teacher in an Italian village, who at one time had been compelled to exist on a plate of macaroni a day. He was born December 7, 1863, the son of a lowly baker at Leghorn. His father, ambitious for the boy, wanted him to study law. Pietro, preferring music, studied that art secretly; in this a sympathetic uncle helped him financially. Several small successes at composition won the favor of Count Florestano de Larderel, a wealthy amateur, who sent him to the famous Conservatory of Milan. There he did not succeed in spite of the sympathetic encouragement of his teachers among whom was Ponchielli; he could not endure the routine studies of counterpoint and fugue and soon ran away from the school. For several years, he was a conductor of obscure travelling opera companies. Finally, he married and settled at Cerignola. In 1889 the music publisher Sonzogno offered a prize for the best one-act opera to be submitted to him. Mascagni obtained the libretto of "Cavalleria Rusticana," and in an incredibly short time set it to music. He submitted his work and with it won the first prize. The opera was performed for the first time at the Costanzi Theatre, Rome, May 17, 1890. Before the performance was half over, the rather small audience was wild with enthusiasm and excitement. The composer's fame was made. Medals were struck in his honor. His native city, Leghorn welcomed him back with torchlight processions and illuminations, and the King of Italy conferred upon him the Order of the Crown of Italy, an honor not bestowed upon Verdi until middle life. Cavalleria was played everywhere

88

in the music-loving world, always with amazing success. The work set a fashion for one-act operas. Most of these, with plots that were more and more melodramatic and sordid, have been forgotten; "Cavalleria" remains. Mascagni has frequently tried to duplicate this first success of "Cavalleria," and has always failed. Those of a critical mind believe even this early work shows traces of weaknesses that developed into great flaws, pompousness, melodramatic treatment of trivialities, love of mere noise, a thinly disguised lack of melodic and rhythmic invention. Yet "Cavalleria" has continued as one of the most popular of operas on the modern stage. It survives because its simple, lurid plot contains genuine drama—Eleonora Duse displayed her great ability as an actress in it as a stage tragedy—and because to this simple colorful story of Sicilian life is wedded music of like colorfulness and passionate intensity.

The entire opera, as given at La Scala in Milan and at the Metropolitan Opera, New York, has been recorded on nine double-faced Red Seal Victor records by distinguished soloists and the chorus of La Scala, under the direction of Carlo Sabajno. Their performance constitutes an important contribution to the growing list of operas recorded in complete form by Victor.

Cavalleria Rusticana—Complete *Famous Soloists, Chorus and Orchestra of La Scala, Milan, under the direction of Carlo Sabajno. Album M-98 (9885-9893) AM-98 (9894-9902) Price $13.50*

CHARACTERS

SANTUZZA *(San-toot'-zah), a village girl*	*Soprano*
LOLA *(Low'-lah), wife of Alfio*	*Mezzo-Soprano*
TURIDDU *(Too-ree'-doo), a young soldier*	*Tenor*
ALFIO *(Al'-fee-oh), a teamster*	*Baritone*
LUCIA *(Loo-chee'-ah), mother of Turiddu*	*Contralto*

Chorus of Peasants and Villagers.

(The name of the opera is pronounced *Kah-vahl-leh-ree'-ah Roos-tih-kah'-nah.* The English translation is "Rustic Chivalry.")

The action is supposed to take place in a Sicilian village at the present time.

THE opera begins with an orchestral prelude that introduces us to the stormy passions we are to witness. The progress of this is interrupted by the voice of Turiddu singing, from behind the curtain, a characteristic Sicilian love song. This "Siciliana," a serenade with guitar-like accompaniment, unites a melody expressive of the amorous longing of Turiddu with dark harmonies that hint at tragedy to follow. *(M 98-1.)*

> O Lola, with thy lips like crimson berries,
> Eyes with the glow of love deepening in them,
> Cheeks of the hue of wild blossoming cherries—
> Fortunate he who finds favor to win them!
>
> On thy threshold blood readily is streaming!
> What do I care if here before thee I perish?
> Yet tho' I died and found heav'n on me beaming,
> Wert thou not there to greet me, grief I should cherish.

Preludio e Siciliana *(Thy Lips Like Crimson Berries)* **Giovanni Martinelli** 8109-2.00

At the end of the prelude, the curtain rises and there is revealed the square of a Sicilian village. On one side is a church, at the other the wine shop and dwelling of Mamma Lucia. It is the dawn of Easter—a time of great rejoicing with the Sicilians *(M 98-2)*. The church bell rings, distant voices are heard singing "Ah!" in Sicilian fashion. The orchestra plays a

Mishkin

GIGLI AS TURIDDU

bright melody in the genuine native style—a joyous care-free melody, expressive of the happiness of the day and of the mood of the people who are now entering the square. There are peasants and villagers, the women singing of the joys of Easter time; the men joining the song, but giving voice to praise the industry and the charm of women *(M 98-3)*.

THE WOMEN

Blossoms of oranges
Sweeten the vernal air,
Carol gay larks mid the
Myrtles in flow'r.
Now all the world is glad!
Murmurs of tender refrains
Tell of plighted vows—
Love's happy hour!

THE MEN

O fair ones, stars of the world, by you we're enraptured
As the bird where the lure tempts, flies and is captured.

Some of the people enter the church, the others go their various ways. *(M 98-4)*. As their voices recede in the distance, the village girl, Santuzza, enters and calls for Mamma Lucia. "What is it?" asks the old woman, coming from her combined house and wine-shop. *(M 98-5)*. "Where is Turiddu?" questions the girl anxiously. Mamma Lucia tries to evade her repeated questions with "Do not ask me . . . I don't know . . . I want no trouble." Santuzza pleads, "Do unto me as Christ did to the Magdalen! Tell me, in pity's name, where hides Turiddu?" Lucia replies that Turiddu has gone to Francofonte for wine. "No," declares Santuzza, "last night he was seen about the village." The older woman's suspicions are aroused, for she, Turiddu's mother, has not seen him. She invites the girl to enter, but this the unhappy Santuzza cannot do, for in this little Sicilian village the moral laws are strict; she is an outcast, excommunicated! "What of my son?" questions the mother, but before Santuzza can reply, the cracking of whips and jingling of bells are heard. *(M 98-6)*. It is Alfio, the village carrier, who is approaching. He is singing a spirited song in praise of a teamster's career, and of his wife's beauty and love. A crowd follows him and joins in his song.

Alfio asks Mamma Lucia if she has on hand some of her usual fine old wine *(M 98-7)*. "Not just now," she tells him, "but Turiddu has gone to buy a supply of it." Alfio exclaims surprisedly, "No, he is here. I saw him this very morning standing in the neighborhood of my cottage." Mamma Lucia is about to express her own astonishment, but Santuzza quickly checks her. Alfio goes on his way.

From the church the voices of the choir are heard singing the "Regina Coeli." The crowd in the square join in the "Allelujas," then kneeling, and led by the voice of Santuzza, sing the Resurrection hymn, "Inneggiamo, il Signor non e morto." *(M 98-8)*. This Easter music has a bright, joyful, but characteristic melody that vividly pictures the importance of religion in the lives of these pastoral people.

> Let us sing our Saviour's wondrous story,
> He hath rended the veil of the tomb.
> Christ our Lord is King of glory,
> He is ris'n! Light conquers gloom!

The people now all enter the church leaving Lucia and Santuzza. The mother asks Santuzza why she signaled her to keep silent when Alfio said that he had seen Turiddu in the village. Santuzza reminds Lucia that Turiddu was engaged to Lola before he went away to serve in the army; but while he was gone Lola married another. When he returned Turiddu consoled himself by courting Santuzza; she returned his love, he betrayed her. Now, Lola has become jealous, and, favored by the frequent absences of her husband, Alfio, has enticed her former lover back to herself. Thus she sings, at first simply, with great pathos, then with growing agitation and finally despair, the aria generally known by the words of its first phrase, "Voi lo sapete, O mamma." *(M 98-9)*.

SANTUZZA: None should go but those who have not sinned!

Well do you know, good mother, ere to the war he departed
Turiddu plighted to Lola his troth, like a man true-hearted.
And then, finding her wedded when he returned, he gladly,
To extinguish the passion that in his breast burned madly,
Loved me!—I loved him!—She coveting what was my only treasure—
Love of him who had been her love—burning with fell displeasure
Enticed him from me! Robbed of my maidenhood's honor my sorrow I keep still!
She and Turiddu love again! I weep and I weep and I weep still!

Voi lo sapete *(Well You Know, Good Mother)* **Maria Jeritza** 1346-1.50

Mamma Lucia is most sympathetic towards the unfortunate girl, who implores her to go into church and pray for her. *(M 98-10)*.

Turiddu now enters the square, also on his way to church. This handsome young Sicilian is surprised at finding Santuzza outside rather than inside the church on Easter Day, and tries to avoid stopping to talk to her. Santuzza upbraids him violently for deserting her to return to Lola, yet when he hints that his life would be in danger if Alfio were to know of these visits to Lola, she is frightened. "Strike me, insult me, still I'll adore you!" she sobs in her mood of mingled love and desperation.

Suddenly the voice of Lola is heard in the distance. She is singing a carefree love song about her "King of Roses" that portrays for us the coquette she is. She enters, and grasps the situation at a glance. *(M 98-11)*. The two girls converse in rather bitter irony; Turiddu is nearly speechless with confusion. Lola does not loiter in this uncomfortable situation but enters the church, asking her lover to follow. Santuzza vehemently detains him, and the quarrel continues. "Do not forsake me," the girl pleads. *(M 98-12)*. "Why do you follow me . . . why play spy at the church door?" is Turiddu's response. The girl's frenzied agony is no less powerful than Turiddu's

SANTUZZA PLEADING WITH TURIDDU

violent anger. Finally, when Santuzza calls him "Braggart," he loosens the hold of this clinging, supplicating woman, casts her roughly to the ground and hurries into the church. Santuzza cries after him, "May you be accursed, accursed at Easter, false one!" then sobbingly yields to her despair.

When she looks up Alfio is approaching. "God himself has sent you!" she exclaims *(M 98-13)*. "At what point is the service?" he asks, intending to enter the church. "It's almost over . . . but I tell you Lola is gone with Turiddu." Then he, in surprise, "What do you mean?" "Turiddu, my lover, my lover, betrayed me! And 'twas your wife enticed him from me!" His anger is immediate and passionate. "If you're lying, I'll pierce your heart!"—but soon he is convinced. Santuzza repents having told him, " 'Twas shameful of me." But the generous-minded Alfio tries to console her, then breaks into sudden fury against Turiddu and Lola. " 'Tis they who are shameful! Revenge I'll have upon them this very day!"

The music of this scene has been alternately tense and tumultuous to portray the various moods of the characters; Santuzza whispers her tragedy in suppressed tremulous tones, then the two have a most vehement duet.

They go out, leaving the square deserted for a few moments. Meanwhile calm, devout music rises from the orchestra, that of the "Regina Coeli" the choir sang earlier. This is followed by a haunting melody, vibrant with a certain religious ecstasy and yet pulsating with tense, fervid passions like unto those of the scenes being unfolded in the drama. This, the famous "Intermezzo," (M 98-14) that made "Cavalleria Rusticana" renowned in even the most remote corners of civilization, provides a moment of relief for which the audience is grateful.

Intermezzo adapted to Ave Maria   *Tito Schipa* 6753-2.00   *Boston "Pops" Orchestra* 4303-1.00   *Victor Concert Orchestra* 20011-.75

As the strains of the "Intermezzo," soar aloft and finally die away, the people begin to come out of the church; soon a jolly crowd is assembled outside of Mamma Lucia's. Turiddu is in especially high spirits, he is with Lola, and Santuzza is not in sight to be reproaching him. (M 98-15). He invites his friends over to his mother's wine shop, their glasses are filled, then he leads in singing a care-free drinking song in which the crowd all join.

Brindisi—Viva, il vino spumeggiante *(Drinking Song—Hail! the Red Wine Richly Flowing)* M98-16   *Beniamino Gigli and Metropolitan Opera Chorus* 8222-2.00

Hail the red wine richly flowing,
In the beaker, sparkling, glowing,
Like young Love, with smiles bestowing,
Now our holiday 'twill bless.
Hail the wine that flows and bubbles,
Kills care, banishes all troubles,
Brings peace, pleasure it redoubles,
Causes sweet forgetfulness!

Alfio enters, is warmly greeted by all, and Turiddu offers him a drink. Alfio refuses . . . he might be drinking poison. (M 98-17). Lola is horrified at hearing this; the women consult together hastily, then leave, taking Lola with them. There are a few brief words between the two men. A challenge is given in the Sicilian fashion, the two men embracing and Turiddu biting Alfio's ear in token of acceptance. Alfio then leaves for the place appointed for the duel.

THE DEATH OF TURIDDU

Turiddu calls his mother; *(M 98-18)* he tells her:

> Exciting
> Surely that wine was.
> I must have taken
> Too many cups while we were drinking!
> For a stroll I am going,
> But first, I pray you,
> Give your son your blessing
> As when I left you
> To become a soldier!
> And listen, mother! This also!
> If I return not, if I return not,
> You must not falter.
> To Santuzza be a mother!
> I have sworn to shield her
> And lead her to the altar.

Mamma Lucia wonders why he speaks so strangely; he continues:

> Oh, nothing! the wine
> Has filled my brain with vapors!
> O pray that God forgive me!
> One kiss, dear mother!
> And yet another!
> Farewell now! If I return not
> Be a mother to my Santa.

He kisses her, then rushes off. Mamma Lucia wanders distractedly about;

Santuzza enters and throws her arms around her. People crowd nervously into the square . . . a rustle of suppressed excitement . . . a murmur of distant voices . . . then from afar the cry of a woman, "Turiddu is murdered!" A group of women enter agitatedly; one of them is shrieking, "Turiddu is murdered!"

Santuzza sinks to the ground in a swoon. The fainting Mamma Lucia is supported by some of the women . . . the crowd is speechless with terror.

Another tragedy of Sicilian life, simple but hot-blooded, has reached its end.

Gems *Victor Opera Company* 35932-1.25

THE SQUARE BEFORE THE PALACE

LE CID

OPERA in four acts; music by Jules Massenet; text by A. D'Ennery, Louis Gallet and Edward Blau, based upon the play of the same name by Corneille. First produced, November 30, 1885, at the Opera, Paris. First performance in the United States, February 23, 1890, at New Orleans.

Nearly all of Massenet's operas deal with the "eternal feminine," but in this case the composer attempted a heroic subject, the great Spanish hero, El Cid (1040-1099). In keeping with his subject he introduced a considerable amount of Spanish "local color" into the opera. This is particularly striking in the very effective ballet music. The name of the opera (from the Arabic, *el seid*, "The Conqueror,") is pronounced, in French, *Luh Seed*, and in Spanish *El Theed*, with the *"th"* as in "thread."

THE Cid has returned from victory over the Moors, and the first act shows him receiving knighthood from King Ferdinand, at the house of Count Gormas, whose daughter, Chimene, is in love with the warrior. The King and his family approve, although the King's daughter herself loves the Cid. The latter match, however, is impossible since the hero is not of royal blood. The King bestows upon Don Diego, father of the Cid, a governorship expected by Count Gormas. The enraged Count insults Don Diego,

96

who, too old to fight, calls upon his son to uphold his honor—without naming his adversary.

Although grieved upon learning his adversary's identity, the Cid is obliged to go through with the duel, and more by accident than design kills the Count. Chimene swears vengeance.

The next scene takes place in the great square before the palace of the King at Seville, where a crowd of merrymakers has gathered, for this is a festival day. As a part of the *fiesta* a group of dancers rush on the scene and perform a series of characteristic dances. The music that accompanies them is peculiarly Spanish in its warmth of melody, striking rhythms, its swift changing moods of gaiety, languor, frivolity, dejection, and utter abandon to the headlong speed of the dance. Naturally this music has won a popular place in the concert hall where its wealth of melody, fiery rhythms, and abundance of orchestral color can better be appreciated than in the opera house.

Ballet Music *Hertz-San Francisco Symphony Orchestra.* *Album M-56* (1406-1408)
Price $5.00

In the midst of the revelry Chimene appears and begs the King to bring revenge upon the Cid. The King refuses, and learning that the Moors are advancing, bids her delay her vengeance until the close of the campaign, for the Cid is to lead the Spanish forces. Before departing, the Cid gains an interview with Chimene, and finds that her love is as strong as her desire for retribution.

At first seemingly near defeat, the Cid prays and resigns his fate to Providence. Then there is a sudden turn of fortune and the Spaniards are victorious.

First reports come that the army has been defeated and its leader slain. Chimene has her revenge, but is prostrated with grief and fervently declares her love. A second report reverses the news and the Cid returns to find his beloved still implacable. The King, shrewdly enough, now promises Chimene he will punish the warrior, but Solomon-like asks her to pronounce the death sentence. This unexpected decision causes her once more to change her mind, and when the Cid draws his dagger and threatens to end his own life if she will not wed him, she is compelled to acknowledge that Love is triumphant.

awkward proposal. She seems to hesitate and yields only on condition that Polkan shall be executed.

ACT III

Dodon and the new Queen are welcomed back to the capital in the most extravagant splendor.

Bridal Cortège   *Albert Coates-London Symphony Orchestra* **9696-1.50**

The bride is already bored by her quavering husband. The Astrologer appears and demands as his reward—the Queen! Dodon begs him to accept, instead, riches or power. The Astrologer is firm; Dodon becomes angry and strikes him with his sceptre. The Astrologer drops dead. There is a sudden thunder storm, the scene grows dark and the Golden Cockerel is heard crowing. The bird flies at Dodon, pecks him on the head and the old ruler falls lifeless. The Queen is heard laughing, and when daylight returns she has vanished. The people sing a weird lament . . . who now will be their King?

EPILOGUE

As the curtains falls the Astrologer again appears, and reminding us that this is merely a fairy tale, says that in Dodon's kingdom only he and the Queen are mortal.

THE RIDE TO HELL—ACT V

LA DAMNATION DE FAUST

(Damnation of Faust)

IN its original form this work is a "dramatic legend" for the concert stage; the music by Hector Berlioz, the words, after Gerald de Nerval's version of Goethe's play, by Berlioz, Gerard and Gandonnière. Adapted for operatic performance by Raoul Gunsberg, and produced by him, February 18, 1893, at Monte Carlo. In New York the work was first performed in its original form under Dr. Leopold Damrosch, February 12, 1880; and in the operatic version, at the Metropolitan Opera House, December 7, 1906.

Berlioz, disregarding Goethe's poem, transferred the action of his "Faust" to Hungary simply to excuse the interpolation of the Rákóczy March. Although the opera as a whole has not retained a permanent place in the repertoire, this national Hungarian March, and the delicate Dance of the Sylphs, have always been concert favorites; in them Berlioz shows his great genius at orchestral writing.

THE aged Dr. Faust pores over his musty volumes and regrets his lost youth. He is indifferent even to the sounds of village gaiety outside; but when he beholds the martial display, watches the soldiers march by preparing for war, and hears the stirring rhythm and melody of the Hungarian March, beloved by all patriots, he is seized for the moment by patriotic ardor.

Rákóczy March *Stokowski-Philadelphia Symphony Orchestra* 6823-2.00

His old depression returns, and he is about to end his life with poison, but is diverted by the sight of a church and the fervor of the devotees. Now Mephistopheles comes and offers to console the unhappy old man by means of pleasure. Faust accepts, but does not make any pledge on his own part.

They visit a den where drunkards are indulging in revelry; Faust soon disgusted with this, asks Mephistopheles if this is the best he can offer. Cannot he give him the greatest prize of all, youth? Mephistopheles agrees and wafts him away to the banks of the beautiful river Elbe, where, a young man again, Faust sleeps on a bed of roses. To exquisite fairy music, sylphs dance and charm him with their seductions.

Ballet des Sylphes *Victor Concert Orchestra 20563-.75*

Faust sees a vision of a beautiful maiden, Marguerite; he calls to her in his sleep.

Mephistopheles conducts Faust to Marguerite's house. The fiend sings a mocking serenade:

> Dear Katherine, why to the door of the lover
> Drawest thou nigh?

Marguerite, likewise in a dream, sees the handsome youth, Faust, and awakens to find him coming to her from the garden. Their love scene is interrupted by Mephistopheles, who tells them that people are wondering what the presence of a man in Marguerite's house at such an hour means. Even now the voices of neighbors are heard outside; Faust escapes through the garden.

But from that night on, Marguerite is forsaken by Faust and, alone in her house, she laments her hopeless condition. Faust has wandered to a remote forest cavern where we find him again voicing his disgust with life. Mephistopheles tells him that Marguerite has been condemned to death, but he will save her if Faust will sign an oath to become his slave in the future. Faust signs and they begin a wild ride at breathless speed; but at the end, amid horrible sights and sounds, they drop into the inferno. After this, angels descend to bear Marguerite to Heaven.

THE SHADOW DANCE

DINORAH

OPERA in three acts; music by Giacomo Meyerbeer; libretto by Barbier and Carré. First produced at the Opéra Comique, Paris, April 4, 1859. First performance in the United States, November 24, 1862, at New York.

"Dinorah" was a great favorite with an earlier generation of opera-goers; now, seldom performed, it is known chiefly through the famous "Shadow Song."

THE homestead of Dinorah's father has been destroyed by storm, and the girl's lover, Hoël, wishes to help the stricken household. Being only a credulous Breton goatherd, he accepts the story of a village soothsayer telling of a vast fortune hidden in the mountains. The treasure can be had, however, only by one who lives for a year in a lonesome glen, and even then the first person to touch it will die. Accordingly Hoël takes with him the half-witted bagpiper, Corentino, hoping he will be the first to touch the treasure.

The opera begins as Dinorah, crazed by the belief that her lover has deserted her, is wandering in the mountains in search of her goat. Finding it asleep, she sings a strange lullaby. The hut of Corentino is nearby, who, when he returns, finds Dinorah and mistakes her for an evil fairy. The demented girl compels the frightened piper to dance for her; he falls exhausted. When she has gone, Hoël appears, telling the bagpiper that the wizard has instructed him to seek for a white goat which will lead him to the treasure. The bell of Dinorah's goat is heard and Hoël goes in pursuit, dragging the terrified Corentino with him.

Dinorah has wandered to an open space in the woods. A clear moon casts a strong shadow upon the ground, and seeing her own form thus fantastically outlined, she regards it as a friend, and sings and dances with her shadow as with a living partner. This is the occasion for the delightful, waltz-like coloratura "Shadow Song."

> Light flitting shadow, companion gay
>   Go not away!
> Play here beside me, dark fears betide me
> When thou dost go far from me!
>
> .   .   .   .
>
> Know'st thou not that Hoël loves me?
> That as his bride he claims me!
> Love well hath known
> Our two hearts to unite!

Ombra leggiera *(Shadow Song)*   *Amelita Galli-Curci* 1174-1.50

The scene changes. A violent storm arises, in the midst of which Hoël still seeks the treasure; but Corentino, having heard from Dinorah that he who first touches it must die, refuses to take the risk, suggesting that the demented maid of the mountains do so in his place. As they go to search for her, a dam bursts high in the mountains and the flood carries away a bridge on which Dinorah is crossing the ravine. Hoël rushes to her rescue.

In the quiet and peacefulness following the storm, Hoël brings the still senseless Dinorah, and lays her among the gathering of herders and huntsmen. Believing her dead, he bitterly reproaches himself. But she revives; reason returns. Hoël gives up the treasure hunt, and the curtain descends upon the preparation for the reunited lovers' wedding.

Photo Lumière

GALLI-CURCI

DON CARLOS AT LA SCALA, MILAN—ACT II, SCENE II

DON CARLOS

OPERA in four acts; music by Giuseppe Verdi; libretto by Méry and Du Locle, based on a tragedy by Schiller. First produced at the Grand Opéra, Paris, March 11, 1867. First performance in the United States, New York, April 12, 1877.

"Don Carlos" belongs to an intermediate stage of Verdi's career as a composer. Coming after the magnificent successes of "Trovatore," "Traviata," and "The Masked Ball," it shows Verdi reaching out towards the fuller, richer style with which he was to astonish the musical world in "Aïda." Schiller's highly dramatic tragedy inspired Verdi to compose some thrilling operatic music; moreover, the fact that he was writing for production at the Paris Grand Opéra, may have influenced him to follow somewhat the example of Meyerbeer in conceiving his work on a grandiose scale. The famous arias that have been recorded for Victor rank among Verdi's great achievements.

DON CARLOS, son of Philip II, King of Spain, is in love with the beautiful Elizabeth de Valois, daughter of Henry II, of France. She returns his affection, but for reasons of state is compelled to marry not Don Carlos, but Philip II himself; thus the young prince finds himself in love with his own stepmother. He confides in his friend, Rodrigo, who advises him to leave the Spanish Court and obtain a commission from his father to go to The Netherlands and relieve the Flemings from some of the cruelties inflicted on them by their Spanish rulers. Don Carlos meets with Elizabeth to gain her influence in obtaining the object of this request from Philip. But as the King is secretly in favor of the method of rule of the Spanish tyrants, the request only angers him and helps estrange father and son. Moreover, as a result of this meeting, the former passion between Don Carlos and Elizabeth returns with even greater intensity.

Don Carlos has a dangerous admirer in Princess Eboli, who learns that the Queen has by no means ceased to love him, and, overcome by jealousy, informs Philip of the state of affairs. At the beginning of the last act, we see the King alone in his library, thinking of his unhappy, loveless condition. It is dawn, and his weary eyes long for sleep. "Yet," he meditates, "I shall sleep only in my royal mantle when the day of my doom shall have come," and sings the beautiful aria beginning with the words, "Dormirò sol nel manto."

Acting on the advice of the Grand Inquisitor, he orders Don Carlos to be thrown in prison. Princess Eboli repents of her rash act and confesses to the Queen. Elizabeth orders her to leave the Court . . . death or exile! Left alone, the Princess pours forth her grief in the air "O don fatale," a melody of great beauty and dramatic force.

O don fatale *(Oh, Fatal Gift)*   *Sigrid Onégin* **7191-2.00**

Rodrigo visits Don Carlos in prison and there is shot by order of the King, who suspects him of aiding the Flemings. He bids farewell to earth in the beautiful melody "O Carlo, ascolta."

Carlos is freed, but in keeping a tryst with Elizabeth is discovered by the King, and handed over to the officers of the Inquisition. They lead him away to death.

THE STATUE

DON GIOVANNI

(Don Juan)

OPERA in two acts by Wolfgang Amadeus Mozart; text by Lorenzo da Ponte. First produced at Prague, October 29, 1787. First performance in the United States, May 23, 1826, at the Park Theatre, New York. The original title was: "Il Dissoluto Punito, ossia il Don Giovanni" (The Reprobate Punished, or Don Giovanni). Da Ponte's libretto was based directly on the Spanish version of the story, called El Convidado de Piedra (The Stone Guest), also the subject for an opera by the Russian, Dargomijsky. Molière, Corneille, and Gluck, also were intrigued by the story, as well as the English laureate, Shadwell, whose "The Libertine Destroyed" appeared in 1676.

"Don Giovanni" is one of the few great operas that were successful from their very first performance, and yet it bids fair to outlast almost all others. It is at once popular with the opera-going public and beloved and admired by connoisseurs. Such widely varied geniuses —to name only a few—have all testified to its greatness: Beethoven and Rossini, Wagner and Gounod! For well-nigh a century and a half it has been an inexhaustible treasure house of melody.

This great opera began its career as an opera buffa, but Mozart was so carried away with the dramatic possibilities of the story that his music makes of it something much greater. For the opening and closing scenes he composed some of the most remarkable dramatic music ever written. The intermediate scenes, treated in a spirit of comedy, are invested with music, charming and gloriously beautiful. Through his melodies, at first seemingly so attractively naïve, Mozart delineates the characters of his drama in a most

107

subtle manner. Where later composers would have needed involved harmonies, poly-
phonic treatment of themes and elaborate orchestration, Mozart uses his incomparable
melodies, and with his simple means attains an equally great effect.

The story is told that at the first rehearsal of this opera, Mozart, who was directing,
was not satisfied with the way in which the actress playing the part of Zerlina gave her
cry of terror from behind the scenes. He left the orchestra, and, ordering a repetition of
the finale of the First Act, concealed himself on the stage behind the wings. There stood
Zerlina, awaiting her cue. When it came, Mozart quickly reached from his hiding place
and pinched her. She gave a piercing shriek. "That's the way I want it," exclaimed the
composer, returning to the orchestra, while the actress in her amazement both laughed
and blushed.

The night before the first performance, friends of Mozart reminded him that the
overture was still unwritten. The composer pretended to grow nervous about it, and
went to his room. About midnight he began work. His wife was at his side and kept
him awake with stories and with punch. At seven in the morning when the music copy-
ists came, the work was done. Nevertheless, this overture, so quickly composed, is no mere
potpourri of chief airs, but a masterly work, charged with the atmosphere of the drama.

CHARACTERS

DON GIOVANNI (*Joh-vahn'-nee*), *a licentious young nobleman*	*Baritone (or Bass)*
DON OTTAVIO (*Ot-tah'-vee-oh*), *betrothed to Donna Anna*	*Tenor*
LEPORELLO (*Lep-oh-rel'-loh*), *servant of Don Giovanni*	*Bass*
DON PEDRO (*Pay'-droh*), *the Commandant*	*Bass*
DONNA ANNA, *his daughter*	*Soprano*
MASETTO (*Mas-set' toh*), *a peasant*	*Bass*
ZERLINA (*Tsair-lee'-nah*), *betrothed to Masetto*	*Soprano*
DONNA ELVIRA (*El-vee'-rah*), *a lady of Burgos*	*Soprano*
Peasants, Musicians, Dancers, Demons.	

The action takes place at Seville, in the middle of the Seventeenth Century.

The opera is known also under the Spanish title, "Don Juan" (*Don Wahn*).

The Overture begins with the solemn music of the banquet scene at which the statue
appears to Giovanni. It is followed by a gay *allegro* movement, a characterization of the
bold, pleasure-seeking Don.

ACT I

SCENE I

LEPORELLO, wrapped in his cloak, is waiting in a garden outside a house
in Seville. He complains that he has rest neither by night nor day, and
he adds, "Gaily he within is sporting, I must keep off all intrusion, for his
lordship needs seclusion!" The complaining servant quickly conceals himself as his master, Don Giovanni, comes excitedly from the house pursued by
Donna Anna. The sounds of their voices bring the Commandant, Donna
Anna's father, to the scene. A duel soon follows and the grey-haired Commandant falls dying from a stroke of the agile Don, who at once flees with
Leporello. Donna Anna has run for aid, and when she returns she is grief-
stricken to find her father dead. With her is her betrothed, Don Ottavio.
Noble youth that he is, he endeavors to calm her despair and joins with
her in swearing vengeance upon the unknown assailant and murderer.

Scene II

While fleeing along a desolate road, Giovanni and his inevitable Leporello espy a woman approaching who seems to be weeping bitterly. Giovanni says that he will go to console her. "As you've done eighteen hundred others," murmurs Leporello. But on drawing nearer the Don starts back in surprise. It is Donna Elvira, whom he has deserted even while eloping with her. She berates him for his deceitfulness; Giovanni attempts to explain his sudden disappearance. If she will not believe him, let her hear what Leporello says about it. While the servant holds her attention for a moment, the deceiver quickly

New York Times
SCHIPA IN DON GIOVANNI

slips away. When Donna Elvira turns to Giovanni, he is gone! Leporello tells her to be comforted, singing:

> Gentle lady, this list I would show you,
> Of the fair ones my master has courted,
> Here you'll find them all duly assorted,
> In my writing, will't please you to look,
> In fair Italy, six hundred and forty,
> Germany two hundred and thirty-one,
> An hundred in France, Turkey, ninety-one,
> But in Spain . . . in Spain . . . one thousand and three!
> Here are Countesses in plenty,
> Waiting maids, nineteen or twenty,
> Rustic beauties, Marchionesses,
> Ev'ry grade his pow'r confesses,
> Here are courtly dames and maidens,
> Young and handsome, old and plain.
>
> The fair one, be she slender,
> He will praise for modest sweetness,
> Then the dark ones are so tender!
> Lint-white tresses show discreetness:
> When 'tis cold he likes her portly,
> In the summer, slim and courtly,
> Tall and haughty, ne'er she alarms him,
> If she's tiny, very tiny, no less she charms him.
> Ripe duennas he engages
> That their names may grace these pages.
> But what most he's bent on winning,
> Is of youth the sweet beginning,
> Poor or wealthy, wan or healthy,
> Stately dame or modest beauty,
> He to win them makes his duty,
> And you know it not in vain!

The music of this aria is a most perfect mingling of grace, sentiment,

irony, and the comic . . . a wonderful expression of the sophistication of the eighteenth century . . . or the twentieth!

After giving her this cynical comfort, Leporello follows his master. Donna Elvira, like Donna Anna, is ready for revenge.

SCENE III

In the country villagers are making merry with singing and dancing, in honor of the forthcoming marriage of Zerlina and Masetto. Don Giovanni joins the the gathering and, having cast covetous eyes upon the village bride, he orders Leporello to invite all to his castle, then cleverly detains Zerlina.

Cliche du Guy

LEPORELLO

Finch' han dal vino *(For a Carousal)* **Ezio Pinza** 1467-1.50

The maiden is greatly flattered by the Don's gallantry and his offer of marriage. The courtly grace of Giovanni and the hesitant yielding of Zerlina are admirably expressed in the duet "La ci darem la mano!" one of the gems of all opera. Just as Giovanni seems to have succeeded, Donna Elvira appears, and by her denunciation shows the noble's real character to Zerlina, who at once hurries to her betrothed. Donna Anna and Don Ottavio also come upon the scene. To them, Don Giovanni so far is merely an acquaintance not associated with any of the dark deeds of the former evening. Donna Elvira's accusations, however, begin to raise suspicions, and in Giovanni's parting words Donna Anna recognizes the voice of her father's murderer. She leaves Don Ottavio, who renews, to himself, his vow to avenge her wrongs, for to him she is all happiness. He sings of his love for her to the exalted beauty of the aria, "Dalla sua pace!"

Dalla sua pace *(On Her All Joy Dependeth)* **Tito Schipa** 1308-1.50

SCENE IV

Don Giovanni has ordered a festival at his palace. Among the peasants in the garden are Zerlina and Masetto. The youth upbraids the girl for her faithlessness in yielding so easily to Giovanni, and tells her to go away forever. She pleads with him, singing the wistful and lovely "Batti, batti, o bel Masetto."

Batti, Batti, o bel Masetto *(Scold Me, dear Masetto)* **Elisabeth Schumann** 7076-2.00
Elisabeth Rethberg 7472-2.00

> Scold me, dear Masetto,
> Scold Zerlina at your will;
> Like the patient lamb I'll suffer,
> Meek and mute and loving still,
> Ah! I see, love, you're relenting,
> Pardon, kneeling, I implore!
> Night and day, to thee devoted,
> Here I vow to err no more.

Then as she thinks of a happy future, the melody grows bright and winsome.

> Peace and joy once more shall bless us,
> Not a frown shall e'er distress us,
> While united and delighted
> All our days shall sweetly glide.

Upon hearing such a plea, Masetto, of course, forgives her. Don Giovanni now approaches, and after an attempt to smooth things over with the jealous husband-to-be, he invites all into the palace. Leporello opens a window for a moment, and we hear the strains of the minuet that is being danced within. As he stands there enjoying the evening air, three masked figures enter the garden, and Leporello, in accordance with the custom of the time, invites them to the festivities. When they have accepted, Leporello goes to admit them. The masked characters are none other than Donna Anna, Donna Elvira, and Don Ottavio, who, before entering the palace, pause to pray for heaven's aid in achieving vengeance.

ACT II

SCENE I

I N Don Giovanni's palace the festivities are progressing merrily. The graceful and courtly minuet is danced to the incomparable music of Mozart.

Minuet *(Harpsichord)* **Wanda Landowska 1199-1.50 *Victor Band* 20990-.75**

During the minuet Giovanni has contrived to lead Zerlina to an adjoining room. Suddenly the dance is interrupted by her screams for help. A moment later, the Don comes in, sword in hand and dragging Leporello. But this ruse fails to convince anybody of Giovanni's innocence. Donna Anna, Donna Elvira, and Don Ottavio unmask and confront Giovanni; but he, ignoring their accusations, draws his sword and forcing open a passageway through the crowd, disappears.

Carlo Edwards
EZIO PINZA AS DON GIOVANNI

Scene II

Even after all this, Donna Elvira cannot quite forget her love. She has taken Zerlina into her care, and it is this magnet that draws Giovanni to Elvira's house. The Don changes cloaks with Leporello, and with the help of darkness and this disguise, the servant succeeds in luring away Donna Elvira, who rejoices that her lover has returned. Meanwhile Giovanni serenades Zerlina in a most ingratiating air:

Deh vieni alla finestra *(Open Thy Window)* **Ezio Pinza** 1467-1.50

Masetto approaches and Giovanni assumes the manner of Leporello. Masetto is hunting for Giovanni to kill him, or at least give him a good beating. But the clever Don administers the drubbing to Masetto instead. Thus Zerlina finds her betrothed lying in the street in a rather amusingly sore and battered condition.

Scene III

Leporello does so well as Giovanni that he cannot get away from Donna Elvira. Before the house of Donna Anna, however, the pair are confronted by the various persons whom Don Giovanni has wronged; Leporello is forced to reveal himself and flee from their wrath. Don Ottavio, who is present, again affirms his intentions of bringing justice upon Giovanni; he then sings the great aria "Il mio tesoro instanti," often regarded as the supreme test of classic song for tenors. It is a most beautiful melody, admirably written for the voice, and provided with an accompaniment exactly adapted to set off its melodic charms.

Il mio tesoro *(To My Beloved)* **Tito Schipa** 1308-1.50

Scene IV

In fleeing from his master's accusers, Leporello chances upon Don Giovanni. It is now long past midnight, and as they grope about in the darkness they come upon a statue erected to the memory of the Commandant. Giovanni orders Leporello to invite it to supper with him at his palace. The statue nods acceptance; Leporello trembles but his master is undaunted.

Scene V

In the palace a banquet is spread. While Giovanni eats, his own private orchestra plays airs from operas of the day. Leporello, looking on rather nervously, comments on the music that is being played; "That's a song I've heard too often!" he says concerning a Mozart number.

The musicians take their leave. Donna Elvira unceremoniously enters, and on her knees, entreats Giovanni to change his ways. He is firm—cold in his refusal. She leaves, hopelessly. In the corridor she screams; she reënters the room and runs out through another door. Giovanni orders Leporello to see what it is; the servant comes back trembling, "The man in stone!" He

ELVIRA, LEPORELLO AND THE DON—ACT II

refuses to open the door. Giovanni boldly takes a candle, draws his sword and goes into the corridor . . . a moment later he backs into the room . . . there follows him, with slow, heavy footsteps the statue of the Commandant. "You have invited me . . . I am here!" it says. Leporello has sought refuge under the table. Giovanni coolly orders him to serve the meal. "No," says the statue, "he who has partaken of heavenly food, desireth not the food of earth! . . . Don Giovanni, I have been your guest, will you be mine?"

"Yes!" replies the Don, still fearless.

"Give me your hand in token of it!"

"There."

The statue's huge hand grasps Giovanni's.

"How deadly cold your hand!"

"Turn from your ways at your last hour!"

"Never!"

"Repent, ere it is too late!"

"No, fool!"

"Repent!"

"No! No!"

A fiery pit opens—demons drag Giovanni down, unrepentant but brave to the end.

DON PASQUALE

COMIC opera in three acts; text and music by Gaetano Donizetti; the libretto adapted from Cammarano's "Ser Marc'Antonio." First produced at the *Théâtre des Italiens*, Paris, January 4, 1843. First performance in the United States, March 9, 1846, at the Park Theatre, New York, in English. Always at his best in his comic operas, Donizetti gave us a masterpiece in his "Don Pasquale." Music and plot are a delight. Both sparkle with genuine humor. (The title of the opera is pronounced, *Don Pahss-quah'-leh*.)

The action takes place in Rome at the beginning of the Nineteenth Century.

While "Don Pasquale" is not in the active repertoire of any American opera company— or perhaps *because* it is not, the company of La Scala, Milan, have added it to their growing list of recorded operas. With seasoned opera enthusiasts it has long been a favorite; with modern recording technique, and the authoritative performance of La Scala, "Don Pasquale" becomes a genuine treasure in recorded music. The recorded version is musically complete, and is done under the direction of Maestro Sabajno.

Complete *Famous Artists and Orchestra of La Scala, Milan* **Album M-187** (11563-11577) **AM-187** (11578-11592) **Price $22.50**

Overture *La Scala Orchestra* **Direction Carlo Sabajno M-187-1 and 2**

Don Pasquale is much displeased with his nephew, Ernesto, who has refused to marry as his uncle wished. He is waiting *(M 187-3)* for his friend, Dr. Malatesta, who himself brings a proposition that Don Pasquale marry, though he is old, fat and unprepossessing. He has in mind a candidate whom he describes *(M 187-4)* in glowing terms. Don Pasquale likes the idea and urges Malatesta to bring the lady, his sister, immediately. Malatesta leaves Don Pasquale *(M 187-5)* in great excitement, in the middle of which the nephew, Ernesto, enters. Pasquale scolds him vigorously, ending his lecture with the startling announcement of his own proposed marriage.

Sogno soave e casto (*Fond Dream of Love*) **Tito Schipa 1282-1.50**

Ernesto is astonished and annoyed *(M 187-6)* and when he hears that Malatesta has advised the marriage he bewails *(M 187-7)* the treachery of one whom he thought was his friend.

The next scene reveals Norina, the lady in the case, who is disliked by Don Pasquale and loved by Ernesto. She is discovered in her room reading a romantic novel *(M 187-8)*. Norina knows that Malatesta has a plan for deceiving Don Pasquale and he *(M 187-9)* now tells her of it. It requires that Norina shall masquerade as the sister of Malatesta and so plague the Don that he will sicken of the idea of marriage and probably force Norina to marry his nephew, Ernesto, which is, of course, exactly what Norina and Ernesto desire. They rehearse *(M 187-10 and 11)* the part Norina is to play when she comes into the presence of Don Pasquale.

The second act, after a short prelude *(M 187-12)*, reveals Ernesto bemoaning his sad fate *(M 187-12 and 13)*. Pasquale, dressed in his finest in preparation for his marriage, appears. Malatesta comes in escorting Norina, who is apparently very shy and bashful *(M 187-14)*. The Don is delighted at her modesty *(M 187-15)* and immediately proposes marriage and after some high pressure salesmanship Norina consents. The notary public is brought in and

Pasquale, with much legal verbiage, *(M 187-16)* dictates the terms of the marriage contract and signs it. Just as Norina is also about to sign it Ernesto is heard without. He enters, recognizes Norina but by frantic gestures and whisperings is persuaded to remain silent and to act as witness *(M 187-17)* to the marriage contract. No sooner has this been done than Norina abandons her affected timidity and turns instantaneously into a vicious termagant. She will have nothing to do with Pasquale and announces her intention to retain Ernesto as usher in her house. The Don objects to this and Norina ferociously reproves and even threatens him *(M 187-18)*. Then in the presence of Pasquale she summons the household staff and outlines a scheme of living so extravagant *(M 187-19)* that her husband-to-be is choked with rage and declares he will not pay her bills.

M. *Camuzzi*

SCHIPA AS ERNESTO

In Act III, Norina, marvelously gowned, is giving audience to a troop of servants *(M 187-20)*, while Pasquale is contemplating the huge pile of unpaid bills his marriage has produced *(M 187-21)*. He attempts forcefully to dissuade Norina from going to the theatre *(M 187-22 and 23)* and for his plans has his ears soundly boxed by his vigorous lady. As she goes on her way she drops a letter which Pasquale discovers to be an appointment for a rendezvous. With jealousy added to his other troubles he is in complete despair.

The plotters now feel that Pasquale has been sufficiently tortured *(M 187-24)*. Malatesta offers to correct matters if Pasquale will give him *carte blanche.* This the Don *(M 187-25 and 26)* is glad to do with only the condition that Norina leave his house at once. Ernesto comes to serenade Norina *(M 187-26)* who presently joins him *(M 187-28)*,

> **Tornami a dir** *(Once Again Let Me Hear Thee)*   *Amelita Galli-Curci, Tito Schipa*
> 1755-1.50

and while they are talking Pasquale and Malatesta approach, and Ernesto withdraws *(M 187-29)*.

Don Pasquale accuses Norina of secreting a lover about the house. She denies this and Pasquale's search for the miscreant discovers no one. The solution comes when Pasquale calls Ernesto, promises him a liberal allowance if he will marry Norina and get out of his house. This Ernesto is only too glad to do and presently *(M 187-30)* it is discovered that Dr. Malatesta's sister and Norina were the same person; that the marriage of Don Pasquale was a mock marriage, and all his misfortune is the result of a mischievous scheme, but the old man is so happy to extricate himself from his troubles that he sends his nephew and the bride away with his blessing.

SAN CARLO OPERA COMPANY SETTING—DON QUICHOTTE

DON QUICHOTTE

HEROIC comedy in five acts; text by Henri Cain after Le Lorrain; music by Jules Massenet. First produced at Monte Carlo, February 19, 1910, Feodor Chaliapin playing the title rôle. It was first performed in the United States, January 27, 1912, at New Orleans.

R AOUL GUNSBOURG, the manager of the Monte Carlo Opera, was so much pleased by Jaques Le Lorrain's play, which he heard in 1904, that he spoke to Massenet of it. The composer was likewise enthusiastic over the play, and with Le Lorrain's consent decided to turn it into an opera. Unfortunately the playwright died soon thereafter; thus it was necessary to engage Henri Cain to write the libretto.

The characters of Don Quichotte and Sancho Panza and the incident of the windmills are from Cervantes' masterpiece; the plot is the work of the Frenchmen. In their story, Dulcinea is a courtesan. The brain-befogged Don Quichotte becomes one of her many admirers and in flowery language proposes marriage. She is greatly amused at this and replies that first he must recover for her a precious necklace stolen by the brigand Tenebrun.

Quichotte sets out enthusiastically to do this accompanied by the faithful

116

Sancho. He mistakes some windmills for giants extending menacing arms, and charges them, with results disastrous to himself.

He comes upon the brigands, who capture, bind, and threaten him with death; finally they are so impressed by his gentleness and lofty ideals that they not only permit him to go his way unharmed, but also give him the necklace stolen from Dulcinea.

The courtesan is overjoyed at the return of her necklace; but when Don Quichotte again proposes marriage, she is deeply moved by his naïve nobility, and she tells him what her real character is. Their marriage would be impossible. Sancho leads away his grief-stricken master.

Critics are agreed that musically the last act, brief though it be, is by far the finest. The entire act, save for a few introductory measures, is included on the record:

Finale—Parts I and II   *Feodor Chaliapin* 6693-2.00

The world's music lovers are indeed fortunate to have thus permanently crystallized the performance of the very great artist who was first to play the rôle of Don Quichotte. This record is, moreover, a valuable tribute to the versatility of Mr. Chaliapin, for in it he sings not only the part of the great Don, but also that of his faithful follower, Sancho; yet such is Mr. Chaliapin's artistry, that these two widely different characters are clearly delineated in voice and expression.

The last act takes place along a road through an ancient forest. It is a starlight night. Quichotte is resting against the trunk of an oak while Sancho watches over him. The orchestra *(beginning of Finale Part I)* plays very softly a quaint melody. Sancho sings a prayer for the repose of his master's soul. Quichotte awakens, his voice is feeble for he is sick unto death. Sancho exclaims in sorrow when his master says that fate has decreed that they must now part. The woodwinds play a little flowing pastorale while Quichotte recalls the village of his childhood. Then he feebly declares that he must die. Sancho sobs in grief.

Suddenly straightening himself while the orchestra plays a bold melody *(beginning of Finale, Part II)* the great Knight-Errant declares that he was the leader in the fight for the helpless. Then he sinks, choked with sudden pain, himself beyond help. After a moment, as his power of speech returns, he recalls vaguely that he has promised to the faithful Sancho, castles, even a fertile island, his heart's desire. Quichotte tells him to take that island, the sole thing he has to give . . . a wonderful, enchanted island . . . the island of Dreams! While the hero sings of this island the orchestra softly plays a wandering, delicate melody that climbs to luminous heights, then subsides. The master sinks dying and asks Sancho to say a Pater-Noster for him. From afar is heard the voice of Dulcinea singing a song of farewell to happiness and love. The Knight is thrilled with ecstasy at the sound of her voice. She is his goddess, his light, his love . . . she has called him and to her he will go. Thus does he die, leaving the disconsolate Sancho to sob out his grief.

117

DULCAMARA EXPOUNDING THE ELIXIR

ELIXIR OF LOVE

(L'Elisir d'Amore)

OPERA in two acts; music by Gaetano Donizetti; text by Felice Romani. First produced, May 12, 1832, at Milan. First performance in the United States at the Park Theatre, New York, June 18, 1838, in English.

The genius of Donizetti shines at its brightest, not in his tragic works, but in his fascinating comic operas, of which "L'Elisir d'Amore" is one of the best. The plot of this comedy possesses amusing possibilities of character and situation that inspired Donizetti to write some of his gayest tunes, as well as a number of most beautiful, more serious melodies.

CHARACTERS

ADINA *(Ah-dee'-nah), a wealthy and independent young woman*   *Soprano*
NEMORINO *(Nem-o-ree'-noh), a young peasant, in love with Adina*   *Tenor*
BELCORE *(Bell-ko'-ray), sergeant of the village garrison*   *Bass*
DOCTORE DULCAMARA *(Dool-kah-mah'-rah), a quack doctor*   *Bass*
A Landlord, a Notary, Peasants, Soldiers, Villagers.

Scene and period: A little Italian village during the Nineteenth Century.

(The Italian name of the opera, "L'Elisir d'Amore," is pronounced *Lay-lee-seer' Dah-moh'-reh.*)

ACT I

SCENE—*The Homestead of Adina's Farm*

IT IS a glorious summer's day, and Adina sits surrounded by her friends, reading a romance. From a distance the love-sick Nemorino gazes in a rapture articulate only in the lovely song, "Quanto e bella."

A burst of laughter from Adina startles everyone. She reads the legend of Tristan and Isolde, in which the knight wins the lady's affection by means of a wonderful elixir. Nemorino sees no mirth in the tale, and sighs heavily for some of the draught.

Martial music is heard, and the dashing Sergeant Belcore appears with a bouquet for Adina. She has but few smiles for him, and Nemorino, somewhat encouraged, renews his suit as soon as Belcore departs. Adina, though respecting this worthy young fellow, finds him rather dull and tells him go visit his sick uncle, for his suit is useless.

A commotion among the villagers is heard, and Dulcamara, a quack doctor, riding in a splendid carriage, appears. He has a whole trunkful of wonderful nostrums whose virtues he extols in song. To Nemorino, the doctor seems heaven-sent, and he immediately petitions him for some love elixir. Although a bit puzzled, the doctor loses no time in producing a bottle of strong wine which he says is the coveted potion. Nemorino gives the doctor his last coin, and, as soon as he sees him depart, drinks the elixir.

Nemorino feels exalted, and begins to sing and dance. Adina, coming in, is astonished to see her love-sick swain so merry. Feeling sure that the potion will bring the lady to his feet, he pays no attention to her, which piques her so much that when the sergeant arrives and renews his suit, she consents to wed him in three days. Nemorino laughs loudly at this, which so enrages the lady, that she sets the wedding for that very day. This sobers Nemorino, who fears that the marriage may take place before the potion works, and he begs for delay, singing his heartfelt plea, "Adina credimi."

> Adina, trust to me, I do entreat thee,
> Thou canst not wed him.
> I tell thee truly, wait, I conjure thee,
> Until tomorrow.
> But one short day, love,
> The future, dearest, thou'lt spend in sorrow,
> If to my suit, love, thou now say'st nay.

Adina credimi (*Adina, Trust to Me*) *Tito Schipa* 1362-1.50

Adina and the others only laugh at him and begin preparations for the wedding.

ACT II

Scene—*Interior of the Farmhouse*

THERE is a great wedding-day feast. The notary arrives, and the party goes to an inner room to sign the contract. Dulcamara, however, remains loyal to the table. To him comes Nemorino, whose uncle is dying, and whose sweetheart is marrying another. And the elixir did not work! Dulcamara produces another bottle, but pockets it when Nemorino is unable to pay for it. Belcore appears, and Nemorino desperately confides his misery to him. Belcore suggests that he enlist as a soldier, for which he will receive twenty crowns.

This colloquy takes the form of a wonderfully melodious duet in which the sly sergeant cajoles the hesitating swain with promises of pay and renown. Finally, Nemorino signs the articles, and each sings of what is uppermost on his mind:

BELCORE:
Your appearance will be splendid,
When the sergeant shall have trained you . . .
Yes, I my rival have enlisted,
Now the field lies fair and free . . .

NEMORINO:
He knows not why my freedom I barter,
Nor e'er can imagine its value to me.
The sun brightly gleaming, our arms gayly streaming,
The name of Adina my bright star shall be.

Nemorino takes the money, runs in search of the doctor, and drinks the second bottle of love potion!

The peasant girls, having heard that the death of Nemorino's uncle has just made him rich, begin to pay him attention. Adina capitulates when she sees her now freshly heartened lover approach surrounded by sixteen girls. Nemorino is thus convinced that the elixir has worked and, moved to compassion at the sight of Adina's tears, sings the romance, "Una furtiva lagrima," a remarkably beautiful melodic inspiration, even for the melodist, Donizetti.

Una furtiva lagrima (*A Furtive Tear*) *Beniamino Gigli* 7194-2.00 *Tito Schipa* 6570-2.00 *Enrico Caruso* 6016-2.00

Down her soft cheek a furtive tear
   Stole from her eyelids dark,
Telling their gay and festive cheer,
   It pained her soul to mark;
Why then her dear presence fly?
   When all her love she is showing?
Could I but feel her beating heart
   Pressing against mine own;
Could I my feeling soft impart,
   And mingle sigh with sigh,
Gladly then I would die,
   All her love knowing!

Adina soon returns, bringing the soldier's contract, and says that Nemorino must not go away. All misunderstandings are now cleared, and Belcore arrives to find his bride-to-be embracing another. He considers the situation with true soldierly philosophy, saying, "There are other women." As he goes off the villagers tell Adina and Nemorino of the latter's good fortune. The doctor claims credit for the reconciliation, and the curtain falls as he is relieving the peasants of their wages in return for bottles of his wonderful Elixir of Love.

THE EMPEROR JONES

OPERA in two acts, a prologue, an interlude and six scenes. After the play by Eugene O'Neill. Libretto by Kathleen de Jaffa; music by Louis Gruenberg (Op. 36). First performed by the Metropolitan Opera Company of New York, at the Metropolitan Opera house, with Lawrence Tibbett in the title role, 1933.

THE opera is based on the story of the powerfully-built negro convict Jones, in the toils of the law for the murder of a friend in a crap-game. While working in a chain-gang, Jones kills a guard, escapes, and stows away on a ship which eventually lands him in Africa. Here his superior sophistication enables him to dominate the natives; he becomes "Emperor" of a tribe, and this position of eminence gives him opportunity to loot, ravish and otherwise exploit his imperial powers. He has a revolver, in which the last bullet is a silver one—the only one potent enough, he tells his subjects, to kill the Emperor Jones. This bullet he will use when, as and if he finds it necessary, but as the opera begins, Jones foresees no imminent need for the silver bullet. In the prologue, however, we are permitted to observe what the Emperor Jones has not yet perceived—that his subjects are weary of his overbearing and cruel rule, and that they are preparing his downfall. "He mus' die, he mus', he mus'," they chant; "he steal our money, he steal our women, he make us bump our heads on de ground to him lik' a god. Huh!"

In the first act Jones confides to Henry Smithers, a cockney trader with whom he is in league and who also is a subject of the Emperor, that he is planning to abandon the tribe, and escape to the coast with much treasure. He says he has câchéd food and other supplies along the trail, and that he will find his way without difficulty to a coastal point where a French gunboat will pick him up and take him to safety, to the riches he has stored in a foreign bank.

Smithers indicates it is high time for this escape, for already the tribe is in revolt. Jones scoffs at this, but finds it alarmingly true when he summons his ministers and court, and no one answers. At this Jones "resigns de job of Emperor" and plans departure immediately. There is an interlude during which the voices of the tribe are heard, savage, determined, and threatening.

The second act deals with Jones' attempted flight through the forest, and his pursuit by his own fears and by the ever-louder, closer and persistent drums of his savage subjects. Frightened by shadows and by his conscience, the Emperor wears himself out in the tangled ways of the jungle. His gorgeous uniform is in

Edwards

TIBBETT AS THE "EMPEROR"

rags; his feet are tortured in his fancy boots, and tortured more terribly when he runs barefoot. Hallucinations bedevil him, and cause him to shoot wildly at shadows, using up all but the silver bullet and incidentally revealing his position to his pursuing enemies. At length the last shred of bravado leaves him, and he breaks down in a plea to the Almighty for mercy. This desperate supplication is a distorted form of an old spiritual which he remembers from his youth—"Standin' in the Need o' Prayer."

Standin' in de Need of Prayer   *Lawrence Tibbett* **7959-2.00**

He confesses his murders and his lesser crime, and begs mercy—but it is too late. The ghosts of his victims appear to him; he shoots wildly, then runs desperately here and there. It is no use; and when, as a final terror, he is confronted by the witch-doctor of the tribe, who summons the avenging natives, Jones, with a last scream of supplication, fires the fatal bullet into his head, and dies. The tribesmen, at first awed, presently gather about and with growing courage abuse the body. They dance in a frenzy of triumphant vengeance, and at length disappear in the forest. The stage is left to Smithers, who, inspecting the body of the Emperor Jones, mutters "Dead as a 'erring. Well, God blimey, yer died in a grand style, anyhow."

ELVIRA'S APARTMENT—ACT I

ERNANI

OPERA in four acts; music by Giuseppe Verdi; words by Piave, after Victor Hugo's drama, "Hernani." First produced at La Fenice Theatre, Venice, March 9, 1844. First performance in the United States, at the Park Theatre, New York, April 15, 1847. Revived by the Metropolitan Opera Company, December 17, 1928, with Ponselle, Martinelli, and Ruffo.

It is interesting to compare this, the earliest of Verdi's operas still to hold the stage, with mature work represented in one of his later operas, such as "Aïda." Although Verdi continually made advances in all features of his art, the earlier work, does, however, display the same genius for melody that ever was his.

Even as a small child, Verdi manifested his passion for music. It is recorded that as a very young boy he was greatly fascinated by the melodies of a passing hand organ, and would follow the player through the streets as far as his own childish strength would permit or his parents allow. There is a certain poetic justice in this happening to the future composer, whose operas were to become the main source of supply for the hand-organ repertoire during the next hundred years.

"Ernani" was a success from its first production, which, however, was not without its excitement. The Venetian police found the conspiracy scene in the tomb of Charlemagne too stirring; it might incite volatile Italians to revolt, for Venice was then under Austrian rule. A nobleman complained of the scene in which Don Silva sounds the hunting horn as a desecration. When "Ernani" was performed in Paris, Victor Hugo more justly resented the melodramatic atmosphere the librettist had thrown around the tragedy. Nevertheless "Ernani" was for its day a fine opera; its melodious arias and dramatic ensembles still endear it to the public. (The name of the opera is pronounced *Ayr-nah'-nee*.)

CHARACTERS

DON CARLOS, *King of Castile*	*Baritone*
DON RUY GOMEZ DE SILVA, (*Day Seel'-vah*), *a Grandee of Spain*	*Bass*
ERNANI, *a bandit chief*	*Tenor*
ELVIRA (*El-vee'-rah*), *betrothed to Don Silva*	*Soprano*

123

Esquires, Attendants, Mountaineers, Bandits, followers of Don Silva, followers of the King. Spanish and German Nobles and Ladies, Electors, and Pages.
The action takes place in Aragon, about the year 1519.

ACT I

Scene I

THE father of John of Aragon has been murdered in cold blood by Don Carlos, King of Castile, and John himself driven from the land of his ancestor. He has taken refuge in the mountains and, under the name of Ernani, has become leader of a band of brigands.

Infelice e tu credevi *(Unhappy One)* **Ezio Pinza** 7552-2.00

Only one thing remains from his past—his love for Elvira; now, he tells his followers, she is to be married to her guardian. The bandits pledge their service and unite in a plan to prevent the wedding.

Scene II

In the solitude of her chamber, Elvira awaits sacrifice, lamenting the loss of her lover. Grief-stricken, she calls to him for aid, though he is far beyond hearing.

> Ernani, fly with me;
> Prevent this hated marriage!
> With thee, e'en the barren desert
> Would seem an Eden of enchantment!
> One nightless, unending day!
> One Eden of enchantment!

Ernani involami *(Ernani, Fly With Me)* **Rosa Ponselle** 6875-2.00

This is a coloratura number, rich in vocal display, but joined with it is a genuine expression of despair. It closes with a brilliant cadenza.

Don Carlos, King of Castile, comes in disguise, to make love to her. He is a fiery lover, and though she repulses him, he is about to drag her off by force when a secret panel opens and Ernani enters. The sounds of their violent argument attract Don Silva, who rushes in, astonished to find two men fighting over his bride on her wedding eve. In violent rage he calls for his armor and sword; then happening to recognize the King, against whom he dare not fight, he bows politely. The King points to Ernani and says that he wishes him to leave. Thus Ernani is temporarily safe, for a noble Spaniard would not leave an enemy for another's vengeance.

ACT II

ELVIRA and Silva are about to be married; Elvira has been told that Ernani is dead. To Silva comes a pilgrim seeking shelter; as the presence of a holy man is supposed to bring blessings on a household sheltering him, he is welcomed. Moreover, under the old law of hospitality he becomes Silva's guest, and therefore entitled to his protection.

Elvira enters in her bridal attire. The supposed pilgrim reveals himself—Ernani! He demands to be given over to the King for he prefers death to life without his beloved. But Don Silva, bound to protect his guest, refuses. The King, however, suddenly arrives and Ernani is concealed in a secret passage. Don Silva will not give up Ernani even at the King's orders; and as the King's soldiers fail to find Ernani when they search the castle, Don Carlos drags away Elvira as hostage.

Don Silva calls Ernani from his hiding and taking down two swords, bids him fight with him to the death. Ernani refuses, for his host has just saved his life at the risk of his own. Let them first unite to save Elvira from the King. Then he will yield himself. As a pledge, Ernani gives Silva a hunting horn, and swears by the memory of his dead father, that when the horn is blown, he shall return to yield his life.

Mishkin

PONSELLE AS ELVIRA

ACT III

CARLOS is conducted by one of his esquires who has been informed of the plot, to the gloomy catacombs of Aix-la-Chapelle, the chosen meeting place of the conspirators. Here is the tomb of Charlemagne, and Carlos, thinking of his great ancestor, is struck with horror and exclaims:

Great Heaven! Is't here upon my father's tombstone they come to whet the knife wherewith to slay me! Sceptre, dominion, ye conquests of glory, pride of youth, vain shows, what are ye? Oh bright and fleeting shadows . . . I bid ye farewell forever. . . . Yet if 'tis the will of Heaven that power be given to me, I'll triumph o'er worldly passions, and win a deathless fame!

He then unlocks the entrance of Charlemagne's tomb and enters. The conspirators forthwith arrive, and at their meeting Ernani is chosen to assassinate the King. A sudden booming of cannon announces that Carlos has been elected Emperor. At the self-same moment Carlos steps forth from his hiding place, and an instant later the electors and a great crowd of nobles appear to acclaim him as Emperor. Carlos immediately condemns the conspirators to death, but, moved by the prayers of Elvira and a wish to begin his new rule by an act of grace, pardons them, and even unites Ernani and Elvira. All join in an impressive chorus in praise of Carlos for his nobility and kindness, all save Silva, who still plots vengeance; his ominous

THE TOMB OF CHARLEMAGNE—ACT IV

mutterings may be heard at times even through this magnificently swelling song of praise.

O **sommo Carlo** (*Oh Noble Carlos*) *De Luca, Tedesco, Anthony, Metropolitan Opera Chorus* 8174-2.00

ACT IV

I N the very midst of the wedding festivities of Ernani and Elvira, a sudden blast from a horn is heard; Don Silva has come to claim his debt. True to his oath, Ernani stabs himself and Elvira falls across his lifeless form. Don Silva has his revenge!

EUGEN ONÉGIN

OPERA in three acts; music by Peter Iljitch Tschaikowsky; text by the composer and Constantine Shilovsky, based on Pushkin's poetic romance of the same name. First produced by students of the Moscow Conservatory in March, 1879. First performance in the United States, March 24, 1920, at the Metropolitan Opera House, New York, in Italian. It had been given in concert form by the Symphony Society of New York, at Carnegie Hall, February 1, 1908.

Not without reason is this the most successful of Tschaikowsky's fairly numerous operas, for Pushkin's elegiac and subjective romance is ideally adapted to this most subjective of composers. Pushkin's story aroused great enthusiasm in Tschaikowsky—the ideal mood for composition, and moreover, inspired him to write music more genuinely Russian in style than is usual in his operas.

The action takes place upon an estate near, and in the city of St. Petersburg during the second decade of the Nineteenth Century.

ACT I

To the dilapidated country house of Mme. Lerin near St. Petersburg, comes her daughter Olga's fiancé, Lenski, and his friend, Eugen Onégin, a Russian gallant, rather bored by rural scenes. Olga's romantic sister, Tatiana, falls in love with the haughty Onégin at first sight, and that night pours out her soul in a letter which she sends to him. Onégin meets her as she has requested, but spurns her confession of love, saying that he has neither time nor inclination for affairs of the heart. Tatiana runs away in utter dejection, overcome with shame.

THE BALL IN HONOR OF TATIANA

ACT II

A BALL is being given in honor of Tatiana's birthday. Here is heard the charming and brilliant waltz, now a concert favorite.

Waltz *Royal Opera Orchestra, Cond. by Eugene Goossens* 9026-1.50

Eugen, who is present, ignores Tatiana, and flirts with her sister, thus arousing Lenski's jealousy who challenges him to a duel. Early the following morning, Lenski awaits Onégin at the place appointed—a mill by a wooded stream. Looking over the desolate winter landscape, Lenski thinks of his youth that seems so remote, and of death that seems so near.

Soon the duel takes place and Lenski falls. Onégin, realizing his folly, is overwhelmed with remorse.

Bains
DE LUCA IN EUGEN ONÉGIN

ACT III

A FTER six years of restless travelling in search of peace of mind, Onégin returns to St. Petersburg and is invited by Prince Gramin to a ball at his palace. Picture his astonishment when he discovers there Tatiana, now the wife of the Prince, a man of distinction and in high favor with the Czar. He promptly falls in love with the beautiful woman whom he once spurned. Seeking her out he declares his passion; but she decides to remain true to her husband, while admitting that she still loves Onégin. Onégin is left despondent, overcome by mingled yearning and cynicism.

EURYANTHE

OPERA in three acts; music by Carl Maria von Weber; libretto by Helmine von Chezy, based on an old French romance, "L'Histoire de Gerard de Nevers. . . ." The opera was written for the Kärnthnerthor Theatre, Vienna, where it was produced, October 25, 1823. Performed at the Metropolitan Opera House, New York, December 23, 1887. A performance is reputed to have taken place at Wallack's Theatre, New York, about 1863. (The title of the opera is pronounced *Oy-rahn'-teh*.)

This opera, which because of its inane libretto seems to hold only a most transient place in the repertoire, is known to the public largely through its overture, which ranks among von Weber's greatest compositions. Like the Overture to Oberon which has a dominant element in the fairy atmosphere, so the Overture to Euryanthe has for its keynote, chivalry. A brilliant introduction is followed by a knightly theme from an air of Adolar's, in which that hero affirms his faith in his bride, Euryanthe. His love is indicated by the use of a melody from another aria of his, as a lyrical, second theme. Then there is heard a *Largo*, symbolical of the ghost of Emma, cause of all the tribulations depicted in the ensuing turbulent music *(beginning of Part II)*. Chivalry and love triumph, however, as is indicated in the joyful return of the earlier themes.

Overture Berlin State Opera Orchestra, Leo Blech, Conductor 9398-1.50

THE STORY

Adolar, Count of Nevers and Rethel, in an argument with Lysiart, Count of Forest and Beaujolais, is led to wager all his possessions on the faithfulness of his bride, Euryanthe. It happens that Euryanthe has become intimate with Eglantine de Duiset, who is herself in love with Adolar, and desiring vengeance, learns from Euryanthe the secret of her sister Emma's suicide, and steals from the girl's tomb a ring. This she gives to Lysiart, who displays it as evidence of Euryanthe's faithlessness. Adolar, deprived of his possessions, abandons his bride, believing her guilty. Eglantine, about to marry Lysiart, sees Emma's ghost, and reveals the plot. In his anger, Lysiart stabs her—for this he is led away to execution. Adolar, his possessions restored, is united to the forgiving Euryanthe.

FALSTAFF—THE FINALE

FALSTAFF

OPERA in three acts; music by Giuseppe Verdi; libretto by Arrigo Boïto, after Shakespeare's "Merry Wives of Windsor" and "King Henry IV." First produced, March 12, 1893, at La Scala, Milan. First performance in the Western Hemisphere, at Buenos Aires, July 19, 1893, and in the United States, February 4, 1895, at the Metropolitan Opera House, New York.

Like the comic hero of his final opera, Verdi once had an unexpected plunge into a stream of water, though for different reasons! When a boy of about ten years, living at the village of Busseto, he held the position of organist at another village several miles distant. The story goes that while walking homeward one Sunday evening, exhausted through lack of food and sleep, he did not observe that he was on the wrong path and fell into a deep canal, where he surely would have drowned for, paralyzed by the bitter cold, he was being rapidly carried away by the current, when a passerby heard his cries through the darkness and brought help. This experience may, indeed, have served to temper his laughter at the fat knight when, years later, he came to set Falstaff's adventure to music.

What a wonder that Verdi, after composing a long line of tragic operas, should end his career with a comedy! That this comic work should be a masterpiece is a tribute to the versatility of his genius; and that the composer was over eighty years of age when writing it is evidence of his inborn energy. The music of "Falstaff" sparkles and bubbles over with high spirits; it combines boyish fun with a Mozartian delicacy and skill in musical technique, remarkable in a man of any age.

It was while singing the rôle of Ford in a revival of "Falstaff" at the Metropolitan Opera House, that Lawrence Tibbett first won fame.

ACT I

THE jovial, fat old rogue, Falstaff, is with his friends, Bardolph and Pistol, at the Garter Inn. Dr. Caius arrives and quarrels with the Knight, but is soon thrown out. Falstaff then writes his extraordinary love letters, one to Mistress Page, the other to Mistress Ford.

In Ford's garden the two women compare the letters, and discovering them to be alike, plan revenge. In this they are joined by the men, Ford, Fenton, and Dr. Caius; even Bardolph and Pistol will help, for they too, having smarted under Falstaff's jibes, want vengeance. Fenton is on hand because he is in love with Mistress Ford's daughter, Anne, even though Ford himself plans to have her marry Dr. Caius. Dame Quickly is sent to invite Falstaff to an interview with Mistress Ford, and meanwhile the men arrange to have Ford introduced to Falstaff under an assumed name.

ACT II

DAME QUICKLY delivers her message, and Ford, introduced as Signor Fortuna, offers money to the fat knight to intercede for him with Mistress Ford. Falstaff says he will be delighted to "intercede," and goes to array himself in his very best attire, leaving the irate husband to swallow his jealousy.

Mishkin

TIBBETT AS FORD

Falstaff arrives at Ford's house, but before he can proceed very far with his interview, Ford is heard coming. Falstaff quickly hides behind a screen. Ford enters with the other men and, hoping to find the rakish knight, begins a search of the house. As soon as the men are out, the women hurriedly conceal Falstaff in a large laundry basket they have thoughtfully provided, pile soiled clothes over him, and fasten down the lid. A moment later Ford returns having thought of the screen. Even as he enters he hears back of it a sound suspiciously like a kiss—Fenton and Anne are having an unrehearsed love scene of their own! Ford rushes out, more enraged than ever.

Thereupon his wife has the servants empty the basket into the Thames, which flows below. Ford returns in time to be shown the knight climbing clumsily from the water, laughed at by all who see him.

ACT III

FALSTAFF is back at the inn, sad and stiff. After much explaining, Dame Quickly consoles him and arranges another meeting. Falstaff keeps this assignation with great trembling, for it is held at midnight at a haunted spot in Windsor Forest. The moment Falstaff begins his awkward love making ghostly sounds are heard; Mistress Ford runs away in mock terror;

Falstaff throws himself face downwards on the ground, for it is fatal to gaze on supernatural beings! The whole company enter, disguised as fairies. They seem to stumble upon Falstaff accidentally, then give this "impure mortal" a sound thrashing until he promises to mend his ways. Ford has definitely agreed to give Anne in marriage to Dr. Caius, but the women, set on helping Fenton's cause, have confused the men in their disguises. Thus when masks are suddenly removed, Dr. Caius finds that he has been making love to Bardolph. In the laughter that follows, Ford agrees to the union of Fenton and Anne, and all ends happily . . . except for Falstaff.

Byron FALSTAFF GETS IN THE BASKET

THE KERMESS (PARIS OPERA)

FAUST

OPERA in five acts by Charles Gounod; words by Barbier and Carré. Produced at the Théâtre Lyrique, Paris, March 19, 1859; first performance in the United States, at the Academy of Music, New York, November 25, 1863, in Italian. It is reputed to have been performed by a German company in Philadelphia, November 18, 1863.

Like many another famous opera, "Faust" received scant success at first, being given only occasionally during the ten years after its production. Gounod revised the score, introducing a ballet in the last act, for performance at the Grand Opéra, Paris, March 3, 1869. From that date the work had such success that during the next eight years it received 1,000 performances at that theatre alone.

Goethe's tragedy, "Faust," is written on too vast a scale for treatment in a single opera; the writers of the libretto for Gounod's work, therefore, wisely limited themselves to the single episode of Faust and Gretchen (Marguerite in the opera). Thus they produced a text, lacking in the literary greatness of the original, but remarkably adapted for effective operatic treatment. And Gounod was the ideal man to set this libretto to music.

Charles Gounod was the son of parents who were gifted in the arts, his father being a painter, and his mother, who gave him his early musical training, a distinguished pianist. Before seriously taking up the study of music, however, he received a thorough classical training. Then, in 1836, he entered the Conservatoire, and three years later won the famous Prix-de-Rome. While continuing his musical career at Rome under the terms of this prize, he became deeply engrossed in the religious music of Palestrina. On his return to Paris he became organist in one of the leading churches, and his interest in religion deepened to such an extent that he at one time studied for the priesthood. He was therefore a combination of churchman and artist, and until "Faust" was produced his sacred music included, perhaps, the best of his work. His secular compositions, however, revealed a power of sensuous melody rather startling in a man of his ecclesiastical tendencies. Thus it was that in "Faust," with its conflicting human passions and religious sentiment, he found the perfect vehicle for his complex nature. Today it remains his masterpiece.

(In French, "Faust" is pronounced *Fohst*; Americans, however, generally give it the German pronunciation, *Fowst*, although giving a French pronunciation to the names of the other characters in the opera.)

This truly great and unfailingly popular opera, with its amazing wealth of melody and invention, its dramatic and colorful orchestral treatment, has been recorded in its entirety for Victor by the artistic forces of l'Opéra, Paris, where, incidentally, its first successful performance was given. The recorded performance is done under the direction of Henri Busser.

CHARACTERS

FAUST *(Fowst)*	Tenor
MEPHISTOPHELES *(Meh-fees-tof-el-layz')*	Bass
VALENTINE *(Val'-en-teen)*	Baritone
BRANDER *or* WAGNER	Baritone
SIEBEL *(See-bel)*	Mezzo-Soprano
MARGUERITE *(Mahr-guer-eet')*	Soprano
MARTHA *(Mar-ta')*	Contralto

Students, Soldiers, Villagers, Sorcerers, Spirits.
The action takes place in Germany during the Sixteenth Century.

Complete Famous Artists and Orchestra of l'Opéra, Paris, Conducted by Henri Busser. Album M-105 (11000-11019) AM-105 (11020-11039) Price $30.00

ACT I

INTRODUCTION *(M 105-1)*

FAUST, hoary and bent with age, is alone in his study poring over an immense volume which lies open on the table before him. By the flickering light of a dying lamp the strange utensils of medieval necromancy scattered about the murky confines of this oppressive chamber are only half discernible. Faust, renowned and learned philosopher though he be, is weary of life *(M 105-2)* and the vain pursuit of knowledge . . . The riddle of the universe is for him still unsolved. He seizes a flask of poison, pours the liquid into a goblet and puts it to his lips. Outside the day has been dawning unobserved in this dusty and closely shuttered cell. The cheerful song *(M 105-3)* of young women passing down the street stops him as he is about to drink. When the song dies away he again raises the goblet and again he is arrested by a song, this time the song of a group of laborers making merry outside. The tune is fresh and spring-like, a pastorale in marked contrast to the gloomy and reflective polyphony of Faust's own music. The sage *(M 105-4)*, overpowered with envy and despair at these evidences of youth and human happiness, curses life with its relentlessly advancing age and calls aloud to Satan for help.

There is a flash of light and through it rises Mephistopheles, the Evil One, clad in the height of fashion as a cavalier. In his sophisticated manner, alternately gay, cynical, and blandly ingratiating, he offers Faust wealth and power *(M 105-5)*. Faust wishes neither without the gift of youth. This boon, too, the tempter will grant, if Faust will sign away his soul. The philosopher hesitates. At a gesture from Mephistopheles a glowing vision is revealed, a beautiful maiden seated at a spinning wheel, with her long blond hair braided and falling down her back. Faust gazes at her in ecstasy. In the orchestra is heard a romantic melody against a shimmering accompaniment while Faust declares that, for such loveliness, he is willing to pawn his immortal soul . . . Men have declared such things with no Mephistopheles at hand. He drinks the magic potion which his new-found friend offers, exclaiming to the vision, "To thee!" As the vision disappears,

Painted by Kreling

FAUST, AGED PHILOSOPHER, WEARIES OF LIFE

Mephistopheles reassures Faust that he will see the maiden again that very day. A supernatural transformation takes place. The philosopher's garb, grey beard, and other evidences of age vanish; instead of the wearied scholar, Faust is now an impetuous youth, elegantly clad, eager for adventure. Faust and Mephistopheles dash out in quest of it.

ACT II

A CROWD has gathered to celebrate at the "Kermess," the fair of a German village. Prominent in the scene is the inn, which bears as a sign a carved image of Bacchus astride a keg. Amid this confusion of humanity are students, soldiers, burghers young and old, maidens, and matrons. Each group is cleverly differentiated in the gay, bantering music *(M 105-6 and 7)*, the chatter of the toothless old men being a clever detail.

> **Vin ou bière** *(The Fair)* **Metropolitan Opera Chorus** 9697-1.50
> **Ainsi que la brise légère** *(Waltz and Chorus)* **Metropolitan Opera Chorus** 9697-1.50

Valentine and Siebel join the crowd. Valentine is pensively examining a medallion which Marguerite, his sister, has given him as a charm to protect him from the dangers of battle. He is to depart with the soldiers that evening and is worried about the welfare of his motherless sister. Siebel, generous

PINZA AS MEPHISTOPHELES

hearted and seriously in love with Marguerite, even though he is a beardless youth too young to go to war, impulsively offers to be her guardian. To a melody of unusual breadth and sweep Valentine prays for heaven's protection on his sister during his absence (M 105-8).

Dio possente (Even Bravest Heart) **Giuseppe de Luca** 7086-2.00 Avant de quitter ces lieux **Tibbett** 8452-2.00

Wagner, one of the students, wishing to banish this solemn mood, jumps onto a table and begins to sing a ribald ditty concerning a rat (M 105-9). Mephistopheles pushes through the crowd, interrupts the song and offers to sing a better one. It turns out to be the fantastic song of "The Calf of Gold," a cynical description of man's worship of Mammon. It ends with a weird dance which Mephistopheles himself leads.

The Calf of Gold *Pinza and the Metropolitan Opera Chorus* 1753-1.50 *Chaliapin, Cozette* 7600-2.00

The crowd is vastly entertained, and the stranger soon finds himself in the middle of an admiring circle, while he tells fortunes and reads palms. Among others he catches Siebel, and succeeds in seriously disturbing him by foretelling that whatever flower he touches will wither in his grasp.

Wagner, delighted with this vivacious newcomer, proposes a drink (M 105-10). Wine is brought, but when Mephistopheles tastes it, he exclaims with displeasure. He offers to give them better wine, strides over to the inn and strikes the sign before it with his sword. A magical liquid gushes forth; from it each one can drink a vintage of his own choosing. Raising his glass, Mephistopheles proposes a toast to Marguerite. Valentine, terrifically enraged and insulted at thus hearing his sister's name flaunted about in public by a stranger, at once draws his sword and makes for him. Mephistopheles quickly traces a magic circle about himself and, when Valentine's sword passes it, the blade breaks. With a quick medieval instinct, Valentine realizes the iden-

Mishkin

TIBBETT AS VALENTINE

136

tity of his opponent, and seizing the sword by its broken end, holds it aloft toward the fiend. The hilt and guard of the sword form an emblem of the Cross. The other soldiers follow Valentine's example, all uniting, meanwhile, in a noble chant, with broad, sustained harmonies, magnificent in strength and simplicity. The Evil One shrinks impotent and in terror from this array of cross-shaped sword hilts.

Such impressive solemnity is quickly forgotten, however, for the crowd returns to take part in the kermess dance *(M 105-11)*. A gay, rippling melody is heard and the people give themselves up to the enchantment of the waltz. The tune, played by the violins, has a captivating lilt and refreshing exuberance; meanwhile the dancers sing yet another melody giving voice to their delight. Marguerite approaches, wending her way rather timidly through the whirl of dancers; she is on her way home from church, prayer book in hand. Siebel wishes to join her, but every time he starts toward her he is confronted by the suave yet ominous figure of Mephistopheles, who always adroitly manages to get in the way. Meanwhile Faust approaches the maiden and respectfully asks her *(M 105-12)* :

> High-born and lovely maid, forgive my humble duty,
> Let me, your willing slave, attend you home today

Overwhelmed with confusion, she modestly, and yet not without a touch of feminine coyness replies:

> No, my lord, not a lady am I,
> Nor yet a beauty;
> And do not need an arm
> To help me on my way.

Then she goes, leaving Faust trembling with ecstasy; music, first of ingratiating charm, then glowingly rapturous, accompanies their meeting. Mephistopheles approaches and laughingly suggests that his aid will be needed in winning Marguerite. The waltz is resumed and soon the square is again filled with a whirling maze of dancers lost in reckless gaiety.

ACT III

THE garden before Marguerite's cottage is a delightfully old-fashioned place with trees, shrubs and flower beds laid out in orderly profusion. Valentine has gone away to the war, and Siebel, in keeping with his promise, is loitering near Marguerite's home. He picks some flowers for her, singing meanwhile a cheerful, rather youthful song, "Le parlate d'amore" *(Flower Song) (M 105-13):*

> Gentle flow'rs in the dew
> Bear love from me,
> Tell her no flow'r is rarer,
> Tell her that she is fairer,
> Dearer to me than all,
> Though fair you be!

137

But suddenly he notices that the flowers are withered in his hand. Greatly perturbed he exclaims:

'Tis withered! Alas! that dark stranger foretold me what my fate must be. . . .
Never to touch a single flower but it must decay. . . .

Then noticing a little font with holy water, he has a happy thought: "Suppose I dip my hand in holy water?" To delicate, reverent, harmonies he meditates:

'Tis here when day is o'er that she prays: Marguerite.
Yes, now I will try, and this moment! Can it be withered?
No! Thou fiend! Thy power is gone!

Again happy, he resumes his song:

Gentle flowers lie there
And tell her from me,
Would she but deign to hear me,
And with one smile to cheer me,
For delight so sweet
I would die at her feet,
I would die for her.

He arranges the flowers in a bouquet which he places on the house steps in hopes that Marguerite will find it. Then he leaves.

He has been watched, however, and now Faust and the grinning

Photo Boyer and Bert   SETTING FOR GARDEN SCENE AT PARIS OPERA

Mephistopheles step from behind the bushes. Faust is dreamy *(M 105-14)*, quiet, distraught, for by this time he is desperately in love with Marguerite. On the other hand, his demoniac companion is in high glee—he is bringing about unhappiness and tragedy in the world. Mephistopheles leaves for a moment to fetch, as he says, a companion to Siebel's bouquet.

Faust's worship extends, lover-like, even to the dwelling which houses his beloved. He sings to it his apostrophe, a melody of exquisite tenderness, a violin obligato wreathed about it.

RETHBERG AS MARGUERITE

> **Salut demeure** *(All Hail, Thou Dwelling)* **Giacomo Lauri-Volpi** 7389-2.00

> All hail, thou dwelling pure and lowly!
> Home of an angel fair and holy,
> What wealth is here, what wealth outbidding gold,
> Of peace and love, and innocence untold!
> Bounteous nature!
> 'Twas here by day thy love was taught her,
> Here thou didst with care overshadow thy daughter
> In her dream of the night!
> Here, waving tree and flower
> Made her an Eden-bower of beauty and delight.

Mephistopheles forthwith returns, bringing a casket of jewels *(M 105-15)*. This he places near Siebel's bouquet. The Tempter knows the heart of a woman as of a man—flowers against gems? At this moment Marguerite enters the garden through the wicket gate and the intruders hurriedly conceal themselves.

Marguerite, lovely and unspoiled, is at the mysterious threshold of life, in mind an unsophisticated child, in body a beautiful woman. A naïve, hesitant melody is heard from the orchestra at her entrance. She seats herself at the spinning-wheel to take up her work and as she starts to spin she begins to sing a simple old song that happens to be floating through her mind. It is a quaint old melody, with words that tell the time-honored legend of the faithful King of Thulé and his golden goblet; the orchestra supplies delicately tinted, archaic harmonies.

Le Roi de Thulé *(The King of Thulé)* **Elisabeth Rethberg** 7179-2.00

The spinning suddenly ceases, the song is broken off in the middle; without her realizing it, her thoughts have wandered to the handsome stranger who addressed her so politely . . . who can he be? With an effort she resumes her work and her song *(M 105-16)*, only to let the second stanza suffer a similar unwilled though not unpleasant interruption. Even the day itself is languid, dreamy, adapted to her mood. She turns slowly towards the house. The bouquet of bright flowers catches her eye. Siebel's, of course, poor boy; but look—a casket! Obviously, she cannot resist the temptation of looking to see what is in it. Jewels! She trembles with delight at the sight of their brilliance. To resist their lure would be to resist nature. She hesitates, then begins to deck herself out with them. Looking at herself and the sparkling gems in the handglass that came with the casket she bursts into the brilliant "Jewel Song" *(M 105-17)*.

Air des Bijoux *(The Jewel Song)* **Elisabeth Rethberg 7179-2.00**

Marguerite, alone in her garden, is at last drawn away from her reserve and carols away with bird-like exuberance.

Soon the patter-tongued matron, neighbor Martha, enters *(M 105-18)*. She goes into raptures over the necklace and other treasures. But this flighty soul's delight is cut short by Mephistopheles, who enters and salutes her gracefully. He brings her the sad news that her absent husband is dead. After a few rather conventional exclamations of grief she ceases to lament, for Mephistopheles behaves so graciously that strange hopes spring up in her own old, foolish heart. Faust gently induces Marguerite to take his arm, and the four promenade the garden, now growing dim under the lengthening shadows of evening. As the couples pass and repass, we catch snatches of their conversation, their voices blending, at times, into a quartet of wonderful harmony *(M 105-19)*. While Martha becomes increasingly persistent in her attentions to the gallant cavalier in red, entirely infatuated with his worldly-wise manner, Marguerite and Faust grow more and more confiding in one another, oblivious to all else. Suddenly Marguerite realizes that it is late, night is at hand; she entreats Faust to leave. He grasps her impetuously, but she flees into the shadows of the garden. Martha crosses the scene searching her demon suitor, who seems to have escaped from her, and whom she now dreams of marrying. Then, safely alone, Mephistopheles appears, and raising his arms solemnly, sings an impressive "Invocation" *(M 105-20)*. He calls upon night to cast its bewitching shadows over the lovers, and upon the flowers to bring, with the subtle magic of their perfume, sorrow to the soul of Marguerite.

The soft, voluptuous darkness of the night envelops the garden. Mephistopheles slinks into

From a Lithograph

THE QUARTET

the shadows, his invocation completed, when the lovers come along the path. Marguerite gently bids farewell to her lover *(M 105-21)*. The enchantment of the night is beginning to work, however, and Faust pleads with her to let him still gaze upon her face. Marguerite naïvely draws the petals from a flower one by one, playing the age-old game of "he loves me—he loves me not." It ends with a little cry of joy, "He loves me." "Believe the flower," Faust exclaims, drawing nearer. Lost in ecstasy, they sing a wonderful duet: music that is vibrant with the expression of the sensuous beauty of human love in all its depth, sincerity and sweetness. Soft chords in the woodwinds, mellow tones of horns and strings blend with the voices of the lovers as the night draws its soft veil about them *(M 105-22)*. Marguerite, breaking away from her lover, runs to the house; but at the door she pauses to throw him a kiss. Faust has a promise to meet her on the morrow, and already he longs for the morning to come.

"Wait!" cries Mephistopheles coming up behind him. "You dreamer, wait and hear what she tells to the stars!"

Indeed, at this very instant, Marguerite opens her casement window, and she pours out to the night the song of her rapture. The melody, borne upward by flute and clarinet, climbs slowly to the heights of ecstatic expression. Almost radiant in contrast with the luxuriant blue darkness which enfolds her, she stands uttering her tremulous cry to the deaf ears of the night. Faust has been listening, shaken with love's agitation. As Marguerite in her impassioned imaginings calls out, "Tomorrow—tomorrow! Ah! hasten thy return, my beloved! Come!" Mephistopheles, who has been holding the youth, now releases him. Faust rushes to the open window, crying out "Marguerite" and clasps the maiden in his arms. The lovers are enveloped in the blackness of night, punctuated only by sardonic laughter from the fiend in the garden.

ACT IV

MARGUERITE sits alone in her room wearily toiling at her spinning. Outside in the street girls of the village pass by making jeering remarks about Marguerite and her lover. Betrayed and deserted, Marguerite trembles with remorse. Of her friends, Siebel alone remains faithful. He comes to console her and offers her his own love. He speaks a word

MEPHISTOPHELES: "Elle ouvre sa Fenêtre"

141

Painted by Kreling
MARGUERITE

against Faust, however, and to that Marguerite of the guileless heart will not listen for she still trusts in her lover.

Marguerite flees to the cathedral for consolation where we behold her kneeling in agonized prayer *(M 105-23)*. In response, she hears the mocking voices of Mephistopheles and a choir of demons who jeeringly call her name from infernal regions, saying that it is too late, prayer is useless. Indeed, the very awesomeness of the dark medieval structure adds to her misery; and the cathedral choir, that might sing of hope and salvation, is now chanting of the dreadful day of judgment when even the just shall tremble *(M 105-24)*.

The oppressiveness of the dark church, the thunderlike tones of the organ, the portentous chant of the choir, the menacing words of the Evil One, and the taunts of the demons, all conspire to torture the soul of Marguerite. Terror-stricken and despairing of peace, she rushes out of the cathedral, crying aloud in her agony.

Again the scene is changed and we see a square before the cathedral in which Marguerite has just prayed so hopelessly; at one side of the square is her house *(M 105-25)*. Martial music is heard. The troops are coming home victorious; they express their happiness in the famous strains of the "Soldiers' Chorus" *(Concluded on M 105-26)*.

Soldiers' Chorus   *Victor Male Chorus* 19783-.75

> Glory and love to the men of old,
> Their sons may copy their virtues bold,
> Courage in heart and sword in hand,
> Ready to fight or ready to die for Fatherland!
> Who needs bidding to dare, by a trumpet blown?
> Who lacks pity to spare, when the field is won?
> Who would fly from a foe, if alone, or last?
> And boast he was true, as cowards might do
> When peril is past?
>
> Now to home again we come,
> The long and fiery strife of battle over;
> Rest is pleasant after toil as hard as ours
> Beneath a stranger sun.
> Many a maiden fair is awaiting here
> To greet her truant soldier lover,
> And many a heart will fail and brow grow pale,
> To hear the tale of peril he has run!
> Glory and love to the men of old,
> Their sons may copy their virtues bold,
> Courage in heart and sword in hand,
> Ready to fight or ready to die for Fatherland!

The rejoicing of the welcome over, the crowd drifts away; Valentine enters his sister's house, and the tranquillity of dusk descends upon the scene *(M 105-27)*. A cynical little strain is heard in the orchestra; Mephistopheles approaches followed by Faust. The fiend would go into Marguerite's house at once, but Faust refuses, for, torn with contrition, he fears that he will bring more unhappiness. How little Faust's grief means to the Tempter, is at once revealed, for he stations himself beneath the window and sings a villainous serenade—the famous "Sérénade de Mephistopheles" *(While You play at Sleeping)*.

Vous qui faites l'endormie *Feodor Chaliapin* 7600-2.00

> While you play at sleeping,
> Close not thus your heart,
> Close not thus your heart,
> Caterina! wake thee! wake thee!
> Caterina! wake! 'tis thy lover near!
> Hearken to my love-lorn pleading;
> Let thy heart be interceding,
> Awaken love, and hear!
> Ha! ha! ha! ha! ha! ha! ha! ha! ha! ha!
> Don't come down until, my dear,
> The nuptial ring appears
> On thy finger sparkling clearly—
> The wedding-ring—the ring shineth clear.
> Ha! ha! ha! ha! ha! ha! ha! ha! ha! ha! ha!
> Caterina! cruel, cruel!
> Cruel to deny to him who loves thee—
> And for thee doth mourn and sigh—
> A single kiss from thy rosy lips.
> Thus to slight a faithful lover,
> Who so long hath been a rover,
> Too bad, I declare!
> Ha! ha! ha! ha! ha!
> Not a single kiss, my dear,
> Unless the ring appear!
> Ha! ha! ha! ha! ha! ha! ha! ha!

This infernal and insulting ditty with its sinister, snarling accompaniment of plucked strings and chuckling woodwinds comes to its end with a hideous mocking laugh. Such gross churlishness at his very door justly brings Valentine rushing out sword in hand. Angry words are exchanged *(M 105-28)*; Faust is perplexed for he would not fight with Marguerite's brother. Valentine is indignant, and Mephistopheles scornful. Valentine attacks the pair, but, of course, has no chance with one of the adversaries, the Master of Black Magic. Valentine falls mortally wounded; his murderers flee.

The sounds of the fight have naturally caught the attention of the townspeople, who begin to hurry into the dark square *(M 105-29)*. They soon find Valentine, writhing in the agonies of death. Marguerite also rushes towards him anxiously. With terrible words he orders her away and calls down the curse of Heaven upon her *(M 105-30)*. The people plead with him, saying

THE DEATH OF LEONORA

LA FAVORITA

(The Favorite)

OPERA in four acts; music by Gaetano Donizetti; text by Alphonse Royer and Gustave Waez, adapted from the drama "Le Comte de Comminges," by Baculard-Darnaud. First produced at the Grand Opéra, Paris, December 2, 1840; New York, Park Theatre, October 4, 1848; New Orleans, February 9, 1843.

Though not so well known as the same composer's "Lucia," "La Favorita" contains some of Donizetti's finest inspirations; and the libretto, compared with those of many an opera of its epoch, is almost a masterpiece of ironic tragedy. The music, always fluent and exceedingly melodious, requires above all else, exquisite singing. Modern opera composers, by means of their skilful orchestration, often make mediocre voices sound excellent. Donizetti gives his orchestra a subdued accompaniment that leaves the voices exposed in their real timbre—the voices and the singing *must* be excellent, and such indeed they are on the records here named.

ACT I

FERDINAND (or Fernando), a novice, is sitting with Baltazar, the Prior, in a cloister, ancient and grass-grown even in this, the year 1340. Ferdinand wishes to renounce his novitiate for he has fallen in love. Singing a broadly flowing melody he describes his beloved as "A virgin, an angel of God," whom he has seen, yet never met.

"Una vergine un angiol di Dio" *(Like an Angel)* **Tito Schipa** 1362-1.50

"Dost thou not know her?" asks Baltazar and Ferdinand exclaims, "I know her not, yet I love her!" At this, Baltazar sternly bids him go and not profane this sacred place; Ferdinand, unhappy at leaving the monastery, pleads for forgiveness and departs to search for the beautiful unknown.

The scene changes to the Island of Leon, where Leonora (The Favorite) lives and whence she has sent for Ferdinand. He is led blindfolded to his destination by a fair guide who refuses to reveal the identity of the lady who has sent for him. Leonora now appears, and a tender love scene follows; but the Favorite is anxious, fearing that Ferdinand will learn that she is the King's mistress. She commands him to leave her forever, and gives him a parchment which she says will insure his future. He wishes to remain, but Inez enters, whispering that the King is at the villa. As Ferdinand leaves he recognizes the monarch, and his hopes fall, for how can a recreant monk now aspire to her hand? He looks at the parchment—his commission as an officer in the army of the King!

ACT II

THE King has just installed himself with Leonora at the Alcazar Palace newly regained from the Moors. Here he is sought out by Baltazar who threatens him with a Papal interdiction for deserting his legal wife, an interdiction that will apply to all the court if the King does not drive Leonora from him. The King, torn between love and fear of the Church, hesitates; he is tempted to brave the Papal denunciation.

ACT III

FERDINAND, returning victorious from the wars, is offered by the grateful King any reward he may desire. The hero asks only for the hand of Leonora, who enters at this very moment. This is a request the King is rather happy to grant for it will relieve him of any further fear of ecclesiastical curses. With the cruelest irony that only Ferdinand is not in a position to grasp, the King bestows the hand of Leonora on the conqueror. Left alone, Leonora meditates on the tragedy of her position; she sings a sustained, melancholy air in which she declares her willingness to sacrifice everything for Ferdinand's sake.

O mio Fernando *(Oh, Dearest Ferdinand)* **Sigrid Onégin** 7191-2.00

She sends her attendant, Inez, to reveal the truth. At the King's order, Inez is intercepted and the wedding takes place at once; then Ferdinand's wrath is aroused by the cold looks and sneers he and his bride receive from the courtiers. Overcome with rage he draws his sword, and bloodshed would soon follow were it not that Baltazar arrives and the shameful truth is revealed to Ferdinand.

147

ACT IV

FERDINAND has fled from the world and sought consolation back in the Monastery. Baltazar and a chorus of monks musically reflect upon the joy and serenity of penitence and salvation.

Splendon più belle *(In Heavenly Splendor)* **Ezio Pinza and the Metropolitan Opera Chorus 7552-2.00**

Before entering the chapel for the final rite which will make him one of the order, he soliloquizes on his unhappy fate. The phantom of love and its illusions are left behind—only memories remain, pale, tranquil, tender, and ineffably sad.

Leonora, stricken unto death, follows him even here and disguised as a novice gains admittance. She is found on the chapel steps by Ferdinand when he comes from the service making him one of the order, and as he lifts her forgivingly in his arms, she dies.

FEDORA

OPERA in three acts; music by Umberto Giordano; text by Colautti after a drama by Sardou. First produced, November 17, 1898, at the Teatro Lirico, Milan. First performance in the United States at the Metropolitan Opera House, December 5, 1906.

ACT I

COUNT VLADIMIR, the betrothed of the beautiful Princess Fedora, is brought to her mortally wounded. It is hinted that Count Loris has committed this murder. Fedora swears vengeance.

ACT II

A MAGNIFICENT reception is being held at the house of Fedora in Paris. She uses all her skill in fascinating Count Loris in the hope that she will find proof of his guilt. He has already fallen madly in love with her, and when they happen to be left together for a few minutes she leads him on, coquettishly, until, growing poetic under her enchantment, he tenderly declares that his love is so great and strong that it compels her to love him. Even now she has pushed him away. Yet her hand is searching his; and while her lips deny it, her eyes confess that she loves him. The melody of this avowal of love is a sustained cantatina; the orchestra supplies a glowing accompaniment.

Amor ti vieta di non amar *(My Love Compels)* **Alessandro Ziliani** 1735-1.50

Outside police are waiting to seize Loris after the guests have departed. Loris weepingly confesses to the murder, and reveals, moreover, that his wife was betrayed and brought to her untimely death by Vladimir. On learning this, Fedora, who herself has fallen in love with Loris, embraces him, and saves him from the police.

ACT III

ALTHOUGH Loris and Fedora are living happily together in Switzerland, he is followed by a police spy. News comes that because of Loris' deed his brother was put into prison, where he died; his mother died of the shock. A message also comes bearing Loris' pardon. Thrilled by conflicting emotions he exclaims, "My dear old mother!" These words are the title of a moving aria.

With the same mail comes a letter revealing that it was Fedora who set the detectives after him. In sudden blind anger, Loris is about to kill her, but she quickly swallows poison. Then he implores her to live. It is too late: she dies in his arms.

Rembrandt

SCENE FROM FIDELIO

FIDELIO

OPERA in two acts; music by Ludwig van Beethoven; libretto by Sonnleithner after Bouilly; first revision by Breuning, second by Treitschke. First produced in three acts, as "Fidelio, or Conjugal Love," at the Theatre on the Wien, Vienna, November 20, 1805. Revised and given a few performances at the Imperial Private Theatre, Vienna, March 29, 1806. Again revised and successfully performed at the Kärnthenerthor Theatre, Vienna, May 23, 1814. First performance in the United States, at the Park Theatre, New York, September 9, 1839, in English. (The name of the opera is pronounced *Fee-day'-li-oh*.)

This story of wifely faithfulness and self-sacrifice from a French book by Bouilly appealed very much to the noble-minded Beethoven as a subject for an opera, even though it had been so used by three other contemporary composers. Inspired by his theme, Beethoven put into the work an amount of loving labor that was unusual even for that most conscientious of men. After two revisions of music and text, the work finally achieved success. Beethoven composed four overtures for the opera, three entitled "Leonore" (the name by which Beethoven desired the opera to be known), and one "Fidelio." Unfortunately the Leonore overtures have not been correctly numbered. That now called No. 2 is the one that was played at the first performance of the opera. The greatest and most famous, now known as No. 3, was next to be composed. The overture known as No. 1 was written later for an intended performance at Prague which never took place. The "Fidelio" overture, intended for the second revision, was not ready in time; the overture to "The Ruins of Athens" was substituted. At present-day performances it is usual to play the "Fidelio" overture before the opera and "Leonore" No. 3 before the final scene.

The Fidelio Overture, while not closely related to the music of the opera thematically, is expressive of the final triumph of the faithful Leonore and the joyful release of her husband. The allegro movement, which follows the stately introduction, has a first theme

150

of unusual loveliness, first played by a French horn. The second theme is played by the strings. At the end, the first theme is developed into an exultant climax.

Fidelio Overture—Parts I and II *British Broadcasting Co. Symphony Orch., Cond. by Bruno Walter* 11809-1.50

Leonore Overture, No. 3—Parts I and II *San Francisco Symphony Orch.* 6906-2.00
Parts III and IV *San Francisco Symphony Orch.* 6907-2.00

The wonderful Leonore overture, No. 3, is in reality a résumé of the entire drama. In it are expressed the devotion, struggle, suffering, and joy of final victory of Leonore and Florestan. As Wagner said, this overture is a drama in itself. It begins with an awesome introduction, like a descent into the gloomy dungeon where Florestan is imprisoned, and a portion of whose lament at the loss of freedom now follows. Next there begins the principal theme of the overture, *allegro,* but very softly, the merest whisper, then growing impetuously in power. Then follows the second theme, which has well been described as "woven out of sobs and pitying sighs." There is twice heard in the distance the trumpet call that in the opera announces the arrival of the freedom-bringing Minister of the Interior. Each time, this is answered by Leonore's song of thanksgiving. The earlier themes are repeated, then the overture comes to its close in the most frenzied jubilation.

CHARACTERS

FLORESTAN, *a Spanish Nobleman*	*Tenor*
LEONORE, *his wife, in male attire as* FIDELIO	*Soprano*
DON FERNANDO, *Prime Minister of Spain*	*Bass*
PIZARRO, *Governor of the Prison and enemy to Florestan*	*Bass*
ROCCO, *chief jailer*	*Bass*
MARCELLINA, *daughter of Rocco*	*Soprano*
JACQUINO, *assistant to Rocco*	*Tenor*
Soldiers, Prisoners, People.	

The action takes place during the Eighteenth Century at a fortress near Seville, Spain.

FLORESTAN, a Spanish nobleman, has incurred the enmity of Don Pizarro, Governor of the State Prison. Pizarro has therefore had him placed in a dungeon and announced his death. But Leonore, wife of Florestan, refuses to believe this report. Disguising herself as a servant, and assuming the name of Fidelio, she secures employment with Rocco, the head jailer. Rocco's daughter falls in love with the supposedly handsome youth. Some amusing by-play is afforded by the turnkey, Jacquino, who was himself high in favor with Marcellina before the advent of his rival.

Mir ist so wunderbar (*It Is So Wonderful*) *Berger, Gottlieb, Wittrisch, Domgraf-Fassbaender* 11826-1.50

Hearing that the Minister of the Interior is coming to the prison to investigate the supposed death of Florestan, the Governor decides to have the prisoner murdered. Since Rocco refuses, the Governor will himself commit the crime. Leonore overhears the plot and when the two men go away she appears from her hiding place and exclaims in a highly dramatic recitative:

Monster! Whither in thy haste? What design breeds thy rage? Nor pity's call, nor humanity's voice, naught moves thy tiger mind. . . . But a ray of hope on heaven's face I still perceive: it brings me calm, restores my soul . . .

151

SENTA AND THE MAIDENS

there accordingly hurried to produce the "Dutchman." After the dazzling, brilliant earlier work, the somber beauty of the "Dutchman," more introspective than objective in its approach, was a disappointment. The work, nevertheless, marks a great step in the development of Wagner's musical and dramatic style; here he first uses leading motives to a great extent, and the orchestra is treated in a more symphonic manner. The genius is beginning to find himself! (The name of the opera in German is Der Fliegende Holländer, *Dair Flee'-gen-deh Hol-layn'-der.*)

THE OVERTURE is in itself a vivid picture of the entire story: The stormy sea, portrayed as no other composer has ever succeeded in doing; the gloomy Dutchman, the curse upon him and his longing for redemption; the tranquil motive of Senta, who shall bring about that redemption; for a moment of relief, the gay song of the Norwegian sailors, soon overwhelmed in the storm; and finally the crashing of the Curse motive displaced by the theme of Senta, glorified and radiant, as it will be heard at the end of the opera, when across the glow of the sunset the figures of Senta and the redeemed Dutchman are seen rising from the sea heavenward.

Overture—Parts I and II *Mengelberg-Philharmonic-Symphony Orchestra of New York 6547-2.00 Berlin State Opera Orchestra 9275-1.50*

THE legend, as told both by Heine and by Wagner, relates to a Dutch sea captain who once swore that in spite of storms and contrary winds he would round the Cape of Good Hope, even in spite of all Hell. As a punishment for his impious vow he was condemned to sail the seas until the crack of Doom. But once in seven years this "Flying Dutchman" was permitted to land; if then he could find a maiden who would be faithful unto death, she would bring relief from the curse. At the opening of the opera, this Dutchman is driven by a storm to seek shelter in the same harbor where Daland, a Norwegian sea captain, has been compelled to put up. Daland, impressed by the apparent wealth of the Dutchman, tells him of his daughter, Senta, and even consents to give her in marriage to him. The second act shows Senta at home surrounded by a crowd of girls who are busily spinning. They sing meanwhile a most melodious, maidenly chorus, the orchestra imitating the whir of the wheels.

Spinning Chorus *Royal Opera Chorus and Orchestra, Covent Garden* 7117-2.00

But Senta is wearied by their constant singing and humming, and sits gazing pensively at a painting of the "Flying Dutchman" that hangs on the wall. She says that she will sing them a song better than theirs, the ballad of the "Flying Dutchman."

Senta's Ballad *(Traft ihr das Schiff)* *Florence Austral with Royal Opera Chorus and Orch.* 7117-2.00

She begins by singing the mariner's wild cry of "Yo-ho, Yo-ho-he." Then, while the orchestra vividly portrays the raging of the ocean, she sings of the Dutchman's attempt to round the cape, his oath, the curse upon him and how he is now driven hopelessly across the seas in a ship with "blood-red sails." Then continuing—to the peaceful theme first heard in the overture—she sings of his possible salvation if anywhere on earth he can find a woman who will be "faithful unto death." In growing agitation she adds that such a woman can be found, and forgetting herself in a final passionate outburst, declares that she herself is that woman—she shall save him from his unhappy fate.

She recognizes the Dutchman the moment she sees him as he enters with her father. She instinctively realizes that hers shall be the task of saving him; love springs up between them and their wedding is announced. Senta has had, however, a youthful lover, who returning from a journey, heaps reproaches upon her for her faithlessness. The Dutchman happens to overhear the unfortunate young man's words, and is struck by a terrible thought. Senta has been faithless to Eric: she will surely be unfaithful to him, a stranger—faithless, as all other women have been!

He hurriedly boards his ship and sets sail. As he embarks a terrifying storm suddenly arises. Breaking away from Eric and her friends who attempt to hold her back, Senta runs to a cliff and casts herself into the sea, crying: "Behold me! Faithful unto death!" With a sudden plunge the Dutchman's phantom ship sinks; the storm quickly subsides; the sea immediately grows calm. The figures of the Dutchman and Senta rise heavenward, clasped in each other's arms.

From an Old Print

THE BETROTHAL

LA FORZA DEL DESTINO

(The Force of Destiny)

OPERA in four acts; music by Giuseppe Verdi; the libretto, which is by Piave, is based on a play, "Don Alvaro o la Fuerzer del Sino," by the Duke of Rivas. First produced at St. Petersburg (Leningrad), November 10, 1862. Revised and performed at La Scala, Milan, February 20, 1869. First performed in New York, February 24, 1865, at the Academy of Music. The second version is described here, that being the one followed in the recordings herewith noted and, generally, in present-day performances.

Destiny, or Fate, seems early to have taken a hand in the life of the composer of "The Force of Destiny," for the story is told that when an infant, in the village of Le Roncole, his life was saved in an almost miraculous way. Italy was at war with Austria and Russia, and when the soldiers of the enemy were pouring into Le Roncole, the women and children sought refuge in the village church. Yet the soldiers entered even there. Verdi's mother, with a sudden, fortunate inspiration, hurriedly concealed herself and child in the belfry, where they remained unobserved, the only ones to escape alive! For this kind act of "Destiny," lovers of Verdi operas assuredly may be grateful!

In "La Forza del Destino" we find the composer making an advance in musical style over the successes just preceding it, "Trovatore" and "Traviata." While in a general sense equally melodious, the music seems possessed of a greater seriousness and depth of purpose. The orchestral accompaniment is at once more full-bodied and colorful; the harmonies richer and more varied. Seldom has Verdi charged a scene with a more genuine feeling of the dramatic, of tragic foreboding, almost "atmospheric" in character, than he has done in the second scene of Act II of this opera. Truly, in "Forza," Verdi seems to be anticipating the later perfection of "Aïda."

DON ALVARO: Solenne in quest'ora

CHARACTERS

MARQUIS OF CALATRAVA (Kal-ah-trah'-vah)
Bass

DONNA LEONORA	his children	Soprano
DON CARLO		Baritone

DON ALVARO (Ahl-vah'-roh) Tenor
PADRE GUARDIANO (Goo-ahr-dee-ah'-no) Bass
FRA MELITONE (May-lee-toh'-ne) Baritone
Muleteers, Peasants, Soldiers, Friars, etc.

Scene and period: Spain and Italy, about the middle of the Eighteenth Century.

(The name of the opera is pronounced Lah Fort'-zah del Des-tee'-noh.)

The Overture that precedes the opera is of exceptional beauty and dramatic appropriateness. After an attention-compelling blast of trumpets, there is heard a restless, sinister melody, that seems to typify the unhappy destiny of the chief characters. This melody recurs frequently throughout the opera. At times it is bold and menacing and at others merely a dark undercurrent to other melodies. After this so-called "Fate" motive, there enter other themes—notably the pathetic, broken air of Alvaro's plea, sung in the third act, and the very beautiful melody of Leonora's prayer, sung during the second scene of Act II. Then are heard other themes from the opera, all combined to form a splendid mood picture of the tragic scenes that are to follow.

Overture—Parts I and II *Victor Symphony Orchestra* 21865-.75

ACT I

SCENE—*Drawing Room of the Marquis of Calatrava*

Don Alvaro is a young prince of an illustrious family in India; but this counts for so little in Spain that the beautiful Leonora, certain that her family will never permit marriage, plans to elope with him. Her father, the Marquis of Calatrava, discovers them, and ignoring their protests accuses them of shameful conduct. Assuming all the blame, Alvaro throws away his pistol and presents his bare breast to the aged noble's sword. But when the weapon strikes the floor it explodes and mortally wounds the Marquis. He dies cursing his daughter.

ACT II

SCENE I—*An Inn at Hornacuelos*

Leonora, in male disguise, has fled from Seville to this mountain hostelry; she is alone and in despair, having lost all trace of Don Alvaro since the fatal night. Her uneasiness increases when she recognizes among the motley crowd her brother, Don Carlo, he too in disguise. She learns from his conversation that he is hunting for the man he believes to be the seducer of his sister and the murderer of his father. She flees in terror.

SCENE II—*The Monastery at Hornacuelos*

Leonora has come to the door of the monastery, where, kneeling in the moonlight she prays for the Virgin's protection. She knocks, and confessing all, begs for protection from the kindly Abbot, Padre Guardiano. He tells her of a deserted cave in the mountains where she may abide as a "hermit" in safety. The doors of the monastery chapel swing open, revealing in the distance the brilliantly lighted great altar. The deep tones of the organ unite with the solemn supplication of the kneeling monks and Guardiano, who prays that a curse *(Maledizione)* descend upon any person who should ever intrude upon or seek to learn the identity of this stranger. Then *(beginning of Record 8097)*, Guardiano bids Leonora depart

Mishkin

PONSELLE AS LEONORA

to her mountain retreat; there none shall ever disturb her although she shall be under the protection of the monastery. The monks join him in praying:

> Let the Holy Virgin
> Cover you with her mantle,
> And the angels of God
> Watch over you.

La vergine degli angeli *(May Angels Guard Thee)* **Rosa Ponselle, Ezio Pinza**
8097-2.00

The prayer, simple yet most impressive in melody and harmony, is repeated, while the voice of Leonora enters and rises above the others in calm, majestic beauty.

ACT III

SCENE—*A Military Camp Near Valletri*

Don Alvaro, believing Leonora dead, has enlisted with the Spanish army. He is tormented by memories of his unhappy fate, and to a tender, melancholy air, soliloquizes *(beginning of Record 6000)*:

Life is misery for the unfortunate. In vain I seek death . . . Seville! . . . Leonora . . . Leonora . . . Oh memories! Oh night! Thou hast taken from me all my happiness! . . . Oh, when will my misfortunes cease?

Then, the melody growing in warmth and intensity until it rises to a splendid climax, he prays to the supposedly dead Leonora:

Thou heavenly one, all beautiful and pure from mortal sins,
Do not forget to look on me a poor sufferer, who without hope eagerly seeks death fighting against destiny.
Leonora, help me and have mercy on my sufferings!

O tu che in seno agli 'angeli *(Thou Heavenly One)* **Enrico Caruso** *6000-2.00

His reveries being interrupted by a cry of distress, he goes out and finds a wounded man . . . Don Carlo, his sworn enemy! Since they have never before met, and since both are going under assumed names, neither recognizes the other, and they become close friends.

Later, Don Alvaro, seemingly mortally wounded in battle, begs Carlo to swear to perform his last request. Carlo, torn with pity, swears that he will do his bidding. Alvaro begs him to search in his effects for a package of letters . . . these he wishes burned without opening. Then, Alvaro says he will die happy, and to a poignant melody sings farewell, while his friend replies with words of comfort—a duet of the most intense emotional fervor.

Solenne in quest'ora *(Swear in This Hour)* **Gigli, de Luca** 8069-2.00 **Caruso, Scotti**
*8000-2.00

Destiny, however, cannot be thwarted, and although Carlo does not open the package, he elsewhere in the wounded man's effects discovers a picture of Leonora. When, contrary to expectations, Don Alvaro recovers and Don

Carlo makes himself known, Alvaro strives to convince Don Carlo that he is guiltless of wrong-doing and worthy of his sister. Intent on avenging his father's death, Don Carlo will not believe him, and insists they fight it out. Alvaro refuses until Carlo threatens to search out Leonora and take her life instead; then Alvaro consents and, in the duel that follows, he wins. Believing that he has killed a second man, he decides to take holy vows and end his days in a monastery . . . He cannot go to Leonora with the blood of both a father and a brother on his hands.

ACT IV

Scene I—*The Monastery of Hornacuelos*

In the five years that have passed, Don Alvaro, now Father Raphael, has become noted for his goodness of life, and his compassionate kindness towards all who suffer. Yet even to the sacred calm of this retreat, Don Carlo comes seeking vengeance. While he awaits Alvaro, he soliloquizes:

> In vain, Alvaro, dost thou hide from the world in hypocrite's garb.
> Only thy blood can cleanse the stain of my outraged honor!

Don Alvaro enters and exclaims in surprise on beholding Carlo whom he thought dead. Carlo coldly presents him with a sword . . . they must fight to the death. Alvaro bids him be gone: he is now a man of peace and cannot fight. To this Carlo replies, "Coward!" The friar, well schooled in ignoring his own feelings, answers, "Thy menaces, wild and angry words, are cast to the winds." His words are sung to the broken, pathetic little melody first heard in the overture.

Alvaro tries hard to convince Don Carlo that vengeance lies with God. In return he receives the most venomous insults. In the music, the pleading accents of the priest are remarkably contrasted with the sinister threats of Don Carlo. Slowly, yet inevitably the benevolent friar becomes again the fiery man of action; he prays for self-restraint . . . Carlo strikes him insultingly . . . Alvaro seizes the weapon and, the convent being no place to fight, the men rush away . . . The music swells with a tumult of wild passion.

Scene II—*A Wild Spot Near Hornacuelos*

The beautiful music of this closing scene is presented on the record:

Pace, pace mio Dio *(Peace, Oh My Lord)* **Rosa Ponselle** 6875-2.00

As the curtain rises we hear in the orchestra the agitated melody first played at the opening of the overture. On this dark night Leonora, pale and worn, yet beautiful, has issued from her desolate cavern to pray, still tormented by memories of her ill-fated love. "Peace, oh my Lord, grant me peace" she implores, to a melody of haunting loveliness that rises more and more poignantly as memories of Alvaro come crowding back. In despair, she

THE WOLF'S GLEN SCENE

ᴅER FREISCHÜTZ

(*The Freeshooter*)

ROMANTIC opera in three acts; music by Carl Maria von Weber; words by Fredrich Kind. First produced June 18, 1821, at Berlin. First American performance, March 2, 1825, at the Park Theatre, New York, in English.

Von Weber, the great pioneer of romanticism in German opera, endeavored, in "Der Freischütz," to escape Italian influence by discarding plots of intrigue, and instead sought material for his opera in the legends of his own country. Thus he opened up the dual paths of romanticism and nationalism which led, eventually, to the monumental "Ring des Nibelungen." Originally written with spoken dialogue (nowadays often sung as recitative) and based on a native subject, "Der Freischütz" is a link between the old "Singspiel" and Wagner.

The title "Der Freischütz" (pronounced approximately, *Dair Fry'-shoots*), means literally, "free-shooter," a term applied to one who used magic bullets. The story of the opera is founded on an old tradition among huntsmen in Germany, to the effect that whoever should sell his soul to Zamiel, the Demon Hunter, would receive seven such magic bullets, which would always hit the mark. But at the seventh bullet, the man must yield up his soul to Zamiel, if he has not in the meantime found another victim for the demon; for every convert his life will be extended and he will receive a fresh supply of bullets.

The Overture, long a concert favorite, reveals Weber, the great romanticist, at his best. It opens in religious calm, with a beautiful melody played by the horns. Then creeps in the fearsome, sinister music of Zamiel and of the terrifying scene in the Wolf's Glen. Opposed to this music of evil *(beginning of Part II)* is heard the triumphant outburst from Agatha's aria: "We Shall Meet in Joy at Last!" In the ensuing struggle between

162

these forces of good and evil, thrillingly depicted in music, good is triumphant, and the overture ends in a mood of rejoicing.

The action takes place in Bohemia about the year 1750.

Overture—Parts I and II   *Alfred Hertz-San Francisco Symphony Orchestra* **6705-2.00**

CUNO, head ranger to Ottokar, a Bohemian Prince, has two assistants, Max and Caspar, both excellent marksmen. Max is in love with Agatha, Cuno's daughter, who has promised to be his bride on condition that he prove himself the best shot at a contest to be held before the Prince. The preliminary trial is won, however, by Kilian, a peasant. Max is found bewailing his bad luck by the dissolute Caspar, whose evil ways have led him to put himself into the power of Zamiel. Caspar sees in Max a chance to extend his own days of grace and induces him to come to the Wolf's Glen, there to receive some magic bullets which never miss their mark.

In the meantime, Agatha is anxiously awaiting her lover, much alarmed at his non-appearance. She bids her cousin, Annie, retire, for her attempts at bringing cheer with a gay song are vain. Left alone, her thoughts revert to her lover *(beginning of Record 6588)*; she opens the window and looking out at the beautiful starlight night, exclaims at the wonder of it, then sings her expressive prayer:

> Softly, softly,
> Still devoutly,
> Let my voice reach realms of light.

Again looking out *(beginning of Part II)* she continues:

> Earth has lulled her cares to rest
> And all nature now seems blest.
> Naught but gently breathing air
> Whispers in mine anxious ear.

Then hearing her lover approaching, she sings the exultant melody first heard in the overture:

> Ah! now each pulse is beating wildly
> And my heart is throbbing high,
> We shall meet in joy at last!

Agatha's Prayer—Parts I and II   *Maria Jeritza* **6588-2.00**

The joy of their meeting is brief, for Max, somewhat embarrassed, says he

must go to bring in a stag he shot near the Wolf's Glen. Agatha begs him not to go near that haunted spot, but he disregards her warnings.

At the Wolf's Glen, Max meets Caspar, and amid a scene of supernatural horror they summon Zamiel and cast the magic bullets.

When the shooting contest is about to begin, the assembled foresters sing a rousing and famous chorus in praise of hunting, "What is so fine as a huntsman's life?"

During the contest Max amazes all with his remarkable skill. At the final shot, Max's seventh bullet, the Prince points to a white dove he has observed hovering above a tree. At that moment Agatha appears from behind the tree and cries out to Max not to shoot, for she is that dove. But it is too late: Agatha sinks in a swoon and Caspar falls mortally wounded from the tree whence he had been watching the contest. He had, in fact, planned to sacrifice Agatha to Zamiel, thereby being permitted to live longer. The demon appears, however, and claims Caspar. Thus the story of the magic bullets is revealed and the Prince banishes Max for his wickedness. A strange hermit opportunely appears, however, revives Agatha, and pleads the cause of Max, declaring that the prayer of Agatha has been answered, Providence using her to restore Max to truth and honor. The young man is therefore forgiven and all ends happily.

PRINCE OTTOKAR PARDONS MAX—FINAL
SCENE OF THE OPERA

THE RELATIONS HEAR THE NEW WILL

GIANNI SCHICCHI

OPERA in one act; music by Giacomo Puccini; libretto by Gioachino Forzano. First produced at the Metropolitan Opera House, New York, December 14, 1918, together with two other one-act operas by Puccini, "Il Tabarro" and "Suor Angelica." There is no connection between their plots: "Gianni Schicchi" is the one most frequently performed.

"GIANNI SCHICCHI" is a shrewd but good-hearted Tuscan peasant of the thirteenth century. His daughter, Lauretta, loves Rinuccio, whose family is at present greatly disturbed because a relative, Buoso Donati, has just died leaving his fortune to a monastery. Schicchi is consulted by the disappointed relatives in the hope that he may prove clever enough to suggest a plan for obtaining the property. As Donati's death has not yet been made public, Schicchi suggests that he himself impersonate the old man and dictate a new will, leaving the estate to Rinuccio's family. Schicchi is placed in the dead man's bed, and a notary summoned. He takes down the new will; after leaving a few worthless trifles to the relatives, he bequeaths the bulk of the property to himself! The relatives are highly indignant, but they dare not expose Schicchi, for in so doing they would render themselves liable to punishment. A minute after the notary and witnesses have gone, they go after Schicchi with cries of "Robber! Traitor! Scoundrel!" But Schicchi seizes a stick, and though his nightgown is torn to shreds in the struggle, drives the cursing relatives from the house. The lovers, who eventually will be Schicchi's heirs, are happily united.

Gerardi

ACT I—LA GIOCONDA AS GIVEN AT VERONA

LA GIOCONDA

OPERA in four acts; music by Amilcare Ponchielli; libretto from Victor Hugo's drama "Angelo"; by Arrigo Boïto (under the pen-name of "Tobia Gorrio"). First produced at La Scala, Milan, April 8, 1876, and with the libretto revised, at Genoa, December, 1876. First performance in the United States, December 20, 1883, at the Metropolitan Opera House, New York.

Amilcare Ponchielli (1834-1886) is an important figure in the history of Modern Italian Opera, for besides being a teacher of Giacomo Puccini, he was one of the leaders in the movement that, aroused by the achievements of Richard Wagner, set itself to work to revivify the lyric stage in Italy. "La Gioconda" is a fine example of this movement; the music is of a more continuous, unified construction, more closely adapted to the action, and the orchestration is richer and more nearly symphonic in texture, than had hitherto been the case in Italian Opera. Yet "La Gioconda" is genuinely tuneful, its melodies, while always in keeping with characters and situations, are in themselves beautiful and call for real *bel canto* singing; thus it remains true to the traditions of Italian opera. Some of the arias and ensembles are of the greatest dramatic power; contrasted with these are many attractive choruses and the ever-popular ballet, "The Dance of the Hours."

CHARACTERS

LA GIOCONDA *(Joh-kon'-dah), a ballad singer*	*Soprano*
LA CIECA *(Chay'-kah), her blind mother*	*Contralto*
ALVISE *(Al-vee'-zeh), one of the heads of State Inquisition*	*Bass*
LAURA, *his wife*	*Mezzo-Soprano*
ENZO GRIMALDO, *a Genoese noble*	*Tenor*
BARNABA, *a spy of the Inquisition*	*Baritone*

A Boatman, Public Letter-writer, Pilot, and chorus of Monks, Senators, Sailors, Ladies, Gentlemen, Populace, Masquers, etc.

ACT I

Scene—*Street Near the Adriatic Shore, Venice*

IT is the afternoon of a spring holiday at Venice, during the glorious, though turbulent, seventeenth century. The Grand Courtyard of the Ducal Palace is ablaze with moving color . . . monks, sailors, masqueraders, shipwrights, townspeople, foreigners . . . all bent on a gay holiday. They sing a merry chorus: *Feste! Pane!* (Games and feasting!)

This festive song is interrupted for a moment by Barnaba, who announces that the regatta is about to begin; then the song dies away as the people go to watch the sports. He disdainfully watches the departing merrymakers and mutters to himself "Dancing above their graves," for he knows that the prisons of the Inquisition are underfoot. La Gioconda, the beautiful and popular ballad singer, approaches, leading by the hand her blind mother, La Cieca, whom she seats at the church steps to enjoy the sun and charity of Venice. Barnaba, grim spy of the Inquisition though he be, is infatuated with La Gioconda, and when she turns to follow the crowd he accosts her. Infuriated at this she dashes away. Barnaba plans a heartless revenge.

When the crowd returns from the regatta, he tells the defeated competitor that La Cieca is a witch who has cast a spell over him, thus causing his failure. The defeated man and his friends attack the blind woman and drag her from the church steps, crying "Kill her! burn her!" Fortunately Enzo, a friend of La Gioconda's, now appears and rushes to the defense of her mother, holds the crowd at bay, and upbraids them for thus attacking a helpless blind woman. The people reply that it is Heaven's will that she be destroyed for she is a sorceress. The music grows to a most dramatic climax.

In the midst of the commotion the doors of the palace suddenly fly open and the Grand Duke Alvise and his wife, Laura, appear. Laura intercedes with her husband on behalf of the aged blind woman, who is therefore released. In gratitude La Cieca gives Laura her rosary. Meanwhile the crafty Barnaba has observed a meaningful glance pass between Laura and Enzo.

The doors of Saint Mark's swing open, and

Bain

DE LUCA AS BARNABA

167

the crowd now enter the jewel-blazing church, but Enzo stands thoughtfully gazing after Laura. Barnaba forthwith approaches Enzo and engages him in conversation—a very dramatic duet, in which the spy makes another move towards achieving his desire.

Enzo Grimaldo, Principe di Santafior *Gigli, De Luca* 8084-2.00

BARNABA (*approaching Enzo*):
Enzo Grimaldo,
Prince of Santa Fior, thou art pensive.
ENZO (*aside*):
I am discovered!
BARNABA:
What magic stupor steals away thy senses?
'Tis of the Lady Laura, Alvise's wife, thou'rt thinking.
ENZO (*astonished*):
Who art thou?
BARNABA (*impressively*):
I know all;
Can penetrate thy thoughts, however secret.
Thy birthplace was Genoa!
ENZO:
Prince I am not, but sailor. Yonder's my ship.
I am Dalmatian, Enzo Giordan.
BARNABA:
For others, but not for me. Proscribed thou wert by Venice,
Yet hither thou art led, by chainless impulse
Thy life to peril. Thou didst love a maiden
Yonder, in thine own Genoa, but she another's bride became.
ENZO:
I have pledged my faith to Gioconda.
BARNABA:
Poor wand'ring ballad-singer!
Her thou dost love as sister, but Laura as thy mistress.
Thou hadst all hope abandoned, dreamed not to see her features.
But here, under her velvet mask, thy beauteous angel saw thee
And recognized thee.
ENZO:
Oh, happiness!
BARNABA:
Love sees through all disguises,
All this night will her husband stay at the Doge's palace,
With the great Council. Laura shall be on board thy vessel,
Love's sweetest consolations await thee!
ENZO:
Ah, with what joy my heart is filled,
Fortune at last is kind!
But who art thou, oh gloomy messenger of joy?
BARNABA:
I hate thee! I am the demon-in-chief
Of the Council of Ten. Read this. Beware thee!
(*Reveals the letters "C. X."—Council of Ten—embroidered in silver on his vest.*)
ENZO (*starting back*):
Oh, horror!

BARNABA (*fiercely*) :
   To thy doom at once I could bring thee, but I spare thee.
   Gioconda loves thee, hates me fiercely;
   I have sworn to crush her heart,
   Enzo's death would little serve me;
   She must learn how false thou art.
ENZO (*aside*) :
   Kind Heaven, to her thy mercy show,
   Save her from grief and pain;
   But ah, sweet Laura, my adored,
   Bring to my arms again!
BARNABA (*to Enzo*) :
   Go! not a moment lose,
   Spread thy white sails to the skies,
   (*aside*)
   I can my triumph read
   In each glance of thine eyes!
ENZO (*going*) :
   When the dark night falls,
   On board my ship I shall await my Laura.
BARNABA (*sneeringly*) :
   Good luck attend you!
ENZO:
   And curses be upon you!

Barnaba at once turns to the public scribe; La Gioconda and her mother
return, and having concealed themselves from the sight of their enemy, they
overhear him dictate an anonymous letter to the secret chief of the Inquisition informing him of the meeting to take place between Enzo and Laura.
At this the soul of the passionate Gioconda is filled with hate against
Barnaba, against Laura, and against Enzo . . . for was he not her lover?

ACT II

SCENE—*A Lagoon Near Venice, Enzo's Ship at the Quay*

THE orchestra supplies a background at once redolent of the soft beauty
of the Venetian night yet with a note of mystery that portends tragedy.
Sailors, singing an occasional "Oh! he!" busy themselves about Enzo's ship
as it rides at anchor. Basses down in the hold sing of the terrors of the sea,
and are answered by sailor boys perched in the rigging, who, replying with
a gay "la la la," call themselves the squirrels of the ocean.

Barnaba, disguised as a fisherman, now appears, with the scribe, whom he
sends back for aid, after having noted the number and disposition of the
crew. He then sings a merry ballad, *Ah pescator!* The sailors aboard Enzo's
ship join in the refrain.

   Ah, pescator affonda l'esca (*Fisher Boy, Thy Bait Be Throwing*) **De Luca-Metropoli-
   tan Opera Chorus 8174-2.00**

The song ended, Barnaba puts off in his boat, and Enzo bids his sailors go
below for he will keep watch himself. In the depths of the slightly clouded

ENZO'S VESSEL—ACT II

Italian Adriatic sky a few stars are visible and, the moon coming out from behind a cloud, the limpid waters of the lagoon sparkle. In the famous aria, "Cielo e mar," Enzo apostrophizes the beautiful scene, then pours out rapturously his love for her whom he awaits.

Cielo e mar! *(Heaven, and Ocean!)* **Beniamino Gigli** 7194-2.00

A boat approaches: it is Barnaba bringing Laura. The lovers greet one another impassionedly; then Enzo goes below to arrange for their departure, and Laura kneels in prayer. La Gioconda unexpectedly appears and is about to stab her rival. She suddenly halts and points to a gloomy boat approaching . . . A vengeance more cruel than her own draws nigh—Laura's husband! The faithless wife, in despair, holds aloft a rosary and implores the Virgin's aid. La Gioconda recognizes the rosary as her mother's and even at peril to her own life, enables Laura to escape in a boat. Soon Enzo comes on deck calling for Laura, he is greeted instead by the vengeful Gioconda. Trapped by Alvise and Barnaba, he sets fire to his ship rather than let it fall into their hands.

ACT III

A FESTIVAL is about to take place at the Ducal Palace, and Alvise, planning a perfect revenge, gives Laura a phial of poison. This she must drink before the end of the serenade that is being sung outside. He at once leaves her, and before she fulfills his command, La Gioconda, who has foreseen all this, enters, and in place of the poison, gives Laura a harmless narcotic, that will produce merely the semblance of death. La Gioconda takes the poison away with her, and Laura drinks the narcotic.

The scene changes to the great hall of the Palace. For the entertainment of his guests, Alvise has provided a splendid ballet, representing the hours and symbolical of the struggle between the powers of darkness and of light.

Dance of the Hours—Parts I and II *Boston "Pops" Orchestra* 11833-1.50 *Victor Symphony Orchestra* 35833-1.25

There is a faint twittering and shimmering in the violins and upper woodwind instruments of the orchestra, and dancers enter representative of the delicate tints of dawn. The music then swells to a sudden climax as the brighter hours of the day appear. They dance to a dainty, well-known melody, then withdraw when the music changes to a more serious minor strain, and the darker-hued hours of the evening approach. These are in turn succeeded by the somber hours of the night, and the music finally sinks to a mere thread of tone. The harp plays tranquil arpeggi, there follows a languorous solo dance and in conclusion all join in an exceedingly rapid and high-spirited *finale*, in which the hours of darkness are vanquished by the hours of light.

At the end of the dance Barnaba rushes in dragging La Cieca, who he says was performing her magical rites; she vows that she was but praying for the soul of the dead. A bell is heard tolling and Barnaba whispers to Enzo, who is among the masquers, that it is for Laura. Believing all is lost, Enzo advances, throws off his mask and reveals himself, the former noble, proscribed and robbed of his betrothed by Alvise. The Grand Duke suddenly draws back a curtain and discloses Laura lying on a bier. Enzo rushes at him but is seized and arrested.

ACT IV

LA GIOCONDA manages to have the unconscious Laura brought to a ruined palace on a deserted island in the Adriatic not far from Venice. She asks the men who have helped her, to seek out her mother whom she fears she will never again see. Left alone, she gazes at the flask of poison and contemplates suicide; then she is tempted to complete Alvise's work and give the poison to Laura, but memories of Laura's kindness to her mother return, and she sobs in despair.

Enzo has been released from prison and now arrives; Laura having revived, Gioconda enables the grateful lovers to escape. Gioconda alone knows at what price Enzo's freedom was purchased . . . the price is Gioconda herself, paid to

THE RUINED PALACE—ACT IV

Barnaba. She is about to swallow the poison when the spy appears demanding his reward. While pretending to adorn herself for him, she picks up a dagger; when he rushes at her she stabs herself, and falls dying at his feet. . . . At first Barnaba thinks this must be a jest . . . when he grasps the reality of it, he exclaims, "Hear this, and die ever damned!" . . . He bends down over her and calls furiously into her ear, "Yesterday your mother offended me: I have strangled her!" . . . But Gioconda no longer hears . . . with a cry of half-choked rage, he rushes from the ruins.

THE GIRL OF THE GOLDEN WEST

Bain
JERITZA AS MINNIE

OPERA in three acts; music by Giacomo Puccini; libretto by Zangarini and Civinini, based on a very successful American play of the same name by David Belasco, which in turn was based on a story by Bret Harte. First produced, December 10, 1910, at the Metropolitan Opera House, New York, with Destinn and Caruso in leading rôles.

The plot is concerned with rather melodramatic happenings during the days of the California gold rush in '49. While remaining true, in general, to his usual melodious style, Puccini has adapted his score to a rapidly moving conversational dialogue. He also shows that he was aware of the musical progress of the times by his use of consecutive and unresolved seventh chords somewhat in the manner of Ravel, and in the employment of Debussian augmented triads. Moreover, for the sake of local color, he introduces melodies and rhythms characteristic of the South and Southwest—of plantations, Mexicans, and Indians.

ACT I

Ashby, agent of the Wells-Fargo Company, enters the "Polka" bar-room, and, joining the miners there assembled, says that he is close on the track of Ramerrez, chief of the band of Mexican outlaws who have recently committed a big robbery. The sheriff, Jack Rance, in talking with the men, boasts of his own love affair with the "girl," Minnie, and says that he is going to marry her. One of the miners disputes his claim and a brawl results. Minnie herself enters and stops it. Minnie runs the "Polka," for she is the orphaned child of the founder of this establishment, and also acts as mother and guardian angel to the miners and cowboys who frequent the place. When Rance proposes to her in his crude fashion, she spurns him and holds him at bay with a revolver. A stranger enters and gives his name as Dick Johnson of Sacramento. The sheriff is suspicious concerning him, but Minnie takes his part, saying that she has met him before. Johnson is in reality none other than the hunted Ramerrez—he has come to rob the saloon. Unaware of this, Minnie recalls with Dick the time they first met and fell in love with one another. The men all go in search of Ramerrez, leaving with Minnie their gold. She declares that if anyone is to steal the gold he must do so over her dead body. Johnson has become more and more enamoured of her and relinquishes his plan of robbery; now he admires her courage. She invites him to visit her in her cabin when the miners shall have returned.

ACT II

Johnson and Minnie meet at her "shack" and sing of their love. Suddenly shots are heard outside in the darkness—the men are again searching for Ramerrez. Not wanting to be found with her lover, she conceals Johnson, then admits the men. They are hunting, they say, for Dick Johnson, who is none other than Ramerrez. Minnie declines their offered protection and they leave. Then she turns upon Johnson with the revelations that she has just heard. Dick acknowledges their truth, but goes on to tell how he was compelled by fate to become a bandit; since meeting her he has resolved to give up his old life, and had prayed, in vain, that she would never know of his past. The tense dramatic atmosphere is reflected in somber chords in the orchestra.

EDWARD JOHNSON
AS DICK JOHNSON

But Minnie cannot forgive him for having deceived her after confessing his love. She sends him out into the night. A moment later shots are heard, Minnie runs to the door, opens it and drags in Johnson, seriously wounded. She hides him in a loft up under the roof. The sheriff soon enters, hot on the trail. Minnie has almost overcome his suspicions when a drop of blood falls from the loft, revealing the wounded man. Knowing that the sheriff is a desperate gambler, Minnie, as a last resort, offers to play a game of poker with him, the stakes to be her own hand and Johnson's life, or else her own and the prisoner's freedom. Minnie cheats, wins the game and her lover.

ACT III

Johnson, nursed back to life by Minnie, is about to be hanged by Ashby's men. He asks one last request. Let her believe that he had gained his freedom and gone away to live the nobler life she had taught him. He touchingly apostrophizes her as the "star of his wasted life." This last request of Johnson's is sung to the most famous melody in the opera; it is, moreover, noteworthy as having been one of the most popular songs among the men in the Italian army during the World War.

Just as the lynchers are about to draw the rope taut, Minnie rushes in on horseback. She at first holds the crowd at bay with her drawn revolver, then appeals to them eloquently, reminding them of her faithful care for their needs; they should not fail her now. The "boys" relent, and in spite of Rance's protests, release the prisoner. Johnson and Minnie bid them farewell and go away together to begin life anew.

Jerome Robinson

(LEFT TO RIGHT) TESSA, GIUSEPPE, CASILDA, MARCO AND GIANETTA AS PLAYED BY MEMBERS OF
THE D'OYLY CARTE OPERA COMPANY

THE GONDOLIERS

or The King of Barataria

COMIC OPERA in two acts by W. S. Gilbert and Arthur Sullivan. The cast:
THE DUKE OF PLAZA-TORO *(a Grandee of Spain)*
LUIZ *(his Attendant)*
DON ALHAMBRA DEL BOLERO *(The Grand Inquisitor)*
MARCO PALMIERI ⎫
GIUSEPPE PALMIERI ⎪
ANTONIO   ⎬ *(Venetian Gondoliers)*
FRANCESCO   ⎪
GIORGIO   ⎭
THE DUCHESS OF PLAZA-TORO
CASILDA *(her Daughter)*
GIANETTA ⎫
TESSA   ⎪
FIAMETTA ⎬ *(Contadine)*
VITTORIA ⎪
GIULIA   ⎭
Chorus of Gondoliers and Contadine, Men-at-Arms, Heralds and Pages

"The Gondoliers," with nearly all the other Gilbert and Sullivan operas, has been
recorded for Victor, in a somewhat condensed version, by the D'Oyly Carte Opera
Company, the original Savoyards. The following story of the opera is keyed to the
complete recording, in Album C16 (11188-11199), Ac16 (11200-11211). Price $18.00.

Overture (C16-1)

174

ACT I

The Piazetta, Venice (Date, 1750)

THE two Gondoliers, Marco and Giuseppe, are so handsome and have such winning ways that they have completely turned the heads (C16-2 and 3) of the pretty contadine. Marco and Giuseppe are nonplussed (C16-4) as to whom to choose as their brides. They decide to solve the problem by allowing themselves to be blindfolded (C16-5), whilst the contadine and their superfluous gondolier admirers dance round Marco and Giuseppe. In the ensuing game Marco (C16-6) catches Gianetta, and Giuseppe, Tessa. The remaining contadine accept their fate and pair off with the previously ignored gondolieri. They all run off merrily to get married. As they disappear (C16-7) a gondola stops before the steps of the Piazetta. From it emerge the Duke and Duchess of Plaza-Toro, their daughter Casilda and their suite, consisting of "His Grace's private drum," Luiz. They are dressed as befits their noble station (C16-8), but their clothes are a little the worse for wear. They have brought their daughter Casilda from Spain. The Duke demands an audience with Don Alhambra, the Grand Inquisitor. While Luiz is on the errand the Duke reveals (C16-9) to Casilda that when she was a six-months-old babe she was married by proxy to the infant son of the wealthy King of Barataria. The King of Barataria subsequently became a Wesleyan Methodist of a most bigoted and persecuting type. The Grand Inquisitor, determined that such an innovation should not be perpetuated in Barataria, stole the youthful heir to the throne and conveyed him to Venice. A fortnight later the Baratarian King and his Court were all killed in an insurrection. Casilda, therefore, is now Queen of Barataria. But the whereabouts of the new King are not definitely known. Casilda, unfortunately, is in love with someone else—her father's "private drum," Luiz—and they are both despondent at the sad thought of what the future must bring. Don Alhambra, the Grand Inquisitor, who now approaches and is introduced to Casilda, explains that when he stole the youthful Prince of Barataria, he brought him to Venice and placed him in the family of a highly respectable Gondolier, who had a son of the same age. The Gondolier, through a fondness for drinking, muddled up the two children, and when the Inquisitor went to fetch the Royal Child he found it impossible to tell which was which. This news is received rather philosophically (C16-10). The only person who can possibly tell is the foster-mother of the Prince, Inez (who is Luiz' mother). Luiz is sent to fetch her. Giuseppe and Marco now return with their new-wed wives (C16-11). Don Alhambra (whom at first they mistake for an undertaker) informs them that either Giuseppe or Marco is the King of Barataria, and that until the mystery is unravelled they must take up the reins of government as one individual. They may take all their friends with them—all, that is, except the ladies, who must stay behind. This is rather a blow (C16-12 to 16), but they are assured that the separation will be only for a short period. A boat is then brought, and the Gondoliers clamber aboard with Giuseppe and Marco, whilst the contadine wave a tearful farewell.

ACT II

A Pavilion in the Court of Barataria
(Three Months Later)

BOTH Marco and Giuseppe, when they were Gondoliers, had ideas on Republican government, and they have reorganized the state on their idealistic principles. The result is somewhat chaotic, but they seem to enjoy it, and as the act opens they (C16-17) are seen cleaning the royal crown and sceptre whilst they sit, clad in magnificent robes, on the royal throne. If they want anything done they have to do it themselves. In a delightful little song, "Of happiness the very pith," Giuseppe outlines his day's work as a monarch about the palace (C16-18). Only one thing is missing, they feel—it is dull without female society. Scarcely have they confessed the fact when the contadine run in, led by Fiametta and Vittoria. Curiosity is the cause of the invasion, though they know they were strictly forbidden to come. They are all very excited. Tessa and Gianetta (C16-19) are anxious to know if their husbands have anyone to mend the royal socks, and if it is known yet which of them is to be queen. In honor of their arrival Giuseppe and Marco announce a grand banquet and dance. In the middle of a brilliant cachucha there is an unexpected interruption. Don Alhambra enters. He is astonished at the scene, and tries, by quoting an example (C16-20), to explain where their theories of government are wrong. He announces the arrival of Casilda. One of them, he says, Marco or Giuseppe (whichever is the real King of Barataria), is married to the beautiful Casilda, and is, of course, an unintentional bigamist if he has married a contadina in the meantime. Poor Tessa and Gianetta are very upset. By the light of this new exposure, one of them is married and one of them is not. But they cannot tell which it is. They burst into tears. Meanwhile Casilda is afraid that she will never learn to love her husband. The Duchess is firm. "I loved your father," she says, and (C16-21) proceeds to explain how she married and "tamed" him. The Duke has turned his social prestige to account and has become a limited company. His daughter feels that there is hope that when the King sees what a shady family he has married into he will refuse to recognize the alliance. Both the Duke and the Duchess repudiate the statement that their transactions are shady in a delightful duet, "To help unhappy commoners" (C16-22). Marco and Giuseppe explain the state of the country and the attitude of their subjects towards them. The Duke, in the famous Gavotte (C16-23), "I am a courtier," instructs them on the correct demeanor of a king, which they try, very awkwardly, to adopt. Marco and Giuseppe are tactfully left alone with Casilda, but Gianetta and Tessa come in, and they all discuss the highly complicated problem of exactly who is married and who is not. They are interrupted by Don Alhambra, who enters, accompanied by the Duke and Duchess and all the court of Barataria. Inez, the foster-mother of the Prince, has been found. She alone can unravel the mystery. Inez is brought forward. She confesses that when she took care of the royal prince, and there was an attempt to steal the child, she substituted her own little boy. The traitorous bands never knew the difference, and the child she slyly called her "son" (C16-24) is none other than the King of Barataria. Luiz is, therefore, the King. Casilda and Luiz are reunited, and everything ends happily, much to the secret relief of Marco and Giuseppe.

Jerome Robinson   *(D'Oyly Carte Players)*
(LEFT TO RIGHT) THE DUKE AND DUCHESS OF PLAZA-TORO, CASILDA AND LUIZ

From the Painting by Czackorski

HAMLET AND THE ACTORS—ACT II

HAMLET

OPERA in five acts by Ambroise Thomas; libretto by Barbier and Carré. First produced, March 9, 1868, at the Paris Académie, and in the United States, March 22, 1872, at the Academy of Music, New York.

The plot of the opera contains several variations from Shakespeare's great tragedy from which it is taken. These blemishes, as well as the loss of Shakespeare's verse, are at least partially atoned for by some musical passages of beauty and dramatic force.

ONLY two months after the death of the King of Denmark, his widow has married his brother and successor, Claudius. Hamlet, son of the Queen and the deceased King, appears at the marriage festivities in deep mourning. Ophelia, his betrothed, worried at his strange behavior, wonders if he has ceased to love her. He reassures her, and on the departure of her brother, Laertes, promises to cherish and care for her.

Informed of a strange nocturnal visitant, Hamlet ascends the battlements of the castle at night. There the ghost of his father comes to him with the dreadful information that he was murdered by Claudius at the instigation of the Queen. The ghost begs Hamlet to take revenge on Claudius but to leave his mother's punishment to Heaven.

In order to watch his uncle more closely and to avoid suspicion because of his actions, Hamlet pretends to grow insane. He plans to have presented before the King, a play, so nearly in accordance with the murder as described by the ghost, that the King will instinctively betray himself. He instructs the assembled players in the plot he has conceived, then calling for wine bids them make merry.

Brindisi—O vin dissipe la tristesse *(Drinking Song—Wine, This Gloom Dispel)*
John Charles Thomas 1639-1.50

O wine! this gloom dispel,
That o'er my heart now weighs;
Come grant me thine intoxicating joy;
The careless laugh—the mocking jest!
O wine! Thou potent sorcerer,
Grant thou oblivion to my heart!

The vigorous rhythm of this song, and its attractive melody, first sung by Hamlet alone, then repeated by the troupe of actors, combine to make this an unusually brilliant number.

The play is given before the King as Hamlet planned. As the action progresses, the guilty monarch shows agitation, and finally in a rage orders the actors to stop and leave at once. Hamlet rushes forward and denounces the murder, but no one will believe him—he is merely a madman!

When alone, Hamlet chides himself on his lack of decision; although he is certain of the King's guilt, he has done nothing to avenge his father. To avoid remorse he contemplates suicide. His mother and Ophelia enter and plead with him to give up these wild imaginings. He nevertheless maintains his old pose of insanity, and, believing that Ophelia is involved in his mother's plot, treats her most harshly.

Hamlet's pretended insanity and his cruel treatment bring upon Ophelia a madness that is all too genuine. She wanders to the shore of a lake where a crowd of peasants are making merry at the arrival of spring.

An exquisite orchestral introduction accompanies her entrance, a strange, wild figure, with flowing hair and torn white dress. Speaking to the amazed peasants she tells them childishly of the lark which she heard at dawn, then launches into a brilliant display of bird-like trills and staccatos.

A STATUETTE OF JOHN CHARLES THOMAS IN THE RÔLE OF HAMLET

Ophelia then turns to the shepherds and asks them to listen to her song, a strange, sad melody, interrupted at intervals by wild laughter and weeping. Presently she seems to forget the others, and placidly plays with her flowers, until the magical siren's song is heard luring her to the water's edge. She plunges in to her death, still singing of Hamlet's vow of love.

In the churchyard Hamlet meditatively watches the grave diggers prepare a last resting place for Ophelia. Soon her funeral train arrives. The ghost also appears and, with his looks of reproach, stirs Hamlet to tremendous excitement. The Prince thereupon rushes at and stabs the guilty Claudius. The ghost then solemnly nominates him as successor to the throne, consigns the Queen to a convent, and disappears as the crowd acclaims Hamlet King.

THE HOME OF THE WITCH

HÄNSEL AND GRETEL

(Hänsel und Gretel)

FAIRY opera in three acts; music by Engelbert Humperdinck; text by Adelheid Wette. First produced, December 23, 1893, at Weimar. First performance in the United States at Daly's Theatre, New York, October 8, 1895, in English.

This most delightful opera came to be written, one might say, almost by accident. The composer's sister, Mrs. Hermann (Adelheid) Wette, had compiled for her children a series of verses based on Grimm's fairy tale of "Hänsel und Gretel" and sent them to her brother to set to music. This he did, arranging the work for a home Christmas celebration. It proved to be so enjoyable that Mrs. Wette and Humperdinck elaborated it into a full-length opera. A success from its first performance, this opera of childhood appealing to grown-ups and children alike, has gone around the world and become a part of the permanent repertoire of nearly every opera house.

The composer could not have captured so well the spirit of the story, had he not possessed a most intimate sympathy with and knowledge of his native folk-lore. Accordingly he has made frequent and appropriate use of German folk-songs in writing his score for the charming version of the old fairy-story provided by his librettist. His music is frankly molded on Wagnerian lines with leading motives and their contrapuntal treatment; yet there is little to suggest Wagner; everything is handled with a captivating lightness and delicacy perfectly suited to the story.

(In this country the opera is generally known under the English name, *Han'-sel and Gret'-el*. The German title, Hänsel und Gretel, is pronounced *Hen'-sel oont Gray'-tel*.)

The Overture, a charming and beautiful preparation for the fairy-story, opens with the melody of the prayer of the children in Act II, now played by the French horns. This theme is contrapuntally developed, soaring in reverent calm up to luminous heights that are broken into by a trumpet call, the "Counter-charm" through which the children overcome the hazards that beset them. Then follows the theme heard when the children are awakened by the Dawn Fairy, music that breathes the cool radiance of an early summer's morning in the woods. The very gay melody heard when all the children are rescued and rush joyfully towards one another, enters next (*Part II*). And now, the composer takes all these themes and combines them with the same remarkable contrapuntal mastery he shows throughout the opera. These themes are heard, sometimes simultaneously, at others playfully bandied back and forth with unexpected changes of tone color, dynamics and harmony. Yet so great is the composer's skill that there are no apparent difficulties, all is natural and spontaneous, and therefore delightful. After a brilliant climax, the "Prayer" returns, growing ever softer until it seems to vanish into the air.

Overture—Parts I and II *Mengelberg-Philharmonic-Symphony Orchestra of N. Y.*
7436-2.00 *Coates-Symphony Orchestra 9075-1.50*

ACT I

IN A cottage by the woods there live a poor broom-maker and his wife with two children—a boy, Hänsel, and a girl, Gretel. One day when the father and mother go away to sell brooms, they leave the children at home to take care of the house. The children soon grow tired of their work and Hänsel begins to cry for hunger. But they can find nothing to eat, so Gretel tries to cheer him up with a song and dance. Hänsel attempts to dance also, but being only a boy his steps are so awkward that Gretel laughs when she watches him. After a time their mother returns. She has not been able to sell any of her brooms and could buy no food to bring home. Therefore, she sends Hänsel and Gretel into the woods to gather strawberries.

The poor mother is so tired that as soon as the children have gone she falls asleep. In the evening when the father returns he awakens her. Fortunately he has sold his brooms and has brought home both arms filled with good things for the children. But now it is growing late and Hänsel and Gretel have not returned. The parents are fearful lest they may have been captured by the dreadful witch who lives in the woods and makes children into gingerbread. They start out to search for them.

ACT II

WHEN Hänsel and Gretel come to the woods they gather strawberries until their basket is full. Then they pick wild flowers to make a wreath for Gretel and sit down to rest. Hänsel tries just one berry and Gretel follows his example. The first is so good that they take another, and another. Before they realize it the basket is empty. Meanwhile the sun has set and it has grown so dark that they cannot see to pick any more berries, or to find the way home. And now

World Wide

HÄNSEL AND GRETEL

the woods that were so cheerful while the sun was shining, have become full of terrors, ghosts and frightful sounds. Still, when the Sandman comes, the children say their prayers and fall asleep. While they sleep angels descend and watch over them.

Dream Pantomime—Parts I and II   *British Broadcasting Co. Symphony Orch., Cond. by Adrian Boult* 11832-1.50

ACT III

IN THE morning when they have been awakened by the Dawn Fairy, the children are greatly surprised for they see a little sugar-candy house nearby. Surrounding it is a wall of gingerbread boys and girls. Hänsel and Gretel are so very hungry that they at once begin to nibble at the gingerbread wall. Suddenly there comes from the house a dreadful witch riding on a broom. She tries to make friends with the children, but they are too frightened. Therefore, she bewitches Hänsel with her magic juniper wand, locks him in the barn, and dances for joy at the prospects of a tasty meal. She feeds Hänsel with good things to make him grow fat. While the witch is busy at this, Gretel takes the magic wand and repeats the spell which had locked Hänsel in the barn. Thus when the witch turns away he is able to escape. The witch orders Gretel to look in the oven to see if the cakes are ready. Gretel pretends to be very dull and asks to be shown. Then as the witch stoops in front of the open door, the children give her a hard push so that she falls right into the oven. Soon the oven falls apart with a crash and all the gingerbread boys and girls are restored to life. The father and mother, who have been hunting all night, come, and are happy on finding that Hänsel and Gretel are safe. From the ruins of the oven the children draw forth the witch, now turned into a great gingerbread cake, and all dance and sing for joy and devout thankfulness.

Larcher　　　　　　　　　THE CHAMBER OF HEROD

HÉRODIADE

OPERA in four acts; music by Jules Massenet; words by Miller and Gremont; based on Gustave Flaubert's Novelette. First produced, December 19, 1881, at the Theatre de la Monnaie, Brussels. First performed in London, 1904, under the name *Salome*, the change of title being ordered by the Lord Chamberlain. This title has also sometimes been used in the United States. First American performance, at the New Orleans Opera, February 13, 1892.

(The name of the opera is pronounced *Ay-rohd-yadd'*.)
The action takes place in Jerusalem, about 30 A.D.

ACT I

SCENE—*The Courtyard of the Palace of Herod*

IT IS dawn and a great horde of merchants, traders and slaves crowd the scene to do their oriental bartering. The Pharisees and Sadducees among them soon begin to argue, then to fight. Phanuel, seer and chief adviser to Herod, attracted by the uproar, enters and bids them cease; the crowd disperses. Phanuel remains musing over the impossibility of a strong Israel with her people thus divided, when he is interrupted by the entry of Salome. She is seeking John, the prophet with a new and rising gospel. She tells Phanuel how when she was a child, John had saved her from the desert; this she narrates in a lovely aria.

Il est doux, il est bon (*He is Kind, He is Good*)　**Maria Jeritza 6604-2.00**

While listening to her sympathetically he marvels that this seemingly in-

183

nocent child does not know who her mother really is. As she leaves, Herod enters, seeking her. He has seen her seldom, yet his passions are inflamed by this new beauty who lives so obscurely in his palace. He is startled from his amorous meditation by the arrival of Herodias, who comes crying out for vengeance; she demands the head of John, who has insulted her by calling her Jezebel. Herod refuses, much to the chagrin of Herodias, his one-time favorite. Her scoldings are in turn interrupted by the entry of John, who denounces the pair in such terrifying language that they flee.

Salome now comes towards the prophet, and frankly confesses her great love for him. He listens understandingly and kindly, but bids her turn to God and dream only of the love that is fulfilled in heaven. But Salome is not able to comprehend why she should not love and be loved on earth as well as in heaven.

ACT II

Scene I—*Herod's Chamber*

HEROD, restless on his luxurious couch, watches the dance of the almond-eyed women whose sole purpose in life is doing his pleasure. He cannot endure their presence now, for his thoughts are of nothing but Salome; he longs for her with the urgent desire that every powerful man has for the unattainable. A serving woman brings him a mysterious potion that will enable him to see a vision of the woman he most loves. Herod hesitates a moment, for fear that it may be a trick to poison him, but desire is too strong. He drinks the potion, and beholds a maddeningly tantalizing vision of Salome.

Vision fugitive (*Fleeting Vision*) **John Charles Thomas 1639-1.50**

The vision passed, he again attempts to sleep; his restless tossings are ended by Phanuel, who comes to warn him that his hold upon the populace is insecure. Even as he speaks, from without there is a great cry for Herod.

Scene II—*A Public Square in Jerusalem*

Local patriots have come to swear their allegiance to Herod in attempting to throw off the yoke of Rome. They are laughed at by Herodias. Soon trumpets announce the approach of Vitelius, and Herod is among the very first to bow the knee to the Roman; only John boldly remains standing before the rulers. Vitelius wonders at this man; Herod, although conscience of what is going on about him, is still under the spell of Salome's beauty. He sees nothing—his eyes are glued on Herodias' daughter as she affectionately watches the prophet, John. Herodias observes everything, and warns Vitelius of John's growing power. The prophet denounces the Romans, saying their glory is but for a day; then, surrounded by his followers, he disappears.

INNER COURT OF THE TEMPLE—ACT III

ACT III

Scene I—*Phanuel's House*

PHANUEL, alone, is gazing out over the city, silent under the starry sky. He wonders about this man John, is he merely man, or a god?

Herodias comes seeking her horoscope; the astrologer finds only blood written there. A star, inextricably linked to hers, serves to remind Herodias of her long-forgotten daughter; she wishes to see her again. Phanuel points from his window down to the gates of the temple. It is Salome they see. Herodias is horrified; hatred and desire for vengeance return. "My Daughter," she cries, "never . . . my rival!"

Scene II—*Inner Court of the Temple*

Salome laments and then falls fainting at the gate of the temple prison where John is confined. Herod, planning how he might release John and use him in his plot against the Romans, forgets all his political ideas when he finds Salome here. She recoils in horror when she realizes that this is the all-powerful Herod making love to her. Priests and people enter and worship at the Holy of Holies; then John is brought out for trial. The priests demand his execution; the crowd is divided. Herod would save John if he will help him in his plot against the Romans. John refuses; the Priests clamor for his execution. Suddenly Salome throws herself at John's feet, and, before the astonished multitude, begs that she may die with him. Herod has found his rival, and condemns the two to death.

ACT IV

Scene I—*A Dungeon in the Temple*

JOHN prays for strength in the ordeal to come, and pleads that he may be freed of the love of Salome which constantly disturbs his soul. When she enters a moment later he believes that this is an indication that heaven approves their love. They clasp one another in a supreme embrace while they sing their duet, "Il est beau de mourir en s'aimant." Priests enter to lead John to death; but Salome is dragged away to Herod's Palace.

Scene II—*The Great Hall in the Palace*

A most luxurious festival in honor of the Roman Empire is in progress. As a part of the festivities a group of Phœnician women perform a languorous oriental dance. Salome runs distractedly before Herod and Herodias again to plead that she may be permitted to die with John. She appeals to the Queen, saying, "If ever thou wert a mother, pity me!" Herodias trembles at the word. Suddenly there appears at the back of the hall an executioner with dripping sword, crying "The Prophet is dead!" From the expression on the face of Herodias, Salome recognizes her as the one responsible for this; she rushes at the woman with drawn dagger. "Spare me!" cries the frightened Herodias, "I am thy mother!" Salome recoiling in horror answers, "If thou be my mother, take back thy blood with my life," then drives the dagger into her own breast.

Cautin & Berger
CALVÉ AS SALOME

186

CASTLE AND GARDENS OF CHENONCEAUX

LES HUGUENOTS

(The Huguenots)

OPERA in five acts; music by Giacomo Meyerbeer; libretto by Scribe and Deschamps. First produced, February 29, 1836, at the Grand Opéra, Paris. First performance in America, April 29, 1839, in New Orleans. Owing to the great length of the opera, the original five acts are usually cut to four, sometimes to three.

Meyerbeer has provided this dramatic story written around the Massacre on the night of St. Bartholomew's with a very effective setting. While his music may at times be trite, yet when well performed in the theatre with appropriate action and settings it is still capable of being tremendously impressive. Even Wagner, who often made light of Meyerbeer, praised some of the greater moments in "Les Huguenots." (The original French title is pronounced, *Lay oog-noh'*; the Italian, Gli Ugonotti, *l'yee oo-goh-not' ti*.)

The action of the Opera takes place during 1572, the first two acts in Touraine, the remainder at Paris.

ACT I

SCENE—*House of the Count of Nevers*

THE Count of Nevers, who is entertaining a party of Catholics, seems so preoccupied that his guests ask the cause. He replies that another guest is coming, the Protestant, Raoul. "A Huguenot!" they exclaim. Although

187

they know that Margaret of Valois, the betrothed of the King, is eager to reconcile Catholic and Protestant, and that he who furthers her purpose is apt to win royal favor, yet they receive Raoul with ironical politeness when he arrives. His frank open nature is undisturbed by this, and when Nevers toasts the ladies and proposes that each tell of some adventure with the fair sex, Raoul willingly complies, although he being the last to arrive is chosen to be first to respond. In a Romanza he tells them of the unknown beauty whom he rescued this very morning from some drunken revellers. He does not know her, but is wildly in love with her because of her beauty.

The applause which greets this romantic recital is interrupted by Raoul's sturdy old Huguenot servant Marcel, who distrusts his master's Catholic friends and sings the Lutheran choral, "A Mighty Fortress is Our God." The guests accept Raoul's apologies for his behavior and ask the old fellow to sing again. He responds with a vigorous Huguenot ditty against the "snares of Rome."

The resulting rather constrained feeling is quickly forgotten when a servant announces that a veiled lady wishes to speak to Nevers, who at once retires to meet her amidst the banter of his friends. All are curious regarding the lady, and Raoul himself joins in peeping behind a curtain. It is none other than the unknown beauty he rescued that morning; at once he believes that some disagreeable liaison exists between this woman and Nevers.

Still another unexpected diversion occurs in the arrival of a page, who, in the very ornate but melodious "Page's Song," informs them that one of their number is addressed with the unusual request to go blindfolded in a carriage wherever his guide may take him.

Nobles seigneurs, salut! *(Noble Sirs, I Salute You!)* **Sigrid Onégin** 7146-2.00

Raoul, though highly puzzled when he learns that the message is addressed to him, gallantly accepts. He also wonders at the sudden respect with which he is treated, for he does not realize that the seal on the letter is that of Margaret of Valois.

ACT II

SCENE—*Castle and Gardens of Chenonceaux*

MARGARET of Valois, surrounded by her maids of honor, rejoices in the pleasant sunny field of Touraine after the stress of life at court. Valentine, daughter of the Count of St. Bris, enters and tells Margaret news—she has succeeded in breaking her engagement to marry the Count of Nevers, news in which both rejoice, for Valentine does not love the man, and Margaret has other plans for her. Valentine and some of the ladies go away as Raoul is brought before Margaret and the bandage removed from his eyes; though astonished to find himself before Margaret of Valois, he gallantly offers her his sword and service. She tells him of her desire for him to marry Valentine and as he knows of Margaret's ambition to reconcile Catholic and Protestant by this union, he consents. The nobles of the Court are summoned and when they appear they gather around the Queen and in commemoration of the union of Raoul and Valentine swear an oath of eternal truce between their parties. Valentine is brought in to be presented to her betrothed, Raoul recoils in horror and exclaims, "I her husband?" for he recognizes in Valentine the woman who called secretly on the Count of Nevers. All present are filled with the greatest consternation; Valentine is overcome with shame, and St. Bris, furious at the insult to his daughter, joins with Nevers in swearing vengeance. Margaret's presence does indeed prevent immediate bloodshed, but her hopes of uniting the warring factions are forever shattered.

ACT III

Scene—*A Square in Paris*

NEAR the entrance to a chapel on the banks of the Seine, a group of Catholic students has gathered about the doors of an inn; and at another inn across the way a number of Huguenot soldiers have met to drink and play dice. Townspeople of all sorts pass to and fro, their many-colored costumes adding glamour to the brilliant sunlight. A bridal procession passes—Valentine and the Count of Nevers are to be married. While the bridal party is in the chapel, Marcel enters with a message for St. Bris, from Raoul. The wedding over, Valentine remains in the chapel to pray

C. Gerardi   THE PUBLIC SQUARE

alone and Marcel presents the message to St. Bris; it proves to be a challenge. The nobles re-enter the chapel.

Twilight falls, the curfew sounds, and the people disperse. Valentine comes from the chapel in deathly terror, for she has overheard the nobles plotting to kill Raoul. She finds Marcel waiting for his master, and warns him of the plan. It is too late for him to see Raoul before the hour of the duel, so he hastily gathers a group of Huguenot friends nearby. The two parties prove to be evenly matched, a serious fray is threatened and, in fact, is prevented only by the arrival of Margaret of Valois, who happens to be passing. Raoul also learns that he has deeply wronged Valentine, for her visit to Nevers was made at the request of Margaret merely to break off the engagement. His remorse comes too late, for now Valentine is married to this man she never loved, and a boat, gay with lanterns and music, has come up the Seine to take her to the Count's home.

ACT IV

Scene—*A Room in Nevers' Castle*

Alone at her new home, Valentine still thinks of Raoul, who suddenly and unexpectedly appears. He so longs to see Valentine that he has entered the castle at the risk of his life; she warns him but he insists on remaining and scarcely has time to hide behind the tapestry before St. Bris, Nevers, and other leaders of the Catholic party, enter. Thus the young Protestant overhears the whole ghastly plot for the massacre of the Huguenots. Nevers alone among them refuses to swear allegiance to the plan; he is led away under guard. While all draw their swords, three Monks who have entered bless them.

Copy't Mishkin
CARUSO AS RAOUL

The crowd having departed, Raoul comes cautiously from his hiding place; he would run to warn his friends. Valentine meets him, and fearing he may kill her father she will not let him go. They sing a surpassingly beautiful duet which is interrupted by the sinister tolling of the great bell of St. Germain, the preliminary signal for the slaughter. Raoul makes an effort to rush to the aid of his people; Valentine clings to him. Pointing to the street below he shows her that the massacre has already begun, then tears himself from her arms and leaps through the window.

In American productions, because of the great length of Meyerbeer's work, the opera usually ends with the shooting of Raoul

190

THE GREAT BANQUET SCENE IN ACT I

by the mob as he leaps from the window; but in the original version a fifth act occurs. In this fifth act Nevers is killed, and Valentine, renouncing her faith, is united to Raoul by Marcel. St. Bris and his party enter the street, and, not recognizing Valentine, fire upon and kill all three. St. Bris discovers too late that in his great zeal he has slain his own daughter.

THE EARL OF MOUNTARARAT, PHYLLIS, AND EARL TOLLOLLER AS PLAYED BY MEMBERS OF THE
D'OYLY CARTE OPERA COMPANY

IOLANTHE

or, The Peer and the Peri

COMIC OPERA in two acts by W. S. Gilbert and Arthur Sullivan. Like most of the Gilbert and Sullivan operas, "Iolanthe" has been recorded for Victor by the D'Oyly Carte Opera Company of London. The story of the opera is keyed to the records in Masterpiece Album C10 (9708-9718), Ac10 (9719-9729). Price $16.50.

Gilbert derived his plot from one of his *Bab Ballads*, "The Fairy Curate." In that poem the odd story is told of the son of a fairy mother and a mortal father, who became a curate. All went well until one day when the Bishop discovered him talking affectionately to his mother, who of course appeared much younger than her son. The Bishop accordingly upbraided him violently. Eventually this curate was obliged to become a mormon. As developed by Gilbert, the story of *Iolanthe* presents his favorite themes of duality and plurality. Strephon is both fairy and mortal; the Chancellor is judge, jury, plaintiff and defendant. As usual with him there is a captivating blending of reality and fantasy, and a view of a world in which things are amusingly "topsy-turvy"—a world in which a lord sings to a maid of lowly birth:

> Spurn not the nobly born,
> With love affected!
> Nor treat with virtuous scorn
> The well connected!

DRAMATIS PERSONAE

THE LORD CHANCELLOR
EARL OF MOUNTARARAT
EARL TOLLOLLER

Private Willis of the Grenadier Guards
Iolanthe, *a Fairy, Strephon's mother*
Strephon, *an Arcadian shepherd*
Queen of the Fairies
Phyllis, *an Arcadian shepherdess and ward in Chancery*
Celia ⎫
Leila ⎬ *Fairies*
Fleta ⎭
Chorus of Dukes, Marquises, Earls, Viscounts, Barons, and Fairies

Overture (C10-1 and 2) *Symphony Orchestra, cond. by Malcolm Sargent*

ACT I

Scene—An Arcadian landscape. In the background a stream is seen. At the raising of the curtain, the Fairies enter, led by Leila, Celia, and Fleta. They trip across the stage, singing (C10-3) as they dance.

At the end of their chorus the Fairies lament that since Iolanthe was banished twenty-five years ago, their revels have lost their former spirit. According to law, Iolanthe's crime—that of marrying a mortal—should have been punished by death. At this point in their conversation the Fairy Queen, entering, herself finishes their story. The Queen, rather than let so dire a punishment be visited on a beloved Fairy, banished Iolanthe, on condition that she never explain to, or communicate with, her husband. The Queen herself laments the loss of Iolanthe, to whom she is deeply indebted. For—and be it known the Queen is built on the most generous proportions—it was Iolanthe who taught her to curl up inside a buttercup, to swing upon a cobweb, to dive into a dewdrop, nestle in a nutshell, and gambol upon gossamer! Leila remarks that Iolanthe certainly did surprising things. The fairies all beg the Queen to restore Iolanthe to them, and the Queen, who is troubled by no small curiosity to know why, of all places, Iolanthe, when banished chose to live in the bottom of the stream, summons her (C10-4). Iolanthe rises from the water. She is clad in tattered and sombre garments. She approaches the Queen with head bent and arms crossed. Her rags fall from her, and she appears clothed as a fairy. The Queen places a diamond coronet on her head and embraces her. The others also embrace her. When the Queen asks why she chose to live in the bottom of the stream, Iolanthe replies that she wished to be near her son, who was born shortly after her banishment. All are curious to see this child, now grown to manhood, who is half fairy and half mortal. At that moment this very youth, Strephon, approaches, singing and dancing, and playing on a flageolet. He does not see the Fairies, who conceal themselves as he enters. From the conversation of Strephon and Iolanthe we learn that he intends to marry Phyllis this very day, even though the Lord Chancellor, whose ward she is, withholds his consent. The Fairies and Fairy Queen come forward and make Strephon's acquaintance before they go (C10-5).

The Queen and the Fairies trip away. Iolanthe, who takes an affectionate farewell of her son, going off last. Phyllis enters, singing and dancing, and accompanying herself on a flageolet. Phyllis recalls that the punishment for marrying a ward of court without the Lord Chancellor's consent is penal servitude for life. She asks if they should not wait for two years until she becomes of age. But Strephon thinks that the House of Lords has become so attentive to her that delays are dangerous, and Phyllis agrees. Trumpets herald (C10-6 and 7) the approach of the Peers. During the instrumental march, they enter in a procession of super-dignity, wearing their gorgeous robes of state. The Earl of Mountararat and the Earl of Tolloller lead the procession. The Lords have been so powerfully affected by the beauty of Phyllis that they have petitioned the Chancellor to bestow her upon whichever one she will select. This is the reason for their visit here. The Lord Chancellor is grieved to have to confess that he is himself so attracted by the girl that he is wasting away under the strain of his position. For if he were to award her to himself, his action might be open to misconstruction. Even though it pains him, he therefore waives all claims for himself. Could he give his own consent to his own marriage with his own ward? Can he marry his own ward without his own consent? And if he did so, can he commit himself for contempt of his own court? It is indeed painful, the Chancellor avers, to have to sit upon a woolsack which is stuffed with such thorns as these.

Lord Mountararat, who has gone to summon Phyllis, returns, followed by the young lady (C10-8 and 9). The Peers depart, marching around the stage with much dignity. The Lord Chancellor separates Phyllis from Strephon, and orders her away. The Lord Chancellor and Strephon remain.

ELIZABETH NICKELL-LEAN OF THE D'OYLY CARTE OPERA COMPANY, AS "IOLANTHE"

The Lord Chancellor asks Strephon what excuse he can offer for daring to disobey an order of the Court of Chancery. Strephon replies that he knows only Nature's acts of Parliament, and since he loves Phyllis, all the voices of Nature—from the brooks to the thunder-storms—have commanded that he marry her. "Are you also Chancellor of birds and trees?" Strephon asks. The Chancellor admits it's a nice point, but doubts that the evidence is conclusive. But an affidavit from a thunder-storm would meet with more attention. Strephon asks if he would apply the prosaic rules of evidence to so poetic a case. The Chancellor answers that he certainly would, for he owes his present distinguished position to the fact that he has always kept his duty before his eyes (C10-10). When he has finished, the Lord Chancellor rushes away, leaving Strephon in tears at his fate. Iolanthe enters, and trying to comfort him, says she will seek help from the Fairy Queen (C10-10). The Peers approach in the background, advancing unseen and on tiptoe. Lord Mountararat and Tolloller lead Phyllis between them, who listens in horror to what she hears. Phyllis rushes forward (C10-11) and reveals herself. Iolanthe and Strephon are much confused. Strephon's claim that Iolanthe is his mother is laughed at, and Phyllis believes him unfaithful. Iolanthe clings for protection to Strephon. Phyllis sings of her distress, and despairingly gives her heart to one of two lords, "I don't care which" (C10-12). Strephon calls the fairies to his aid. They come, and the situation is explained to them (C10-12). The Peers and Lord Chancellor attempt to dismiss them (C10-13) but the daring Fairy Queen will not budge until she has pronounced sentence on their stupidity. She threatens them (C10-14) and tells them their fate (C10-14); Strephon shall be sent to Parliament, and every bill he wishes shall be passed by magic. But the Peers are defiant.

ACT II

SCENE—The Palace Yard, Westminster, Westminster Hall at the left. Private Willis is discovered on sentry, at the right. Night. He muses upon politics and its stupidity (C10-15). The Fairies enter, singing of the mischief Strephon has caused in Parliament. Meanwhile the Peers are terrifically upset because Strephon is about to carry his bill to throw the peerage open to competitive examination. The Fairies claim the honor for this, saying that they influence the members to vote for any bill Strephon wishes. Lord Mountararat retorts "This comes of women interfering in politics." He adds that if there's any British institution not susceptible of improvement, it's the House of Peers (C10-16). The Chorus of Peers go away. Lords Mountararat and Tolloller remain with the Fairies to plead with them to stop their mischief. The latter refuse, although Leila has been much attracted (C10-17) by the Peers, and Celia also is moved to exclaim, "For self-contained dignity, combined with airy condescension, give me a British representative peer!"

Lords Mountararat and Tolloller go, and the Fairies remain looking wistfully after them. The Fairy Queen enters (C10-18), and scolds them for their faithlessness to the fairy law, reminding them of the death penalty for those who marry a mortal. They must subdue their weakness! The Queen admits that she herself is not insensible to the effect of manly beauty. Pointing to Sentry Willis, who remains motionless at his post, she says he has the most extraordinary effect upon her. If she yielded to her impulse she would fall down and worship him. But she mortifies that inclination. The Fairies go away sorrowfully, led by the Fairy Queen. Phyllis enters in tears, for she finds herself engaged to two noblemen at once, neither of whom she loves. Lords Mountararat and Tolloller enter, each wanting to embrace her, and claiming her as his own. Phyllis finds them both equally wealthy and equally plain, so that there is nothing to choose between them. She says that if one of them would forego his title and distribute his estates among the Irish tenantry, then she could see a reason for accepting the other. But although they have been friends since boyhood, neither can quite persuade the other to make such a sacrifice (C10-18). Enter the Lord Chancellor, very miserable, singing the celebrated "nightmare song," (C10-19).

During the last lines of the song, Lords Mountararat and Tolloller have entered. They gaze sympathetically upon the Lord Chancellor's distress. At the end of his song they approach him and express their sympathy. His situation is most difficult: firstly, he is Lord Chancellor, entrusted with the guardianship of Phyllis; secondly, he is her suitor. And he confesses, "In my latter capacity I am overawed by my dignity in my former capacity; I hesitate to approach myself—it unnerves me." The others urge him to take courage (C10-20). They go away, dancing together, arm-in-arm. Phyllis and Strephon, both of whom are wandering about disconsolately at this hour of the night, enter. Phyllis' taunt about his young mother, leads Strephon to explain that he is only half mortal. Phyllis bursts into tears saying that she would rather have half a mortal she loves than half a dozen that she does not love. Strephon thinks she had better stick to her mortals for there would be too many difficulties with him . . . his grandmother and his aunts look as young as his mother! Phyllis says that she understands; whenever she sees him kissing a young lady she'll know it's an elderly relative. So they agree (C10-20) to get married at once—before they change their minds—saying ". . . we'll get married first—and change our minds afterward." Iolanthe enters and they ask her to intercede for them with the Lord Chancellor. That exalted personage also arrives on the scene, exulting over the great victory he has won with himself—he has at last succeeded in persuading himself to give his consent to his marriage with Phyllis! The young people withdraw, and Iolanthe appeals to the Chancellor (C10-21). The rather complicated plot begins to clear.

The Peers and Strephon enter (C10-22). The Queen raises her spear. The Lord Chancellor and Strephon implore her mercy. Leila and Celia rush forward. Leila cries, "Hold! If Iolanthe must die, so must we all, for as she has sinned, so have we." And so it is revealed that all the Fairies have now married Peers. The Queen is forced to admit that she cannot "slaughter the whole company." Yet, she says as she unrolls a scroll, the law is clear: Every fairy must die who marries a mortal! The Lord Chancellor with his keen legal mind, is equal to the emergency. He suggests, "Let it stand that every fairy shall die who *don't* marry a mortal!" This pleases the Queen, and she alters the scroll in pencil. Then to save herself she must needs—though gladly enough—summon Private Willis to her aid. She asks if he'll marry her at once. True British soldier, he is ever willing to "save a female in distress." Now by her Majesty's command wings spring from the shoulders of Private Willis and all the Peers—they too have become immortals—and the Queen cries, "Away we go to Fairyland!"

THE JEWELS OF THE MADONNA

(I Giojelli della Madonna)

OPERA in three acts by Wolf-Ferrari; plot by the composer, verse by C. Zangarini and E. Golisciani. First produced at the Kurfuersten Oper, Berlin, December 23, 1911; in the United States, by the Chicago Opera Company, at the Auditorium Theatre, Chicago, January 16, 1912. In this opera the composer forsakes the charming style of his earlier works, such as "Le Donne Curiose" and "Il Segreto di Susanna," for a bold attempt in the blood-ridden realist school. Though the opera has a plot that is over-exaggerated in its melodramatic features, it presents a colorful picture of Neapolitan life and contains some very effective music, notably the delicate intermezzi, the touching duet of mother and son, the orgiastic apache dance, and the finale with its glowing fervors.

(The original Italian name of the opera is "I Giojelli della Madonna," pronounced *Ee-Joh-yel' lee del-lah Mah-don -nah.*)

ACT I

THE action takes place at the present time in Naples. We are introduced to the life of the poorer sections of that teeming city—a life crowded with spectacular religious ceremonies, gross superstitions, reckless gaiety and sordid animal love along with fierce hatred and jealousy. Maliella *(Mah-lee-el'-lah)* is beloved of the simple Gennaro *(Jen-nah'-roh)* and the bold Rafaele *(Rah-fah-el'-leh)*, leader of the dreaded secret order of Camorristi. The latter, with his reckless bravado, appeals much more to this high-spirited girl; he boasts that he would do anything to win her love . . . he would even steal the jewels from the holy image of the Virgin that has just been carried by in solemn procession. But

THE GARDEN SCENE—ACT II

the gentle Gennaro has heard of this boast, and, stung by the taunts of Maliella, breaks into the church and secures the jewels.

ACT II

A BEAUTIFUL orchestral intermezzo, with the warmth of its orchestral colors and the passionate intensity of its melody, creates the mood of soft voluptuousness characteristic of a Neapolitan night.

Intermezzo *(Act II)* **Ormandy-Minneapolis Symphony Orchestra 1742-1.50** *Victor* **Symphony Orchestra 35976-1.25**

Maliella, lingering among the shadows of her moonlit garden, is serenaded by Rafaele; she promises to come to him the next day. When he has
left, and she remains alone in the garden, her whole being still vibrating
under the passion that Rafaele has aroused in her, Gennaro comes with the
jewels and spreads them before her. She gazes at them in a rapture, mystical
yet sensuous, and when Gennaro clasps her in a passionate embrace she
yields herself to him, utterly, still thinking of Rafaele.

ACT III

A SECOND intermezzo precedes the last act—an orchestral version of Rafaele's
serenade, typically Neapolitan in the impetuousness of its melody, the
verve of its waltz-like rhythm, and the lightness of its accompaniment.

Intermezzo *(Act III)* *Ormandy-Minneapolis Symphony Orchestra* 1743-1.50 *Victor*
Symphony Orchestra 35976-1.25

At a den of the Camorristi the companions of Rafaele hold their dissolute
revels, dancing the "Tarantella" and "Apache." Rafaele toasts Maliella as
the girl who will give herself only to him. Maliella breaks into this scene;
she is as in a trance. Crying out in agony she makes her way to Rafaele
through the maze of dancers. She attempts to explain that in giving herself
to Gennaro she was dazed, and confused the two men. The coarse women
laugh derisively at Rafaele; burning with rage, jealousy and disdain, he
flings Maliella to the ground . . . the jewels fall, scattering over the floor
. . . the crowd draw back in superstitious awe and the unhappy girl runs
screaming from the place to drown herself in the bay. At Rafaele's command
the crowd disperses, but Gennaro, who was pointed out by Maliella as the
thief, remains. He reverently gathers up the jewels, places them before the
crude fresco of the Madonna, then in expiation for his enormous sin plunges
a dagger in his heart.

THE JUGGLER SEES BONIFACE

LE JONGLEUR *DE* NÔTRE *DAME*

(*The Juggler of Notre Dame*)

OPERA in three acts; music by Jules Massenet; libretto by Maurice Lena. The story, first published by Gaston Paris as "Le Tombeor de Nostre Dame" in the review, *Romania*, during 1874-75, and later in his "Etude sur la Poésie Française au Moyen Age," is better known through the version included by Anatole France in his "Etui de Nacre." The opera was first produced at Monte Carlo, February 18, 1902, and was first performed in the United States at the Manhattan Opera House, New York, November 27, 1908.

This opera is said to owe its existence to the fact that a certain *concierge*, or hall porter, in Paris, fell ill and took a "day off," thereby obliging M. Massenet to collect his own mail. Otherwise, the libretto would have gone the way of hundreds of libretti continually showered upon the successful composer. For Massenet, it is a unique work; excepting the brief passage for angels, it is written entirely for men's voices. Massenet had written such a long line of heroine operas—Thaïs, Herodias, Manon—that he was accused of being an *effeminate* composer. Perhaps, as Mr. Henry T. Finck suggests, he was piqued at this, and wished to show his critics he could write an opera omitting the fair sex. If that be true, there is irony in the fact that at the Manhattan performance Mr. Hammerstein assigned the rôle of Jean to Mary Garden, and that since that date the work—like many another of Massenet's—has become familiar to American audiences as a prima donna opera.

(The name of the opera is pronounced *Luh-Jon-glur'duh Noh-tr Dam*, and when literally translated reads "Our Lady's Juggler.")

The action is supposed to take place at Cluny, near Paris, during the Sixteenth Century.

ACT I

French Poster
DEATH OF THE JUGGLER

IT IS May Day at Cluny, and a merry crowd is gathered before the gates of the monastery. Jean, announcing himself as "King of Jugglers," haggard and worn from illness, and weak from lack of food, begs leave to entertain them. They scoff at his sorry appearance; nor do they wish his tricks; instead they demand his famous "Hallelujah of Wine," a sacrilegious mock-litany. At the height of the performance, the Prior of the monastery appears and wrathfully disperses the crowd. After threatening Jean with the torments of Hell, he suggests that the mountebank enter the monastery. Although Jean loves his freedom, the sight of Boniface, cook at the abbey, leading home a mule heavily laden with good things for the table of the brothers, is too much; he is soon converted.

ACT II

LIFE in the abbey agrees with him physically, but his constant jests and gross delight in the things of the table scandalize as well as amuse his fellow-monks. He strives to sing with the choir, but he cannot grasp the Latin . . . how should a poor juggler know the language of the saints? The monks, striving in vain to teach him their various arts, fall to quarreling as to which is the greater, painting or sculpture; the good prior is obliged to conduct them to the chapel, there to study art in a spirit of prayer and devotion. Poor Jean is grieved by his ignorance; to console him the cook tells him that anything done well is good in the sight of the Lord. To convince him of this he sings the Legend of the Sagebrush.

Légende de la sauge (*Legend of the Sagebrush*) **Marcel Journet 6785-2.00**

The eyes of the old monk soften as he tells the quaint story of the rose that refused to shelter the little child Jesus from the wrath of Herod for fear of staining its lovely petals, and the humble sageflower that undertook the task cheerfully and became blessed among flowers. Jean listens openmouthed . . . is it possible that even the low gift of the juggler may be acceptable in the eyes of the Blessed Virgin?

ACT III

JEAN appears before the altar in the dim chapel. Dressed in his juggler's costume he performs his tricks and sings his villainous songs; finally he breaks into a wild dance. The good Boniface, understanding the feverish earnestness of the juggler's manner, has, with difficulty, been restraining the horrified monks who have been looking on. As Jean collapses in prayer before the altar, Boniface points to a strange glow of light upon the face of the Virgin, who slowly stretches forth her hands in benediction. "A miracle!" cry the monks, devoutly sinking to their knees. The chapel is flooded with a mystic glow . . . the face of Jean is transfigured . . . while the monks pray for the passing of a soul, from above floats the chanting of angels, *Kyrie eleison* . . . "At last," cries the dying juggler, "at last I can understand Latin!"

MARTINELLI AS ELEAZAR

LA JUIVE

(The Jewess)

OPERA in five acts by Jacques Halévy; book by Scribe. First produced at the Académie de Musique, Paris, February 23, 1835; first performance in America, February 13, 1844, at the Théâtre d'Orléans, New Orleans. Though the libretto of this opera was originally written for him, Rossini refused it; the subject appealed to Halévy, whose real name was Levi, and, coupled with the music he wrote, won him fame. Caruso made his last public appearance playing the rôle of Eleazar in this opera, at the Metropolitan Opera House, New York, on Christmas Eve, 1920. He had first played the part two years earlier; at that time those of his admirers who had come to hear him and who did not know the opera, were rather startled when that great artist appeared wearing a long white beard and a false nose, his figure bent and footsteps tottering. While Halévy's music may at times seem antiquated, a number of the airs, notably those of the aged Eleazar, are humanly pathetic and touching, and the brilliant pageantry of some of the scenes is most

impressive. Wagner was enthusiastic over "La Juive" when he first saw it, and it probably inspired him in the writing of "Rienzi." (The title of the opera is pronounced
La Ju-eev'.)

The action takes place in Constance, during the year 1414.

ACT I

THE City of Constance is in festivities over the recent victories of the
Prince of the Empire, Leopold. In the great cathedral a Te Deum is
being sung; in the spacious square before it a brilliant crowd is making
merry holiday. But the wealthy old Hebrew, the goldsmith Eleazar, stays
industriously at work in his shop at the corner. Such conduct naturally
arouses the indignation of this rather medieval throng. They drag him and
his beautiful young daughter, Rachel, from the shop and would no doubt
lead them to death. But at that moment the Cardinal, happening to come
from the church, calms the excitement. The Cardinal and Eleazar at once
recognize each other. From their hastily whispered conversation we learn
that at Rome the Cardinal, then a private citizen, had led in the persecution
of the Jews resulting in the death of Eleazar's sons; shortly thereafter, the
Cardinal's home was mysteriously burned and his wife and daughter lost.

Now a prince of the Church, he kindly orders Eleazar and Rachel released,
and proposes that they forget their enmity; but the aged Jew refuses, still
filled with thoughts of vengeance. The Cardinal, in a stately cavatina, prays
heaven to pardon these non-believers and lead them to the true faith. His
magnanimity is acclaimed by the populace.

This cavatina affords the singer playing the part of the Cardinal an opportunity to display a great vocal range extending from the resonant upper to
the extreme lower register.

ACT II

A GROUP of faithful Jews, gathered at Eleazar's house, are seated around
the table. Eleazar leads in singing their prayer, "O God of Our
Fathers."

Leopold, in love with Rachel and disguised as a young Jew, has also come
to her home, but when the sacred bread is eaten he secretly casts his portion
aside. Continuing his prayer, Eleazar sings:

> "Oh, may my trembling voice,
> Ascend to Thee on high,
> Stretch out Thy mighty hand
> To Thy afflicted children. . . ."

The assembly is startled by a sudden knocking at the door; all the Hebraic
tableware is hastily put out of sight, then they admit . . . the Princess
Eudoxia! Leopold turns away in distress. Eudoxia has come to order a very

precious jewel for one she names as a great hero. Rachel justly demands an explanation of his conduct from Leopold, and when the others have left, he reveals to her that he is a Christian. Both are in terror, for the penalty is death both to the Jewess who loves a Christian and to the Christian who loves a Jewess. Yet so great is Rachel's love that she is about to elope with Leopold when they are discovered by Eleazar. On hearing that the young man is not a Jew he would kill him but is restrained by his daughter.

ACT III

MARJORIE LAWRENCE
IN LA JUIVE

BRILLIANT festivities are being held in the great hall of the Palace. The Princess receives from the hands of Eleazar a gorgeous chain and amid the acclamation of the crowd she bestows it upon Leopold, who kneels at her feet. She proclaims him as one of the greatest of heroes and her betrothed husband! Rachel, blind with jealousy, accuses the hero of treachery and of being the lover of a Jewess. The Jewess, she adds, to the consternation of the assemblage, is herself! To terrifying dramatic music the Cardinal calls down the curse of heaven upon the Jews, excommunicates Leopold, and orders all three to prison. All are horrified at his pronouncement:

You, who have the clemency
Of loving heaven outraged,
Are now by heaven denounced!

. . . . . .

And when life's spark is fled
May their last remains
Be left without a tomb,
And let no prayer be offered up
For them, to outrage heaven,
Whose gates to them are closed!

ACT IV

RACHEL, who still loves Leopold, yields to Eudoxia's plea to save him by declaring him innocent. The kindly disposed Cardinal tries to save Eleazar by urging him to become a Christian, but the devout Jew is resolved to die true to his faith. Moreover he threatens to take a cruel vengeance upon the Cardinal, whom he reminds of the day when he lost his wife and child by fire. Eleazar tells him he saved the child, she is still alive, but he refuses to reveal her dwelling-place. The Cardinal leaves, broken with sorrow. Alone, Eleazar prays for heaven's guidance . . . shall he sacrifice Rachel? Though she is the Cardinal's child, yet he loves her as his own.

Singing a most pathetic melody, *Rachel, quand du Seigneur,* he meditates:

> Rachel, when the grace of the Lord
> Entrusted thee to me,
> I vowed life's aim should be thy welfare and protection,
> And 'tis I who yield thee now to death,
> But a voice upon my ear is ringing,
> "Save thou me from the fatal decree.
> I am young, and to the world still clinging,
> Father spare me, thy daughter set free.
> Save me!"

ACT V

THE Jews must die a frightful death, thrown in a cauldron of boiling oil; but, as a result of Rachel's statement of his innocence, Leopold's sentence has been changed to banishment. Eleazar, hesitating, again asks Rachel if she is willing to become a Christian and save her life. She bravely says that she would rather die with him than give up her faith. They are led to their doom and as Rachel is thrown into the boiling cauldron, Eleazar calls out to the Cardinal, "Behold your child!" then resolutely plunges to his own death.

THE STRELTSY

KHOWANTCHINA

MUSICAL folk-drama in five acts; libretto and music by Modeste Moussorgsky. An amateur performance (Rimsky-Korsakow's version), by the Musical and Dramatic Union, at St. Petersburg, November, 1886. First production, November 7, 1911, at the Marie Theatre, St. Petersburg, Chaliapin playing the rôle of Dositheus. First performance in the United States, April 18, 1928, by the Pennsylvania Grand Opera Company, Philadelphia.

Like Boris Godounow, Khowantchina has for the basis of its text events in the history of Russia, in this case the struggle between the old and the new that took place at the close of the seventeenth century. A variety of typical characters are brought into relief: Dositheus, the sincere and devout leader of the sect of "Old Believers"; Ivan Khowansky, representative of the half-oriental, fanatical and conservative Russia; Galitsin, who strives for the introduction of European culture in his country; Martha, the passionate and mystical "Old Believer"; the dissolute Andrew Khowansky; Emma, the German girl; the fierce Streltsy; the down-trodden and suffering populace. The "Old Believers," around whom much of the action centers, were a sect, who, clinging to the old, though inaccurate version, broke away from the Orthodox church when a revision of the Bible was introduced in 1655. Also during this period the Czars were removing many of the privileges that had formerly been granted the nobility. This was resented and was fought against by the nobles. Hence the struggle of the Prince Khowansky and his bodyguard, the Streltsy. The score was not quite complete at Moussorgsky's death, although it had already grown to monumental length. Rimsky-Korsakow therefore revised, completed, orchestrated, and reduced it to a length suitable for performance; tasks for which his great knowledge of orchestration, his practical stage experience, and his intimate friendship with the composer made him eminently fitted. Certainly, whatever the ultimate verdict on Rimsky-Korsakow's work as a reviser may be, none can deny him the deepest gratitude for having thus made available some of Moussorgsky's most beautiful and characteristic pages.

("Khowantchina" is pronounced *Khah-vahn'-tschee-na*, the initial "K" being in reality a "hard h," and the succeeding "o" being sounded as "ah.")

ACT I

THE orchestra plays a brief prelude—a remarkable musical picture, thoroughly Russian in character, of dawn in Moscow. The first scene shows the Red Square in the Kremlin. Here are gathered a group of Streltsy, one of whom, lying near a pillar, mumbles sleepily about an attack of the previous evening in which many deeds of violence took place. A scribe enters to take up his daily stand; after making a few gibes at his expense, the Streltsy leave. The Boyard Shaklovity enters and bribes the scrivener into writing a denunciation of the Khowanskys for plotting against the throne. In a short time the elder Khowansky (Ivan) arrives and shows by his arrogant commands that he is indeed ambitious. After the crowd has departed Emma runs in. This girl is hotly pursued by the younger Khowansky (Andrew), whose attentions she in vain tries to avoid. At the climax of their scene, Martha, a discarded love of Andrew's, enters, protects Emma from his unwelcome embraces, and in one of her strange trances prophesies his ultimate fate. The elder Khowansky returns, takes a fancy to Emma and orders his followers to arrest her. Father and son quarrel jealously over the girl. Fortunately Dositheus enters at this moment, rebukes the men for their violence, and restores peace.

ACT II

PRINCE GALITSIN, in spite of his European education, is superstitious and has Martha summoned to tell his horoscope.

Martha, having filled a silver goblet with water, calls upon the spirits of the underworld in the uncanny, mysterious first part of her "Divination." Then, gazing into the bowl, she foresees Galitsin's future: his power and riches will avail him naught, for he shall be overcome by poverty and sorrow. Galitsin is frightened at this and secretly orders a servant to drown Martha in a marsh nearby. Khowansky enters and their ensuing bitter dispute is quelled only by the timely arrival of Dositheus.

ACT III

MARTHA, having escaped the drowning ordered for her, is seated near the home of Andrew Khowansky, and recalls her passion for him. Susan, a fanatic Old Believer, reproves her for singing shameless love songs, and threatens to denounce her as a witch. Dositheus again restores peace. Night falls, and along the street, now deserted, comes Shaklovitoff *(Shakhlov-vee'-toff)*. Gazing over the slumbering city, he exclaims: "Yes, the Streltsy are sleeping"; then thinking of his harassed country, he continues, saying, "Sleep thou, O Russia, thy enemies awaken . . . the enemy who will come to strike you down without mercy!" Then, singing a broad, noble melody of the greatest beauty, he prays for divine guidance for his native land.

The Streltsy now enter and are encountered by their women folk, who soundly berate them for their conduct. The quarrel is interrupted by the scribe, who runs in breathlessly, to report that the revolt of the Czar's guard has been suppressed . . . foreign troops and Peter the Great's bodyguard have arrived—the cause of Old Russia is lost. The Streltsy kneel in prayer.

ACT IV

PRINCE IVAN KHOWANSKY is at his country house, being diverted by the songs of his serving maids and the wild, impassioned dances of his Persian slaves.

Dances of the Persian Slaves—Parts I and II   *Coates-London Symphony Orchestra* 11135-1.50

Shaklovitoff appears summoning him to the Tsarevena's council. As Prince Ivan, in his robes of ceremony, crosses the threshold, he is stabbed and drops dead.

The scene changes. From the orchestra is heard mournful music, a solemn processional, of the most intense expressiveness. The curtain rises slowly revealing the square before the bizarre church of Vassily Blajeny. Forcing a way through the lamenting populace comes Galitsin, led under guard into exile—Martha's words are being fulfilled. The people follow the procession, the music dies away, and the square remains empty. The orchestral music of this scene is highly descriptive of the action.

Dositheus approaches, soliloquizing on Russia's unhappy condition. Martha comes to him with the news that the foreign mercenaries have been ordered to trap the Old Believers in their meeting place and execute them. Dositheus declares that they would sooner immolate themselves; he charges Martha to bring Prince Andrew among them. When, however, the Prince learns that Emma has been safely married to her lover, he curses Martha as a witch and vainly attempts to summon the Streltsy to put her to death. Vainly, for the Streltsy, themselves condemned, enter bearing axes and blocks for their own execution; at the last moment word comes that the Czar has pardoned them.

ACT V

THE Old Believers have assembled by moonlight at their meeting place in the woods near Moscow. Dositheus urges them to remain faithful and Martha prays for the soul of her beloved Andrew, who, urged by her great devotion, mounts the pyre which the white-robed Brethren have built for themselves. The soldiers are heard approaching, and Martha lights the pyre. The soldiers recoil in horror at the sight of the self-immolation of the Old Believers, who continue their chant until overcome by the flames, while a blare of trumpets announces the passing of the old and the dawn of a new day for Russia.

THE COURT OF KING EADGAR

THE KING'S HENCHMAN

OPERA in three acts; music by Deems Taylor; libretto by Edna St. Vincent Millay. First produced, February 17, 1927, at the Metropolitan Opera House, New York.

Deems Taylor, born December 22, 1885, in New York, began his career, not as a musician, but rather as a journalist, connected with various New York newspapers. He had, however, studied piano, harmony, and counterpoint, and though self-taught in composition, several cantatas and orchestral works brought him a growing reputation as a composer, a reputation that developed into fame with the success of the "The King's Henchman." Just credit must also be given to Edna St. Vincent Millay, one of the most prominent of contemporary poets, for the librettist's share of this success. Miss Millay, well known and justly beloved for her beautiful "Renascence," here shows her ability as a dramatic poet. The plot, said to be based on an early Anglo-Saxon chronicle, is appropriately narrated in an old Saxon style of language; there is effective characterization, an abundance of humorous detail, and genuine poetic beauty. Mr. Taylor has provided music, modern, though not ultra-modern, in character, and splendidly orchestrated. His score is adapted closely to the action after the manner of Wagner, and at times, of Debussy, and, particularly in the last act, is of great beauty and dramatic force.

It is gratifying to note that this, one of the most successful of American operas, had as its first performance American artists in the principal rôles, including Edward Johnson as Æthelwold and Lawrence Tibbett as Eadgar.

The action takes place in England during the Tenth Century.

ACT I

GREAT feasting and revelry are in progress at the court of King Eadgar. Maccus is singing a rugged old lay of warriors and battle and in return receives praises of the courtiers. King Eadgar, long a widower, has heard of a wonderful beauty, Ælfrida, who lives at Devon, and has determined to make her his wife and queen, should reports of her beauty be true. The kingdom is in such turmoil, however, because of an ecclesiastical disturbance, that Eadgar cannot well leave his court. He has therefore determined to send his friend and foster-brother, Æthelwold, a brave warrior, but young and inexperienced in the ways of women. For this reason Æthelwold is reluctant, but finally, because of his affection for the King, promises to go. Eadgar and Æthelwold pledge friendship according to the old Saxon rite, both drinking from the same cup of wine. Day is beginning to break, and there is a sudden stir as the men of Æthelwold's retinue ride past the door. In the excitement of departure, Maccus begins a song, bold in melody and sturdy in rhythm; Æthelwold and the courtiers join in the refrain.

Oh! Caesar, Great Wert Thou! *Lawrence Tibbett and the Metropolitan Opera Chorus and Orchestra* 8103-2.00

The song, while celebrating the prowess of various Cæsars, concludes with the characteristic sentiment that Cæsar's day is over while that of Britain has just begun. The song ended, Æthelwold and Maccus mount their horses and ride away, while the courtiers sing "Farewell."

ACT II

DURING a dense fog, Æthelwold and his trusted friend and servant, Maccus, become separated from their men and lost in the forest. They wander for hours mistakenly believing themselves far from their destination. Finally, Æthelwold lies down to sleep while Maccus continues searching for their followers.

Ælfrida approaches, a bit frightened, it is true, although she is accompanied by her serving woman, Ase. It is Hallowe'en, and she has come to

Mishkin

TIBBETT AS THE KING

perform certain charms, hoping thus to avoid marrying some suitor of her father's selection, and to procure instead a lover of her own choice. Having found a suitable spot nearby, she sends Ase away, and sings an incantation. While she sings, the fog clears and she beholds Æthelwold asleep on the ground. The charm has worked! Trembling with fear, yet fascinated by this handsome youth, she bends over him and kisses him.

Æthelwold awakens, greatly startled, and likewise believes that this is some supernatural creature whom he sees, and whose presence has aroused a strange emotion in him. When the two have convinced one another that they are both mortal, they find themselves already desperately in love. Their happiness in one another's arms, is cut short, however, by Ase, who from a distance calls Ælfrida by name.

Ælfrida hurries away for a moment, and Æthelwold, shaken with horror and dismay at learning her identity, would hurry off never to return; but while he is yet near Ælfrida calls him. He is powerless to go on. He bids Maccus go to the King and say that Ælfrida is indeed not beautiful, but being rich, Æthelwold, who is poor, craves the King's consent to marry her.

ACT III

THOUGH seeming to be happily married, Æthelwold is secretly tormented by thoughts of his treachery to his friend and King; and for Ælfrida the first charm of marriage has begun to fade, she is discontented in spite of her love for Æthelwold. She had expected that with the King's foster-brother for a husband, she would at least go to the Court, not remain thus buried at her father's house in Devonshire. Now, on this spring morning, Æthelwold yields to her entreaties, and with a show of his former decisiveness, promises he will take her away; they shall go to the great city of Ghent in Flanders, a city of Ælfrida's dreams. Yet close upon this resolve, Maccus enters saying that the King approaches with his retinue. In dismay, Æthelwold confesses his deception, and begs Ælfrida for the sake of their love to disguise herself as though she were both ugly and crippled, then to remain in her chamber under the pretext that she is ill; he will conduct Eadgar there to see her. Ælfrida is angry for a moment . . . she might have had the King for husband . . . and now she will not even be seen by him in her real beauty! Yet, fearing for Æthelwold's safety, she promises. Ase, who has overheard their conversation, whispers to Ælfrida not to be so weak as thus to ruin her chances; but Ælfrida replies that she will keep her promise, and the two go to her room.

A crowd of villagers hurry in, excited at the thought of seeing the King. Soon after, Eadgar arrives with his retinue. He has come on a friendly visit, not even suspecting Æthelwold's deception. After a few words of greeting they turn to go to Ælfrida's chamber. At that moment, the door opens, and before them stands Ælfrida, proud and radiantly beautiful in her fairest gown and jewels. Eadgar is at first dazed; then realizing the truth, grieves at his friend's faithlessness. In the deepest remorse, Æthelwold draws his dagger and stabs himself. As he falls dying, the faithful Maccus catches and gently supports him, while Eadgar, who has not stirred from the spot where he stood when first he beheld Ælfrida, solemnly walks over and gazing down upon his friend, bids Maccus lay him down. He sings a noble threnody for the departed; the people reply in a beautiful refrain. While they sing the body of Æthelwold is taken up and borne away in great solemnity, but Ælfrida is left to follow alone, in contrition and despair.

Nay, Maccus, Lay Him Down *Lawrence Tibbett and the Metropolitan Opera Chorus and Orchestra* 8103-2.00

PONS
AS LAKMÉ

LAKMÉ

OPERA in three acts; music by Leo Delibes; libretto by Goudinet and Gille (from the book Le Mariage de Loti). First produced, Paris, Opéra Comique, April 14, 1883; in the United States by the Abbot Opera Company, 1883, and at the Academy of Music, New York, March 1, 1886, under Theodore Thomas, in English.

(The title of the opera is pronounced *Lak-may'*.)

ACT I

SCENE—*A Garden in India*

THE fanatical Brahman priest, Nilakantha, stands before the temple he guards and exhorts the gathered worshippers to have courage and await the day when the English invaders shall be driven from the land. From the temple is heard the voice of a maiden in prayer, "O Durga! O Shiva! Mighty Gansea, created by Brahma!" . . . the worshippers echo it devoutly. It is Lakmé, the daughter of Nilakantha, who is praying.

Scarcely have these persons left the scene when an English sightseeing party approaches. They are charmed by the exotic beauty of the temple and the luxuriant growth of trees and flowers surrounding it. Against the advice of Frederic, an English officer, they break down the frail fence and make a way into the garden. Some of the girls admire especially the wonderful white blossoms. "Those are *daturas*," explains Frederic, "they are dazzlingly beautiful—and deadly poisonous!" Soon they happen to find some jewels left by Lakmé, and decide to leave this spot where they are evidently trespassing. Gerald, another officer, insists on remaining to sketch the design of the jewels, for it has caught his fancy. His fiancée, Ellen, goes on with the others. Left alone he contemplates the jewels with pleasure that finds expression in a charming air with phrases like exclamations, typical of a poet's wayward fancy.

Fantaisie aux divins mensonges *(Idle Fancies)*   *Tito Schipa* 1187-1.50

Lakmé returns and is so fascinated by the appearance of this handsome stranger of a race she is supposed to hate, that she is powerless to summon the guards from the temple—they would kill him instantly. In dismay, she tells him to leave; his reply is a rhapsody of love. She is deeply affected but succeeds in persuading him to go before her father returns. The aged priest, finding the fence broken, declares that the intruder must die.

ACT II

SCENE—*A Street in an Indian City*

NILAKANTHA and Lakmé mingle with the variegated crowd at a bazaar. He, armed with a dagger, is disguised as a beggar, she, as a street singer.

He believes that on hearing Lakmé's voice the intruder will surely betray himself. Therefore, he orders her to sing the legend of the Pariah's daughter.

Là-bas, dans la forêt *(In the Forest)* **Lily Pons** 1502-1.50

Down there, where shades are glooming,
What trav'ler's that, alone, astray?
Around him flame bright eyes, dark depths illuming,
But on he journeys, as by chance, on the way!
The wolves in their wild joy are howling,
As if for their prey they were prowling;
The young girl forward runs, and doth their fury dare.
A ring in her grasp she holds tightly,
Whence tinkles a bell, sharply, lightly,
A bell that tinkles lightly, that charmers wear!
(She imitates the bell)
Ah! Ah! Ah! Ah!

While the stranger regards her
Stands she dazed, flush'd and glowing,
More handsome than the Rajahs, he!
.   .   .   .
And to heaven she soars in this holding,
It was Vishnu, great Brahma's son!
And since the day in that dark wood,
The trav'ler hears, where Vishnu stood,
The sound of a little bell ringing,
The legend back to him bringing.

Où va la jeune hindue *(Indian Bell Song)* **Lily Pons** 1502-1.50

Morton

SETTING FOR THE BAZAAR—ACT II

214

The music makes such exceedingly great demands upon the technical ability of the singer that this number is rightly classed as one of the most difficult of coloratura arias: but its peculiar oriental quality, the use of bells, the very touching similarity of the story of the Indian maid beloved by a god to Lakmé's own fate, serve to give this "Bell Song" an emotional appeal that is altogether unusual.

Nilakantha recognizes Gerald, rushes to him stabs him, then escapes.

ACT III

MARTINELLI AS FREDERIC

LAKMÉ and her slave have carried Gerald to a hut hidden deep in the forest. During his recovery from the wound he has become more than ever enamoured of Lakmé. She goes to bring water from a sacred spring, one that has been blest of the gods so that lovers who drink thereof will always remain faithful. While she is gone, Frederic comes reminding Gerald of his duty, his regiment has been ordered away. Lakmé returns and the lovers drink of the sacred water, but even as they drink the martial music of Gerald's regiment is heard in the distance. He starts up eagerly. Knowing that her hold on him is now broken, Lakmé secretly gathers some of the deadly datura blossoms. Nilakantha discovers the lovers. In terrific rage he would kill Gerald, but Lakmé warns her father, Gerald has drunk of the sacred spring, to harm him would be sacrilege. Lakmé has again saved the life of her beloved; she dies, happy, in his arms.

German Tourist Information Office

THE SWAN CASTLE—SCENE OF WAGNER'S "LOHENGRIN"

LOHENGRIN

OPERA in three acts; words and music by Richard Wagner. First produced at Weimar, Germany, August 28, 1850, under the direction of Liszt. First American production, New York, April 2, 1871, at the Stadt Theatre, in German.

Wagner's "Rienzi" had been very successful when produced at the Dresden opera; "The Flying Dutchman" had been something of a failure, and "Tannhäuser" had appealed even less to early audiences. Thus Wagner could not succeed in having his next opera, "Lohengrin," produced there, even though he held the post of royal conductor at that very theatre. He had completed the score in August, 1847, and when in 1849 the wave of social unrest that was sweeping over Europe reached Dresden, believing that a more democratic form of government might improve artistic conditions, he joined the popular uprising. This "May Revolution," apparently successful at first, was soon suppressed by the military forces, and Wagner was compelled to make his escape from the country in disguise. An exile in Switzerland, he wrote to Liszt the following April and begged him to produce "Lohengrin." It is hard to realize at the present time the moral courage necessary for a man like Liszt to sponsor a work of Wagner's—Liszt, courted by kings, greatest of pianists, universally acknowledged, yet subject to endless criticism; Wagner, a political exile and comparatively unknown. Thanks to his friendly support, "Lohengrin" was produced at Liszt's artistic center at Weimar, and with more success than Wagner might have expected. The opera grew in popularity, and was performed throughout Germany, so that in the course of time, Wagner, still an exile, was able to say with some ironic truth, that he was the only German who had not heard "Lohengrin." Not until 1861, when, through the intervention of the Princess Metternich he was permitted to return to Germany, was the composer enabled to hear his own opera, fourteen years after completing the score!

To us the beauty of this music is familiar enough, but in the day of its origin it must have seemed like a strange language—this music which shows Wagner making another step in advance of "Tannhäuser" in the development of his style even as in "Tannhäuser" he had progressed beyond "The Flying Dutchman." Here Wagner also reveals his ability as a dramatist, for he has made of the old legend with which he dealt a much more dramatic and human story than one would imagine possible. The character, Lohengrin, is a symbol of the man who, in Wagner's own words, seeks "the woman who would not call for explanations or defense, but who should love him with an unconditioned love."

CHARACTERS

HENRY THE FOWLER, *King of Germany*	*Bass*
LOHENGRIN *(Lo'-en-grin)*	*Tenor*
ELSA OF BRABANT	*Soprano*
DUKE GODFREY, *her brother*	*Mute Personage*
FREDERICK OF TELRAMUND *(Tel'-rah-moond), Count of Brabant*	*Baritone*
ORTRUD *(Ohr'-trood), his wife*	*Mezzo-Soprano*
THE KING'S HERALD	*Bass*

Saxon, Thuringian and Brabantian Counts and Nobles, Ladies of Honor, Pages, Attendants. *The action takes place at Antwerp during the first half of the Tenth Century.*

The Prelude, an epitome of the entire opera and one of Wagner's great inspirations, has for its one and only theme the "Grail," the sacred vessel of the Last Supper. The "story" of the prelude, briefly told, is this: In the wonderful blue of the sky, a vision appears: angels bearing the Grail. Gradually coming earthward, its effulgent glory is shed on the worshipper who kneels transported in ecstasy. The celestial vision then recedes and disappears into the blue of the sky. This is wonderfully expressed in the prelude with its gradual crescendo, magnificent climax and ethereal close.

Prelude *Leopold Stokowski-Philadelphia Symphony Orchestra* 6791-2.00 *Arturo Toscanini-Philharmonic-Symphony Orchestra of New York* 14006-2.00

ACT I

O N THE green banks of the River Scheldt, seated upon a throne beneath the Oak of Justice, sits Henry the Fowler, King of Germany. On one side of him are gathered the knights and nobles of Saxony and Thuringia; opposite them are the counts and nobles of Brabant, headed by Frederick of Telramund; beside him, his wife, Ortrud. The King has come to gather an army together, but he finds the people of Brabant torn in dissension. The trouble is due to the disappearance of young Duke Godfrey of Brabant, who with his sister, Elsa, lived under the care of Telramund, who was to have married the girl. Telramund, however, charges that Elsa herself has

RETHBERG AS ELSA

killed the boy in the hope that she would succeed to his estates. So certain is he of Elsa's guilt, says he, that he has married Ortrud instead. Telramund is indeed a knight of proven courage and loyalty, for in a fight against the Danes, he saved the life of the King. Yet Henry the Fowler is loath to believe the monstrous charge of fratricide against the girl, and commands that she shall be brought before him. Elsa, accompanied by her women attendants, approaches as one in a dream, a mystic look in her deep blue eyes. Replying to Telramund's charge, the King decrees that justice shall be done through ordeal by battle. Elsa is asked to name her champion. She at first declines, and when urged, replies by telling of a wonderful, mysterious dream she had, in which a knight in shining armor came to her protection. The soft, ethereal music of the Grail accompanies her words, its shifting and shimmering tone color and harmonies a perfect representation of her vision. Elsa exclaims in her ecstasy that this glorious knight shall be her champion.

Elsas Traum (*Elsa's Dream*)   *Maria Jeritza* **6694-2.00**   *Elisabeth Rethberg* **6831-2.00**   *Kirsten Flagstad* **14181-2.00**

Four trumpeters blow a summons to the four points of the compass, and the Herald calls, "Who will do battle for Elsa of Brabant?" There is no answer. Elsa exclaims that her champion abides afar; let the summons be repeated. Ortrud watches Elsa's growing agitation with an evil smile, but the King is touched by the girl's trust. The summons is repeated. Still the very heavens seem silent. "She is doomed," murmur the nobles. Elsa falls to her knees in prayer. Soon there is a commotion among the men nearest the river (*beginning of Record 9017*). Excitedly they exclaim, "Look . . . a marvel . . . a swan . . . a swan drawing a boat . . . a warrior upon the prow!" The radiant theme of the Deliverer heard in "Elsa's Dream" sounds in the orchestra. The people grow more and more agitated, and hurry to the river bank to watch this strange knight in shining armor approach in a swan-drawn boat. As he reaches the shore they exclaim:

Weirich, Festspielhaus, Bayreuth
MAX LORENZ AS LOHENGRIN

> All Hail, thou hero from on high!
> Be thou welcome!
> Heav'n hath sent thee here!

Then as the knight moves to step from the skiff, all are silent in rapt expectancy. With one foot still resting in the boat he leans forward towards the swan and bids it farewell:

> I give thee thanks, my trusty swan!
> Turn thee again and breast the tide.
> Return unto that land of dawn
> Where late we did in joy abide.
> Well thy appointed task is done!
> Farewell! Farewell! my trusty swan!

Mercè, Mercè, cigno gentil! *(Swan Song) (In Italian)* *Aureliano Pertile* **6904-2.00**

A mysterious mood of awe settles over the assemblage and, as the swan now disappears from view, the people, in a chorus of impressive beauty, sing:

> Doth he not seem from heav'n descended?
> His radiant mien holds me enthrall'd!
> Valor and grace in him are blended,
> To deeds of glory he is call'd!

Swan Chorus *(In English)* *Chorus and Symphony Orchestra, Conducted by Albert Coates* **9017-1.50**

The stranger knight, having made obeisance to the King, advances to Elsa and, his eyes resting upon her radiant beauty, tells her that he has come at her summons, and asks if she will accept him as her betrothed.

She humbly exclaims, "All that I have, all that I am, is thine!" Continuing, he declares in the utmost solemnity that if he should succeed as her champion and become her husband there is one promise she must make; she must never ask whence he came, his rank, or his name.

She promises, demurely. Again he repeats his charge; Elsa whole-heartedly accepts.

Then the King sings a majestic prayer:

> O King of kings, on Thee I call;
> Look down on us in this dread hour!
> Let him in this ordeal fall
> Whom Thou know'st guilty,
> Lord of Pow'r!
>
> To stainless knight give strength and might,
> With craven heart the false one smite;
> Do Thou, O Lord, to hear us deign,
> For all our wisdom is but vain!

Königs Gebet *(King's Prayer)* *Marcel Journet* **1274-1.50**

"ALL HAIL, THOU HERO FROM ON HIGH!"

The nobles warn Telramund that he may not hope to worst such a heaven-sent champion; but Telramund, urged on by his wife, will not assent. A field of battle is measured off by six nobles who solemnly stride forward and plant their spears to form a complete circle. The King beats three times with his sword upon his shield and the fight begins. The white knight succeeds in striking Telramund to earth, but mercifully spares his life. Her innocence proved, Elsa plights her troth to the stranger amid the cheering of the crowd, while Telramund, unobserved and in disgrace, drags himself to the feet of Ortrud, who is still uncowed.

ACT II

IT IS night: the moon precipitates gloomy shadows off the battlements of the great castle that rises in the background. On the steps of the chapel, at the right of the courtyard, Telramund and Ortrud, clad in the habiliments of disgrace, crouch dejectedly. Telramund irritably blames his wife for having deceived him. Skilfully she replies that this strange knight has won by magic; if he could be compelled to divulge his name and state, his power would cease. Elsa alone has the right to compel him to reveal this secret. Possessed of it, Telramund can freely fight him again, for the first loss of blood will weaken him forever. Through her magical practices she has divined all this. The last of her race, Ortrud clings to the old religion of the ancient gods, Wotan and Freia, whose wrath she now calls down upon Elsa and her champion. Telramund has listened breathlessly.

Elsa comes to her window at the left of the courtyard and confides to the wandering breezes her happiness. Ortrud bids Telramund be gone, then imploringly calls Elsa's name. The girl is startled at hearing her name through the darkness; Ortrud feigns repentance, and begs for protection, both of which, in her new-found happiness, Elsa grants. At the same time Ortrud succeeds in implanting the seeds of doubt in the girl's heart, hinting at mystery and magic . . . things easily believed under the circumstances. But outwardly Elsa rejects all suspicion and takes Ortrud with her into the palace.

Trumpets answering one another from the turrets of the castle announce the dawn of Elsa's wedding day. With the growing light, the courtyard begins to bustle with preparations. Servitors pass hurriedly . . . then come knights glittering in their armor, and nobles arrayed in festive attire . . . a blazing pageant in the sunlight. A herald announces that Telramund has been banished, and that the mysterious champion, having refused the Dukedom, has been proclaimed leader of the country's forces.

The orchestra begins a soft, graceful melody while a long procession of women, dressed in the gorgeous court robes of the period, come gradually from the palace and, slowly crossing the courtyard, group themselves around the doorway of the church.

Procession to the Cathedral   *Chorus and Symphony Orchestra, Conducted by Albert Coates* 9017-1.50

Then Elsa appears, and the nobles deferentially bare their heads and make a way for her through their midst, meanwhile softly singing:

> May ev'ry joy attend thee,
> And heav'n its blessing lend thee,
> And angels guard thee round!

As Elsa approaches the church, all joyfully shout "Hail! Elsa of Brabant!" and voices and orchestra swell in a climax of radiant beauty.

Just as Elsa sets foot on the church steps, Ortrud springs before her—a very different Ortrud from the suppliant of a few hours previous. She now demands priority over the bride-elect of a nameless knight. Her stormy outburst causes considerable excitement; soon the King and Elsa's champion appear. Ortrud is silenced; the knight supports his trembling bride, and the procession is resumed. Suddenly from behind a buttress where he has been lurking, Telramund steps out before them, and wildly proclaims that this unknown knight is a sorcerer . . . the swan-drawn boat is evidence enough . . . He demands his name. But the King will not listen, and the banished pair are driven away in disgrace. Elsa, her wedding processional twice interrupted, is trembling with fear and grief, yet she affirms her trust in her defender. The procession is again resumed and the music grows to a splendid climax as they enter the cathedral.

Juley

ACT III—THE BRIDAL CHAMBER

ACT III

SCENE I

BEFORE the rise of the curtain, the orchestra plays the throbbing "Epithalamium" prelude. The joyous burst of strings, wood-wind and brass, the crash of cymbals, the masculine strength of the theme for the trombones, the feminine grace of the middle portion, are all well known to concert and opera goers. Never has a wedding festival been more happily, riotously expressed in music!

Prelude   *Coates-Symphony Orchestra* 9005-1.50   *Chicago Symphony Orch., Cond. by Stock* 7386-2.00   *Arturo Toscanini and the Philharmonic-Symphony Orchestra of New York* 14007-2.00

The music grows softer, the curtain rises upon the bridal chamber, the great doors at the rear fly open, and the bridal procession enters. The ladies are leading Elsa, the King and the nobles conducting the bridegroom. They sing the familiar "Bridal Chorus."

Bridal Chorus   *Metropolitan Opera Chorus* 11249-1.50   *Chorus and Symphony Orchestra, Conducted by Albert Coates* 9005-1.50   *(Organ) Mark Andrews* 20036-.75   *Victor Herbert's Orchestra* *55048-1.50

The procession encircles the chamber. Then, after saluting the bridal pair, depart; their song gradually dying away in the distance.

Now it is that Elsa first shows the doubt in her heart:

How sweet my name as from thy lips it glided!
Canst thou deny to me the sound of thine?

222

The stranger knight gently reproves her. She scarcely hears, for the poison instilled into her mind is at work . . . She grows more and more insistent, her own curiosity strengthened by her lover's kind protests. She fears that he will be lost to her, that he will return to the unknown land whence he has come—even now she thinks she sees the swan returning for him . . . In a sudden frenzy she demands to know his name. At this very moment Telramund rushes into the chamber, his sword drawn. Elsa quickly hands her husband his sword, and with the weapon he strikes the would-be assassin dead.

SCENE II

At the Oak of Justice, the king and the nobles await the knight and, when he appears, the nobles hail him as their leader. Their rejoicing gives way to amazement as they see the body of Telramund being borne along, and Elsa approaching, her face pale as death. The knight explains the slaying of Telramund; now he is compelled to answer the question Elsa has asked. From the orchestra are heard the ethereal harmonies of the Grail, and the knight begins his narrative:

> In distant land, by ways remote and hidden,
>   There stands a mount that men call Monsalvat;
> It holds a shrine, to the profane forbidden;
>   More precious there is naught on earth than that,
> And thron'd in light it holds a cup immortal,
>   That whoso sees from earthly sin is cleans'd;
> 'Twas borne by angels thro' the heav'nly portal,
>   Its coming hath a holy reign commenc'd.
> Once every year a dove from Heav'n descendeth,
>   To strengthen it anew for works of grace;
> 'Tis called the Grail; the pow'r of Heav'n attendeth
>   The faithful knights who guard that sacred place.
> He whom the Grail to be its servant chooses
>   Is armed henceforth by high invincible might;
> All evil craft its power before him loses,
>   The spirits of darkness where he dwells take flight.
> Nor will he lose the awful charm it blendeth,
>   Although he should be called to distant lands,
> When the high cause of virtue he defendeth:
>   While he's unknown, its spell he still commands.
>
>   .   .   .   .
>
> If known to man, he must depart and flee.
>   Now mark, craft or disguise my soul disdaineth,
> The Grail sent me to right yon lady's name;
>   My father, Percival, gloriously reigneth,
> His knight am I, and Lohengrin my name!

Lohengrin's Narrative *(In Distant Lands)* **Richard Crooks** 7105-2.00 *Aureliano Pertile* 6904-2.00

The people, in a chorus of remarkable beauty, express their awe at his wonderful narrative. The swan is seen approaching and Elsa gives way to

TIBBETT AS TELRAMUND

her grief. Lohengrin bids her farewell most tenderly, and leaves with her his horn, his sword and his ring—for her brother, should he ever return. As Lohengrin steps aboard his boat, Ortrud suddenly appears from among the crowd and with a cry of triumph exclaims that her magic is superior, for it was she who changed Elsa's brother into the swan that is now to draw Lohengrin away . . . Had the knight stayed a year longer, he would have been able to release the boy from the spell . . . Thus have Ortrud's gods rewarded Elsa's faithlessness! But she has spoken too soon. Lohengrin kneels for a moment in prayer while all eyes are instinctively turned upon him. The white dove of the Holy Grail flutters down from above . . . the swan sinks, and in its place, Lohengrin raises from the water a boy in shining raiment and lifts him to land. "Behold the ruler of Brabant!" cries he. The boy rushes into Elsa's arms, while the dove mysteriously draws the boat on its course to Monsalvat. Lohengrin is seen, ere he disappears in the distance, his head bent sorrowfully, leaning upon his shield. "My husband! My husband!" cries Elsa, and sinks back lifeless in her brother's arms.

Photo Byron   THE KING DENOUNCING TELRAMUND—ACT II

ACT II—STREET SCENE

LOUISE

A MUSICAL romance in four acts; libretto and music by Gustave Charpentier. First produced, February 2, 1900, at the Opéra Comique, Paris. First performed in the United States, at the Manhattan Opera House, New York, January 3, 1908.

Probably the most popular of French operas since Carmen, and one of the few of any nationality to deal with contemporary life—such are two of the distinctions of Louise. Its real distinctions lie, however, in the music, pulsating with the life and the conflicting human emotions of a great city, and in the vivid and touching manner in which the life of that city is revealed. Truly the heroine of the opera is not Louise, but Paris. For external details we have the street cries of Paris realistically reproduced, and the magnificent panorama of her innumerable lights seen from Julien's house on the top of Montmartre. Even more representative of the City of Light are the scenes in Louise's garret home, the various strange characters of the night with their own poignant or ironic tragedies, the awakening city, the workshop, the festival on Montmartre, the conflict of Louise with old restraints and new freedom. Above and through all this does the city brood, and to all this does Charpentier's music give life. Through his music float a few short motives, briefly heard, disappearing, then reappearing, quite a different matter from the elaborate symphonic treatment of themes used by Wagner. This is music that is French of the French, vivacious, light, subdued, high-spirited, or tensely dramatic—the soul of a great city and of an epoch made manifest in music.

It was as Louise that Mary Garden made her début—and on Friday, the thirteenth! (April, 1900.) At that time she was in Paris studying; the singer who was taking the rôle of Louise became ill during a performance. Miss Garden was called upon to sing the third act, and was acclaimed with the utmost enthusiasm. Since that time her interpretation of the rôle of Louise has come to be ranked as one of the greatest.

ACT I

SCENE—*The Garret Home of Louise*

THE gay "Bohemian" poet, Julien, calls secretly to see Louise. Her parents are so bitterly opposed to him that they will not acknowledge a letter he has written. Louise has promised, should they treat his second letter similarly, that she will elope with him. As they have known each other intimately for only a short time, Louise asks Julien how he happened to fall in love with her. He replies in the charming passage beginning "Depuis longtemps j'habitais cette chambre."

Depuis longtemps j'habitais cette chambre (*A Long, Long Time I Have Lived in This Room*) *Edward Johnson* 9293-1.50

He tells her how he had lived in a room in the house next door for a long while without realizing that there was such a beautiful girl near him. But when he happened to meet Louise, life awoke for him with new hope, and his heart was inspired to new songs of love. The two become so enrapt in recounting their love adventures that they are for a long while unaware that Louise's mother has entered and is listening to them. Finally, rather amusingly startled by her presence, the lovers separate. The mother violently upbraids Louise for her conduct, sarcastically quoting some of Julien's words. Louise believes herself old enough to make up her own mind, and she strenuously defends Julien's character from the vituperation and villification of her mother. Their angry words are interrupted by the entry of Louise's father. His joy and contentment at returning from a hard day's work are cut short by a renewal of the argument, for he has just received Julien's second letter asking to marry Louise. The father, who is very fond of his daughter and takes a sympathetic attitude towards the match, suggests that they look into the young man's character, but the mother absolutely refuses. The father tenderly asks Louise to read from the evening paper to him. Louise begins reading—by chance—an article describing the arrival of spring and the gay festivities accompanying it at Paris.

ACT II

SCENE I—*A Street at the Foot of the Hill of Montmartre*

A LIGHT mist rests over the city which is gradually coming to life, though still dark with the obscurity that precedes the dawn. While the varied characters of the night creep away, laborers of the ruder sorts, men and women, cross the scene on their way to work. Paris awakens with its myriad cries and noises. The mother accompanies Louise to work but as soon as she has left, Julien, who has come with a crowd of his easy-going companions, brings Louise back from the work-shop. Her parents have refused his second request, and now, recalling her promise, he passionately urges her to run away with him. Springtime, youth, love, all conspire together to make Louise yield; finally, however, her sense of duty prevails and she refuses, saying that sometime later she will be his wife. Julien is left alone despairing, and again are heard the street cries of Paris—the voice of the city.

Scene II—*A Dressmaker's Work Room*

(This scene is often omitted in American performances.)

The girls are singing and joking, and, noticing that Louise seems quiet, they make fun of her, saying that she must be in love. She denies it. Julien comes with his comrades and sings a serenade from the courtyard below. At first the girls are delighted, then as his serenade changes from its popular love-song air to an impassioned reproach for his beloved's faithlessness, the girls become bored and mock him. Louise, overwhelmed by her emotions, says she is sick and must go home. The girls

K. P. Studios

HELEN JEPSON AS LOUISE

tend to believe her; then, as they look out the window and see her going away with Julien, they all laugh—it's a great joke.

ACT III

Scene—*A Garden and House on the Side of the Hill of Montmartre. In the Background the City Is Spread Out in a Great Panorama*

LOUISE, in the garden with Julien as twilight falls over the city, is telling how happy she has been since she came away with him. Her whole being vibrates with the delicious rapture of love; all nature and life seem to unite in her happiness. Her emotions are beautifully expressed in a lovely air.

Depuis le Jour (*Ever Since the Day*) **Lucrezia Bori 6561-2.00 Helen Jepson 14153-2.00**

While the countless lights of the city gradually begin to pierce the darkness, the lovers unite in an ecstatic duet expressive of their great happiness and their mutual love . . . an apotheosis of the pulsating life of the city that lies spread out before them. Scarcely have they gone into their little house before a gay Bohemian crowd arrives. They decorate the yard with lanterns, summon the lovers, crown Louise Queen of Montmartre, and make merry with songs and dancing. In the midst of the festivities Louise's mother appears. The crowd having left in precipitous haste, she tells Louise that her father is ill, dying from sorrow over the loss of his daughter. Only her return may save him. Louise is grief-stricken at this news, for she loves her father deeply and, as her mother promises that she will be free to return to her lover, Julien consents to her departure.

ACT IV

SCENE—*Louise's Garret Home*

THE father, though still weak, has recovered sufficiently to be able to work; Louise is already becoming sullen under the restraints of home life. Her father, resting from his day's toil, draws his complaining child to himself and, while she rests on his knees, sings a tender lullaby as to a slumbering infant. A quaint, haunting melody pervades the orchestra, while the father in a melodious recitative tries in vain to recall the peace and contentment of a bygone day.

Berceuse *(Lullaby)* **Marcel Journet 6785-2.00**

Louise, looking up quietly, suggests that the child would be content if her father did not cause her so much sorrow: he is unable to understand how she can be unhappy when her parents are doing everything possible to make her happy. She does not wish to be kept as a bird in a cage; she desires the freedom that was promised her. Her parents' pleading only serves to develop an argument that grows more and more heated. Finally, in a delirium of excitement, Louise calls out that it is only her Julien and the free life of Paris she desires: her father, violent with rage, opens the door and orders her out. She rushes away. Then, suddenly realizing what has happened, he calls after her, but in vain. Broken by this new grief he looks for her from the window. He beholds only the city into which she has disappeared, stretches forth his hand towards it menacingly and cries out, "O Paris!"

THE LOVE FOR THREE ORANGES

BURLESQUE opera by Serge Prokofieff in a prologue and four acts, text by the composer after Carlo Gozzi's *Fiaba dell' Amore delle Tre Melarancie*. First produced, December 30, 1921, at the Chicago Auditorium, by the Chicago Opera Company, the composer conducting. It was on this occasion that Nina Koshetz made her American *début*, playing the rôle of Fata Morgana.

Prokofieff, one of the advance guard of musical futurism, has given us in this work an immensely clever and diverting satirical burlesque opera. The music, while not so extreme in its modernity (that is, in its use of dissonance) as one might expect from this composer, is, nevertheless, exceedingly amusing in its witty treatment of this fantastic legend.

THE opera opens with a prologue, wherein are shown four groups of personages: the somber-robed Glooms, who urge that the forthcoming play be a tragedy; the Joys who wish for a comedy; the Empty Heads who want only farce; and finally, the Jesters (sometimes called the Cynics) who enter and quell the hubbub of the quarreling groups. All take refuge in towers at the side of the stage, whence, like the Chorus of Greek Drama (but without its dignity), they make comments on the play that is enacted.

The Three Oranges are really princesses imprisoned by a wicked sorceress,

Fata Morgana. To release them is the wish of the handsome Prince, who is ill, seemingly beyond cure. The physicians declare to his anxious father that the only effective remedy will be to make the Prince laugh; but that is well-nigh impossible, for he has no sense of humor. The King orders his magician to prepare a gay masquerade. The scene grows dark, fire and smoke rise from the earth and the wicked witch, Fata Morgana, appears amidst thunder and lightning. Swarms of little devils enter and place a table between the magician and Fata Morgana, who begin a game of cards. While they play, the devils dance wildly about them. This scene is graphically depicted in the modernistic music of the "Waltz Scherzo."

Waltz Scherzo *(Fiends Infernal)* *Coates-London Symphony Orchestra 9128-1.50*

The witch is successful at the game, playing for the Prime Minister against the magician who plays for the King. Laughing in triumph she sinks into the ground and the devils vanish. Now it is revealed that, if the Prince dies, the Prime Minister will become his successor.

A buffoon tries vainly to make the Prince laugh. Then hearing festival music, he carries him away to the festivities. While the scene is being changed the orchestra continues with the brilliant and bizarre march music.

March and Scherzo *Koussevitzky-Boston Symphony Orchestra 7197-2.00* **Coates-London Symphony Orchestra 9128-1.50**

In the grand court of the palace, the merrymakers attempt to make the Prince laugh, but they fail, for the evil Fata Morgana is among them. The guards seize her and try to throw her out. In the struggle she turns an awkward somersault, a sight so ridiculous that even the Prince breaks into laughter. All rejoice, but the base Fata Morgana returns and pronounces a terrible curse upon the Prince: he may not be happy until he has fallen in love with three Oranges and has had his love returned.

In the desert, the magician Tchelio meets the Prince and pronounces an incantation against the cook who guards the Oranges. The Prince continues his search. While the scene is being changed the orchestra plays the fantastic Scherzo. The Prince and his companion arrive at the weird castle where the Oranges are kept and, after overcoming many great hazards, obtain them. The Prince's companion is seized by a terrific thirst; in order to quench it they open one of the monster fruits. A beautiful Princess steps forth, but as it had been decreed that the Oranges are to be opened only at the water's edge, she at once drops dead. The second Princess likewise succumbs. The spectators in the towers excitedly argue over the fate of the third Princess. Released from her Orange she falls dying as did the others; the Jesters, however, rush to the rescue with a bucket of water, then capture and carry away the ugly sorceress, Fata Morgana. Thus the Prince and the Princess are enabled to live ever happily.

THE LOVE OF THREE KINGS

(L'Amore dei Tre Re)

OPERA in three acts; music by Italo Montemezzi; text by Sem Bennelli, from his tragedy of the same title. First produced at La Scala, Milan, April 10, 1913. First performed in the United States at the Metropolitan Opera House, New York, January 2, 1914.

The action takes place during the Tenth Century in a remote portion of Italy, forty years after a Barbarian invasion led by Archibaldo.

ACT I

THE scene shows an immense hall in a somber medieval castle at the hushed hour that precedes dawn. Through the curves of arches one can look across a terrace out into the night penetrated only by the reddish light of a signal lantern. The aged and blind Archibaldo, restless and unable to sleep, is led into the hall by the servant, Flaminio. He has been stirred by recollections of the time forty years earlier when he led his soldiers into Italy, subdued the people and became ruler of Altruria. Flaminio, one of the conquered natives, recalls that it was for the sake of peace that Fiora, the intended bride of the local Prince, Avito, was given to the conquerors to marry Archibaldo's son, Manfredo. The old man is expecting the return of his son, now away at war, and it is for him that the signal light burns. As dawn is approaching, Archibaldo has Flaminio extinguish the light; then both return to the blind man's apartment.

From another room now comes forth Avito, the Prince of Altruria, stealthily looking about to see if anyone is in the hall. He is followed by Fiora who would have him linger yet longer. Avito is fearful lest the door to the aged Archibaldo's room be open, but Fiora assures him it is tightly closed. She says that there is great peace in her soul; Avito exclaims that he knows no peace when parted from her lips. Entirely overcome by the power of their mutual infatuation, the two embrace passionately, heedless of the growing daylight. Suddenly, perceiving that the signal lantern has been extinguished and thereby knowing that someone has already been there at this early hour, Avito flees in terror. Archibaldo has entered just at this moment, and though Fiora would escape silently, he is, with a blind man's sure instinct, aware of her presence and her excited condition. He orders her to stay, and fain would learn who was with her. She insists that she has been alone, and then with shockingly deceitful naïveté, adds that she came out on the terrace because she could not sleep for thinking of her husband. Archibaldo, justly horrified by her duplicity, orders her to her room.

Manfredo's return is announced by the sound of trumpets outside of the castle, and in a few moments he is warmly welcomed by his father. Manfredo has been looking forward to this return with all the fervor of a young husband. Fiora enters and greets him with a cruel coldness that the noble

Manfredo neither realizes nor comprehends. As they leave, Archibaldo exclaims to himself, "O God, since Thou hast taken away mine eyes, let me indeed be blind!"

ACT II

THE second act takes place on a terrace at the top of the castle walls. The afternoon sky is covered with fleeting clouds. Below, trumpets sound a retreat. Manfredo, about to leave again for the wars, is bidding Fiora a most affectionate farewell, and begs some little token of her that he may keep near him while away. Failing in this, he pleadingly asks that she remain on the summit of the castle wall a little while and wave her scarf in greeting to him. Fervently he adds that, as he is riding away with his soldiers and looks back, it will seem to him that she is drying the tears upon his heart. Fiora, moved with sincere pity, promises that it shall be done.

No sooner has Manfredo left her, and Fiora gone to the summit of the battlement to watch his departure, than Avito, disguised as Flaminio, stealthily approaches. Fiora bids him leave her forever, though he begs for her compassion. They are interrupted for a moment by the arrival of a servant who brings Fiora a casket containing a scarf from Manfredo. This she very slowly removes from the casket. Then falteringly, she reascends the stairs to the parapet and endeavors to wave the scarf. After three attempts, her arm drops wearily to her side. Avito comes from his hiding place saying he is going, never to return, but he longs to see her for this last farewell, and begs a parting kiss. Fiora tries to ward away his advances and feebly attempts to resume waving the scarf. Yielding, she says that he may kiss the fringe of her garment, which she has herself embroidered. Avito runs to her hastily, seizes her dress and feverishly kisses it. Fiora would again wave the scarf, but her arms droop helplessly; she is overcome by the thought of the contrast between her real desire and her husband's ideal. Fascinated by Avito, she gradually yields herself to him. They kiss and, lost in the ecstasy of love, they remain in a close embrace, oblivious to all around them. They do not even hear the approach of Flaminio and Archibaldo, who calls "Fiora." The lovers suddenly awaken from their trance. Avito rushes with drawn dagger at the blind man. He is warded off by the servant and, at a sign from Fiora, escapes silently. Manfredo is heard returning in the distance, and Archibaldo orders Flaminio to go meet him, thus giving himself a wished-for chance to be alone with Fiora. He denounces the faithless woman, demanding to know the name of her lover. First denying, then acknowledging her guilt, she refuses to name the man who has just left her. Overpowered by his rage, Archibaldo seizes her as she lies on a bench, and half conscious of his actions, he chokes her until life itself is gone. Manfredo has returned for, seeing that Fiora no longer waved from the parapet, he fears that she might have fallen. He is appalled to find her dead, his father proclaiming her guilt and acknowledging himself the murderer.

ACT III

IN THE somber light of the crypt in the chapel of the castle, the body of Fiora is seen reclining, clothed in long white garments. From the chapel itself are heard the voices of the choir, singing a dirge. In the crypt are a group of mourners, old men, women and youths, standing at a respectful distance from the corpse and lamenting the loss of their beloved princess. Thinking how Fiora has been cruelly murdered, the mourners grow angry and call for vengeance, but under the spell of the solemnity of the place and the impressive chanting in the chapel, their wrath subsides, and singing an eternal farewell they depart. As they are going they notice the arrival of the Prince of Altruria, Avito, who likewise has come to bid Fiora adieu. The mourners gone, he speaks to Fiora as though she were yet alive; then, with a sudden realization of her eternally silent condition, he weeps in agony. Perhaps a breath of her dear soul yet remains in her body, he thinks; and desperately he kisses her now icy lips. His body is shaken by a strange sensation; he believes himself dying and, even in the sudden death pangs, rejoices. As he staggers away, Manfredo enters, recognizes him, and reveals the fact that in order to trap Fiora's lover, a powerful poison was placed on her lips—a desecration of which Archibaldo alone was capable. Manfredo is not happy in the death of his rival, he only sorrows that Fiora should have had so great a love for another than himself; and as Avito breathes his last, supports him gently as he sinks lifeless to the ground. Then, turning to Fiora, he throws himself over her, kisses her also on the lips, and remains there quivering while the deadly poison creeps through his veins. Nor has the poison quite finished its work when Archibaldo enters, groping his way through his own eternal darkness. He approaches the bier and, thinking he has caught the guilty man, shouts triumphantly; then, hearing the voice of his own son, dying, the old ruler cries out in the utmost agony and despair.

LILY PONS AS LUCIA

LUCIA DI LAMMERMOOR

OPERA in three acts; music by Gaetano Donizetti; text by Salvatore Cammarano, after Sir Walter Scott's novel, "The Bride of Lammermoor." Produced at the San Carlo Theatre, Naples, September 26, 1835; first performance in America, December 28, 1841, at the Théâtre d'Orléans, New Orleans.

This work, when first produced, won for its composer the appointment to the position of Professor of Counterpoint at the "Real Colegio di Musica" at Naples; moreover, it gained for him an abiding place in popular affection. It is the habit of some modernists to scoff at this, Donizetti's masterpiece; it is performed too often and regarded merely as a vehicle for showing off some popular prima donna. In reality its melodies are fresh, and though simple, possess genuine beauty; even in the ornate passages they are basically expressive of the situation in which they are placed in the drama. The ensemble numbers, including the world-renowned sextette, rank among the finest in Italian opera.

The rôle of Lucy has been a favorite with many coloratura prima donnas, including Patti, Melba, Sembrich, Tetrazzini and Galli-Curci. Galli-Curci first sang the rôle in the United States at Chicago, November 21, 1916. A list of the great interpreters of the character of Edgar would certainly include the names of Caruso and Gigli.

CHARACTERS

LORD HENRY ASHTON, *of Lammermoor*	*Baritone*
LUCY, *his sister (in Italian, Lucia, Loo-chee'-ah)*	*Soprano*
EDGAR, *Master of Ravenswood*	*Tenor*
LORD ARTHUR BUCKLAW	*Tenor*

RAYMOND, *Bide-the-Bent, chaplain at Lammermoor*   *Bass*
ALICE, *companion to Lucy*   *Mezzo-Soprano*
NORMAN, *follower of Lord Ashton*   *Tenor*

The action takes place in Scotland near the close of the Sixteenth Century.

ACT I

SCENE I—*A Wood Near Lammermoor*

IN THE somber gardens of Lammermoor Castle, the guards and their leader, Norman, are discussing a stranger who has been seen prowling around the place, perhaps on secret mischief. The guards leave hurriedly to search for him, but Norman remains behind to suggest to Lord Henry Ashton, who now enters, that the intruder may very likely be none other than Edgar of Ravenswood. Lord Henry is Edgar's mortal enemy and has recently acquired through treachery the Ravenswood estates. The talkative Norman further narrates, in the hearing of the kindly disposed Bide-the-Bent, that one day Lord Henry's sister, Lucy, was saved from the attack of an angry bull by some unknown person. She has fallen in love with him and secretly meets him every day. Lord Ashton's anger grows even more intense when the guards report that they saw the intruder and were able to recognize him as the hated Edgar. Ashton vows speedy vengeance.

From the Painting by Millias
THE PARTING OF LUCY
AND EDGAR

SCENE II—*A Park Near the Castle*

Lucy, accompanied by her maid, Alice, awaits Edgar at their daily trysting place. She looks with dread at a fountain nearby and tells Alice the legend of a Ravenswood who stabbed his sweetheart beside it. To a wistful, pathetic melody she vows that she has seen in the dark waters, an apparition of the murdered woman.

> Silence o'er all was reigning,
> Dark was the night and low'ring,
> And o'er yon fountain her pallid ray
> Yon pale moon was pouring,
> Faintly a sharp but stifled sigh
> Fell on my startled ear,
> And straightway upon the fountain's brink,
> The specter did appear!
> But slow on high its skeleton hand,
> Threat'ning it did uprear,
> Stood for a moment immovable,
> Then vanish'd from my view!
> Oh, what horrid omen is this?

234

> I ought to banish from my heart this love,
> But I cannot; it is my life,
> And comfort to my suff'ring soul!

Edgar arrives, a gloomy figure with black-plumed cavalier hat and cloak of sable. This, he tells her, must be their last meeting for he has been ordered to France. But he proposes first to go to Henry and endeavor to end the mortal feud which exists between the two families. Lucy, knowing her brother only too well, declares that it would be useless, and entreats Edgar to keep their love secret lest they will be forever parted. Such information causes Edgar again to renew his vow of vengeance. Then, as they begin their lovely duet of parting, "Verranno a te sull'aura," Lucy asks, "Wilt thou send a token that thou remainest faithful; while I sigh for thy return my heart will live on that hope." Edgar tenderly replies, "While life is mine, on thy memory I'll live." Then to a gentle, swaying melody, Lucy continues:

> Borne on the sighing breeze
> My ardent prayers to heav'n ascending,
> Each murm'ring wave shall echo make
> How I thy absence do mourn, love!
> Ah! think of me when far away,
> With naught my heart to cheer;
> I shall bedew each thought of thee
> With many a bitter tear!

Edgar repeats this charming melody and these words. Then both impassionedly unite in again repeating their vow of faithfulness. Edgar dramatically urges "Remember me, thou hast given thy promise!" and they unite in a last farewell, "Addio!"

ACT II

Scene I—*An Anteroom in Lammermoor Castle*

EDGAR was mistaken in his supposition that Lord Ashton's conduct is entirely a matter of hatred. In reality Ashton is in desperate straits and his only chance to improve his fortune is to have Lucy marry Lord Arthur Bucklaw. He intercepts all of Lucy's and Edgar's letters, and now he has forged in Ravenswood's handwriting a letter which seems to prove beyond doubt that Lucy is betrayed, her lover having deserted her for another. Ashton heaps upon her his scorn for having dared love his enemy and asserts that he will be disgraced and ruined unless she consents to marry Lord Arthur Bucklaw, as he has arranged. The unfortunate girl, stricken nearly dumb with grief, finally consents to the sacrifice.

Scene II—*The Great Hall of the Castle*

In the great armorial hall of the castle, knights and ladies are assembled to witness the wedding, and sing a gay chorus of welcome; but the pale, agitated appearance of the bride gives the lie to their joyful song. Lord Ashton tries to explain away her condition by saying that she still mourns her mother. Wan and almost fainting, she is escorted to the table where a notary is preparing the marriage papers; then with trembling hands she signs the document that makes her Lady Arthur Bucklaw. No sooner has she set down the pen, than a stranger enters the room. All eyes are turned upon him in fear and amazement. Edgar of Ravenswood, sword in hand, pistol in belt, stalks boldly toward the table. At this most dramatic moment begins the famous sextette. Its flowing melody, majestic rhythm, gorgeous harmonies and soaring climax are known to all; but only those who know the action of the opera can fully realize how magnificently it expresses in sound the conflicting emotions of this scene. It begins with Edgar and Henry; Edgar wonders why he has not rushed ahead to claim his vengeance and, on beholding the despairing Lucy, realizes that he still loves her. Henry fears for his own future and the effect that this excitement may have on his sister. The voices of Lucy and Bide-the-Bent enter, Lucy expressing her despair that death has not come to save her from this grief and shame, Bide-the-Bent kindly praying that heaven will aid and protect her. Now the voices of Alice and the attendant knights and ladies unite in this prayer, but above the outpouring of all these conflicting feelings rise the tones of Lucy's lament, forming a climax of vibrant, soul-stirring beauty.

Sextette—**Chi mi frena** *(What Restrains Me?)* **Galli-Curci, Egener, Caruso, de Luca, Journet, Bada** *10000-3.50 **Galli-Curci, Homer, Gigli, de Luca, Pinza, Bada** 10012-3.50 **Creatore's Band** 35850-1.25

The eternal enemies, Edgar and Ashton, rush at one another with drawn swords but Bide-the-Bent restrains them, bidding them both, in heaven's

C. Gerardi. FAGINOLI'S SETTING FOR A VERONA PERFORMANCE OF LUCIA

THE SEXTETTE

name, sheathe their weapons. Coldly asking Edgar the reason for his unwelcome visit, Ashton shows him the marriage contract. Unable to believe his eyes, Ravenswood turns to Lucy for confirmation; forlorn and in misery she tremblingly nods assent. Edgar, in furious rage, calls down the curse of heaven on Lucy and all her hated family and rushes away.

ACT III

Scene I—*The Tower of Ravenswood Castle*

ASHTON comes to the gloomy Ravenswood Castle and there challenges Edgar to a duel to take place at dawn. Amid the terrors of a terrific storm they unite in an agitated duet, praying that the vengeance-bringing morn may soon arrive.

Scene II—*The Hall at Lammermoor Castle*

Meanwhile, at the castle, the wedding guests are still feasting and making merry. Suddenly the laughter ceases and the song dies upon their lips as Raymond enters, horror-stricken, and cries out that Lucy has gone mad and slain her husband. An instant later Lucy herself appears, pale and lovely, robed in white, her hair loose upon her shoulders. In her eyes gleams an unnatural light and her face bears the tender, questioning expression of one who strives to recall a dream. Her brain unable to endure a suffering too intense, Lucy is mad, indeed; but she is happy in her madness, for she

237

believes herself with her lover. Singing a melody of great sweetness she imagines that she and Edgar are being married.

Mad Scene—Ardon gl' incensi *(The Burning Tapers)* **Lily Pons 7369-2.00**

> Round us, the guests assembled, waiting, I see them. The priest is ready!
> "With this ring I wed thee!" Oh day of rapture, oh rapture!
> At last I'm thine, love, at last thou'rt mine, love,
> Heav'n smiles upon us,
> And love's delights have won us.
> Ah! we're no more divided, no, no more divided,
> 'Tis heav'n to be with thee,
> My own forever,
> By heav'n to me thou wert guided,
> And smiling before us brightly dawns the future, without a cloud.

Mishkin

GIGLI AS EDGAR

Heard apart from the opera, this number seems hardly more than an unusually brilliant coloratura aria. But in its proper setting, carolled out by the demented Lucy amid the startled retainers, it takes on an ironic character quite its own. The scales and fioritura seem what they are, the audible wanderings of a mind distraught. The flute joins her in these difficult cadenzas, forming an ensemble effect of great brilliance and loveliness. After a brief interruption by Ashton, she resumes her song. Still imagining that Edgar is with her, she kneels and begs him not to leave; then requests "Cast on my grave a flower."

Mad Scene—Spargi d'amaro pianto—Part II *(Cast on My Grave a Flower)* **Lily Pons 7369-2.00**

> Cast on my grave a flower,
> But let there be no weeping,
> When 'neath the turf I'm sleeping,
> Let not an eye grow dim,
> For 'mid the fields of azure,
> I go to wait for him. Ah!
> I go to wait for him.

She sings this to a whimsical melody, half sad, half gay. Then growing more and more agitated at the thought that she will await her beloved in heaven, her voice rises ever higher in tones of great purity and beauty, until at the end she falls swooning into Alice's arms.

SCENE III—*The Tombs of the Ravenswoods*

As the night wears on, the lights still winking gaily from the castle at Lammermoor convey to the silent watcher who stands amid the graves of the Ravenswoods no knowledge of these tragic events. In somber meditation, he soliloquizes:

> Tomb of my sainted fathers, open your portals;
> I, the last of my kindred, am come to rest beside them.

Then, his thoughts instinctively turning toward Lucy, Edgar continues:

Ungrateful maiden! While I despairing, mourn that my hopes have perished, beside thy chosen consort thou art beaming with pleasure! Thou full of hope and gladness, I die despairing!

To a pensive but hauntingly lovely melody he gives voice to his despair:

> To earth I bid a last farewell,
> The tomb will soon close o'er me. . . .
> Forget the grave that hides me,
> But ne'er, thou false one, near it stray,
> With him whose joy derides me.
> Ah! nor vex the spirit's last repose
> Of him who died for thee.
> Oh faithless maid, I die for thee.

Yet even as he, in self-pity, heaps reproaches upon the absent Lucy, he remarks a train of mourners coming from the castle. He interrupts their solemn measured dirge, exclaiming, "Why lament ye!"

Giusto cielo! Rispondete (*Why Lament Ye!*) *Beniamino Gigli, Ezio Pinza* 8096-2.00

Singing their stately strain, the mourners tell him of Lucy's madness and of her love for him. She lies, they say, in the castle at the point of death. Even as they rehearse the story, the sound of a tolling bell brings word that Lucy's gentle soul has passed. Now, Edgar would rush to her side. He cannot quite believe that the death knell is hers; the mourners and Bide-the-Bent restrain him. "Speak, where is she?" asks the distressed Edgar. "In heaven," is the awesome affirmation of Bide-the-Bent. "My Lucy is no more!" cries Edgar, the reality of the tragedy beginning to dawn upon him.

Tu che a Dio spiegasti (*Thou Hast Spread Thy Wings*) *Beniamino Gigli, Ezio-Pinza* 8096-2.00

As dawn approaches, Edgar of Ravenswood sings his own dying prayer, that his soul may join his beloved in realms remote from the gloomy halls of Lammermoor. "Thou hast spread thy wings to heaven" sings he, in a melody of wonderful pathos. Edgar draws a dagger from his belt, and declaring that life is hateful where Lucy is not, stabs himself. "Fatal rashness!" exclaims the sympathetic Raymond, who has tried to stay Edgar's act.

Victor George

GALLI-CURCI AS LUCIA

A 'cello whispers out the melody and Edgar, his voice broken by grief and pain, sobs, "None shall part us, belov'd *(A te vengo o bell'alma)*, while Raymond and the horror-stricken retainers unite in praying for heaven's forgiveness. The song grows increasingly agitated under the stress of the catastrophe, Edgar's voice soaring above the others to a splendid climax, as, thinking only of the departed Lucy, he declares that he cannot live without her. Suddenly, he falls to the ground dead . . . the lovers are at last united.

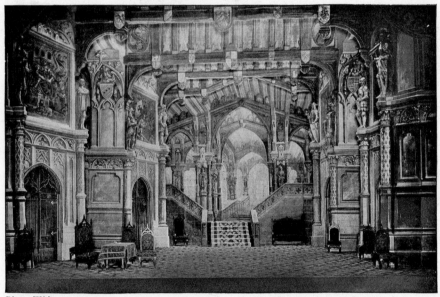

Photo White THE HALL IN LAMMERMOOR CASTLE (METROPOLITAN OPERA SETTING)

OUTSIDE PINKERTON'S HOUSE

ƆMADAMA ᏮBUTTERFLY

OPERA in three (originally two) acts; music by Giacomo Puccini; libretto by Illica and Giacosa. First produced at La Scala, Milan, February 17, 1904. First performance in the United States, at Washington, D. C., October 15, 1906, in English. First performed at the Metropolitan Opera House, February 11, 1907, with Farrar, Homer, Caruso and Scotti.

Early in 1900 an American producer needed a play with which to save a rather disastrous season, and finding possibilities in John Luther Long's short story, "Madame Butterfly," he fashioned from it a drama in the short space of two weeks. His season was saved, for the play was a success, the all-night vigil making a particularly great appeal. Soon the play was produced in London, where the manager of Covent Garden saw it, and knowing that Puccini needed a successor to "La Tosca," he wired him. Puccini came to London immediately, and was charmed with "Madame Butterfly" as an operatic possibility, even though, it is said, he did not at that time understand a word of English.

At its first performance the opera was a distinct failure. Perhaps the strangeness of a Japanese setting antagonized the audience; the second act, moreover, with its miniature all-night watch, so successful in the drama, became too long in the opera. The opera was withdrawn, Puccini made a few slight changes, and through necessity ruthlessly interrupted the vigil, making two parts of the second act (now often given as Acts II and III). Produced three months later at Brescia, Madame Butterfly was a success, and since that day has become one of the most popular of operas.

While much of this success is due to the dramatically conceived play, much more is due to Puccini's music. For the sake of local color the composer has introduced a number of genuine Japanese melodies—melodies that he was enabled to obtain exactly from Victor records made in Japan. Puccini also shows that he was aware of musical progress in the rest of the world, when, for instance, at the entrance of Butterfly, he effectively makes extensive use of augmented triads after the fashion first brought into prominence by

affirms her belief (in a famous aria), that some day *(Un bel di)* a great ship will appear far in the horizon . . . the boom of cannon will announce its arrival in the harbor . . . they will see *him* coming from a distance . . . climbing the hill. Butterfly will hide for a moment just to tease him . . . he will call for her by the old names of endearment . . . so let fears be banished, Butterfly declares, utterly carried away by the joy of her anticipation, for he will return, she knows it!

Un bel di vedremo *(Some Day He'll Come)* **(M97-15)** *Lucrezia Bori* 6790-2.00
Margherita Sheridan 7102-2.00

At the moment she has finished this declaration of her trust, Sharpless appears (M-97-16). Goro, who has conducted him here, waits outside. "Madame Butterfly," he calls. "Madame B. F. Pinkerton, beg pardon!" the wife corrects, then turning and recognizing her visitor, greets him cheerfully. He has a letter from Pinkerton, he tells her. She is the most happy of women, she replies, and then without waiting for Sharpless to read she asks him when the robins build their nests in America . . . for, she continues, Pinkerton had said that he would come back in the happy season when the robins return . . . now, for the third time the robins are building their nests. Sharpless, in his embarrassment, is forced to reply that he never studied ornithology. Goro laughs outright at this. The marriage-broker now presents (M-97-17) Yamadori, a wealthy suitor, who, though he has had many consorts and divorced them all, says that he is madly in love with Butterfly and will swear eternal faithfulness to her. She repulses him and his proffered wealth, for she is married to an American, and in his country people remain

Castagneri

BUTTERFLY'S HOUSE

faithful! Broker and suitor disposed of (M-97-18), Sharpless attempts to resume reading the letter; everything he reads is interpreted by Butterfly into some happy assurance that her husband will soon return. The consul has not the heart to go on, he asks Butterfly what she would do if Pinkerton were never to come back to her. As if struck by a death-blow Butterfly gravely replies that she might again become a Geisha or she might kill herself (M-97-19). Sharpless is horrified and advises her to marry Yamadori. This greatly insults Butterfly . . . ordering Suzuki to bring in "Trouble," the name she has bestowed on her little son, she points to the child in agitated pride, and exclaims "And this? Can such as this be forgotten?" She asks Sharpless to write to her husband and tell him what a beautiful son he has. Thus does the consul learn to his surprise that unknown to Pinkerton there is a child. In true motherly joy (M-97-20), her attention concentrated entirely on little "Trouble," she bids him not to believe the bad man when he says that father will not return, but leave them to wander through the streets for a living.

RETHBERG AS BUTTERFLY

Sharpless leaves, fearful for the future. Soon after he has gone a cannon shot is heard booming from over the harbor, announcing the arrival of an American warship (M-97-21). With the help of a telescope Butterfly spells out its name—"Abraham Lincoln," Pinkerton's ship!

So, then, the agony of waiting is over! He has come with the robins—her lover, her husband, her adored one! In a moment the two women are feverishly rushing to the garden to gather cherry blossoms to deck the house. They sing the joyous "Duet of the Flowers" (M-97-22), throbbing with the excitement and exultation of the rejoicing Butterfly, who then hastens to put on the wedding dress she wore on that day long ago (M-97-23), so that she may greet her lover as he first knew her. Little "Trouble," too, is arrayed in his finest.

Flower Duet and Letter Scene *Victor Salon Orchestra* 24856-.75

Night has been falling; the servant closes the shosi (M-97-24) and brings in several Japanese lanterns which cast a dim glow over the darkened room. But they must await Pinkerton's return . . . be ready to welcome him. In her anxious, joyful expectancy Butterfly has pierced three little holes through the wall so that they may watch for him. "Trouble" sits before one, supported by cushions; at another kneels Suzuki; close up against a third stands Butterfly, rigid and motionless . . . watching . . . waiting . . . A wonderful melody (M-97-25) first heard during the reading of the letter, floats across the scene, softly hummed from a distance. "Trouble" soon nods, then falls asleep . . . next Suzuki . . . Butterfly keeps her vigil alone (M-97-26).

ACT III

THE grey light of dawn begins to enter the room. Butterfly still stands, motionless, watching; Suzuki and "Trouble" still sleep, profoundly (M-97-27). The lanterns become even more dim while the day grows brighter; like the morning sunlight the music sparkles with vagrant Japanese melodies. Suzuki having awakened and begged her to lie down to rest awhile, Butterfly takes little "Trouble" and goes with him into an inner room. No sooner has she gone than Sharpless and Pinkerton arrive. Suzuki is overjoyed at seeing them, but they motion her to keep silent. She points out how Butterfly has decorated the house, and tells how she waited all night. The servant, on opening the shosi, exclaims in surprise for she notices a strange woman in the garden. Fearfully she asks who it is. Pinkerton's wife, Sharpless explains. Suzuki cries out in grief.

Sharpless asks Suzuki to prepare Butterfly for this bitter revelation and tells her that the American woman has come to adopt the child (M-97:28-29). Pinkerton, overwhelmed with remorse, leaves the house after asking Sharpless to console Butterfly the best he can. A moment later Butterfly rushes in, joyfully expecting to find Pinkerton (M-97-30). Instead she sees Sharpless, a foreign woman, and Suzuki in tears. She begins to realize the heartless truth. She asks if *he* is alive, her voice hushed with expectant fear. Only Suzuki's broken "yes" is needed, and she knows that she has been deserted. Mrs. Pinkerton expresses her helpless sympathy, and asks to take the child. Butterfly, having listened in pathetic dignity, replies that only to Pinkerton will she yield her son . . . she will be ready in half an hour. Sharpless and Mrs. Pinkerton take their leave; Butterfly orders Suzuki to go into another room with the child (M-97-31).

Photo Hall
THE DEATH OF BUTTERFLY

Then she takes from its sheath the dagger with which her father had fulfilled the law of his race, and reads the inscription written upon its blade: "To die with honor when one can no longer live with honor." She raises the knife to her throat (M-97-32). At that instant, the door opens and little "Trouble" runs to her with outstretched arms. She drops the knife, impetuously seizes the child and covers

BUTTERFLY PREPARES FOR PINKERTON'S RETURN

him with kisses. Having bade him a heart-rending farewell, she gives her son a doll and an American flag, urges him to play with them, then gently bandages his eyes. Again she takes the dagger, goes behind the screen. A moment later the blade is heard falling to the floor. Butterfly staggers forward groping her way to her child, takes its hand, and smiles feebly. She scarcely has strength to give her son one final embrace, then falls beside him, dead.

Pinkerton is heard calling her name. A moment later he rushes into the room followed by Sharpless. He kneels beside Butterfly sobbing with grief and shame; Sharpless takes the child and turns away.

The orchestra thunders out a solemn Japanese melody . . . over and above the very last note of that melody there sounds a poignant, questioning chord, as though this tragedy were not yet, nor ever would be, ended.

Fantasie—Parts I and II *Victor Symphony Orchestra* **35786-1.25**

melody, descending to the lower register of the bass voice, has for a background, solemn harmonies and the dark hues of the deeper-toned orchestral instruments.

O Isis und Osiris *(Chorus of Priests)*　**Alexander Kipnis and Chorus 1738-1.50**
Metropolitan Opera Chorus 4027-1.00

The Prince and Pamina gladly go through many hazardous trials for the sake of their love.

In diesen heiligen Hallen *(Within These Sacred Halls)*　**Alexander Kipnis 8684-2.00**

During one of these trials it chances that Pamina becomes lost from Tamino. Hearing him playing the flute she rushes to him joyfully, but Tamino heeds her not.

Ah! je le sais *(Ah! I Knew It)*　**Lily Pons 8733-2.00**

Willinger

PAPAGENO

Moved to despair she sings a poignant lament declaring that her love can be ended only by death.

The melody, calm, dignified, and seemingly of no great complexity, is of the most intense expressiveness, and requires a consummate vocal mastery to be perfectly interpreted.

Finally, however, in spite of the constant interference of the Queen of the Night, the lovers emerge from their trials victorious. The clownish Papageno also succeeds in finding a mate for himself in the person of Papagena, a bird-woman. The wicked Queen disappears, let us hope, forever; and the lovers are married in the great Temple of the Sun.

MANON—ACT I

MANON

OPERA in four acts; music by Jules Massenet; libretto by Meilhac and Gille, after the novel by the Abbé Prévost. First produced, January 19, 1884, at the Opéra Comique, Paris. First performance in the United States, December 23, 1885, at the Academy of Music, New York.

Much of this opera was composed by Massenet during the summer of 1882, at The Hague, in the very room in which the Abbé Prévost had dwelt. Perhaps the surroundings may have inspired Massenet to achieve his delicately moulded score, which, while of necessity departing from the details of the Abbé's romance, pictures the story of the beautiful though misguided Manon with great charm and pathos.

CHARACTERS

CHEVALIER DES GRIEUX (*Shev-al-yay' day Gree-uh'*)	*Tenor*
COUNT DES GRIEUX, *his father*	*Bass*
LESCAUT (*Les-koh'*), *Manon's cousin, one of the Royal Guards*	*Baritone*
GUILLOT MORFONTAIN (*Jwee-yo' Mohr-fon-ten'*) *a roué, Minister of France*	*Bass*
DE BRETIGNY (*Duh Bray-tee-nyee'*) *a nobleman*	*Baritone*
MANON (*Ma-non'*), *a school girl*	*Soprano*

People, Actresses, and Students.

The action takes place in Amiens, Paris, and Le Havre, about the year 1721.

ACT I

AMONG the variegated crowd gathered at the courtyard of an inn at Amiens to meet the arrival of the coach, is Lescaut, member of the Royal Guard . . . and soldier of fortune. He has come to meet his cousin,

SCHIPA AS DES GRIEUX

Manon, and is to escort her to a convent. He is pleasurably surprised to find her as charming as she is unsophisticated. He accepts her proffered lips in cousinly greeting, then hastens within to engage rooms.

No sooner has he gone than the old roué, Guillot Morfontain, trots out into the courtyard and begins to pay marked attention to the girl, who is thereby amused and a trifle flattered. There are some among the crowd who make game of the old libertine. Though undaunted, he is soon called back to the inn by his travelling companion, de Bretigny. Among those haunting the courtyard are three girls of doubtful character, but brilliantly costumed. Their fine apparel is not lost on Manon, who thinks between sighs and tears of her own sad lot and her approaching gray life in a convent. Her musings are interrupted, for the handsome Chevalier des Grieux, son of the Count des Grieux, has entered, and, struck by Manon's beauty, addresses her. They become quickly acquainted and, ere they know it, deeply in love.

A carriage previously placed at the disposal of the girl by the infatuated Guillot unexpectedly draws near; intoxicated with her new-found love, she suggests that they fly together to Paris. Des Grieux joyfully agrees, and they sing rapturously of the life they will live together there. Suddenly Manon hears the voice of her cousin, Lescaut; the lovers jump into the carriage and disappear.

Lescaut comes out wrathfully; there has been gambling in the inn and he has lost his money . . . now he learns that he has also lost his cousin. Guillot appears anticipating another *tête-à-tête* with Manon; instead he is accused by Lescaut of having abducted the girl. A crowd assembles watching the growing argument, which is calmed by the observing innkeeper, who says that Manon departed with a young man . . . in the distance they hear the departing coach.

ACT II

MANON and des Grieux are together in their apartment in Paris. Des Grieux is writing to his father and trembles for fear the old man may read in anger what he writes from the heart. "Afraid?" says Manon, who stands looking over his shoulder, "then we'll read together." She takes the letter and begins to read: "She is called Manon . . . is young and fair . . ." Some little glint of the girl's weakness is visible in her response to his glowing phrase, "In her eyes shines the tender light of love." "Is this true?" asks Manon. Des Grieux will soon ask himself the same question. But now he continues reading his poetic rhapsody: "Her lips, like flowers, smile and speak to the zephyrs that kiss them in passing." He is certain that his father will give his consent and they embrace tenderly. As he passes to go out, he notices a bouquet of flowers mysteriously left for Manon. She returns only an evasive answer to his questions. As the perturbed des Grieux opens the door to leave, Lescaut and Bretigny enter. Lescaut demands satisfaction for the abduction of his cousin. Des Grieux takes him aside, and shows him the letter to his father as proof of his honorable intentions. Bretigny, left with Manon, makes the best of his time; he says that des Grieux is to be carried away by his own father that night and urges her to fly with him. Knowing that Bretigny can give her the pretty things for which her heart longs,

Payton

BORI AS MANON

Manon hesitates—and is lost. Lescaut, now seemingly appeased, departs with Bretigny, and des Grieux goes out to mail his letter. Left alone, Manon struggles with herself and sings a charming farewell to the little table at which des Grieux and she have been so happy. When he returns he finds her in tears which she cannot quite conceal. Seeking to comfort her, he tells her of his dream: singing a sweet, rapturous melody, while the orchestra supplies a softly murmuring accompaniment, he describes the little home he plans to share with her.

Il sogno *(The Dream)* **Tito Schipa** 1183-1.50 *Richard Crooks* 8421-2.00 *Beniamino Gigli* 1656-1.50 *Edmond Clement* *6062-2.00

A knock at the door halts the dream; Manon starts guiltily. She tries to prevent him from opening the door, but he insists—is captured and borne off. Now Manon is in despair.

ACT III

M ANON and Bretigny mingle with the merrymakers that crowd the streets of Paris on a festival day. They are met by the Count des Grieux, an old acquaintance of Bretigny. He tells them that his son is at St. Sulpice, about to enter the priesthood. This revives all Manon's love, and forsaking Bretigny, she hurries to St. Sulpice. The Count, however, arrives there before her, and attempts in vain to persuade his son to abandon this rash resolve. Left alone, des Grieux sings a fervent song of renunciation, declaring that he will now seek the peace of mind which only heaven can give.

Ah! Dispar, vision *(Depart, Fair Vision)* **Tito Schipa** 8422-2.00

When he has gone his way, Manon arrives. Chameleon soul that she is, she is greatly affected by the sacred surroundings . . . in the distance the choir

253

is heard singing a *Magnificat* . . . Manon prays . . . and by the time des Grieux comes to the ante-room to meet her, she is in a fine mood of repentance . . . and even more fascinating than usual. After a struggle with himself, des Grieux yields to her entreaties, and, forsaking the seclusion of the priesthood, goes with her into the world.

ACT IV

DES GRIEUX and Manon come to a fashionable gambling house in Paris. After much persuasion, the Chevalier, hoping to win riches for Manon, consents to play. He has remarkable luck, and after continuous winning from Guillot, is falsely accused of cheating. A brawl results and des Grieux and Manon are both on the point of being arrested by the police when the Count appears, and protects his son. Manon, however, as an "abandoned woman," is captured and exiled.

Carlo Edwards
CROOKS AS DES GRIEUX

ACT V

LESCAUT and des Grieux are hiding by the road to Le Havre, along which Manon will pass on her way to exile. Des Grieux bribes a soldier and is thus able to talk to Manon. He begs her to try to escape with him, but she is too weak from fatigue. After entreating him to forgive her for her unworthiness, she dies in his arms.

THE HAVRE HARBOR—ACT III

MANON LESCAUT

OPERA in four acts; music by Giacomo Puccini; libretto (founded on Abbé Prévost's novel) is by the composer, assisted by a committee of friends. First performed at Turin, February 1, 1893. First performance in the Americas, at Buenos Aires, June 9, 1893; in the United States, at the Grand Opera House, Philadelphia, August 29, 1894, in English. Produced at the Metropolitan, January 18, 1907, with Caruso, Cavalieri and Scotti, under the direction of the composer, who then visited America for the first time.

Manon Lescaut is the earliest of Puccini's operas to hold a permanent place in the repertoire in this country. In Manon Lescaut, Puccini gives promise of the genius for effective operatic composition that was to flower three years later in La Bohême, and eventually to win him the rank of the foremost of modern Italian opera composers. In writing Manon Lescaut, Puccini also displayed a certain boldness of spirit, for only a few years previous Massenet had written his own most successful setting of Prévost's novel, while Puccini was himself still a young and relatively unknown composer. It seems inevitable to compare the two works: Puccini's presents four relatively detached scenes that follow the novel rather closely; Massenet's departs somewhat from the novel in order to present a more unified drama; Puccini's makes no attempt to be anything other than Italian opera; Massenet's is thoroughly French in character; both remain favorites.

CHARACTERS

MANON LESCAUT (*Mahn-on Les-koh'*)	Soprano
LESCAUT, *Sergeant of the King's Guards*	Baritone
CHEVALIER DES GRIEUX (*day Gree-uh'*)	Tenor
GERONTE DE RAVOIR (*day Rah-vwar'*), *Treasurer General*	Bass
EDMUND, *a student*	Tenor

An Innkeeper, a Dancing-master, a Sergeant, a Captain, Singers, Beaux and Abbés, Girls, Citizens, Students, People, Courtesans, Sailors.

The action takes place at Paris and vicinity during the second half of the Eighteenth Century.

ACT I

STUDENTS are singing and whiling away the time in front of an inn at Amiens. Des Grieux, pensive and lonesome, enters but does not join heartily in their revels. Manon, with her brother Lescaut, and a chance acquaintance, Geronte, alight from a coach; and while the men are busied with arrangements at the Inn, des Grieux speaks to her. She is, she tells him, on her way to a convent, rather against her will; just then her brother calls her from the inn, but she will return later. Left alone des Grieux meditates on the beauty of the woman he has just seen, singing an air in which he declares that he has never before seen such a wonderful beauty.

Donna non vidi mai *(Maiden So Fair)* **Beniamino Gigli** 1213-1.50 **Alessandro Ziliani** 1735-1.50

Geronte, an old libertine, secretly orders a swift horse and carriage with which he intends to abduct Manon, but Edmund, a student friend of des Grieux, overhears the plot. Warned by Edmund, the young people elope and leave the irate Geronte to be consoled by Lescaut's suggestion that they will be found in Paris . . . it will be easy to lure a woman from a poor student.

ACT II

THE opening of the second act reveals that Lescaut's prophecy has come true, Manon was found and has been Geronte's mistress so long that she

Copy't Mishkin

CARUSO AS DES GRIEUX

is already beginning to weary of the luxuries with which she is surrounded. A group of musicians, sent by Geronte, come and sing for her entertainment; they are followed by the aged gallant himself and a crowd of his cronies. Manon delights them all by dancing a Minuet under the guidance of the dancing-master. Then all but Manon leave for some brilliant party; she will follow in a moment. She is surprised by the arrival of des Grieux. He reproaches her for her faithlessness, singing the aria, "Ah! Manon, mi tradisce." He is soon overcome by her great beauty and earnest pleadings, and the two sing a passionate love duet.

They are found by Geronte, who returns to see the cause of Manon's delay. He con-

ceals his anger under the cold polished manner of the man of the world, pretends to forgive the couple, and leaves them with apparently ironical indifference. Soon, however, Lescaut rushes in with the news that the police have been summoned; they must save themselves quickly. Again her love of pretty things is her undoing, for Manon stops to gather up her finery, and when des Grieux rushes her to the alcove, the way is barred by the police.

ACT III

Banished from France as an abandoned woman, Manon is to embark for the French province of Louisiana. Des Grieux and Lescaut bribe the guard, and are prevented from rescuing her only by the sudden arrival of the ship's captain. Des Grieux would follow when Manon is led away with a crowd of women who are also to be deported, but is restrained by the guard. In desperation he pleads with the captain, singing an intensely fervent aria. The captain is sympathetic and finally consents to smuggle him aboard.

ACT IV

The last act takes place on a great open space near the territory of New Orleans. It is a barren and uneven country with a remote horizon, and the darkness of approaching night is made still more gloomy by low overhanging clouds. Even in the New World beauty has brought importunate solicitations; to escape these Manon and des Grieux have fled to this desolate spot. They wander about, vainly seeking shelter until Manon is exhausted, then des Grieux continues the search alone. When he returns Manon sinks, dying, into his arms.

Gottscho

FROM A JUILLIARD PRODUCTION OF
THE MARRIAGE OF FIGARO

THE MARRIAGE OF FIGARO

(Figaros Hochzeit) (Le Nozze di Figaro)

OPERA in four acts; music by Wolfgang Amadeus Mozart; libretto by da Ponte based on the second of a trilogy of Figaro comedies by Beaumarchais. This trilogy includes *The Barber of Seville*, basis of Rossini's charming opera of that name, *The Marriage of Figaro*, and *The Culpable Mother*. Mozart's opera was first produced, May 1, 1786, at the Burgtheater, Vienna, the composer conducting. The date of the first performance in the United States is disputed, although this masterpiece is reported to have been sung as early as 1799 in New York under the title *The Follies of a Day*. A performance in English at the Park Theatre, New York, May 10, 1824, was advertised, however, as "the first time in America."

"Public performance forbidden by the police" sounds very much like New York in this present age, yet such was the decree—in Paris!—against Beaumarchais' rollicking and now classic comedy, "The Marriage of Figaro." The work was condemned not because of moral scruples, however, but because it too truthfully revealed the life of the nobility. Never before had the exalted of estate been so pictured! In that day, only a scant decade before the Revolution, government officials were already conscious of gathering storms, and made out that such a production at such a time would serve less as a warning to a Court apparently bent on riding to its destruction, than as a simple means of developing resentment against a cynical and conscienceless aristocracy. The inevitable happened: "The Marriage of Figaro" took on the charm of forbidden fruit. In place of public performances, private "rehearsals" were given, at which no less a personage than Marie Antoinette—always liberal in matters of art—delighted in being present.

The well known dramatist, Lorenzo da Ponte, proposed to Mozart for musical setting his version of Beaumarchais' famous comedy, but it was only with difficulty that Mozart was able to obtain the Emperor's consent to do this piece of work. Yet, like the play before it, the opera was an instant success. The singer, Kelly, who took the double rôle of Basilio and Don Curzio at that memorable first production, writes of it thus: "Never was anything more complete than the triumph of Mozart and his 'Nozze di Figaro,' to which numerous overflowing audiences bore witness. Even at the first full band rehearsal, all present were aroused to enthusiasm, and when Benucci came to the fine passage, 'Cherubino, alla vittoria, alla gloria militar,' which he sang with stentorian lungs, the effect was electric, for the whole of the performers on the stage, and those in the orchestra, as if actuated by one feeling of delight, vociferated, 'Bravo! Bravo! Maestro! Viva, viva, grande Mozart!' Those in the orchestra I thought would never have ceased applauding by beating the bows of their violins against the music desks. And Mozart? I never shall forget his little, animated countenance, when lighted up with the glowing rays of genius. It is as impossible to describe it as it would be to paint sunbeams."

Yet this very popularity worked to Mozart's injury, for other musicians, jealous at the composer's success, started a cabal against him with the result that "The Marriage of Figaro" had soon to be withdrawn from the stage at Vienna. Still more bitterly tragic is the fact that this apparently great success brought only empty glory, for Mozart still had to struggle on for a mere existence—a struggle which hastened his premature death only five years later.

"The Marriage of Figaro" remains one of the greatest masterpieces of comedy in music. Mozart's melodies, with all their charm, perfection of form, apparent naïveté, and utter spontaneity, are most masterful in their subtle psychological fidelity to character and situation; and moreover, they sparkle with all the wit and rapid care-free fun-making of Beaumarchais' comedy. Well indeed does this opera deserve its fame and popularity!

The opera is also known under the Italian title, "Le Nozze di Figaro," *(Leh Not'-zeh dee Fee'-gah-roh)*, and the German, "Figaros Hochzeit," *(Fee'-gah-rohs Hohk'-zyt)*.

The Overture is a gem of sheer humor. Without drawing on any of the music of the following scenes, it is literally alive with the spirit of the comedy. The chattering violin figure in octaves at the opening is justly famous. Equally charming is the second subject in which a half-serious ascending figure in the bases and bassoons only provokes a laughing echo in the violins. All this merriment frolics to a climax . . . a glorification of care-free existence and the untrammeled joy of motion.

Complete—in 3 albums *Glyndebourne Festival Opera Company with orchestra conducted by Fritz Busch* **M-313 (14042-14047) AM-313 (14048-14053) $12.00 M-314 (14054-S-14059) AM-314 (14060-S-14065) $11.00 M-315 (14066-14070) AM-315 (14071-14075) $10.00**
Overture *Minneapolis Orchestra, Eugene Ormandy conducting* **8458-2.00** *Vienna Philharmonic Orch., Cond. by Clemens Krauss* **11242-1.50**

ACT I

FIGARO, in high spirits, is preparing the room assigned to him and his bride, Susanna; he remarks how convenient it will be for him to wait on his master the Count, and yet equally convenient for Susanna to attend her mistress, the Countess. Susanna suddenly dampens his ardor by remarking that the Count has had a more subtle reason in giving them a room so near his own. She calls Figaro a "goose" for not observing this or realizing that the Count was moved by anything other than generosity in paying her dowry. So soon has the gallant young Count Almaviva grown faithless to his wife, the formerly beloved Rosina! Still further troubles are to beset the erstwhile Barber of Seville, for old Dr. Bartolo, whom he outwitted in former days, still bears a grudge against him. Bartolo discovers that in a weak moment Figaro promised to marry the aged Marcellina, and that the old dame wants to compel him to fulfill the contract. Susanna fortunately overhears the plotting of this unseemly couple. When they have gone, the adolescent Cherubino enters, who is at the tender age susceptible to anything feminine, and has fallen deeply in love, if you please, with no less a personage than the Countess herself. He describes his feelings in a remarkable aria.

Photo White
SUSANNA, COUNTESS AND CHERUBINO IN
ACT I

Non so più cosa son *(I Know Not What I Am Doing)* **Elisabeth Schumann** 1431-1.50

Suddenly the Count is heard approaching, and Cherubino hastily conceals himself behind a large arm-chair. The Count has come to complain against Cherubino whom he suspects of paying attention to the Countess. But even as he speaks a knock is heard. The Count hastily hides behind the same chair as the page, who

260

cleverly darting around out of the Count's way, sinks into the depths of the chair. Susanna quickly covers him with a dress that happens to lie at hand. The busybody Basilio enters and taunts Susanna for flirting with the Count, then twits her about Cherubino. As soon, however, as Basilio mentions Cherubino's name in connection with that of the Countess, Almaviva, unable to stand it longer, jumps from his hiding place and demands an explanation. He goes on to tell how a short while ago he discovered the boy concealed under a table flirting with Basilio's cousin, Barbarina. In order to demonstrate how he found the youth when he lifted up the table-cloth, the Count goes over to the arm-chair and pulls away the dress. And lo! there again is Cherubino! The Count is beside himself with rage; then a sudden inspiration comes to him. There is a commission vacant in his regiment; Cherubino shall have it. He must go at once. Figaro laughingly sings to the page that now instead of tender love-making he will have weary marching.

ACT II

Scene—*Apartment of the Countess*

THE Countess and Susanna are in despair because of the Count's wayward affections. The resourceful Figaro suggests a plan for reawakening the Count's interest in his wife—make him jealous by letting him discover a note arranging a rendezvous between the Countess and a lover. They plan to send Susanna in the Countess' place, and Cherubino, dressed as Susanna, to meet the Count. Thus it is hoped that through ridicule the Count will be persuaded to remain faithful to his Countess.

Cherubino comes, delighted at the thought of seeing the Countess before his departure. He sings "Voi che sapete," one of the most famous arias in the opera, a wonderful delineation of the vague emotion characteristic of early youth:

What is this feeling makes me so sad?
What is this feeling makes me so glad?
Pain that delights me—How can it be?
Pleasure that pains me—
Fetter'd though free!
Whence, too, these yearnings,
Strange to myself?
Tell me their meaning, spirit or elf!
Why am I burning? Why do I freeze?
Restless, forever, never at ease.
All is so altered, nothing's at rest,
Or are these changes but in my breast?
Gentler the forest, greener the hill,
Soft, too, the music flows from each rill.

Voi che sapete (*What Is This Feeling?*) *Elisabeth Schumann* 7076-2.00 *Ria Ginster* 7822-2.00

Continuing with their plot, the women proceed to dress him in the maid's gar-

CHERUBINO'S BALLAD

ments. Susanna sings a fascinatingly humorous aria in which she coquettishly bids him kneel before her and tells him first to turn one way and then another while she adapts the feminine apparel to his person.

Venite, inginocchiatevi (*Now Pray Bend Down Upon Your Knees*) **Elisabeth Schumann** 1431-1.50

The Countess happens to notice Cherubino's officer's commission, and observes that the seal to it has been forgotten. Suddenly her husband is heard angrily knocking outside. Cherubino scurries into hiding in a closet. The Count enters just in time to hear him upset a chair in his blind haste, and, observing his wife's confusion, he demands admission to the closet. Susanna, concealed in an alcove, hears the Countess refuse on the ground that her maid is in the closet dressing. The suspicious Count, however, goes out for a crowbar to break down the door and insists on taking the Countess with him. As soon as they have gone Cherubino emerges and escapes through the window; Susanna quickly hides in the cabinet in his place. When the Count returns, prepared to batter away, the Countess finally confesses that Cherubino is there. Thus she is quite as startled as her husband when Susanna suddenly appears! The Count is almost penitent when a half-drunken gardener arrives to complain that somebody has dropped on his flower-bed from the window and broken a valued flowerpot. Luckily Figaro turns up just then and stills the Count's reawakened suspicions by announcing that it was he who jumped through the window. The gardener spoils this by producing a paper that was dropped by the fugitive; the Count says that he will believe Figaro's story if he is able to tell what this paper contains. Through a quick whisper from the Countess passed along by Susanna, Figaro learns it is Cherubino's commission. This would make things look rather bad for the Countess, but the quick-witted Figaro, again prompted by the women, declares that he had the commission in his pocket in order to have it looked after, for it lacked a seal. The day is saved, but Figaro now has a worse problem to face. Marcellina enters with her lawyer and demands that Figaro shall keep his promise to marry her. The Count, rather wanting to settle accounts with the valet, says that he will look into this!

ACT III

COUNT ALMAVIVA plans to force Susanna to accept his attentions by threatening to make Figaro wed the aged Marcellina; and Susanna, wishing to further the plans of her mistress, seems to surrender. As he goes away, rejoicing in his triumph, the Count overhears Susanna exclaim to Figaro "our cause is victorious." Growing suspicious, the Count resolves to punish Figaro at once and deal with Susanna later.

Accordingly, Marcellina, her lawyer, the Count, and Bartolo, arrive to inform Figaro that he must marry as he has promised, or pay damages. Figaro thinks he may be rich enough to pay the damages, for he has just discovered clues that suggest that he may be of noble birth. While he is

ACT III—AT THE MUNICH OPERA

explaining, Marcellina suddenly asks if he has a spatula mark upon his right arm. He has. By this she knows him to be her long-lost son; the Count's plans are spoiled! Mother and son embrace and are so discovered by Susanna, who is much distressed until matters are explained. At last Susanna and Figaro are free to go ahead with preparations for their wedding.

Continuing with the plot, Susanna meets with the Countess and at her dictation writes a letter to the Count fixing exactly the time and place of their rendezvous. The letter is sealed with a pin which the Count is to return as a sign that he will keep the appointment. Rather than send Cherubino, the Countess herself has decided to go disguised as Susanna.

The wedding of Susanna and Figaro forthwith takes place, and Susanna contrives, even during the ceremony, to slip the letter to the Count, who pricks his finger on the pin. Figaro observes this without, however, suspecting anything.

ACT IV

Scene I—*A Room in the Castle*

BARBARINA, the gardener's daughter, is looking for a pin she has lost, the pin with which Susanna had sealed her letter to the Count, and which Barbarina had been entrusted to return. Figaro learns of this from the unsuspecting child, and hastily decides that Susanna actually is faithless and intends to yield to the Count that very evening.

Scene II—*The Garden of the Château*

Night in the park of the Château, just such a night as is made for love and intrigue. Figaro has come to the rendezvous intending to spy on the supposed infidelity of his bride; he conceals himself just as the Countess and Susanna enter. The mistress hides, too, and the maid, awaiting the Count, and knowing that her husband is listening, sings a wonderfully beautiful soliloquy addressed to her supposed lover. She does this with the quaintly humorous idea of harassing her husband.

Cherubino, having an appointment with Barbarina, suddenly appears on the scene, and seeing the Countess, whom he believes to be Susanna, attempts to kiss her. The Count arrives, just in time to see this, and stepping between them, unexpectedly receives the kiss himself. He gives the boy a violent box on the ear, and the youngster flies, his head ringing. The Count then proceeds to make ardent love to his wife, whom he believes to be Susanna, so cleverly does she imitate her maid's voice and manners.

Figaro, wild with fury at this spectacle, unexpectedly meets Susanna, who similarly is impersonating the Countess. He accordingly tries to awaken the jealousy of the supposed Countess by telling her of her husband's conduct. Susanna, however, reveals herself; and the Count, seeing Figaro apparently embracing the Countess, promptly forgets the supposed Susanna, and violently seizing Figaro, calls for help. Explanations follow, and the Count, perceiving himself outwitted, begs his wife's forgiveness.

Painted by Becker

THE MARRIAGE OF FIGARO AND SUSANNA

HELEN JEPSON AS LADY HARRIET

MARTHA

OPERA in four acts; music by Friedrich von Flotow; words by Wilhelm Friedrich Riese. First produced at the Kärnthnerthor Theatre, Vienna, November 25, 1847. First performed in the United States, November 1, 1852, at Niblo's Garden, New York, in English.

Martha perhaps of all operas most deserves the appellation of an "old favorite." The composer was born in 1812, the son of the Baron von Flotow, of Mecklenburg, who had intended to have him follow a diplomatic career. When the boy was about fifteen years old, he went to Paris, and the brilliant artistic life of that capital awakened in him a consciousness of his own talent. He took up the study of composition with Reicha, and spent a considerable portion of his life, at various intervals, in Paris. "Martha" had its origin as a ballet, "Harriette, ou la Servante de Greenwiche," text by Vernoy and St. George. That work was designed for the Grand Opéra, and as it was needed on very short notice, each of its three acts was assigned to a different composer, the first falling to the lot of Flotow. Of this ballet, intended for a French dancer and a French audience, Martha is a development. This fact, together with the composer's Parisian residence and training, may account for the music of "Martha" having an elegance and vivacity that are thoroughly French in character, although some students believe they find equally characteristic German traits in the score.

Overture—Parts I and II *Victor Symphony Orchestra* 35916-1.25

After a brief, tragic-seeming introduction there is heard a lovely horn solo, the melody of the dramatic finale of Act III. It grows to a climax played by the full orchestra. There follows (*beginning of Part II*) a restless little melody, not without a touch of cheerfulness. It develops into a passage of boisterous gaiety that is in turn followed by a rustic tune with the accompaniment of a jangling tambourine, the song of the servant girls at the Fair. These themes are then repeated and developed, the theme of the horn solo and the agitated melody above mentioned being cleverly combined. All ends in merriment.

ACT I

SCENE I—*Boudoir of Lady Harriet*

THE young and beautiful Lady Harriet, maid of honor to Queen Anne, has grown weary of the elaborate monotony of court life. Admirers without number, dresses, jewels, flowers, social position, the distractions of the court, all have become for her an empty show. Her faithful maid, Nancy, discovers her weeping and tries to comfort her. Lady Harriet knows not why she weeps.

Harriet has a cousin, Sir Tristan Mickleford, a gay but rather tottery old beau. Skilled in the ways of women, he now proposes a new list of amusements, but Harriet rejects them all; moreover, the absurd airs of the old fop cause her to break into gales of laughter. Hearing, through the open window, the song of the servant maids on their way to Richmond Fair, Harriet has a characteristic inspiration—she will go with them! Nancy and Tristan object, but she orders them along with her. Another brilliant idea— Harriet remembers the peasant costumes they wore at the Queen's ball last week—they will wear these. Sir Tristan will assume the name "John," Nancy will go as "Julia," Harriet will be "Martha."

SCENE II—*The Fair at Richmond*

The fair is in full swing—crowded with farmers and their wives, and servants in search of work; for it is the custom of the age for farmers to seek their hired help at the fair. Two young farmers, Lionel and Plunkett, appear in the crowd. From their conversation we learn that Lionel is Plunkett's adopted brother and that Lionel's father, a mysterious stranger—passing through the neighborhood, left behind him a ring with instructions that if

Mishkin

GIGLI AS LIONEL

his son ever found himself in danger or difficulty he should present it to the Queen. Lionel is such a firm friend of Plunkett and has been so happy in his country life that he has had no desire to see the court or to test the ring's potency.

Soon the disguised ladies appear with the harassed Tristan. The two young farmers see the girls, and attracted by their obvious good looks, offer to hire them. Carried off by the spirit of their prank, the two "girls" accept in spite of Tristan's remonstrances. They take the money proffered them, not knowing that by doing this they legally bind themselves to serve their masters for a year. Tristan wishes the girls to return with him, but he is hooted off the grounds, and the now terrified "servants" are led away by the two farmers. Work threatens!

ACT II

SCENE—*A Farmhouse*

WHEN the two young men get their new servants home they soon discover that they have some unexpected characters to deal with. They show the girls the room that is to be theirs, and at once the fair young things exclaim that they are tired and propose to shut themselves up in it. The farmers have to remind them that there is work to be done first. Plunkett wishes to have his orders carried out at once, but Lionel, who seems to have an inborn gallantry, is touched at the sight of the unhappy beauties, and in order to let them down easily, suggests that they first do some spinning. "Spinning?" They don't know how! The men have to sit down to show them! The orchestra begins a merry tune that continues at its breakneck speed throughout this entire number. Rapid scales and darting staccato passages are illustrative of the bustle of getting out the spinning wheels and fetching chairs to place beside them. The men sing brr—brr—in imitation of the hum of the wheels: the girls lift their voices in song telling of their delight at watching the skill of the men in this operation of spinning, doubtless something heretofore unknown to them. Nancy brings the lesson to an unexpected close by upsetting Plunkett's spinning wheel and running out of the room. Plunkett dashes after her.

This gives the susceptible Lionel an opportunity to declare his feelings to Martha. Although he assures her that he will be a kind and gentle master to her, she smilingly replies that she will not be a good servant, for she knows how to do nothing except to laugh and joke. That matters not to Lionel. He wishes her to be happy, laughing and singing always. He begs her for one little song now, and in his elation he snatches a rose she is wearing. This gives her a cue, and she sings to him "The Last Rose of Summer." (This is an old Irish melody, "The Groves of Blarney," to which Tom Moore adapted his poem.)

Last Rose of Summer *Amelita Galli-Curci* 1355-1.50 *Victor String Ensemble* 24114-.75

The young man is apparently hypnotized by her song, and in ecstasy kneels before her and cries out that he no longer thinks of her rank, love has elevated her to his position. Martha bursts out laughing at the thought of *her* being raised to a farmer's rank. Her laughter drives the smitten Lionel to distraction.

Fortunately this strained situation is broken up by the noisy return of Nancy and Plunkett. A saucy little melody is played by the orchestra as they return *(beginning of the Quartetto Notturno)* and Plunkett exclaims to Nancy, whom he is holding fast, "Don't you try this game again, girl!" Then

267

SCHIPA AS LIONEL

he continues to Lionel, "Where do you suppose she was? This vixen was in the kitchen breaking glasses, dishes and bottles . . . spilled all our wine . . . at last I've caught her!" Nancy insists, "Let me go!" The two begin a genuine combat; Nancy is no weakling, a worthy opponent of the farmer. Luckily before any harm is done the clock strikes and all exclaim in their surprise, "Midnight!" Lionel sings a beautiful melody, wishing them all good night, and pleasant dreams. Nancy replies, "Yes, good night! such night as never we have lived to see before; if I were only away from here, I'd never play the peasant any more!"

Then as the young men demurely take their leave, all four of the young people unite in a final quartet of great loveliness wishing one another good night.

Left alone for the first time, the girls hold a hurried consultation and agree that they must get out of this escapade at once—how? What would the Queen say if she were to hear of it? They tremble at the thought. There is a stealthy tap at the window, Sir Tristan has come to their rescue. He has a carriage waiting, and the supposed servants make their escape.

ACT III

Scene—*Hunting Park in Richmond Forest*

THE young farmers have come to watch the Queen and her train at the hunt, in the hope that thereby they may forget the fascinating servants who so mysteriously left them. Plunkett is at an Inn with a crowd of his peasant friends and leads in a song praising that good old English beer-like drink called porter; a rousing tune, sturdy as an English oak, and with these words:

> I want to ask you, can you not tell,
> What to our land, the British strand
> Gives life and power? say!
> It is old porter, brown and stout,
> We may of it be justly proud,
> It guides John Bull, where'er he be,
> Through fogs and mists, through land and sea!
> Yes, hurrah! the hops, and hurrah! the malt,
> They are life's flavor and life's salt.
> Hurrah! Tra, la, la, la, la, la, la, la!
> And that explaineth where'er it reigneth
> Is joy and mirth! At ev'ry hearth

Resounds a joyous song.
Look at its goodly color here!
Where else can find you such good beer?
So brown and stout and healthy, too!
The porter's health I drink to you!

The farmers and Plunkett go away leaving Lionel alone, pale and distracted, to meditate on his hopeless love. Forgetting the praises of porter, he sings "M'appari," one of the most popular of operatic songs:

Like a dream bright and fair,
Chasing ev'ry thought of care,
Those sweet hours pass'd with thee
Made the world all joy for me.
But, alas! thou art gone,
And that dream of bliss is o'er.
Ah, I hear now the tone
Of thy gentle voice no more;
Oh! return happy hours
Fraught with hope so bright.
Come again sunny days of pure delight
Fleeing vision cloth'd in brightness,
Wherefore thus, so soon depart?
O'er my pathway shed thy lightness once again,
And glad my heart.

M'appari *(Like a Dream)* **Tito Schipa 6570-2.00   Enrico Caruso 7720-2.00   Beniamino Gigli 7109-2.00   Anthony Galla-Rini** *(Piano-accordion solo)* **25413-.75**

Lady Harriet now comes wandering to this place. A member of the royal hunting party, she is again unhappy in her gay court life and has wandered off in order to be alone and pine over her loveless fate, for truly, Cupid must have been at that farmhouse and wounded all four of the young

Photo Byron   THE FAIR SCENE

people. Though surprised at seeing her in the garb of a lady of the court, Lionel at once declares his love. Disregarding the promptings of her heart, Harriet pretends that she has never before seen him. In his excitement, Lionel goes so far as to remind her that by law she is his bound servant. She calls aloud to the other hunters for help and declares to them that this man must be insane. Lionel is arrested, but before he is led away, he gives to Plunkett his ring requesting him to give it to the Queen, whose approach is now announced.

ACT IV

Scene I—*Plunkett's Farmhouse*

ALTHOUGH the ring has wrought a great improvement in Lionel's fortune, yet his unhappiness is by no means over. The ring has proved that he is the son of the late Earl of Derby whose title and estate he now inherits. But of what use is that, for the cruel treatment of Harriet has turned his mind. The Lady, now that Lionel's high station has been revealed, is quite willing to indulge in her love for him. She comes to him at his farmhouse and in hopes of restoring his reason, sings again "The Last Rose of Summer." Even this fails. She avows her thorough repentance and pleads for forgiveness; Lionel's clouded mind can think only of one thing, her heartless, cruel treatment; the former gentle gallant hurls reproaches at her and rushes from the room leaving her in tears.

Nancy has no such hindrance as lofty birth to keep her from returning Plunkett's proffered affection. Their friendship for Lionel and Harriet, in fact, helps bring these two obstreperous souls together, as they lay a plan for attempting to reunite their friends.

Scene II—*A Representation of the Richmond Fair*

The scene changes and we behold a part of Lady Harriet's private grounds where a crowd of merrymakers is trying to reproduce the Richmond Fair as exactly as possible. Farmers and their wives and maid-servants are all there in the midst of their bargaining. Into this Lionel is gently led by the trusty Plunkett. The well-remembered sights and sounds work like a magic potion on the befogged brain. Lionel is himself once again. An instant later and his "Martha" is in his arms; Nancy likewise yields to Plunkett; meanwhile all join in singing heartily the melody of "The Last Rose of Summer," but with the words, "The Spring Has Returned, Fresh Roses Now Bloom."

METROPOLITAN SETTING FOR THE MASKED BALL

THE MASKED BALL

(Un Ballo in Maschera)

OPERA in three acts; music by Giuseppe Verdi; words by Somma, after Scribe's libretto for Auber's "Gustave III, ou Le Bal Masque." First produced, February 17, 1859, at the Apollo Theatre, Rome. First performance in the United States, February 11, 1861, at the Academy of Music, New York.

The opera has some historical foundation in that Gustavus III, of Sweden, was assassinated during a masked ball at Stockholm. As luck would have it, while rehearsals of Verdi's opera were in progress, an Italian revolutionist made an attempt on the life of Napoleon III. Naturally the authorities forbade a performance of the opera. The composer refused to adapt his music to an entirely different libretto. As a result great excitement prevailed in Naples. Crowds of people paraded, shouting "Viva Verdi!" using the popular composer's name as a slight disguise for the fact that they were favoring a united Italy under Victor Emanuel, thus: Vittorio Emmanuele Re D'Italia (Victor Emanuel, King of Italy). A strange use for the letters of a composer's name! As a way out of the difficulty, the censor at Rome suggested that the title be changed and the scene transferred to Boston. The assassination of a governor in provincial Boston would not disturb the authorities. A colonial governor singing on the Italian operatic stage is an amusing thing for an American to contemplate, and Europe having recovered from its fear of royal assassinations, the scene of the opera is now frequently placed in Naples.

(The name of the opera is in Italian, "Un Ballo in Maschera," *Oon Bahl'-loh in Mahs'-keh-rah,* although literally "A Masked Ball" has come to be known as "The Masked Ball.")

271

The action takes place in Boston (or Naples), during the late Seventeenth (or middle Eighteenth) Century.

Among the assembly gathered at the house of Richard, Count of Warwick and Governor of Boston, are two of his enemies, Samuel and Thomas. Many of the others are friendly towards the Governor, however, and when he enters sing his praises. He greets them with assurances of his interest in their welfare. Then his page, Oscar, presents him with a list of the guests invited to the Governor's ball. Richard reads the list until he comes to one name that makes him start with delight; he exclaims:

> Amelia—dear sweet name!
> Its mere sound fills my heart with joy!
> Her beauteous, charming image
> Inspires my soul with love . . .

Meanwhile Oscar and the people unite in singing the praises of the Governor—"Our welfare and protection are still his sole desire," and the conspirators, headed by Samuel and Thomas, agree that:

> The hour is not propitious
> To carry out our mission;
> From this unsafe position
> 'Tis better to retire.

These varied sentiments are expressed in a highly melodious quartet and chorus.

A negro woman, Ulrica, is brought in and accused of being a witch. Richard laughs at the accusation and dismisses the woman. He calls his courtiers around him, and suggests that for a lark they go disguised to the hut of the sorceress and consult her. All agree, his enemies seeing a chance to further their plan.

The Governor, dressed as a sailor, arrives at the witch's cottage with his companions. While they are conversing a knock is heard. At Ulrica's request all leave the hut—all save Richard, who conceals himself in a corner. A veiled woman enters. It is none other than Amelia whom Richard loves. She returns his affection, although she is the wife of Reinhart, the Governor's secretary and most trusted friend. She desires to remain a loyal wife and asks the sorceress to give her peace of mind by banishing a love which she cannot control. Ulrica tells her of an herb from which can be brewed a magic potion; to be effective it must be gathered only at night near a gallows.

Amelia departs, the people re-enter, and Richard, in his sailor's disguise, asks to be told his fortune. The request takes the form of a barcarolle—a favorite type of sea-song. This barcarolle is famous for its rollicking swing and bantering humor—a number which Caruso sang with inimitable style.

> Declare if the waves will faithfully bear me;
> If weeping the lov'd from whom I now tear me,
> Farewell to me saying, my love is betraying.

Ulrica rebukes him, and examining his palm, tells him he is soon to die

272

by the sword of that friend who shall next shake his hand. Oscar and the courtiers exclaim in horror at her pronouncement *(beginning of the famous Quintet, "E scherzo")*. Ulrica insists that such is the decree of relentless fate. Samuel and Thomas are fearful lest their plot be discovered, although Richard sings jestingly:

> But food for mirth and mocking,
> This prophecy so shocking,
> In faith perforce it makes me laugh,
> Their woeful looks to note.

Reinhart enters anxious for the safety of Richard, for he has learned of the conspiracy. Happy at finding him, he greets him with a vigorous shake of the hand. Richard tells the witch she is a poor fortune-teller, for this is the best friend he ever had, and throws her a fat purse. For his bravery and gallantry he wins the applause of the people.

Amelia goes by night to seek the magic herb at the foot of the gallows. She sings a dramatic aria, praying heaven to release her from her hopeless love. A clock striking midnight, she fancies that she sees a phantom rising before her.

> When at last from its stem I shall sever
> Yonder weed of dread virtue enchanted,
> From my tempest-torn bosom forever
> That image so ethereal shall perish . . .
> Come, oh, Death, let thy merciful dart,
> Still forever my poor throbbing heart!
>
> Hark! 'tis midnight! Ah, yon vision!
> Moving, breathing, lo! a figure,
> All mist-like upward wreathing!
> Ha! in those orbits baleful anger is seething;
> Fix'd on me they angrily burn!
> Deign, oh, Heaven, Thy strength to impart
> To this fainting, fear-stricken heart.

The vision resolves itself into Richard, who now approaches. Although she confesses her love, she begs him to leave. Reinhart suddenly appears; he has come to warn the governor that his life is in danger; he must escape down a side path. Reinhart consents to Richard's request to conduct this veiled lady back to the city without speaking or otherwise trying to learn

Copy't Mishkin
TOMASO

her identity. He is prevented from doing so by the arrival of the conspirators, who, enraged at the escape of the governor, tear the veil from the woman's face. Reinhart beholds his wife! Filled with terrific rage, he arranges for a secret meeting with the conspirators.

At home with Amelia, he assails her with the most bitter fury, and is at the point of killing her. She swears that she is innocent and begs for a moment's respite to bid farewell to their child. This request he grants.

human and amusing "Meistersinger." Because of this very human quality and thoroughly good humor, "Die Meistersinger" early became one of the most popular of Wagner's works and has continued to grow in public favor.

Instead of his usual legendary source, Wagner depends upon actual history to furnish him the basis of his comedy. He at first conceived the work as a sort of humorous after-piece for "Tannhäuser." In that opera Wagner had treated of the Medieval Minnesingers, who were nobles and sang poetically of exalted love—German counterparts of the French Trouvères. But like the chivalry of which they were an expression, the Minnesingers disappeared with the coming of the Renaissance. In their place there arose among the middle class trade guilds, bands of singers who, patterning themselves after the Minnesingers, took the name Mastersingers (Meistersinger). In order to become an acknowledged member of one of these groups of "Mastersingers," the ambitious youth, while learning his trade, was obliged also to study the arts of singing and poetry and, by dint of passing various examinations, work his way up through the several degrees of "Scholars," "Schoolmen," "Singers," "Poets," and finally "Masters." The purpose of the guild, to foster a love of the best in art, was indeed noble; but in the course of time, The Mastersingers' Guild quite naturally arrogated to itself an undeserved importance, and ascribed an undue value to pedantic and traditional rules. Most famous of the Mastersingers was Hans Sachs, cobbler, poet and dramatist, who lived at Nuremberg (1494-1576).

Wagner undoubtedly made a thorough historical research before he wrote this life-like picture of life in Nuremberg, crowded with amusing and picturesque details. Even two of the musical motives, "The Banner" and "The Art Brotherhood," are gleaned from some "Prize Master Tones" included in an old book by J. C. Wagenseil, printed at Nuremberg in 1697. Yet Wagner does not thrust his history upon us; it forms a diverting background for the story he has to tell. Likewise his music, uniting an amazing wealth of the most clever contrapuntal detail, perhaps intentionally reminiscent at times of one of the great Organ Fugues in C major by J. S. Bach, ranking among the most inspired compositions ever written, grows from Wagner's high conception of the poetic idea embodied in his narrative. This poetic idea is represented in the struggle between the liberal-minded young Walter, who, reformer-like, would cast aside every tradition in order to express his thoughts freely, and Beckmesser, who, like the hidebound conservative critics, opposes all progress in the arts. The fair-minded Hans Sachs represents enlightened public opinion, respectful of the great masters, yet open to acknowledge valuable and justifiable innovations.

Certain portions of the opera have become favorites on concert programs, notably the Overture, called by Wagner simply *Vorspiel*.

CHARACTERS

The Mastersingers (or Die Meistersinger, pronounced *My-ster-zing-er*):

HANS SACHS, *cobbler*	*Bass*
POGNER, *goldsmith*	*Bass*
BECKMESSER, *town clerk*	*Bass*

VOGELGESANG, *furrier;* NACHTIGAL, *buckle maker;* KOTHNER, *baker;* ZORN, *pewterer;* EIS-SLINGER, *grocer;* MOSER, *tailor;* ORTEL, *soap boiler;* SCHWARZ, *stocking weaver;* FOLZ, *coppersmith*

SIR WALTER VON STOLZING, *a young Franconian knight*	*Tenor*
DAVID, *apprentice to Hans Sachs*	*Tenor*
EVA, *Pogner's daughter*	*Soprano*
MAGDALENA, *Eva's nurse*	*Soprano*

Burghers of all Guilds, Journeymen, Apprentices, Girls and People.

Scene: Nuremberg in the middle of the Sixteenth Century.

The Overture begins at once with the theme of the Mastersingers, assertive, pompous,

THE MASTERSINGERS

even stolid, but nevertheless of genuine worth and beauty.

After these characteristics of the Mastersingers have been emphasized by repetition, the

WAKING LOVE

placid, spring-like motive of "Waking Love" is heard in the wood-wind. This soon gives

THE BANNER

way before the proud "Banner" of the Mastersingers, emblem of all the self-complacent pride of that group of tradesmen-musicians. Closely joined with it is the suave theme of

THE ART BROTHERHOOD

the "Art Brotherhood," the melody with which the citizens of Nuremberg hymn their praise of all that is finest in their native art. This is developed to a magnificent climax;

LOVE CONFESSED

then follows a motive expressive of Walter's love, the motive of "Longing." This leads directly into the beautifully lyric theme that will finally blossom in its fullest glory during the "Prize Song," the theme of "Love Confessed." It, in turn, grows directly into the more impassioned motive of "Love's Ardor." These melodies are then combined, and,

LOVE'S ARDOR

"Love's Ardor" seemingly in the ascendancy, developed into a climax. This climax is suddenly broken off and we hear the pompous theme of the Mastersingers, parodied in a perkish manner by the wood-wind. Into this the motives of "Love's Ardor," "The Art Brotherhood" and "Longing" make various attempts to enter. In the bass is heard the

RIDICULE

derisive theme of "Ridicule." "Love's Ardor" again triumphant, there is a dazzling climax during which the motive of the "Mastersingers" sounds forth in the bass, like a call to arms. As this tumult subsides we hear in broad, magnificent phrases the theme of "Love Confessed," veritably sung by the violins, while far below, like the most solid of foundations, is played the motive of the "Mastersingers"; at the same time, wood-wind instruments in the middle voices chatter along with the "Banner"—one of the most remarkable feats of combining themes ever achieved; yet there were once musicians who said that Wagner knew no counterpoint! These various motives are then heard separately, in ever-growing sonority and richness, until the very end of the overture.

Overture *Karl Muck-Berlin State Opera Or. (Included in Album M-37) Frederick Stock-Chicago Symphony Orch. 6651-2.00 Leopold Stokowski and the Philadelphia Orchestra* (In Preparation).

277

Landesman

THE CHURCH OF ST. CATHERINE (CLEVELAND SYMPHONY ORCHESTRA PERFORMANCE)

ACT I

WITH the very last chord of the overture, the curtain rises and we behold the Church of St. Catherine in Nuremberg, and hear the people there gathered for a service, singing a fine, stately choral to Saint John, for this is the eve of that Saint's day.

Only a few of the last rows of pews are visible. One of them is occupied by Eva and her nurse, Magdalena. At one side, leaning against a pillar, is Walter von Stolzing. According to a custom of the period, at the end of each line of the choral that is being sung, long pauses occur; during these pauses, Walter and Eva exchange glances. The knight is evidently much enamoured of the girl, and she, though very modest, betrays considerable interest in him. Their pleasant agitation is beautifully expressed by the orchestra during these pauses.

Kirchenchor *(Church Scene)* **Berlin State Opera Chorus-Orch. 9160-1.50**

When the choral is ended and the congregation leaves, Walter, who is a stranger in Nuremberg, for the first time learns that Eva's father has a singular plan in view: he intends to give his daughter as bride to the winner of the song-contest on the morrow, in which none but a Master of the guild may compete.

Walter promptly decides to become a Master and win the contest, though he has not the slightest idea of the necessary process involved. Magdalena is called to assist, and she in turn calls upon David, the young apprentice, who on pain of his sweetheart's displeasure, is to try to instruct Walter in the

278

rules of the art of the Mastersingers' Guild. As there is to be a test immediately, David begins instruction at once, while his brother apprentices are arranging the chairs and furniture for the Guild meeting. But David, an apprentice cobbler as well as musician, so mixes his instructions concerning the rules of art with comment concerning the rules of his trade that Walter is more confused than helped.

In due course the Mastersingers arrive and their roll is called. Pogner addresses them, saying that he offers his daughter, Eva, in marriage to the winner of the coming contest, provided that he also meets with her approval.

Das schöne Fest, Johannistag *(The Feast of St. John)* **Alexander Kipnis 7894-2.00**

Walter asks to be given a trial for admission to the Mastersingers' Guild. The Masters consent, although surprised at his boldness.

Am stillen Herd *(By Silent Hearth)* **Max Lorenz 11162-1.50**

Beckmesser, their duly appointed "Marker," takes his place in the enclosed stand erected for him. Besides being a formidable stickler for rules, he is also eager to wed Eva; the result can well be imagined. Walter's freely improvised song

Fanget an *(Now Begin)* **Max Lorenz 11162-1.50**

is constantly punctuated by the sound of the scratching of the pencil on a slate as the Marker notes down his "errors." At the end of the first verse the Masters refuse to hear any more. Hans Sachs alone is willing to go further,

German Railroads Information Office

BECKMESSER SERENADES EVA DISGUISED AS MAGDALENA

279

for, being a Master of true worth, he has detected in the song a touch of genuine inspiration. He admits that it may disregard the "rules" of the Guild, but suggests that it may be governed by other rules justified by its character. He is shouted down, however, and the indignant young knight is dismissed amid the jeers of the apprentices. Thus the trial has ended in confusion, and Sachs turns away in a mood half-humorous, half-despairing.

ACT II

A Street in Nuremberg. The Houses of Pogner and Hans Sachs, separated from each other by a Narrow Alley, but both facing the same Broader Street, which is shown sectionally across the stage

As night falls over the town the apprentices are busily putting up the shutters on the quaint old Nuremberg houses. Meanwhile they sing in joyful anticipation of the midsummer festival. They are disposed to ridicule David, who has suffered Magdalena's ire as a result of Walter's failure. Sachs drives them away, chasing David off to bed, but first he has his workman's bench so placed that at the same time he can work at his cobbling and still watch the street. But work he cannot, for the beauty of the summer's evening and recollections of Walter's song haunt his mind. The orchestra murmurs, like a merest breeze stirring the summer air, and Sachs, putting aside his work, meditates:

> The elder's scent is waxing
>   So mild, so full and strong!
> Its charm my limbs relaxing:
>   Words unto my lips would throng.
>   . . . . . .
> But I'd better stick to my leather
> And let all this poetry be!—
> *(He tries again to work.)*
> And yet—it haunts me still.—
> I feel, but comprehend ill:—
> Cannot forget it, and yet cannot grasp it.—
> I measure it not, e'en when I clasp it.
> But how then would I gauge it?
> 'Twas measureless to my mind;
> No rule could fit it or cage it,
> Yet there was no fault to find.
> It seemed so old, yet new in its chime,—
> Like songs of birds in sweet May-time:—
> Spring's command
> And gentle hand
> His soul with this did entrust:
> He sang because he must!
> His power rose as needed;
> That virtue well heeded.
> The bird who sang today
>   Has a throat that rightly waxes;
> Masters may feel dismay,
>   But well content with him Hans Sachs is.

Was duftet doch der Flieder (*How Sweet the Elder's Scent*) **Kein' Regel wollte da passen** (*I Found No Rule That Would Fit It*) **Friedrich Schorr 7425-2.00**

Now Eva appears. Despairing of being able to win Walter for a husband, she half suggests that Sachs might be a welcome suitor.

Gut'n Abend, Meister! (*Good Evening, Master*) **Schorr-Ljungberg 7680-2.00 Ich seh'! 'swar nur** (*I See How It was*) **Schorr-Ljungberg 7680-2.00**

She has known and loved him from childhood, and is aware of his essential worth. Indeed, Sachs, a middle-aged widower, has had dreams of winning Eva for himself, but realizing full well that her deepest love is for Walter, this kindly soul will not put himself forward. He shakes his head over the turn of events, Eva leaves him, and he resumes his work. Soon he notices Walter and Eva across the street, talking together; they decide to elope, but Sachs "accidentally" places his lamp where the light will fall upon them, and they are deterred for fear of being seen. While they debate, however, a stranger approaches, and they draw back into the shadow. It is Beckmesser, who has come to serenade his mistress with the song he hopes to sing on the morrow. Sachs, hearing him tinkle on his lute, breaks in with a lusty song of his own, and Beckmesser is greatly discomfited.

Jerum! Jerum! (*Cobbler's Song*) **Friedrich Schorr 7426-2.00**

He pretends that he has come to inquire about a pair of shoes, and Sachs declares he is working on them. In the meanwhile, Magdalena appears at the window, by prearrangement in Eva's stead, and Beckmesser, thinking her to be Eva, wishes to sing more than ever. He pretends that he wants Hans Sachs to criticize the song, and Sachs agrees to act as "Marker," hammering on the shoe for every mistake. In this way, Beckmesser proceeds. In his agitation, however, his song runs wild, and Sachs hammers loudly. The thumping becomes more and more vehement as the mistakes of the now irate Beckmesser increase. The disturbance naturally arouses the neighbors, who begin peering through the windows. David also is awakened, and seeing the Town Clerk apparently serenading Magdalena, who is still at the window, he vows vengeance, and jumping quickly from his room, he proceeds to give the astonished Beckmesser a sound beating. Magdalena screams aloud at seeing her David fighting thus, and the townspeople, still in their curious nightgowns, hurry to the street. The trade-guild men, seeing two of their members fighting, follow their example and soon the street is in an uproar. Walter and Eva, who have been in hiding, decide that this is a good opportunity to elope; but the observant Sachs seizes the pair by the arm and pushes Eva in the door of Pogner's house. Then with a well-placed kick he sends David scurrying into his own house, whither he follows, drawing Walter after him. Meanwhile the good women of the town, distressed at the behavior of their husbands and sweethearts, suddenly throw water from the windows above down upon the fighters, who immediately scatter to the safety of their homes. At the self-same moment the night-watchman is heard sounding his horn in the distance. But when he reaches the scene of the disturbance all is quiet. He announces the hour, singing in a quavering voice his antique ditty:

> Hark to what I say, good people!
> Eleven strikes from every steeple;
> Defend you all from specter and sprite,
> Let no power of ill your souls affright.
> Praise the Lord of Heaven.

His horn is again heard in the distance as he wanders off, staff and lantern in hand, through the slumbering streets.

ACT III

SCENE I—*Interior of Sachs' Workshop*

Prelude *Leopold Stokowski and the Philadelphia Orchestra* 1584-1.50

THE third act is preceded by a remarkably beautiful prelude. It is built principally from the theme of Sachs' monologue, in which, during a moment of despair, he declares that all things human are but vanity; and from the fine choral with which the people greet him in the closing scene.

Landesman SACHS AND HIS APPRENTICE (CLEVELAND ORCHESTRA PRODUCTION)

The early morning sun streams through the window at which Sachs sits, so engrossed in reading a large folio that he does not notice when David enters with a basket of good things to eat. David has patched it up with Magdalena and he is, in consequence, happy; only he is fearful that his part in last night's disturbance will bring down a beating from his master. He begins to explain, declaring the night before was just a "polterabend"—a night of merrymaking on the festival of St. John. Sachs appears not to notice; but suddenly he asks the wondering youth to sing the song of the day—a carol of St. John. This tells the story of the child of a woman of Nuremberg christened in the River Jordan by Johannes, the saint, for whom he was named; but on his return to Nuremberg the name was abbreviated to "Hans." David is struck with a sudden thought, and exclaims joyfully, "Hans! Hans! why then it's your name day too, master!" and in almost childish glee offers Sachs the flowers and cakes that Magdalena had bestowed on him. Sachs kindly declines, and though still preoccupied, understands the 'prentice's hopes and desires, and dismisses him with a pleasant word. Sachs then sits in meditation—a meditation which becomes vocal in the stirring lines beginning with the words "Wahn, wahn, Ueberall Wahn."

Wahn! Wahn! Ueberall Wahn! (*Mad! Mad! The Whole World Is Mad!*) **Friedrich Schorr** 7319-2.00   **Ein Kobold** (*An Impish Spell*) **Friedrich Schorr** 7319-2.00

Walter, who has just awakened, enters from an adjoining room.

Grüss Gott, mein Junker! (*Greeting, Sir Knight*) **Schorr-Laubenthal** 7427-2.00

He is full of a wonderful dream he has had in which a marvelous poem and melody have sung their way into his heart. Sachs desires to hear it.

Mein Freund, in holder Jugendzeit (*My Friend, in My Bygone Youth*) **Schorr-Laubenthal** 7427-2.00

He is struck with amazement at its beauty and inspiration, and he tactfully instructs the young poet-composer in the technical requirements necessary to make it satisfactory to the judges.

After they have written down the poem they leave the room. Beckmesser enters, and notices the song, which he believes to be by Hans Sachs himself. After the manner of plagiarists the world over, he pockets it for his own use. When Sachs returns, the Town Clerk scolds him for planning to enter the contest. Sachs denies this. Beckmesser accordingly produces the manuscript, and Sachs, perceiving the man's mistake, does not undeceive him. On the contrary, he divines the fact that Beckmesser desires the poem, and knowing the Town Clerk incapable of making good use of it gives it to him, promising not to claim to be the real author. Beckmesser leaves greatly delighted.

Eva next enters, in festival attire.

Sieh' Ev'chen! (*Where Was Eva?*) **Rethberg-Schorr** 8195-2.00

Her shoe pinches, and Sachs, knowing well what is in her heart, pretends to busy himself adjusting the offending shoes. Walter enters, likewise in the most gorgeous of knightly costume. On seeing his adored one, he stands as in a trance, and softly sings the last stanza of his song. Overwhelmed with emotion, Eva sinks weeping into Sachs' arms. He also has been so deeply moved that, giving her into Walter's care, he needs must burst into a stanza of his sturdy cobbler's lay in order to control himself.

Hat man mit dem Schuhwerk! *(A Shoemaker's Life)* **Rethberg-Schorr 8195-2.00**

Eva vows her gratitude and love to her old friend, but Sachs sagaciously replies that he would avoid the fate of King Mark. At this the orchestra knowingly quotes a phrase from Tristan and Isolde. David and Magdalena now appear, also in gala attire. Hans invites them to a christening—he seeks to name Walter's song, a witness is needed, and as a mere 'prentice will not suffice, the kindly cobbler, with twinkling eyes, gives David his freedom, making him a full journeyman-cobbler by means of the customary box on the ear. David is overjoyed for now he will be able to marry his Magdalena. These five characters now give voice

Quintet—Selig wie die Sonne *(Brightly as the Sun)* **Schumann, Melchior, Schorr, Parr, Williams 7682-2.00**

to their mingled emotions of happiness, love, and for Sachs, mild sorrow, in an indescribably lovely quintet. Then they leave for the contest, David carefully closing the door after them.

Scene II—*A Field on the Shores of the River Pegnitz*

In an open meadow on the banks of the river, a great crowd of people assemble for the song-contest. The various trade guilds arrive in procession

ACT II—DR. HERBERT GRAF'S PRODUCTION AT SALZBURG, ESPECIALLY ARRANGED FOR TOSCANINI

. . . tailors . . . shoemakers . . . bakers. The band of youthful apprentices
is there also. A gaily decorated boat filled with girls arrives. The apprentices
hurry to help them ashore, then at once begin dancing with them, the orchestra accompanying with a most delightfully rustic, waltz-like tune. David
seizes a pretty girl and starts to dance with her; the other 'prentices frighten
him by saying his 'Lena is watching.

Dance of the Apprentices *Coates-Symphony Orchestra* **9060-1.50 Aha! da streicht
die Lene!** (*There's Magdalena*) *Friedrich Schorr* **7681-2.00**

Finally the Mastersingers arrive in great pomp, their banner with its picture of their patron, King David, carried at the head of the procession;
Pogner is leading Eva. All take their places on a raised platform at one side.
Sachs comes forward to address the assembly. At the sight of him the crowd
rises exultantly and breaks into a magnificent choral, the words (in quota-
tion) being taken from a poem by the historical Hans Sachs:

> "Awake! draws nigh the break of day:
> I hear upon the hawthorn spray
> A bonny little nightingale;
> His voice resounds o'er hill and dale.
> The night descends the western sky
> And from the east the morn draws nigh,
> With ardor red the blush of day
> Breaks through the cloud-bank dull and grey."
>> Hail, Sachs! Hans Sachs!
>> Hail Nuremberg's darling Sachs!

Wach' auf! es nahet gen den tag (*Awake! The Dawn of Day Draws Near*) *Berlin
State Opera Chorus-Orch.* **9160-1.50**

Sachs, deeply impressed, thanks them for their kindness, and announces
the terms of the contest.

Euch macht ihr's leicht (*Words Light to You*) *Friedrich Schorr* **7682-2.00**

Beckmesser, being the oldest of the contestants, is selected to begin. Still
sore from his beating of the previous night, grievously flustered, and with
his stolen song only half-learned, he attempts to wed the poem to his own
serenade-melody. The result is a hopeless jumble which first excites the
wonder, then the derision of the audience. Beckmesser, enraged, declares the
song is not his own but the work of Hans Sachs. The Masters believing this
a spiteful joke, call upon Sachs for an explanation. He then insists that the
song is good when properly sung, and persuades them to let it be interpreted
by the author, Walter von Stolzing. The crowd listens in wondering silence
as the young knight begins:

> Shining resplendent in dawn's rosy light,
> Air filled with bloom and sweet perfume,
> Where joys outmeasure
> Dreamed of pleasure,
> A garden doth invite.

And there beneath a magic tree,
Of fruits hung rich with treasure,
In blessed dream of love I see
What ardent thirst for pleasure
With promise doth entice,
The fairest maid:—
Eva in Paradise!

Closed round by shadows, surrounded by night,
By pathway steep
I reach a deep
And noble fountain on a mountain
Whose waves smile on me bright.
And there beneath a laurel tree
Through which the stars are gleaming,
The noblest woman's form I see
In waking poet dreaming,
While she with holy, gracious mien
My brow bedews.
Parnassus' sacred muse!

Most blessed day
When I from poet's dream awake!
Now what I dreamed of Paradise,
Divine in fresher glory, lies
Before my eyes,
While smiling still the fountain shows the way,
The maid Elysian
I saw in a vision,
She whom my heart doth choose,
Earth's fairest, and my muse,
So holy, grave, and good,
By me is boldly wooed,
Here by the day's bright sun,
By power of song is won
Parnassus and Paradise!

Prize Song *Richard Crooks* 7105-2.00 *(Violoncello)* **Pablo Casals** 6620-2.00
Mischa Elman 7649-2.00 *Marek Weber's Orchestra* 24773-.75

The beauty and expressiveness of the melody are beyond all description; around it a glowing orchestral accompaniment seems lovingly to entwine itself.

Abendlich glühend *(The Light of Evening)* **Schorr-Melchior-London Symphony** *Orchestra* 7681-2.00

The people listen with growing enthusiasm, and at the close of the song the Masters rise and acclaim Walter as victor. Eva confers on her lover a wreath of laurel and myrtle, then leads him to her father, before whom they both kneel. Pogner extends his hands over them in benediction and presents the emblem of the Masters' guild to the young knight. But Walter, remembering his reception of the day before, and conscious also of his noble birth, refuses the honor. In consternation, all turn towards Sachs. The poet-cobbler

FINALE FROM THE HERBERT GRAF PRODUCTION IN SALZBURG; TOSCANINI CONDUCTING

goes to Walter, takes him impressively by the hand, and, while the orchestra brings in review many of the motives first heard in the overture, says:

Disparage not the Masters' ways,
But show respect to Art!

*   *   *   *   *

Not through your ancestors and birth,
Not by your weapons' strength and worth,
But by a poet's brain
Which Mastership did gain,
You have attained your present bliss;
Then think you thankfully on this:
How can you e'er the Art despise
Which can bestow so rare a prize!

*   *   *   *   *

If not so honored as of yore,
When courts and princes prized her more,
In troublous years all through
She's German been and true;
And if she has not won renown
Beyond this bustling, busy town,
You see she has our full respect:
What more from us can you expect?
Beware! Bad times are nigh at hand.

*   *   *   *   *

Our native Art will fade from hence
If 'tis not held in reverence.
So heed my words:—
Honor your German Masters
If you would stay disasters!

287

For while they dwell in every heart,
Though should depart
The pride of holy Rome,
Still thrives at home
Our Sacred German art!

Verachtet mir die Meister nicht *(Disparage Not the Masters' Ways)* **Was Deutsch
und echt** *(Our Native Art Will Fade)* **Friedrich Schorr** 9285-1.50

Walter now is willing to accept the Mastersingers' emblem. Sachs embraces the couple, who then remain standing beside him, Walter at one hand, Eva at the other. Before this group Pogner kneels as if in homage. Thus the cobbler-musician and the two lovers become symbols of Art and Life, enshrined in the incomparable splendor of the song of the people *(closing portion of Record 9285-B)* who repeat the final words of their beloved cobbler-poet, and shout exultantly:

Though should depart
The pride of holy Rome,
Still thrives at home
Our Sacred German art!
Hail Sachs! Hans Sachs!
Hail Nuremberg's darling Sachs!

PURIFICATION BY FIRE

MERRY MOUNT

OPERA in four acts, five scenes. Music by Howard Hanson; libretto by Richard L. Stokes. First produced, 1933, at the Metropolitan Opera House, New York, by the Metropolitan Opera Company, with Lawrence Tibbett in the leading rôle.

THIS is one of the operas staged by the Metropolitan in response to continued demand for native American works. Indigenous operas have not always been happily chosen, and seldom have enjoyed a happy fate. While on one side there is a vociferous group demanding that native talent be exploited in the creative field as well as in the sphere of interpretation, there is another group, quietly and stubbornly satisfied with the standard operatic repertoire, and stubbornly uninterested in anything new. Furthermore, the hybrid art that we call opera cannot be said to be *en rapport* with the spirit of American life, and while we can understand it as a manifestation of life in foreign countries, we find it difficult to accept as a product of our own habit of thought and living. Doubtless it is for this reason also that the demand for opera in English makes so little progress.

"Merry Mount" has a certain historical basis, but a sketchy one, which need not concern us here. The *locale* is near what is now the city of Quincy, Massachusetts,—virtually the gateway to Cape Cod. The time is May, 1625. The characters are Puritans, Indians, and a group of Cavaliers, whose ideas are anything but puritanical. The story revolves about the conflict between these groups; the tyrannical asceticism of the Puritan clergyman, wrestling Bradford; his—to his mind—sinful passion for Lady Marigold Sandys; witch-

289

craft, and the penitential suicide of Bradford by fire, into which he leap
with Lady Marigold in his arms.

The single aria by which the opera is represented on Victor Records, i
drawn from Act I. In it, the preacher Bradford, tormented night and day—
but especially at night—by his blind and half-understood passion, declaim
of a world that is full of demons, of evil and of temptation—mostly in th
form of fair women.

'Tis an Earth Defiled   *Lawrence Tibbett* 7959-2.00

𝒜MIGNON

OPERA in three acts by Ambroise Thomas; libretto based on Goethe's "Wilhelm Meister,
by Barbier and Carré. First produced, November 1′
1866, at the Opéra Comique, Paris. First performe
in the United States, at the Academy of Music, Nev
York, November 22, 1871. Revived by Metropolita
Opera Company, March 10, 1927, with Marion Talle
Lucrezia Bori, Beniamino Gigli and Clarence White
hill.

PINZA AS LOTHARIO

Charles Louis Ambroise Thomas, born at Met
August 2, 1811, came honestly by his creative talen
for he was the son of a musician. Like Gounod b
was an artist, poet and author, a man of unusu
versatility. In 1871 he was appointed director of th
famous Conservatoire at Paris; he filled this post wit
great distinction until his death, February 12, 189
Thomas possessed an inborn instinct for the stag
was a master of all moods, and displayed remarkab
skill in his orchestration. Had he only possessed
little more individuality and daring in the concep
tion of melody, he would probably rank among th
great musical leaders of his epoch. Nevertheless w
can gladly give him all credit due for his music
style—easy, fluent and brilliant.

CHARACTERS

MIGNON *(Meen'-yon), a young girl stolen by gypsies*   Mezzo-Sopran
PHILINE *(Fee-leen), generally known under the Italian name,* FILINA *(Fil-leé-nah), a*
  actress   Sopran
FREDERICK *(Fray-day-reek), a young nobleman*   Buffo Tenor or Contralt
WILHELM *(Veel-elm), a student on his travels*   Ten
LAERTES *(Layr'-tayz), an actor*   Ten
LOTHARIO *(Loh-tah'ree-oh), an Italian nobleman*   Basso Cantant
GIARNO *(Gee-ahr-no), a gypsy*   Ba
Townsfolk, Peasants, Gypsies, Actors and Actresses.

*The scene of Acts I and II is laid in Germany; Act III in Italy. Time: Late Eighteent
Century.*

290

THE OVERTURE, well known the world over as a concert piece, is a typical example of that grace and delicacy so characteristic of the French school of operatic music. It opens with a tranquil introduction in which a harp cadenza occupies a position of prominence, reminding us of the minstrel Lothario. There follows in the luscious tones of a horn *solo*, the melody, "Knowest Thou the Land?" This is taken up by the violins, fading away in calm, mysterious heights. Next is heard a brilliant polonaise, or polacca movement, "I'm Fair Titania," vivacious and frivolous like Filina herself, and the overture concludes in gaiety.

Overture *Frederick Stock-Chicago Symphony Orch.* 6650-2.00

ACT I

SCENE—*Courtyard of a German Inn*

MIGNON, daughter of noble parents, has been stolen from her home by gypsies. Soon thereafter, her mother dies of grief, and her father, Lothario, driven nearly mad by the loss, wanders abroad as a minstrel in search of his child.

At the opening of the opera, Lothario has found his way to the courtyard of a German inn where a crowd of people are having a gay time drinking and feasting. Now broken with age, Lothario's memory has left him, so that his name and home are forgotten; yet he is still blindly seeking his lost daughter whom he vaguely believes to be alive.

Into the courtyard comes a troupe of gypsies. Giarno, their mercenary leader, orders Mignon to dance for the crowd. Mignon, now grown to a singular, half-boyish looking figure, has become tired of her master's insolent commands and refuses to go through her performance. Giarno at once threatens to beat her. Lothario, stirred with a sudden sympathy for this young girl, runs to protect her, but the feeble old man is powerless before the gypsy. Thus it happens that a young student, Wilhelm, who is looking on, rushes to the rescue, and with his pistol forces Giarno to release the girl. In gratitude she divides a bouquet between her rescuers. Wilhelm receives the applause of the bystanders, including a troupe of travelling actors among whom is Filina. This beautiful young actress of designing temperament succeeds in attracting Wilhelm's attention, much to the jealousy of Frederick, a young nobleman.

Curious about the girl he has rescued, Wilhelm questions her regarding her childhood. She remembers nothing except that she was captured when a child by gypsies in some far away country that she describes in the very charming air, "Connais tu le pays?" One of the most well loved melodies in the entire range of opera, it begins thus:

Peyton

BORI AS MIGNON

291

The passionate longing of the orphan for the home of her infancy is expressed in a fine climax:

Connais-tu le pays? *(Knowest Thou the Land?)* *Lucrezia Bori* 1361-1.50

Knowest thou yonder land where the orange grows,
Where the fruit is of gold, and so fair the rose?
Where the breeze gently wafts the song of birds,
Where the season round is mild as lover's words?
Where so calm and so soft, like heaven's blessing true,
Spring eternally reigns, with the skies ever blue?
Alas, why afar am I straying, why ever linger here?
'Tis with thee I would fly!
'Tis there! 'Tis there! my heart's love obeying,
'Twere bliss to live and die!
'Tis there my heart's love obeying,
I'd live, I would die!

Moved to pity, Wilhelm arranges to buy the girl's freedom from her master. Mignon is entirely infatuated with her rescuer and wishes to follow him on his travels, but Wilhelm, rather embarrassed, suggests she remain in the village with some kind-hearted people. At this Mignon is very unhappy, and agrees to accompany the aged Lothario, who, moved by some subtle parental instinct, has come back to bid her good-bye. Realizing the impracticability of that, Wilhelm yields to the girl's entreaties—she may go with him disguised as a servant.

Filina receives an invitation to visit the castle of Prince Tieffenbach with the troupe of actors and any guests she may care for. She promptly invites Wilhelm, whom she desires to captivate. He willingly accepts her invitation to go as poet of the company.

ACT II

Scene I—*A Boudoir in the Tieffenbach Castle*

The second act is preceded by the very popular Intermezzo, a dainty Gavotte.

Intermezzo *(Gavotte)* *Stokowski-Philadelphia Orchestra* 7456-2.00 *Florentine Quartet* 20443-.75

FILINA sits at her mirror, considering her charms and laying on cosmetics. She is thinking of Wilhelm, for she is much infatuated with this handsome, romantic student. Soon he enters, accompanied by Mignon, who is greeted by the actress with civil yet subtly "cattish" remarks. The poor girl does not resent this, however, and curling up in a great chair by the fire, apparently goes to sleep. Yet she observes, under half-closed lids, that Wilhelm is paying court to the actress, to whom he has given the bouquet of blooms presented to him by Mignon herself. Presently Filina and Wilhelm leave, and Mignon, dreaming that she may equal the actress' charm, goes to the adjoining room to try on one of Filina's many gowns. Frederick leaps in through the window (*beginning of Record 1361*). "I'm here," he exclaims; "I've broken all the rules of etiquette, but I'm here!" Then he begins to sing the ever-popular Gavotte telling of his rapture at being in his beloved Filina's room.

By Hans Printz

MIGNON AND LOTHARIO

Gavotte—Me voici dans son boudoir (*Here Am I in Her Boudoir*) *Lucrezia Bori* 1361-1.50

Wilhelm unexpectedly enters, in search of Mignon. Jealous accusations concerning affairs with Filina are exchanged by the young men. In the heat of their quarrel they draw swords, but Mignon rushes in between them. Frederick recognizes Filina's gown on her and goes away laughing. Wilhelm has realized the difficult situations that may arise from having the girl following him about, and has come to tell Mignon that they must part. She begins to cry, saying that it is Filina who has persuaded him to drive her away. He tries to calm her fears singing:

> Farewell, Mignon take courage.
> Nay, never weep!
> In the bright days of Youth sorrow lingers but briefly:
> Kind heav'n will thee console!
> With thee my thoughts will go!
> Thy tears control!

Addio, Mignon! (*Farewell, Mignon!*) *Beniamino Gigli* 6905-2.00

Filina, now re-entering, utters some sarcastic remarks about Mignon's borrowed raiment, words that bring a flush of anger to the girl's cheeks. She rushes from the room, dons her old gypsy costume, and returns just in time to see Wilhelm leading away the actress on his arm. She cries, "That woman! I detest her!"

Scene II—*The Gardens of the Castle*

Thinking her love for Wilhelm hopeless, Mignon is about to drown herself when she hears the strains of a harp. It is the minstrel Lothario; he now enters and listens sympathetically to the girl's tale of sorrow and desire for vengeance. The half-crazed old man starts curiously when she expresses the wish that heaven's lightning would strike and burn down the castle. He goes away muttering her words to himself.

The performance in the theatre having ended, the players and guests come out into the garden. Filina, who is still in her costume of the Fairy Queen in "A Midsummer Night's Dream," has made a brilliant success, and flushed with triumph sings "I am Titania." The rhythm is that of a polonaise; the melody, dashing and showy, places this number high among coloratura songs.

Polonaise—Io son Titania (*I'm Fair Titania*)   *Amelita Galli-Curci* 7110-2.00

> I'm fair Titania, glad and gay,
> Thro' the world unfetter'd I blithely stray.
> With jocund heart and happy mien,
> I cheerily dance the hours away,
> Like the bird that freely wings its flight.
> Elfin sprites around me dance.

Lothario returns and whispers to Mignon that she need not grieve, her vengeance will be complete, for he has set fire to the castle. Happening to notice Mignon, Filina is moved by a cruelly jealous thought. She orders the girl to bring from the castle a bouquet she has forgotten. Since Filina knows that the flowers were given by Mignon to Wilhelm there is malice enough in her request; yet Mignon goes gladly. Immediately word comes that the castle is on fire. Wilhelm, realizing that Mignon is in danger, rushes off to her rescue. He returns with the unconscious girl in his arms; she is still clasping the bunch of withered flowers. Wilhelm exclaims that he has rescued her against her will.

ACT III

SCENE—*Count Lothario's Castle in Italy*

WILHELM has brought Mignon and Lothario to an old castle in Italy, one that he is half inclined to purchase. Mignon is recovering from a dangerous illness and Wilhelm comes to take Lothario's place watching outside her sickroom. The latter, satisfied that he has quieted the restless girl, sings "J'ai calmé la fièvre."

De son coeur j'ai calmé la fièvre (*Soothed Is Now Her Sorrow*) (*Berceuse*)   *Ezio Pinza* 6642-2.00

Meditating over her guileless heart and faithfulness, and his final realization that he loves her deeply, he sings a Romance—a melody of the utmost simplicity, naïve as Mignon herself. It rises to a passionate climax as the young man exclaims: "Gentle Spring! give her one balmy, caressing kiss; O, my heart give her one fond sigh of love!"

Ah! non credevi tu (*Ah! Little Thought the Maid*)   *Beniamino Gigli* 6905-2.00

Mignon comes with feeble steps to the balcony, and when she looks out
n the landscape she is stirred by strange memories. On seeing Wilhelm she
ecomes very agitated, fearing that Filina may be with him. He soothes her
vith the assurance that he loves her alone, but she insists that only Lothario
s faithful. Meanwhile a strange thing has happened—being again in familiar
urroundings, Lothario's reason and memory are restored. He is Count
Lothario and the Castle is his. His only regret is the loss of his daughter,
perata. At the sound of that name, the floodgates of memory are opened
n Mignon's perturbed consciousness, and when Lothario shows her the
ewels and prayerbook of his lost daughter, she not only recognizes them but
lso begins unconsciously to sing the prayers of her early childhood. Thus
ather and daughter are reunited, and Wilhelm being admitted to the family
ircle, their happiness is complete.

Camuzzi

SCHIPA IN MIGNON

SYLVIA CECIL OF THE D'OYLY CARTE OPERA COMPANY AS YUM-YUM

THE MIKADO

Or, The Town of Titipu

COMIC opera in two acts; text by W. S. Gilbert; music by Sir Arthur Sullivan. First produced at the Savoy Theatre, London, March 14, 1885. First performance in the United States, July 6, 1885, at the Museum, Chicago.

Not without reason is this one of the most popular of the long line of "Savoy Operas," for Gilbert's text is a masterpiece of comic writing to which Sullivan's ever tuneful music is perfectly adapted, serving in a remarkable manner to set off the amusing character of the words. The Japanese setting supplies a refreshingly colorful background, although, of course, the characters are by no means Japanese, but ourselves in a very thin disguise.

THE MIKADO ON VICTOR RECORDS

This classic among comic operas has been completely recorded in Album C-26 (11961-11971) AC-26 (11972-11982) —$16.50. The following account of the opera is keyed to these records.

The performance was recorded in Europe under the direction of Mr. Rupert D'Oyly Carte, with the following cast of

CHARACTERS

THE MIKADO OF JAPAN	George Baker (*Bass*)
NANKI-POO, *his son, disguised as a minstrel*	John Harrison (*Tenor*)
KO-KO, *Lord High Executioner of Titipu*	Ernest Pike (*Baritone*)

POOH-BAH, *Lord High Everything Else*   Robert Radford *(Baritone)*
YUM-YUM   } *Wards*   {   Violet Essex *(Soprano)*
PITTI-SING   } *of*   {   Violet Oppenshaw *(Contralto)*
PEEP-BO   } *Ko-Ko* {   Bessie Jones *(Contralto)*
KATISHA, *an elderly lady, in love with Nanki-Poo*   Edna Thornton *(Contralto)*
PISH-TUSH, *a Noble Lord*   Edward Halland *(Tenor)*
Schoolgirls, Nobles, Guards and Coolies. Chorus of Ladies and Gentlemen.

ACT I

AFTER the captivating overture composed of some of the choicest melodies from the opera, the curtain rises on the courtyard of Ko-Ko's palace at Titipu. Japanese nobles who are gathered there sing a lively chorus revealing their identity:

> If you want to know who we are,
> We are gentlemen of Japan . . .

Nanki-Poo enters excitedly, carrying a native guitar and a bundle of ballads. He asks to be directed to the maiden Yum-Yum, the ward of Ko-Ko. In turn the nobles ask his own identity. He replies with the song, "A Wandering Minstrel I." He offers them his wares, that is, his songs—sentimental, patriotic or nautical. Pish-Tush asks his business with Yum-Yum. Nanki-Poo replies that a year ago he saw Yum-Yum and immediately fell in love with her, but at that time she was betrothed to her guardian, Ko-Ko. Now, having heard that Ko-Ko is condemned to death for flirting, he has come to see Yum-Yum. Pish-Tush replies that Ko-Ko has been pardoned and made Lord High Executioner; this happened under the remarkable circumstances he relates in the song, "Our Great Mikado." Thereupon, the Lord High Everything Else, Pooh-Bah, enters and, singing the song, "Young Man, Despair," tells him to give up hope, for Yum-Yum is to marry Ko-Ko this very day. Nanki-Poo's lament is cut short by the arrival of Ko-Ko himself, entering in state with his attendants who sing the rousing chorus "Behold the Lord High Executioner!" Thanking them for their reception, he sings the amusing song, "I've got a little list of society offenders who might well be underground"—possibilities for his own professional employment! Soon there enters a procession of Yum-Yum's school-mates singing their girlish chorus "Comes a train of little ladies from scholastic trammels free." Immediately after appears Yum-Yum herself with her two sisters, Peep-Bo and Pitti-Sing, "Three little maids from school." The girls happen to offend the haughty Pooh-Bah, so are obliged to beg his pardon, singing "So please you, sir, we much regret if we have failed in etiquette." Then all depart, save Nanki-Poo and Yum-Yum. The young man at once declares his love and reveals to Yum-Yum that he is none other than the son of the Mikado. He has assumed this disguise in order to avoid marrying an elderly lady of the court, Katisha, who has claimed him. The couple sing their duet, "Were you not to Ko-Ko plighted," saying that if Yum-Yum were not engaged to Ko-Ko they would

Photo Valentine
DARRELL FANCOURT
AS THE MIKADO
(D'OYLY CARTE OPERA COMPANY)

fondly kiss one another, and audibly demonstrate how it would be done. Then each goes away sorrowfully. Pooh-Bah and Pish-Tush enter with a letter for Ko-Ko from the Mikado who, struck by the fact that no one has been beheaded in Titipu for a year, threatens to abolish the office of Lord High Executioner unless somebody is executed within a month. In the trio they sing, "I am so proud," each of the men declines the honor of decapitation, Ko-Ko because of his duty to Titipu, Pooh-Bah because he must mortify his family pride, and Pish-Tush really doesn't greatly care. Curiously enough, at this moment Nanki-Poo enters, carrying a rope with which he intends to hang himself for sorrow at the loss of Yum-Yum. Ko-Ko suggests that Nanki-Poo allow himself to be executed instead. After some argument Nanki-Poo consents, on condition that he be permitted to marry Yum-Yum at once—the execution to be a month later.

Ko-Ko reluctantly agrees. The nobles and ladies enter to learn the decision; Ko-Ko announces that Yum-Yum is to marry Nanki-Poo, and all rejoice, singing merrily "The threatened cloud has passed away." Suddenly the dreaded Katisha appears, declaring melodramatically, "Your revels cease." She balefully claims Nanki-Poo her own, but Pitti-Sing laughing replies that they are not concerned with her connubial views—

> For he's going to marry Yum-Yum
> Your anger pray bury,
> For all will be merry,
> I think you had better succumb.

The tottering and wicked Katisha then turns to Nanki-Poo, declaring: "Oh, faithless one . . . I'll tear the mask from your disguising!" But as soon as she begins her denunciation, "He is the son of your . . ." Nanki-Poo and Yum-Yum interrupt, singing Japanese words loudly and drowning out her voice. Thus repeatedly foiled, Katisha furiously vows vengeance, while all the others sing merrily, "For joy reigns everywhere around!"

ACT II

Yum-Yum is attended by her maidens who, while preparing her for the wedding, sing the graceful chorus, "Braid the raven hair," and Pitti-Sing interpolates a short solo, "Sit with downcast eye. . . . Try if you can cry." Yum-Yum, gazing in the mirror, is thrilled by her own loveliness and expresses her appreciation of it in the song:

> The sun whose rays
> Are all ablaze
>   With ever-living glory,
> Does not deny
> His majesty,
>   He scorns to tell a story!

Reminded that her married happiness is to be "cut short," Yum-Yum bursts into tears; Nanki-Poo enters and tries to console her. With a forced, melancholy laugh, Yum-Yum, Pitti-Sing, Nanki-Poo, and Pish-Tush attempt a cheerful quartet, "Brightly dawns our wedding day," but each time their "Sing a merry madrigal—Fal-la!" ends in sorrow. Their unhappiness is further augmented when Ko-Ko enters with the exciting news that a law has just been discovered which decrees that when a married man is beheaded his wife is to be buried alive. So far the law has never been put into force, for the only crime punishable with decapitation is flirting, and of course, married men never flirt. Yum-Yum complains that burial alive is such a stuffy death: yet if Nanki-Poo releases her she will have to marry Ko-Ko. With reason do they break into the incomparable Trio, "Here's a how-de-do!" A moment later the stately Japanese melody played at the opening of the overture is heard, and a procession enters, singing Japanese words, "Miya sama," announcing the arrival of the Mikado, who enters, accompanied by Katisha, "His daughter-in-law elect." The Mikado introduces himself with the song, "A more humane Mikado never did in Japan exist," having a delicious Gilbertian refrain:

> My object all sublime
> I shall achieve in time—
> To let the punishment fit the crime.

Pooh-Bah now comes forward to assure the Mikado that his wishes have been respected, the execution has just taken place; Ko-Ko, Pitti-Sing, and Pooh-Bah describe it graphically in their song, "The criminal cried." Although the Mikado is gratified at the news, this was not the purpose of his coming; he really is seeking his son, who is reputed to be in Titipu, disguised under the name of Nanki-Poo. At this moment Katisha, who is reading the death certificate, finds the name there—Nanki-Poo beheaded! Ko-Ko, Pooh-Bah, and Pitti-Sing pretend to be dismayed to think that they have executed the Heir Apparent. The Mikado reminds them that they will have to be punished for this; he is not the least angry, but the laws decree that "compassing the death of the Heir Apparent," they shall be punished by boiling in oil, or by some similar protracted torture. Such is the injustice of Fate, of which they sing in the Glee, "See how the Fates their gifts allot." The Mikado and Katisha go away, and while the trio remain bemoaning their luck, Nanki-Poo and Yum-Yum appear, ready to start on their honeymoon. The unlucky trio attempt to persuade Nanki-Poo to "come back to life," but the Prince, wishing to be free of Katisha, refuses unless Ko-Ko will himself marry her; then, he says, life will be as

299

welcome as "The flowers that bloom in the spring." Ko-Ko replies with
the unforgettable lines:

> The flowers that bloom in the spring,
>   Tra la,
> Have nothing to do with the case.
> I've got to take under my wing,
>   Tra la,
> A most unattractive old thing,
> With a caricature of a face . . .

All go out and Katisha enters, singing "Alone, and yet alive!"

To her now comes Ko-Ko, declaring a passionate love for her. When she
sternly refuses him, he sings the pathetic story of a bird's unhappy affection,
"Willow, tit-willow." Katisha is so moved by his song and his threatened
death from a broken heart that she yields, and even asks if he does not
mind that she is the least wee bit bloodthirsty. Ko-Ko finds beauty even
in bloodthirstiness, and the two sing their duet, "There is beauty in the
bellow of the blast," then go away together joyfully. The Mikado now
enters ready to behold the execution of the three culprits.

A moment later they rush in, but Katisha is with them, and implores
mercy for she has married Ko-Ko. The Mikado hesitates since the law must
be enforced. The situation is saved by the appearance of Nanki-Poo whose
non-execution is marvelously explained, all then taking their turns in the
exhilarating finale, "For he's gone and he's married Yum-Yum!"

Gems *Victor Light Opera Co.* **35796-1.25** *Light Opera Co.* **36148-1.25**

Stage Photo Company

"MERCY! EVEN FOR POOH-BAH!"
(D'OYLY CARTE OPERA PRODUCTION)

NORMA: "Now, for your judgment, a new victim is offered—I am guilty!"

NORMA

OPERA in four (originally two) acts; music by Vincenzo Bellini; libretto by Felice Romani, founded on a tragedy by Soumet played at the Théâtre Français, Paris, about a year before the first production of the opera, which took place December 26, 1831, at Milan. First performance in the United States, February 25, 1841, at the Park Theatre, New York. Revived at the Metropolitan Opera House, New York, November 16, 1927, with Rosa Ponselle (Norma), Lauri-Volpi (Pollione), Telva (Adalgisa), and Pinza (Oroveso).

Bellini's opera, "Norma," appeared the year after "La Sonnambula" had won exceptional favor, and it was no less successful. The technique of the work is that of the older Italian Opera School, in which airs and ensemble numbers, based on the simplest harmonic and melodic architecture, are plentiful. This does not mean, however, that emotional quality is absent, or even meager; and such numbers as "Casta Diva" or the great duet "Mira o Norma" are remarkable for sincerity of emotional expression, notwithstanding their clear simplicity of style, and recent revivals of the opera have proved that they still are effective. Those who weary of declamatory modern opera, in which the music is constantly changing in agreement with the most swift and subtle moods that emotion throws upon the stage, at the expense of clearly defined melody, will have no quarrel with the simplicity of "Norma." Certainly the part of Norma ranks as one of the very greatest and most difficult of coloratura soprano rôles and has been a favorite with many generations of singers. Among the great sopranos who have sung the rôle are Jenny Lind, Grisi, and Lilli Lehmann; and in our own day Rosa Ponselle has achieved one of her greatest successes in the part of the Druidical priestess.

THE OVERTURE introduces us to the prevailing moods of the opera. After a few introductory measures of a martial character, the first theme is heard, agitated and in minor. This is followed by the melody of the opening chorus of Druidical soldiers. From this material the overture is built.

The action takes place in Gaul during the Roman occupation, about 50 B. C.

Overture *Victor Symphony Orchestra* 21669-.75

ACT I

IN THE dark forests, Oroveso *(Or-oh-vay'-soh)*, the Arch-Druid, and the Druidical Soldiers and Priests, await the rising of the moon, at which mystic hour Norma is to perform the sacred rite of cutting the prophetic bough of mistletoe. They sing a sturdy chorus, swearing vengeance upon their Roman oppressors.

The Druids having gone away, Pollione *(Pol-lee-oh'-neh)*, the Roman proconsul and his lieutenant, Flavio, approach. From their conversation we learn that Norma, the daughter of Oroveso and Druidical high priestess, has fallen in love with Pollione, and violating her vows of chastity has borne him two sons. Now, however, Pollione is secretly in love with Adalgisa *(Ah-dahl-gee'-sah)*, one of the virgins of the temple; and that he is conscience stricken he reveals in his cavatina:

Chicago Civic Opera
ROSA RAISA AS NORMA

With me in Rome, before the shrine
Was Adalgisa bending.
When an unearthly, awful shade,
Fashion'd itself from nothing,
Daylight shrank out all sickly. . . .
Vainly I sought the gentle one,
There at the altar kneeling,
Mocking my search, a stifled moan
On the sad air came stealing;
While in a deep mysterious tone
Reëcho'd thro' the temple,
"Norma thus makes example
Of traitors false to Love."

The narrative suddenly interrupted by the sounds of the approaching Druids, the two Romans conceal themselves. Norma appears before her people, and fearing for the life of her lover, addresses them, saying in her recitative *(beginning of Record 8125)*, that the time is not yet ripe to arise against their oppressors; then, in a famous aria she prays for peace, and in the second part of the aria gives voice to her unhappy love while the Druids hymn the day of their vengeance:

Queen of Heaven, while thou art reigning
Love upon us is still remaining,
Clad in pureness, alone disdaining
Grosser earth's nocturnal veil.

302

Queen of Heaven, hallow'd be thy presence,
Let its holier, sweeter essence,
Quelling ev'ry lawless license,
As above, so here prevail!

(PART II)

All is ended; be now the forest
Disencumber'd of aught mortal.
When our godhead's thirsting anger
Wills the life-blood of the stranger,
From our temple's awful portal
My command then thunders forth.

. . . . . .

The bloom of life is lying
As flow'rets pale when dying,
The zephyr's softly sighing,
A coldness ever blows;
Restore to mine affection
One smile of love's protection,
My heart in thy affection
Its only summer knows.

Casta Diva *(Queen of Heaven)* **Rosa Ponselle, Chorus and Orchestra of the Metropolitan Opera 8125-2.00**

Adalgisa meets Pollione in the forest, and after much persuasion, consents to elope with him the following night; they plan to seek safety and happiness in Rome.

ACT II

STILL hesitant, the distraught Adalgisa tells her trouble to her High Priestess. Norma, thinking of her own love affair, is at first disposed to release the girl from her vows, but when she learns that the lover is Pollione, her soul is filled with a passion for vengeance.

ACT III

NEARLY crazed with anger, Norma plans to kill her husband and children and let herself be burned on the funeral pyre. Only thus can she atone for her secret marriage since death is the punishment laid on any priestess who dares break her vow. She advances with uplifted dagger toward her sleeping children, but the sight of her innocent victims overcomes her. Then she summons Adalgisa and, urging her to marry Pollione, begs her to care for the children following her death. Moved by her generosity, Adalgisa entreats Norma not to do this, and the two unite in a well-known duet.

ADALGISA:
Hear me, Norma, before thee kneeling,
View these darlings, thy precious treasures;
Let that sunbeam, a mother's feeling,
Break the night around thy soul.

303

NORMA:

> Wouldst win that soul, by this entreating
> Back to earth's delusive pleasures,
> From the phantoms, far more fleeting,
> Which in death's deep ocean shoal?

ADALGISA:

> Ah, be persuaded.

NORMA:

> Deceive me not, His passion—

ADALGISA:

> Dies in repentance . . .
> Either I shall restore thy husband,
> Or with thee seek oblivion
> Far from the haunt of men.

NORMA:

> Thou hast conquer'd . . . embrace me now,
> Life is mine own again.

Mira Norma *(Hear Me, Norma)* **Rosa Ponselle, Marion Telva** 8110-2.00

ACT IV

THE assembled Druids sing of the day when their wrath will be turned against the Romans.

Copy't Mishkin
PINZA AS OROVESO

Oroveso continues this mood with his stately air in which the soldiers join, declaring:

"Soon shall Rome by Heaven's permission melt as breath from off the plain!"

Oh del Tebro *(Haughty Roman)* **Ezio Pinza and Metropolitan Opera Chorus** 1753-1.50

Adalgisa having failed in her attempt to persuade Pollione to return to Norma, the Priestess, now infuriated, calls her people to revolt against the Romans, and when Pollione is discovered in the midst of their soldiers as a spy, she claims the right to kill him. She finds, however, that she is powerless to drive her dagger into one she loves. But Pollione still refuses to give up Adalgisa; therefore Norma confesses her guilt to the astonished priests, and claims purification by death upon the sacrificial pyre. Moved by her devotion, Pollione's love for Norma returns, and he begs and receives permission to die with her. Norma confides her children to her father's care, and the reunited lovers go to meet their death.

FINAL SCENE—OBERON

OBERON

(Or, The Elf-King's Oath)

OPERA in three acts; music by Carl Maria von Weber; text by James Robinson Planché. First produced at Covent Garden, London, April 12, 1826, in English, under the Composer's direction. First performance in the United States, October 9, 1827, at New York. Revived at the Metropolitan Opera House, New York, December 28, 1918, in English.

Weber's "Der Freischütz" immediately became so popular that the composer was soon commissioned to write an opera for Covent Garden, London. After many difficulties with librettist and singers, the opera was ready. Weber was in an advanced stage of consumption, however, and by the time of the first performance he was nearly too exhausted to conduct. It was a great success; but within less than two months the unfortunate composer died. In this work Weber's genius for interpreting the romantic and eerie shows itself at its best; thus, from a historical point of view, he is the forerunner of all the wonderful music of the supernatural that has been written since that time.

THE OVERTURE takes us from the very start to that elfin-land we all at some time or other long to visit. The delicate though golden tones of Oberon's fairy horn summon the Elf-King's subjects, who come tripping to the fluttering passages of the wood-wind. The brilliant march of Charlemagne follows, and as a closing theme the violins sing the ecstatic melody of Rezia's song, when, shipwrecked on a desert island, she beholds a sail approaching.

Overture   *Albert Coates-Symphony Orchestra* 9122-1.50

QUEEN TITANIA, having quarreled with her husband, Oberon, the King of the Elves, says she will not speak to him until he shows her two lovers who, despite all obstacles, remain faithful to one another.

divine music, legend tells us, trees uprooted themselves and rocks became loosened from their ledges in order to follow the wonderful sounds; and well may legend tell the truth, for Orpheus is the son of Apollo, god of music, and Calliope, muse of epic poetry. Amor, the god of love, is so touched by the deep, sincere grief of Orpheus that he tells him he may descend to the nether world, the dark realm of Pluto, there to seek the shade of Eurydice. One condition, however, is attached: if Orpheus would have Eurydice return to earth with him, he must not look at her until he has recrossed the River Styx.

In the awesome depths of Tartarus, the frightening bark of Cerberus is heard, and Furies join in a grotesque dance. Although they at first endeavor to frighten him away, Orpheus moves even these dark spirits to pity with the song of his grief, and they allow him to continue his quest.

In the happy Elysian fields beneath cheerful skies, the Spirits of the Blest dance to the song of birds and the murmur of brooks. Gluck's music is marvelously descriptive of the chaste beauty and the tranquil felicity of these happy spirits; a flute solo of indescribable loveliness accentuates the mood of classical antiquity.

Ballet Music *(Dance of the Spirits)* ***Toscanini-Philharmonic-Symphony Orchestra of N. Y. 7138-2.00***

Here Orpheus finds his beloved, clasps her joyfully to his breast, begs her to follow him, but never looks upon her face.

As they mount higher and higher Eurydice is more and more grief-stricken because Orpheus seems no longer to love her. Not once have their eyes met. She would rather remain below than return to earth without his love. Orpheus is bound by the conditions not to reveal the cause of his apparent indifference. When they are almost in sight of the land of the living, she cries out with such heart-rending pathos, that, in a moment of forgetfulness, Orpheus looks back upon her, only to see her sink lifeless to the ground. Now his sorrow is even more profound than before. Utterly disconsolate his grief finds expression in a melody of deathless beauty and pathos, not gloomy and poignantly tragic, but colored with an ineffable feeling of sadness. This music is equaled only in the lines of Virgil:

> Vox ipsa et frigida lingua,
> "Ah! miseram Eurydicen," anima fugiente, vocabat;
> "Eurydicen," toto referabant flumine ripae.

Translated by Dryden:

> E'en then his trembling tongue invok'd his bride;
> With his last voice, "Eurydice" he cried,
> "Eurydice," the rocks and river banks replied.

Che farò senza Euridice *(I Have Lost My Eurydice)* ***Sigrid Onégin 6803-2.00 Maria Olczewska 7115-2.00***

Amor, who has been watching Orpheus, is so deeply moved by this threnody that he restores Eurydice to life and permits the rejoicing lovers to proceed to the world above.

THE GREAT HALL OF THE CASTLE

OTHELLO

OPERA in four acts; music by Giuseppe Verdi; libretto by Arrigo Boïto after Shakespeare. First produced February 5, 1887, at La Scala, Milan. First performance in the United States, April 16, 1888, at the Academy of Music, New York. Revived at the Manhattan Opera House, New York, 1908, with Zenatello in the title rôle.

Sixteen years after "Aïda" had seemed to be the crowning glory of Verdi's long musical career, the great composer astonished the musical world with "Othello." At the age of seventy-four he showed, past all doubt, that the fierce creative spirit which burned within him was not only alive, but still glowing brightly. In that sixteen-year interval Verdi had kept close touch with the development of music. "Othello," therefore, is essentially modern in spirit and technique. The characterization is marvelous, there are no set airs or ensembles, the scenes fusing into each other without a break. Its power and almost youthful energy, set upon a lifetime of practical musical and dramatic experience, give the work a unique place in music. Verdi, greatly daring, successfully achieved what few have attempted; he measured skill with Shakespeare himself. (The opera is also known under the Italian title, Otello, *Oh-tel'-loh*.)

The action takes place at a seaport in Cyprus towards the end of the Fifteenth Century.

Complete *Famous Artists, Chorus and Orchestra of La Scala, Milan,* **Album M152 (11363-11378) Am-152 (11379-11394) Price $24.00**

309

ACT I

SCENE—*Othello's Castle in Cyprus*

A STORM rages and the angry sea is visible in the background *(M 152-1)*. A group of Venetian citizens and soldiers watch the vessel bearing the victorious Othello as it struggles with the storm. His vessel arrives safely, and amid great rejoicing the Moor announces a complete victory over the Turkish fleet.

When he has entered the castle *(M 152-2)*, the soldiers begin drinking in celebration of the victory. Among them is Iago, who is secretly smarting with a desire for revenge since his comrade in arms, Cassio, has been promoted to a higher rank than himself by Othello. Iago is, moreover, greatly incensed that this Moor should have risen to be a general in the Venetian army, and now be honored by being made Governor of Cyprus. He finds a willing ally in Roderigo, who loves Desdemona, and still desires her, even though she has married Othello *(M 152-3)*. Iago, therefore, induces Roderigo to help in plying Cassio with wine.

Cassio at first refuses to drink, knowing his own particular weakness; but when Iago toasts Desdemona, he is obliged to respond. He is soon hopelessly befuddled, grows hilarious, finally quarrelsome *(M 152-4)*. Iago now cunningly manages to have him pick a quarrel with Montano, Othello's predecessor in the government of Cyprus *(M 152-5)*. Swords are drawn, Montano is wounded, and Iago fans the disturbance into a small riot.

This is put down by the appearance of Othello, who is enraged that his own soldiers should thus be fighting among themselves, and deprives Cassio of his command. Iago's crafty planning has already begun its work!

The crowd departs, leaving Othello alone with his wife, the gentle Desdemona *(M 152-6)*. They sing a version in duet form of the lines in Shakespeare's play where Othello describes how Desdemona, hearing him tell of his hardships and dangers in battle, came to love him:

> Wherein I spake of most disastrous chances,
> Of moving accidents by flood and field,
> Of hair-breadth 'scapes i' the imminent deadly breach,
> Of being sold to slavery, of my redemption thence. . . .
> And often did beguile her of her tears,
> When I did speak of some distressful stroke
> That my youth suffered. My story being done,
> She gave me for my pains a world of sighs!
>
> .   .   .   .   .   .
>
> She loved me for the dangers I had pass'd,
> And I loved her that she did pity them.

Their duet continues with a splendid musical setting of the scene between Othello and Desdemona in Shakespeare *(M 152-7)*:

310

OTHELLO:

>   . . . If it were now to die.
>   'T were now to be most happy, for I fear
>   My soul hath her content so absolute
>   That not another comfort like to this
>   Succeeds in unknown fate.

DESDEMONA:

>   The heavens forbid
>   But that our loves and comforts should increase
>   Even as our days do grow!

OTHELLO:

>   Amen to that, sweet powers!
>   I cannot speak enough to this content;
>   It stops me here; it is too much of joy;
>   And this, and this, the greatest discords be
>   (Kissing her)
>   That e'er our hearts shall make!

As Othello kisses her the orchestra plays an impassioned phrase that will be repeated with telling effect at the end of the opera. Husband and wife now turn to re-enter the castle . . . the peace of a starlight night envelops the scene. . . .

ACT II

SCENE—*A Room in the Castle*

IAGO plays still more subtly upon the unsuspecting Cassio; he advises him to beg Desdemona to intercede with Othello to give him back his command (M 152-8). Cassio goes in search of her, and, well satisfied with his work, Iago gazes after him, soliloquizing on his own philosophy of life (M 152-9). Like a true believer he begins by saying that he believes in one God . . . but a cruel God, who has fashioned mankind on his own vile image . . . that life is made but to feed death . . . and heaven's only a lie. Verdi has matched this grim confession of faith with a remarkable musical portrayal of Iago's heartless cynicism.

Credo (*Iago's Creed*) **Lawrence Tibbett** 14182-2.00   *Titta Ruffo* *8045-2.00

As soon as Iago sees Cassio in conversation with Desdemona, he hurriedly calls Othello (M 152-10 and 11) and sows in the heart of the Moor the first seed of jealousy, bidding him watch his wife carefully. Othello, much troubled, finds Desdemona and questions her (M 152-12 and 13). As she at once begins to plead Cassio's cause, his suspicions are more fully awakened; and when she seeks to wipe his perspiring brow with a handkerchief that was his own first gift, he tears it from her. It is picked up by Emilia, Desde-

311

mona's maid and Iago's wife. While Othello roughly berates his alarmed Desdemona, Iago forces Emilia to give him the kerchief.

Left alone with Iago, Othello *(M 152-14 and 15)* gives expression to his grief, singing a fervent and heart-broken air in which he bids farewell to peace of mind, ambition, and the glory of conquest.

Now Iago, the Iago that Othello knows only as "honest Iago," pours fuel on the flame of jealousy *(M 152-16)* by avowing that he has seen Desdemona's handkerchief in Cassio's room. He also declares that he has heard the sleeping Cassio speak of her in his dreams.

Othello becomes frantic with rage *(M 152-17)*; Iago offers to help him to vengeance. Uniting in a most impressive duet they call on all the heavenly bodies to witness this solemn oath in which they swear never to relent or pause until the guilty shall have been punished.

Crimella

MARTINELLI IN THE TITLE ROLE

Si pel ciel *(We Swear by Heaven and Earth)* **Caruso, Ruffo** *8045-2.00

ACT III
SCENE—*The Great Hall of the Castle*

OTHELLO seeks Desdemona, and contrives an excuse to borrow her handkerchief. She offers it, but he says it is not the one . . . he wants the one which he had given her *(M 152-18 and 19)*. Though inwardly trembling at its loss, she says it is in her room; she will go fetch it. But Othello at once denounces her and sends her rudely away, astonished and grief-stricken *(M 152-20)* at this strange, sudden jealousy. He remains looking after her in the deepest dejection and sings a sorrowful soliloquy, declaring that nothing that fate might have done to mar his fame or fortune would have been so terrible a blow as this *(M 152-21)*.

Cassio enters, and Iago, bidding Othello watch and listen from behind a pillar, goes to the demoted young officer, and with fiendish ingenuity induces him *(M 152-22)* to talk of his affairs with a woman of the town, Bianca. But Othello does not hear the name, in fact is only able to grasp a part of this half-whispered, rather lewd conversation. Cassio produces the fatal handkerchief, telling Iago that he had found it in his room; he wonders who placed it there. Othello sees the handkerchief; he sees Cassio laughing; and though he does not hear all that is said, this is indeed proof enough of Desdemona's guilt *(M 152-23)*. By the time Cassio has left, Othello is insane with jealousy and rage; he asks Iago to procure him poison wherewith to kill Desdemona. Iago craftily evades being involved, by suggesting that she had better be strangled in the bed she has dishonored; but he will "take care" of Cassio himself. Othello agrees.

The Venetian ambassador, Lodovico, arrives in state, to inform Othello that he has been recalled to Venice, while Cassio is to be Governor of Cyprus in his stead (M 152-24). Desdemona, who has also entered, weeps for pity at seeing her lord's distress. Her every remark brings a rebuke from Othello, who believes that she weeps because of the approaching separation from Cassio. He announces his departure on the morrow, then, unable longer to contain his smouldering anger, he publicly insults Desdemona and flings her to the ground (M 152-25). Overcome with his own feverish emotion he falls to earth in a swoon (M 152-26). Meanwhile, the public outside, hearing that new honors have fallen to their hero, shout "Hail, Othello! Hail to the Lion of Venice!" But Iago points with horrible triumph to the prostrate Moor, and cries "Behold your Lion of Venice!"

ACT IV

SCENE—*Desdemona's Bedroom*

DESDEMONA is preparing to retire (M 152-27), assisted by Emilia. She tells Emilia of an old song she heard in her childhood that keeps coming into her mind this evening. The words tell of a girl who, like herself, loved

From the Painting by Becker   OTHELLO AND DESDEMONA

Schwalb

"I KISSED THEE ERE I KILLED THEE"

too well. She sings *(M 152-28)* this pathetic song for Emilia—the melody is that of a very ancient folk-song.

Salce, Salce *(Willow Song)* **Elisabeth Rethberg** 7393-2.00

When Emilia has bid her good night and gone, she kneels before the image of the Madonna and begins her prayer "Ave Maria . . . " *(M 152-29)* at first in a whispered monotone, then in a noble melody soaring aloft in tones of ecstatic loveliness as she prays for the Virgin's protection.

Ave Maria *Margherita Sheridan* 7102-2.00   *Elisabeth Rethberg* 7393-2.00

Scarcely has this wonderful melody died away before Othello appears at the threshold *(M 152-30 and 31)*. He stands for a moment brooding over the couch where his wife sleeps. He kisses her and she awakens. He asks her if she has prayed . . . he would not kill her soul. Again he accuses her of being the paramour of Cassio. Denials are useless. As he repeats charge after charge, Othello's jealous rage mounts, and the horrified woman cries aloud for help as he takes her by the throat. Emilia hears and knocks at the door, but when she is admitted, it is too late. In reply to her shrieks, the people rush in. Othello denounces as a faithless wife the woman he has slain, and when the others demur, he exhibits the handkerchief as proof. Emilia thereupon tells how this murderous emblem was taken from her by Iago, and thus Othello learns of his false friend's duplicity.

Very soft solemn chords are heard in the orchestra. Othello whispers to the bystanders *(M 152-32):*

> Be not afraid, though you do see me weapon'd;
> Here is my journey's end,
> Where should Othello go?

314

(He turns towards the bed and gazes at Desdemona)
How dost thou look now? . . .
Pale as thy smock! . . .
Cold, cold, my girl!
O Desdemona! Desdemona! dead!

The music swells to a sudden terrifying climax; Othello furtively draws his dagger, stabs himself, and falls at the side of Desdemona. The orchestra whispers the melody we first heard during the love duet, while the dying Othello, his voice half choked with grief and pain, calls to his unhearing wife:

I kiss'd thee ere I kill'd thee; no way but this,
Killing myself to die upon a kiss.

Copy't Mishkin
SCOTTI AS IAGO

his wife down from the cart, but Tonio, the misshapen clown, is there before him, much to the amusement of the crowd. Canio pays him for this with a hearty box on the ear. Tonio slinks off back of the stage muttering to himself while the villagers rock with laughter.

One of the men suggests they go for a drink. Canio calls to Tonio to come along, but the clown answers that he must stay to rub down the donkey. A villager jestingly hints:

> Careful, Pagliaccio!
> He only stays behind
> To make love to Nedda!

At once on the alert, Canio exclaims, "Eh! What!—You think so?" Then, with a wry smile, he continues:

THOMAS AS TONIO

> Such a game, well, I'd have you know,
> 'Twere better not to play it on me, my neighbors;
> To Tonio, aye, to all I say it!
> For the stage there and life, they are different alto-
> gether!
>
> . . . . . .
>
> If up there,
> *(Pointing to the theatre.)*
> Pagliaccio his lady should discover
> With some fine fellow in her room,
> He'd give the two a rating . . . or resign himself,
> And take a jolly beating! And the crowd would ap-
> plaud:
> *(With a sudden change of tone.)*
> But if Nedda I really should surprise so,
> What came after were a far different story!
> *(Resuming his sarcastic tone.)*
> That's a game there, you take my word,
> 'Twere better not to play, sir!

Nedda understands very well the cause of her husband's black looks yet exclaims to herself, "What does he mean?" The villagers are somewhat puzzled and ask if he is serious. He rouses himself with an effort and says lightly, "Not I—I love my wife most dearly," and thereupon he kisses her on the forehead.

A troupe of bagpipe players passes, suggested in the orchestra by the oboe, and church bells are heard ringing in the village; towards it the people now turn, slowly, in couples. As they go they sing the famous "Chorus of the Bells," a charming melody with something of the spirit of Italian folk-song. Imitating the sound of the bells they sing:

> Ding dong, 'tis the vesper song,
> So come along! Ding dong!

The voices fade away in the distance and Nedda is left alone to muse over the jealous fire she saw in Canio's eyes *(beginning of Record 6578)*. "If he were to catch me!" she shudders. The bright summer sunlight soon drives away these ominous thoughts and looking up to the sky she exclaims:

Ah! ye birds without number!
What countless voices!
What ask ye? Where away? Who knows?
My mother, she that was skilful at telling one's fortune,
Understood what they're singing,
And in my childhood, thus would she sing me:
Ah! There on high they cry,
In freedom flying,
Launched on the wing, like arrows they fly!
The clouds and e'en the fierce glowing sun defying,
And onward thro' the pathless sky!

　　·　　·　　·　　·

Storms may be raging and winds may howl around them,
Nor rain nor lightning nothing can restrain them.

　　·　　·　　·　　·

Far off they go! toward unknown countries striving,
Land of their dreams, that perchance they seek in vain
These Bohemians of heav'n some pow'r is driving,
A pow'r whereof they know not:
To go, still on, and go, and go!

The orchestra supplies a shimmering, twittering background while she sings a care-free melody that waltzes along to the most luminous heights of the soprano voice. Nedda has forgotten her tawdry world!

Ballatella—Che volo d'augelli! (Ye Birds Without Number!) **Mary Lewis** 6578-2.00

Her musing is interrupted by the unwelcome reappearance of Tonio. He tells her that he could not resist her singing; she laughs at him, saying he talks like a poet. He knows that he is ugly and deformed yet he cannot help loving her, desiring her, violently. Nedda orders him to go or she will call Canio. "Not before I have kissed you!" he cries rushing at her. She darts away, picks up a whip and strikes him across the face, shouting, "You cur!" Tonio screams with pain, then cries, "By the Blessed Virgin of the Assumption I swear you'll pay me for this!"

No sooner has Tonio gone than a more welcome lover approaches. He vaults lightly over the wall and greets Nedda with a laugh. It is Silvio, one of the villagers, whom she has met on previous visits and found much to her liking. She is alarmed at the sight of him during broad daylight, but he reassures her, for he has left Canio with Peppe at the tavern, where they are drinking and likely to remain.

Nedda tells Silvio of the clown's threats, bidding him be cautious; but the young villager laughs at her fears, and consoles her by

TIBBETT AS TONIO

321

pleading his own love with great earnestness. He begs her to run away with him to some place where they can be happy. Nedda is greatly fascinated, yet remains fearful; she is so charming when she implores him not to tempt her, that he only grows more impetuous in his love-making. He reproaches her for her coldness, until at last, throwing discretion to the winds, she yields herself to the bliss of the moment and consents to go. They are so lost in the ecstasy of their passion that they do not observe Canio, who, warned by the over-observant clown, approaches just in time to hear Nedda's parting exclamation, "Till tonight, then! and forever I'll be thine!" Canio is unable to restrain a subdued "Ah!" Silvio disappears over the wall, and Canio, who has not seen his face, runs to follow him. Nedda bars the way. Canio thrusts her aside in fierce anger and leaps over the wall in pursuit. He is too late, for Silvio knows a path hidden by the brush, and Canio fails to discover it. Tonio, who is looking on, laughs in glee, and to Nedda's scornful "Bravo! Well done, Tonio!" replies that he will do better next time. Canio returns out of breath, exhausted, trembling with anger.

The outraged husband commands his wife to pronounce the name of her lover, but she proudly refuses. Wild with jealousy he rushes at her with drawn dagger. Peppe, who has returned unobserved, runs forward and holds him back. People are coming from church, he says, it will soon be time for their performance; they must hurry and dress for it. Nedda, glad for an excuse, disappears into the tent-like stage; Peppe and Tonio go on about their work.

With bowed head, worn out by passion and jealousy, Canio remains alone to consider his fate. Heavy chords are played by the orchestra as he meditates:

> To go on! When my head's whirling with madness, not knowing what
> I'm saying or what I'm doing! Yet I have got to force myself!
> Pshaw! Can't you be a man?—You're a Pagliaccio!

He continues, singing a melody of heart-rending pathos:

> Put on your smock now, smear your face with the powder—
> The people pay you, and they must have their fun.
> If Harlequin your Columbine take from you,
> Laugh loud, Pagliaccio,
> Change into laughter your sighing and weeping!
> Hide then your grief and your sobbing, play the part, Ah!
> Laugh then, Pagliaccio, for your love that is broken,
> Laugh for the pain that now is breaking your heart!

He moves slowly towards the theatre, sobbing. When reaching the curtain which opens on the little stage, he pushes it roughly, as if not wanting to enter; then, seized by a new fit of sobbing, he again buries his face in his hands. Finally he takes several steps towards the curtain from which he had recoiled in fury, enters and disappears.

Vesti la giubba (*On With the Play*) **Giovanni Martinelli** 6754-2.00 **Enrico Caruso** 7720-2.00

ACT II

IT IS the hour appointed for the performance. Tonio is beating the drum to summon the villagers—it would seem rather to
drown out their animated chatter as they rapidly congregate. Silvio also arrives, to feast
his eyes on Nedda, greeting his friends among
the spectators as he takes his seat. All are excited: some exclaim as they enter, "Let's try to
put ourselves well up in front there!" Others,
true villagers impatient for the show, ask,
"What are you waiting for? Why this delay-
ing? Ev'ry one's here!" Then as the play begins all shout, "Keep quiet! Be still!"

HELEN JEPSON AS COLUMBINE

The curtains of the theatre are drawn
aside, revealing this scene, roughly painted: A small room with two side
doors and a window at the back. A plain table and two ordinary chairs are
at the right. Nedda is there alone, dressed in the costume of Columbine.
She seems to be nervously awaiting someone, although she informs her
audience that her husband will not be home till late this evening. From
outside comes the sound of a guitar, and Columbine (Nedda) rushes towards the window with a little cry of joy. The voice of Harlequin (Peppe)
is heard without, singing a serenade; the Italianate melody is at once dainty
and sentimental; the words, a bit extravagant, are perfectly in keeping with
the character and the occasion.

Serenata d'Arlecchino *(Harlequin's Serenade)* *Tito Schipa* 1183-1.50

> O Columbine, your Harlequin is here with you,
> Tender and true!
> Here am I crying, and am sighing, put your face to view!
> Then show that little face to me, so that I may without delay,
> Press it with kisses,
> Love's torture this is!
> Love's torture this, and I am in dismay!
>
> O Columbine, thy little window, dear undo!
> I'm here for you!
> For you I'm crying!
> For you I'm sighing,
> So tender and so true!
> I'm here for you!
> Yes, for you!

Before Harlequin can enter, however, Taddeo arrives (this clownish rôle
is justly assigned to Tonio), bearing a basket. He sings a pompous greeting,
which brings a roar from the assembled villagers. He forthwith begins to
make love to Columbine. Her reply is a demand for the chicken he had been
sent to fetch; Taddeo kneels before her, holding up the fowl in grotesque

323

devotion. His buffoonery is cut short by Harlequin, who enters and leads him out by the ear—to the delight of the village audience.

With Taddeo banished, the lovers can make merry. Harlequin gives his Columbine a little vial, saying:

> Take this little sleeping-draught;
> 'Tis for Pagliaccio!
> Give it him at bedtime,
> And then we'll fly!

Columbine assents. Suddenly the clown reappears, bawling out in mock alarm:

> Be careful! Pagliaccio is here!

The "lovers" simulate the greatest alarm, while the spectators applaud lustily. Harlequin leaps from the window just as Pagliaccio enters. At that moment Columbine (Nedda) calls to Harlequin the very words:

> "Till tonight, then; and forever I'll be thine!"

This is almost too much for Canio, who forgets for a moment his part of Pagliaccio. Then recalling that he is supposed to be acting he continues with his lines, "Who has been here with you? Tell me his name?" She insists that it was only Taddeo, the clown who, having rushed into hiding, now calls from the closet, "Believe her, sir, she is faithful! Ah, they could never lie, those lips." . . . There is more laughter from the spectators *(beginning of Record 6754).*

Again Canio forgets his part; he demands, "Woman, 'tis thy lover's name I want!" Nedda, still boldly playing Columbine, replies jokingly, "Pagliaccio! Pagliaccio!" This reminder of his part only angers the jealous actor; throwing aside his rôle he answers, to music of unusual ominous force:

No! Pagliaccio no more! I am a man again,
With aching heart and anguish deep and human,
Calling for blood to wash away the stain,
Thy foul dishonor, thou shameless woman.
No, Pagliaccio no more! Fool that I sheltered thee!
And made thee mine by every tender token!
Of the love that I gave thee, what is there left to me?
What have I now, but a heart that is broken?
No, Pagliaccio, I'm not!
Aye, if my face be pale, 'tis shame that makes it so and vengeance twists my features!
I recover my manhood,
The heart that bleeds for blood is seeking to purge its honor, most vile of creatures!
No! Pagliaccio I'm not!
I am that foolish man who in poverty found and tried to save thee!
Nearly dying of hunger, he gave a name to thee, a burning love that was madness he
  gave thee!

Overwhelmed, he sinks on the chair by the table. The spectators murmur at the intense realism of the acting; Silvio exclaims to himself, "This is too genuine!" Canio continues:

THE COMEDY IS ENDED

I hoped—ah! I was blinded indeed in my madness;
If not for love, for charity, and all my life to thee I sacrificed with gladness!
Full of hope, and believing far less in God than thee!
But evil only dwells in thy distorted nature,
For feeling hast thou none, but sense thy only law.
Go! thou'rt not worth my grief,
O thou abandoned creature,
And now with contempt I'll crush thee under heel!

No, Pagliaccio non son! (*No! Punchinello No More!*) **Enrico Caruso** *6001-2.00
Giovanni Martinelli 6754-2.00

The audience, not knowing that this has no part in the play, cries "Bravo!"
Pale, but courageous, Nedda continues the rôle of Columbine; to a frivolous
gavotte tune she remarks that the man who was with her was only the harmless Harlequin. The villagers start to laugh, but stop short on seeing the
expression on Canio's face. They begin to realize that this is no mere play.
The faithful Peppe approaches in the background; he would interfere, but
Tonio craftily holds him back. Canio, crazed with anger and jealousy, again
demands her lover's name; again Nedda refuses, boldly declaring, "I will not
speak! No not even if you kill me!" In their excitement, the villagers have
risen to their feet, overturning benches; some of the women run away. Silvio
draws his dagger, but the men near him, not understanding his excitement,
hold him back. Nedda tries to escape towards the spectators, but Canio is too
quick. With lightning speed he seizes her. There is a sudden flash and he
plunges his dagger into her heart, crying, "Take that . . . and that!" She
shrieks, then falls with a choking sound. Making a last faint effort she calls,
"Help me, Silvio!" The young villager breaks away from the men holding
him and runs to his beloved. Muttering, " 'Twas you!" Canio springs forward and strikes the dagger into him. Then as if stupefied he lets the knife
fall, and addressing his audience for the last time, says with most bitter
irony, "*La commedia è finita!*—The comedy is ended!"

Gems *Victor Opera Company* 35932-1.25

ᑫPARSIFAL

FESTIVAL drama in three acts; words and music by Richard Wagner. First produced at Bayreuth, July 28, 1882. First performance elsewhere, December 24, 1903, at the Metropolitan Opera House, New York. Because of its sacred character, the composer expressed a wish that this work should not be performed as a part of the everyday repertoire of opera houses; he hoped that it would ever remain as a "Stage-consecrating Festival Drama," played only at his own theatre at Bayreuth. Accordingly "Parsifal" was not produced elsewhere until 1903. Then, in spite of the legal protest of Wagner's widow, the Metropolitan Opera Company was enabled to give "Parsifal" its first performance outside of Bayreuth, some technicality in connection with the copyright having been discovered. In Europe, however, "Parsifal" was not performed outside of the composer's theatre until after the expiration of the copyright in 1913.

Parsifal has always held a unique position in the world of opera, partly because of the religious nature of the story, partly because of its being the last of the composer's works, and partly because of the singular beauty of the music. Certainly no other work for the musical stage has been the cause of so long continued controversy, and in the case of no other work is a just appraisal so difficult—difficult because of sentimental reasons associated with the composer's last work, difficult because of its religious nature. On the one hand, it makes a very pretty theory to say, here is Wagner's final opus, here the master hand reached the culmination of its skill and achieved its ultimate perfection: on the other hand, it makes an equally pretty theory to say that here at last are signs of weakening, the waning powers of old age, even in Wagner. Before attempting a final appraisal, however, "Parsifal" should be considered in the light of Wagner's peculiar genius, remembering his uncanny and unequaled ability to enter into and be absorbed by the dramas upon which he was working; how for him the drama was thought of in terms of music, and the music took its form, even down to the minutest details of modulation and or-

German Railroads Information Office

THE TEMPLE OF THE GRAIL

chestration, from the drama; and yet, how each music-drama has a specific character of its own growing from the very idea back of its action. All this is just as true of "Parsifal" as of the other music-dramas; music and drama are perfectly welded together, yet all is keyed to the glowing mysticism of the Grail legend. Thus it may well be that those who are sympathetic towards religious mysticism will find in Parsifal a masterword, those who are not will remain unconvinced. Certain it is that this is no mere "opera" for everyday entertainment; Wagner did not so conceive it, and, in fact, added to "Parsifal" the subtitle, "Stage-consecrating Festival Drama." If the youthful exuberance of "Siegfried" is not in evidence it may be because such overflowing life would be out of "key" here, rather than because Wagner was no longer possessed of such vitality. Yet the converse, as Mr. Ernest Newman has pointed out, may be true, that when Wagner wrote "Siegfried" he was not yet ready for "Parsifal." Certain it is that for some twenty years the "Parsifal" theme, as narrated in the poem of Wolfram von Eschenbach, had been germinating in

Weirich, Festspielhaus, Bayreuth
AMFORTAS

Wagner's mind before it was sketched in 1865, when the "Ring" was well on the road to completion. Evidently during all this time, the composer had been more inclined towards other subjects—perhaps subconsciously felt himself still unripe for the "Parsifal" theme. The text was not completed until 1877 and the music all written until 1882. Whatever the ultimate verdict of the worth of "Parsifal" may be, opinion is now nearly unanimous that portions of the work rank with the most sublime and beautiful music ever written, notably the remarkable Prelude, the lovely "Good-Friday Spell," and the majestic music of the scenes in the Hall of the Grail.

CHARACTERS

TITUREL *(Tee'-too-rel), a Holy Knight*	Bass
AMFORTAS *(Ahm-for'-tas), his son*	Baritone
GURNEMANZ *(Goor'-ne-mahntz), a veteran knight of the Grail*	Bass
PARSIFAL *(Pahr'-see-fahl), "a guileless fool"*	Tenor
KUNDRY *(Koon'-dree)*	Soprano

Knights of the Grail, Klingsor's Flower-Maidens, Youths and Boys.

The action takes place during the Middle Ages, in Spain, at Monsalvat, near and in the Castle of the Holy Grail, and in Klingsor's enchanted garden and castle.

The Prelude is conceived with a simplicity and dignity of form worthy of the lofty subject of the drama. Without any preliminaries, without any accompaniment, the motive of the "Last Supper" rises, calm and reverent, yet most poignant in its tone color. It is repeated with an accompaniment that induces an aspect of awesome mystery. Then is heard the tranquil motive of the "Grail." Its mood of subdued veneration is soon effaced by the motive of "Faith" which is pealed out in the most solemn majesty by the orchestral

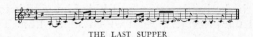

THE LAST SUPPER

brasses. These themes are at once repeated in the loveliest of the softer orchestral voices.

bles his pride in his archery, his eyes fill with tears and he throws away his arrows and breaks his bow. When questioned he betrays the astonishing fact that he knows neither his own name nor that of his father. His mother he left only recently and, wandering about aimlessly, has come to this sacred domain. Kundry listens to his narrative with marked interest, displays some knowledge with his history and startles the youth by informing him that since he left his home, his mother has died. He is so overwhelmed by grief that he seems about to faint, and Kundry revives him with water.

ENCHANTMENT

Then, while the weird theme of "Enchantment" is heard in the orchestra, she sinks down unable to withstand the trance-like sleep which overcomes her. Gurnemanz, thinking that this boy may be the Promised One, turns to conduct him to the castle of the Grail. As they walk, the scene moves, forming a shifting panorama until they enter the great hall of the Grail. (At many performances this moving background is omitted and the curtain merely lowered while the scenes are being changed.)

The music assumes a stately and solemn character as the aged Knight and the boy enter the sanctuary. The Hall is at first empty, but is gradually filled with knights who enter in a dignified procession and take their places at the tables which are ranged around an altar beneath the great central dome. It is the hour of the sacred rite, and while the song of the liturgy echoes throughout the Hall, Amfortas is carried in and assisted to a couch at the altar. From a nearby recess, the voice of Titurel is heard speaking as though from a tomb. He bids his son uncover the Grail. But Amfortas cries out in agonized protest, for this sight which brings joy and peace to others only increases his suffering, and sending the blood coursing wildly through his veins, causes the wound to break out afresh. He sinks down exhausted, but presently yields to the command of his father. The shrine is uncovered disclosing a crystal Cup, and the Hall is permeated by a mysterious darkness. Soon an increasingly dazzling light falls from above, and as the Grail becomes radiant with a soft glow, Amfortas lifts the sacred vessel and slowly moving it from side to side consecrates the bread and wine. The heavenly light gradually vanishes, the Grail is again enclosed in its shrine, and daylight returns. The Knights and Esquires sing a reverent hymn while the consecrated elements are distributed; but the exaltation which filled Amfortas during the ceremony passes, his wound breaks out afresh, and falling back weakly, he is carried from the Hall. The Knights follow and only Gurnemanz and his companion remain. The youth has stood watching the ceremony, silent and motionless, nor does he reply when the veteran Knight questions him concerning what he has seen. Irritated at his apparent stupidity, Gurnemanz opens a side door and turns him out, saying: "Thou art but a fool . . . begone . . . hereafter leave our swans alone, and seek thyself, gander, a goose." He closes the door angrily . . . voices are heard from the heights of the dome singing a lovely cadence . . . the curtain falls.

ACT II

THE Prelude to the Second Act with its sinuously winding theme of "Enchantment" and the wild crying of "Kundry" transports us to an entirely different world. At the rise of the curtain we discern vaguely the keep of Klingsor's castle so shrouded in gloom that the strange instruments of necromancy scattered about can hardly be seen. Klingsor himself is nearly invisible in the mysterious blue smoke that comes from the magic flame at which he stands invoking some unearthly power. He summons Kundry, who rises from the shadows still in her trance-like slumber and awakens with a terrible cry. Klingsor mocks her for her devotion to the knights of the Grail whenever he releases her from his spell; yet he says, she was a priceless aid to him in overpowering Amfortas. She struggles against these remorse-bringing memories and curses the very thought of them. Yet Klingsor proudly tells her that a more splendid victory shall be hers today. There is but one obstacle between him and the attainment of his ambition and that is the stainless youth who even now is approaching. Let her successfully tempt him as she did Amfortas and the battle will be won. Crying out in the wildest agony, Kundry refuses to obey, but Klingsor's magic is the stronger, and at last she disappears to carry out his will. From the parapet of the tower,

German Railroads Information Office

THE GARDEN SCENE—FROM A LITHOGRAPH

Klingsor watches the enemy scale the ramparts and overcome the castle's defenders.

Suddenly, the tower and magician sink into the earth and instead there rises from the ground an enchanted garden filled with flowers of weird, exotic beauty. On the wall surrounding the garden stands the strange, little-knowing youth whom we saw ejected from Monsalvat. As he gazes about bewilderedly, there come from all hands the beautiful denizens of the place, Klingsor's Flower-Maidens, clad in their flowing, diaphanous garments. They approach hurriedly, at first singly, then in groups. They are in alarm for they have discovered that some of their lovers have been slain by an unknown foe. Seeing the stranger they accuse him. He innocently claims the victory, saying that had he not conquered he never could have entered their lovely domain. They soon accept him as a friend; they dance about him, touching his cheeks with their soft hands, and seeking to arouse him to a sense of their beauty. But one more lovely than they approaches. Beholding Kundry, fair beyond the dreams of men, they depart, laughing at the youth for his naïve response to their allurements—he has grown angry and turned to flee. "Tarry, Parsifal," Kundry calls, and the astonished youth remains rooted to the spot; now he remembers that once in the dim past his mother called him by that name. Kundry draws nearer through the luxuriant foliage. She tells the wondering youth

Ich sah' das kind (*I Saw the Child*) **Frida Leider** 7523-2.00

that it was she who first gave him the name of Parsifal, an inversion of the Arabian *"Fal parsi"*—"guileless fool." She tells him of his father, the Knight Gamuret, and of how he was slain in battle before the birth of his son: how Herzeleide (Heart's Sorrow), Parsifal's mother, reared him in the forest, far from the ways of men; and how, her son having departed, she pined away and died. Parsifal is naturally greatly affected and bows in grief. Kundry takes him in her arms caressingly, and while he is still shaken with emotion tells him that she comes to him as his mother's last gift. She bends over him and presses a long kiss upon his lips. Kundry's carefully thought out plan seems to have succeeded, but only for a moment. Suddenly Parsifal starts up, crying out, "Amfortas! the Spear-wound!" He beholds as in a vision the scene in the Hall of the Grail and understands for the first time its significance. Kundry's endeavors to lead his mind back to thoughts of passion only reveal to him more clearly the nature of Amfortas' temptation, and he pushes her angrily away. Now she appeals to his pity by telling him of the curse under which she lives: ages ago she saw Him staggering under His Cross and laughed; His look fell upon her and since that hour she has wandered over the earth vainly seeking to see Him again; now she has found Parsifal, her deliverer—if he will but embrace her, salvation shall be hers. Parsifal rebukes her, saying that deliverance is not won by indulgence, and adds that he now seeks the way back to Amfortas. Turning upon him with the full hatred of thwarted desire, Kundry curses him—may he never find his

GURNEMANZ' HERMITAGE

homeward road. She calls Klingsor to come to her aid, and the sorcerer immediately appears on the ramparts of his castle. He flings the sacred Spear at the youth. And now a miracle happens. The Lance, changed from its course, hovers over Parsifal. He seizes it and makes with it the sign of the Cross. As with an earthquake the castle falls into ruins, the garden withers to a desert, and Kundry sinks down with a cry. In turning to depart, Parsifal exclaims to her: "Thou knowest where only we shall meet again!"

ACT III

ON VICTOR RECORDS

Act III (with the exception of a brief portion at the beginning of the opening scene) has been completely recorded for Victor by renowned Wagnerian artists and the chorus and orchestra of the Berlin State Opera, conducted by Karl Muck. The rôles are distributed as follows: Parsifal, Gotthelf Pistor; Gurnemanz, Ludwig Hofmann; Amfortas, Cornelis Brongeest. The performance is recorded on eight Victor Records. M-67 (7160-7167), AM-67 (7168-7175), $16.00. The following description is keyed to these records.

The prelude to the Third Act (Records 1 and 2), at once plunges us into the gloom and desolation that have now fallen over the Knights of the Grail. The themes of "Kundry," "The Lance," "The Grail," "The Promise" and "Enchantment" all enter but in a somber broken form. At the rise of the curtain we are shown the rude hut where Gurnemanz now makes his solitary abode. The early light of a spring morning is breathing through the leaves of the forest as the faithful Knight, now bent and hoary with age, issues from his dwelling. A strange moaning from a woodland thicket nearby has aroused him; he approaches and discovers Kundry, unconscious, yet crying out as though troubled by some frightful dream. Tending her carefully, he restores her to consciousness. She is less savage but even more wan in her appearance than when we last saw her serving the Knights of the Grail at Monsalvat. She at once resumes her humble duties and in bringing a pitcher of water from the spring observes a new arrival at the domains of the Grail. It is a knight in black armor, with visor closed; Parsifal, weary from long searching, has at last found Monsalvat. Gurnemanz asks him to remove his armor, for this is holy ground and should not be profaned, least of all on this, the most holy of days, Good Friday. Parsifal complies, and striking the Lance which he carries into the ground, kneels before it in fervent prayer. Gurnemanz and Kundry, now recognizing Parsifal, are filled with mingled emotions. Parsifal, rising from his meditations *(Record 3)*, tells Gurnemanz of his joy at seeing him, of the many hardships that beset his path, of the wounds and suffering which he endured during the long search for Monsalvat—hardships all brought about because of a curse which had been placed on him. Gurnemanz is profoundly stirred on beholding again the sacred Lance *(Record 4)*. He tells Parsifal of the sad estate of the Knighthood: Amfortas, driven by his intense sufferings of body and soul, longs only for death and refuses to fulfill his holy office; deprived of the heavenly sustenance of the Grail, the Knights are powerless. No longer, he continues *(Record 5)*, do they journey forth in holy warfare; Titurel, deprived of the vision of the Grail, has died. Parsifal cries out in grief, accusing himself of being the cause of all these misfortunes, and sinks back fainting. Kundry brings water, but Gurnemanz reproves her gently saying that the sacred spring itself would be better. To it they now lead Parsifal *(Record 6)*. On reviving he asks to be conducted to Amfortas. Gurnemanz assures him that this shall be done, for this very day the obsequies of Titurel are to be celebrated, and Amfortas will again, and according to a vow he has made, for the last time unveil the Grail. Now Kundry, eager and humble, bathes his feet, and Gurnemanz, taking water from the spring, baptizes him, pronouncing the solemn words of invocation. Kundry takes a golden vial from her bosom, and pouring a part of its contents over Parsifal's feet, dries them with her hair, hastily unbound *(Record 7)*. Parsifal, who has been observing these ministrations in deep emotion, takes the vial from Kundry, and giving

PARSIFAL

it to Gurnemanz, bids the Knight anoint his head; thus it is that Gurnemanz consecrates Parsifal as King of the Grail, while in the orchestra the theme of "Parsifal" is proclaimed with great majesty.

As a first act of compassion, the New King baptizes Kundry, who falls weeping to the ground. Now the soft weaving of the theme of "Good Fri-day" rises in the orchestra and Parsifal, looking out over the woods and meadows exclaims *(Record 8)*:

GOOD FRIDAY

How fair the woods and meadows seem today!
Many a magic flow'r I've seen
Which sought to clasp me in its baneful twinings:
But none I've seen so sweet as here,
These tendrils bursting with blossom,
Whose scent recalls my childhood's days
And speaks of loving trust to me.

Gurnemanz explains, saying, "That is Good Friday's spell, my lord!" Parsi-fal continues:

Alas, that day of agony!
Now surely everything that thrives,
That breathes and lives and lives again,
Should only mourn and sorrow!

Gurnemanz explains that this beauty of the woods and fields is caused by the spell of Good Friday, and that the flowers and trees, watered by the tears of repentant sinners, express by their luxuriance the redemption of man. He says:

Thou see'st that is not so.
The sad repentant tears of sinners
Have here with holy rain
Besprinkled field and plain,
And made them glow with beauty.
All earthly creatures in delight
At the Redeemer's trace so bright
Uplift their pray'rs of duty.
(End of Record 8, beginning of 9.)

To see Him on the Cross they have no power:
And so they smile upon redeemed man,
Who, feeling freed, with dread no more doth cower,
Through God's love-sacrifice made clean and pure:
And now perceives each blade and meadow-flower
That mortal foot today it need not dread;
For, as the Lord in pity man did spare,
And in His mercy for him bled,
All men will keep, with pious care,
Today a tender tread.
Then thanks the whole creation makes,
With all that flow'rs and fast goes hence,
That trespass-pardoned Nature wakes
Now to her day of Innocence.

335

PARSIFAL, KUNDRY AND GURNEMANZ ENTERING THE CASTLE

Kundry has slowly raised her head again, and gazes with moist eyes, earnestly and calmly beseeching Parsifal. He speaks *(Record 10)*:

> I saw my scornful mockers wither;
> Now look they for forgiveness hither?
> Like blessed sweet dew a tear from thee too floweth:
> Thou weepest—see! the landscape gloweth.
> *(He kisses her softly on the brow.)*

A distant tolling of bells being heard, Gurnemanz says:

> Mid-day: the hour has come.
> Permit, my lord, thy servant hence to lead thee!

Gurnemanz has brought out a coat-of-mail and mantle of the Knights, which he and Kundry put on Parsifal. As they go their way, the landscape gradually changes until finally they disappear in the rocky entrance to the castle *(end of Record 10; beginning of Record 11)*. Processions of Knights are seen in the long arched passageways; the tolling of bells constantly increases. At last the great Hall becomes visible, but the tables are no longer there, and the place is dimly lighted. There enter two processions of Knights singing to one another antiphonally:

> FIRST TRAIN *(with the Grail and Amfortas)*:
> To sacred place in sheltering Shrine
> The Holy Grail do we carry;
> What hide ye there in gloomy shrine
> Which hither mourning ye bear?

SECOND TRAIN *(with Titurel's bier)*:

> A hero lies in this dismal shrine
> With all this heavenly strength,
> To whom all things once God did entrust:
> Titurel hither we bear.
>> *(End of Record 11, beginning of 12.)*

FIRST TRAIN:

> By whom was he slain, who by God himself
> Once was ever sheltered?

SECOND TRAIN:

> He sank beneath the mortal burden of years,
> When the Grail no more he might look on.

FIRST TRAIN:

> Who veiled then the Grail's delights from his vision?

SECOND TRAIN:

> He whom ye are bearing: its criminal guardian.

FIRST TRAIN:

> We conduct him today, for here once again.
> —And once more only—
> He fulfilleth his office.

SECOND TRAIN:

> Sorrow! Sorrow! Thou guard of the Grail!
> Be once more only warned of thy duty to all.

The bier is placed at one side, and Amfortas is helped to his throne back of the altar. He exclaims weakly at his misfortune, then *(Record 13)* breaks into his agonizing prayer:

> My father!
> Highest venerated hero!
> Thou purest, to whom once e'en the angels bended!
> Oh! thou who now in heavenly heights
> Dost behold the Saviour's self,
> Implore Him to grant that His hallowed blood,
> (If once again his blessing
> He pour upon these brothers)
> To them new life while giving,
> To me may offer—but Death!
> My father! I call thee.
> Cry thou my words to Him:
> "Redeemer, give to my son release!"

But the Knights pressing nearer to Amfortas, exclaim *(Record 14)*:

> Uncover the shrine!
> Do thou thine office!

337

PATIENCE

(or, Bunthorne's Bride)

COMIC OPERA in two acts. Libretto by W. S. Gilbert; music by Arthur Sullivan. Recorded completely in Victor Record Album C-14 (11070-11079) AC-14 (11080-11089) $15.00, by the D'Oyly Carte Opera Company. The story of the opera is keyed to the records.

DRAMATIS PERSONAE

COLONEL CALVERLEY
MAJOR MURGATROYD   *Officers of Dragoon Guards*
LIEUT. THE DUKE OF DUNSTABLE
REGINALD BUNTHORNE *(A Fleshly Poet)*
ARCHIBALD GROSVENOR *(An Idyllic Poet)*
THE LADY ANGELA
THE LADY SAPHIR
THE LADY ELLA   *Rapturous Maidens*
THE LADY JANE
PATIENCE *(A Dairy Maid)*
    Chorus of Rapturous Maidens and Officers of Dragoon Guards

OVERTURE *(C 14-1)*

ACT I

THE opening scene is laid at "Castle Bunthorne," where Bunthorne, aesthetic poet, is explaining to twenty love-sick maidens *(C 14-2)* the mysteries of love, which, he asserts, can be cured by proper medical treatment. They listen to him with adoration, but he remains insensible to their passion. He loves Patience, they declare.

De Bellis

MARTYN GREEN OF THE D'OYLY
CARTE OPERA COMPANY AS
BUNTHORNE

Patience, a simple dairy-maid *(C 14-3)*, has never loved anyone except an aunt, and learns that true love must be "utter unselfishness." The previous year the officers of a regiment of Dragoon Guards, whose colonel now introduces himself and them in a rollicking, boastful song *(C 14-4)*, has been much beloved by the twenty maidens, but now they are accorded a different welcome. *(C 14-5 and 6.)* Bunthorne has "idealised them" and "their eyes are opened." When alone, he admits being a sham —only feigning aestheticism to gain admiration. *(C 14-7.)*

Patience remembers a boy who was her child-companion, and when Archibald Grosvenor appears she discovers it is he. They love

340

each other, but Patience, in her belief that true love is "utter unselfishness," thinks she cannot marry one so perfect. (*C 14-8 and 9.*)

Bunthorne, returning, has decided to put himself up to be raffled for (*C 14-10*), and just as the lot is to be drawn, Patience in her "utter unselfishness" says that she will marry him because "she detests him so."

The disappointed maidens then return to the Dragoons, but when they see Archibald Grosvenor, immediately transfer their affections to him because "he is aesthetic!" Bunthorne is jealous, and the Dragoons disgusted. (*C 14-11, 12, 13 and 14.*)

ACT II

A "RURAL GLADE." The unattractive Jane, bewails the lot of maidens who have been in that state too long. (*C 14-15.*) Grosvenor is now adored by all the maidens. He is somewhat annoyed by their attentions for they have followed him since Monday. (*C 14-16.*) He pleads for "the usual half-holiday on Saturday." Patience, meanwhile, muses upon love. (*C 14-17.*)

Bunthorne, deserted and consumed by jealousy, has still one faithful admirer—the portly Lady Jane (*C 14-18 and 19*), whose charms decrease as her size increases. She implores him not to wait too long, but Bunthorne is determined to beat Grosvenor on his own ground.

At last the rival poets meet. Bunthorne threatens to "curse" Archibald unless he consents to cut his hair and become quite commonplace. Grosvenor outwardly appalled, but secretly relieved, consents to become an "every day young man" (*C 14-20*).

Now that Bunthorne is happy, Patience, in her "utter unselfishness," breaks her engagement. Upon Archibald Grosvenor's return, in a tweed suit, she realizes that since he is now a commonplace young man, she can marry him.

Bunthorne finds that the twenty love-sick maidens have returned to their soldier-lovers. He then decides to console himself with the portly Lady Jane. But the Duke of Dunstable, desirous of marrying a plain woman, has already claimed Lady Jane, so Bunthorne is left without a bride!

Lucas-Pritchard
SYLVIA CECIL (D'OYLY CARTE OPERA COMPANY) AS PATIENCE

ZURGA PRONOUNCES JUDGMENT UPON LEILA AND NADIR

LES PÊCHEURS DE PERLES

(The Pearl Fishers)

OPERA in three acts; music by Georges Bizet; libretto by Carré and Cormon. First produced September 29, 1863, at the Théâtre Lyrique, Paris. First performed in the United States at the Grand Opera House, Philadelphia, August 25, 1893.

Not until the success of "Carmen" did the world ask, too late for Bizet to hear, what other operas this brilliant composer might have produced. "The Pearl Fishers" had previously met with little success, but once revived, it revealed a wealth of unregarded, almost unsuspected, beauty. Based on an Oriental theme, it is picturesque and colorful, even though it lacks the dash and electric thrill of "Carmen." Its lovely melodies are coming into the better appreciation they deserve.

The original French name of the opera, "Les Pêcheurs de Perles," is pronounced *Lay Peh-shur duh Pairl*; the Italian, "I Pescatori di Perle," *Ee Pes-kah-toh'-ree dee Pair'leh.*

The action is supposed to take place in Ceylon during barbaric times.

ACT I

SCENE—*The Coast of Ceylon*

Z URGA, the newly selected leader of the little world of Cingalese fishermen, has scarcely been inaugurated when Nadir, a long lost friend of his youth, appears. After greeting one another with affection, they recall the time when they were foolish enough to quarrel over a beautiful priestess in the temple of Brahma, Leila. In the duet, "Del tempio al limitar," they sing of the moment when they saw her, and both fell in love with her as she was revealed to them for an instant in the dim, incense-clouded temple. Believing themselves cured of the old infatuation they swear eternal friendship—blood-brotherhood.

Del tempio al limitar *(In the Depths of the Temple)* **Beniamino Gigli, Giuseppe de Luca 8084-2.00**

A veiled priestess approaches on her way to the temple to pray for the success of the fishermen. Every year she comes thus, mysteriously; none have dared gaze upon her countenance for she is held to be sacred to Brahma. She is about to swear to Zurga's charge of chastity and of faithfulness in prayer for her people when she happens to see Nadir and is greatly startled. She is reminded by the High Priest, Nourabad, that she may revoke her vows, but this she refuses and enters the temple. The people disperse, leaving Nadir alone. Agitated by the discovery that he still loves Leila, he sings an air, pathetic yet beautiful, in which he describes the lovely girl as he once saw and heard her singing among the palms on a star-lit tropical night. Around this truly haunting melody, tinged with a faint Oriental color, the orchestral strings weave a fascinating atmospheric background.

Mi par d'udir ancora *(I Hear as in a Dream)* **Beniamino Gigli 1656-1.50 Je crois entendre encore** *(I Hear as in a Dream)* **Enrico Caruso 7770-2.00**

He is about to go to warn Zurga of all this; but overcome with weariness, falls asleep on the temple steps. There Leila finds him, and while seeming to continue the prayer to Brahma, she subtly makes known her love for him. Nadir, completely under the sway of his former passion, forgets Zurga and, under cover of the encroaching darkness, hastens to his love.

ACT II

SCENE—*A Ruined Temple*

L EILA, about to begin her lonely watch, is reminded by Nourabad of her vow and the punishment that is certain to overtake her should she in the least violate her solemn oath. She replies that she is in no danger of so doing for once when a child she swore to protect a fugitive who implored her aid. Even though his enemies threatened to kill her, she kept her vow. He was enabled to escape and in gratitude he gave her a golden chain as a

343

remembrance. Nevertheless she is now left trembling by the priest who again threatens her with the doom certain to be hers should she prove unfaithful.

But her fears are forgotten at the arrival of Nadir, and soon the two are completely lost in the ecstasy of their love. They are surprised by Nourabad who alarms the people. The fishermen advance with drawn swords, demanding death for the couple. Zurga, mindful of his pledge of friendship with Nadir, intervenes in the couple's behalf until Nourabad draws aside the veil from the girl's face. It is none other than Leila, the very woman Nadir has sworn with Zurga to forget. Enraged at his friend's treachery, the chieftain condemns the guilty pair to death.

ACT III

Scene I—*The Camp of Zurga*

Leila pleads with Zurga for the life of her lover, but Zurga only reveals his own jealousy. Too proud to sue for her own life, the condemned priestess increases the chieftain's wrath by scorning him. Nourabad enters to announce the execution and to him Leila gives the golden chain of the fugitive with the plea that he send it to her mother.

Scene II—*The Place of Execution*

Just as the lovers are about to mount the funeral pyre, a distant glow, at first thought to be the dawn, is seen. Zurga rushes in crying out that the camp is on fire. When the people have scattered to save their goods and children, Zurga explains to the couple that he has set fire to the camp in order to save them, for he has recognized Leila's golden chain. It was he who gave it to her years ago when she had saved his life. The lovers escape.

When the people return, Nourabad denounces Zurga, for he has again been eavesdropping and overheard all that has taken place. Zurga is compelled to mount the funeral pyre. As the flames roar about him, it is seen that the forest itself is ablaze, and, surrounded and overcome by this sea of flames, the people fall prostrate before the wrath of Brahma.

PÉLLÉAS AND MÉLISANDE

OPERA in five acts; music by Claude Debussy; text by Maeterlinck. First produced, April 30, 1902, at the Opéra Comique, Paris, with Mary Garden and Jean Perier in the title rôles. First performance in the United States, at the Manhattan Opera House, New York, February 1, 1908.

Maeterlinck's drama, Pélléas and Mélisande has for the basis of its plot such a simple form of the eternal triangle, that a mere recital of it fails to convey any of the play's great poetic charm and beauty. In fact, stripping the plot of the subtle symbolism of the lines is like trying to present the wonderful impressionistic colors of a Monet painting in a black and white copy.

For this very subdued and appealing drama, Debussy has supplied music of great delicacy and subtly suggestive power. Often the orchestra furnishes a decorative background while the voices sing in a recitative style that closely follows the natural inflections of the speaking voice. At times of climax, the music rises to greater prominence and attains remarkable beauty and emotional force, though still serving to underline the poetic sentiment of the text.

J. Quentin Jaxon

PÉLLÉAS AND MÉLISANDE

AN ALBUM OF PÉLLÉAS RECORDS

An exceptional treat is provided for lovers of Debussy's music in this album —eight Victor records of many of the most beautiful passages in the opera, including the orchestral interludes, the duet at the fountain, the scene at the tower, and the parting of Pélléas and Mélisande. The orchestra is conducted by Piero Coppola and the artists are M. Panzéra (Pélléas), Mme. Yvonne Brothier (Mélisande), M. Tubiana (Arkel), and M. Vanni-Marcoux (Golaud), all of the Opéra Comique, Paris, the theatre at which Pélléas was first performed. They interpret Debussy's music with remarkable finish and in a truly authoritative style; and every nuance of the score is faithfully reproduced on these Victor records. Musical Masterpiece Series, M-68 (4174-4176, 9636-9639, 1444) Price $10.50.

(It is usual in American opera houses to perform the first two scenes of Act IV as one scene and to omit entirely the third scene in which Yniold watches a flock of sheep. Thus what was originally Scene IV of Act IV becomes Scene II, and in the following account of the opera it is so numbered.)

CHARACTERS

ARKEL *(Ahr-kel'), King of Allemonde*   *Bass*
GENEVIÈVE *(Zhahn-viev'), Mother of Pélléas and Golaud*   *Contralto*

345

PÉLLÉAS *(Pay-lay-hss')* ⎫   *Grandsons*   ⎧   *Tenor*
GOLAUD *(Goh-loh')*   ⎬   *of Arkel*   ⎨   *Baritone*
MÉLISANDE *(May-lee-sand')*   *Soprano*
YNIOLD *(Een-yawld')*   *A Child's Voice*
A Physician, Servants, Poor People.

ACT I

SCENE I

GOLAUD has lost his way in the depths of the forest and while wandering aimlessly about, finds a beautiful young woman weeping at the edge of a spring. Her answers to his questions are so vague and mysterious that he cannot learn whence she came, how she happens to be there, or why. She has dropped a golden crown in the spring, but will not permit him to recover it for her; nor will she allow him to come near. She does, finally, tell him her name, Mélisande. Then, as it is growing dark and Golaud insists that they seek shelter, she follows him nervously at a distance, like a timid, frightened animal.

SCENE II

The change of scene is accompanied by a beautiful orchestral interlude in which is heard prominently a theme associated with the unhappy fate of the lovers. Six months are supposed to have elapsed and the curtain rises disclosing the room in the somber castle of Arkel, King of Allemonde. Geneviève is reading to the King a letter that Pélléas has just received from his brother, Golaud, telling of his marriage to Mélisande. Golaud fears that Arkel will not forgive him for having thus married without his consent when a union of political importance had been planned for him. Pélléas enters to ask the King's permission to go to visit a dying friend. But the father of Pélléas also is ill, and Arkel, reminding him of this, bids him place a signal light for Golaud and remain at the castle until his brother's return.

SCENE III

Again a beautiful interlude accompanies the change of scene. Mélisande, Geneviève, and Pélléas having come out of the gloomy castle to watch the ocean at sunset, see a ship that bravely embarks in spite of the threatening storm. Night approaches suddenly, and Geneviève, hurrying off to take care of her little grandson, Yniold, asks Pélléas to conduct Mélisande back to the castle. To Pélléas' seemingly casual remark that on the morrow he must leave, Mélisande responds with the childlike cry, "Why must you go?"

ACT II

SCENE I

TO ESCAPE the stifling summer noon's heat at the castle, Pélléas and Mélisande have come to an ancient, deserted fountain in one of the most remote and silent parts of the woods. After asking, "Do you know where I have brought you?" Pélléas tells her of this fountain (*Vous ne savez pas*). It is reputed to have had miraculous powers. Once it is said to have restored sight to the blind; but now even the King is nearly sightless, and not a soul comes to the place. Mélisande is fascinated by the water; she tries to reach it as she sits on the edge of the well, but only her long, loose-flowing hair is able to penetrate beneath its surface. Pélléas recalls it was beside a spring that Golaud found Mélisande (*C'est an bord d'une fontaine aussi*). Now, Mélisande begins to play with a ring—a ring that Golaud has given her. She throws it up in the air, high up so as to see it sparkle in the few rays of sunlight that manage to penetrate through the dense foliage. Pélléas begs her to be careful; suddenly the ring slips through her fingers into the dark waters of the well. They think they can see it glisten as it sinks. It never will be recovered for the well is immeasurably deep. Moreover they cannot stop longer now, for Pélléas heard twelve o'clock being struck just as the ring disappeared, and they will be sought at the castle.

SCENE II

The change of scene is accompanied by an orchestral interlude in which the bright, flowing music of the fountain sinks down and vanishes beneath the stern tread of the motive of "Fate."

Golaud is lying on his bed in a room in the castle; Mélisande is at the bedside. All is going well now, he remarks, while telling her how he came to be injured. (*Ah! Ah! Tout va bien.*) He cannot understand how it was that just as he finished counting the twelve strokes of noon, the horse on which he was riding at the hunt ran wildly away, for no apparent reason. His injuries were not serious, however, and he tenderly bids Mélisande go to sleep for the night. Suddenly she bursts into tears; and to Golaud's anxious questions she only replies that she is not happy there—it is no one's fault, not the King's, not Golaud's mother, Pélléas, no—it is not Pélléas', it is the darkness of the place: one never sees the blue sky. Golaud tries to console her. Tenderly he takes her hands, and then he notices that the ring he gave her is missing. Instantly he is alarmed. To his insistent questions she replies with childishly evasive answers, finally saying that she dropped the ring in a grotto by the sea. Golaud orders her to go at once to find it, even in the darkness of night. Pélléas will conduct her safely.

SCENE III

During the orchestral interlude, the gentle theme associated with Mélisande is heard in poignant, sorrowful form and the rippling music of the fountain enters briefly. Then all is broken by an eerie formlessness and the curtain rises on a dark cavern by the sea.

Pélléas and Mélisande come groping their way like children through the dense obscurity. Pélléas leads Mélisande into the grotto so that in case Golaud asks she will be able to describe the place. The roar of the sea echoing through the grotto makes it seem even more dismal and terrifying. The moon throws a sudden flood of light into the cavern and reveals a group of paupers who have sought shelter there, for now a famine is raging in the land. Mélisande is so greatly frightened that Pélléas has to hurry back to the castle with her.

ACT III

SCENE I

MÉLISANDE is at a window, up in one of the towers of the castle. While she combs her unbound hair, arranging it for the night, she sings some ancient song that quaintly lists a number of saints. Pélléas comes up the watchman's path around the tower. He halts beneath the window, for tomorrow he must leave. (*Il fait beau cette nuit.*) Again in her childish way she tells him he must not leave—she will not let him take her hand to kiss it in farewell if he goes. Pélléas promises to delay his departure; she leans far out of the window so that he can reach her hand. In so doing her long, magnificent hair comes streaming down over Pélléas, overwhelming him with delicious excitement at the touch of her glorious tresses. In his ecstasy he exclaims that he will hold her thus forever. (*Je les tiens dans les mains.*) Some frightened doves fly out of the tower and hover around them in the darkness. Golaud comes silently around the path. He is agitated at finding Pélléas and Mélisande thus, and laughing nervously, scolds them for playing like children in the night—both children.

SCENE II

The "Fate" motive is heard. It grows suddenly to a climax at which the expressive "Mélisande" theme enters. This in turn subsides and the interlude closes with the ominous theme of "Vengeance."

Golaud has led Pélléas down into the subterranean vaults beneath the castle to see the stagnant pool that lies there. He bids Pélléas let him hold his arm, and then lean out over the chasm. Does he smell the death-like stench that rises? Pélléas is alarmed at the way Golaud's hand holding aloft the lantern trembles; the two hurry out in silence.

SCENE III

The brothers come out from the vaults; Pélléas is happy again to breathe the pure air from the sea. (*Ah, je respire enfin.*) Golaud cautions Pélléas about continuing such childish play with Mélisande as took place the night before. She may become a mother soon and must be spared any shock. Almost threateningly he warns Pélléas to avoid Mélisande as much as possible —though not too markedly, he adds.

SCENE IV

Golaud brings Yniold, his little son by a former wife, out before the castle, and by repeated questioning, tries to learn more of the state of affairs between Pélléas and Mélisande. But the child's answers are so vague that they only tantalize Golaud's suspicions. A light appears in Mélisande's window and Golaud holds Yniold up high so he can look in the room. Yes, Pélléas is there with Mélisande, but they do not speak. No, they do not come near one another, and they do not close their eyes. Then the child becomes frightened and is about to cry aloud so that the unhappy Golaud has to go, his suspicions only partly confirmed.

ACT IV

Scene I

PÉLLÉAS meets Mélisande along a corridor in the castle, and certain that he will leave on the morrow, he begs and obtains a rendezvous with Mélisande—midnight at the well of the blind. The two go their separate ways: Mélisande returns after a moment with Arkel. The old King is filled with sympathy and kindness for her; he hopes that now since the father of Pélléas has recovered, the castle will seem less gloomy and that she will be happier *(Maintenant que le Père de Pélléas est sauvé)*. Half soliloquizing, he says he believes that a young, fair and joyful being will create an atmosphere of joy around itself. In the utmost tenderness, as if speaking to a grandchild, he asks to kiss her . . . the aged need to be reminded of youth in order to drive away for a time the menaces of death. Golaud enters searching for his sword. He rebukes Mélisande for her nervousness; he cannot endure the gaze of her great open eyes. Arkel says he sees in them only a great innocence. This releases the flood of Golaud's pent-up fury. In cruelest irony he cries, that God himself might take a lesson in innocence from her eyes—one would say that the angels were continually baptizing themselves in that innocence. *(Une grande innocence.)* He seizes Mélisande by her long hair—at last it has a use—and drags her savagely to and fro across the floor. Arkel restores quiet; if he were God, he says he would have pity on the hearts of men!

Scene II

An interlude of unusual length and of great expressiveness accompanies the change of scene: the "Fate" motive, played with passionate intensity . . . then the theme of Mélisande for a moment as the music subsides . . . another tense climax . . . finally gloom and foreboding.

In the uncanny silence and obscurity of midnight the desolate fountain of the blind seems doubly mysterious and supernatural. There Pélléas now awaits Mélisande. He reflects how he has played with the forces of destiny; perhaps it would be better if he never again saw her. Yet it seems that a century has passed since last they met. Soon he forgets his fears under the thrill of his excitement at her approach. Mélisande recalls that they came here once long ago *(Nous sommes venus ici il y a longtemps)*. Tenderly she asks why he must leave. He hesitates, saying, "It is because" . . . then he

349

kisses her suddenly, "I love you." Mélisande answers quietly, "I also love you." Pélléas is overwhelmed with the frenzy of love, exultant in the thought that Mélisande loves him, remorseful that they must part. They hear the castle gates being closed for the night; rather than be afraid they rejoice that they are together. (*Quel est ce bruit? On ferme les portes.*) Mélisande believes that she hears Golaud behind them among the trees; Pélléas thinks that is only the wind in the leaves; an instant later they are sure that it is he crouching in the darkness. They would conceal themselves among the shadows; but they realize Golaud has seen all; he carries his sword, Pélléas has not his. Then, filled with a sudden desperate abandon they embrace wildly—it seems that the stars of the whole heavens are falling upon them. Golaud rushes out, sword in hand, stabs Pélléas and pursues the fleeing Mélisande.

ACT V

Mélisande is lying on a bed in a room in the castle; Arkel, Golaud and a physician are watching. The physician says that it is not of the very trifling wound Golaud gave her that she is dying—perhaps, indeed, she may recover. The others having left him alone with Mélisande in response to his earnest entreaties, Golaud begs her forgiveness. Anxiously he asks her if she will answer just one question and tell the exact truth. Then, on her assent, he asks excitedly, "Did you love Pélléas?" With the utmost naïveté she replies, "Yes, indeed, I loved him. Is he here?" Golaud believes she does not understand. Again she replies that their love was not guilty; the childlike simplicity of her manner racks the soul of Golaud. Impassionedly he demands to know the truth; Arkel and the physician reënter, and the despairing Golaud remains as one blind. Though the air is cold, Mélisande wishes the window left open so that she may watch the setting sun. She scarcely seems to realize that she has a little daughter; when Arkel gently shows the child to her she quietly remarks, "She is very tiny, she is going to weep also. . . ." The serving-women of the castle gradually enter the room and take their places along the wall, where they remain waiting, silently. They have not been sent for, why do they come? They make no reply to Golaud's excited questions. Mélisande stretches forth her arms—it is the struggle of the mother. . . . Suddenly the serving-women drop to their knees. "What is it?" asks Arkel. The physician goes over to Mélisande, then replies, "They are right." Arkel speaks to the sobbing Golaud, "Come, now she needs silence . . . she was such a quiet, timid creature, a mysterious being, as is everyone . . . Come, we must not leave her child in this room; it must live on now and take her place . . . it's the turn of the poor little one. . . ."

(LEFT TO RIGHT) LITTLE BUTTERCUP, HEBE, SIR JOSEPH PORTER, RALPH RACKSTRAW, AS PLAYED
BY MEMBERS OF THE D'OYLY CARTE COMPANY

PINAFORE

COMIC opera in two acts; music by Sir Arthur Sullivan; text by W. S. Gilbert. First produced at the Opéra Comique, London, May 28, 1878. The first American performance, New York, 1878, was unauthorized; the first important American production took place November, 1897, at the Boston Museum.

The success of "Pinafore" seems to be as lasting as the mighty deep itself, and nearly as widespread; certainly wherever the English language is spoken it is one of the most popular of comic operas. It sprang to instant popularity in the United States, its success being rivaled among Gilbert and Sullivan's works only by the "Mikado." Its popularity is well deserved for it contains some of Gilbert's most clever sallies of wit and some of Sullivan's most charming melodies. Moreover, the former's satire on matters nautical in England during Victorian days and the latter's parody of "sea music" can be as well appreciated and enjoyed now as ever.

CHARACTERS

RT. HON. SIR JOSEPH PORTER, K. C. B., *First Lord of the Admiralty*	*Baritone*
CAPTAIN CORCORAN, *Commanding "H. M. S. Pinafore"*	*Baritone*
RALPH RACKSTRAW, *able seaman*	*Tenor*
DICK DEADEYE, *able seaman*	*Bass*
TOM TUCKER, *midshipmate*	*Tenor*
JOSEPHINE, *the Captain's daughter*	*Soprano*
HEBE, *Sir Joseph's first cousin*	*Mezzo-Soprano*
LITTLE BUTTERCUP, *a bumboat woman*	*Contralto*

First Lord's Sisters, his Cousins and Aunts, Sailors, Marines.

The action takes place on the Quarterdeck of "H. M. S. Pinafore," 1878.

351

"H. M. S. Pinafore" has been recorded in its entirety by the famous D'Oyly Carte Opera Company, the records being included in the album set C-13. The precise enunciation of this notable group, and the fact that English of the choicest and wittiest kind is the language of the opera, make it unnecessary to key the records to the following story of the opera.

Rupert D'Oyly Carte Opera Company Album C-13 (9937-9945) AC-13 (9946-9954) Price $13.50

ACT I

HIS Majesty's Ship, "Pinafore," is anchored in the harbor at Portsmouth. The sailors are busy scrubbing the decks for the expected arrival of Sir Joseph Porter, K. C. B. Little Buttercup, a bumboat woman who is by no means as small as her name would imply, comes aboard with a stock of "snuff and tobaccy and excellent jacky," not to mention "excellent peppermint drops." It transpires that a handsome young sailor, Ralph, is in love with the Captain's daughter, Josephine. She, however, is to be betrothed to Sir Joseph Porter, who duly arrives attended by "his sisters and his cousins and his aunts." In the meantime, Ralph plans to elope with Josephine, the crew assisting. The plot is overheard by Dick Deadeye, the lugubrious boatswain.

ACT II

CAPTAIN CORCORAN is alone on deck and sings to the moon. Little Buttercup comes to him and reveals her affection. He tells her that because of

DARRELL FAUCOURT AS DEADEYE

his rank he can only be her friend; but she hints darkly that a change is in store for him, saying that "things are seldom what they seem." Sir Joseph returns, complaining that Josephine does not favor his suit. The Captain comforts him by averring that she is awed by his lofty station and suggests that he plead his cause on the ground that love levels all rank. Still Josephine does not respond, for her heart is set upon Ralph. Dick Deadeye reveals the elopement plan, and he and the Captain lie in wait for the crew, "carefully on tip-toe stealing." The elopers are captured, and the Captain is so exasperated that he actually swears, using a "big, big D" which is overheard by Sir Joseph Porter. For this serious breach of morals, a horrible example of depravity before the whole crew, the Captain is ordered to his cabin. Affairs are interrupted by Little Buttercup, who discloses a secret, telling how the Captain and Ralph had been accidentally exchanged while they were both babies.

EVELYN GARDINER AS LITTLE BUTTERCUP

Whereupon, Sir Joseph, with true Gilbertian logic, sends for Ralph and makes him Captain, and at the same time reduces Corcoran to Ralph's former humble grade of "able seaman." Now, since it is out of the question for one of Sir Joseph's exalted station to marry the daughter of a mere seaman, his Lordship nobly consents to the marriage of Ralph and Josephine. The erstwhile Captain consoles himself with Little Buttercup.

Gems from Pinafore   *Victor Light Opera Company 35386-1.25*

seaside spot. They mention the fact that their father, because of his age, has been left far behind. . . . But Isabel says, "Oh, he will be here presently." The girls now decide to go in wading, and are in the act of taking off their shoes and stockings, when Frederic comes forward from the cave. He admits he is a pirate *(C 6-6)* and none of the girls will marry him to reform him except, finally, Mabel, daughter of a major-general. Frederic and Mabel make love, the other girls pretending not to notice. *(C 6-7 and 8)*. The pirates enter stealthily, and each embraces a girl for his bride. *(C 6-9.)* At this point Major-General Stanley enters, identifies himself, and protests the union of his daughter and his wards with a band of pirates. *(C 6-10.)* After Major-General Stanley has introduced himself to the Pirates, he demands an explanation of what is transpiring. Samuel tells him that they intend to marry his daughters. The General does not recognize their uniform, and is startled to learn that they are the famous Pirates of Penzance. He says that he objects to pirates as sons-in-law. . . . And the Pirate King—in turn—retorts that they object to Major-Generals as fathers-in-law, but they'll waive the objection. Then the Major-General has an idea. He tells the pirates that he is an orphan, and asks them if they know what it means to be an orphan. The pirates are much disgusted seeing their prey slip through their fingers in this fashion. (They are partial to orphans —you know—because they are all orphans themselves.) There is an argument between the Pirate King and the General over a misunderstanding as they confuse the words "often" and "orphan." Then the Major-General addresses the pirates *(C 6-11)* explaining the situation in detail, and winning permission to depart with his wards from the pirates' haven. *(C 6-12.)*

ACT II

SCENE—A ruined chapel by moonlight on the estate of Major-General Stanley. Crumbling pillars and arches at the sides. Ruined Gothic windows at back. General Stanley is discovered seated pensively at the right, surrounded by his daughters; presently Mabel and Frederic join them. *(C 6-13.)* Mabel asks Frederic if he cannot in any way comfort her father. Frederic asks the General why he sits "in this draughty old ruin." The reply is that he has come to humble himself before the tombs of his ancestors in atonement for the lie he told the pirates—for he is not an orphan. Frederic reminds him that he only just purchased this estate, wondering how he can refer to those buried on it as "his ancestors." The General answers that he does not know whose ancestors they are, but that he feels he is their descendant "by purchase." Frederic endeavors to console him, but is unsuccessful. The General learns that Frederic will lead an expedition against the pirates at eleven o'clock that night. He inquires if Frederic's followers have arrived. . . . And the latter replies—"They are; they only await my orders." So, the General expresses the desire to give them his blessing but even in spite of it, they show great reluctance to leave. *(C 6-14.)*

Mabel tears herself from Frederic and departs, followed by her sisters who try to console her. The General follows the police. Frederic remains alone and sits musing on his fate until interrupted by the appearance *(C 6-15)* of the Pirate King and Ruth at a window. Instead of shooting him they explain that he is still bound to them, because having been born on February 29, he has only served five, and not twenty-one years of his contract —counting only birthdays, of course. This situation seems to amuse all three to an extraordinary degree. Frederic exclaims that, on that basis, he must go with them . . . for "at any cost, I will do my duty." Then, he is suddenly reminded that as a member of the pirate band, he must now divulge the truth about General Stanley. So he tells the Pirate King that the General only used the *orphan* story as a ruse to save himself and his daughters. . . . "General Stanley is no orphan," he says. "More than that, he never was one!" Upon this disclosure the Pirate King announces that

De Bellis

THE PIRATE KING AND SAMUEL
(D'OYLY CARTE COMPANY)

his vengeance on General Stanley will be swift and sure. He and his pirates will attack the General's castle *(C 6-16)* that very night. Frederic tries to plead with him—but in vain. Ruth and the Pirate King depart, and Mabel enters, finding Frederic alone. He is determined to rejoin the pirates, and despite her pleading, says farewell after promising *(C 6-17)* to return for her in 1940, if he lives. Mabel, left alone, decides to be as dutiful as her lover *(C 6-18)* and she addresses the Sergeant of police telling him how Frederic, who was to have led the police against the pirates, has once more joined his old associates. She says that she loves him all the more for his heroic sacrifice to duty. But, he has made himself her foe . . . so she will do *her* duty, and regard him in that light. She bids the police do theirs . . . and departs. The policemen do not understand the situation. But, their "course is clear." They must capture the pirates. The Sergeant bemoans their daily task of depriving erring fellow-creatures of liberty.

The Pirates are heard approaching, singing gaily *(C 6-19)*, and the police conceal themselves. Frederic peers through a keyhole at the General, who evidently *(C 6-20)* suspects something is afoot. Mabel and all the general's daughters enter *(C 6-21)* curious to know why he is up so late. The Pirates and police struggle, the former winning. The General is promised swift death for his "orphan" lie, but when it is disclosed *(C 6-22)* that the Pirates themselves are not orphans but noblemen gone wrong, everyone forgives everyone else and the ex-pirates win the girls after all.

357

Vandamm   CATFISH ROW

PORGY AND BESS

OPERA in three acts and nine scenes; music by George Gershwin, story by DuBose Heyward, founded on the play of the same name. Libretto by DuBose, Dorothy Heyward and Ira Gershwin. First performed in October, 1935, under the auspices of the Theatre Guild with an all negro cast, under the direction of Alexander Smallens.

"Porgy and Bess," an American opera based on the play "Porgy," established over night the standing of George Gershwin as a pioneer toward a new, a distinctly American opera. The sensationally successful play, "Porgy," smelled of the soil and glowed with the rich primitive colors of American life. One of the most amazing things about George Gershwin's thoroughly amazing score is the fidelity with which it reflects and expresses and intensifies the dramatic elements of DuBose and Dorothy Heyward's play. What is even more important is the fact that Gershwin has written a work which not only marks a tremendous stride in his own development, but brings opera definitely and thoroughly down to earth.

The score of "Porgy and Bess" is filled with sing-able, hum-able and whistle-able tunes—melodies to which a star of the first magnitude, Lawrence Tibbett, is proud to bring the full measure of his unique talent; melodies which at the same time appeal so strongly to the "man in the street" that he leaves the theatre after the first thrilling performance humming them to himself. One of the vital qualities of any artistic work is that of universality and this quality, almost invariably lacking in contemporary art, is present to an astonishing degree in Gershwin's music. For once the highbrow, the middle and low, come together in agreement upon music and we have in "Porgy" a musical drama that gives every indication of being the first valid American folk-opera.

The sensation of its first presentation, with lyrics by DuBose Heyward and Ira Gershwin, sets by Serge Soudeikine, and direction by Rouben Mamoulian, with the distinguished conductor, Alexander Smallens, will not be soon forgotten. We are fortunate in having Mr. Smallens and the original orchestra and chorus of "Porgy and Bess" collaborating in the records of "Porgy and Bess," and American music lovers will be more than delighted to find the incomparable Tibbett, as well as the lovely and highly captivating Helen Jepson, both of them stars of the Metropolitan and of the movies, singing the principal roles. Album C-25 (11878-11881) Price $6.50.

THE scene is laid in Catfish Row, a section of Charleston, South Carolina, formerly occupied by the aristocracy but now a negro tenement. As the curtain rises the night life of this little backwater of negro life is revealed. There is impromptu dancing, and a mother sings a lullaby to her baby while among the men a red hot game of dice is going on ("Summertime" and "Crap Game"—Helen Jepson, Lawrence Tibbett, chorus and orchestra under direction of Alexander Smallens. Record 11879 $1.50). Among the crap players are Robbins and Crown, a stevedore who is the great lover of the community. Crown quarrels with Robbins and attacks the latter, killing him in the subsequent fight. Crown escapes. Sporting Life, the neighborhood high-liver, lover and dope peddler, attempts to induce Bess, Crown's girl, to go to New York with him, but she refuses and, parted from Crown after his flight, Bess seeks sanctuary in Porgy's room. Sporting Life puts his philosophy of life in a devil-may-care song entitled "A Woman Is a Sometime Thing" (Record 11879 Lawrence Tibbett $1.50).

In Act 2 we are shown Catfish Row at morning. Fishermen are working about at odd jobs and Porgy, contented with his life with Bess, sings a song of his complacence entitled "I Got Plenty o' Nuttin' " (Record 11880, Lawrence Tibbett, with chorus and orchestra $1.50) as well as a thrilling duet in which he and Bess express their mutual love ("Bess, You Is My Woman Now"—Lawrence Tibbett-Helen Jepson, with chorus and orchestra. Record 11879 $1.50). A buzzard flies over the court and the bird of ill omen fills all the negroes with premonitions of evil. In the original version of the opera there is a "Buzzard Song" which has been recorded but this number, unfortunately, was deleted from the opera in its final form (Record 11878—Lawrence Tibbett, with chorus and orchestra $1.50). This is the day of the lodge picnic held on Kittiwah Island. One of the most entertaining items of the picnic is the singing and dancing of Sporting Life, who testifies to his skepticism about spiritual things in the highly amusing song called "It Ain't Necessarily So" (Record 11878. Lawrence Tibbett, with chorus and orchestra $1.50). Unknown to anyone, Crown, who has fled after murdering Robbins, is in hiding on the island and at an opportune moment appears, catching Bess alone and persuading her to stay with him in his hiding place on the island. A few days later she returns to Porgy's room, emotionally upset and delirious. She recovers, confesses that she has promised to join Crown when he comes out of hiding, but finally agrees that she really loves Porgy and wants no one but him.

A bell sounds, giving warning of a hurricane. All the women are terrified, for their men are out fishing and in great danger. Clara particularly is thinking of her husband who is far out at sea and suddenly is convinced that he is in imminent danger. No one but Crown has the courage to go to his rescue and Porgy and Bess sit together, sure that even so mighty a man as Crown could not survive the storm on the island. They are to be free of him at last. At this moment the door bursts open and Crown enters. He ridicules Porgy, who is a cripple, for being half a man and rushes out to the rescue.

Act 3 shows Catfish Row at night. From Porgy's room Bess sings a "Lullaby" (Helen Jepson Record No. 11881 $1.50). It is learned from Sporting Life that Crown is still alive. Presently he appears on the scene and crawls towards Porgy's room. Porgy observes him as he is about to enter and leaning out of his window stabs him to death. The police cannot find out anything about the murder, but suspect Porgy and demand his presence at the inquest to identify the body. Porgy refuses to look at his victim and is dragged off to jail. Bess, ("My Man's Gone Now" Helen Jepson Record No. 11881 $1.50) in confusion and distress, is approached by Sporting Life who offers her dope and tries to persuade her to run away with him. He is at first unsuccessful but leaves a package of dope on the step to tempt her. When he has departed she takes the package and carries it into her room. A week later, Porgy returns from jail in high spirits and bringing presents for all his friends. The gaiety does not appear to be contagious for his friends stand about in great embarrassment, which Porgy doesn't notice because of his own high spirits. Presently he calls for Bess and she doesn't answer. He demands information as to where she has gone and finally learns that, seduced by Sporting Life, she has left for New York ("Where Is My Bess?" Record 11880 Lawrence Tibbett, with chorus and orchestra $1.50). Porgy asks how far it is to New York and when he is told that it is a thousand miles away, he calls for his goat and cart and starts out on the road to find Bess.

THE ROGUES DESERT IGOR'S ARMY

PRINCE IGOR

OPERA in a prologue and four acts; music by Alexander Porphyrievitch Borodin; libretto by the composer and his friend Vladimir Stassoff, based on "The Epic of the Army of Igor," an old historical Russian chronicle. First produced at the Imperial Opera House, St. Petersburg, October 23, 1890. First performance in the United States, December 30, 1915, at the Metropolitan Opera House, New York. The opera was unfinished at the composer's death, and was completed by Rimsky-Korsakow and Glazounow. Borodin had not put the overture into notation, but Glazounow, who had often heard him play it on the piano, wrote the composition from memory and orchestrated it.

The popular theory that a musician, and above all, a composer, is necessarily unsuited for practical affairs, finds convincing rebuttal in the life and work of Borodin. Borodin was one of the great scientific figures of his generation; two of his chemical treatises have become standard: "Researches upon the Fluoride of Benzole," and "The Solidification of Aldehydes." He was a professor of medicine and an early advocate of the emancipation of women. Always equally fond of his science and of music, as a matter of duty he chose the former for his career, and remained only a music lover until the age of twenty-eight, when he met Balakirew and began to devote all of his spare time to music. In that famous circle of "five" of which Balakirew was the inspiring genius—Balakirew, Cui, Moussorgsky, Borodin, and Rimsky-Korsakow—Borodin was certainly one of the most highly endowed with the "vital spark," according to various musicians and critics ranking next, above or below, Moussorgsky. Because of his many activities connected with his profession, his musical compositions are, unfortunately, few—two symphonies, two string quartets, a number of songs and piano pieces, and his one opera, "Prince Igor." In all of these works, however, he shows a remarkable energy and wholesomeness that remind one of Beethoven. Though not by any means a dramatic story, "Prince Igor" furnished Borodin splendid opportunities for effective treatment—the contrast of Russian and Oriental music, scenes of comedy, tragedy, and love, and the fiery dances of the Polovetzki. Unlike Moussorgsky he was not especially gifted in the writing of recitative, and therefore writes his opera largely in a lyrical style, after the manner established in Russian opera by Glinka in "Russlan and Ludmilla."

THE OVERTURE is permeated with Borodin's characteristic energy. After an impressive introduction an allegro movement enters, impetuous with the vigor of a Russian folk-dance; next is briefly heard a phrase of the music associated with the oriental Polovetzki; this is followed by the beautiful, lyrical theme of Igor's aria, "No Sleep, No Rest." These themes are developed and repeated in a most spirited manner, the overture closing with a jubilant climax.

Overture—*Albert Coates-Symphony Orchestra* 9123-1.50

PROLOGUE

SCENE—*The Market-Place of Poultivle*

PRINCE IGOR is about to start out on a campaign against the Khan of the Polovetzki, and the people are giving him a rousing farewell, when suddenly an eclipse of the sun happens to occur. Frightened by this unnatural darkness that seems an ill omen, the people, joined by Igor's wife, the Princess Jaroslavna, beg him to postpone his departure. Entirely undaunted, he entrusts the affairs of government to his brother, Prince Galitsky, and departs accompanied by his son, Vladimir. Two rogues, Scoula and Erochka, are so disinclined towards the hardships of war that they desert Igor's army and plan to take more agreeable service under Prince Galitsky.

ACT I

SCENE I—*The Courtyard of Prince Galitsky's House*

THERE is feasting and carousing at Galitsky's. The Prince himself sings a reckless song, a wild, typically Russian air with words expressive of the Prince's philosophy—he hates a dreary life, if he were governor he would give all a merry time, for state and power are nothing to him if they do not bring revelry.

Song of Prince Galitsky   *Feodor Chaliapin* 1237-1.50

A group of young girls enter bewailing the fact that one of their friends has been abducted. Their prayers for her restoration are so coldly mocked by the Prince, who boasts himself to be the abductor, that they leave greatly frightened. The lusts of Galitsky's followers again appealed to, they shout that they will set him up as ruler in place of Igor.

SCENE II—*A Room in the Palace of Prince Igor*

The Princess Jaroslavna is brooding in loneliness over the absence of her husband and praying for news of his safety. She sings of her forlorn hope in a beautiful and intensely expressive aria.

Arioso of Jaroslavna   *Nina Koshetz* 9233-1.50

JAROSLAVNA

Her thoughts are interrupted by the entry of the same group of maidens who appeal to her for protection from Galitsky. Then as that Prince himself enters and bids them begone, they flee in terror. Jaroslavna upbraids her brother-in-law for his shameless conduct, and as he in turn taunts her for being cold and censorious, she reminds him that Igor's authority is legally invested in her, commands him to release the abducted maiden, and orders him from her sight. Scarcely has he left when Boyards enter, bringing word that Igor has met with defeat and is held captive along with his son—the enemy are even now marching towards the city. Their loyalty aroused by this news of disaster, the Boyards swear to defend their Princess and the city with their lives.

ACT II

SCENE—*The Camp of the Polovetzki*

PRINCE VLADIMIR, prisoner in the camp of the enemy, has fallen in love with Kontchakovna, the daughter of the Polovetzkian chief, and now comes to serenade her. He tells her that Igor disapproves of their attachment although her father favors it. Their meeting is cut short by the entrance of Igor, who appears, soliloquizing on his unhappy condition, unable to sleep because of his fate. As his thoughts turn to his wife, he sings the beautiful melody first heard during the overture, saying: "My thoughts fly to thee, oh, beloved; thou alone will weep over my hapless fate!"

KHAN KONTCHAK

Yet when Ovolour, a captive who is on guard, offers him a horse as a means of escape, Igor refuses for he does not believe flight a fair way of treating his captor. A moment later the chief of the Polovetzki, Kahn Kontchak, approaches *(beginning of Record 6867)* and greets Igor:

How Goes It Prince? *(Aria of Khan Kontchak)* *Feodor Chaliapin* **6867-2.00**

How goes it, Prince?
Why so sad, my guest?
Are your nets torn?
Aren't your hunting-vultures savage enough?

363

Do they not catch the flying prey?
Better take mine!

Igor replies *(also sung by Mr. Chaliapin on Record 6867):*

The net is strong
And the vultures are true,
But the falcon cannot be
Deprived of freedom . . .

Kontchak continues:

You still persist in calling yourself a prisoner!
But do you really live like one?
Aren't you my guest?
You get all honors due,
As if you were a Khan,
Your son is with you, your yeomen too . . .
All are afraid of me
And tremble under my yoke!
But you were not afraid to fight . . .
I'd like to be your faithful ally . . .
Believe me, Prince!

Do you want a captive girl?
My harem is full of beauties,
Their tresses fall on their shoulders like snakes,
Their dark eyes are like velvet . . .
Why are you silent?
If you care, make your choice,
Any one is yours . . .

The generous Khan promises Igor his freedom if he will agree never to fight the Polovetzki again. This Igor refuses, saying that if he were free he would bring a larger army and subdue them—frankness that the Khan admires. At his command the Polovetzki slaves enter and begin to sing and dance for Igor's entertainment. At first slow and languorous, their dance gradually develops to a climax of the most turbulent, almost savage, excitement.

Polovetzki Dance *Stokowski-Philadelphia Orchestra* **6514-2.00** *Coates, Chorus, London Symphony Orchestra* **9474-1.50**

ACT III

SCENE—*Another Part of the Camp of the Polovetzki*

AT THE sight of the Polovetzkian soldiers returning from their attack on Poultivle carrying spoils, Igor, filled with pity for the misfortunes of his wife and people, consents to flee. In order to aid him, Ovolour gives the soldiers greater quantities of koumiss (wine) as they divide their spoils. After a drunken orgy, the entire camp falls asleep. The chief's daughter has discovered the plot and comes to beg Vladimir not to leave her. Her passionate entreaties so stir him that he is on the point of yielding when his father

DANCE OF THE POLOVETZKI

arouses in him again the sense of duty. Kontchakovna's ardent Oriental love cannot be so easily balked, however, and when Igor gives the signal to escape, she sounds an alarm and clings desperately to her lover until it is too late for him to leave. The Polovetzkian soldiers rush in and would kill Vladimir in revenge for his father's escape, but the chief enters and forbids them from following Igor or slaying Vladimir. He rather admires Igor's brave attempt, and, as he philosophically remarks, they can chain the young man to them by giving him a mate. This decision is, of course, most agreeable both to Vladimir and Kontchakovna.

ACT IV

JAROSLAVNA stands on the terrace of her ruined palace gazing over the once fertile plains, now barren under the ravaging of the hostile army. Her sorrow is soon changed into joy by the unexpected arrival of her husband. As they enter the great church of the Kremlin at Poultivle, the merry rogues, Scoula and Erochka, who have just been singing a song in ridicule of Igor and praise of Galitsky, now, in order to save their own hides, hurriedly set the town bell ringing to summon the people. Thus their villainy is forgotten in the great rejoicing that welcomes the rightful and justly beloved Prince.

take her place? This, of course, is just what Lady Blanche wants, and she takes the opportunity to indulge in a little abstract philosophy. So the Princess yields to Hilarion, Lady Psyche to Cyril, and Melissa to Florian. Lady Blanche is left, having achieved her heart's desire to be the principal of the "University." She promises the other three that they shall return to their former positions should they ever desire to do so, and the opera ends in general joy.

LE PROPHÈTE

(The Prophet)

OPERA in five acts; music by Giacomo Meyerbeer; libretto by Scribe. First produced, April 16, 1849, at the Grand Opéra, Paris. First performance in America, at New Orleans, April 2, 1850. Revived at the Metropolitan in 1918, with Caruso and Matzenauer, and again in 1927 with Martinelli and Matzenauer. The plot is based on the uprising of the Anabaptists of the Sixteenth Century. This was a semi-religious, semi-social movement characteristic of the early Renaissance period. It knew some qualities which appealed to the downtrodden masses, but it was badly marred by the charlatanry of its leaders, including John Leyden, whose character appears to be the foundation for the Prophet of the present work. The music was completed with most lavish care by

JOHN AND FIDÈS

Meyerbeer, and it includes some of his best-known numbers, such as the famous contralto aria, "Ah, mon fils," and the "Coronation March," which is still considered one of the great processional marches, and frequently is used as such both in Europe and America.

(The original French name of the opera, "Le Prophète," *Luh Pro-feht'*, is in Italian "Il Profeta," *Eel Pro-fay'-tah*, and in English "The Prophet.")

Scene and period: Holland and Germany; in 1543, at the time of the Anabaptist uprising.

ACT I

SCENE—*A Suburb of Dordrecht*

BERTHA, a subject of the domain of Count Oberthal, is betrothed to an innkeeper at Leyden named John. As she is compelled by law to obtain the Count's permission to marry, she has come with John's mother, Fidès (*Fee-dez'*), so to do. At the same time three somber Anabaptists arrive and

370

exhort the people to revolt against the tyranny to which they are subjected. But the trouble they arouse is easily suppressed on the appearance of the Count, who recognizes in one of the Anabaptists a former servant who had been discharged from his service for dishonesty. When Bertha makes her plea the Count is so impressed with her beauty that, desiring her for himself, he orders the girl and John's mother cast in the dungeon of his castle.

ACT II

SCENE—*The Inn of Fidès in the Suburbs of Leyden*

DRIVEN from the castle, the three Anabaptists enter the Inn of Fidès, where, on seeing John, they are at once struck with his resemblance to the portrait of the guardian saint, David, at Munster. Recognizing him as a possible tool who might pass with the crowd for a reincarnation, they try to persuade him to become a leader in their movement. He once had a dream, he says, in which he was venerated by a great crowd of people at an immense cathedral. The Anabaptists try to use this dream to work on his feelings, but John refuses because of his love for, and approaching marriage to, Bertha.

Scarcely have they departed when Bertha, herself having escaped, rushes in, and tells John of the Count's dastardly act. He hardly has time to conceal her before the Count enters with his soldiers, bringing Fidès as a prisoner. John's mother will be slain if he will not give Bertha up; he hesitates, but in the struggle filial loyalty prevails and he yields his betrothed. The released Fidès sings her gratitude in an aria of deep pathos.

> Ah! My son! my son! may you be this day blessed,
> Thy poor mother was dearer to thee
> Than Bertha and thy love.
> You have given up for your mother's sake
> More than life, by sacrificing thy happiness.
> May my prayers ascend to heaven,
> And thou be blessed, my son—
> Blessed in the Lord.

Ah, mon fils! *(Ah! My Son)* **Sigrid Onégin 6803-2.00**

Now it does not take the Anabaptists long to persuade John to join them, as a means of wreaking vengeance on the Count. It being necessary for the success of their plans that every one, even his mother, believe that he is dead, some of John's clothes are stained with blood and left behind, when, after having sworn a solemn oath of secrecy, they depart.

ACT III

SCENE—*The Camp of Anabaptists*

THE people, easily persuaded that John is indeed the Prophet, have followed his leadership in rising up against their oppressors. They now are encamped before the walls of Munster where provisions are brought them by skaters. The Count is captured and reveals to John that Bertha has escaped and is now in Munster. The three Anabaptist leaders would put the Count to death at once, but John orders him spared—Bertha shall be his judge. Angered at John's assuming so much authority these leaders organize an attack of their own on Munster and meet with defeat. The rabble led by them is now furious to the point of mutiny, they would even murder John.

JOHN DENYING HIS MOTHER
ACT IV—SCENE II

He, however, is able to rally the crowd to his support, and by the force of his personality and the glamour of an assumed divine inspiration leads them to victory.

ACT IV

Scene I—*A Public Square in Munster*

FIDÈS, reduced to poverty, has come to Munster to beg. Here she meets Bertha and tells her that John is dead. Ignorant of the state of affairs, Bertha believes that John's death was caused by the Prophet and on him she swears vengeance.

Scene II—*The Munster Cathedral*

The victorious John, about to be crowned King, is led in a procession of the greatest pomp and brilliancy into the church for the Coronation.

Coronation March   *Mengelberg-New York Philharmonic-Symphony Orchestra* 7104-2.00

Fidès suddenly appears from behind a pillar and in a transport of joy greets him as her son. To acknowledge this would be to repudiate the divine origin ascribed to the Prophet. John is, therefore, compelled to deny his mother. To save her from execution he pronounces her insane and has her kneel before him; then standing over her with hands upraised he bids the soldiers draw their swords and run them through his breast if this beggar woman again affirms that she is his mother. Seeing the swords ready to pierce John, Fidès at once answers that he is not her son—she was deceived by her age-dimmed eyes. All exclaim, "A miracle!" believing her miraculously cured of her insanity. Thus has the Prophet strengthened his power.

ACT V

Scene I—*The Crypt of the Palace*

AT John's secret command soldiers conduct Fidès to the dungeon of the palace. As they leave her there in the darkness, she exclaims, "O priests of Baal, where have ye led me?" beginning a grand "Scene, Cavatina and Aria" of the most elaborate Meyerbeerian proportions, well known as a concert aria under the name "Prison Scene." Stricken with grief and shame at her son's denial of her, she cries out to heaven to strike him with its lightning; then suddenly relenting, prays for its mercy on him.

> My beloved, heaven on thee
> Have pity, thou gavest the heart;
> I have given my cares
> That thou may'st be happy,
> Now would I give my life,
> And my soul exalted,
> Will wait for thee in heaven.

An officer enters for a moment to announce the arrival of the Prophet. Greatly agitated Fidès continues with her exuberant coloratura aria:

> He comes!
> I shall see him, delightful hope!
> Oh! truth! daughter of heaven,
> May thy flame, like lightning,
> Strike the soul of an ungrateful son!
> * * * * *
> Immortal grace, oh! conquering come;
> Let thy light pierce this ingrate son,
> Conscience riven, his soul soften,
> Like brass in furnace fierce,
> That he may ascend and reign in heaven!

O Prêtres de Baal (*Prison Scene*)　**Sigrid Onégin 7146-2.00**

Nevertheless, when John enters, runs to her, throws himself at her feet and begs forgiveness, she assumes a severe manner, renounces him and orders him away. He pleads in vain until he has succeeded in persuading her that he has been impelled to his bloody deeds and usurpation of power only because of his desire to avenge Bertha's wrongs. Then she forgives him, but only on condition that he return to Leyden. This he promises, now fully repentant.

They are joined by Bertha, whose joy at meeting her lover is short-lived, for at the same moment a captain comes to announce to John that he has been betrayed—the Emperor's forces are even now at the castle gates. Horrified at this sudden revelation that the loathed Prophet and John are the same person and unable to endure the conflict of love and hatred, Bertha plunges a dagger in her heart and dies cursing her lover.

373

Scene II—*The Great Hall of the Palace*

After the Emperor's troops, under the leadership of the Count, have forced an entrance to the castle, John secretly orders the gates closed. When the Count, source of all John's misfortunes, comes to him saying, "You are my prisoner," John answers, "Nay, ye are all my captives." Life being for him devoid of hope, he has laid a terrific plan for revenge. It is now consummated; the fire he has set causes a terrific explosion, a wall falls and flames leap out on every side. Amid this scene of lurid destruction a woman with disheveled hair runs to John. "My Mother!" he cries. Forgiving him all his wrong-doing she has come to share his fate. They die together, singing "Welcome sacred flame!"

CHICAGO CITY OPERA COMPANY SETTING FOR RIGOLETTO

RIGOLETTO

OPERA in four (originally three) acts; music by Giuseppe Verdi; libretto by Francesco Mario Piave, founded on Victor Hugo's play, "Le Roi s'Amuse." Produced, Venice, March 11, 1851; first performance in the United States, Academy of Music, New York, February 19, 1855. In present-day performances the two scenes of what is Act I in the original score are usually presented as separate "acts," thus making of Rigoletto a four-act opera. Following the example of the Metropolitan Opera Company we are so listing the scenes in the following description.

Greatly desiring a new libretto for the La Fenice Theatre, Venice, Verdi requested Piave to adapt Victor Hugo's play, "Le Roi s'Amuse," which, in spite of its morals, was recognized by the composer as possessing operatic possibilities. A libretto was soon written, the suggestive title being changed to "La Maledizione" (The Curse). A new work was desperately needed by the management of La Fenice and dismay followed the flat refusal of the police to grant permission for the performance of a work in which a king was shown in such dubious character. It will be remembered that Venice was then in Austrian hands, and but a short time previously, 1848-49, there had been an Italian insurrection. As Verdi refused to consider any other plan, the management was in despair. Help arrived from an unexpected quarter, for the Austrian police chief, Martello, was an ardent musical and dramatic enthusiast, and a great admirer of Verdi. He perceived that by substituting the Duke of Mantua for François I, and by changing the title to "Rigoletto" and arranging that all the curses should fall upon the duke of a small town, the work could be presented without any material changes in the original dramatic situations. Verdi accepted this proposal. He went to Buseto, near his birthplace in the moun-

375

tains, and came back within six weeks with the completed musical score. The new work was a brilliant success, and thus the situation was saved for the management of the theatre.

A remarkable feat of rapid composition, being written in less than forty days, Rigoletto still holds a firm place in the repertoire of all opera houses after three-quarters of a century. Not without reason has it held this popularity, for Victor Hugo's drama, even with the numerous alterations of Piave, makes a most effective opera libretto. Moreover, it supplies three characters of interest: the hunchback, Rigoletto, a vital centralizing dramatic figure that appeals to audiences and singers alike; the Duke, a brilliant tenor rôle and a debonair and cynical characterization; Gilda, the heroine, beloved by all coloratura sopranos. These characters have, indeed, been favorites with many of the greatest singers: Patti sang in the opera for the first time at New Orleans, February 6, 1861; Caruso made his American début singing the rôle of the Duke at the Metropolitan Opera House, New York, November 23, 1903; Ruffo first appeared in the United States as Rigoletto, November 4, 1912, at Hammerstein's Metropolitan Opera House, Philadelphia; and on November 18, 1916, occurred the triumphal first American appearance of Galli-Curci when she sang the rôle of Gilda with the Chicago Opera Company. Musically, "Rigoletto" ranks with "Il Trovatore" and "La Traviata" as representing a second and higher stage in the composer's development. These compositions possess expressiveness of melody, variety of harmony, color and richness of orchestration, and subtleties in the presentment of character beyond his previous work.

RIGOLETTO ON VICTOR RECORDS

Lovers of Italian opera are enthusiastic over the complete recording of Rigoletto made by artists and members of the chorus and orchestra of the famous La Scala Opera House, of Milan, Italy. The performance, conducted by Maestro Carlo Sabajno, is completely recorded (with conventional cuts) on fifteen Victor Records, and is issued as Album M-32 (9525-9539) in the Musical Masterpiece Series, with descriptive booklet, listed at the price of $22.50. In the following account of the opera, the number of each of these records is given, in parentheses, at the point where it begins in the narrative. The distribution of the rôles in the La Scala recording is indicated in the following cast—

CHARACTERS

RIGOLETTO (Ree-goh-let'-toh), a hunchback, jester to the duke	Sr. Piazza, *Baritone*
GILDA (Jeel' dah), his daughter	Sra. Pagliughi, *Soprano*
GIOVANNA (Jee-oh-vahn'-nah), her nurse	Sra. Brambilla, *Mezzo-Soprano*
DUKE OF MANTUA	Sr. Folgar, *Tenor*
SPARAFUCILE (Spahr-ah-foo-che'-leh), a hired assassin	Sr. Baccaloni, *Bass*
MADDALENA (Mahd-dah-lay'-nah), his sister	Sra. de Cristoff, *Mezzo-Soprano*
COUNT CEPRANO (Chay-prah'-noh)	Sr. Menni, *Bass*
COUNTESS CEPRANO	Sra. Brambilla, *Mezzo-Soprano*
COUNT MONTERONE (Mon-ter-on'-nay)	Sr. Baracchi, *Baritone*
BORSA	Sr. Nessi, *Tenor*
MARULLO	Sr. Baracci, *Baritone*
CHORUS OF COURTIERS	*Chorus of La Scala,* Milan

The action takes place at Mantua during the Sixteenth Century.

ACT I

AFTER a short, ominous prelude *(Record 1)* the curtain rises and we behold a fête in progress at the Ducal Palace. Courtiers and ladies move gaily through the great ballroom. Through the large archway at the rear we can look into other luxurious apartments, all brilliantly lighted. Pages hurry to

White

and fro. From an adjoining room come bursts of music and laughter. Amid all this bustle and gaiety and to a frivolous light-hearted orchestral accompaniment the Duke enters with one of the courtiers, Borsa. He confides to him that he is pursuing an unknown beauty whom he has seen in church every Sunday during the past three months. He has followed her to her house in a remote part of the city, where, he has discovered, a mysterious man visits her every evening. At this moment a group of knights and ladies happen to pass by. "What beauties," exclaims Borsa. "Ceprano's wife is the loveliest of all!" replies the Duke. His listener warns him that the Count might hear, but the Duke shrugs his shoulders indifferently and *(Record 2)* gives vent to his philosophy in the aria, "Questa o quella." The melody is smooth, it seems to float through the air, yet there is irony concealed beneath its gaiety.

Questa o quella *('Mid the Fair Throng)* **Enrico Caruso** *500-1.50 **Tito Schipa** 1282-1.50

His words, too, display his character:

> 'Mid the fair throng that sparkle around me,
>   Not one o'er my heart holds sway;
> Though a sweet smile one moment may charm me,
>   A glance from some bright eye its spell drives away.

377

All alike may attract, each in turn may please;
  Now with one I may trifle and play,
Then another may sport with and tease—
  Yet all my heart to enslave their wiles display.
As a dove flies, alarm'd, to seek shelter,
  Pursued by some vulture, to bear it aloft in flight,
Thus do I fly from constancy's fetter:
  E'en woman's spells I shun—all their efforts I slight.
A husband that's jealous I scorn and despise,
  And I laugh at and heed not a lover's sighs:
If a fair one take my heart by surprise,
  I heed not scornful tongues or prying eyes.

The courtiers dance a minuet, accompanied by music, graceful and not inappropriately reminiscent of the minuet in "Don Giovanni." The Duke dances with the Countess, closely watched, however, by Ceprano; the fervent manner in which he kisses her hand is not lost on the jealous husband, nor does it escape the court jester, the hunchback, Rigoletto. The Duke leads away the Countess and Ceprano follows them, but not before the jester has launched a cutting taunt at the enraged Count.

Rigoletto forthwith saunters off, seeking other victims. As soon as he is out of sight he in turn becomes the object of similar jests. The gossip Marullo enters with "Great News" *(Record 3)*; Rigoletto, he has discovered, keeps a mistress . . . visits her every night. There are shouts of delight at the thought that the pander of the Duke's romances, Rigoletto himself, is now in love. The merriment is cut short by the re-entry of the Duke followed by Rigoletto. The Duke is saying he would like to get rid of Count Ceprano so that he might have the beautiful Countess. Rigoletto banteringly suggests that he run off with her . . . then he mentions the possibility of prison for the Count . . . or exile . . . or beheading. This sarcasm of the misshapen jester disgusts even the Duke; Ceprano is boiling with rage at such boorish jesting and bids the courtiers who likewise have smarted under Rigoletto's ribaldry meet him the following night, then they shall have their revenge.

The festival music of the band on the stage supplies a flippant background to the badinage of this scene; then, while the Duke and Rigoletto continue their discussion, and the courtiers and Ceprano plot their revenge, the music grows to a climax, suddenly interrupted by the voice of someone outside struggling for admission. A moment later the aged Count Monterone bursts in *(Record 4)*. His daughter has been dishonored by the Duke; now before the entire assembly he denounces that profligate ruler. The Duke at once orders his arrest; Rigoletto mocks him. Monterone, justly incensed with this injury doubled with insult, again reviles the Duke, and turning towards Rigoletto, cries, "As for you, serpent! You who can laugh at a father's anguish, a father's curse be on your head!" Monterone is led off by guards; the courtiers return to their festivities; but Rigoletto cowers, trembling with fright at Monterone's curse.

ACT II

A FEW somber chords are heard in the wood-
wind *(Record 5)* . . . then a subdued,
rather suave melody in keeping with the
scene—the end of a deserted street, sinister
under the darkness of night . . . at the left a
small, humble-appearing house with a wall-
enclosed courtyard . . . across the street a
very high wall and beyond it a corner of
Count Ceprano's palace.

TIBBETT AS RIGOLETTO

Rigoletto, wrapped in his cloak, comes
shambling down the street, but before he can
turn in towards the house at the left he is
accosted by an ominous black-robed figure,
who offers his services, should they be desired,
in putting rivals or enemies out of the way
. . . charges reasonable. The hunchback does not need him now, but asks
where he may be found. This assassin for hire tells his lodging, then departs,
making known his name, Sparafucile.

Rigoletto stops meditatively at the doorway leading into the courtyard.
Thus he soliloquizes, to music that varies with his shifting moods *(Record 6)*:

> Yon assassin is my equal
> He stabs in darkness,
> While I with a tongue of malice
> Stab men by daylight!
> > *(He thinks of Monterone's curse.)*
> He laid a father's curse on me . . .
> > *(Continuing in a burst of rage.)*
> Oh hideous fate! Cruel nature!
> Thou hast doom'd me to a life of torment.
> I must jest, I must laugh,
> And be their laughing-stock!
> Yonder the Duke, my master,
> Youthful and brilliant, rich and handsome,
> Tells me, between sleeping and waking:
> "Come, buffoon, I would laugh now!"
> Oh shame, I must obey him!
> Oh life accursed! How I hate ye,
> Race of vile and fawning courtiers!
> 'Tis my only joy to taunt ye!
> For if I am vile, 'tis to your vice I owe it.
> > *(Growing calm for a moment.)*
> In this abode my nature changes . . .
> He laid a father's curse on me!
> It disturbs me, it haunts me everywhere,
> I would forget it! Is it an evil omen?
> Ah no! that is a foolish thought!

He enters the courtyard *(Record 7)*; at the same moment a young woman

ENRICO CARUSO AS THE DUKE
OF MANTUA

comes from the house and runs to him. They embrace joyfully. "Gilda!" he exclaims; "Father!" she sighs in response. A cheerful orchestral melody accompanies their meeting. Knowing well the hazards of life with courtiers and Duke so near, and perhaps, the curse still ringing in his ears, he again for the thousandth time, warns and solemnly enjoins her to remain strictly within the house and never to venture into the town. He even questions her to know if anybody has followed her to church; but Gilda, with some qualms of conscience, keeps silent regarding the stranger she has met there. To reassure himself further, Rigoletto calls the servant and questions her *(Record 8)*.

Suddenly thinking he hears someone in the street, Rigoletto hurriedly opens the door in the courtyard and goes out to look. The Duke has been loitering outside, and while Rigoletto is in the street, he quietly glides into the courtyard, and throwing a purse to the servant with a sign to keep silent, conceals himself. This action takes place to an agitated orchestral accompaniment, the frightened Gilda exclaiming meanwhile, "Heaven; if he should suspect me!" Rigoletto must leave, and returns *(Record 9)*, saying, "My daughter, farewell!" "His daughter!" exclaims the Duke to himself, surprised at this revelation. "Farewell, oh my father!" *(Addio, mio padre)*, is Gilda's reply. Father and daughter then continue in a lovely duet, Gilda saying that they need not fear, for her mother, as an angel in heaven, is watching over them, while Rigoletto continues his charge to the servant, "Safely guard this tender blossom."

As soon as Rigoletto has departed, the Duke, who, of course, is in disguise, comes from his hiding place *(Record 10)*. Gilda, alarmed, bids him be gone; but he knows well how to calm her fears. He sings a gently swaying melody *(Record 11)*, saying:

> Love is the sun which lights our souls.
> Its voice is the beating of our hearts.
> Fame and glory, power and throne are but human frailties.
> Such joy not even angels can emulate.
> Love me, then, and I shall be the most envied of men.

Soon Gilda is heard singing as if to herself: "Ah! This is the dear voice of my dreams!"

È il sol dell'anima *(Love Is the Sun)* **Galli-Curci, Schipa** 1755-1.50

Gilda desires to know his name; "Walter Malde" he finally admits, adding that he is only a poor, struggling student. Then as he leaves they sing a tender farewell. Gilda remains pensive, dreaming of her wonderful lover in an air that is always a favorite. "Caro Nome" *(Record 12)*. This melody, with delicate accompaniment and flute passages, is one of the most exacting of coloratura arias, calling for extraordinary skill if its fioriture are to be performed with the grace they demand.

While she is yet singing, conspiracy is at work. Under cover of night a band of masked courtiers, led by Ceprano, has come for vengeance *(Record 13)*. Rigoletto, unexpectedly returning, runs into them, and is much alarmed to find them in his neighborhood. His fears are somewhat calmed, however, when the courtiers declare that they are bent on stealing Ceprano's wife for their friend, the Duke. Rigoletto points out Ceprano's house, and offers help. They insist that he must be disguised, give him a mask, and then as if to fasten it securely, tie it with a handkerchief which they pass over the holes pierced for the eyes. Confused and blinded, Rigoletto holds the ladder against what he believes to be the wall surrounding Ceprano's house *(Record 14)*. By it the abductors climb over his own wall, enter his house, seize, gag, and carry away his daughter. Thus after a few minutes Rigoletto finds himself left entirely alone holding the ladder. Becoming suspicious he tears off the mask. The door to his courtyard is open. On the ground he finds a scarf of Gilda's. Frantic with fear he rushes into the house . . . Gilda has disappeared. He staggers under this disaster which he has helped bring on himself. In agony, he cries out, "Ah, the curse!"

ACT III

A salon in the ducal palace . . . at the back large folding doors . . . on the walls portraits of the Duke and the Duchess . . . ideal duchess for, like her portrait that looks down mute upon her husband's philanderings,

CHICAGO CITY OPERA COMPANY
ACT III—RIGOLETTO

DE LUCA AS RIGOLETTO

she makes no comment and does not enter into the action.

The Duke is very much upset; he has returned to Rigoletto's house and found it deserted . . . the bird flown. He laments his loss in a very effective aria, so effective that we nearly feel sorry for him! *(Record 15).*

Parmi veder le lagrime *(Each Tear That Falls)* **Enrico Caruso** *6016-2.00

Marullo and the courtiers enter with some amusing news *(Record 16).* In a rousing chorus, that has a most fascinating swing, they narrate their exploits of the previous night when they captured Rigoletto's "mistress."

Scorrendo uniti remota via *(Chorus of Courtiers— On Mischief Bent)* **Metropolitan Opera Chorus** 4027-1.00

The Duke is amused at the details, laughing at the brilliant idea that made Rigoletto himself a party to the abduction. Knowing well that the woman in question is assuredly his latest inamorata, he is delighted when they inform him that they have brought her to the palace—they left her in the very next room. He hurries to her.

No sooner has he gone than Rigoletto enters *(Record 17)* pitifully striving to conceal his deep distress under a laughing exterior. "Poor Rigoletto" sing the courtiers, enjoying his discomposure at the loss of one they still believe to be only his mistress. The music is remarkably descriptive of Rigoletto's anxiety, as under the disguise of cynical indifference, singing "Tra-la-la," he searches furtively about the room for some evidences of Gilda's presence. A page enters to ask for the Duke; the courtiers tell him meaningly that his lordship cannot be disturbed now. The hunchback at once grasps the situation. "She must be here, in the next room!" he cries, then making no further attempt at concealment, he pleads, "Give me my daughter." He attempts to force an entrance, but the courtiers bar his efforts. Giving way to his feelings he rages among the Duke's followers *(Record 18):*

> Race of courtiers, vile rabble detested,
> Have ye sold her, whose peace ye molested?
> Where is she? do not rouse me to madness—
> Though unarm'd, of my vengeance beware,
> For the blood of some traitor I'll pour!
> *(Again making for the door.)*
> Let me enter, ye assassins, stand back!
> That door I must enter!
> *(He struggles again with the courtiers, but is repulsed and gives up in despair.)*

Ah! I see it—all against me—have pity!
Ah, I weep before ye, Marullo—Signore,
To others' grief thou'rt ever mindful,
Tell me, where have they my daughter hidden?
Is't there? say in pity—thou'rt silent—why?
                    (In tears.)
Oh, my lords, will ye have no compassion
On an old man's intercession?
It costs you nothing to restore her,
Yet to me she's more than all the world.

Lawrence Tibbett has given us a matchless record of this passionate protest.

Cortigiani, vil razza dannata *(Vile Race of Courtiers)* **Lawrence Tibbett** 14182-2.00

The courtiers at first laugh at, then grow indifferent to, Rigoletto's plea, but their curiosity is again piqued as Gilda emerges from the Duke's apartment *(Record 19)*, runs to her father, and throws herself in his arms. Rigoletto orders the courtiers to go. Somewhat abashed, they leave the hunchback and his daughter together. Gilda tells him of the lover who followed her from church.

Tutte le feste *(On Every Festal Morning)* **Lily Pons** 7383-2.00

Rigoletto does his best to comfort the girl, clasping her to his bosom with a tenderness and love that do much to atone for his vileness. "Weep, my child," he sings, to a melody of unusual beauty and pathos *(Record 20)*. Gilda replies, and their voices unite in a duet of most touching, exquisite loveliness—music that expresses in a wonderful manner the delicate, poignant tragedy of the scene.

RIGOLETTO:

"Weep, my child, my little girl, weep . . .
Though bitter the tears that fall on my heart."

GILDA:

"Father! In you speaks a consoling angel!"

By a singular chance, Count Monterone passes through the hall *(Record 21)*, being led to execution. He pauses before the Duke's portrait, exclaiming, "No thunder from heaven has yet burst down to strike you!" As he passes on, Rigoletto watches him grimly. Her father's stern demeanor frightens the girl for he is vowing a terrible vengeance on the Duke.

ACT IV

THE abode of Sparafucile, the assassin . . . an ancient inn, so ruined that one can see the broken staircase which leads to the loft, and even a couch within the loft itself. Near the inn is the river; beyond, the towers of Mantua reach towards the scudding clouds. Sparafucile is indoors seated by the table polishing his belt, unconscious that Rigoletto and his daughter are without, the latter dressed as a young cavalier, for it is her father's wish that she shall leave the city in disguise this very night.

He asks her if she still dreams of the Duke *(Record 22)* and she confesses that she still cherishes the student who came to her so full of romantic protestations. Thinking to cure her of this affection, he leads her towards the inn, so that she may peer through the dilapidated door and see the erstwhile "student" in his real character. The Duke, disguised as a soldier, enters the tavern and calls loudly for wine. While he is being served by Sparafucile, he sings one more song of the love of women. It portrays, clearly as words and music may, the indolently amorous young noble and his views of womankind, whom he charges all and sundry with his own worst failing.

La donna è mobile *(Woman is Fickle)* **Tito Schipa** 1099-1.50 **Giovanni Martinelli** 1208-1.50 **Enrico Caruso** *500-1.50 **Enrico Caruso** 1616-1.50 **Beniamino Gigli** 1704-1.50

> Woman is fickle, false altogether,
> Moves like a feather borne on the breezes;
> Woman with guiling smile will e'er deceive you,
> Often can grieve you, yet e'er she pleases,
> Her heart's unfeeling, false altogether,
> Moves like a feather borne on the breeze!
>
> Wretched the dupe is, who when she looks kindly,
> Trusts to her blindly. Thus life is wasted!
> Yet he must surely be dull beyond measure,
> Who of life's pleasure never has tasted.
> Woman is fickle, false altogether,
> Moves like a feather, borne on the breeze!

THE QUARTET

384

The murderous innkeeper brings the wine *(Record 23)*, and then, as he goes out, knocks on the ceiling, a signal for his sister, Maddalena, to descend. This flirtatious, almost coarse, gypsy girl is the bait that has been used to lure the Duke to the inn. She is wise in the ways of men, and thus, for a time, laughingly evades the Duke's caresses.

The emotions of these four characters so widely different in sentiment are expressed in the wonderful quartet *(Record 24)*.

Quartet—Bella figlia dell'amore *Galli-Curci, Homer, Gigli, de Luca* 10012-3.50
   Galli-Curci, Perini, Caruso, de Luca *10000-3.50   *Creatore's Band* 35882-1.25

In a most suave, ingratiating melody, the Duke sings to Maddalena:

> Fairest daughter of the graces,
> I, thy humble slave, implore thee,
> With one tender word to restore me,
> End the pangs, the pangs of unrequited love.
> Of my anguish see the traces,
> Thee I treasure, all above,
> With one tender word to joy restore me,
> End the pangs, the pangs of unrequited love.

Maddalena coquettishly replies:

> I appreciate you rightly,
> All you say is but to flatter.

Observing all this the heartbroken Gilda, concealed in the darkness outside, exclaims:

> Ah! to speak of love thus lightly!
> Words like those to me were spoken!
> He is false, my heart is broken,
> 'Twas in vain for bliss I strove.

The stern voice of Rigoletto is added to the others, saying:

> Silence, thy tears will not avail thee,
> It were baseness to regret him.
> Thou must shun him and forget him,
> Thy avenger I will prove.
> The strength to punish shall not fail me,
> That I vow to ev'ry pow'r that rules above.

The voices joined in simple though effective polyphony, mount to a splendid climax, one of the finest pieces of ensemble writing in all Italian opera.

Rigoletto then bids his daughter go with all speed to Verona *(Record 25)*, where he plans to follow. He forthwith summons Sparafucile and gives him half his assassin's fee, the remainder he will pay when the Duke's body is delivered, in a sack, at midnight. Sparafucile offers to throw the body in the river, but Rigoletto wishes that grim satisfaction for himself; he will return.

While these business transactions have been taking place outside, within the flirtation has grown more intimate. A storm gathers and the Duke de-

SCHIPA AS THE DUKE

cides to stay at the inn for the night. On Sparafucile's re-entry, he whispers to the girl that he
will return to her soon, and ascends to the loft.

Even the professional coquette has fallen in
love with the handsome Duke. Therefore, as
soon as she is alone with her brother she suggests *(Record 26)* that he kill the hunchback
rather than her Apollo. But the honor said to
exist among thieves is, apparently, found
among murderers too, for Sparafucile refuses
to betray his employer. His sister pleads with
such urgency, however *(Record 27)*, that
finally he agrees that if another guest shall
arrive before midnight, he will slay him instead of the Duke, so that Rigoletto will at
least have a corpse for his money.

Meanwhile the storm has been drawing
nearer, adding its terrors to those of the night.
In spite of the darkness, Gilda has crept back
to the inn, irresistibly drawn to the haunts of
the man she loves. Thus it happens that, hearing this extraordinary agreement, she sees a
way to save the life of her beloved and end
her sorrow.

The storm bursts in a sudden and overwhelming fury; the moaning of the wind, the
long rush of the rain, the blinding lightning and crash of thunder are but outward
symbols of the emotions of Gilda. Summoning up her disconsolate courage,
she knocks at the door. Even the assassin seems startled that anyone should
come at such a time. Sparafucile holds his dagger ready; Maddalena runs to
open the door. Gilda enters. Between the lightning flashes her form is barely
discernible . . . there is a quickly stifled outcry . . . then darkness and
silence.

The storm's fury abates *(Record 28)*, though occasional lightning flashes
illuminate the dreary scene. Rigoletto returns. He pays off the assassin and
in return is given the sack with its gruesome contents. The murderer again
offers to throw the body in the river; again the Jester claims this privilege.
Left alone he gloats over his vengeance *(Record 29)*, then starts to drag the
body towards the river. At that moment he hears a sound that makes his
blood run cold. The Duke has awakened, and is again singing "Woman Is
Fickle." Rigoletto trembles. Who, then, has he in the sack? He tears it
open. A sudden flash of lightning reveals the form of Gilda. The unfortunate
girl, wounded unto death, begs her father's forgiveness *(Record 30)*, singing
with him a duet of farewell, "In heaven beside my mother, I'll pray for

thee." Rigoletto implores her not to leave him thus alone on earth. A little cry of pain, and Gilda falls back dead. "Ah! The Curse—*La Maledizione!*" sobs Rigoletto.

The music of Monterone's curse upon the Jester, now weeping over the corpse of his own despoiled daughter, thunders forth in the orchestra, an appalling triumph.

Introduction and Minuet from Act I *Creatore's Band* 35882-1.25

DER RING DES NIBELUNGEN

(The Ring of the Nibelungs)

DAS RHEINGOLD, DIE WALKÜRE, SIEGFRIED, DIE GÖTTERDÄMMERUNG

THE "Ring"—a work without a parallel in the whole realm of music for grandeur and breadth of conception, occupied Wagner's ever active mind for more than twenty-six years. While he was still a conductor at the Dresden Opera he had become greatly interested in the ancient Scandinavian, Germanic and Icelandic sagas. There resulted a poem, "Siegfried's Death," written in November, 1848. Then, while in exile, realizing that one drama would be inadequate for the proper presentation of so vast a legend, he wrote another poem as an introduction, named "Young Siegfried" (1851). Similarly, the following year, he prefaced this with "The Valkyrie" *(Die Walküre),* and this in turn with "The Rhinegold," *(Das Rheingold).* Wagner then set to work upon the music in the proper order of the dramas, and by 1857 had completed the score through part of the second act of "Siegfried" (originally "Young Siegfried"). By this time even the undauntable Wagner had, as he termed it, grown tired of "piling one silent score upon another." Thereupon he turned to what he almost naïvely considered the more practicable "Meistersinger" and "Tristan." Not until 1869, encouraged by the patronage of the King of Bavaria, did Wagner resume work on "Siegfried." The entire "Ring" was eventually finished, with the completion of the orchestration of the "Dusk of the Gods" *(Götterdämmerung),* originally "Siegfried's Death," in 1874. Wagner termed his vast work a trilogy, considering "The Rhinegold," brief as it is, a preface to the story narrated in the three following music-dramas, "Die Walküre," "Siegfried," and "Götterdämmerung"; modern writers, however, believing all four dramas of equal importance, frequently refer to the series as a tetralogy.

No greater evidence of Wagner's ability as a dramatist can be found than the skill with which he has molded the old legends into a plot; a comparison

of the sagas, beautiful as they may be as poems, and Wagner's well motivated drama is proof enough of this remarkable feat. Due to the order in
which the text of "The Ring" was written, redundancies naturally occur; to
remove them was a labor from which even the active composer shrank. Into
this mighty epic Wagner crowded the wealth of philosophical ideas that
constantly interested him. In keeping with the legendary epoch of his story,
he casts his dramas into an alliterative form of verse, similar to that of the
sagas, but exceedingly difficult to translate into English. And by means of
his music and his verse, Wagner creates and sustains the atmosphere and
spirit of a dim and remote mythological age.

With the very opening of "Das Rheingold"—revolutionary as that magnificent opening must have been in its day—we realize that we are musically in
a different world from that of "Lohengrin," which just preceded the "Ring"
in time of composition. After long thought, Wagner had decided that if the
art of combined music and drama were to progress beyond old-time opera in
expressiveness it would be necessary to adapt to the theatre the forceful
method of thematic development perfected in the symphony under Beethoven. An opera so written would no longer be opera, but "music-drama,"
since, for Wagner, drama and music were conceived together, the nature of
the melodies, the harmonies, every turn of the modulations, the very orchestration growing out of the characters and action of the drama. Wagner's
music gains greatly in expressiveness and in unity through his use of "leading motives"—in the "Ring" they are almost innumerable. A complete cataloguing and naming of all was probably not contemplated by the composer,
and certainly is not necessary for the listener; some knowledge, however, of
the more prominent themes does give an added pleasure and understanding;
the details are for the future. As the Odes of Horace, translated laboriously
in youth, recur to one in later life with unsuspected beauty and meaning, so
"The Ring," after repeated hearings and long acquaintance, assumes new
beauties, and reveals hitherto unnoticed details that surprise the listener
with their dramatic force and loveliness.

In keeping with the magnitude of the trilogy, Wagner makes use of a
gigantic orchestra, nearly unprecedented in size. For special effects he introduced four of a family of instruments that he invented for the "Ring."
These instruments, now known as "Bayreuth tubas" or "Wagner tubas,"
are in reality a hybrid, uniting features of the French horn and trombone.
Their timbre, of unusual nobility and pathos, is peculiarly adapted for the
occasional use to which Wagner puts them—that of intoning the leading
motives of "Valhalla" and "The Wälsungs."

The "Ring" as a whole was first performed at Wagner's own theatre at
Bayreuth, August 13, 14, 16, 17, 1876, the crowning achievement of a lifetime of struggle. In the United States, the "Ring" was first performed at
the Metropolitan Opera House, New York, March 5, 6, 8 and 11, 1889,
performances of the individual dramas having been given at earlier dates.

An undertaking of such size has naturally enlisted the services of many of the world's greatest conductors and singers. At the first Bayreuth performances, 1876, Hans Richter was the conductor and Anton Seidl and Felix Mottl, assistants; while among the singers were Lilli Lehmann, Albert Niemann and Amalie Materna. In 1896, Mme. Schumann-Heink sang the rôles of Erda and Waltraute at Bayreuth. At the first performance of the entire "Ring" cycle at the Metropolitan Opera House, Anton Seidl was the conductor and among the principals were Lilli Lehmann, Max Alvary and Emil Fischer. The late Theodore Thomas was a Wagnerian pioneer in this country, in the days when it was heresy to play or like Wagner. Among the other great Wagnerian singers it is possible here to name only a few: Nordica, Ternina, Fremstad, Gadski, Eames, Homer, Jean de Reszke, Matzenauer, Van Rooy, Whitehill, and, among those of more recent times, Kirsten Flagstad, Marjorie Lawrence, Elisabeth Rethberg, Lauritz Melchior, Frida Leider, Friedrich Schorr and Florence Austral. At the "Ring" cycle given at the Metropolitan Opera House in 1929, Mme. Schumann-Heink sang the rôle of Erda—the occasion for a triumphal return after many years of absence.

An interesting recording of the most important "motives" used in the Ring operas is found on Victor Records Nos. 11215 and 11216.

Ring of the Nibelungs *Motives Nos. 1 to 48—11215* Ring of the Nibelungs *Motives Nos. 49 to 90—11216 Lawrence Collingwood-London Symphony Orch.* Price $1.50 each

German Railroads Information Office

THE FESTSPIELHAUS (BAYREUTH), SCENE OF MANY FAMOUS
PERFORMANCES OF THE "RING" OPERAS

Hans Makart　　　　　　THE THEFT OF THE RHINEGOLD

DAS RHEINGOLD

(The Rhinegold)

MUSIC-DRAMA in four scenes, prelude *(vorabend)* to "Der Ring des Nibelungen"; text and music by Richard Wagner. First produced, September 22, 1869, at Munich. First performance in the United States, January 4, 1889, at the Metropolitan Opera House, New York.

CHARACTERS

Gods

WOTAN *(Vo'-tahn)*	Baritone-Bass
DONNER *(Dohn'-ner)*	Bass
FROH *(Froh)*	Tenor
LOGE *(Loh'-ga)*	Tenor

Giants

FASOLT *(Fah'zohlt)*	Bass
FAFNER *(Fahf'-ner)*	Bass

Nibelungs (Gnomes)

ALBERICH *(Ahl'-ber-ich)*	Baritone
MIME *(Mee'ma)*	Tenor

Goddesses

FRICKA *(Frik'ah)*	Soprano
FREIA *(Fry'-ah)*	Soprano
ERDA *(Air'-dah)*	Contralto

The Rhine-Maidens

WOGLINDE *(Vog-lin'-da)*	Soprano
WELLGUNDE *(Vell-goon'-da)*	Soprano
FLOSSHILDE *(Floss-hill'-da)*	Contralto

390

(The German title is pronounced *Dass Rine'-goldt*.)

The action takes place during legendary times in the bed of the Rhine, at a mountainous district near that river, and in the subterranean caverns of Nibelheim.

Some of the loveliest music of Das Rheingold, including the Prelude, the Rainbow Bridge, and the Entrance of the Gods into Valhalla, is to be found in the excerpts by Leopold Stokowski and the Philadelphia Orchestra.

Excerpts *Leopold Stokowski-Philadelphia Orchestra* Album M-179 (7796-7798)
    AM-179 (7799-7801) $6.50
Prelude *Albert Coates-Symphony Orch.* 9163-1.50

FROM the depths of the orchestra is heard a long sustained tone, calm and motionless. After a time another is added and sustained with it; these tones will continue through the entire prelude, firm as the everlasting rock. In the midst of this stream of sound, other tones soon become audible, moving slowly upwards. This upward motion grows more and more continuous until it is transformed into a constant and overlapping series of gentle undulations. In time these undulations are imbued with a more fluid motion and rise gradually higher. The motion now grows more rapid, surging ever upwards, in great waves of tone, until the entire orchestra is participating in this onward flowing movement. We are hearing a semblance of what we actually behold at the rise of the curtain—the depths of the mighty river Rhine as it glides over the immovable rocks in its course through the earth.

THE RHINE

Here, through the greenish twilight of the waters at the bottom of the river, the three Rhine-maidens sing their nonsensical and care-free song of "Weia! Waga!" as they playfully swim about. Their games are interrupted, however, by the crouching dwarf Alberich, who approaches and attempts to

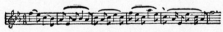

THE SONG OF THE RHINE-MAIDENS

make love to the graceful maidens. One by one, after urging him on with fair words, they laugh scornfully at the misshapen dwarf and swim away, eluding his grasp as he clambers over the rocks, endeavoring to catch one of them. Finally he is forced to remain gazing after the maidens in angry despair, thwarted in his attempt at love-making. But now the light of the sun begins to penetrate the waters and there is reflected from the pinnacle of one of the rocks a bright golden gleam. Against a shimmering accompaniment of violins we hear the motive of "The Rhinegold." The maidens, rejoicing in the radiance, sing their exultant song in praise of the gold.

391

THE GOLD

THE ADORATION OF THE GOLD

On questioning them, the greatly interested Alberich learns that this gleaming substance is the Rhinegold of which the maidens are the guardians

THE POWER OF THE RING

for, though valueless enough here, if forged into a ring, the gold would give the possessor unlimited wealth and power over gods and men. But in order to be able to forge such a ring, the owner must first renounce love. All this the chattering Rhine-maidens carelessly reveal . . . they have nothing to fear for no being would ever renounce love, least of all this passion rent Alberich. Therefore, they swim about light-heartedly. The heedful Alberich, however, whose proffered affection has been scorned by the maid-

THE RENUNCIATION OF LOVE

ens, rapidly climbs up among the rocks; the maidens, thinking he is pursuing them, swim away, shouting in mock-terror; he forever renounces all love, seizes the gold and disappears. The maidens follow in a vain attempt to catch the thief. The music rushes wildly downwards; the waters, bereft of the gold, are left in total darkness, a darkness that becomes like a dense cloud which in time dissipates itself into a light mist.

As the mist vanishes in the morning sunshine, a lofty mountain top is revealed and on another mountain in the distance, across the valley of the Rhine, is seen a mighty castle with high towering pinnacles. From the orchestra is heard the wonderfully majestic "Valhalla" motive. As the day grows brighter, we behold Wotan, chief of the gods, and his consort, Fricka, who are just awakening from

Weirich, Festspielhaus, Bayreuth
WOTAN

392

sleep. The great castle, Valhalla (in German, Walhalla), has been builded for the gods by the giants, Wotan having recklessly promised in payment the beautiful goddess of love, Freia. Even while his wife upbraids him for

VALHALLA

his rashness, Freia rushes to them for protection, in precipitous flight from the giants, who follow claiming their due reward. Freia's cries for help bring her brothers, Froh and Donner, hurrying to the scene, Wotan is faced

FREIA   FLIGHT

with a dilemma: it is Freia who keeps the golden apples which enable the gods to live in perpetual youth, without her they will grow old and perish; yet Wotan has promised her to the giants, swearing by the sacred runes of his spear. As guardian of the law through which alone the gods remain

WOTAN'S SPEAR—THE TREATY

gods, he is compelled to respect his oath. He has hoped to find some substitute acceptable to the giants in place of Freia, and has sent Loge, the tricky god of fire, over the earth to search for such a substitute. Just as the indignant giants are about to drag away the weeping goddess, Loge appears.

LOGE—FIRE

This subtle diplomat says that in all the earth he found none who did not cherish youth and love. As he sings of the universal sway of love, the orchestra sounds the theme of Freia, glowing in great beauty. The giants seem triumphant.

Wotan turns to Loge in rage—is this his promised help? Then Loge remembers the dwarf Alberich who did forswear love and, having stolen the Rhinegold and forged of it a ring, now is amassing a vast treasure in the lower world. The giants say that this treasure will be acceptable to them in place of the goddess, whom, no longer trusting Wotan, they take as hostage until they shall be paid. Bereft of her presence, the gods immediately grow pallid and weak; the mountain top becomes clouded in a mist. Wotan stands lost in thought and finally resolves to descend to Nibelheim and wrest the treasure from Alberich. Preceded by Loge he enters a cavern leading to the underworld. Sulphurous vapors arising from the cavern obscure the scene,

THE NIBELUNGS (THE FORGE)

and as they mount rapidly higher the theatre seems to descend into the earth. The orchestra accompanies with a finely descriptive passage, the leading motives of "Loge," "Gold," and "Flight" being beautifully woven into the symphonic web. In the course of time a red glow shines from a distance and the sound of hammering on innumerable tiny anvils comes near, then recedes. The motive that now dominates the orchestra is associated both with the idea of a "Forge" and the "Nibelungs" who are the smithies.

Hugo Braune

WOTAN AND FRICKA CONTEMPLATE
VALHALLA

As the clanging of anvils dies away we see a great subterranean cave—the abode of Alberich. Through the power of the ring he has enslaved all the dwarfs of Nibelheim, mercilessly compelling them to amass the treasures concealed in the bowels of the earth; and through the power of the ring he has compelled his brother-dwarf, Mime, the skillful craftsman, to forge for him a magic Tarnhelm that will enable the wearer to change his form or render himself invisible. Now, having thus made himself invisible, he beats his slaves and the grovelling

THE TARNHELM

Mime most cruelly. Wotan and Loge approach, flatter Alberich on his power and cunning, and cleverly lead him on to exhibit the magic of the Tarnhelm. At Loge's suggestion, he first transforms himself into a dragon;

Loge pretends great terror, then says that he doubts that Alberich can turn himself into something very small, a toad, for instance. This too, Alberich does—Wotan quickly puts his foot on the toad. Thus Alberich is captured, bound, and dragged back to the upper world.

On the mountain top the enfeebled gods are still waiting in gloom and silence when Wotan and Loge return with the cowering dwarf. Alberich is forced to order his slaves to bring up from the underworld all his amassed wealth; he is compelled to part with the Tarnhelm and even the Ring, the source of his power—these Wotan wishes to keep. Alberich trembles with rage at this loss. When he is released, he pauses before going away and utters a terrific curse upon the Ring: may it bring death and destruction to whomsoever possesses it. Thus will he annihilate the gods who have robbed him of his power.

Now, while the baleful motive of the "Curse" is still ringing in our ears, the Giants return with Freia. The treasures are heaped before her since it is

THE CURSE

agreed that not until the goddess of Love is concealed by the gold, will the Giants give her up. Yet with all the treasure, and even the Tarnhelm added, Fasolt still sees Freia's eye shine through the pile; the Ring is needed, but this Wotan refuses to sacrifice. Now, in a misty light, there rises from the mountain, Erda, the all-knowing, all foreseeing goddess of the earth. With the utmost solemnity she warns him:

> Yield it, Wotan, yield it!
> Quit the Ring accursed!
> Ruin and dismalest downfall wait thee in its wealth.
> Whatever was, was I; what is, as well;
> What ages shall work—all I know;
> The endless world's all-wise one, Erda, opens thine eyes.
> Three, the daughters born to me
> E'er the world was made; all I learn
> Nightly thou know'st from the Norns.
> But hither in dire danger haste I to thy help.
> Hear me! Hear me! Hear me!
> All that exists, endeth!
> A dismal day dawns for the Aesir:
> O render wisely the Ring!

Wotan would detain her to learn more, but she sinks again into the earth, exclaiming:

> I've warned thee now; thou wott'st enough;
> Pause and ponder truth!

Weiche, Wotan, Weiche! *(Yield it, Wotan!)* *Ernestine Schumann-Heink* 7107-2.00

Urged by her warning of the impending doom of the gods, Wotan casts the Ring on the heap; Freia is released and the Giants, starting away with

Painted by Echter
THE CAPTURE OF ALBERICH

their treasure, at once quarrel over the Ring. Fafner kills his brother, Fasolt—the curse on the Ring, its gold, and its power, is at work. But the mountains still remain shrouded in murky clouds. These, Donner, god of thunder, summons to himself, and swinging his mighty hammer, disappears in a storm. *(Beginning of 9100-A.)*

Entrance of the Gods Into Valhalla Coates-Symphony Orchestra 9109-1.50 Abendlich strahlt der Sonne auge *(The Golden Sunlight Gleameth)* **Schorr-Berlin State Opera Orchestra** *(with assisting artists)* **6788-2.00**

Now gleaming in the light of the setting sun, Valhalla is visible, and like a bridge across the valley there rests a glowing rainbow. A theme of great magnificence is heard in the orchestra. *(Beginning of 6788-A.)* Turning to Wotan, Froh says:

> This bridge home will bring you,
> Light but hardy of hold.
> So tread undaunted
> Its terrorless height!

The god, lost in contemplation of the castle, sings:

> See how at eve
> The golden sunlight gleameth
> And with golden touch gilds turret and tower!
> In the morning glamour, manful and glad,
> It bided masterless, mildly beck'ning to me.
> From morning till evening thro' mighty ills
> I won no way to its wonders!
> The night is nigh; from all annoy
> Shelter it shows us now.
> So hailed be the fort; sorrow and fear it heals!
> *(Turning to Fricka)*
> Wend with me, wife,
> In Valhalla, safe shall we dwell.

Fricka asks why he so names the castle *(beginning of 6788-B)*, and Wotan replies, enigmatically:

> What might 'gainst our fears
> My mind may have found,
> If proved a success
> Soon shall explain the name.

The gods proceed towards the bridge, but Loge, remaining behind, looks after them and meditates:

> To their end they even now haste
> While esteeming their strength overwhelming.
> Ashamed am I
> Their acts to have share in.
> A feverish fancy
> Doth woo me to wander
> Forth in flickering fire;
> To burn and waste them
> Who bound me erstwhile,
> Rather than be
> Thus blindly engulfed—
> E'en were they of gods the most godlike—
> There seems sense in the scheme!
> I'll study on it!
> Who asks what I do?

He follows the gods unconcernedly. From the valley the Rhine-maidens are heard lamenting their lost gold *(beginning of 9109-B)*: "Rhinegold! Rarest gold! . . . for thee now we implore . . . O give us our glory again!" Wotan is annoyed by the sound of their plaint; at his command Loge calls down to them: "Ye in the water! Disturb us not . . . If the gold gleams no longer upon you, then bask in the gods' augmented grandeur!" The gods laughingly turn again towards the bridge while the lamenting Rhine-maidens reply:

Rhinegold! Rarest gold!
O might but again
In the wave thy pure magic wake!
What is of worth dwells but in the waters!
Base and bad those who are throned above.

Wotan halts for a moment as if seized by a sudden mighty thought; from the orchestra there thunders

Panel by Hugo Braune
THE GODS ENTER VALHALLA

forth in an impressive cadence, the motive of the "Sword"—the sword

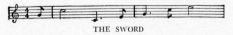
THE SWORD

through which the god hopes to win his salvation. Then, while the gods continue across the bridge towards Valhalla, the theme of the "Rainbow" is heard, majestic and glowing in iridescent beauty.

Golden

FRIEDRICH SCHORR
AS WOTAN

SIEGMUND WITHDRAWS THE SWORD FROM THE TREE

⹁DIE WALKÜRE

MUSIC-DRAMA in three acts; the "first day," of the "Ring des Nibelungen"; text and music by Richard Wagner. First produced, June 25, 1870, at Munich. First performance in the United States, April 2, 1877, at the Academy of Music, New York. (Die Walküre is pronounced *Dee Vahl-kue'-reh* and is Anglicized *The Valkyrie*.)

DIE WALKÜRE ON VICTOR RECORDS

Some of the most remarkable and desirable records in the entire Victor catalog are those of portions of Die Walküre. There is a virtually complete recording of the opera, with a distinguished roster of singers; to this recording (Album M26 and M27) the following story of the opera is keyed.

There is also a complete recording of Act I, presenting the incomparable voices of Lotte Lehmann, Lauritz Melchior, and Emanuel List. These records are found in Album 298.

One of the most wonderful of all Victor Recordings is that which includes the famous Ride of the Valkyries, Wotan's Farewell to Brünnhilde, and the evocation of the Magic Fire. Here we have Leopold Stokowski and the Philadelphia Orchestra, with Lawrence Tibbett marvelously portraying the role of the stern yet saddened Wotan in the farewell and magic-fire scenes.

Finally, there are occasional recordings from the opera, all of unusual power and beauty; these are indicated in the story of the opera as they appear.

Famous Artists of Germany and England M26 & M27 $10.50 each

Act I complete *Lotte Lehmann, Lauritz Melchior, Emanuel List, Vienna Philharmonic Orchestra* M 298 $16.00

Excerpts *Leopold Stokowski and the Philadelphia Orchestra, with Lawrence Tibbett* M 248 $8.00

CHARACTERS
IN THE RECORDING M 26-27

BRÜNNHILDE *(Bruen-hill'-da)*
SIEGLINDE *(Zeeg-lin'-da)*
SIEGMUND *(Zeeg'-moond)*
WOTAN *(Voh'-tahn)*
HUNDING *(Hoond'-ing)*
THE EIGHT OTHER VALKYRIES

Mmes. Frida Leider and Florence Austral, *Soprano*
Gota Ljungberg, *Soprano*
Walter Widdop, *Tenor*
Friedrich Schorr, *Baritone*
Howard Fry, *Bass*
Chorus from the State Opera, Berlin

With the London Symphony Orchestra conducted by Albert Coates and the Orchestra of the State Opera, Berlin, conducted by Dr. Leo Blech.

ACT I

THE orchestral prelude *(Record M 26-1)*, one of Wagner's most descriptive passages, is a vivid portrayal of a tempest: the steady beating of the rain, the crash of thunder, and the hurried tread of a solitary man in flight through the forest.

The storm subsides and the curtain rises, disclosing the interior of Hunding's dwelling—a curious abode of hides and crudely hewn timber, built around the stem of a great ash tree. A fire glows on the hearth. Suddenly the door opens, Siegmund appears, staggers weakly to the fireside and falls exhausted before it, exclaiming, "Whoever may own this house, here must I rest!" *(End of M 26-1.)*

Sieglinde enters from another room; thinking she has heard her husband return, she is surprised to find a stranger lying at the hearth. At his request she hurries to bring him a draught of water. Siegmund revives and they converse, finding a mysterious sympathy in one another. Siegmund would

LOVE

hurry away for he has ever brought misfortune with him; Sieglinde replies that he can bring no misfortune to this abode of unhappiness. He decides to wait for her husband, Hunding, who soon arrives. During the evening meal which Sieglinde prepares, Siegmund tells of his distressful life; how, when a boy, returning with his father Wälse from the chase, he found his home burned, his mother slain, and his twin sister vanished. This crime was done by the Neidungs who from that time relentlessly pursued father and son. Then one day the elder Wälse himself disappeared. And now, wandering alone through the forest, Siegmund has attempted to rescue a girl whose family were about to give her up to a hated lover, but overwhelmed by numbers, he was forced to flee. Thus it is that Hunding recognizes in him the enemy whom he and his kinsmen have been pursuing. Now, however, though weaponless in his enemy's house, Siegmund is his guest and therefore safe, under the ancient law of hospitality. With a threat as to what dawn will bring, Hunding retires for the night, preceded by Sieglinde.

Setzer, Wien
LEHMANN AS SIEGLUNDE

Alone in the room, now entirely dark save for the glow on the hearth, Siegmund broods on his hapless fate (M 26-2). Then, as for a moment he thinks of the beautiful woman who showed him compassion, the motive of their love is heard in the orchestra. Lamenting that she should be the thrall of his enemy, he cries out "Wälse, Wälse, where is thy sword?" for he remembers that his father had promised him a weapon for the time of his sorest need. At this moment the fire on the hearth happens to flicker up, and a ray of its light falls on the hilt of a sword plunged into the stem of the ash tree. Siegmund ponders what this gleam might be, then the glowing embers fade, and he lies down to sleep.

A moment later the door opens, and Sieglinde comes stealthily into the room. (M 26-3). She whispers the information that she put an opiate in her husband's evening draught in order that she might be able to reveal a weapon to the stranger. In explanation she tells of her forced marriage to Hunding: How, while her kinsmen sat at the wedding feast a stranger entered the hall . . . an old man with one eye hidden by his hat, and the gleam of his single eye struck terror into the hearts of all except Sieglinde. Disdaining the assembly the old man drew a sword from his belt and with a mighty swing thrust it deep into the trunk of the ash tree. There the sword remains, for though many tried, the stranger decreed that only one, a great hero, should withdraw it. "Oh, that I might find that man," Sieglinde exclaims, "for in him also should I find the one who shall rescue me from my woe!"

Siegmund, holding Sieglinde in an ardent embrace, replies, "The man for whom the sword and the wife were decreed holds you in his arms!" (M 26-4.) Suddenly, the great door of the house swings wide open; Sieglinde starts back in fright. "Who went?" she cries. Siegmund, drawing her tenderly in his arms again, tells her that no one went but that spring entered. The intoxicating beauty of the moonlit woods pervades the room, and Siegmund, gazing rapturously upon Sieglinde, apostrophizes the spring night, singing the lovely melody well known as the "Spring Song."

> Winter storms have waned to the winsome moon,
> In mild ascendance smileth the Spring,

With balmy breezes, soft and soothing,
Wonders weaving, on he wends,
Through wood and meadow wafts his breathing,
Wide and lustrous laughs his eye;
In songs of birds his silv'ry voice resounds,
Wondrous fragrance he outbreathes;
From his living blood the loveliest flowers are blooming
Leaf and spray spring forth at his voice.
With gentle sceptre's sway he ruleth the world;
Winter and storm wane as his strength awakes;
By dint of his hardy striving
The stoutest doors he is cleaving,
Which, stubborn and strong, once held us from him!
To greet his sister swiftly he flies;
Thus Love the spring hath allured.
Within our bosoms Love lay asleep
That now laughs out to the light.
The bride and the sister is freed by the brother;
Destroyed the walls that held them apart;
Joyous meet now the youthful pair,
United are Love and Spring!

—Copy't Oliver Ditson Co.

In her rapture, Sieglinde answers *(M 26-5)*: "Thou art the Spring for which I have longed in frosty Winter's spell. At thy first glance my pulses leaped. I knew that in thee all that lay hidden in my breast was awakened!" Tenderly Siegmund replies: "Oh sweetest wonder! Woman above all! . . . What has entangled my heart now do I know! I stand and gaze upon thee in wonder!"

Sieglinde looks at Siegmund with increasing amazement *(M 26-6)*; his features awaken a memory of the past. She has seen her own face reflected in the forest stream, and now when she looks upon Siegmund it is as if she regarded her own countenance. Siegmund replies that he has long had a dream image of her in his heart. In growing excitement Sieglinde asks, "Was Wälse thy father? Art thou a Wälsung!" On learning this, Sieglinde, carried away with her ecstasy, cries: "Struck then for thee was the sword! Now may I name thee, as thou hast ever been known and loved . . . Siegmund! So name I thee!"

Springing from Sieglinde's arms, Siegmund runs to the tree and places his hands upon the hilt of the sword which lies buried there, exclaiming, "Nothung! (Needful) so now I name thee, Sword! come from thy scabbard to me!" *(M 26-7.)* With a powerful effort he draws out the sword and brandishes it before Sieglinde, who utters a cry of joy. "Siegmund of the Wälsungs stands before thee! As bridal gift he brings this sword. Let us fly from this house, into the laughing world of Spring!" Embracing fervently they rush away into the forest to the accompaniment of a pulsating and exultant passage in the orchestra.

Weirich, Festspielhaus, Bayreuth   WOTAN AND BRÜNNHILDE

ACT II

THERE is an agitated orchestral prelude descriptive of the flight of the
Wälsungs through forest and mountains *(M 26-8).* After a time a new
theme, "The Valkyries," enters proudly in the bass, for at the rise of the
curtain, Brünnhilde, the favorite of Wotan's Valkyries, is seen. She is clad
in battle array and stands on a cliff over a rock-strewn mountain pass.

THE RIDE OF THE VALKYRIES

Wotan, also fully armed, comes up the pass and addressing her, orders her
to defend Siegmund in the coming struggle. The Valkyrie springs up the
rocky height singing the battle-cry of the Valkyries: "Ho-yo-to-ho!"

Ho-yo-to-ho *(Brünnhilde's War Cry)* **Kirsten Flagstad** 1726-1.50 **Maria Jeritza**
7268-2.00

On reaching a high peak, she looks around her, then calls back to Wotan:
"Take warning, Father, prepare yourself for strife! Fricka approaches
stormily . . .

THE SHOUT OF THE VALKYRIES

403

Der alte Sturm! Die alte Müh' (*The Usual Storm and Strife!*) **Schorr, Leisner** 7742-2.00

"I leave you to her, I prefer the fighting of heroes!" Resuming her wild cry, she disappears over the mountain (*end of M 26-8*).
Fricka is thoroughly enraged

So ist es denn aus, mit den ewigen Göttern? (*Have the gods, then, come to this?*) **Schorr, Leisner** 7742-2.00

because of the illegal love of the Wälsung pair; the offended Hunding has prayed to her for justice, and as Goddess of Marriage she must punish the guilty. In vain does Wotan tell why he became the father of these Wälsungs —how, enjoined from wresting the treasure from Fafner, he had hoped to raise up a hero who of his own free will would recover the Ring and prevent its falling into the hands of Alberich. Fricka demands righteousness:

Mit tiefem Sinne willst du mich täuschen? (*Wouldst thou deceive me?*) **Schorr, Leisner** 7743-2.00

Siegmund must fall before Hunding, and Wotan, again compelled to uphold the law which gives him his power, is obliged to agree.

Was verlangst du? (*What then, wouldst thou?*) **Schorr, Leisner** 7743-2.00

As Fricka goes away, proud in her triumph, Brünnhilde returns to receive Wotan's further commands. She asks him the cause of his dejection. Wotan springs to his feet with an outburst of deepest intensity (*M 26-9*): "Oh infinite shame!" Brünnhilde is frightened and entreats him, "Tell me, what so distresses thee?"

Wotan dejectedly narrates to her the story of the heroes he has had gathered in Valhalla by his Valkyrie daughters. Brünnhilde asks, "Have we ever failed?" Wotan continues, saying that the danger lies with Alberich's hosts, who in revenge for the loss of the Ring are working to overthrow the gods. He exclaims: "Fade splendor of godhood! . . . one thing only I await . . . the downfall . . . the end!" In the utmost bitterness he cries out (*M 26-10*): "Blessings on thee, Nibelung son! May thou inherit the empty pomp of the gods!"

"What must I do, then?" asks Brünnhilde in alarm. "Fight for Fricka," he replies. "Ah, but you love Siegmund and him will I shield!" Again Wotan commands, "Siegmund must fall." Brünnhilde, ever mindful of Wotan's inmost will, exclaims: "I will shield him thou hast taught me to love!" Infuriated by her defiance, Wotan's wrath blazes forth: "Dost thou scorn me? Siegmund shall fall, this be thy task!" He storms away up the mountain leaving Brünnhilde confused and frightened. She disheartenedly takes up her weapons and enters a cavern overlooking the mountain pass.

A tumultuous orchestral passage calls to mind the flight of the Wälsungs (*M 26-11*); a moment later they appear, faltering and exhausted. Yet in her anxiety Sieglinde has run ahead of Siegmund and would go even farther.

He lovingly calls to her, "Here rest a while, Siegmund will guard thee safe." He overtakes her and embraces her tenderly while she gazes into his eyes. Then she starts away in sudden remorse, crying: "Away, away! Fly from the profane one." Her mood suddenly changing, she confesses: "Within your arms I found all that had awakened my love!" Again she draws back overwhelmed with horror, pleading, "Leave me, lest I bring dishonor upon thee!" *(M 26-12.)* Siegmund exclaims: "Fly no farther, Nothung, my sword shall pierce the enemy's heart!" Sieglinde does not hear him; in her apprehension she believes Hunding and his kinsmen are approaching for vengeance. She cries out in delirious terror, then gazing vaguely about, whispers, "Where art thou, Siegmund?" For a moment she rests on his bosom, then starts up, exclaiming, "Hark!

Franklin & Rayon
MELCHIOR AS SIEGMUND

Hunding's horn . . . you fall . . . the sword is in splinters!" She sinks fainting in Siegmund's arms.

And now Brünnhilde appears from the cavern *(M 26-13)*. The ominous "Fate" motive and "Death Song" are heard, stern, and cold as steel. "Siegmund," she calls, "look on me . . . the messenger of death to warriors!

FATE

THE DEATH SONG

Wotan awaits thee in Valhalla!" Siegmund asks whom he will find in Valhalla *(M 26-14)*. Brünnhilde answers: "Wotan . . . glorious heroes . . . wish maidens . . . but Sieglinde, no, she must remain on earth." Siegmund bids her greet Valhalla for him; he will not go where Sieglinde is not. In her astonishment Brünnhilde asks, "Dost thou prize Valhalla so lightly?" Siegmund raises his eyes to Brünnhilde in scorn *(M 27-1):* "Thou seemst fair and young, now I know thee hard and cruel. Feast on my distress!" Deeply moved Brünnhilde asks to guard his bride. "None other than I shall shield her . . . may Death unite us!" cries Siegmund drawing his sword as if to run it through Sieglinde's heart. Brünnhilde, thrilled at such devotion, impulsively springs forward. "Stop! Ye both shall live, triumph shall be yours!" and so saying, she vanishes up the mountain.

Siegmund remains lost in thought *(M 27-2)*. Storm clouds cover the mountain. Hunding's horn call is heard. Siegmund kisses the sleeping Sieglinde in farewell, then calling a challenge, rushes after the enemy and disappears among the clouds. Sieglinde restlessly dreams of her home, her father, her mother, the ominous stranger, the house in flames; she awakens in fright, calling "Help, Siegmund!" She can see nothing but the dark clouds through which are heard the voices of the combatants still seeking one another, and finally meeting on the summit of the mountain (M 27-3). Sieglinde staggers toward them; a sudden flash of lightning and she falls back. Brünnhilde's clarion voice is heard urging Siegmund to attack Hunding. Yet even as Siegmund wields his sword, a ruddy glow in the clouds reveals Wotan stretching forth his spear; on it the sword is shattered. Hunding strikes the disarmed Siegmund dead; at the terrible sight Sieglinde falls fainting. Brünnhilde leaps from the rocky cliff, snatches up the pieces of the broken sword, and lifting the fainting Sieglinde before her on the saddle, vanishes down the gorge. Wotan, in grim dejection, turns upon Hunding: "Go, slave, tell Fricka that I have avenged her!" And at the god's gesture of contempt Hunding falls dead. Then, bursting into terrible wrath, Wotan cries: "But, Brünnhilde, the disobedient, vengeance upon her!" and disappears in a storm of thunder and lightning.

ACT III

OﾠNE of Wagner's most remarkable descriptive passages is heard at the beginning of this act—the famous "Ride of the Valkyries" (M 27-4). It pictures with amazing vigor and realism the wild neighing and rapid galloping of the magic steeds of the Valkyries as they dash through the storm-filled air to their retreat.

Ride of the Valkyries *Coates-Symphony Orchestra* 9163-1.50 *Stokowski-Philadelphia Orchestra*—in Album M-248 (8542, 8543) 2.00 each

Their meeting place is the summit of a mountain, rocky and barren, with a dark cavern beneath its highest peak; below, a somber forest. In the wide yawning space beyond the precipitous edge of the mountain-top clouds are driven before a storm. On the uppermost peak, four of the nine Valkyries stand awaiting their sisters, whom they signal with their savage war cry, "Ho-jo-to-ho!" Two others answer the call as they arrive, galloping through the air on their steeds, fleet as the clouds, and wild as the lightnings that play about them. The six that have now arrived join in the war cry as they hear Roseweisse and Grimgerde approaching (M 27-5). They laugh wildly at their jests, then seeing they are but eight, ask, "Where is Brünnhilde?" Suddenly Waltraute sees her coming, riding in terrifying haste and carrying not a warrior but a woman. All run forward to meet Brünnhilde. "Sister, what has befallen," they cry out in horror at her daring. Sieglinde, who has aroused from her swoon, urges Brünnhilde to escape; as for herself, she would rather be united in death with Siegmund. Brünnhilde, however, commands her to live for she will be the mother of a child by Siegmund.

SIEGLINDE AND SIEGMUND

Thrilled with a new desire to live, Sieglinde cries, "Rescue me!" *(M 27-6.)* The Valkyries know of a place in the forest to the east where a dragon guards Alberich's ring; there Wotan never goes, and Sieglinde will be safe. No time must be lost, the clouds grow darker, Wotan approaches. Brünnhilde urges Sieglinde: "Fly to the eastward! be brave to endure all ills . . . remember only: you bear in your womb the world's most glorious hero!" She gives her the splinters of Siegmund's sword, saying, "I saved these from his father's death-field . . . he shall wield the sword reforged . . . Sieg-

SIEGFRIED

fried let him be called!" To the ecstatic melody of "Redemption through Love," Sieglinde, who is deeply moved, replies: "O radiant wonder . . . farewell . . . I go to save the loved one for him we both loved . . . be blessed in Sieglinde's woe!" Sieglinde then hurries away. A moment later,

REDEMPTION THROUGH LOVE

Wotan, drawing near in the lowering storm clouds, calls, "Stay, Brünnhilde!" The Valkyries cry out in terror, but generously conceal the recreant in their midst. Wotan strides upon the scene, fiercely demanding, "Where is Brünnhilde?" *(M 27-7.)* The terror-stricken Valkyries try to evade his question.

407

Sternly he commands: "Shield her not . . . Brünnhilde, come forth!" The warrior-maid comes slowly from among her sisters, saying meekly, "Here am I . . . pronounce my punishment." Wotan answers: "I will not chastise thee . . . Thou art no longer a child of my will . . . no longer a Valkyrie!"

Brünnhilde anxiously asks *(M 27-8)*, "Dost thou cast me off?" Wotan explains sadly: "No more will I send thee from Valhalla . . . thou art forever banished from my sight. Bereft of thy godhood thou shalt be as other women . . . to be claimed by the first passing churl." The other Valkyries are loud in their lamentations; Wotan commands them to flee the spot forever, or share a like doom, and they ride quickly away still grieving. Wotan and Brünnhilde remain in silence, the Valkyrie prostrate before her father. Slowly she raises her head, and timidly asks *(M 27-9)*: "Was it so shameful, what I have done, that my offenses are so sternly punished?" She whispers to Wotan the secret of the Wälsungs—no craven will come from that race *(M 27-10)*. "Name them not, they are outcasts with thee!" cries Wotan. He decrees that she shall be chained in sleep, a wife for the first passing stranger who wakens her. "Let horrors ward off all but a fearless hero!" pleads Brünnhilde.

Brünnhildes Bitte *(Brünnhilde's Plea)* **Maria Jeritza 7268-2.00**

"Too much thou askest!" "Then crush out my life, but let me not suffer such shame!" Seized by a sudden inspiration, Brünnhilde implores: "Oh, enkindle a fire around this rock to sear the craven who dares approach!"

Overpowered with emotion, Wotan turns eagerly toward her, raises her to her feet and gazing lovingly into her eyes, sings his wonderfully expressive farewell *(M 27-11)* (also by Lawrence Tibbett and the Philadelphia Orchestra in Album M-248, 2 records, $4.00):

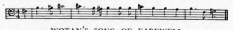

WOTAN'S SONG OF FAREWELL

Farewell, my brave and beautiful child!
Thou once the light and life of my heart!
Farewell! Farewell! Farewell!
Loath I must leave thee; no more in love
May I grant thee my greeting;
Henceforth my maid no more with me rideth,
Nor waiteth wine to reach me!
When I relinquish thee, my beloved one,
Thou laughing delight of my eyes,
Thy bed shall be lit with torches more brilliant
Than ever for bridal have burned!
Fiery gleams shall girdle the fell,
With terrible scorchings scaring the timid
Who, cowed, may cross not Brünnhilde's couch:
For one alone freeth the bride;
One freer than I, the God!

Brünnhilde sinks transfigured on Wotan's breast; then looks into his face with deep emotion while he continues *(M 27-12):*

Those eyes so lustrous and clear,
Which oft in love I have kissed,
When warlike longings won my lauding,
Or when with lisping of heroes leal thy
　honeyed lips were inspired;
Those effulgent, glorious eyes,
Whose flash my gloom oft dispelled,
When hopeless cravings my heart discouraged,
Or when my wishes t'ward worldly pleasure
　from wild warfare were turning.
Their lustrous gaze lights on me now as my
　lips imprint this last farewell!
On happier mortal here shall they beam;
The grief-suffering god may never henceforth
　behold them!
Now heart-torn, he gives thee his kiss,
And taketh thy godhood away!

SLEEP

He places a long kiss on Brünnhilde's eyelids; she sinks gradually into a deep slumber and, as she loses her powers, he assists her to lie down on a grassy mound over-shadowed by a great fir tree *(M 27-13).* He gazes sadly upon her, closes her war helmet, and covers her with her great shield. Then he

Painted by Delitz
WOTAN'S FAREWELL

moves slowly away, pausing to look back once again. He goes decisively to a large rock that juts from the summit of the mountain, and striking it with his spear, he summons Loge:

Loge, hear! Listen and heed!
Appear, wavering spirit, and spread me thy
Fire around this fell!
Loge! Loge! Loge!

As Wotan strikes the rock for the third time, flames pour forth and spread rapidly.

Wotan's Farewell and Magic Fire Music *Coates-Symphony Orchestra* **9006-1.50**
Leopold Stokowski and the Philadelphia Orchestra in **Album M-248 8545-2.00**

The music of Loge, God of Fire and of Deceit, flares upward with a roar, then assumes a constantly flickering form. As the flames surround Wotan *(M 27-14)*, he commandingly directs them to encircle the mountain top. Once again holding out his spear he utters a spell:

He who my spear feareth
Never shall cross this fiery wall.

He casts one sorrowful glance at the sleeping Brünnhilde and turns slowly to depart. As he reaches the fire he again looks back, then disappears

BRÜNNHILDE'S SLEEP

through the flames. Meanwhile, against the music of the "Fire," and the theme of "Brünnhilde's sleep," the melody of "Wotan's Farewell" is heard, in deepest pathos; next the motive of relentless "Fate" is sounded, then only "Fire" and "Brünnhilde's Sleep" remain and tranquillity pervades the scene.

Veirich, Festspielhaus, Bayreuth

SIEGFRIED APPROACHES BRÜNNHILDE

SIEGFRIED

MUSIC-DRAMA in three acts; the "second-day" of the "Ring des Nibelungen"; words and music by Richard Wagner. First produced, August 16, 1876, at Bayreuth. First performance in the United States, November 9, 1887, at the Metropolitan Opera House, New York.

CHARACTERS

SIEGFRIED *(Zeeg'-freed)*	*Tenor*
MIME *(Mee'-ma)*	*Tenor*
WOTAN *(disguised as the* WANDERER) *(Voh'-tan)*	*Baritone-Bass*
ALBERICH *(Ahl'ber-ich)*	*Baritone-Bass*
FAFNER *(Fahf'-ner)*	*Bass*
ERDA *(Air'-dah)*	*Contralto*
BRÜNNHILDE *(Bruen-hill'-da)*	*Soprano*
FOREST BIRD	*Soprano*

SIEGFRIED ON VICTOR RECORDS

Several groups of recordings of the greatest interest have been made by Victor from the opera "Siegfried." Though no absolutely complete recording of the work exists, three masterpiece sets encompass all of the most absorbing portions of the work, and present it to us as performed by such eminent artists as Lauritz Melchior, Florence Easton, Albert Reiss, Friedrich Schorr, and others under the direction of Albert Coates and Robert Heger. These records are catalogued in three groups: M 83, which is a condensed version of the whole opera; M 161, which gives us the major portions of Acts I and II; and M 167, which deals entirely with Act III except for its inclusion of the Prelude to Act I.

The following story of the opera is keyed to these three groups of records.

411

Famous Wagnerian Singers and Orchestras Album M-83 (9805-9814) AM-83 (9815-9824) Price $15.00 *Acts I and II* Tessmer, Melchior, Schorr, Habich, London Symphony Orchestra Album M-161 (7691-7696) AM-161 (7697-7702) Price $12.00 *Act III* Melchior, Easton, Royal Opera Orchestra Album M-167 (7762-7765) AM-167 (7766-7769) Price $8.00

ACT I

A DARK, sinister orchestral prelude, built largely from motives associated with Alberich and Mime *(M 167-8)*, prepares us for the opening of the first act. In a large cavern Mime has set himself up a smithy. In this, his gloomy abode, he sits busily working at his anvil, soliloquizing meanwhile on his unhappy lot *(M 161-1)*: no matter how strong a sword he makes, the boy Siegfried breaks it asunder. Yet he cannot succeed in welding together the fragments of Siegmund's broken sword, "Nothung"; with that for a weapon Siegfried could easily triumph over Fafner, who, transformed by the magic of the Tarnhelm into a dragon, still guards the Ring; and with his subtle cunning, Mime could then easily obtain the Ring from the unsophisticated Siegfried. And now *(M 161-2)*, that joyous youth enters from the sunlit woods, clad in his rude forest garb, and leading a bear by a rope towards Mime. The dwarf runs in precipitous haste to hide himself. Siegfried laughs, and then, having driven the bear off to the woods, demands his new sword from Mime. The dwarf timorously gives it to Siegfried who shatters the weapon with one blow and complains of this "silly switch." Mime brings food as a peace offering; Siegfried, sprawling on a mossy couch, kicks the food aside—he will prepare his own meals. Why does he continue to come here, he asks, when he feels such a loathing for this grovelling dwarf. Mime attempts to persuade *(M 161-3 and 4)* him that it is because he is his father; Siegfried scornfully refuses to believe him. Now he will have the truth, and nearly throttles the dwarf in his endeavor to gain it. Mime

World Wide

MIME

confesses that the boy is the son of an unfortunate fugitive who, overwhelmed with sorrow, sought refuge here, and died in giving birth to him. Siegfried shows great emotion, then fearing lest the crafty dwarf be deceiving him, demands evidence *(M 161-5)*. Mime produces the fragments of "Nothung." Siegfried, thrilled with the thought of owning his father's weapon, orders Mime to forge the pieces into a sword and runs back into the forest.

While the dwarf is still brooding over this impossible task, Wotan appears disguised as a Wanderer *(M 161-6)*. Mime is appalled as the one-eyed warrior looms above him, especially when the Wanderer carelessly touches the earth with his long spear and a soft roll of thunder follows. The dwarf vainly suggests to the Wanderer that he go else-where. The visitor insists on remaining; he will answer at the price of his life any three questions Mime can propose *(M 161-7)*. After successfully answering three riddles regarding the Nibelungs *(M 161-8)*, the giants, and the gods, the Wanderer asks three himself at the same price. Mime success-fully answers the first two regarding the birth of Siegfried, but is terrified at the third: who will repair Nothung? This is the one thing Mime wishes to know, yet, foolishly neglected to ask. As the Wanderer departs he says:

> He who never felt fear
> Will forge Nothung again.
> Guard well your head from today,
> I leave it a prize for him
> Who has not learned to fear.

Mime remains a prey to the wildest imaginings, and when Siegfried re-turns he finds the dwarf hiding behind the anvil. When he asks for the reforged sword of his father, Mime replies by asking what would a sword avail him if he know not fear? Moreover, the dwarf says, the dying Sieglinde bade him teach her son to fear ere he ventured into the world. Siegfried is impatient to learn this mysterious thing. Has he never felt a strange trem-bling in the depths of the forest as night falls, asks the dwarf *(M 83-1)*, then Mime will take him to the great dragon, Fafner; there Siegfried shall learn to fear. The youth is enthusiastic, but first he must have his sword. Mime is compelled to confess that it is impossible for him to forge the broken pieces. Siegfried then says he will himself reforge his father's broken weapon! In joyous excitement he files the pieces into powder, pours this into a crucible and places it on the forge. Then while he lustily blows the fire with the bellows, he sings for sheer youthful exuberance; the orchestra furnishes a wonderful picture of the fire as it flames up, casting off glowing sparks *(M 83-2)*.

> Nothung! Nothung!
> Marvelous sword!
> Why wert thou thus dissevered?
> To shreds I've shattered
> Thy shining blade,
> The fire shall melt now the fragments!
> Hoho! Hoho!
> Hahei! Hahei!
> Bellows blow!
> Brighten the glow!
> Wild in woodlands
> Waved a tree,
> Which I in the forest felled.
> The brown-hued ash
> I baked into coal,
> On the hearth it lies now in heaps.
>
> Hoho! Hoho!
> Hahei! Hahei!

Bellows blow!
Brighten the glow!
Nothung! Nothung!
Marvelous sword!
I've smelted thy steely shreds.
In thine own sweat
Thou swimmest now;
I soon shall call thee my sword!

Mime realizes that the sword will be forged—the Ring will fall into Sieg
fried's hands. While the youth continues with the making of the sword
pouring the molten metal into a mold, plunging that into cold water, the
hammering the newly formed blade on the anvil, Mime sets about to pre
pare a poisonous brew *(M 83-3)*. He will offer this to the boy as soon as h
has slain the dragon, the thirsty youth will drink, and the Ring and it
power will be Mime's! *(M 83-4.)* Siegfried brandishes his newly refashione
weapon and with one blow cleaves the anvil from top to bottom before th
amazed and terrified Mime. The motives of "The Sword" and "Siegfried"
Horn Call" rush into a jubilant *prestissimo* while the hero holds aloft th
sword, shouting with glee.

ACT II

THE orchestra plays another ominous prelude in which, against the shud
dering of violins, is heard the theme of the giants, distorted to represen
Fafner, the dragon. There also enters the menacing motive of the "Curse."

Weirich, Festspielhaus, Bayreuth

ALBERICH AND MIME QUARRELING

414

In the almost ink-like blackness of night we scarcely are able to discern the author of that curse *(M 161-9)*, Alberich, as he sits gloomily watching before Fafner's cave in the depths of the woods, still hoping to regain the Ring. Here arrives the Wanderer, accompanied by the lightning and thunder of a sudden storm. Alberich accuses the god of coming to interfere in the course of events. This Wotan denies *(M 161-10)*, saying that it is only Mime who desires the Ring, not Siegfried or himself, and in proof of this suggests to Alberich that he should call the dragon and offer to save his life in exchange for the Ring. But Fafner, aroused from his tranquil slumber and warned of the approach of his doom at the hands of a youth, refuses to give up any of his hoarded treasure. Then Alberich and the Wanderer go their separate ways and as dawn creeps through the woodland, Mime and Siegfried approach. Now, says the dwarf, Siegfried shall learn to fear, but his prating of love and gratitude only awakens the boy's anger, and Mime slinks off muttering to himself, "Would that Siegfried and Fafner might kill each other."

Siegfried stretches himself out comfortably under a tree, and looking after the departing Mime, exclaims that he is happy that Mime is no father of his *(M 83-5)*. In the orchestra there is heard gradually rising like a faint whisper, the wonderful music descriptive of the murmuring of the leaves of the forest. Siegfried continues his meditation:

> My father—what semblance was his?
> Ha!—no doubt like myself; for, were there of Mime a son
> Must he not look
> Mime's likeness?
> *(He leans back and looks up through the trees.)*
> Surely my mother,
> What semblance had she?
> I—cannot imagine it ever!
> Like soft fallow doe's deeply would shine
> Her soft languishing eyes—
> Only more lovely!
>
> When in sorrow she bore me
> Why must she have died withal?
> Do thus all mortal mothers
> Leaving their dear ones
> Lonely behind?
> Sad were such a world, sure!
> Oh! might I my mother see!
> My own—mother!
> A mortal's bride!

As he thinks of his mother there is heard in the most delicate of orchestral

THE BIRD

tints, the expressive theme of "Filial Love." Siegfried leans back lost in silent contemplation while the murmuring of the forest grows more fulsome around him. Finally his attention is attracted by the song of a bird *(M 83-6)*. He playfully tries to

SIEGFRIED'S HORN CALL

answer it on a reed. He decides he can do better on his horn, and sounds a rousing call. This awakens Fafner who comes clumsily from his cave, and the youth, laughing at the sight, resolutely places himself in the dragon's path *(M 161-11)*. In the battle that ensues, Siegfried, avoiding the lashing tail and venomous teeth, deftly plunges his sword into the monster's heart. Fafner admires the bravery of the young man, and cautions him, "He who led thee blindly to do this deed, surely plots for thy death!" and sinks dying to the ground.

Weirich, Festspielhaus, Bayreuth
THE WANDERER

In withdrawing his sword, Siegfried receives a drop of the dragon's blood on his hand. Involuntarily he carries his hand to his lips. The result of having tasted the dragon's blood is that he can understand the song of the birds. The bird who sang for him before, now tells him clearly of the Tarnhelm and the Ring. Siegfried enters the cave to search for these treasures. While he is gone, Alberich and Mime come forth from the hiding places whence they have been looking on. Their bitter quarrel *(M 161-12)* as to who shall claim the Ring is ended abruptly by the reappearance of Siegfried. Alberich vanishes with a dark threat, and Mime, with seemingly fair words, tries to induce the young hero to partake of a supposedly refreshing drink. Siegfried, however, having tasted of the dragon's blood, can understand the significance of Mime's fawning deceit, and in a final burst of anger, draws his sword and kills the dwarf. He drags Mime's corpse and also the body of the dead dragon into the cave *(M 83-7)*. He soon returns, and exclaiming at the heat of the midday which sends the blood coursing through his head, throws himself down to rest under a tree. Looking up he notices the bird twittering about with its "brothers and sisters," and is reminded that he has none *(M 83-8)*.

> Friendliest warbler,
> I would fain demand,
> Grant unto me a gracious friend.
>
> .   .   .
>
> Already rightly thou'st told me;
> Now sing! I list to thy song.

His new-found friend tells him of a wonderful maiden who sleeps on a

416

mountain top girt round by protecting flames. With a shout of joy, Siegfried asks to be shown the way, and as the bird flutters off, he follows in eager pursuit.

The motive of the "Bird" dominates this scene. Mingled with it are heard the themes of "Fire," "Siegfried," his "Horn Call," and an often repeated impetuous passage, expressive of Siegfried's youthful ardor. As the hero runs away excitedly following the bird, the music swells to an exuberant climax and comes to a close with a brief passage that flutters captivatingly upwards.

Forest Murmurs (Waldweben) *Mengelberg-New York Philharmonic-Symphony Orchestra* 7192-2.00

This beautiful concert favorite is an orchestral version of the music of the scene immediately preceding the slaying of the dragon, and also of the subsequent dialogue between Siegfried and the bird.

ACT III

A TEMPESTUOUS orchestral prelude of unusual magnificence introduces the third act. The rhythm of "The Ride," and the motives of the "Distress of the Gods," "The Rhine," "The Fall of the Gods," "Alberich," "Sleep," "Fate" and "Wotan's Spear," all enter, with singular beauty and appropriateness. As we hear the mysterious harmonies of "Sleep," the curtain rises, revealing a savage, barren and rocky country, shrouded in obscurity. Wotan, the Wanderer, halts before a cave in the mountain-side, and with great solemnity invokes the goddess of the Earth (M 83-9).

The cavern begins to glow with a bluish light, and Erda slowly rises from the earth, her hair and garments shimmering as with hoar-frost. Dreamily she asks who wakens her (M 83-10). Wotan replies that he has come to her, the wisest of all beings, to learn her counsel. She wearily answers that her sleep is dreaming, dreaming that brings wisdom; but the Norns are ever awake, weaving the rope of fate from her knowledge; let him seek their counsels. Wotan, however, would not know the future, he would alter its course. Then Erda calls to mind that she once submitted to Wotan's will, bore him a daughter, the Valkyrie; why does he not seek the far-seeing Brünnhilde? The god informs her (M 83-11) of the punishment that he has been compelled to inflict on the rebel warrior-maid; can he consult her who is no longer one of the gods? Erda is unwilling to counsel him who punishes the Valkyrie for having done his will; who, a god, the upholder of truth, holds his sway through falsehood. She would return to her sleep. Wotan is resolved to accept his fate (M 83-12), to welcome his doom. The world, which in

MELCHIOR AS SIEGFRIED

417

anger he had left to the Nibelung, he now bequeaths to the son of the Wälsungs. The splendid theme of "The Heritage of the World" is heard briefly in the orchestra. This hero, Wotan says, having gained the Ring, will

THE HERITAGE OF THE WORLD

awaken Brünnhilde, and she shall win the world's freedom. Gladly will Wotan yield to the eternally young. "Away, then," he says, "mother of all fear, to endless sleep, away, away!" Erda sinks into the earth.

Wotan awaits Siegfried, who appears with the approach of dawn and demands right-of-way from this stranger barring his path. Wotan questions him good-humoredly and learns of the death of Fafner. He asks, too, whence comes the sword, and Siegfried answers he has forged it from a broken weapon. "Who was it first made that sword?" pursues Wotan. Siegfried answers that he cares not since a broken weapon is useless until repaired. Wotan laughs, but Siegfried becomes insistent to know the way to the fiery couch of Brünnhilde, the bird that directs him having flown. Wotan confesses that the black ravens that always accompany him have frightened the bird away, and adds that *(M 83-13)*, although he has always loved Siegfried's race, he was once compelled to shatter the sword of that youth's father; now he bids him beware and not arouse his ire, lest the sword be again so shattered. Siegfried cries out for joy, thinking that he has discovered his father's enemy and thus his own. Wotan angrily bars the path with his spear. Siegfried severs the weapon with a mighty blow of Nothung *(M 83-14)*, and hurries excitedly up the mountain side. Wotan turns gloomily away.

The themes of "Fire," "Sleep" and "Siegfried's Horn Call" blend in a magnificent tumult while flames rise up and obscure the scene from view. When the music and the flames subside, we again behold Brünnhilde still locked in her magic sleep on the desolate mountain top. Siegfried approaches, wonderingly *(M 83-15)*, and seeing what he believes to be a sleeping knight in armor, raises the

SIEGFRIED AWAKENING BRÜNNHILDE

HAIL TO THE WORLD

shield, removes the helmet, and cuts through with his sword the fastenings of the breastplate. This discloses Brünnhilde in woman's dress *(M 83-16)*, and Siegfried starts back in right. Now for the first time, the hero is shaken with fear *(M 83-17).* He attempts vainly to arouse her from her sleep, and at last kisses her on the lips. This breaks the spell and Brünnhilde slowly awakens, while we hear in the orchestra the luminous chords of "Hail to the World."

She greets the sun *(M 83-18) (M 167-1),* the light, the radiant day, and asks who wakened her. The youth gazing at her, transfixed with rapture, answers that it is Siegfried *(M 167-2, 3)* who has released her from the spell. Brünnhilde continues her apostrophe:

> Hail, ye gods all!
> Hail, thou world!
> Hail, ye glories of nature!
> Unknit is now my sleep;
> I stand awake;
> Siegfried 'tis
> Who breaks the spell.

Then, in music of glowing fervor, they sing together:

> O hail to her
> Who gave me to life!
> Hail to earth,
> My fostering nurse!
> That I should e'er have seen
> The sight that smiles on me here!

Siegfried *(M 167-4)* seizes Brünnhilde impetuously; she springs up, repulses him and flies in the utmost terror to the opposite side of the mountain-top. She cries out in fright and shame—no god's touch has she felt! Siegfried's ardor is unabated, and already the godhood in Brünnhilde is waning. She pleads gently with the hero, calling to mind happy days that are vanished *(M 83-19) (M 167-5):*

> Deathless was I,
> Deathless am I,
> Deathless to sweet
> Sway of affection—
> But deathless for thy good hap!
> . . . . .
> O Siegfried! happiest
> Hope of the world!
> Leave me in peace!
> Press not upon me
> Thy ardent approaches!

Siegfried replies *(M 167-6):*

> I love thee:
> O lovest thou me?
> I have no more self:
> O had I but thee!
> The grandest of floods
> Before me rolls,
> And all my senses

419

Seize on the sight,
O would that its waters
In bliss might embrace me.

Brünnhilde, no longer the icy goddess, surrenders to her love for Siegfried. She is overcome with emotion and in a beautifully lyric passage
answers. "Thine, O Siegfried, have I ever been!" *(M 83-20.)* The lovers
embrace in rapture, and sing their exultant duet, throbbing with the high
ecstasy of the theme, "The Decision to Love" *(M 167-7):*

THE DECISION TO LOVE

Farewell grandeur
And pride of gods!
Here still is streaming
Siegfried, my star.
He is forever,
My own, my only,
And my all.—
Love that illumines,
Laughing at death.

Weirich, Festspielhaus, Bayreuth
SCENE FROM ACT II AS GIVEN AT BAYREUTH

DIE GÖTTERDÄMMERUNG

MUSIC-DRAMA in three acts with prologue, the "third day," of the "Ring des Nibe-lungen"; text and music by Richard Wagner. First produced, August 17, 1876, at Bay-reuth. First performance in the United States, January 25, 1888, at the Metropolitan Opera House, with Lehmann, Niemann and Fischer.

"DIE GÖTTERDÄMMERUNG" ON VICTOR RECORDS

These new records of "Die Götterdämmerung"—among the outstanding recording achievements of recent years—represent the chief portions of the music-drama, performed by some of the greatest of living Wagnerian artists and recorded on sixteen Victor Records. While, of course, these records do not include all of Wagner's five-hour music-drama, they are so well chosen that they do represent all the great moments of the music and completely outline the action of the drama. Besides including the magnificent im-molation scene, the funeral music, the "Rhine Journey," the fascinating scene of the Rhine-maidens, the parting of Siegfried and Brünnhilde, the stirring wedding music and the dramatic scene of the conspiracy, this set of records also contains the impressive music of the scene of the Norns at the opening of the Prologue and the very beautiful scene between Brünnhilde and Waltraute—some of Wagner's most glowing pages, yet because of the length of the music-drama, seldom heard in our opera houses. Thus this set of records is of unusual significance to all opera lovers. The beautiful and intricate orchestral score is performed by the Orchestra of the Berlin State Opera, conducted by Dr. Leo Blech and the London Symphony Orchestra, conducted by Albert Coates and Lawrance Collingwood; the Chorus is that of the Berlin State Opera. The records are issued as Album M-60 (and in automatic sequence AM-60) in the Musical Masterpiece

Series, Price, $24.00. The accompanying description of the music-drama is keyed to these records and the names of the artists are given with the following cast of—

CHARACTERS

BRÜNNHILDE *(Bruen-hill'-da)* · Florence Austral, *Soprano*
SIEGFRIED *(Zeeg'-freed)* Walter Widdop and Rudolf Laubenthal, *Tenor*
GUNTHER *(Goon'-ter)*, *Chief of the Gibichungs* Messrs. Zador and Fear, *Bass*
ALBERICH *(Ahl'-ber-ich)*, *the Nibelung* *Baritone*
HAGEN *(Hah'-gen)*, *son of Alberich, half-brother to Gunther*
Messrs. List, Andresen and Collier, *Bass*
GUTRUNE *(Goot-troon'-a)*, *Gunther's sister* Goeta Ljungbeg, *Soprano*
The Rhine-Maidens
WOGLINDE *(Vo-glin'-da)* Mme. de Garmo, *Soprano*
WELLGUNDE *(Vell-goon'-da)* Mme. Kindeamann, *Soprano*
FLOSSHILDE *(Floss-hill'-da)* Mme. Marker, *Mezzo-Soprano*
THE THREE NORNS, Mmes. Eadie, Arden and Palmer, *Contralto, Mezzo-Soprano, Soprano*

(Title of the opera, pronounced "Dee Goe-ter-daym'-mer-oong," is translated, "The Dusk of the Gods.")

PROLOGUE

A BRIEF though impressive orchestral prelude prepares us for the scene. In it are heard the themes of "Hail to the World," and "The Rhine" in somber hues. "Fate" sounds darkly, and the curtain rises showing the Valkyrie's rock, now shrouded in the obscurity of night *(M 60-1)*. The three Norns, the Fates of Scandinavian mythology, sit gloomily winding the rope of destiny. As they speak of the fire which Loge maintains around the mountain, the theme of the magic flames is heard, vague like a distant glow in the orchestra. The first Norn, unwinding a golden cord and fastening it to the fir tree, recalls that once it was a joy to perform her task, sheltered by the

Weirich, Festspielhaus, Bayreuth
HAGEN

branches of the mighty world-ash at the foot of which flowed the spring of wisdom. Wotan came to drink of the waters, she continues *(M 60-2)*, giving in payment therefor, one of his eyes; he tore a branch from the world-ash to make his spear. From that time the tree withered and fell in decay, and the spring became dry at its source. She then adds, "Sing, sister, for I throw thee the rope . . . knowst thou what next befell?" The Second Norn takes the rope, and having fastened it to a rock, sings as she weaves. She tells how Wotan graved on his spear the runes of the treaties which gave him his power; how this weapon was shattered when the god opposed a young hero; how Wotan then commanded the warriors of Valhalla to destroy the world-ash. "What next is decreed?" she asks, throwing the rope to her sister. The third Norn

422

continues the narrative *(M 60-3)*: In Valhalla Wotan and his heroes sit in state; around the castle is piled the wood of the world-ash. If that should be set afire, the gods will be destroyed. "Know ye more?" she asks, throwing the rope back to the Second Norn, who in turn throws it to the First. Here eyes are dimmed by sorrow and, wondering whether it is the dawn or the magic fire she sees, asks what happened to Loge. The Second Norn replies telling how Wotan subdued Loge by means of his spear and bound him around Brünnhilde's rock. "Knowst thou what then will befall?" she asks. The Third Norn foresees that Wotan will plunge the broken pieces of his spear into the fire and then will cast the blazing spear into the heaped up boughs of the ash tree. "If thou wouldst know when this shall come to pass, give me the rope," cries the Second Norn *(M 60-4)*. The First Norn has it, however; "The night wanes," she sings, "I can grasp nothing more. I feel no longer the strands, the threads are broken . . . a dreadful sight overwhelms my senses . . . the Rhinegold that once Alberich stole . . . know ye what came of that?"

The Second Norn takes the rope again, fastening it to a rock. She cries in alarm, "The rope is breaking, cut by the rock! It is the curse of the Nibelung's Ring which gnaws at the strands! Knowst thou what will hap?" The Third Norn takes the rope. It is too slack, and as she stretches it, it breaks. The three sisters cry out in terror. They bind themselves together with the pieces of the broken rope. "Ended is eternal wisdom!" they lament, "the world shall hear us no more!" then sink into the earth to seek Erda, their mother *(end of M 60-4)*.

Dawn begins to break and the music swells into a fine climax developed on a theme associated with Brünnhilde, now a mortal. As the sunshine floods the mountain top, the melody of Siegfried's horn call is heard, changed

BRÜNNHILDE

into a serious, heroic form *(M 60-5)*, and Siegfried and Brünnhilde come out of the cave. "To deeds of valor, I must send thee forth!" cries Brünnhilde. She has bestowed on him all the wisdom that she had known as one of the gods, yet thinks her gift too little. Siegfried replies passionately that though he may have been a poor scholar, he has learned well ever to remember her. She earnestly charges him not to forget the fire he crossed to win her and the love and faith they have vowed. "I must leave thee here," Siegfried exclaims *(M 60-6)*, "guarded by the fire. For all thy runes I give thee now this Ring won from a dragon." Joyfully Brünnhilde replies, "For the Ring, take now my horse! Once he flew with me through the heavens, with me he lost his magic powers . . . guard him well . . . speak to him oft Brünnhilde's name!" Siegfried answers rapturously, "Upon thy horse I shall fight, with thy shield ward me, then shall I no longer be Siegfried,

Brünnhilde's arm shall I be!" Brünnhilde calls upon the gods, "Apart, who shall divide us? Though divided, ne'er shall we be parted!" They unite in their ardent duet, "Hail rapture of loving! Hail rapture of living! Hail!" *(End of M 60-6.)* Siegfried leaps on Grane's back and rides quickly down the mountain. Brünnhilde stands watching him, as he disappears. At the moment of parting the motives of Siegfried and Brünnhilde are played brilliantly by the full orchestra, then as the music grows quieter Siegfried is heard joyfully sounding his horn call from the mountain side. Brünnhilde, standing far out on the cliff, catches sight of him again and waves delightedly before he finally vanishes from her sight *(beginning of M 60-7, and Record number 6859).* The motives of "Flight" and "The decision to love" enter in the orchestra, and then as the curtain falls, these motives are marvelously combined together with that of the "Magic Fire." At the moment of climax, there is a sudden change of key, the music associated with the Rhine enters, and in a burst of special magnificance, the "Adoration of the Gold" is combined with Siegfried's horn call, and "Gold." The music, growing quieter and more somber, is then pervaded by the theme of the "Ring" the "Gold," and the "Renunciation of Love" *(end of M 60-7).* And now the wonderful exuberance and youthful joyousness having vanished, the "Bondage" motive, associated with Alberich, is heard.

Siegfried's Journey to the Rhine *Karl Muck-Berlin State Opera Orchestra (6859—in Album M-37)* **Albert Coates-Symphony Orchestra 9007-1.50**

The recording by Albert Coates (in two parts) is a favorite concert piece especially arranged. It includes besides the Rhine Journey proper, the beautiful music of the dawn preceding the entry of Siegfried and Brünnhilde, the great climax heard as Siegfried rides away, and closes with the final gloomy measures that, in the music-drama, lead directly into Act I. The most recent, most complete and finest recording, however, is found in Album M-188, 7843-7844, $10.00 by Leopold Stokowski and the Philadelphia Orchestra.

ACT I

O N THE banks of the Rhine is the kingdom of the Gibichungs, of whom Gunther is the chief. He is now in consultation with his sister, the fair Gutrune and his swarthy half-brother, Hagen. The latter, while extolling their prowess, laments that neither Gunther nor Gutrune is as yet married. He tells Gunther of the sleeping goddess, Brünnhilde, who can be won only by a fearless hero who will penetrate a wall of flames. Gunther would like to win Brünnhilde, yet he knows well that he cannot pass through the fire. Hagen then tells of Siegfried, the fearless hero who slew the dragon Fafner; he it is who might be persuaded to win Brünnhilde for Gunther. Moreover, Siegfried would be a worthy husband for Gutrune; should her beauty not succeed in winning his love, a magic potion will easily do so. Scarcely has this plan been devised, when Siegfried arrives in his quest for adventure. He is welcomed effusively by Gunther (M 60-8). Then Hagen suggests, "Rumor has it that you are the ruler of the Nibelung treasure?" and Siegfried admits he had forgotten all about that. "Took you none of it?" asks the wondering Hagen. "Only this," replied Siegfried, pointing to the Tarnhelm, "this of which I know not the use!" Hagen explains to him the mystery of the Tarnhelm, then asks, "Was there nothing else?" "Only a Ring," Siegfried answers, "which now a glorious woman guards for me."

At this moment Gutrune enters the hall and advances to Siegfried bearing a filled drinking-horn. "Welcome to Gibich's house, as our guest take thou this drink!" she exclaims. Bowing to her kindly, Siegfried takes the drinking horn, which he holds before him meditatively. "If lost were all that thou hast taught me, one lesson I shall ne'er forget . . . this draught, the first my lips e'er tasted, Brünnhilde, I drink to thee!" (End of M 60-8.) No sooner has he finished this magical draught of forgetfulness, than he is fired with a sudden passion for Gutrune. When he learns that Gunther is unmarried, but desires for his wife a noble maiden who lives on a mountain top surrounded by fire, he at once suggests that they go together to win her as a bride. They swear blood-brotherhood and set out immediately. Should they succeed, Siegfried shall be granted Gutrune's hand in marriage.

Hagen, now alone in the hall, broods over his sinister plan while the orchestra supplies a background remarkable for its unmitigated gloom (M 60-9):

> Here I sit and wait, watching the hall,
> Warding the house from all foes.
> Gibich's son is wafted by winds;
> A-wooing forth is he gone.
> And fleetly steereth a stalwart man,
> Whose force all perils can stem.
> His own the bride he brings down the Rhine:
> But he will bring *me* the Ring.
> Ye gallant partners, gleeful companions,
> Push ye then merrily hence!
> Slight though your natures,
> Ye still may serve the Nibelung's son!

The curtain is lowered for a few moments, while the orchestra continues playing in this mood of fateful brooding. When the curtain is raised we are again at the Valkyrie's rock. Brünnhilde is sitting at the mouth of the cave contemplating Siegfried's Ring, which she covers with kisses as though lost in happy memories. Suddenly she is startled by a distant roll of thun-

Painted by Echter
ALBERICH URGES HAGEN TO RECOVER
THE RING

der, then another, nearer. A Valkyrie is approaching. A cry is heard from the distance, "Brünnhilde! Sister!" Soon the Valkyrie reaches the mountain top, it is Waltraute. Brünnhilde is so enrapt with her own felicity, that she does not notice Waltraute's agitation, but asks, "Did my happiness lure thee from Valhalla?" Waltraute exclaims, "Share thy madness! Not for that did I break Wotan's ban!" For the first time observing Waltraute's perturbed condition, Brünnhilde questions, "What woe troubles thee?" "Heed well what I say!" answers Waltraute.

Höre mit Sinn, was ich dir sage! *(Harken with Heed to What I Tell Thee!)* **Ernestine Schumann-Heink** 7107-2.00

"Since Wotan bade thee farewell, no more has he sent the Valkyries to battle" *(M 60-10)*. She tells how he roamed, lonely and restlessly over the world and returned to Valhalla, his spear shattered. How he then commanded his heroes to hew down the world-ash and pile the fragments about the castle. How he now sits in state surrounded by his warriors; ever silent and gloomy, no more does he eat of Freia's apples. The other gods sit near him in silent terror. He has sent his two ravens over the earth, continues Waltraute *(M 60-11)*. Should they return with good tidings, the god will face his doom smiling. The Valkyries sit tremblingly at his feet. Waltraute tells how once in tears she clasped herself closely against Wotan's breast, then she hesitates as she continues— "Wotan's face grew softer—he thought, Brünnhilde, of thee!" And from the orchestra there is heard the motive of "Wotan's farewell," a whisper of ineffable pathos, like a faint echo from a vanished day. Waltraute continues, "Sighing deeply, he murmured as in a dream, that shouldst thou give back the Ring to the Rhine-maidens the gods and the world would be released from the curse!" When Waltraute heard this she stole secretly away through the waiting ranks of silent warriors and came here *(M 60-12)*. "End the grief of the gods!" she entreats, prostrating herself before her sister. Brünnhilde replies that she understands nothing for Valhalla knows her no longer. "The Ring," cries Waltraute, "cast it far from thee, to the Rhine-daughters give it!" "The Ring?" asks Brünnhilde in amazement, "Siegfried's love token! Art thou mad?"

"Oh hear me!" pleads the unhappy Waltraute. "The woe of all the world is caused thereby! Throw the ring into the waters, so shalt thou end Valhalla's grief!" "You know not what this Ring is to me," cries Brünnhilde.

426

"More than the wonder of Valhalla, more than the immortal pleasures of the gods! . . . Siegfried loves me! Oh that I could teach this rapture to thee!" "Go, then!" continues Brünnhilde *(M 60-13)* "to the gods in council arrayed, and say that never shall I give up love! Nor shall they steal it from me, though proud Valhalla fall!" Crying out in anguish, Waltraute mounts her steed and rides away in a storm cloud. Brünnhilde quietly contemplates the evening landscape, and the flames that glow in the distance at the foot of the mountain.

Suddenly the fire springs up brightly, a horn call is heard. "Siegfried!" exclaims Brünnhilde excitedly, "up to greet him, clasped in the arms of my god!" The flames mount higher and higher; suddenly there springs on to the mountain top a strange figure. Brünnhilde shrieks in terror and cowers tremblingly, murmuring, "Who dares approach?" *(End of M 60-13.)* The stranger is, of course, Siegfried, transformed by the magic of the Tarnhelm into the likeness of Gunther. He claims Brünnhilde as his bride and though she resists him, he quickly overpowers her, takes the Ring from her finger, and orders her into the cave. He then calls Nothung to witness his faithfulness to Gunther, whose wooing he is accomplishing.

ACT II

Hagen is on watch outside of the hall of the Gibichungs. In the darkness there crouches near him the dwarf Alberich. From their conversation we learn that Alberich, having renounced love, was able to marry only after finding a woman who would accept him because of his proffered gold. Of this loveless union Hagen is the offspring. Urged on by his father, Hagen swears to recover the Ring before Siegfried learns of its power or is persuaded to restore it to the Rhine-maidens. Alberich goes his way as dawn approaches. Siegfried soon arrives, now in his natural form, no longer wearing the Tarnhelm. After being greeted by Hagen and Gutrune, he tells how he penetrated the wall of flames; and adds that Gunther now follows with the bride there won for him.

Hagen mounts a rocky cliff overhanging the river near the hall *(M 60-14)*. "Hoi-ho!" he calls, "Ye vassals! Bring weapons, come armed for war." Hurrying to the scene, they ask "Who is the foe?" He replies that Gunther comes bringing a wife and bids them make sacrifices unto the gods that the marriage might be blessed. He

Cliche Hans Brand
SETTING OF ACT II AT BAYREUTH

orders them to fill their drinking-horns, and drinking freely, give honor due to the gods (*M 60-15*). The vassals laughingly answer, "Good fortune indeed greets the Rhine if Hagen, the grim one, makes merry!" But Hagen, still grave, warns them, "Greet now Gunther's bride. Be loyal to the lady; should she be wronged swiftly avenge her!" Gunther's boat now approaches down the Rhine, and the vassals cheer wildly, "Hail! Welcome!" Gunther leads Brünnhilde ceremoniously forward, and the vassals bowing respectfully, sing a stately "Hail, Gunther! Health to thee and thy bride!" (*End of M 60-15.*) Brünnhilde, however, has remained with downcast eyes, as one in a trance, but on hearing Siegfried's voice, she is startled with sudden amazement. Noting on Siegfried's finger the Ring which she believed was taken from her by Gunther, she divines that it was Siegfried who came to her on the mountain top, and blazing forth in terrible anger, denounces him, and declares that she is his wife. Siegfried protests this, saying that he will swear that he has not betrayed Gunther. He asks on whose weapon he shall take oath. Hagen advances saying, "On my spear shall it be sworn!" Siegfried, placing two fingers of his right hand upon the spear point, declares (*M 60-16*), "On your point, shining spear, I take my oath! . . . Whatever strikes me—if ever weapon do, yours be the point, should I have betrayed my brother!" Brünnhilde rushes forward and strikes Siegfried's hand from the spear. "Holy spear!" she cries, "witness my eternal oath. I pray that he may perish by thy point, for here he has sworn falsely an oath." The vassals in their astonishment call for the help of Donner. Siegfried tells Gunther to care for his "wild mountain maid" well; she is still bewildered and angry and knows not what she is saying. Then he takes Gutrune's hand and bids the vassals and their women follow into the hall for the feasting (*end of M 60-16*). The procession moves away leaving only Hagen, Brünnhilde and Gunther, all absorbed in gloomy meditation.

"What crafty thing lies hidden here?" mutters Brünnhilde to herself (*M 60-17*), lamenting the cruelty of the man who casts her aside after having accepted her love and wisdom. "Who bringeth me a sword that I may cut my bonds?" Hagen, coming near, whispers, "Trust in Hagen! He will wreak vengeance on him who betrayed thee!" Turning towards him, Brünnhilde exclaims, "On whom? On Siegfried!" and adds with disdain, "One glance of the hero and thy might would be turned to terror!" "Yet was not his falsehood sworn on my spear point?" Hagen asks. "Truth and falsehood are but words," answers Brünnhilde, "seek stronger cause ere striking the strongest!" Hagen with suave friendliness now questions, "Tell me, then, how may I slay him?"

Brünnhilde cries out in sorrow (*M 60-18*), "Oh thankful! shameful return! All the art known to me have I employed to guard his life; my spells hold him safe from harm!" "Can nothing wound him?" asks Hagen. "In battle, no," she replies, "but . . . if thou shouldst strike at his back . . . well I know that he will never turn his back on the foe . . . and so . . . no spell guards him there!" "And there striketh my spear!" Hagen cries, and turning towards Gunther continues, "Up, noble Gibichung! Here stands thy warrior bride! Why so sad?" But Gunther responds with an outburst of grief at his dishonor; and Brünnhilde turning upon him exclaims, "Low indeed has fallen the race that bore such faint heart as thou!" Gunther, overwhelmed, continues, " 'Tis I the betrayer who am betrayed . . . help me, Hagen!" "Naught helps save Siegfried's death!" And though Gunther is appalled at the thought, remembering the oath of blood-brotherhood, Hagen insists that the oath has been broken and calls for blood.

Brünnhilde exclaims (M 60-19), "He betrayed thee, and me ye all now betray!" Hagen whispers to Gunther, "His death brings our gain if we secure the Ring!" But Gunther is stricken with remorse, and answers: "He has wedded Gutrune, how can we face her with his blood on our hands?" Brünnhilde starts up in sudden rage, exclaiming, "Once it was revealed that I should be robbed of my hero by a spell named Gutrune! Woe to her!" Hagen now counsels Gunther, "If his death grieve Gutrune, we will hide the deed . . . we hunt tomorrow . . . a wild boar shall kill him!" "So may it be!" repeat Brünnhilde and Gunther. And the voices of the conspirators unite briefly in a magnificent passage: Brünnhilde and Gunther call upon the gods to aid their revenge, and Hagen mutters, "Alberich, father, again shalt thou be lord of the Ring!" The wedding procession of Siegfried and Gutrune comes from the hall and is joined by Gunther and Brünnhilde. The joyful music of the marriage feast sounds out brilliantly in the orchestra, but mingled with it as a strange undercurrent is the ominous motive of "Revenge."

ACT III

AGAIN we are at the banks of the Rhine, this time at a point where it flows through a woods. In the waters swim the three Rhine-maidens singing their fascinating song (M 60-20):

> Kind lady sun, send us thy beams;
> Night lies in the depths of the Rhine.
> Once they were bright with the Rhinegold's rays . . .
> Weialala, weialala heia leia wallala . . .

They pause for a moment and listen as a hunting-horn is heard, echoing in the distance. Then joyfully splashing about in the water, they resume their song:

> Kind lady sun, send us soon the hero
> Who shall give us again our gold.
> Rhinegold! How fair would be thy gleam!

Again a horn call is heard (M 60-21), and the Rhine-maidens dive down into the water to take counsel and await Siegfried, who, having lost his way in the hunt, soon appears on the banks of the river. The Rhine-maidens rise to the surface and call him by name. He asks where they have hidden his quarry, the bear. They say they will tell if he will give them the Ring

Ferd. Leeke

SIEGFRIED:

If you threaten my life.
Hardly you'll win from my hand
the ring!

which he wears. "The Ring I slew a dragon to win? that for a worthless bear-skin?" "What so mean? so miserly?" the daughters of the Rhine exclaim. "Thou shouldst be ever generous with maidens!" "If I wasted my goods on ye, my wife might scold!" replies Siegfried. "Is she a shrew? Does she strike thee? Has the hero so soon felt her blows?" the Rhine-maidens laugh. Siegfried retorts that their mocking will never win the Ring. "So fair . . . so strong . . . so made for love . . . how sad that he is such a miser!" cry the maidens laughingly, as they dive down under the water. Sieg-fried descends nearer the water's edge (M 60-22). Pained by their teasing and moved by a sudden impulse, he takes the Ring from his finger, and holding it up, cries, "Hey! Hey! ye water-maidens! Come! I'll give you the Ring." The Rhine-maidens return, no longer laugh-ing. "Keep the Ring," they answer, "till thou learn'st its curse; fain wouldst thou be freed by us!" Siegfried, quietly replac-ing the Ring, says, "Tell me all ye know." They warn him, "Siegfried! Evil lies in store for thee! The Ring bears a curse! Ever it brings death to its owner! So shalt thou this day be slain! Only the waters of the Rhine can remove the curse!" But Siegfried is not frightened; he is less stirred by their threats than their wiles, and declares that he would sooner yield his life than the Ring. "Come, sisters!" lament the Rhine-maidens, be-wailing the hero's presumptuous daring (M 60-23). "Farewell, Siegfried!" they sing. "Today a proud woman will inherit thy treasure . . . more will-ingly shall she grant what we ask!" The maidens turn and swim away sing-ing their song, "Weialala . . ." (end of M 60-23).

The hunting party is heard sounding the hunting horns and calling. Siegfried answers their call, and soon they appear—Hagen, Gunther and a crowd of vassals. They put down their game and prepare for a repast. Sieg-fried says that he found no game—only "water fowl" who foretold his death. This gives Hagen a cue, and he asks Siegfried to tell them how he came to understand the song of birds. Siegfried tells

Mime heiss ein murrischer Zwerg (Mime was a crabbed old dwarf) Melchior, Helgers, London Symphony Orchestra 7659-2.00

of his life with Mime (M 60-24), the forging of Nothung, the slaying of the dragon, the dragon's blood which enabled him to understand the song of birds, and the Ring and the Tarnhelm of which a bird told him. Hagen offers a drinking horn to Siegfried saying that the mead will help rekindle his memory. Hagen has secretly put into the mead the juice of an herb. When the hero drinks of it, the effects of the earlier potion which made him forget Brünnhilde are removed. Siegfried continues his story *(M 60-25)*.

In Leid zu dem Wipfeln *(In Grief to the Branches)* **Melchior, Helgers, London Symphony Orchestra 7659-2.00**

He tells of the forest bird's promise to lead him to Brünnhilde, of his passing through the flames. He becomes more and more enraptured as he recalls the sleeping maiden he found, his awakening kiss—"Then like flames enfolded me beautiful Brünnhilde's arms!" Gunther, rising in horror, cries, "What says he!" At this moment two ravens circle around over Siegfried ere they fly away through the gathering twilight.

"What do these ravens say?" demands Hagen. Siegfried turns to look. "Vengeance they say to me!" cries Hagen. And with a fearful thrust he plunges his spear into Siegfried's back. Siegfried turns and raises his shield, intending to crush Hagen, but falls unconscious. Gunther and the vassals stand appalled, muttering, "What deed is this?" Hagen answers, "Falsehood do I avenge!" then walks gloomily away.

Gunther bends down sorrowfully at the side of the stricken man, surrounded by the sympathetic vassals *(M 60-26)*. Siegfried, opening his eyes, whispers, "Brünnhilde! holiest bride!" The orchestra echoes the glowing music of Brünnhilde's awakening. "Awake! . . . thy awakener came . . . awakened thee . . . broke thy bonds . . . blissful surrender . . . Brünnhilde awaits me!" And he falls back lifeless. Sadly the body is lifted and carried in solemn procession to the Gibichungs' hall while mists rising from the Rhine obscure the scene *(M 60-27)*. But the music of the orchestra continues, attaining a height of tragic expression seldom equalled by any artist. Siegfried's Death Music is included in Album *M 188-7845*, Leopold Stokowski and the Philadelphia Orchestra. Contrasted with the ominous, relentless pulsating of the rhythm of "Death" are heard the themes associated with the Wälsungs, Siegfried's parents, melodies of great simplicity, yet of

DEATH

most touching pathos. Then there gleams out the motive of the "Sword," brightly, but with a new breadth and solemnity. And now *(M 60-28 and also Part II of 6860)*, we hear the rhythm of "Death" swelling out in tones of overwhelming power and grandeur, soon to be joined by the motives of "Siegfried" and of "Siegfried's Horn Call," glorified in the most transcendent majesty. Then suddenly all the splendor of heroism fades and again the music is veiled with grief. The motive of "Brünnhilde" is heard sorrowingly; the rhythm of "Death" persists, now somber-hued, and "The Curse" sounding darkly, the music subsides in the deepest gloom.

Siegfried's Rhine Journey and Death; Brünnhilde's Immolation *Leopold Stokowski-Philadelphia Orchestra, Album M-188 (7843-7847), AM-188 (7548-7852)*, Price $10.00 Siegfried's Funeral March *Coates-Symphony Orchestra 9049-1.50 Karl Muck-Berlin State Opera Orchestra (6860—in Album M-37)*

When the mists clear we find that the scene has changed to the Hall of the Gibichungs. In the darkness the hall and the river beyond it are barely discernible. Gutrune is anxiously awaiting the return of the huntsmen for she has been haunted by dreams of evil foreboding. Suddenly Hagen enters in agitation, and bids her prepare lights for her lord's return . . . then adds that Siegfried is dead, slain by a boar. The body is brought in; Gutrune falls fainting. Gunther would tend her, but she repulses him, and he reveals to her that it was Hagen who murdered her husband. Hagen, unashamed, approaches claiming Siegfried's Ring. Gunther opposes him, they fight, and Gunther falls dead from a stroke of his brother's sword. Still undeterred, Hagen reaches for the Ring, but Siegfried's arm rises threateningly; Hagen recoils in horror and the terror-stricken women shriek. At this moment Brünnhilde enters *(M 60-29)*. "Silence your wailing!" she exclaims. "Children I heard whining the loss of their milk, yet heard I not lament worthy of the highest of heroes!" Gutrune rises in a sudden burst of passion: "Ah, Brünnhilde, thou it was who for envy of me set the men against Siegfried." Brünnhilde gazes sadly at her and replies, "Thou wert ne'er wife of his . . . his troth he plighted me long ere he saw thy face!" The unhappy Gutrune denounces Hagen for having brought the potion which caused Siegfried's forgetfulness.

Brünnhilde remains lost in deep contemplation, then stirred with a sudden exaltation, she turns to the vassals and commands: "Build up a mighty pile of logs by the river's edge! High and bright kindle a fire that in it may be consumed the body of the noblest of heroes! Bring his steed," she continues *(M 60-30)*, "that with me the horse may

GUTRUNE: "Welcome, O Guest, to Gibich's House!"

432

follow his lord. . . ." Then gazing on Siegfried's face, she sings, "Truer than he was none! None more faithfully held promises! Yet oaths and vows hath he betrayed! . . . Ye gods, guardians of all oaths, witness now my distress; behold your eternal disgrace . . . Wotan, hear me! . . . on him, the hero who wrought thy will, thou dost lay the curse which fell upon thee! Yet he must betray me, that all I might comprehend! . . . Rest, then, thou god!" (M 60-31.) At a sign from Brünnhilde the vassals place Siegfried's body on the pyre which is now completed. Brünnhilde takes from Siegfried's hand the Ring, and looking at it thoughtfully exclaims, "Ye Rhine-maidens who so long have lamented the gold . . . take from my ashes the Ring! The fire which consumes me shall cleanse away the Curse! Guard well, then, the gold!" She takes a firebrand from one of the men. "Fly home ye ravens!" she cries, "tell Wotan what ye have here seen. And bid Loge hasten to Valhalla, for at last the day of the gods reaches its twilight!" So saying she flings the torch upon the funeral pyre, which quickly breaks into flames, and Wotan's ravens, flying up from the river bank, disappear in the distance. Brünnhilde's horse has been led in.

"Knowst thou whither we go?" she exclaims (M 60-32). "There lies thy master . . . wouldst thou follow him in the flames? In my heart flames, too, are glowing, fast to embrace him, with him forever made one . . . Siegfried, Brünnhilde greets thee in bliss!"

The Immolation Scene is superbly presented by Leopold Stokowski and the Philadelphia Orchestra, Agnes Davis as Brünnhilde, in Album M-188.

Closing Scene *Stokowski-Philadelphia Orchestra* 6625-2.00

She swings herself on Grane's back and at her urging, the horse leaps forward into the burning funeral pyre. The flames, growing constantly more violent, mount upwards and overrun the hall, until the very building seems ablaze. The terrified Gibichung vassals draw back, huddled together in a corner. Suddenly the flames die down, the smoke drifts away, and the river Rhine, having overflowed its banks, submerges the embers in an instant. The Rhine-maidens appear where last the pyre was seen blazing. Hagen, who has been anxiously watching, throws off his armor and plunges into the flood, shouting, "Back from the Ring!" Now for the last time, the motive of the "Curse" is briefly sounded. But the Rhine-maidens have recovered the Ring; then seizing Hagen, they drag him down into the depths. The Rhine returns to its normal course, and as the Rhine-maidens swim away rejoicing, the melody of their song is heard. Soon there enters with it the majestic theme of "Valhalla," while on the distant horizon is seen a red glow—Valhalla and its assembled gods and heroes are passing away in flames. Yet above these two themes is heard the ecstatic melody of "Redemption through Love" swelling into a transcendent apotheosis; for though the gods be destroyed and though the Gold, bereft of its might and its curse, be restored to its unsullied condition in the depths of the Rhine, there remains one power to govern the world—Love.

433

ROBERTO IL DIAVOLO

(Robert the Devil)

OPERA in five acts; music by Giacomo Meyerbeer; words by Scribe and Delavigne. Produced at the Grand Opéra, Paris, November 22, 1831; Park Theatre, New York, April 7, 1834. The production of Robert Le Diable, as this work is named in the original French, was such a success that it made the fortune of the Grand Opéra. Striking scenic effects, powerful contrasts, brilliant orchestration, effectively dramatic recitatives, and melody that was attractive and, although it contained many traces of the old Italian opera conventionalities, at times rose to a vivid dramatic power, unexpected and until then unknown, all combined to win universal approval, for there was something to please every taste. Meyerbeer's music certainly saved the libretto, for in it the melodramatic and grotesque are carried to the point of absurdity. The opera has a certain historical interest in that, being the first of Meyerbeer's works after his arrival in Paris, it shows the beginning of his later style; Italian influences are still strong, but there is also evidence of his study of French style. From a broader historical point of view "Robert the Devil" is also of interest, for it contains some of the earliest signs of the influence of the Romantic movement on French dramatic music.

(The Italian title, Roberto il Diavolo, is pronounced *Roh-berh'-toh eel Dee-ah'-voh-loh*, the French, Robert le Diable, *Roh-bare' luh Dee-abl'*; the translation is Robert the Devil.)

ROBERT, Duke of Normandy, is really the son of the Devil by a mortal woman, the chaste Princess Bertha of Normandy. Disguised and under the name of Bertram, the fiend follows his son about, constantly leading him into temptation in hope of winning his soul for Hell. The mother's good influence clings to Robert in the form of a foster-sister, Alice. Banished from Normandy because of evil deeds inspired by Bertram, Robert has come to Sicily where he has fallen in love with the beautiful princess Isabella, and she with him. Bertram does his best to interfere with the match, and by his wiles keeps Robert from attending the tournament, the winner of which is supposed to have the right to claim Isabella's hand. Having thus seemingly lost his chance to win her honestly, Robert is led by Bertram to a ruined convent at midnight. There Bertram summons the ghosts of faithless nuns, singing the impressive invocation: "Suore chi riposate."

The ghosts dance about Robert in wild diabolical revelry. With a magical branch he obtains here, Robert puts to sleep Isabella's guards and tries to force her to his will, but she pleads with him so earnestly that he breaks the branch and thus loses its supernatural power. Once more Bertram tempts Robert and tries to induce him to sign a contract yielding his soul; he reveals himself as his father and the young man, overcome by emotion, is about to sign. But Alice repeats the last words of his mother, warning him against the fiend and thus delays the signing of the pact until the clock strikes twelve. The spell is broken, Bertram disappears to the nether regions, and Isabella is revealed in her bridal robes waiting at the altar for the redeemed Robert.

La Scala, Milan

ACT I—ROMÉO ET JULIETTE

ROMÉO ET JULIETTE

(Romeo and Juliet)

OPERA in five acts; music by Charles Gounod; words by Barbier and Carré, after Shakespeare. First produced at the Théâtre Lyrique, Paris, April 27, 1867. First performance in the United States, at the Academy of Music, New York, November 15, 1867. Revived at the Metropolitan Opera House, New York, with Galli-Curci as Juliet in 1922.

Gounod's sweetly sentimental setting of this great love story is second in popularity only to his "Faust." Not unjustly has it been called a "love duet with occasional interruptions." The action of the opera follows in the main Shakespeare's tragedy; but several of the Shakespearean personages have been omitted from the opera cast, and a new character, the page, Stephano, has been added. Moreover, to allow for the greater length of time required to sing instead of to speak a text, omissions were necessary. If, in addition, it is borne in mind that Shakespeare's beautiful English verse had first to be turned into French, the French into opera-librettese, and that retranslated into English so as to fit Gounod's music, it will be readily understood that the opera-libretto of Romeo and Juliet may offer a few surprises to the Shakespearean student.

(The French name of the opera, "Roméo et Juliette," is pronounced *Roh-may'-oh ay Joo-lee-et'*; and the Italian, "Romeo e Giulietta," *Roh-may-oh ay Joo-lee-et' tah*.)

The action takes place in Verona.

PROLOGUE

The orchestra supplies solemn chords, while from behind the curtain voices are heard singing of the tragedy that is about to be performed—a version of Shakespeare's lines:

Two households, both alike in dignity
In fair Verona, where we lay our scene,
From ancient grudge break to new mutiny,
Where civil blood makes civil hands unclean.
From forth the fatal loins of these two foes
A pair of star-cross'd loves take their life;
Whose misadventur'd piteous overthrows
Do with their death bury their parents' strife.
The fearful passage of their parents' rage,
Which, but their children's end, naught could remove,
Is now the two hours' traffic of our stage:
The which if you with patient ears attend,
What here shall miss, our toil shall strive to mend.

ACT I

SCENE—*Ballroom in Capulet's House, Verona*

CAPULET, a Veronese noble, is giving a masked fête in honor of his daughter Juliet's entrance into society. When the guests have gone to the banquet hall, Juliet lingers behind and gives expression to her girlish joy in the famous waltz song.

Valse *(Juliet's Waltz Song)* **Sofía Del Campo 9206-1.50**

She is about to leave when Romeo enters, having ventured with some of his comrades, all masked, into the house of their enemy. It is a case of love at first sight, but the tête-à-tête is cut short by the entrance of Juliet's hotheaded cousin, Tybalt. He recognizes Romeo through his mask and denounces him as a member of the hated house of Montague. A general fight is prevented only by the entrance of Capulet, who, loath to have the festivities spoiled, permits Romeo and his friends to go in peace.

ACT II

SCENE—*Capulet's Garden; Juliet's Apartment Above*

ROMEO braves the displeasure of his enemies in the hope of seeing Juliet again, and gazing up at her balcony, sings his lovely serenade:

Arise, fairest sun in heaven!
Quench the stars with thy brightness,
That o'er the vault at even
Shine with a feeble lightness.
Oh! rise again! Oh! rise again!
And banish night's dark shades.
She is watching, ah! ever untwining,

Lumiere

GALLI-CURCI AS JULIET

From their bonds her tresses shining!
Now she speaketh. Ah! how charming!
By her beauty's brilliant ray,
As burneth, ashamed and jaded,
A lamp by the light of day!
At her window, on her fair hand,
See how she leaneth her cheek.
On that hand, were I a glove,
That I might touch that cheek!

Juliet appears on the balcony and the two sing a love duet. Juliet's nurse calls for her, and the girl reënters her apartment. After a few minutes she returns to bid Romeo good night. He exclaims:

Ah! linger yet a moment,
Let me yet hold thy dear hand in my own!

Taking up the melody, Juliet replies:

Silence! a step is near us,
Someone I fear will hear us,
Let me at least take my hand from thy keeping.
Good night, love.

ROMEO:

Good night, love.

BOTH:

Good night! Dearest, this fond good night is such sweet sorrow
That I would say good night, till it be dawn!

ROMEO:

Soft be thy repose till morning!
On thine eyes slumber dwell, and sweet peace
In thy bosom: would I were sleep and peace
So sweet to rest!

ACT III

SCENE I—*The Cell of Friar Laurence*

THE secret marriage of Romeo and Juliet takes place in the cell of Friar Laurence, who hopes that the union will reconcile the rival houses. Juliet then returns to her home.

SCENE II—*A Street in Verona*

Romeo's imprudent page, Stephano, having come in search of his master, sings an impertinent song before the Capulet house, which soon brings out Gregorio, angry at having been awakened. He scolds the troublesome youth, and when he recognizes him as having been the companion of Romeo on the night before, a fight results. They are interrupted by Mercutio and Tybalt, who immediately join the quarrel. Romeo enters and tries to act as peacemaker—he cannot well fight with the relatives of his bride. He is unsuccessful; the fight is resumed and Romeo's friend, Mercutio, is wounded. Believing him dead, Romeo cannot resist fighting to avenge him. Thus he happens to kill Tybalt, and for this he is banished by the Duke of Verona.

ACT IV

SCENE—*Juliet's Room*

ROMEO has found a way into Capulet's house, at imminent risk of death, and has penetrated to the room of his bride. He bids her a tender farewell. After he has departed, Friar Laurence enters, to tell the girl that it was Tybalt's dying wish that she marry Paris, and that the wedding is to be hastened. Counselling the despairing Juliet to be patient, he gives her a potion which he tells her to drink when the marriage ceremony is about to take place. It will throw her into a death-like trance for forty-two hours; after that she may escape from her tomb and fly with Romeo.

The good priest leaves her. Soon she sees her father and Paris approaching; she drinks the contents of the phial, and growing faint, apparently expires in Capulet's arms.

ACT V

SCENE—*The Tomb of Juliet*

IN THE silent vault of the Capulets, Juliet lies on the bier, still in her trance. Having failed to receive Friar Laurence's message, Romeo forces in the door to gain one last glimpse of the bride whom he believes dead. Awed by the gloomy solemnity of the place he exclaims:

> All hail, oh tomb! somber and silent!
> A tomb! No, no! Oh yet lovelier a dwelling
> Than yon fair abode in the skies!
>
> *　*　*　*　*
>
> Come, funeral light! Show her face to mine eyes!
>
> *　*　*　*　*
>
> Oh beloved! Wife too soon forsaken!
> E'en Death, who so untimely thy sweet life hath taken,
> Can naught of thy beauty deny.
>
> *　*　*　*　*
>
> Less have I dreaded thee never,
> Tomb where I shall at last repose, no more to grieve:
> Oh my arms! This embrace shall be your last forever!
> My lips, take ye now a long farewell to love!

ACT V—SETTING BY N. BENOIS

He embraces her, then drinks a deadly poison. No sooner has he swallowed it than he is startled to behold signs of life in the body of Juliet. Too late! They have time only to say farewell. Presaging some need, Juliet has concealed a dagger among her grave-garments. With it she stabs herself. Romeo and Juliet enter into their eternal sleep clasped in one another's arms.

439

LA RONDINE

LYRIC comedy in three acts; music by Giacomo Puccini; book by Giuseppe Adami. First produced, March 27, 1917, at Monte Carlo. First performance in the United States, March 10, 1928, at the Metropolitan Opera House, New York, with Gigli and Bori in the leading rôles.

While attending a light opera at Vienna in 1912, Puccini was approached by an Austrian publisher with a magnificent offer for a similar work. Then came the war, Austria and Italy were at arms, and Puccini lost all hope of ever receiving the $40,000 that had been offered. As completed the opera differed from what had been originally planned, yet in the delicacy and lightness of the music as well as in the effective employment of waltz rhythms, it is possible to imagine something of Viennese influence—perhaps, also, emulation of Strauss' "Der Rosenkavalier."

Not yet so well known as Puccini's earlier operas, "La Bohême" and "Madame Butterfly," "La Rondine" reveals the composer, though in a lighter mood, still a master at writing pleasant melody. The Italian title, La Rondine *(Lah Rohn'-dee-neh)* means, literally, The Swallow.

The action takes place at Paris and Nice during the Second Empire (mid-Nineteenth Century).

MAGDA, the beautiful demi-mondaine, lives under the care of a rich banker, Rambaldo, but is unable to forget her first love who was a poor young student. While a reception is taking place at her apartment, there appears a new arrival from the provinces, Alfred, son of an old friend of Rambaldo's. All the frivolous guests suggest various cabarets as suitable places for his introduction to Paris. Magda names the "Bal Bullier," the boy goes there, and when her guests have departed, she follows him. At the "Bal Bullier," they meet, and fall seriously in love. Deserting her banker, Magda goes with Alfred to Nice, where they intend to live an idyllic existence. Alfred has written his parents describing Magda in glowing terms. They reply that if she be good and virtuous she will be received with open arms. Like Violetta in "Traviata" she now believes herself unworthy, and not willing to spoil Alfred's future she leaves him, to return, swallow-fashion, to Rambaldo.

Ellinger   (*Herbert Graf Production*)

THE PRINCESS (LOTTE LEHMANN) AND HER SERVANT

DER ROSENKAVALIER

(The Cavalier of the Rose)

"A COMEDY for music by H. von Hofmannsthal . . . music by Richard Strauss," thus reads the title page of the score, an indication of the poet's importance. First produced, January 26, 1911, at the Royal Opera House, Dresden. First performed in the United States, December 9, 1913, at the Metropolitan Opera House, New York.

The questionable morals of Strauss' "Salome" and the shockingly harsh dissonances of his "Electra" may operate against their permanence in the repertoire, but all are agreed that "Der Rosenkavalier" is a lasting delight. The libretto, by one of the most prominent of contemporary Continental authors, is in itself a masterpiece, combining elements of the comedy of intrigue, the comedy of manners, a bit of farce, and satire, all held together by the blended humor and pathos of Hofmannsthal, the symbolist and poet. For this, Strauss has supplied thoroughly captivating music. Although, from a historical point of view, a bit of an anachronism, he has made frequent use of the ever-delightful waltz, securing thereby an inimitable atmosphere of lightness and romance. A number of these waltz melodies, worthy descendants of the waltzes of the great Viennese Strauss family of composers (of which, however, Richard Strauss is not a member), have been combined to form the record hereafter listed, entitled "Waltz Movements."

Although making use of innumerable leading motives, Strauss has revealed a wealth of beautiful straightforward melody, hitherto unsuspected of the composer of the great Symphonic Poems. The purely orchestral music recorded is of especial interest in that it comes from the special orchestral arrangement of his score, prepared by Strauss for a motion-picture version of "The Rose Cavalier," which was first produced at one of the great cinema palaces in London, "The Tivoli," April 12, 1926. Strauss visited London for the occasion, and the following day himself conducted the especially augmented Tivoli orchestra while making certain of these records, which are therefore of a double historic and artistic interest.

No one who was present can ever forget the incomparable performances of "Der Rosenkavalier" given by the Philadelphia Orchestra association, November 30, December 1 and 4, 1934, under the direction of Fritz Reiner, with the peerless Lotte Lehmann starring. Here was one of the most extraordinary confluences of talent ever witnessed on any operatic stage. Mme. Lehmann, as the world knows, occupies a place of solitary splendor in the art of song—and furthermore is a personality of such charm, wisdom and grace as to assure a penetrating and sympathetic performance. Fritz Reiner is second to no conductor in the world in the field of opera. The Philadelphia Orchestra is universally admitted the peer of any in the world. In addition, there was stage direction by Dr. Herbert Graf, the brilliant young Viennese whose services have just been acquired by the Metropolitan; production by the gifted Donald Oenschlager.

It is a matter of both pride and pleasure to note that Lotte Lehmann is the star of a complete recording of "Der Rosenkavalier." The Philadelphia Orchestra is not here, nor the settings and costumes of that memorable production—but Lotte Lehmann *is* here, and here is Strauss' most endearing music.

Famous Artists and Vienna Philharmonic Orchestra, conducted by Robert Heger, Album M-196 (7917-7929), AM-196 (7930-7942), Price $26.00 Herr Kavalier *(Letter Scene and Waltz)* **Kipnis, Ruziczka-Berlin State Opera Orchestra 7894-2.00 Suite—Presentation of the Silver Rose and Ochs' Waltz** *Vienna Philharmonic Orchestra, conducted by Karl Alwin* **11217-1.50 Suite—Breakfast Scene and Trio; Closing Duet** *Vienna Philharmonic Orchestra, conducted by Karl Alwin* **11218-1.50**
Introduction to Act I *Tivoli Orchestra* **9280-1.50 and also on M 196-1**
Octavian and Sophie Duet *Tivoli Orchestra* **9283-1.50**

The action takes place at Vienna during the reign of Maria Theresa, Eighteenth Century.

"Der Rosenkavalier" begins with an orchestral introduction *(M 196-1)*, typical of Richard Strauss, yet sounding the mood of the work: impetuous, capricious, and witty. It grows to an impassioned climax (according to Strauss' directions, "parodied"). The music then subsides to a mood of tranquillity mingled with tender yearning. This introduction, together with music from the opening love scene, is included on the record.

ACT I

SCENE—*The Bedroom of the Princess*

MORNING sunlight is streaming into the room as the very youthful Octavian kneels at the feet of the Princess von Werdenberg and declares *(M 196-2)* a great love for her. She returns his passion, but alas, sounds which the lovers believe to be her husband unexpectedly *(M 196-3 and 4)* returning, disturb them. Octavian quickly conceals himself and puts on the dress of a lady's maid. Meanwhile the fears of the Princess are turned into amusement, for the person who arrives is the boastful and debauched *(M 196-5)* Baron Ochs of Lerchenau. He noisily enters the room to ask the assistance of the Princess in his approaching marriage with Sophie Faninal. When Octavian, in his maid's disguise, has emerged from hiding, the observing Baron at once begins to flirt and *(M 196-6)* invites "her" to supper with him. Meanwhile, the Princess has her usual morning interviews and is entertained by a flute player and an Italian tenor.

The Baron leaves with the Princess a silver rose, which he requests her to have delivered to his bride, according to a custom of the day. He then departs *(M 196-7)*, and in a moment of quiet and sadness the Princess meditates *(M 196-8 and 9)* that soon her charms shall have faded and she will no longer hold her lover. Octavian also goes, bidding her a tender farewell *(M 196-10)*. When he has gone, the Princess, suddenly remembering the rose, hurriedly sends a servant to him with it, for him to deliver.

ACT II

A LL is excitement *(M 196-11)* at the Faninal household for Sophie is to marry a real notable, and now the ceremony of the presentation of the rose is to take place. Octavian enters *(M 196-12)*, radiant in garments of white and silver. The music glistens and scintillates even as the "Knight" and the rose he bears. Each of the young people is overwhelmed by the beauty of the other *(M 196-13)* and is able to speak only in the most hesitant fashion, yet they are already deeply in love.

Left alone for a moment, they confess their mutual affection, and forgetful of all else sing of the rapture of their love *(M 196-14)*.

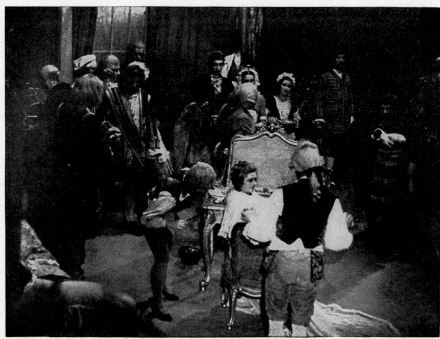

Otto Skall   THE PRINCESS' BOUDOIR   *(Herbert Graf Production)*

They are discovered in each others' arms, and in the subsequent duel Octavian slightly wounds the Baron's hand. Sophie, disgusted with the Baron's crude, blustering manner, refuses to marry him; but her father, seeing his social ambitions for a noble alliance broken, declares she shall marry the Baron or take the veil *(M 196-15)*. Meanwhile Octavian has set his wits to work and now the Baron receives a note *(M 196-16)* from the waiting maid of the Princess . . . the Baron thinks with delight of the dinner he is to have with "her."

ACT III

OCTAVIAN, again in disguise as a maid, keeps the rendezvous at an inn *(M 196-18)*. There such a host of tricks of Octavian's devising are played on the Baron *(M 196-19)* that he believes himself mad. Faces appear from blank windows and trapdoors. Suddenly a woman with a horde of screaming children enters, claiming the Baron as husband and father! In the midst of this turmoil come the police; they arrest the Baron as a seducer of women. Faninal is furious to discover his prospective son-in-law in this brawl; Sophie renounces him *(M 196-20)*. Upon the arrival of the Princess, the police withdraw, and Octavian reveals himself to the Baron in his usual male attire *(M 196-21)*. The Baron begins to perceive how he has been duped, and is presently the butt of the mockery of everyone present *(M 196-22)*. The Princess brings together the youthful lovers *(M 196-23)*, and to the glowing music of the Trio and Finale expresses her sorrow and finally, her resignation *(M 196-24)* at the loss of her youthful admirer, while Sophie and Octavian rejoice in dream-like *(M 196-25)* happiness. The Princess takes her leave; the glittering music of the "Presentation of the Rose" returns in the orchestra, and Sophie and Octavian linger for a moment to tell one another yet again that each loves only the other *(M 196-26)*. Then they also go . . . the room is empty and in semi-darkness . . . an amusing, twittering melody darts up and down through the orchestra . . . the door opens, a little black servant boy runs in, picks up a handkerchief that Sophie has dropped, trips lightly out again . . . the curtain falls.

Rosenkavalier Waltzes *Eugene Ormandy and the Minneapolis Symphony Orchestra*
1758-1759. $1.50 each.

TWO POPULAR SAVOYARDS AS SIR DESPARD MURGATROYD AND MAD MARGARET

ℛUDDIGORE

(or The Witch's Curse)

COMIC opera in two acts by W. S. Gilbert and Arthur Sullivan.

"Ruddigore" has been recorded for Victor by the D'Oyly Carte Opera Company in Album C-19 (11510-11518) AC-19 (11519-11527) $13.50, and the recorded version is keyed to the following story of the opera.

DRAMATIS PERSONAE

SIR RUTHVEN MURGATROYD, *Disguised as Robin Oakapple, a Young Farmer*
RICHARD DAUNTLESS, *his Foster-brother, a Man-o'-war's-man*
SIR DESPARD MURGATROYD OF RUDDIGORE, *a wicked Baronet*
OLD ADAM GOODHEART, *Robin's Faithful Servant*
ROSE MAYBUD, *a Village Maiden*
MAD MARGARET
DAME HANNAH, *Rose's Aunt*
ZORAH, *Professional Bridesmaid*
Chorus of Officers, Professional Bridesmaids, Villagers and Ghostly Ancestors.

ACT I

Overture (C 19-1).

THE scene opens in the pretty little Cornish fishing village of Rederring, showing the harbour and Rose Maybud's cottage. The village possesses an endowed corps of professional bridesmaids, who are languishing in idleness, there having been no weddings for at least six months *(C 19-2)*. The village beauty, Rose, will have none of her many suitors, and, in desperation, the Bridesmaids, fearful of losing their endowment, endeavour to persuade Dame Hannah, Rose's Aunt, to marry old Adam, Robin Oakapple's faithful servant.

Hannah is, however, pledged to eternal maidenhood. Years ago, she was betrothed to a youth who woo'd her under an assumed name, but on the day when they should have been married, she discovers that he was no other than Sir Roderic Murgatroyd, one of an accursed race. She tells the girls how his ancestor, Sir Rupert Murgatroyd *(C 19-3)*, employed his time in persecuting witches, and that one of his victims, in mortal agony at the stake, laid this curse on him: "Each lord of Ruddigore, despite his best endeavor, shall do one crime, or more, once every day, for ever." The penalty for defying the curse is death by torture on the day the crimes cease, and each lord of Ruddigore has so died.

Hannah chides Rose for not returning the love of "some gallant youth," and Rose explains that her difficulty is that the youths of the village are bashful, and it would not be becoming for her to make advances *(C 19-4)*. Rose is a foundling, and bases her ideals on a book of etiquette which, with a change of baby-linen, were her only possessions when she was discovered in a plated dish-cover suspended to the knocker of the workhouse door.

Robin enters and would fain consult Rose on the predicament of a friend who is in love with a maid, but is too diffident to tell her. Rose similarly wishes to ask his advice as to *her* friend, and they "consult" accordingly in a charming duet *(C 19-5)*, without, however, mending matters.

Robin Oakapple is really Sir Ruthven Murgatroyd, but in horror at the prospect of inheriting the title and the curse, he had fled his home and taken an assumed name. His younger brother Despard, believing him to be dead, had succeeded to the title. Old Adam enters and informs Robin that his foster-brother Richard is home from sea. This news is quickly followed by the entry of Richard himself *(C 19-6)*. He kisses all the girls, spins them the yarn of the "Bold Mounseer," and dances a Hornpipe as an appropriate climax.

Dick and Robin exchange greetings, and Robin, on being upbraided for being sad, tells his foster-brother of his love for Rose, and of the shyness that prevents him from declaring it *(C 19-7)*. Richard consults "the dictates of his heart," and his heart tells him to speak up for his friend. Robin is overjoyed and sings a song, the burden of which is that, "If you wish in the world to advance . . . you must stir it and stump it, and blow your own trumpet."

Dick goes off on his self-imposed mission, but no sooner does he see Rose than his heart "dictates" once again, and says: "This is the very lass for *you*, Dick." So he forgets Robin, and makes love, very successfully, on his own account.

Robin enters with the Bridesmaids, and is astounded at the unexpected turn events have taken. Still, he has sworn to stand up for Dick through thick and thin. Therefore, while pretending to agree, he "gets his own back" by making many disquieting insinuations regarding the less respectable aspects of a sailor's life. This clever move turns the tables on Richard, and Rose forsakes him for Robin.

A new character (C 19-8) is introduced—Mad Margaret—whose wits have been crazed by the cruel treatment of Sir Despard Murgatroyd—the "Bad Baronet." She is actually trying to find Rose Maybud, of whom she is jealous, having heard that Sir Despard intends to carry her off as one of his daily "crimes." Rose tells her, however, that she need not fear, as she (Rose) is pledged to another.

Despard Murgatroyd and his following of "Bucks" and "Blades" now appear.

They are welcomed (C 19-9 and 10) by the Bridesmaids, who are tired of village swains, and are delighted with the swaggering newcomers in their gorgeous military uniforms.

Despard bewails his lot, as one who, being really thoroughly good, is condemned to be thoroughly bad. He tries to balance his account of evil and good by getting his crime over the first thing in the morning, and then being good for the rest of the day. For example, in the morning he steals a child, and then builds an orphan asylum.

Richard enters, and to pay off his score against Robin, he reveals his secret to Despard (C 19-11), who is overjoyed to learn that he is not the real heir, but that his elder brother is still living.

They determine to act without delay, for Rose and Robin, with the Bridesmaids, have entered for the wedding ceremony. A lovely Madrigal is sung, followed by a Gavotte, and the procession is about to start for the church, when Despard enters, and challenges Robin, claiming him (C 19-12) as his elder brother Sir Ruthven Murgatroyd, rightful heir to the Baronetcy of Ruddigore. He cannot deny the fact, and Rose, in spite of Richard's blandishments, forsakes him, and offers herself to Despard (C 19-13). This offer is refused, for Despard, once again virtuous, keeps his vow to Margaret. Rose returns to Richard, and Robin, now the "Bad Baronet," falls senseless to the ground.

ACT II

THE scene changes to the Picture Gallery in Ruddigore Castle. Round the walls are full-length portraits of the Baronets of Ruddigore from the times of James I—the first being that of Sir Rupert, alluded to in the legend: the last, that of the latest deceased Baronet, Sir Roderic.

Sir Ruthven and Adam enter melodramatically (C 19-14). They are greatly altered, Sir Ruthven looking haggard and guilty, and Adam filling the part of steward to such a wicked man. They hate the life, but there is no help for it, and they are trying to think of new crimes to commit. Adam suggests that as Richard has come to the Castle with Rose Maybud to ask

447

for Sir Ruthven's consent to their marriage, a really excellent crime would be to "poison their beer!" This is too much for Sir Ruthven, who has not yet reached the requisite state of "badness."

Rose and Richard enter happily, and Sir Ruthven, thinking he has her in his power, threatens to immune her in a dungeon, and calls for assistance. He is foiled by Richard, who produces a small Union Jack, which even a "Bad Baronet" cannot defy. Rose pleads with Sir Ruthven, who yields to her entreaties, gives his consent and allows them to leave unmolested *(C 19-15)*.

The scene darkens, and when it becomes lighter the Pictures are seen to have become animated. A soft chorus of men's voices is heard, and the ghosts of the ancestors step from their frames and march round, the last to descend being Sir Roderic *(C 19-15 and 16)*.

They reproach Sir Ruthven for having failed to fulfill the curse, and Sir Roderic sings an eerie song, "The Ghosts' High-noon." Sir Ruthven realizes who they are, and makes many weak excuses. For instance he committed no crime on Monday because it was a Bank Holiday. On Tuesday he made a false Income Tax return, on Wednesday he forged his own Will, and so on. These do not satisfy the ghosts, who after giving him a taste of the torture which will follow if he fail to commit some real crimes, allow him one more chance, and command him to carry off a lady at once.

Sir Ruthven yields, and the ghosts, having made him pardon them ("for having agonized him so"), return to their frames. The low, soft chorus is heard again and the Gallery assumes its normal aspect.

Sir Ruthven bids Adam go at once to the village and carry off a maiden. Despard and Margaret now appear *(C 19-17)*. They, too, are changed, both being dressed in sober garments of a formal cut. They run a National School, and Margaret is a District Visitor. They have come to urge Sir Ruthven to abandon his wild courses. Despard points out that although Sir Ruthven has only been a Bad Baronet for a week, he is responsible, in the eyes of the law, for all the crimes committed by him, Despard, during the past ten years. This so appalls Sir Ruthven that he determines to reform and take the consequences.

Meanwhile Adam has returned, bringing with him Dame Hannah, who seizes the sword from a suit of armour on the wall, and makes for Sir Ruthven. He, in an agony of terror, invokes the aid of his uncle, Sir Roderic, who once again steps from his picture.

Lucas-Pritchard
MISS BRENDA BENNETT OF THE
D'OYLY CARTE COMPANY AS
ROSE MAYBUD

He and Hannah, who, it will be remembered were lovers before his death, ten years before, recognize each other. Sir Ruthven is ordered by his uncle to leave them together, Hannah sings (C 19-18) of her old love for him and bursts into tears, but at this moment, Sir Ruthven rushes in excitedly, followed by all the other characters and the chorus of Bridesmaids. An idea has occurred to him. Since a Baronet of Ruddigore can only die through refusing to commit a daily crime, the refusal is tantamount to suicide. But suicide being itself a crime, Sir Roderic ought never to have died. This is all very satisfactory; Rose returns to her first love, Sir Ruthven, and Richard has to take Zorah, the chief bridesmaid, and the opera ends with a joyful chorus.

RUSSLAN AND LUDMILLA

OPERA in five acts; music by Michael Ivanovitch Glinka; text after Pushkin's poem of the same name. First produced 1842 at St. Petersburg.

Not without reason is Glinka considered the "Father of Russian music." In his first opera, "A Life for the Czar," he introduced a national style into operatic music, and in his orchestral works he anticipated later developments of Tschaikowsky and Rimsky-Korsakow. In his second opera, "Russlan and Ludmilla," he introduced for the first time in Russian music, effects of oriental color. His orientalism is so spontaneously introduced, however, that it seems perfectly natural; the importance of this can be appreciated when we consider the long line of famous Russian compositions in which oriental effects are prominent, to mention only a few: Balakirew's "Islamey," Rimsky-Korsakow's "Scheherazade," "Sadko," and "Coq d' Or," and Strawinsky's "Fire-Bird."

Although the opera has not as yet been played in the United States, the brilliant and melodious overture has become a favorite as a concert number. It begins with the music of the final apotheosis and the song of thanksgiving on Ludmilla's recovery, then follows the melody of one of the hero's arias. These themes are developed and repeated. Near the end is heard, descending in the bass, a whole-tone scale, which in the opera is associated with the wicked dwarf Chernomor. This is one of the earliest instances of the use of the whole-tone scale—a device that became well known a half century later through its effective treatment by Debussy. But this suggestion of Chernomor is quickly routed and the overture closes in rejoicing.

Overture   Frederick Stock-Chicago Symphony Orchestra 7123-2.00

FESTIVITIES are being given by Prince Svetozar in honor of his daughter's suitors: Russlan, a Russian Knight; Ratmir, a Tartar Prince, and the timorous Varangian chief, Farlaf. But as the beautiful Ludmilla favors Russlan her father orders the marriage to take place at once. Scarcely has the god of love, Lel, been invoked, when the scene is shrouded in the darkness of a sudden storm. When the light returns the Princess is missing. Svetozar vows to bestow her hand in marriage on the one who will restore her. The suitors at once begin their search.

Russlan learns from a friendly sorcerer, Finn, that Ludmilla was abducted by the dwarf Chernomor. Finn warns Russlan against the sorceress, Naina.

On a deserted battlefield Russlan gains possession of magical weapons with which to free his beloved.

Naina, having promised to help Farlaf, traps Ratmir in her enchanted abode. There Persian maidens tempt him with their sirens' song. Here also Gorislava, whom he has cruelly deserted, appears and pleads earnestly with him to return to her. The melody of her entreaty has a breadth and dignified beauty that remind one of Händel. He hears her appeal, but is again soon lured away by the maidens. Russlan enters and is rescued from a similar fate only by the timely intervention of Finn.

Russlan discovers Chernomor's enchanted domain and aided by his magical sword conquers the dwarf. At the appearance of Russlan, Chernomor casts Ludmilla into a trance from which the hero is unable to awaken her. He meets Ratmir and Gorislava, now reconciled, and on their advice sets out for Kiev.

Aided by Naina, Farlaf steals Ludmilla from Russlan.

Rondo of Farlaf *(Patter Song)* **Feodor Chaliapin** 7704-2.00

He returns her to her father at Kiev, but it is impossible to arouse her from the trance. At last Russlan arrives bringing Finn's magic ring with which he releases his bride and the opera ends in rejoicing.

THE HALL OF THE MERCHANTS' GUILD

SADKO

OPERA in seven tableaux; music by Nicholas Rimsky-Korsakow; text by the composer after several variants of the legends concerning the Eleventh Century minstrel-hero, Sadko, notably the "Cycle of Novgorod."

First produced, January 6, 1898, at the Private Opera House, Moscow. Portions have been sung in concert form in the United States, but the opera as a whole was announced for its first American performance by the Metropolitan Opera Company during the season 1929-30. The accompanying illustrations are of the productions at the Imperial Opera House, St. Petersburg, in 1901 and 1906.

The ever-stormy North Sea that inspired Wagner in the writing of his "Flying Dutchman" also supplied Rimsky-Korsakow with a background for his sea music that figures prominently in "Sadko" as well as "Scheherazade" and other works. Wagner's wonderful sea music, of course is profoundly subjective; Rimsky-Korsakow's, also very beautiful, is equally objective in character. In fact, Wagner's dictum regarding Mendelssohn, "A landscape painter in tones," might well be paraphrased for Rimsky-Korsakow, "A seascape painter in tones." His knowledge of the sea was intimate, for during a number of years he was an officer in the Russian navy. In his very interesting autobiography he even describes his visits to American ports; and he writes of the North Sea in its wild, changeful moods, in a most entertaining manner.

In the legend of Sadko, Rimsky-Korsakow found material perfectly adaptable to his genius, which was always at its best in the treatment of nature, the fantastic and the legendary. His interest in the pantheism and legends of his country, charmingly revealed in the fanciful "Snow Maiden," was here offered a broader canvas for its expression. The text, written by the composer with the aid of Bielsky, was taken from the several versions of the Epic of Sadko; moreover, expressions and decorative and scenic details have been

451

preserved exactly as they are in the old legends and songs. A youthful symphonic poem, "Sadko" was the basis of a ballet of that name danced in this country by Diaghileff's company in 1916.

Musically, "Sadko" is a thorough blending of the two contrasting styles that have persisted throughout the history of Russian opera: the lyrical manner of Glinka, and the declamatory style inaugurated by Dargomyzsky (Dargomijsky). The thoroughly Russian flavor of the music is remarkable throughout the opera. For special effects other styles are contrasted with it: the vigorous and characteristically Scandinavian melody and harmonies of the song of the Viking merchant . . . the oriental song of the Hindu, long one of the most popular of concert numbers with singers and violinists, under the name "Song of India" . . . and the delightfully Italianate barcarolle of the Venetian. The opera is orchestrated in Rimsky-Korsakow's most glowing colors, one of the striking features of the orchestration is the clever imitation of the sound of the gousli by means of a combination of piano and harp. The gousli (pronounced goo-slee') is a native Russian instrument that in its primitive form dates back to the most remote antiquity. It is probably allied to the family of the cembalo or dulcimer.

CHARACTERS

THE KING OF THE OCEAN	*Bass*
VOLKHOVA *(Vol-khoh-vah'), his favorite daughter*	*Soprano*
SADKO, *singer and gousli player at Novgorod*	*Tenor*
LUBAVA *(Liu-bah'-vah), his wife*	*Mezzo-Soprano*
NEJATA *(Neh-jah'-ta) (French "j"), gousli player from Kiev*	*Contralto*
A VIKING ⎫	⎧ *Bass*
A HINDU ⎬ *Foreign merchants*	⎨ *Tenor*
A VENETIAN ⎭	⎩ *Baritone*
AN APPARITION: *a great hero in the garb of an old pilgrim*	*Baritone*
THE TWO ELDERS, *chiefs among the merchants of Novgorod*	*Tenor and Bass*
BUFFOONS	*Two Mezzo-Sopranos, Tenor and Bass*

Chorus: men and women, citizens of Novgorod; merchants of Novgorod and foreign lands; the companions of Sadko; the daughters of the King of the Ocean.

Ballet: the Queen of the Ocean; the brooks and rivers, and all the marvelous inhabitants of the realm of the King of the Ocean. According to a note in the score, the seven tableaux may be presented in three or five acts, thus: I and II; III and IV; V, VI, and VII; or, I, II and III; IV; V and VI; VII.

It is customary to Anglicize the name Sad'ko. The Russian pronunciation is Sahd-ko'; the "s" very sharp, the "d" light, the "o" as in gloss, but very short; the accent on the final syllable.

TABLEAU I

THE members of the merchants guild of Novgorod sit at their richly laden tables in their sumptuous hall. They sing a lively song "Drink the sparkling wine from distant lands," and praise the prosperity and freedom of their own country in which neither king nor soldier is the ruler, but the merchant. The two elders ask Nejata, singer and gousli player from Kiev, to sing a song of old heroic times. When he has finished the merchants applaud, then ask for a singer who will praise their own Novgorod. At this moment, Sadko appears, his gousli hung from his shoulder. He essays to comply with their request, but he sings rather a song telling of his own strange ideas. Novgorod, he says, is merely on a lake; he would have their ships carried to the ocean, whence they could sail away and return with fortunes from all the world. This Sadko would do and in doing become the richest in all Novgorod. The merchants discuss his idea, but the elders are opposed to such an innovation. Sadko, laughed at with scorn, bids the proud merchants farewell and departs with his faithful gousli. The merchants continue their festivities and are entertained with a comic song and the dance of buffoons.

Carlo Edwards
SWARTHOUT AS NEJATA

TABLEAU II

CLEAR summer night reigns over Lake Ilmen, the crescent-shaped moon is sinking toward the horizon. Sadko approaches, playing upon his gousli; he sings of his unhappiness and implores aid even from the murmuring waters of the lake.

Suddenly a breeze springs up, the waters are agitated, and a group of swans appear, coming from the distance. As they draw near they are transformed into young maidens; Volkhova, the Sea Princess, is among them. They have been fascinated by Sadko's singing, and at the request of the Princess, Sadko sings them a dance-like song; the sea-maidens dance away into the woods, and the Princess sits near the marvelling Sadko, weaves him a garland, confesses her love for him, and claims him as her own. Dawn approaches, however, and, in parting, she promises Sadko that he will catch three golden fish in the lake; he will journey to distant lands; she will await him faithfully for many a year; he will come to her. Now her father, the mighty King of the Ocean, summons his daughters back to his realm. The sea-maidens swim away over the lake . . . disappear . . . the sun rises.

TABLEAU III

LUBAVA stands before the little window of her room, awaiting the return of her husband, Sadko. She sings despairingly . . . all night has she waited, now the bell for matins is sounding . . . she fears that he has been moved by an ambition to seek adventure in distant lands . . . yet only yesterday he vowed his love for her . . . played for her his gousli . . . and sang for her his songs . . . he comes not . . . love is ended.

Then, suddenly seeing Sadko coming in the distance, she sings joyously and runs to meet him. As he enters, he thrusts her rudely aside. The song of the sea-maidens is still ringing in his ears, nor can he forget it. The sound of a bell reminds him that now the service is ended, people will be coming out from church; this is the time to make use of his secret. Pushing

THE PORT OF NOVGOROD

away the lamenting Lubava he shouts, "Farewell!" and rushes away as though mad.

TABLEAU IV

THE port of Novgorod on the shores of Lake Ilmen . . . ships lie at the quay . . . the merchants and people of Novgorod swarm around the merchants from foreign lands—Viking, Venetian and Hindu . . . among the crowd are two soothsayers . . . Nejata sits alone at one side holding his gousli. With the song of the people are mingled the chant of pilgrims, the ribald lay of the buffoons and the voices of the two elders consulting the soothsayers. Sadko appears and all greet him with derisive laughter. Saluting them respectfully, he declares that he knows a deep secret: fish of gold can be caught in Lake Ilmen. The elders laugh . . . that is no secret, it is only a dream. Sadko wagers his head against all the wealth of the haughty merchants that he can prove his claim. A boat is launched, a net lowered. All await in hushed expectancy. From the depths of the lake is heard the voice of the Sea Princess repeating her assurance. The net is raised, Sadko takes from it three golden fish, and is acclaimed victor. He summons all adventurous young men to join him in his exploits. While they are away preparing themselves, Nejata leads in the singing of the symbolical legend of the nightingale that became a great merchant.

Sadko and his followers return in gala attire, ready for the voyage. Sadko announces that he will restore the merchants their shops and goods—he desires only their ships. He asks three foreign merchants to sing of their own lands that he may decide to which he should go. First the Viking (Varangian) replies, singing of a rugged coast on which breaks a stormy sea,

454

the swords and arrows of the Norsemen which spare not the enemy, Odin their great god, and the sea, their destiny!

Song of the Viking Guest   *Feodor Chaliapin* 6867-2.00

The people, with hushed voices, counsel Sadko not to visit that habitation of brigands. Next the Hindu sings his exotic lay: India, land of incalculable gems, land where the maiden-faced Phoenix sings and hovers over the gleaming ocean . . . and the hearer forgets the world as in a dream.

Song of India   *Amelita Galli-Curci* 1524-1.50   *Beniamino Gigli* 1570-1.50   *Boston "Pops" Orchestra* 4303-1.00   *Whiteman's Orchestra* 20200-.75   *Ganz-St. Louis Orchestra* 45531-1.00

"Do not go there!" the people murmur. Now the Venetian sings a barcarolle, telling of his city, its wealth, its beauty—"Venice, Queen of the Ocean." Thither Sadko will go. Requesting the Novgorodian merchants to care for Lubava, he bids her an affectionate farewell, and sets sail . . . the ships disappear in the red glow of the sunset.

TABLEAU V

CALM in mid-ocean . . . Sadko's ship, "The Falcon," slowly draws near . . . the other ships of his fleet pass by . . . "The Falcon" remains becalmed, twilight falls over the sea.

Now, after twelve years, says Sadko, they are returning laden with gold and jewels, but they have not yet sacrificed to the King of the Ocean. Therefore sailors pour overboard great treasures. Still they remain becalmed. Another gift is desired. At Sadko's order, logs are cast into the water . . . all float away except Sadko's, which plunges directly to the bottom of the ocean. The sailors are overawed. A ladder is lowered, as Sadko has commanded, and that hardy mariner-minstrel, gousli in hand, descends to a plank that has been thrown overboard. Immediately a breeze springs up and "The Falcon" sails away. Sadko, abandoned in mid-ocean, begins to play his gousli . . . the Sea Princess is heard calling . . . there is a sudden surging of the waters and Sadko is drawn down into the deep . . . clouds obscure the scene and when they clear away we behold—

SADKO

TABLEAU VI

THE palace of the King of the Ocean . . . azure, iridescent and transparent, rising in the dim, blue-green light at the bottom of the sea. The King and Queen are on their thrones, Volkhova at her wheel spinning

455

SHIPS LIE AT THE QUAY

sea-weeds. The sea-maidens are weaving wreaths of flowers. Sadko appears, greets the King, and at Volkhova's request, sings for him. In reward he is promised the hand of the Princess in marriage. Summoned by a blast of trumpets, there comes a great procession of wedding guests: the elder daughters of the King—the swift rivers; his nieces—the clear brooks; white water nixies; fish of gold and silver, and other wonders of the deep. The whale guards the entrance. All take their places according to their rank, and the marriage of Sadko and Volkhova is celebrated with song and dance. The clear brooks and little springs perform their lightly flowing divertissement; then follow the fish of gold and silver with their gayer movements. At the King's request, Sadko begins to play his gousli and sing; the inhabitants of the deep waters dance, gracefully, undulantly. Such is the charm of the minstrel's music, that the King and Queen cannot resist joining the dance. Gradually the music and the movements of the dancers grow faster and faster, and, at length become so frenzied a tumult that the waters of the ocean are stirred; a storm is raised on the surface of the sea and great ships are sunk. Suddenly an apparition of an old legendary hero appears, strikes the gousli from Sadko's hands . . . the dance ends with a crash. The apparition speaks, saying that the reign of the King of the Ocean must end and that Sadko must return to Novgorod. Sadko and Volkhova seat themselves in a shell and are drawn away by sea gulls while the palace and all the court vanish in obscurity.

456

TABLEAU VII

THE prelude pictures the voyage of Sadko and the Princess as they are drawn with lightning speed across the ocean.

In the grey light of early morning Sadko is seen asleep by the shore of Lake Ilmen. Around him rushes sway lightly in the breeze, and Volkhova watches over him, singing a lullaby:

Sleep came to the shores of the lake;
To his garden the god of dreams.
Sleep then went to the god and asked,
In this manner questioned him:
"Hast thou seen where Sadko sleeps?"
Minstrel fair and brave is he.
Slumber deep, my beloved, slumber deep, my beloved!

On the shore nearby the mead,
On the feath'ry moss he sleeps;
Rushes round him lend their shade,
Make for him a restful bed.
Who will watch him as he sleeps?
'Tis my love and tenderness.
Slumber deep, my beloved, slumber deep, my beloved!

Grow around him high, oh reeds,
Guard him safe in verdant bed!
Ye green rushes do not sway,
Watch his sleep most tenderly!
Well I know what fate is mine,
Yet his singing charms my soul!

Berceuse *Nina Koshetz* 9233-1.50

Now the rosy light of dawn creeps over the waters of the lake. The Princess sings the sleeping minstrel a touching farewell, vanishes in a mist and is converted into the mighty river Volkhova, flowing from Lake Ilmen to the sea. Thus will she be forever faithful to her singer, forever near his songs!

Lubava, still lamenting her husband, approaches the lake distractedly. Great is her happiness and amazement on finding Sadko; and he, awakening, greets her affectionately and joyfully. He believes the past years a dream until he sees his fleet coming up the newly created river—an outlet to the ocean for Novgorod.

The people hurry from the city to welcome their singer, become the wealthiest of merchants.

A BUFFOON

Even the Hindu, Viking and Venetian, each singing the melody of his own country, join in the chorus of salutation. And Sadko, now happily reunited to his wife, leads in the hymn of praise for the hero of olden times who calmed the ocean's storm, and for Volkhova, the Princess, now their river.

SALOMÉ

OPERA in one act and four scenes. Music by Richard Strauss, libretto based on the poem by Oscar Wilde. First performance at Dresden, December 9, 1905.

More than once in his extraordinary career Richard Strauss has shocked the musical public. He administered the greatest shock of all, however, with the one act opera, "Salomé"; but it was the text and the action rather than the music which in this instance offended a certain section of the public. Music suggesting the ecstasies of physical love is not new or in itself offensive, but the horror and morbidity of certain scenes in "Salomé," accompanied by music that is sometimes highly suggestive, touched with no gentle hand the sensibilities of opera goers in a more conservative day. The Dance of the Seven Veils has become a symbol and a synonym for voluptuousness, but surely this is a case of "honi soit qui mal y pense" because it is highly improbable that any operatic Salomé has ever been sufficiently gifted as a dancer or sufficiently shapely to delineate the psychopathic voluptuousness of Herodias' daughter.

The story of the opera deals with the passion of Salomé for Iokonaan (John the Baptist) who has been imprisoned by Herod, vice regent of Palestine, because he had publicly reproached Herod for marrying his brother's wife, Herodias. Iokonaan is kept imprisoned in a well in the courtyard of Herod's palace. Salomé, passing by, hears the prisoner's voice as he foretells a great catastrophe. Infatuated with the voice she asks the guards to let her see the prisoner. They obey unwillingly as they have orders to let no one see Iokonaan. When he is brought from the cistern Salomé is immediately possessed of a fierce desire for him, but her brazen advances are repulsed; Iokonaan curses her, comparing her unfavorably with her wicked mother, and counsels her to seek out the Lord and ask forgiveness for her sins. She begs stubbornly for kisses but the prophet refuses to let her touch him and descends again into his subterranean cell.

Iokonaan Descends into the Cistern   *Coppola with Pasdeloup Orchestra* 4283-1.00

Narraboth, an officer in charge of the guard over Iokonaan is in love with Salomé, and, hearing her passionate entreaty to Iokonaan, is suddenly filled with despair and kills himself at her feet. At this moment Herod and his wife, with their court, appear. Herod, already distracted by troubles with the Jews, with his wife, and with a passion for Salomé, his step-daughter, is deeply disturbed upon finding the dead body of the young soldier. He orders it removed and to soothe his tormented soul asks Salomé to drink from his cup, to eat with him, to show some sign of interest in him. She refuses. Iokonaan from his cistern is heard declaiming against the evils of Herod's family and Herodias demands that Herod silence the pris-

oner and hand him over to the Jews for punishment. Herod is unwilling to do this because
he fears Iokonaan. Again the voice of the
prisoner resounds foretelling the coming of
the Saviour. When Herod asks who the Saviour
might be he is told that he has already come
and that he has raised the dead and performed
other miracles.

With fear added to his other troubles, Herod
asks Salomé to dance, hoping to be distracted
from his ominous forebodings. Salomé refuses
until Herod promises to grant anything she
will ask if she will dance for him. Inspired with
a horrid thought, Salomé performs the seductive Dance of the Seven Veils.

When it is over she throws herself at the
feet of Herod and then demands her fee—
the head of Iokonaan, brought to her on a
silver platter. Herod is horrified and offers her
instead all his wondrous store of jewels and
riches. Stubbornly Salomé insists that he keep
his oath and give her what she wishes. Egged
on by his wife, Herod finally acquiesces and
orders Iokonaan beheaded.

Lorette & Rudolph (Paris)
MARJORIE LAWRENCE AS SALOMÉ

Salome's Dance *Stokowski and Philadelphia Orchestra* 7259-7260-2.00 each

Swordsmen descend into the well and Salomé eagerly listens for the sound
of the death stroke. Presently the head is brought to her on a great silver
tray. In a hideous ecstasy compounded of amorousness, vindictiveness, of
satisfied revenge, and unsatisfied passion Salomé fondles and kisses the lips
of the dead man's head, singing wildly of his beauty and of her triumph.

Herod, suddenly disgusted with the cruelty and insatiable passions of
Salomé, tells his wife that her daughter is a fiend. Commanding that the
lights be extinguished, he suddenly orders his soldiers to kill Salomé. They
instantly crush her to death beneath their shoes.

Thou Wouldst Not Suffer Me to Kiss Thy Mouth *Ljungberg* 9786-1.50
Thy Tongue Speaks No More and **Thou Wouldst Not Suffer Me to Kiss Thy Mouth**
Lawrence 8682-2.00
I Have Kissed Thy Mouth and **Wherefore Didst Thou Not Look?** *Marjorie Lawrence*
8683-2.00
Thy Body Was a Column of Ivory *Gota Ljungberg* 9786-1.50

459

THE BACCHANALE

SAMSON ET DALILA

OPERA in three acts; music by Camille Saint-Saëns; libretto by Ferdinand Lemaire. First produced at Weimar under Liszt, December 2, 1877. First performed in the United States as an opera at New Orleans, January 4, 1893; sung in concert form at Music (Carnegie) Hall, New York, March 25, 1892. Produced at the Metropolitan Opera, New York, in 1915, with Caruso, Matzenauer and Amato.

In spite of his unusually brilliant early success as a composer, Saint-Saëns had difficulty in finding a way for his Biblical opera, "Samson and Delilah." The difficulty was largely due to factional disturbances which divided Paris at the time, a result of the then revolutionary musical doctrines of Richard Wagner; and although Saint-Saëns is now regarded as one of the arch-conservatives, at that epoch he was ranked among the radicals. A powerful friend came to the composer's aid in the person of Franz Liszt, who never missed a chance to give possible genius a hearing. Saint-Saëns was invited to the pianists' Mecca, Weimar, where the work was produced with a success which made performances elsewhere inevitable; and today "Samson" ranks as an operatic classic. Of Saint-Saëns' many operas it is the only one which seems permanently to hold the stage; perhaps the Biblical subject made an especially strong appeal to the composer—he was for many years organist at the Church of the Madeleine, Paris. The score is an excellent piece of workmanship, with its Hebrew chants vividly contrasted with the sensuous music of the pagan Philistines— Delilah's voluptuous songs, including the ever-popular "Mon cœur s'ouvre à ta voix," and the wildly oriental Bacchanale. (The original French name of the opera, "Samson et Dalila," is pronounced *Sahn-so'hn* (nasal) *ay Da-lee'la*.)

460

ACT I

BEFORE the rise of the curtain an invisible chorus of Israelites is heard bewailing their bondage and imploring Jehovah for release. At the rise of the curtain they are vaguely seen, for it is early morning; they are gathered in a public square in the city of their conquerors, Gaza, lamenting their servitude. Samson comes forward and in stirring tones urges his countrymen to arise and cast off the Philistines' yoke.

At first they continue with their lamentations, but his vigorous proclamation of faith finally sets fire to their souls, and the Israelites exclaim: "It is the Lord who speaks through him! Let us follow Samson and Jehovah be our guide!" Their ringing shouts soon bring forth from his palace, Abimelech, the Satrap of Gaza, with his bodyguard. He taunts the Israelites: they are helpless; what avail their prayers to Jehovah . . . did He deliver them in the day of battle? Better turn to Dagon, the greatest of gods. This blasphemy moves Samson to stand forth declaring himself the inspired leader of the chosen people . . . they join him in singing a spirited battle hymn: "Arise, Oh Israel, and break asunder the chains that bind you! Let righteousness be victorious!"

Abimelech cannot tolerate this and attacks Samson with drawn sword. Samson wrests the weapon from him and runs him through. The Satrap falls calling for help. This is but the signal for revolt and the Israelites follow Samson in a struggle for freedom. When they have disappeared, the gates of the temple of Dagon swing open and the High Priest approaches with his attendants. He is horrified at the sight of the murdered ruler and, seeking vainly to rally his panic-stricken followers, he calls down a curse on Samson, his people and his God. The High Priest and his followers are forced to flee with the body of Abimelech as the victorious Hebrews return, chanting hymns of praise. It is Samson's great hour.

Once more the gates of the temple of Dagon open, but this time the seductively beautiful priestess, Delilah, appears. While the maidens who accompany her bearing garlands of victory sing and dance, she exerts her allurement upon the hero. "I come to celebrate the victory of him who reigns in my heart," sings this worldly-wise priestess. An old Hebrew solemnly warns Samson; but the chosen leader is already vanquished although he still prays for divine power to resist the enchantress. While the young girls continue their dance, Delilah sings to Samson her fascinating "Song of Spring."

Printemps qui commence *(Delilah's Song of Spring)* **Sigrid Onegin** 7320-2.00

> Spring voices are singing,
> Bright hope they are bringing,
> All hearts making glad.
> And gone sorrow's traces,
> The soft air effaces
> All days that are sad.
> The earth glad and beaming,
> With freshness is teeming.

461

In vain all my beauty:
I weep my poor fate!
(She gazes fondly at Samson)
When night is descending,
With love all unending,
Bewailing my fate,
For him will I wait.
Till fond love returning,
In his bosom burning
May enforce his return!

Delilah returns to the temple with her dancing girls, not forgetting one last coy glance at the conqueror who gazes after her; for, as it is written, in the hour of his triumph, the heart of Samson is shaken within him.

ACT II

NIGHT is descending upon the valley, and Delilah, more sumptuously clad than ever, waits outside her dwelling for the approach of Samson. She calls upon Love to come to aid her in achieving a victory over this man, whom, as a leader of a despised people, she in reality hates above all others.

Amour, viens aider ma faiblesse *(Love Come Aid My Weakness)*   **Gladys Swarthout** 14143-2.00

The High Priest comes to Delilah, enjoining her not to fail in her purpose. After he has gone, Samson approaches to keep the rendezvous hinted at by Delilah in her "Spring Song"; slightly hesitant, his last struggling sense of duty is being hopelessly overcome by irresistible temptation. And with her allurements, tears and protestations of love Delilah plays havoc with the man's emotions. No wonder! Hearing such a melody as her *"Mon cœur s'ouvre à ta voix,"* could any man resist?

Mon coeur s'ouvre à ta voix *(My Heart at Thy Sweet Voice)* **Sigrid Onegin** 7320-2.00 **Louise Homer** 1422-1.50 **Gladys Swarthout** 14143-2.00

My heart at thy sweet voice opens wide like the flower
Which the morn's kisses waken!
But, that I may rejoice, that my tears no more shower,
Tell thy love still unshaken!
O say thou wilt not now leave Delilah again!
Repeat thine accents tender, ev'ry passionate vow,
O thou dearest of men!
(Copyright, 1892, G. Schirmer.)

During this exquisite melody a storm has gathered, the swift pattering of the rain being suggested in the accompaniment. Delilah strives her utmost to persuade Samson to betray the secret of his miraculous strength; the increasing fury of the storm seems symbolical of the increasing turmoil of his emotions. Delilah alternately threatens and pleads . . . if he will not share his

SAMSON: Sore my distress, my guilt and anguish,
Have pity, O Lord, in misery I languish!

(Act III)

secret with her he does not really love her. Though weakening, Samson refuses, praying for strength. Seemingly in despair, Delilah runs into her house, crying out that he is a coward, and his a heart without love. Trembling with his emotion, Samson raises his arms hopelessly to heaven, then hurries after her. The storm breaks over the scene in all its fury. Philistine soldiers approach stealthily . . . Delilah appears at the terrace for a moment and summons them . . . Samson is vanquished.

ACT III

SAMSON, slayer of thousands, now is helpless. Blinded, shorn of his long locks and weighed down with chains, he slowly turns the mill which grinds corn for the Philistines. Out of the depths of his misery he calls upon the Lord for mercy . . . nearby his fellow-countrymen sing: "For love of a woman he sold his power . . . and made us captives!"

Samson is led away and the scene changes. From the orchestra are heard soft chords and harp arpeggios, mild like the first glow of dawn which penetrates the temple of Dagon, crowded with rejoicing Philistines. Repeating

463

Copy't White

SAMSON:

Lord, thy servant remember now,
For one moment make him strong!
(Act III)

the dainty melody sung by the dancing girls in the First Act, they sing the praises of dawn which puts darkness to flight, and of Love, which alone brings happiness.

As they finish singing, an oboe plays a weirdly exotic cadenza; the orchestra sounds a dance rhythm and a group of dancers rush forward beginning their bacchanalian-like evolutions. The music, at times softly yet luxuriantly voluptuous, grows to a climax of the most frenzied, oriental abandon.

Bacchanale *Leopold Stokowski-Philadelphia Symphony Orchestra* 6823-2.00

The dance ended, Samson is led in by a child. All mock him with the cruelest scorn; Delilah even derisively sings at him some of the phrases of her former love song. Then all turn their attention to the morning sacrifice to the god Dagon, whom the High Priest and Delilah invoke in broad, canonic phrases. Meanwhile Samson has let himself be led between the two massive pillars which support the roof of the temple. His unceasing prayers are answered . . . he feels his old strength return. While all are lost in the ecstasy of worship he seizes the pillars with a mighty effort . . . they break . . . the roof crashes to earth . . . Samson is buried with his enemies.

LA SONNAMBULA

(The Somnambulist)

OPERA in three acts; music by Vincenzo Bellini; libretto by Felice Romani. First produced at the Teatro Carcano, Milan, March 6, 1831. First performance in America, at the Park Theatre, New York, November 13, 1835, in English.

During the mid-nineteenth century this was one of the most popular of operas; a favorite with our grandparents and many a famous prima donna, including the beloved Jenny Lind. The succeeding era of Wagnerianism and modern complexities made light of Bellini's elegiac, delicate melodies, his vocal frills, and above all, of his thin orchestration. Revived in recent years, this very simplicity proved its charm once more, and came as a refreshing relief in an age given to the bizarre and overly complex.

(The name of the opera is pronounced *Lah Son-nahm'-boo-la*.)

The action takes place in a Swiss village.

ACT I

THE betrothal of the charming Amina to Elvino is being merrily celebrated on the village green when a handsome stranger arrives asking the way to the castle. As it is a considerable distance he decides to put up in the village inn over night. The sight of these surroundings revives memories that find their expression in his aria, "Vi ravviso."

Night is approaching and Amina's foster-mother, Teresa, declares that it is time for all to go to their houses lest the phantom that has lately been haunting the neighborhood appear. The people depart, and the stranger enters the inn, not from fear of the specter, but through desire for rest.

Lande

TERESA'S MILL—ACT III—SCENE II

465

THE SORCERER

COMIC OPERA in two acts by W. S. Gilbert and Arthur Sullivan. First produced at the Opéra Comique, London, November 17th, 1877. "The Sorcerer" followed "Trial by Jury" (1875), and as the latter is more of a Cantata we may name "The Sorcerer" as the first of the Gilbert and Sullivan Operas. It was also the first production of the syndicate formed by the late Richard D'Oyly Carte. Although it may lack something of the practiced technique of the later Gilbert and Sullivan operas, "The Sorcerer" has a delightful freshness and easy flow. There is abundance of fun and some charming music, of which a generous selection has been made and is now presented as an abridged version on six Victor records. The story following will enable the listener to fill in the gaps. Album C-21 (4258-4263) AC-21 (4264-4269) Price $6.50

DRAMATIS PERSONAE

SIR MARMADUKE POINTDEXTRE, *an Elderly Baronet*
ALEXIS, *of the Grenadier Guards, his Son*
DR. DALY, *Vicar of Ploverleigh*
NOTARY
JOHN WELLINGTON WELLS, *of J. W. Wells & Co., Family Sorcerers*
LADY SANGAZURE, *a Lady of Ancient Lineage*
ALINE, *her Daughter, betrothed to Alexis*
MRS. PARTLET, *a Pew Opener*
CONSTANCE, *her Daughter*
Chorus of Villagers.

ACT I

IT IS mid-day and the villagers of Ploverleigh are assembled in front of the Elizabethan Mansion of Sir Marmaduke Pointdextre, voicing their joy at the betrothal of Sir Marmaduke's heir Alexis to Aline *(C 21-1)*, the only child of an equally aristocratic neighbour, the Lady San-

gazure. There is one present, however, who does not share in the general joy. Constance, the daughter of Mrs. Partlet, the worthy Pew Opener, is downcast and confesses to her mother that she loves (vainly, it seems) the Vicar, Dr. Daly. On his appearance they withdraw and Dr. Daly sings the notable ballad, "Time was when Love and I were well acquainted" *(C 21-2)*, in which he laments the days now

SULLIVAN

gone when, as a pale young curate, he had the adoration of the maidens of his flock. Mrs. Partlet, anxious to help Constance, comes forward and leads the conversation to the subject of marriage, but it is obvious from his replies that he looks on himself as a confirmed bachelor, and Constance is led away sobbing by her mother.

The Vicar now turns to welcome Sir Marmaduke and Alexis in weighty language, and with a touch of allegory that pleases Sir Marmaduke, who is a great admirer of the school of stately compliment, and a stickler for "blue blood." He claims that his own family is directly descended

GILBERT

from Helen of Troy, and is all for a marriage of pedigree, regarding love as a comparatively unimportant accessory.

Aline makes her appearance *(C 21-3)* and is greeted by the village girls. She acknowledges their good wishes, and her mother, Lady Sangazure, adds her congratulations. The men now welcome Alexis and the lovers greet each other with ecstasy. Then follows a stately duet *(C 21-4)* ("Welcome joy, adieu to sadness") between Sir Marmaduke and Lady Sangazure, who were lovers in their young days. The stately gavotte measure is punctuated by their dreams of what might have been.

A notary has now arrived, all is prepared for signing the marriage contract *(C 21-5)*. This done, Alexis and Aline are left together. Alexis does not agree with the views of his father, and, believing that men and women should be coupled in matrimony without distinction of rank, has done some propaganda on the subject. So far, however, his ideas have only been welcomed by the humbler classes. His own happiness seeming assured, he reveals his scheme for making the whole village happy. He has engaged John Wellington Wells, a Sorcerer, to administer secretly a love-philtre to all the others, which will first send them to sleep, and on their awaking cause them to fall madly in love with the first person of the opposite sex they may see who has also drunk the potion. It has no effect on those already married.

Mr. Wells is introduced in the well-known patter song *(C 21-6)*, and then details are discussed. It is decided that the philtre shall be placed in a large teapot which will be used for the "banquet" to follow. Mr. Wells then proceeds to his horrific Incantation *(C 21-7)*, and after the Fiends have disappeared, the villagers return, make merry *(C 21-8)*, and each drinks of the enchanted tea. The act closes as, after struggling vainly against the charm, all present save Alexis, Aline and the Sorcerer fall insensible.

ACT II

IT is midnight, and the villagers are still lying where they have fallen. Mr. Wells, with a great sense of fitness, has had the more exalted members taken home and put to bed "respectably."

As the villagers wake, each falls in love with the first person of the opposite sex visible, Constance and the Notary making one couple.

Alexis is so pleased with his success that he urges Aline to join with him in drinking the philtre, in order that nothing may be left to chance. She refuses, and they quarrel *(C 21-9)*. The remaining characters begin to arrive: first Dr. Daly, the worthy Vicar, who is puzzled because, in a village hitherto rather slow in the matter of marriage, he has suddenly had a request for hasty weddings from everyone—even Sir Marmaduke. Alexis is none too pleased when he finds that the philtre has led the Baronet to fix on Mrs. Partlet, the Pew Opener. Still, he must live up to his opinions, and there is a congratulatory quintet *(C 21-10)* from those concerned. Mr. Wells, having caused the mischief, falls a victim to his own spell, for Lady Sangazure, entering, sees him and at once adores him. He, on the other hand, not having drunk the philtre, does not reciprocate, and in an amusing duet endeavours to dissuade her *(C 21-11)*. Without success, however, for she threatens to bury her woe in her family vault.

Aline, having pondered the matter, has decided to fall in love with her lover's wish, and drinks the philtre. Immediately afterwards, she catches sight of Dr. Daly and of course falls in love with him. He is delighted at his good fortune, but Alexis, coming in full of remorse, is astounded to find his embraces repulsed. Explanations ensue, and the Vicar obligingly offers to quit the country and bury his sorrow "in the congenial gloom of a Colonial Bishopric."

This is not enough, for Aline is still under the influence of the philtre, and no longer loves Alexis. They appeal to Mr. Wells, who reveals that there is one way only in which the spell can be revoked. Either he or Alexis must sacrifice himself to Ahrimanes. Argument ensues, and the issue is put to popular vote; John Wellington Wells loses and disappears into the earth to the sound of a gong *(C 21-12)*.

All quit their temporary partners to rejoin their old lovers, and Sir Marmaduke, claiming Lady Sangazure, invites them all to another feast in his mansion.

Gems *Light Opera Company* 36147-1.25

THE LEGEND OF KLEINZACH

THE TALES OF HOFFMAN

(Les Contes d'Hoffmann)

OPERA in three acts, with Prologue and Epilogue; music by Jacques Offenbach; libretto by Jules Barbier. First produced, February 10, 1881, at the Opéra Comique, Paris. First performance in the United States, October 16, 1882, at the Fifth Avenue Theatre, New York, by Maurice Grau's French Opera Company upon their first American appearance.

Although Offenbach wrote many a successful *opéra comique*, this fantastic opera is now ranked as his masterpiece. Without being pretentious as music, the score has a delicacy, grace, and poetic feeling perfectly adapted to the fanciful imagination of Hoffman's "Tales."

Offenbach began his work during the summer of 1880, but even before it was completed he became seriously ill. Believing it to be his finest piece of work, he was anxious to witness the first performance; unfortunately, he died, October 5, 1880, some four months before the work was first produced.

CHARACTERS

HOFFMAN, *a poet*	Tenor
NIKLAUS, *his friend*	Contralto (or Baritone)
OLYMPIA, GIULIETTA, AND ANTONIA, *the poet's loves*	Sopranos
COPPELIUS, DAPERTUTTO, AND MIRACLE, *a magician under various names*	Baritone
SCHLEMIL	Bass
SPALANZANI	Tenor

PROLOGUE

THE crowd of students in "Martin Luther's Wine Cellar" at Nuremberg sing the praises of the master of the tavern, but Hoffman, who is among them, seems despondent. Upon the students' request for a song, however, he begins the weird Ballad of Kleinzach, but soon wanders off into a song in praise of a beautiful woman. The students jest with him saying that he is in

love. He replies that he has given up all such matters, but will tell them of three of his own unfortunate love adventures. Each of the succeeding acts of the opera reveals one of these.

ACT I

THE famous scientist Spalanzani has a beautiful daughter, Olympia. She is, however, not really his daughter but a wonderful mechanical doll, made by the scientist and his friend, Coppelius. Hoffman has seen this automaton through the window, and now comes to Spalanzani's house, ostensibly as his pupil, but really to make love to Olympia. Coppelius has persuaded him to wear a certain pair of spectacles with which to look at the girl. At an entertainment given by Spalanzani, Olympia sings her oddly mechanical coloratura song with its bird-like rondelays. At one point the song seems about to stop, a servant touches her shoulder, the sound of a spring is heard, and the song continues.

Olympia's Aria *(Doll Song)* **Miliza Korjus** 11921-1.50

Hoffman is so enraptured by her beauty and by her singing that he will not listen to his friend Niklaus when he tries to enlighten him; and so carried away is he that when he tells the doll of his passion he believes she returns his affection, although she only says, "Yes, yes," whenever he happens to touch her shoulder. This odd couple begin a dance which grows faster and faster until Hoffman falls to the floor in a swoon, thereby breaking his spectacles. Now also Coppelius enters in a great rage, for Spalanzani has bought Olympia and paid for her with a worthless draft. In his anger, Coppelius breaks the priceless doll to pieces. Spalanzani and Coppelius quarrel and the guests laugh at Hoffman, whose first love has ended in disillusionment.

ACT II

AT Venice, city of enchantment, is the palace of Giulietta, overlooking the Grand Canal. Niklaus sings with her the gently swaying and ever famous Barcarolle. Hoffman also is here, and in spite of the warning of

Barcarolle, Belle Nuit *(Oh, Night of Love)* **Lucrezia Bori, Lawrence Tibbett** 1747-1.50 *Victor Concert Orchestra* 20011-.75 *International Concert Orchestra* 35839-1.25

Niklaus, he allows himself to become fascinated by Giulietta. This beautiful courtesan is really under the sway of the magician Dapertutto; for him she has stolen the shadow of her lover Schlemil, for him she now similarly sets out to ensnare Hoffman in order to steal his reflection in a mirror.

Surprised by the jealous Schlemil, Hoffman fights a duel with him, using

Dapertutto's proffered sword. Schlemil is killed and Dapertutto disappears. A moment later Giulietta passes in her gondola, leaning on Dapertutto's arm and singing a mocking song at Hoffman. Thus the second love affair ends in disappointment.

ACT III

Hoffman is engaged to marry Antonia, daughter of Rath Krespel in Munich, at whose house we now see him. Antonia, like her mother before her, has a remarkably beautiful voice, and, also like her, is afflicted with consumption. Although singing gives her great happiness, Krespel forbids her so taxing her strength since he knows it will be fatal to her. At first Hoffman is delighted to hear her sing when alone with her, but after he has overheard a conversation between Krespel and Dr. Miracle and learns of the danger, he makes Antonia promise never to sing again. When, however, Krespel and Hoffman have gone, Miracle, the evil genius that has haunted Hoffman as Coppelius and as Dapertutto, returns, and summoning the spirit of Antonia's mother, whom he has likewise killed, he persuades the girl to sing. Finally she falls exhausted, and when Hoffman and Krespel return, she sinks dying in her father's arms. So ends in tragedy Hoffman's third love story.

EPILOGUE

The boon companions thank Hoffman for his Tales and take their leave. The Muse of Art now comes to console Hoffman, and for a moment he is aroused to great ecstasy, then he falls, face forward, across the table . . . asleep? "Dead drunk," remarks one of the students in departing; but Stella, the girl who leans upon his arm, pauses as she goes out and throws a flower from her bouquet at Hoffman's feet.

Photo White

THE BARCAROLLE

TANNHÄUSER AND VENUS

TANNHÄUSER

OPERA in three acts; words and music by Richard Wagner. First produced, October 19, 1845, at the Royal Opera House, Dresden. First performance in the United States, April 4, 1859, at the Stadt Theatre, New York.

The first of Wagner's operas to be performed in the United States, it is still one of the most popular.

When "Tannhäuser" was having its first performances it aroused the most violent discussion. Some there were who found the new work beautiful; but the majority were disappointed, for them the opera was either meaningless or too full of dissonance. The overture was declared to be devoid of melody by a Parisian critic, and one of the best orchestras in Germany found it too difficult to play. A prominent musician admitted that the "Song to the Evening Star" was a good tune, but declared that it was improperly harmonized, and wrote "correct" harmony for it. How time has reversed these decisions! Today "Tannhäuser" is one of the most beloved of operas, the overture is in the repertoire of every symphony orchestra, the harmonies of "Evening Star" having long since ceased to be daring.

All of Wagner's works for the stage possess either a legendary or historical foundation; Tannhäuser rests on both. According to medieval romance, the gods and goddesses of antiquity did not die, but took refuge in the underworld. Thus it was believed that the Goddess of Love, Venus, had established her court near the Wartburg beneath a mountain which came to be known as the Venusberg, there to prey upon the souls of men. The Landgraves who ruled in Thuringia were patrons of the arts and held contests of song. The minnesingers, a class of lyric poets and musicians, generally of noble birth, who sang of idealized love and beauty, were at their height in Germany from about 1150 to 1350 and often took part in such contests. Those appearing in the opera were actual characters. The historical Tannhäuser seems to have been too fond of the good things of this world, and thus the legend arose concerning him that he had dwelt in the Venusberg. As treated by Wagner, the legend becomes symbolical of the struggle between the lower and the higher in human nature.

For the famous and stormy production at Paris, Wagner wrote a new version of the opening scene, making more dramatic the discussion between Venus and Tannhäuser, and greatly elaborating the wild revels of the denizens of the Venusberg. This version is frequently used, though not universally, in present-day performances of the opera. In this version the overture, having its final portion omitted, leads directly into the opening ballet—for such it really is—the music of which has become well known in the concert hall under the name of "New Venusberg Music" or "Bacchanale."

CHARACTERS

HERMANN, *Landgrave of Thuringia*	*Bass*
TANNHÄUSER *(Tahn'-hoy-zer)*	*Tenor*
WOLFRAM VON ESCHENBACH *(Vohl-frahm)*	*Baritone*
ELISABETH, *Niece of the Landgrave*	*Soprano*
VENUS	*Soprano*

The other minstrel knights: WALTER VON DER VOGELWEIDE (Tenor), BITEROLF (Bass), HEINRICH DER SCHREIBER (Tenor), REIMAR VON ZWETER (Bass).

Chorus of Thuringian Nobles and Knights. Ladies, Elder and Younger Pilgrims, Sirens, Naiads, Nymphs, Bacchantes.

The action takes place in the vicinity of Eisenach at the beginning of the Thirteenth Century.

Wagner himself wrote for the orchestra at Zurich an explanation of the meaning of the overture. Greatly abridged, it runs as follows:

To begin with, the orchestra leads before us the Pilgrim's Chant alone; it draws near, then swells into a mighty outpour, and finally passes away.—Evenfall; last echo of the chant. As night breaks, magic sights and sounds occur, a rosy mist floats up, . . . the whirlings of a fearsomely voluptuous dance are seen. These are the "Venusberg's" seductive spells, that show themselves at dead of night. . . . Attracted by the tempting show, a comely human form draws nigh; 'tis Tannhäuser, Love's minstrel. He sounds his jubilant "Song of Love" in joyous challenge, as though to force the wanton witchery to do his bidding. Wild cries of riot answer him: the rosy cloud grows denser round him, entrancing perfumes steal away his senses.

In the most seductive of half-lights, his wonder-seeing eye beholds an alluring female form; he hears a voice that sweetly murmurs the siren-call . . . Venus herself it is . . . Then heart and senses burn within him: . . . before the goddess' self he steps with that canticle of love triumphant, and now he sings it in ecstatic praise of her . . . The wonders of the Venusberg unroll their brightest before him; tumultuous shouts and savage cries of joy mount up . . . in drunken glee Bacchantes drive their raging dance and drag Tannhäuser to the warm caresses of Love's Goddess, who bears him where no step dare tread . . . A scurry, like the sound of the Wild Hunt, and speedily the storm is laid. Only a wanton whir still pulses in the breeze, a wave of weird voluptuousness . . .

But dawn begins to break already; from afar is heard again the Pilgrims' Chant. As this chant draws closer . . . as the day drives farther back the night, that whir and soughing of the air—which had erstwhile sounded like the eerie cries of souls condemned—now rises, too, to ever gladder waves; so that when the sun ascends at last in splendor, and the Pilgrims' Chant proclaims in ecstasy to all the world, to all that lives and moves thereon, Salvation won, this wave itself swells out the tidings of sublimest joy . . .

Overture and Venusberg Music *Leopold Stokowski and the Philadelphia Orchestra* M-78 (7262-7264) AM-78 (7265-7267)-6.50 Overture *Coates-Symphony Orchestra* 9059-9060-1.50 each

475

THE HALL OF SONG—ACT II *(Direction Herbert Graf)*

ACT I

THE immense cave-like grotto, illuminated by mysterious multi-colored lights, where Venus holds her court—the Venusberg. Here languorous youths, urged on by the enticements of Nymphs, lead in a wild dance. Into their midst dash a throng of Bacchantes who cause the dance to grow even more riotous. Satyrs and Fauns appear from the clefts in the rock walls of the cavern and running headlong after the Nymphs bring the dance to a tumult of frenzy; and with the increasing madness of the dance, the music has grown to a climax of the wildest voluptuousness. The three graces vainly attempt to quell the riot. They awaken sleeping cupids, who fly above the tumult and shoot their arrows at the surging crowd below. Stricken with the pangs of love, the wounded take flight. The music subsides from its impassioned turbulence and glowing with a wonderful, silvery iridescence, sinks into a profound calm. A rosy mist falls over the cave until only Tannhäuser, Venus and the three graces are visible in the foreground. And now through the mist there appears a cloud picture of the abduction of Europa . . . from a remote portion of the grotto is heard the song of sirens:

> Come to these bowers,
> Fragrant with flowers . . .

The vision fades, and another is revealed: the soft glamour of the moon, Leda and the swan at a woodland pool. This vision also disappears, the graces withdraw, and Venus and Tannhäuser remain silent and motionless. The music dies away in a final languorous sigh.

Venusberg Music and Bacchanale *Coates-Symphony Orchestra* 9027-9028-1.50 each

Tannhäuser starts up, suddenly, as from a dream. He has grown weary of the soft, sensuous life of Venus' Court, and although the Goddess of Love herself uses all the fascinations in her power, each time he begins to sing his hymn in her praise he forgets his theme and tells of his longing for earth with its mingled joys and sorrows. When she finds that the allurements of herself or her realm avail nothing, the goddess threatens him, saying that on earth he will be scorned, an outcast among men. Tannhäuser replies that he trusts in Mary. At the name of the Blessed Virgin, Venus and all her kingdom instantly disappear and Tannhäuser finds himself standing in a valley near the Castle of the Wartburg.

It is a bright spring morning; a shepherd plays on his pipe and sings merrily while nearby can be heard the tinkle of his flock's bells; a band of pilgrims on their way to Rome pass by singing their chant. Tannhäuser, shaken with emotion, falls on his knees in devout thankfulness. While he is yet kneeling, the sound of hunting horns is heard gradually drawing nearer, and soon the Landgrave and a party of minnesingers come along the path. They recognize Tannhäuser and greet him joyfully. When they ask where he has stayed for so long, he vaguely replies that he wandered far, that he is unhappy and would still continue his wanderings. Nor can all their entreaties and promises cause him to return to them, until the noble-hearted Wolfram reminds him that here lives Elisabeth, and adds that she has sorrowed greatly since his departure. Deeply moved, Tannhäuser consents to remain.

ACT II

THE hall of the singers at the Wartburg is in readiness for a contest. Elisabeth enters, singing to it her joyful greeting.

> Oh, hall of song, I give thee greeting!
> All hail to thee thou hallowed place!
> 'Twas here that dream so sweet and fleeting,
> Upon my heart his song did trace.
> But since by him forsaken
> A desert thou dost seem—
> Thy echoes only waken
> Remembrance of a dream.
> But now the flame of hope is lighted,
> Thy vault shall ring with glorious war;
> For he whose strains my soul delighted
> No longer roams afar!

Dich, teure Halle (*Oh! Hall of Song*) *Elisabeth Rethberg* 6831-2.00 *Kirsten Flagstad* 14181-2.00

Wolfram enters conducting Tannhäuser to her. She is overjoyed, but modestly refrains from revealing her happiness too openly. When she asks where he has been so long, he again vaguely says that he wandered in a distant land, only by a miracle did he escape; and, he adds, it was she who caused him to return. They sing a duet in praise of this power which has

477

reunited them, then Tannhäuser leaves to prepare for the contest. Elisabeth's uncle, the Landgrave, enters and informs her that he will offer her hand to the singer she crowns as victor in the contest. At this moment a trumpet fanfare announces the arrival of the time appointed; a hurrying figure, as of pleasant agitation, is played by the strings; then a broad, magnificent march theme is announced. Elisabeth and her uncle welcome their guests as they enter. The chorus of voices singing "Hail, bright abode, Landgrave Hermann, Hail!" swells in power and brilliance even as the number of those assembled constantly grows. Finally, when the hall is filled with the gorgeously attired nobles, the march comes to a dazzling close.

Procession of the Guests in the Wartburg *Berlin State Opera Chorus-Orchestra* 9161-1.50 **Fest March** *Chicago Symphony Orchestra* 7386-2.00 *Banda di Chieti* 36169-1.25

The Landgrave addresses them in welcome, states the theme of the contest, "Love," and pages collect lots to determine the beginner. The minnesingers hymn the praises of virtuous love.

Blick' ich umher *(Gazing On This August Assembly)* *Friedrich Schorr* 7426-2.00

Tannhäuser, growing more and more agitated, replies to each of them, singing of the delights of merely sensual passion. Finally, inspired by some unnatural force, he bursts into his hymn in praise of Venus, those who know her not, know not love! The women hurry from the hall as from a place unholy; the men, drawing their swords, rush at Tannhäuser. Elisabeth, though heartbroken at her betrayal, throws herself before him, and pleads that they allow him to seek Heaven's forgiveness. The Landgrave consents on condition that Tannhäuser will seek pardon from the Pope. A group of younger pilgrims are heard singing as they start on their journey to Rome. Stricken with remorse, Tannhäuser rushes out to join them.

Prelude to Act III *Albert Coates-Symphony Orchestra* 9028-1.50

ACT III

REMINISCENCES of the Pilgrims' Chorus, the music of Tannhäuser's pilgrimage to Rome, and the Venusberg music first heard in the Overture are combined into a prelude of somber beauty.

In the Valley of the Wartburg stands a crucifix; before it Elisabeth, arrayed in white, kneels in prayer. From a distance is heard the song of returning pilgrims, gradually drawing nearer.

Once more with joy, oh, my home, I may meet thee;
Once more, ye fair flow'ry meadows, I greet ye;
My pilgrim staff henceforth may rest,
Since Heav'n's sweet peace is within my breast.
The sinner's plaint on high was heard,
Accepted by a gracious Lord;
The tears I laid before His shrine
Are turned to hope and joy divine . . .
Hallelujah eternally.

Lande

SETTING OF ACT III AT THE METROPOLITAN

Pilgrims' Chorus *Berlin State Opera Chorus-Orchestra* 9161-1.50 *(In English)*
Victor Male Chorus 20127-.75

Elisabeth rises and scans them in the greatest anxiety as they pass by and disappear in the distance. *He* is not among them. She sinks once more before the crucifix and in the greatest agony of soul sings her prayer:

> Oh, blessed Virgin,
> Hear my prayer!
> Here in the dust I bend before thee,
> Now from this earth, oh set me free!
> If vain desires and earthly longing
> Have turned my heart from thee away,
> The sinful hopes within me thronging,
> Before thy blessed feet I lay;
> And on thy bounty I will call,
> That heavenly grace on him may fall!

Elisabeths Gebet *(Elisabeth's Prayer)* *Maria Jeritza* 6694-2.00 *Kirsten Flagstad* 8920-2.00

Wolfram has been standing at a distance, sorrowfully watching, and when Elisabeth rises and starts to return to the castle, he gently asks if he may not accompany her. By her gesture she declines. Meanwhile night has fallen over the valley and the evening star glows on high. Thinking of

479

FLAGSTAD AS ELISABETH

Elisabeth, Wolfram sings a wonderfully expressive apostrophe to the star, accompanying himself on his minstrel's harp.

> O thou sublime sweet evening star!
> Joyful I greet thee from afar;
> O greet for me as passing by,
> From earth's green valleys to the sky;
> One to whom all my heart was given,
> An angel soon to be in Heaven.

Evening Star *Reinald Werrenrath* **6563-2.00** *Marcel Journet* **1274-1.50** *Lawrence Tibbett* **8452-2.00** *John Charles Thomas* **7605-2.00** *('Cello) Pablo Casals* **6620-2.00**

A gloomy motive is heard in the orchestra and Tannhäuser appears, haggard and weary. In a broken voice he asks of Wolfram the way to the Venusberg. Wolfram recoils in mingled horror and pity. He urgently questions Tannhäuser, who then tells of his pilgrimage: how he suffered every privation and hardship over dangerous mountains and rock paths; how he

Inbrunst im Herzen *(Yearning for Pardon)* and **Da sah ich ihn** *(Then I Saw Him)* **Melchior 9707-1.50**

prostrated himself before the Pope, and in deepest contrition confessed his sin; and the terrifying response:

> Thou art for evermore accursed!
> And as this barren staff I hold
> Ne'er will put forth a flow'r or leaf,
> Thus shalt thou never more behold
> Salvation or thy sin's relief!

He fled from Rome in despair. Now, without hope of salvation, he seeks forgetfulness at the Venusberg. A ruddy glow illuminates the recesses of the mountain; the song of the sirens and the voluptuous music of the Venusberg are heard; Venus appears holding out her arms to welcome Tannhäuser. Wolfram pleads with him, but the minstrel spurns his entreaties. At this moment when Venus seems to have won her prey, Wolfram recalls to Tannhäuser the name "Elisabeth." The Knight stands as if spellbound. Recognizing her defeat, Venus vanishes with all her magical companions. Bells are heard tolling, for Elisabeth has died during the night and now the mournful music of her funeral train draws near. As the procession of mourners enters the valley carrying the bier, Tannhäuser, broken with grief and exhaustion, sinks dying beside Elisabeth. As his soul takes its flight, the second band of pilgrims arrives. They carry the papal staff which has brought forth green leaves—a miracle revealing that Tannhäuser has been pardoned.

THAÏS

OPERA in three acts; music by Jules Massenet; libretto by Louis Gallet, after Anatole France. First produced March 16, 1894, at the Opéra Comique. First performance in the United States, November 25, 1908, at the Manhattan Opera House, New York. At the first production of Thaïs the title rôle was sung by the American, Sibyl Sanderson, for whom Massenet had especially written the opera. Mary Garden, who is ranked as one of the greatest living interpreters of this rôle, is herself a pupil of Sibyl Sanderson and made her American début singing Thaïs at its first American performance.

The libretto of the opera is after—indeed, a considerable way after—the novel by Anatole France. Massenet's music of saccharine sweetness is perfectly adapted to the action, and with reason has won the opera world-wide popularity. The symphonic interlude, the "Meditation," first played during a change of scenes in Act II, is world-famous and has become beloved as a violin solo. This same music, slightly extended and modified, occurs at the death of Thaïs; accordingly the finale of the opera has been given this same title.

The action takes place in Alexandria and the Egyptian Desert during the Early Christian Era.

CHARACTERS

THAÏS *(Tah-ees')*	Soprano
ATHANAËL *(A-tan-a-ell)*	Baritone
NICIAS *(Nee-see-ass)*	Tenor
PALEMON *(Pal-ay-mon)*	Bass
ALBINE *(Al-bee-ne)*	Mezzo-Soprano

Apex

SCENE FROM ACT II—THAÏS

481

CROBYLE *(Kro-beel)*   *Soprano*
MYRTALE *(Meer-tal)*   *Soprano*
Monks, Nuns, Citizens, Servants, Dancers, etc.

ACT I

SCENE I

IN A time when Alexandria is wrapped in luxury and profligacy, Thaïs, a priestess of Venus, is recognized as the most beautiful of women. Athanaël, a Cenobite monk, who has been to the city in an effort to preach the gospel, returns to his devout associates with strange stories of Alexandria's wickedness. Even though wearied by his journey, his sleep is troubled by a vision of Thaïs, posing in the Alexandrian Theatre before a great throng who noisily applaud her beauty. Awaking with a start, he is determined to "reform" her, and against the advice of the aged monk, Palemon, he sets out upon this mission.

SCENE II

In Alexandria, Athanaël has a friend of his former unregenerate days named Nicias, whose palace occupies a commanding situation. Nicias greets his old friend with courtesy, but is moved to laughter at his apparently whimsical notion of reforming the lovely Thaïs, upon whom Nicias himself has squandered a fortune. Willing to help for old times' sake, however, he has his household slaves array Athanaël in rich robes, concealing his monkish habit. When at last Thaïs herself arrives she is at first repelled yet intrigued by this austere visitor. Athanaël tells her that he has come to bring her to the only true God, as whose humble but jealous servant he stands before her. Thaïs' reply is characteristically pagan—she believes in the joy of living; but she is none the less impressed. Athanaël leaves, horrified, as Thaïs begins to disrobe, to pose as Venus.

ACT II

SCENE I

IN HER room lies Thaïs. The floor is carpeted with precious rugs from Byzantium, the air laden with the exotic perfumes of flowers in vases of agate . . . incense burns before a statue of Venus . . . yet Thaïs is wearied of the world, her luxury . . . the words of the strange monk haunt her memory . . . she fears that beauty and happiness will quickly fade. Taking a mirror, she contemplates herself, and begs it to assure her that she shall be forever beautiful.

Dis-moi que je suis belle *(Mirror Song)*   **Helen Jepson** 14153-2.00

At this moment comes Athanaël, who speaks to her of life everlasting, and eternal beauty of the spirit. She at first tries to triumph over him with her allurements, then succumbs to fear. The inexorable Athanaël leaves, declaring, "On thy threshold till dawn I shall await thy coming." The curtain falls, but the orchestra continues playing the famous "Meditation," symbolical of the conversation of Thaïs. To a harp accompaniment, a solo violin plays a melody of indescribable sweetness and expressiveness.

Meditation *Fritz Kreisler* 6844-2.00 *Mischa Elman* 7392-2.00 Boston *"Pops" Orchestra* 11887-1.50 *(Organ) Jesse Crawford* 22155-.75 *(Organ) Charles R. Cronham* 35858-1.25

SCENE II

True to his word Athanaël waits before her house. From another house nearby come sounds of revelry. Towards dawn, Thaïs appears, worn and repentant after a night of emotion, ready now to follow her holy guide into the wilderness. She leaves everything behind, and begs only for a small statue of Eros—love himself, for she says, love has long been a rare virtue, and begs that they may take the statue along to set up in some monastery as an emblem of the love celestial.

Athanaël listens patiently enough until she remarks that this was a gift from Nicias. Thereupon, Athanaël immediately seizes the statue and casts it to the ground, shattering it into a thousand fragments. They enter her palace to destroy the treasures—relics of "hell" there guarded; Thaïs accepts this sacrifice without demur.

As soon as they have gone, Nicias appears, having won heavily at the games. He orders dancing, wine and music. When Thaïs and the stern monk return, they are greeted by a scene of revelry. This quickly changes to a near riot, for the companions of Nicias are enraged at the prospective loss of Thaïs, and at Athanaël, for in his zeal he has set fire to her palace. The crowd are about to seize and kill the monk. To save him, Nicias throws gold coins among them, and as the people scramble for the money, Athanaël and Thaïs depart for the desert and a life of repentance.

ACT III

SCENE I

White

JERITZA AS THAÏS

TORTURED by lack of water, and weary from her long journey across the desert, Thaïs nearly faints although the journey is almost over. The monk remorselessly drives her on, bidding her "mortify the flesh," and she goes willingly. Finally, however, she staggers with weakness, and Athanaël, moved to pity, allows her to lie down while he bathes her feet, and gives her fruit and water from the oasis at which they have arrived.

Thaïs now seems uplifted, beyond the do-

483

minion of flesh, into great spiritual exaltation; she is glad when the Abbess Albine and the White Sisters come to lead her into a cell in the convent, a short way off. She has found that peace for which her soul craved. Only Athanaël is troubled.

SCENE II

Back among the brethren at the Cenobites' camp, Athanaël is compelled to confess to the aged Palemon that he has saved Thaïs at the cost of his own soul. Passionately raging at himself, he strives to cast out of his mind the memories of her human weakness and of her intoxicating beauty. Yet he longs for her . . . in his sleep, a vision comes to him of Thaïs, lovely, self-sure, mocking, as he first beheld her in Alexandria; then the vision changes . . . her face lighted with the fervor of religious mysticism as she lies dying in the convent. With a cry of terror he awakens and rushes out into the darkness.

SCENE III

Thaïs, worn with repentance and self-denial, is dying surrounded by the White Sisters, who respectfully withdraw when Athanaël enters. Utterly distraught, the monk implores Thaïs to return with him to Alexandria, there they shall live happily . . . all that he has taught her has been lies.

Meditation *Mary Lewis* 6578-2.00

The ecstatic music of the "Meditation" soars calmly aloft in the orchestra, and Thaïs, heedless of the words of Athanaël, sings of the gates of heaven opening before her . . . the smiles of angels . . . the beating of their wings. Suddenly she falls back dead, and Athanaël, cheated by himself, cries out in despair.

Ben Pichot

JEPSON AS THAÏS

Castagneri
THE CHURCH OF ST. ANDREA

TOSCA

OPERA in three acts; music by Giacomo Puccini; text by Illica and Giacosa, after Sardou's drama. First produced, January 14, 1900, at the Constanzi Theatre, Rome. First production in the Americas, at Buenos Aires, June 16, 1900; in the United States, February 4, 1901, at the Metropolitan Opera House, New York.

This gruesome tragedy by Sardou, at first seems scarcely suitable for musical setting. Yet such is Puccini's genius for the theatre that his music not only is equal to the demands of the action, but adds to the tensely dramatic atmosphere. Moreover, at every opportunity for lyrical expression, the composer has given us melodies, unmistakably Puccinian in character and warmth of feeling.

The opera has been recorded, in the version generally performed, by distinguished soloists, the chorus and orchestra of La Scala, Milan, under the direction of Carlo Sabajno. A modern recording, revealing some of the finest operatic voices in Italy, this album of Victor Records makes possible the possession of still another musical treasure in permanent form. The recording, contained in Masterpiece Album M 84, is keyed to the story of the opera given here.

CHARACTERS

FLORIA TOSCA *(Floh'-ree-ah Toss'-kah), a celebrated singer*	*Soprano*
MARIO CAVARADOSSI *(Mah'-ree-oh Cav-a-rah-doss'-ee), a painter*	*Tenor*
BARON SCARPIA *(Scar'-pee-ah), chief of police*	*Baritone*
CESARE ANGELOTTI *(Chay-zahr'-ay Ahn-jel-lot'-tee)*	*Bass*
A SACRISTAN	*Baritone*
SPOLETTA *(Spo-let'-tah), a police agent*	*Tenor*
SCIARRONE *(Shar-rohn'-nay), a gendarme*	*Bass*

485

Judge, Cardinal, Officer, Sergeant, Soldiers, Police Agents, Ladies, Nobles, Citizens.
The action takes place at Rome, June, 1800.

Famous Artists *Chorus and Orchestra of La Scala, Milan, Album M-84* **(9758-9771),**
AM-84 **(9772-9785), Price $21.00**

ACT I

As the curtain rises three somber chords are thundered out *(M84-1)* by
the orchestra, and we behold the high vaulted interior of the church
of St. Andrea. Angelotti enters, pale, dishevelled, panic-stricken, in prison
garb. He barely has time to conceal himself before the Sacristan appears,
going about his duties. A moment later Cavaradossi enters, returning to
work. He has been painting a fair-haired, blue-eyed Madonna, using for
his model an unknown worshipper in the church, whose beauty has impressed him. He is unaware that she is the sister of his friend, Angelotti,
for his interest is purely artistic. Drawing from his bosom a miniature of his
beloved, the dark-eyed Tosca, he sings of the strange manner in which the
various features of her loveliness blend into a harmonious whole. *(M84-2)*

Recondita armonia *(Strange Harmony)* **Beniamino Gigli 1213-1.50 Enrico Caruso**
*511-1.50

The Sacristan goes, after a covetous glance at Cavaradossi's lunch basket.
(M84-3) A moment later the wild-eyed Angelotti appears, relieved at finding
his old friend, who promises him aid in escaping. Tosca is heard calling
outside for her "Mario." Cavaradossi gives the fugitive a few hurried directions and Angelotti disappears, taking with him a woman's dress left as a
disguise for him by his sister.

Tosca enters. The temperamental singer is angry at Mario's delay in
admitting her, and suspicious, having heard voices. *(M84-4 and 5)* The

LEHMANN AS TOSCA

painter quiets her jealous fancies and they arrange to meet that evening. Tosca leaves, and
Mario *(M84-6)* goes to aid Angelotti further
in his escape.

The members of the choir *(M84-7)* enter,
hurriedly preparing for a festival to celebrate
Napoleon's defeat. Their excitement is suddenly hushed at the entrance of Scarpia, the
dreaded chief of police. The escaped prisoner
has been traced to the church. *(M84-8)* A fan
is discovered belonging to Angelotti's sister,
and overlooked by the prisoner in his haste.
Tosca, still doubting her lover, returns to
church under some trivial pretext. *(M84-9)*
She is greeted not by Mario, but by Scarpia,
who approaches her courteously. Flatteringly

ACT II—TOSCA

saying that she comes to church devoutly, to pray, not like other women who come to distribute their favors, he shows her the fan. Tosca becomes greatly excited *(M84-10)* with jealousy and leaves the church weeping. Scarpia orders three of his agents to follow her. *(M84-11)* The cardinal and a great procession now enter the church, advancing towards the High Altar and a Te Deum is sung. The voices of the choir mount in sacred song, and Scarpia, kneeling in mock devotion, can be heard muttering to himself while he gloats over the anticipated destruction of his rival and the moment when Tosca shall be his own. At this thought he joins with the final magnificent outburst of the choir, *"Te aeternum Patrem omnis terra veneratur!"*

Te Deum **Lawrence Tibbett and Metropolitan Opera Chorus** 8124-2.00

ACT II

In his apartments in the Palace Scarpia restlessly awaits news of his prey—Cavaradossi and Angelotti. Hearing Tosca's voice *(M84-12)* in the Queen's apartment nearby, he sends a message to her saying that he has received word of her lover. This will be bait enough for Tosca, tormented as she is with jealousy; again Scarpia rejoices *(M84-13)* at the thought of his conquest. Yet a moment later he is angered, for Spoletta, his agent, brings word that Angelotti cannot be found. He is quickly consoled, however, on hearing that Cavaradossi has been captured. *(M84-14)* The painter, when brought in, refuses to divulge Angelotti's hiding place. Accordingly he is consigned to the torture chamber—just as Tosca appears. Scarpia greets

487

Carlo Edwards
TIBBETT AS SCARPIA

her *(M84-15)* with gruesome courtesy, and bluntly tells her that her lover is in the next room being tortured; for each refusal the pain-producing instrument is tightened. Tosca trembles with anxiety and Scarpia opens the door so that she may hear Mario's stifled cries. *(M84-16)* The artist urges her to reveal nothing. Scarpia bids her look at her lover; one glance and Tosca cries out in horror; even the hardened Spoletta is appalled at this abominable double torture. The ever augmented pain brings a suppressed cry from Mario; Tosca can endure this no longer and tells Scarpia *(M84-17)* where Angelotti is hidden. Cavaradossi is then brought in, still racked with pain, near fainting. Suddenly word comes that the reported defeat of Napoleon was a mistake, he was really the victor. Scarpia stands abashed, but Mario, in spite of his weakness and Tosca's whispered admonition to remain silent, gives a shout of victory—joy at promised freedom from the tyrannical Scarpia. The enraged official orders Cavaradossi to prison and death.

Landesman   THE EXECUTION   *(Cleveland Orchestra)*

When Mario has been taken away, Scarpia begins his cruel love-making; *(M84-18)* he has long adored Tosca, has sworn to possess her; he will brook no refusal. Her spirit crushed, Tosca weeps for shame and sings *(M84-19)* her famous plea, "Vissi d'arte." She has devoted her life to art and love, has gone regularly to church and been generous in bestowing charity, how can she deserve this cruel treatment?

Vissi d'arte *(Love and Music)*   **Maria Jeritza** 1346-1.50   **Helen Jepson** 14184-2.00

Scarpia replies to her impassioned prayer cynically, *(M84-20)* and at last in desperation Tosca says that she will yield to his unholy demand if he will rescind the order of execution and write a passport giving Mario and herself safe-conduct to leave the country.

Scarpia is overjoyed. He informs her that a mock execution will be necessary, summons Spoletta for a moment to give him some secret instructions, *(M84-21)* then turns to his desk to write the required papers. Meanwhile Tosca surreptitiously takes from the table a sharp knife and conceals it. Scarpia advances towards her, overpowering in his triumph. He takes her in his arms; Tosca drives the knife into his body, crying, "Thus will Tosca yield her kisses!" He falls lifeless. With grim reverence, she extends the corpse upon the floor, places lighted candles at the head, and a crucifix on the bosom, crosses herself, and steals noiselessly away.

ACT III

Mishkin

MARTINELLI AS MARIO

MARIO is brought out from his cell to the terrace of San Angelo Castle. *(M84-22 and 23)* The city is still in darkness although the sound of sheep-bells on the distant hill-sides and the clanging of the great bells in the church tower announce the approach of dawn. Told that he has only one hour to live, Cavaradossi sings a touching farewell to his dreams of art and to his beloved, recalling their former meetings on starlight nights in quiet gardens. *(M84-24)*

E lucevan le stelle *(Stars Were Shining)*   **Giovanni Martinelli** 1208-1.50   **Beniamino Gigli** 1704-1.50   **Enrico Caruso** *511-1.50

He is suddenly startled by the arrival of Tosca. She tells *(M84-25)* him of the death of Scarpia and he commends the gentle hands that struck the blow even though regretting that they should have had to soil themselves with the blood of such a scoundrel. *(M84-26 and 27)* The soldiers come, the shots of the

TOSCA AND SCARPIA

supposedly mock execution are fired, and Mario falls. Tosca, waiting till the firing party has gone, bids him rise—"Now, Mario, all is safe." He does not answer. (M84-28) She rushes to him . . . Scarpia has tricked her. Mario is dead. She throws herself on the body in an agony of grief. Spoletta and the soldiers approach to seize her as Scarpia's murderer. Before they can realize her intention she evades them, quickly climbs the parapet of the castle and leaps to freedom—and death.

LA TRAVIATA

OPERA in three acts; music by Giuseppe Verdi; text by Francesco M. Piave, after the play "La Dame aux Camelias," well known in English under the name "Camille," by Alexandre Dumas, *fils*. First produced, March 6, 1853, at La Fenice Theatre, Venice. First performance in the United States, December 3, 1856, at the Academy of Music, New York. Revived for Caruso and Sembrich at the Metropolitan in 1909. Galli-Curci first sang the rôle of Violetta in the United States, in Chicago, December 1, 1916.

When first produced, "La Traviata" was a failure. This may have been due to the fact that, being based on a contemporary drama and performed in modern costume, it rather dazed an audience habituated to operas played only in the guise of bygone times. Other causes contributed to the failure. The leading tenor was hoarse; the soprano who played Violetta weighed several hundred pounds. Naturally, in the last act, when the doctor declared that this heroine was dying of consumption, the audience roared with laughter. A year later, "La Traviata" was again played at the same Opera House; at that time the costuming was changed to the period of Louis XIV. The performance was very successful, and since then "La Traviata" has grown to a world popularity, rivaling that of "Il Trovatore." The whole nature of the plot, however, is so typical of the time originally assigned to it, 1850, that in most present-day performances the opera is so staged.

"Traviata" is one of the most durable of favorites in the field of opera. For that reason, among others, it has been included among the operas chosen for recording completely. A group of distinguished soloists, the chorus and the orchestra of La Scala, Milan, were assembled for this recording under the direction of Carlo Sabajno, one of the world's great authorities on the Italian opera. The following outline of the story of "Tra-

Castagneri

ACT I—TRAVIATI

491

Peyton

BORI AS VIOLETTA

viata" is keyed to the records, which are contained in Masterpiece Album No. M112.

CHARACTERS

VIOLETTA VALERY *(Vee-oh-let'tah Vah-lay-ree), a courtesan*	*Soprano*
FLORA, *friend of Violetta*	*Mezzo-Soprano*
ALFREDO (ALFRED) GERMONT *(Ahl-fray-do Zhair-mon'), lover of Violetta*	*Tenor*
GIORGIO GERMONT *(Jor-jo), his father*	*Baritone*
BARON DOUPHOL *(Doo-fohl), a rival of Alfred*	*Baritone*

Ladies and Gentlemen, Servants, a Doctor, Masquers.

Scene and period: Paris and environs, about the year 1850 (sometimes 1700).

Famous Artists Chorus and Orchestra of La Scala, Milan, Album M-112 (11105-11117), AM-112 (11118-11130), Price $19.50

ACT I

Prelude *Toscanini, Philharmonic-Symphony Orchestra of New York* 6994-2.00
Victor Symphony Orchestra 35879-1.25

THE prelude *(M112-1)* begins with very soft tranquil harmonies, high in the strings, similar to the prelude to the scene of Violetta's death. There follows a haunting melody, passionate, yet sentimental—the melody of the heroine's parting in the second act. This melody is repeated by the violoncellos while the violins play Italianate embroidery above. At the close the prelude fades gently away, making all the more striking the contrast with the brilliant music of the opening scene.

The elaborately furnished salon of Violetta is the meeting place of the gayer element of Parisian life. *(M112-2)* Tonight an unusually lively entertainment seems to be taking place. Alfred Germont is introduced to Violetta as another of her admirers, and at her request he sings a jovial drinking song *(M112-3)* in which Violetta and the guests join. The energetic rhythm and lively melody of this number cause it to be ranked high among operatic drinking songs.

> Where beauty and mirth are beckoning,
> Seize we the swift winged hours,
> Let joy crown the cup with flowers,
> And life's a dream of bliss.
> While youth's swift fire within us burns,
> Shall love's delight inspire us,
> With such bright eyes to fire us,
> *(Indicating Violetta.)*
>
> What joy can equal this?
> Then quaff we the wine-cup when love is beckoning,
> Life is a short dream of bliss.
>
> *(The guests take up the refrain, then
> Violetta rises and replies):*
>
> My days shall pass in a dream of ecstasy,
> By joyous friends surrounded.
> Give me a measure of rapture unbounded,

There is no life but this.
While envious time flies swiftly on,
Enjoy the time of flowers,
Too soon will fade the bowers,
Then vain to sigh for bliss,
Enjoy while pleasure and mirth are beckoning
There's no life but this.

Music is heard from the adjoining ballroom *(M112-4)* towards which the guests proceed. Violetta is seized by a sudden faintness, an ominous fore-warning of consumption, but at her request the guests continue into the ballroom; Alfred, however, remains behind. Violetta cannot quite under-stand why a young man of such evidently good standing should be concerned with her—a mere butterfly. He confesses *(M112-5)* that he loves her, has loved her since the day when first he happened to see her a year ago. At first Violetta thinks his protestations mere banter; when she begins to realize their seriousness she is profoundly moved and begs him to go . . . she is unworthy, he must forget her. Alfred's tender confession of love and Violetta's nervous response are beautifully expressed in their duet.

Un di felice *(Rapturous Moment)* **Amelita Galli-Curci, Tito Schipa** 1754-1.50

One phrase of Alfred's avowal will recur frequently throughout the opera as a love theme:

Through all the world, through creation wide, extended,
Oh power mysterious, power yet uncomprehended!

The rosy light of dawn begins to penetrate the curtained windows, put-ting to shame the erstwhile brilliant candles. The guests take their leave; Alfred follows. Violetta is left alone in the room, which is now in disorder and tawdry under the growing daylight.

She meditates on the night's happenings, saying to herself, in recitative:

How wondrous! his words deep within my heart are graven!
And would it bring me sorrow to love sincerely?
No love of mortal yet hath moved me;
Shall I dare to disdain it, and choose the empty follies that now surround me?

Then singing a hesitant but most expressive little air, she continues: *(M112-6)*

The one of whom I dreamed when in the throng of pleasure,
I joy'd to shadow forth him whom alone I'd treasure.
Ah, now I feel that it is love, and love alone,
Mysterious power, guiding the fate of mortals
Sorrow and sweetness of this poor earth.

An instant later she becomes suddenly transformed, for, thinking that her dreams are hopeless, she begins a dazzling coloratura aria, singing: *(M112-7 and 8)*

494

What folly! What folly!
For me there's no returning!
In ev'ry fierce and wild delight
I'll steep my sense and die!
I'll fulfill the round of pleasure,
Joying, toying from flower to flower,
I will drain a brimming measure from the cup of rosy joy.

Ah, fors'è lui *(The One of Whom I Dreamed)* **Lucrezia Bori** 7438-2.00 *Helen Jepson* 14184-2.00

ACT II

Scene I

VIOLETTA and Alfred have been living a life of idyllic happiness in a little country house near Paris. *(M112-9)* Poetical young man that he is, Alfred is enraptured at having found in Violetta a true mate. Singing a very melodious aria, he tells of his happiness in this haven of peace and love, and contrasts it with his own turbulent youth.

The practical affairs of life, however, recall him from his amorous dreams; for the maid enters, and upon questioning her, Alfred learns that Violetta has secretly had all her jewels sold in order to keep this secluded home. He is much ashamed on thus suddenly realizing his position, and hurries to the city to obtain funds. *(M112-10)*

Violetta enters; no more is she the painted courtesan of the city, but a gracious, modest young wife. On reading an invitation to a party at the home of a former friend, Flora, she smiles in refusal . . . such things do not interest her now. Alfred's father, the elder Germont, appears and makes himself known. He is none too polite in his greetings for he has been greatly distressed at what he conceives to be a boyish entanglement. Violetta maintains such dignity, however, that he is soon charmed and abashed, especially when he learns that, far from being dependent upon Alfred, she has sold her property to support him. Thus abandoning his former attitude he throws himself wholly on her mercy. *(M112-11)* Alfred has, it seems, a younger sister, whose marriage to a noble will be jeopardized if this scandalous mésalliance continues in the Germont family. Violetta at first refuses to give up her lover, then, as the father continues to plead, she begins to realize that her union with Alfred will ultimately react to his disadvantage. She finally yields, singing through her tears: *(M 112-12)*

JOHN CHARLES THOMAS
AS GERMONT

495

Say to thy daughter dear, guarded and cherish'd,
That one unhappy heart for her hath perish'd.
One single hope had she, but one single hope e'er did bless her,
That blessed hope she hath now sacrificed for her sake.

Germont replies:

Bitter, bitter sorrow speaks in thy words. . . .
Thy noble heart heav'n will never forsake!

Violetta continues, saying, "Now command me." *(M112-13)* Germont answers, "Say you do not love him." She replies, "He'll not believe me." Violetta thinks of a plan; but she is shaken with sobs and pleads for consolation; she will need courage in order to go through with her resolve. The father comforts her tenderly, then leaves.

The music of this scene represents Verdi at his best. The melodies are lovely, yet appropriate to the situation and characters and the changing sentiments of the text.

As soon as Germont has gone, the unhappy Violetta writes *(M112-14)* a note of farewell to Alfred and makes ready to leave for Paris. Alfred returns, and is mystified by her confusion. His father has written him a stern letter demanding an interview—Alfred expects him at any moment. Not even suspecting that Violetta and his father have ever met, he believes that the charm of her bearing and personality will cause the elder Germont to

Copy't Georg
GALLI-CURCI AS VIOLETTA

relent. Violetta begs to be excused for a time, saying that she will return and throw herself at his father's feet, he will forgive them, they will then be happy forever! But before she goes out she questions Alfred with such extreme anxiety, "Do you love me? Do you truly love me?" *(M112-15)* and says "Farewell" with such tenderness that her lover is deeply moved.

In a very few moments a servant comes with a note for Alfred. It is in Violetta's handwriting. He tears it open, staggers as he realizes its meaning. His father has entered unobserved, and tries to console his son by recalling their home, singing "Di Provenza il mar." *(M112-15)* In spite of the declaration of critics that it is trite and inappropriate, an example of Verdi in a weaker moment, this melodious aria remains one of the most popular in the opera.

Di Provenza il mar *(Thy Home in Fair Provence)* **Giuseppe de Luca** 7086-2.00
John Charles Thomas 7605-2.00

The father appeals to Alfred to return to his home in vain. Gazing vaguely about the room, Alfred notices Flora's letter and on reading it concludes that, having abandoned him, Violetta will make her plunge back into a life of gaiety at Flora's fête. Burning with anger and jealousy he rushes out to seek revenge.

SCENE II

The scene changes. Festivities are being held in the richly furnished and brightly lighted salon in Flora's palace. The first feature of the entertainment is a masquerade. The music ripples along with the utmost frivolity, gypsies *(M112-16)* appear and contribute to the gaiety with their jangling tambourines and a little by-play at fortune telling. They are followed by another group dressed in Spanish costume who sing a festive song of Matadors. *(M112-17)*

To this party now comes Alfred, who remarks with assumed indifference that he knows nothing of Violetta's whereabouts. The primary feature of the entertainment being gambling rather than dancing, he joins the game, and oddly enough is extremely lucky in his winnings. When Violetta arrives leaning on the arm of Baron Douphol she is shocked at seeing Alfred present. *(M112-18)* Pretending not to notice her, Alfred remarks, "Misfortune in love brings luck at cards." The Baron is plainly disturbed at Alfred's presence, cautions Violetta not to speak to him, then goes over and joins the game. Again Alfred wins; angry words follow between Alfred and the Baron that threaten to lead to a duel. The tension is relieved, fortunately, by a servant's announcement that the banquet is ready. All withdraw to the adjoining salon.

Violetta returns immediately, *(M112-19)* followed by Alfred, whom she has asked to see privately. She begs him to leave the house at once, thus he will avoid further trouble. He will go only on one condition—that she come with him. Though her heart is breaking she remembers her promise to the elder Germont and says she cannot—she is bound. "To whom?" questions Alfred anxiously, "To Douphol? then you love him!" With a painful effort she replies "Yes!" Trembling with fury, Alfred flings wide the doors and calls back the astonished guests. Before them all he denounces Violetta, and shouting "I call on you to witness that I have paid her back!" he flings a purse at her feet. She sinks fainting in the arms of Flora. All are shocked at Alfred's outrageous conduct. *(M112-20)* Germont enters at this moment, in search of his son. He alone realizes the full significance of the scene, but for the sake of his daughter he cannot reveal it.

ACT III

SCENE—*Violetta's Apartment*

Prelude to Act III *Toscanini-Philharmonic-Symphony Orchestra of New York* 6994-2.00

The tranquil beauty of the prelude is a fine introduction to the mood *(M112-21)* of the closing scene of Violetta's unfortunate life. She has been

Canuzzi

SCHIPA AS ALFRED

living for some time in her modest apartment. Now she is a mere shadow of her former self, for her unhappiness has greatly aggravated her illness. *(M112-22)* Although the doctor reassures Violetta, he whispers to the faithful maid that her mistress has not long to live. Left alone, Violetta reads a letter she has received from Germont, meanwhile the orchestra whispers touchingly a strain of the first duet of the lovers: *(M112-23)*

"You have kept your promise. The duel took place, and the Baron was wounded, but is improving. Alfred is abroad. I myself have revealed your sacrifices to him. He will return to implore your pardon. I also shall come. Hasten to recover; you deserve a bright future." —Germont.

"Too late!" is her comment in a hollow voice. Then she rises, saying, "I've trusted, and waited, but alas, he comes not!" She pauses to look at herself in the mirror. "Oh, can I be so altered! and the doctor said that I would soon recover . . . but this faintness tells plainly all is hopeless." She continues, singing a beautiful and pathetic farewell to this "fair world of sorrow." *(M112-23)* The melody, of a fragile delicacy like the wasted heroine herself, rises at its close to clear high tones of poignant loveliness as she exclaims, "Now, all is over!—*Tutto Finè!*"

Parigi o cara *(Far from Gay Paris)* **Galli-Curci-Schipa** 1754-1.50

A moment later the door opens and Violetta is transported to the heaven of her lover's arms. *(M112-24)* In contrition Alfred begs forgiveness; it is at once joyfully granted. Violetta's health seems to return with her happiness, even Alfred is for a moment deceived. They plan *(M112-25)* a bright future . . . the quiet country life in which they first found happiness. The joy of the meeting has been too much; soon she collapses into her lover's arms. Germont enters with the physician. The father blames himself for having brought all these sorrows on his son and Violetta. Again the melody of the lovers' duet is heard, whispered by the violins in ethereal, tremulous beauty, as from another world. *(M112-26)* Violetta no longer feels pain; she rouses herself with an unnatural return of strength and cries, "I live! I have again returned to life!" With this she falls back upon the couch—dead.

TRIAL BY JURY

DRAMATIC Cantata; text by W. S. Gilbert; music by Sir Arthur Sullivan. First produced, March 25, 1875, at the Royalty Theatre, London.

This delightful work was the first product of the regular collaboration of Gilbert and Sullivan. Though called a "Dramatic Cantata," it is, in its perfect union of tuneful music and clever words, a direct forerunner of the more famous later successes of this inimitable pair, and is equally well worth knowing. Lovers of Gilbert and Sullivan will therefore rejoice in the complete recording of "Trial by Jury" made for Victor by the D'Oyly Carte Opera Company under the supervision of Rupert D'Oyly Carte. It is interesting to note that Mr. Rupert D'Oyly Carte is the son of Richard D'Oyly Carte, the impresario who first brought Gilbert and Sullivan together, and whose company first performed the long line of famous comic operas written by this remarkable team.

"Trial by Jury" is their only work entirely without spoken dialogue. Therefore this complete recording, on four Victor Records Album C-4 (9314-9317, and in automatic sequence 9318-9321) includes everything that is heard at an actual performance. The records are issued in a special album with a complete libretto. Price, $6.00. The following is the cast of—

CHARACTERS

THE LEARNED JUDGE	Leo Sheffield, Baritone
COUNSEL FOR THE PLAINTIFF	Arthur Hosking, Tenor
THE DEFENDANT—EDWIN	Derek Oldham, Tenor
FOREMAN OF THE JURY	T. Perry Hughes, Bass
USHER	George Baker, Baritone

D'Oyly Carte Production   THE PLAINTIFF AND THE JUDGE

THE PLAINTIFF—ANGELINA   *Winifred Lawson, Soprano*
            Chorus of Jurymen, Bridesmaids, Barristers, Attorneys, Etc.

The Chorus of the D'Oyly Carte Opera Company.
Scene: A Court of Justice. Curtain rises on Chorus of Barristers, Attorneys, and Jurymen
with Ushers.

THE chorus, in their sturdy song, make known the course of events *(Records 9314-A and 9318-A)*:

> For, today, in this arena,
> Summoned by a stern subpoena,
> Edwin—sued by Angelina—
> Shortly will appear.

The Usher, having marshaled the Jurymen into the Jury-box, gives them the judicial counsel to heed the plaintiff, "The broken-hearted bride," and not "the ruffianly defendant," for,

> From bias free, of every kind,
> This trial must be tried.

The Defendant appears, asking "Is this the Court of the Exchequer?" and is greeted with scorn: "Monster, dread our damages!" The Defendant explains *(Records 9314-B and 9319-A)* that happiness with the Plaintiff having palled, he became "another's love-sick boy." The Jury admit that once they were like that, but now they're respectable and have no sympathy with the defendant. The Usher orders silence, for the Judge approaches. The Chorus greet him with churchly song, "All hail, great Judge!"

The Judge, having thanked them *(Records 9315-A and 9320-A)* proceeds to tell how he reached his exalted station. When young, he was an impecunious lawyer,

> So, he fell in love with a rich attorney's
> Elderly, ugly daughter.

The attorney turned plenty of cases over to him, and when he had grown "rich as the Gurneys'" he threw over the "Elderly, ugly daughter." But now he's a Judge, "it was managed by a job," and ready to try this breach of promise case.

Then, at the Judge's order, the Usher swears in the Jury *(Records 9315-B and 9321-A)* and summons the Plaintiff, Angelina. A chorus of Bridesmaids enter as her escort. While they are singing the Judge sends a "mash note" to the first Bridesmaid by the Usher, but when Angelina sings her graceful air, he transfers his attention to her. He even admits *(Records 9316-A and 9321-B)* that he never saw "so exquisitely fair a face"; and the Jurymen too, profess great admiration for the Bridesmaids, then address the Defendant as "Monster." The Counsel for the Plaintiff makes his appeal to the Jury telling how the Defendant

> . . . deceived a girl confiding,
> Vows, et cetera, deriding.

And when the Plaintiff wished to name the day, he left her,

> Doubly criminal to do so,
> For the maid had bought her trousseau!

Counsel and Jurymen join in singing to the Plaintiff "Cheer up!" while she sighs "Ah me!" à la Italian opera. The Plaintiff reels as if to faint *(Records 9316-B and 9320-B)* and falls sobbing on the Foreman's breast, but when the Judge approaches she leans on him instead. Edwin attempts to defend himself from their charge of "Monster!" saying,

> Of nature the laws I obey,
> For nature is constantly changing.

and concludes by granting that

> If it will appease her sorrow,
> I'll marry this lady today,
> And marry the other tomorrow!

This seems reasonable to the Judge, but the Counsel, on referring to his books, finds that to marry two wives at a time is a serious offense, "Burglaree!" This dilemma is discussed in a splendid burlesque of an Italian opera sextet *(Records 9317-A and 9319-B)*. The Usher having restored silence in court, Angelina proves her loss: crying "I love him" she embraces the Defendant, then adds:

> Oh, see what a blessing, what love and caressing
> I've lost, and remember it, pray,
> When you, I'm addressing, are busy assessing
> The damages Edwin must pay.

The Defendant counters by saying that he is a bad lot, given to liquor, he's sure he would beat her, and that she couldn't endure him very long; the Jury should remember this when assessing the damages. These conflict-

(D'Oyly Carte Production)
SYDNEY GRANVILLE AS THE JUDGE

ing statements are developed in a dramatic ensemble. The Judge therefore suggests *(Records 9317-B and 9318-B)* that they make the Defendant "tipsy" and see if his assertions be true. But to this proposition all save the Defendant object. Thereupon, the Judge is in a terrible rage for he is in a hurry to get away; he settles the case quickly by declaring that he'll marry Angelina himself! And thus the "Trial" ends in a mood of general rejoicing, while the Judge makes his concluding comment:

> Though homeward as you trudge,
> You declare my law is fudge,
> But of beauty I'm a judge.

To this all reply:

> And a good judge, too!

ON BOARD TRISTAN'S SHIP *(Herbert Graf Production)*

TRISTAN AND ISOLDE

(*Tristan und Isolde*)

MUSIC-DRAMA in three acts; words and music by Richard Wagner. First produced at Munich, June 10, 1865. First performance in the United States, at the Metropolitan Opera House, New York, December 1, 1886.

Among all the stories that have been told of unhappy love there are a few, handed down for generations, that seem well-nigh immortal. Among these is the legend of Tristan and Isolde, a story that has been narrated in a variety of forms by a number of the greatest of poets from medieval times to the present. Gottfried von Strasburg, Matthew Arnold, and Swinburne present the drinking of the love-potion as a purely accidental affair; thus Tristan and Isolde are irresponsible for their love. Omitting the love-potion, Tennyson makes the passion between the two entirely guilty. With Wagner, the love exists between Tristan and Isolde before the drinking of the potion, which does not so much cause the love as it causes forgetfulness of restraints of society. Accordingly the fate of the lovers does not seem unjustly harsh, yet wins for them our sympathy. In so planning his tragedy, Wagner attains a nobility of conception approaching that of the dramatists of ancient Greece.

Writers on esthetics are fond of pointing out how "Tristan and Isolde," having none of the elaborate staging or violent action that is a part of the "Ring," more nearly attains the ideal condition of a perfect music-drama. Yet this very absence of outward action in "Tristan and Isolde" may, at first, be a stumbling block. Few works for the lyric stage are so highly charged with drama, but it is an inward, psychological drama, though intensely absorbing and profoundly moving. Wagner was at the summit of his powers, when, having the "Ring" half finished, he turned aside to write this more practical music-drama. How "practical" it was in that day is illustrated by the fact that at Vienna, after more than fifty rehearsals, the work was abandoned as impossible! With time, however, Wagner's glowing pages have won the recognition they deserve. This tense, fervid, truly impassioned music is built from a wealth of leading motives, flowing together in a most wonderful manner and forming a continuous commentary on the action. But since these motives are themselves so largely subjective in character and associated with emotions or states of mind, the names given them can be little more than convenient means of identification. This music that follows closely every changing mood of the drama, grows in intensity as the tragedy unfolds, and attains an almost incredible poignancy and beauty in the last act. This act, sung by famous Wagnerian artists, has been recorded for Victor. The music-drama closes with Isolde's wonderful scene, well known as a concert number under the name "Liebestod," or "Love-Death," a title first applied to it by Franz Liszt.

THE ORCHESTRAL MUSIC OF TRISTAN

Perhaps the most effective music of the entire opera has been woven together in the form of a tone-poem, a synthetic symphony, by Leopold Stokowski. This music is not a condensed orchestral version of the opera; rather it is a great, free dramatic utterance in music, burdened with the most intense and passionate expression of love that music has ever been able to achieve. This music need not and should not be considered with relation to the dramatic action of the opera; it is, rather, a distillation and a sublimation of certain elements of the opera, combined in a new entity with its own artistic and musical validity and integrity.

In his "symphonic synthesis" Mr. Stokowski has combined the Prelude, the Love Music from the second act, and Isolde's "Liebestod." This is contained, on four records, in Masterpiece Album M-154, (7621-7624) (and in automatic sequence AM-154, 7625-7628). Further material germane to this has been recorded by the Philadelphia Orchestra under Mr. Stokowski's direction, and will in due course be made available to the public.

CHARACTERS

TRISTAN, *a Cornish knight, nephew of King Mark (Triss'-tan)*	Tenor
KING MARK OF CORNWALL	Bass
ISOLDE, *Princess of Ireland (Ee-sohl'-da)*	Soprano
KURVENAL, *Tristan's servant (Koor'-vee-nahl)*	Baritone
MELOT, *one of King Mark's courtiers*	Tenor
BRANGÄNE, *Isolde's friend and attendant (Brahn-gay'-na)*	Soprano

A Shepherd, a Steersman, a Sailor Lad; Chorus of Sailors, Knights, Esquires and Men-at-Arms.

The action takes place during legendary times, at sea, in Cornwall and in Brittany.

LEGENDARY EVENTS PRECEDING THE MUSIC-DRAMA

Isolde, Princess of Ireland, was betrothed to Sir Morold, who in fighting in the war against Cornwall, was slain by Tristan. This heartless adversary sent the head of the slain warrior back to the Princess, who discovered in it a splinter of steel from the sword of her lover's murderer.

Tristan, however, had also been gravely wounded in the fight, and his wound would not heal. Having learned that the Princess of Ireland was skilled in magic balms and

THE LOVERS DRINK THE POTION

potions, he disguised himself, assumed the name of Tantris, and went to Ireland to seek her aid. Moved by his suffering, Isolde tended him; then, one day, she was horrified to discover that she was sheltering her betrothed's slayer, for the splinter of steel exactly fit a notch in the stranger's sword. Fired with a desire for revenge she raised the weapon about to kill the stricken man. At that moment their eyes met. Powerless against the supplicating appeal of his glance, she let fall the sword, and concealing the secret of his identity, continued to tend him. The knight recovered and departed with many declarations of gratitude.

He soon returned, this time under his true name of Tristan, as an emissary to demand the hand of Isolde for his uncle, King Mark. Her parents assented, believing as did Mark, that this alliance would end the long strife between Ireland and Cornwall. Although grieving bitterly, for she secretly loved Tristan and believed that he loved her, Isolde was compelled to follow the knight to Cornwall. Such are the events that are supposed to have taken place before the beginning of the music-drama.

The Prelude to "Tristan and Isolde" is one of Wagner's most glowing, impassioned compositions, built marvelously from a few brief themes which will be of prominence during the course of the action. It begins with a mere whisper, like a sigh of deepest yearning, played by the violoncellos, the motive of "The Confession to Love." The effect of this is heightened by the poignant interrogation of "Desire" which immediately follows. After a reiteration there enters the eloquent theme of "The Glance," expressive of the origin of the mutual passion of Tristan and Isolde. This is followed by the suave motive of the "Love Philtre." There now begins a gradual crescendo in which the theme of "Deliverance by Death" is heard, growing to a climax of indescribable vehemence. The tumult of emotions finally wanes, and while the prelude comes to its close in a mood of expectancy, the curtain rises.

Prelude *Hertz-San Francisco Symphony Orchestra* 6585-2.00 *(Piano) Paderewski* 7324-2.00

ACT I

O N BOARD Tristan's ship is a magnificent pavilion, erected on the deck to house Isolde. From above in the masthead, a sailor sings of his "Irish Maid, wild and amorous maid," a song that only increases Isolde's unhappiness. The ship is now nearing Cornwall, and the Princess is growing indignant at Tristan's persistent refusal to see her, and desperate at the thought of her enforced loveless marriage. Her maid, Brangäne, suggests that with the aid of a magic potion she can win the love of the King after she is married to him. Isolde bids her bring the casket containing the potion, then she selects not the love-philtre, but a swift death-bringing poison, and commands the maid to prepare a draught. Vengeance and surcease of her sorrows shall be attained, for she will die and Tristan with her!

She summons Tristan, and at first declares to him that she should be the avenger of her murdered lover, Morold. Tristan boldly offers her his sword;

he is ready to die. Isolde refuses, saying that she ought not deprive her husband-to-be of his most trusty knight; therefore she suggests that as a pledge of peace, they drink a cup of reconciliation and forgetfulness. While outside the sailors are shouting joyfully at the approach to land, the trembling Brangäne sets about to prepare the drink. Isolde presents the cup to Tristan, who resolutely accepts it; he divines her intentions, yet is glad indeed if he will be able thus to end the grief with which his heart is oppressed. He drinks, but before he has finished, Isolde snatches the cup from his hands and drains it to the dregs.

In this manner would the two meet their doom; but they are granted not the longed-for death and end of sorrow, but life and unhappiness; for Brangäne, unwilling to see her mistress die, has substituted the love-potion for the poison. Overcome with emotion they gaze longingly at one another, then sink into each other's arms, while a great shout outside announces the arrival of the ship at Cornwall. King Mark approaches for his bride!

ACT II

Isolde is waiting impatiently before her dwelling. The King has gone on a hunt—through the soft air of this lovely summer's night, the sound of the hunting horns can be heard, growing fainter in the distance. Brangäne is fearful lest the hunt be merely a ruse, planned by Melot, ostensibly a friend of Tristan, but who, she thinks, suspects the true state of affairs. Heedless of the admonition, Isolde gives the signal for Tristan to come, by extinguishing the torch burning at her doorway, then excitedly waves her scarf to her hurrying lover. While Brangäne watches from the tower,

ISOLDE GIVING THE SIGNAL—ACT II (COLOGNE FESTIVAL PRODUCTION)

singing a song in warning at the approach of day, the lovers rapturously embrace, oblivious to all else. They sing of their love,

Isolde! Tristan! Geliebter! *(Isolde! Tristan! Beloved!)* **Frida Leider, Lauritz Melchior** 7273-2.00

of bliss-bringing night,

Doch es rächte *(But it's vengeance)* **Leider, Melchior 7273-2.00**

of their hatred for day which causes sorrow and separation,

O sink' hernieder, Nacht der Liebe! *(Descend upon us, O night of love!)* **Leider, Melchior 7274-2.00**

of death which would bring freedom, and of their utter felicity—"Love's Peace." As their ecstasy reaches its very summit, Brangäne cries out,

Soll ich lauschen? *(Shall I listen?)* **Leider, Melchior 7274-2.00**

and Kurvenal rushes in, calling, "Save thyself, Tristan!" The King enters with his courtiers and Melot. The King is deeply grieved that he should have been so betrayed by his most trusted of knights, and reproaches Tristan for his faithlessness. Melot rushes at Tristan with drawn sword. Tristan pretends to respond to the attack of his treacherous friend, but lets his sword fall. He is mortally wounded.

ACT III

COMPLETE ON VICTOR RECORDS

The third act, the culmination of the entire drama, has been recorded by Victor. The performance is sung by famous Wagnerian singers including Walter Widdop as Tristan and Gota Ljungberg as Isolde, and accompanied by the London Symphony Orchestra, conducted by Albert Coates, and the Berlin State Opera Orchestra, conducted by Dr. Leo Blech. This remarkable recording, on five Victor Records, is issued as Album M-41 (9265-9269) in the Musical Masterpiece Series, Price, $7.50. The following account of the third act is keyed to these records.

A N ORCHESTRAL prelude *(M 41-1)* pictures wonderfully the desolation of Tristan's castle, the knight's suffering, and the wide expanse of the ocean. The scene shows the garden of Tristan's ancestral castle in Brittany. It is situated on rocky cliffs overlooking the sea. A shepherd who is on watch, looks over the wall and asks Kurvenal about Tristan *(M 41-2)*. But the servant, refusing to disclose the cause of his master's distress, orders the shepherd back to his watch and instructs him to play a lively melody the moment he sees a ship. After scanning the sailless horizon, the shepherd begins to play a plaintive melody on his reed-pipe and disappears down the cliff. Tristan awakens and upon hearing the mournful tune, exclaims dejectedly, "Ever the sorrowful melody!" At the sound of Tristan's voice, Kurvenal is thrilled with the most joyous agitation. "Life returns to my Tristan!" he exclaims. His master, still only half-conscious, asks "Where am I?" Kurvenal assures him that he is in Kareol, in his own castle, surrounded by his faithful followers (M 41-3). Still his enthusiastic picture does not arouse Tristan's memory. He knows not whence he came nor whither he goes, he longs only for death, for in oblivion he will be united to Isolde. Kurvenal assures him that he has sent

THE CONFESSION TO LOVE   DESIRE

MELCHIOR AS TRISTAN

for her, but this only serves further to excite the delirious man. He works himself up into a frenzy of anticipation believing that he sees the ship bringing his beloved. Then the mournful tune of the Shepherd's pipe is heard, and Tristan, in despair and exhausted by his fevered imaginings, falls back as though lifeless. Kurvenal fears that he is dead, and bends over to hear his breathing (M 41-4). While Tristan slowly revives and dreams of a vision of Isolde, the motives of "Desire" and "Love's Peace" are heard in the orches-

LOVE'S PEACE

tra. Again he imagines that his beloved is approaching (M 41-5). This time he is not deceived for as he exclaims, "The ship! Isolde's ship!" the shepherd begins a lively tune. Kurvenal runs to the watchtower and describes the approach of the vessel while Tristan listens nervously from his couch. When the ship is hidden for a moment behind the cliff, Tristan is alarmed, for there the rocks are dangerous. "Who is the helmsman?" he cries, "some accomplice of Melot's? Dost thou also betray me? Dost thou not yet see her? . . . All's lost then!" A moment later the ship comes in view. Isolde is on the deck waving to them. In a delirium of joy, Tristan sends Kurvenal to meet her.

Now alone, Tristan tosses on his couch in great agitation (M 41-6). Soon he raises himself, tears the bandage from his wound and staggers forward to meet Isolde. He hears her voice, and his dazed mind thinks of it as the light of the torch which once summoned him to her. "Hear I the light?" he cries. He has overtaxed his vanishing strength, and he sinks dying into the arms of his adored one, able only to cry a heart-rending "Isolde!" In vain Isolde calls to him: he cannot return even for an hour (M 41-7). She distractedly cries that she will heal his wounds, then realizing that he is forever silent, she falls unconscious.

The shepherd hurries in and calls softly to Kurvenal that another ship has come (M 41-8). Recognizing it as King Mark's, and believing that the sovereign has come to attack Tristan's castle, he summons his men to its defense. Brangäne is heard calling her mistress from a distance. Melot, too, approaches, and Kurvenal rushing at him savagely strikes him down as he enters the gate. Having thus avenged his master, Kurvenal attacks the others of the King's retinue. Brangäne rushes in to tend Isolde, and Kurvenal, deeply wounded, totters towards his master. And with his dying breath he entreats, "Chide me not, O Tristan, if I try to follow thee!"

King Mark is deeply sorrowful at the loss of Tristan, once his most faithful of knights (M 41-9). Vainly does he call "Awake, and hear my grief!" Brangäne, having revived Isolde, pleads for forgiveness, saying that she has told the King of the love-potion. Mark continues, "When I understood what I had failed to grasp before, how glad I was to find that my friend was blameless! . . . So to unite ye, I hurried with flying sails . . . Yet I only added to the harvest of Death, Error increased our woe!" Brangäne asks pleadingly, "Doest thou not hear, Isolde?"

Unconscious of all around her, Isolde gazes upon Tristan. She imagines him as living, transfigured (M 41-10). The "Song of Death" is heard, at first somber, then transformed, growing ever lighter. As Isolde becomes more

THE SONG OF DEATH

and more carried away with her vision, the theme of "Ecstasy" enters, constantly growing more agitated, swelling toward a climax only to begin anew. Isolde exclaims: "Hear ye not . . . round me flowing . . . growing nearer . . . clearer . . . the wondrous melody?" The music, having reached its culmination, seems to burst in overwhelming glory, then melt away in

ECSTASY

deepest calm, while Isolde breathes her last: "In the billowy waves, in the resonant harmony, in the life-breath of creation, drink deep and drown in dreamless sleep, purest bliss!" As though glorified, Isolde sinks in the arms of the faithful Brangäne and dies upon Tristan's body. King Mark raises his arms in blessing over the dead.

Isolde's Love-Death *Maria Jeritza* 1363-1.50 *Frida Leider* 7523-2.00 *Kirsten Flagstad* 8859-2.00 *Hertz-San Francisco Symphony Orchestra* 1169-1.50

THE GARDENS OF ALIAFERIA

IL TROVATORE

(The Troubadour)

OPERA in four acts by Giuseppe Verdi, libretto by Salvatore Cammanaro, based on Spanish drama of the same title by Antonio Catteerea. First produced at the Apollo Theatre, Rome, January 19, 1853. First performance in the United States, at the Academy of Music, New York, May 2, 1855. Some notable revivals at the Metropolitan Opera House, in 1908, with Caruso, Eames and Homer; and in 1914, with Destinn, Ober, Martinelli, Amato and Rothier.

Ever since its first production, "Il Trovatore" has ranked as one of the most popular of operas. With reason it is such, for its music is melodious and its action swift. The plot, it is true, is over-melodramatic and not so very clearly expressed, yet the irrepressible verve of the master's music sweeps all else before it; even without knowing the plot one can feel the dramatic force of many of the scenes. "Il Trovatore" is, indeed, a triumph of the composer's uncanny skill in expressing the dramatic; here, at times, on a mere dance rhythm, such as a waltz or mazurka, he develops melodies of passionate beauty and dramatic appropriateness. "Il Trovatore" preaches no moral and cloaks no philosophy; it aims only to tell an exciting story of a gypsy's vengeance, and in that it succeeds admirably.

In fact, "Trovatore" succeeds too well. Its melodies have been played and sung in every conceivable arrangement until their spontaneity has largely been worn away. Particularly is this true of the remarkable ensemble known as the "Miserere," really a most telling piece of dramatic music, but heard so often, that if we do not pause to give it thought we are likely not to appreciate fully its excellent qualities. The fact that it is still effective is in itself a tribute to Verdi's genius and, indeed, when sung by great artists such as have recorded it for Victor it still is wonderfully thrilling.

The tenor aria, "Di Quella Pira" (Tremble Ye Tyrants), a truly stirring and dramatically appropriate number, also deserves a word of apology. A "high C" that Verdi never wrote and the cause of much argument has been introduced in it for so many operatic generations that it has become a firm tradition. A noted vocal authority informs us that by means of a very intricate apparatus photographs were made of the vibrations produced by Caruso's voice as he sang and held this "high C." The chart gives a record measuring fifty-eight feet in length, scientific evidence of the splendid manner in which Caruso took and held this tone.

According to a custom of the mid-Nineteenth Century, each act of the opera is given a title. (Il Trovatore is pronounced *Eel-Troh-vah-toh-reh*.)

CHARACTERS

LEONORA *(Lay-oh-noh'-rah), a noble lady of the Court of an Aragon Princess*   Soprano
AZUCENA *(Ahz-you-chay'-nah), a wandering Biscayan Gypsy*   Mezzo-Soprano
INEZ *(Ee'-nez), attendant of Leonora*   Soprano
MANRICO *(Man-ree'-koh), a young chieftain under the Prince of Biscay, of mysterious birth, and in reality a brother of the Count di Luna*   Tenor
COUNT DI LUNA *(dee-loo'-nah), a powerful young noble of the Prince of Aragon*   Baritone
FERRANDO, *a captain of the guard and under di Luna*   Bass
RUIZ, *a soldier in Manrico's service*   Tenor
AN OLD GYPSY   Baritone
Also a Messenger, a Jailer, Soldiers, Nuns, Gypsies, Attendants, etc.

Scene and period: Biscay and Aragon; middle of the Fifteenth Century.

This opera, hardiest of perennials and a favorite all over the world, has been recorded in conventional entirety for lovers of music in its permanent form. To Americans, probably no opera is so well known—though it is perfectly possible that many of us who hum and whistle the melodies of this grand old work, or hear them poured lustily from the hurdy-gurdy of some itinerant son of Italy, are not conscious of their operatic source.

This is opera in the old tradition—almost folk-opera. The most important sources of drama in the life of the old-school Italian peasant—the church, the prison, the military and the aristocracy, the quick violence and passionate love, the romance attached to gypsies—all are satisfactorily and almost conventionally present. Around them Verdi has woven a chain of melody that commends itself to us all, however sophisticated we may think we are.

The complete recording has been done by the staff of that great home of Italian opera, La Scala of Milan, under the direction of its distinguished conductor, Maestro Carlo Sabajno. The story of the opera which follows is keyed to the records, in Masterpiece Album M 106. (11040-11054) automatic sequence (11055-11069) Price $22.50.

EVENTS PRELIMINARY TO THE OPERA

The old Count di Luna, now long since dead, had two sons of almost the same age. One night, while they were still infants, asleep under a nurse's charge, a Gypsy hag who had stolen unobserved into the old Count's castle, was discovered bending over the cradle of the younger child. She was instantly driven away, yet because the child grew wan and pale afterwards she was believed to have bewitched it. She was caught and after the fashion of the times burned to death at the stake.

Her daughter Azucena, then a young Gypsy woman with a child of her own, witnessed the execution. She swore vengeance. The following night she crept into the castle and stole the younger child of the Count from its cradle. Then she hurried back to the scene of the execution, where the fire that had consumed her mother still raged. She intended to throw the Count's child into it, thus securing her vengeance. Blind, half crazed with the horror of the sight she had witnessed, she hurtled into the flames *her own child*. Her vengeance temporarily thwarted, Azucena fled with the Count's child and rejoined her Gypsy tribe. She reveals her secret to no one, brings the infant up as her own son, and though she grows to love him, still cherishes the thought that through him she may wreak vengeance upon his family. When the opera opens this child has grown up, known by the name of Manrico, the Troubadour. Azucena has become old and wrinkled, but still thirsts for vengeance, and the old Count has died, leaving his elder son, the Count di Luna appearing in the opera, sole heir to his title and possessions.

MARTINELLI AS MANRICO

ACT I

The Duel

THE retainers of Count di Luna are keeping guard in an outer chamber of Aliaferia Palace *(M 106-1)*. The captain of the guard, Ferrando, passes away the time with a story *(M 106-2 and 3)* of the gypsy who was burned for casting a spell on one of the children of the former Count, and of her daughter, who for vengeance stole the present Count's brother and is believed to have burned him to death at the place of her mother's execution. He relates his lurid story while singing a markedly rhythmical melody, expressive of the weird horror of his narrative. A clock strikes midnight and the retainers, already frightened by the gruesome tale, rush out in terror.

In the gardens of the palace the fair Leonora strolls with her attendant and companion, Inez. To her she confides her interest in an unknown knight *(M 106-4)*, victor at a recent tourney. She knows that her love has been requited, for the hero has since serenaded her. Thus it is that they refer to him as "The Troubadour," *Il Trovatore*. She tells of his serenade and the emotions it has awakened, in an aria of unusual beauty and expressiveness.

Tacea la notte placida *(Peaceful Was the Night)* **Amelita Galli-Curci 7652-2.00**

> The joy which then I knew,
> Angels in heaven alone can feel!
> My heart was raised from earth to highest heaven!

Leonora's companion speaks of an evil presentiment *(M 106-5)*, and begs her lady to forget her hero, but Leonora cannot.

The ladies enter the palace just as the Count di Luna *(M 106-6)* comes into the garden. He has barely appeared before the voice of the Troubadour

THE CONVENT NEAR CASTELLOR

is heard from a nearby clump of bushes, singing his serenade. Leonora again comes out of the palace. Mistaking the Count in the shadows of the trees for her Troubadour, she hurries towards him *(M 106-7)*. At that moment the moon happens to emerge from behind the dense clouds that are hurrying across it. Leonora then realizes her mistake, sees the Troubadour, and rushes to him declaring her love for him. The Count is in a terrible rage; and demands to know the intruder's identity. Unmasking, the Troubadour reveals himself as Manrico, a follower of the Prince of Biscay, and thus proscribed in Aragon. Unable to restrain their jealousy the two men draw their swords and rush away to fight a duel. Leonora falls fainting.

ACT II

The Gypsy

DAWN at a gypsy camp in the Biscay Mountains *(M 106-8)* . . . a ruined house at the foot of a mountain . . . in it a bright camp fire . . . groups of gypsies scattered about . . . Azucena hovers near the fire . . . Manrico at a distance holding his sword at which he looks thoughtfully.

As the daylight grows brighter the gypsies bestir themselves about their duties; working at the forges they swing their hammers and bring them down on the clanking metal while they lustily sing the famous "Anvil Chorus."

Anvil Chorus *Victor Mixed Chorus* 20127-.75 *Arthur Pryor's Band* 19879-.75

Who cheers the life of the roving gypsy?
The gypsy maiden! The gypsy maiden!

The aged Azucena has been gazing abstractedly at the blaze of the camp fire. When the gypsies pause to rest a moment from their labors, she begins to sing, as to herself, of the vision that surges in her memory as she watches the blaze. The gypsies draw near and attentively listen to her song, a melody perfectly in keeping with the character of this wild gypsy woman and of the harrowing scene she describes *(M 106-8 and 9)*.

> Upward the flames roll; the crowd presses fiercely on,
> Rush to the burning with seeming gladness;
> Loud cries of pleasure from all sides reëchoing!
> By guards surrounded—forth comes a woman!
> While, o'er them shining, with wild, unearthly glare,
> Dark wreaths of flame curl, ascending, to heaven!
>
> Upward the flames roll! on comes the victim still;
> Robed in dark garments, ungirt, unsandal'd.
> Fierce cries of vengeance from that dark crowd arise;
> Echo repeats them from mountain to mountain,
> O'er them reflecting, with wild, unearthly glare,
> Dark wreaths of flame curl, ascending to heaven!

Stride la vampa! *(Fierce Flames Are Soaring)* **Louise Homer** 1422-1.50

When she has finished the gypsies depart, the echoes of their song becoming fainter and fainter from down the mountains. Azucena is still trembling with the horror of the memory she has revived . . . still seems to hear the command, "Avenge thou me!" As in a trance, not realizing what she is saying, she continues her narrative *(M 106-10)*, describes her attempt at revenge and her frenzied error when she destroyed her own child instead of her enemy's.

Castagneri

PERTILE AS MANRICO

The story sets Manrico thinking. "If your son perished," he asks *(beginning of Record 8105)*, "whose child am I?" *(M 106-11.)* The gypsy woman with a quick instinct for prevarication, avoids the question, claiming him as her son. She changes the subject by reminding him how she had nursed him back to life

513

Azucena, in her anxiety to see her son, has attempted to get through the besieging forces (M 106-18). She is captured and brought before the Count as a possible spy. Questioning brings out the story of her past and her connection with the episode of the Count's childhood (M 106-19). Ferrando swears she is the murderess of di Luna's long-lost brother. Azucena, in her extremity, cries out the name of Manrico, and the Count on finding that she claims the Troubadour as her son, vows upon her a double vengeance. She is bound and dragged away.

Within the stronghold of Castellor, Manrico and Leonora (M 106-20) await the hour appointed for their marriage. Their happiness is troubled, however, by the fear that the Count di Luna may soon attack the castle. Thus it is that Manrico attempts to quiet Leonora's alarm, singing a beautifully lyrical melody and declaring:

> Oh come, let links eternal bind the vows we fondly plighted,
> My soul is strong to dare ev'ry foe, with thee united!

As he finishes this declaration of love the solemn music of the organ in the adjoining chapel announces the beginning of the ceremony. Manrico takes his bride's hand to lead her to the altar. At that very moment Ruiz enters with the news that Azucena has been captured by the besiegers (M 106-21). Already fagots are being heaped together for she is to be burned at the stake as was her mother. Delay would be fatal. Manrico drops Leonora's hand, draws his sword, and while his soldiers are being summoned, gives vent to his rage and horror in a famous aria—a *tour de force* for operatic tenors (M 106-21).

> Tremble, ye tyrants, I will chastise ye,
> My flaming beacon ye have uprais'd!
>
> She was my mother ere I ador'd thee,
> I'll not desert her, though my heart break.
> Farewell, belov'd one, I, who implor'd thee,
> My dear old mother cannot forsake!

He then rushes away to the rescue followed by his soldiers.

Di quella pira (*Tremble, Ye Tyrants*) **Martinelli, Metropolitan Opera Chorus** 8109-
2.00

ACT IV

The Penalty

DEFEATED by Count di Luna and his forces, Manrico has been taken captive and cast into the dungeon tower of Aliaferia, where Azucena has already been chained. Outside of these frowning battlements Leonora lingers (M 106-22), for on this clouded night she has come with a despairing hope of saving her lover. She wears a poisoned ring so that if need be she can take her own life. Her thoughts turn towards Manrico, and she sings

(M 106-23) a poignantly expressive melody declaring her hope that love may even penetrate into his dungeon.

> A breath of hope, oh send thou,
> His lonely hours attend thou,
> In memory, oh waft him
> The visions of our happy days.
> But tell him not my heart will break,
> If fate our hope betrays.

D'amor sull' ali rosee *(Love, Fly on Rosy Pinions)* **Amelita Galli-Curci** 7652-2.00

Within the tower voices begin a solemn chant of "Miserere" *(M 106-24)*, praying for heaven to have mercy on the soul of him about to perish. Meanwhile a deep-toned bell tolls out the announcement of Manrico's impending doom.

LEONORA: What voices of terror! For whom are they praying?

Miserere *Caruso, Alda, Metropolitan Opera Chorus* *8042-2.00 *Ponselle, Martinelli, Metropolitan Opera Chorus and Orchestra* 8097-2.00 *Creatore's Band* 35850-1.25

> Pray that peace may attend a soul departing,
> Whither no care or thought of earth can follow;
> Heav'nly mercy allays the pangs of parting,
> Look up, beyond this life's delusions hollow.

The mournful ecclesiastical chant, and the tolling knell sounding from the tower across the blackness of the night, fill Leonora with terror; while the orchestra accompanies with shuddering chords in slow but irresistibly reiterated rhythm, like the approach of doom, she exclaims:

> What voices of terror! for whom are they praying?
> With omens of fear unknown they darken the air.
> New horrors assail me, my senses are straying,
> My vision is dim, is it death that is near?
> Ah, is it death, is it death that is near?

From his prison the Troubadour, seemingly unconscious of all that is taking place around him, sighs forth his plaint:

> Ah! send thy beams, Aurora,
> Light me to early death,
> Waft her my longing,
> Waft her my latest breath!
> I leave thee, Leonora, ah, I leave thee!

While the voices resume their chant and the bell continues tolling, Leonora exclaims:

> Forget thee can I never!
> I'm thine, I'm thine for ever!

AZUCENA

Then Manrico resumes his song. To it the voices of the chanting priests supply a funereal background and interwoven with it is the cry of Leonora; a marvelously impressive ensemble.

The Count enters, Leonora begs mercy for Manrico, but he refuses *(M 106-25)*, gloating over his triumph. As a last resource she offers to marry the Count if her lover may go free. So great is di Luna's passion for Leonora that he agrees *(M 106-26)*. While he is giving orders to one of the guards, Leonora swallows the poison she has concealed on her ring, muttering, "Thou shalt have me, but cold and lifeless!"

In the gloom of their prison Manrico and Azucena await execution *(M 106-27)*. The gypsy pictures to herself the horror of the flames leaping around herself even as they did around her mother. She falls overwhelmed with terror, and Manrico tries to comfort her, saying:

> If any love remains in thy bosom,
> If thou art yet my mother, oh hear me;
> Cease thy terrors to number,
> And seek repose from thy sorrows in soothing slumber.

Azucena replies, singing a serious melody, tranquil yet with an undercurrent of agitation:

> Yes, I will rest, for my soul is weary,
> Let me forget that the past is dreary,
> But if the visions fearful that haunt me
> Darken my slumber, wake me, my son.

Manrico reassures her, saying:

> Sleep, oh my mother, and may heaven grant thee rest from thy sorrows ere day is done.

Then thinking of the happy days that are past, Azucena meditates *(M 106-28)* as in a dream:

> Home to our mountains thou yet shalt take me,
> No fear or sorrow there shall o'ertake thee;
> In happy slumber lull me with singing,
> As in those blessed days, I shall have rest.

Again Manrico tries to comfort her, then their voices are heard together, while Azucena falls asleep, still thinking of her gypsy home. Thus closes in reposeful beauty this justly beloved duet.

Ai nostri monti *(Home to Our Mountains)* **Schumann-Heink, Caruso** *8042-2.00
Homer, Martinelli 8105-2.00

Leonora enters *(M 106-29)* with news of Manrico's freedom. His joy, however, is turned to desperation as he learns the price to be paid. In a sudden frenzy he accuses Leonora of betraying his love: "Thou hast sold thyself," he shouts. At this moment the poison begins to claim its victim *(M 106-30)*. Leonora sinks to the floor at Manrico's feet, in death agony. The lover, who now realizes the full extent of her sacrifice, is all contrition and pleads for forgiveness. The Count suddenly appears, pausing on the threshold. Leonora confesses to the Troubadour, "Rather than live for another, I have preferred to die for thee!" and sinks lifeless to the ground.

Perceiving that Leonora has cheated him, di Luna orders Manrico to instant execution, and drags Azucena to the window to witness the death of her son. The old gypsy is crazed with excitement, blind to the external world. "It is ended," the Count exclaims when the executioner's work is done.

"He was your brother!" With a last effort to her passionate soul she shrieks, "Thou art avenged, O mother!" then falls lifeless.

The Count, overwhelmed with horror, exclaims, "And yet I live!"

THE ARENA DI VERONA

TURANDOT

OPERA in three acts; music by Giacomo Puccini; libretto by Simon and Adami, based on Carlo Gozzi's fairy play of same name, which was adapted from an Eastern legend. First produced at La Scala, Milan, April 25, 1926. First performance in the United States, at the Metropolitan Opera House, New York, November 16, 1926, with Jeritza in the title rôle and Lauri-Volpi as Calaf.

Puccini unfortunately died before completing this, the last of his operas. The unfinished portion, the last part of Act III beginning at Liù's suicide, was completed from the composer's sketches by Alfano. When this point was reached at the first production, the performance came to a dramatic close. Toscanini, who was conducting, put down his baton, and turning to the audience said that there the opera ended, for the composer died when he had written thus far. In "Turandot" Puccini advanced beyond any of his previous work in harmony, orchestral color and choral writing, even introducing poly-harmony; yet in its wealth of melody the opera is distinctly Puccinian.

The action takes place during legendary times, in Pekin, capital of China.

ACT I

Amid the confusion of the listening crowd that has gathered at the Imperial Palace, an old man makes his way, supported and guided by a young girl, Liù. Suddenly a youth hurries towards them from the crowd. Their whispered conversation reveals that the old man is the dethroned King of the Tartars, the youth, his son, Calaf, called the "Unknown Prince." Soon there is a movement of agitation in the crowd, because the Prince of Persia, attempting to solve Turandot's riddles, and failing, as all others have done, is now being led to execution. For the Princess Turandot has decreed that whosoever would win her hand must solve three riddles, and failing, suffer death. The people, moved by the youthfulness of the Persian Prince, cry for mercy. But Turandot, when she appears upon the balcony, silences them by the mere sight of her matchless beauty. The thud of the executioner's axe is heard, then the head of the Persian Prince is seen, raised on a pike over the city gates.

The Unknown Prince is greatly thrilled by the beauty of Turandot. Forgetting her cruelty and heedless of the prayer of his father and Liù, and of the warnings of the ghosts of Turandot's executed lovers, and unmindful of the counsels of the three Court Officials, Ping, Pang, and Pong, he determines to brave the Princess' enigmas, and in token thereof sounds the great gong that hangs at the palace gate.

ACT II

ACCORDINGLY there assembles a multitude of great personage on the staircase that leads to the Imperial Palace. Turandot, coming before them, tells of her grandmother, the chaste Princess Lo-u-ling, who, ravished by the invading Tartars, died most unhappy. To avenge her ancestor's wrongs, Turandot has meted out a cruel fate to all who would be her suitors. She turns to the Unknown Prince, and propounds her direful enigmas. One by one the Unknown Prince answers them, boldly, and correctly; he is greeted by shouts of joy from all except Turandot. The Princess, weeping, begs to be saved from the stranger; but her father, Emperor and guardian of the law, decrees that her word must be held sacred. Turandot therefore pleads with the conqueror for her freedom, and he answering, says that he will indeed release her from her vow and give up his life even as though he had failed in the trial, should she be able to call his name ere the morrow.

ACT III

THUS it comes about that during the entire night heralds search through all the city, but none they find who can rightly name the Unknown Prince. Someone then whispers that an old man and the girl, Liù had been seen with him. They are brought to the Palace, but Liù cries out that she alone knows the Prince's name, and then, fearing she may reveal the secret during the tortures to which she will be subjected, she quickly seizes a dagger from one of the soldiers and plunges it into her heart. Turandot is troubled—what moved the girl to such self-sacrifice? The Prince, reproaching Turandot, clasps her passionately. Thus is the Princess vanquished, and she confesses that she loves the Unknown Prince. He likewise, says that such is his love that he would be happy to die for her, and reveals his name; at this, the cold pride of Turandot returns, and dawn now approaching, she leads him to the Palace to announce her victory and his doom. At the throne of the great Emperor she cries out that she has found the stranger's name; then looking at Calaf, she is shaken by a strange emotion, and murmurs, "His name is Love!" And the multitude that has assembled sings for joy that the heart of the cruel Turandot has been vanquished by the Unknown Prince.

WERTHER

LYRIC drama in four acts; music by Jules Massenet; libretto by Edouard Blau, Paul Milliet and George Hartman, founded on Goethe's melancholy and romantic story of his own life, *The Sorrows of Werther*. First produced at the Imperial Opera House, Vienna, under the composer's direction, February 16, 1892. First performed in the United States at the Auditorium, Chicago, March 29, 1894.

De Bellis

SCHIPA AS WERTHER

Although not Massenet's most popular work, many critics believe that "Werther" is in many respects his best, the subject, particularly adapted to the composer's genius, inspired him to write some of his finest melodies. The fact that the remarkable baritone, Battistini, recorded a number from what was originally a tenor rôle, will be understood when it is explained that Massenet so admired Battistini's singing that he especially rewrote the part for this famous artist.

The action takes place in Germany in 1772.

CHARLOTTE, surrounded by her brothers and sisters, is preparing the noonday meal. Werther, a serious-minded young man, comes to the house with Albert, who is betrothed to Charlotte. Werther falls in love with the girl, who returns his affection, but feels it her duty to marry Albert in order to fulfil a promise made to her dying mother. She begs Werther to leave the village.

At Christmas time Werther returns and visits Albert and Charlotte, who now are married. He is filled with delight on viewing the familiar household, and noticing the poems of Ossian, he begins to read one of that famous poet's stanzas; but as he sings, the poem becomes an expression of his own despairing love. The melody is one of great beauty and passionate intensity.

Ah! non mi ridestar! *(Do Not Wake Me!) In Italian* **Tito Schipa** 8422-2.00 **Chant d'Ossian** *(Ossian's Song) In French* **Tito Schipa** 1187-1.50

The song so plays upon the emotions of Charlotte, that her very agitation is an avowal of her secret love. She entreats Werther to go away forever. Later, a servant brings a letter for Albert from Werther, saying that he is about to go on a long journey, and requesting the loan of Albert's pistols. Charlotte reads the letter, and, greatly worried, hurries at midnight through a blinding snow-storm to Werther's residence. Mortally wounded, he dies in her arms. She faints, overcome with grief. Outside, bells peal joyfully and children sing Christmas carols.

De Bellis   "I HAVE A SONG TO SING, O!"   *(D'Oyly Carte Players)*

THE YEOMEN OF THE GUARD

(Or the Merryman and His Maid)

COMIC OPERA in two acts, by W. S. Gilbert and Arthur Sullivan.

DRAMATIS PERSONAE

SIR RICHARD CHOLMONDELEY *(Lieutenant of the Tower)*
COLONEL FAIRFAX *(under Sentence of Death)*
SERGEANT MERYLL *(of the Yeomen of the Guard)*
LEONARD MERYLL *(his Son)*
JACK POINT *(a Strolling Jester)*
Chorus of Yeomen of the Guard, Gentlemen, Citizens, etc.
WILFRED SHADBOLT *(Head Jailer)*
ELSIE MAYNARD *(a Strolling Singer)*
PHOEBE MERYLL *(Sergeant Meryll's Daughter)*
DAME CARRUTHERS *(Housekeeper to the Tower)*
KATE *(her Niece)*

The opera has been recorded for Victor by the D'Oyly Carte Opera Company in Album C-17 (11220-11230), in automatic sequence AC-17 (11231-11241). Price $16.50 and the records are keyed to the following story of the opera.

ACT I

COLONEL FAIRFAX, a man of science, but formerly a soldier of great and dashing bravery, is confined in the Tower of London. He is under sentence of death as a sorcerer. Although he is a student of alchemy,

Fairfax is still young and handsome, and Phoebe has lost her heart to him, for she sees him occasionally taking exercise on the Beauchamp Tower.

As the curtain rises the unhappy girl is discovered sitting at her spinning wheel sighing over her hopeless love for the prisoner. *(C 17-2 and 3.)* Wilfred Shadbolt, head jailer and assistant tormenter, is greatly put out, for Phoebe will have none of him, though before the arrival of Fairfax she had not been so averse to his attentions. Dame Carruthers, the housekeeper to the Tower, believing Fairfax to be guilty, resents Phoebe's praise of him, and her criticisms of the Tower. The Dame was born in the old Keep, and the Tower is very dear to her; she leaves no doubt of her sentiments in the noble air *(C 17-4),* "When our gallant Norman foes." Sergeant Meryll, of the Yeomen of the Guard, is saddened by the thought of the approaching execution of Fairfax. He greatly admires Fairfax for his brilliant career as a soldier and not even the imminent arrival of his son, Leonard Meryll, can raise his despondent spirits, though there is a hope that Leonard may bring a reprieve from Court with him for Fairfax. Leonard arrives even while Phoebe and her father are discussing the sad case of the unfortunate prisoner; there is no reprieve. None saw him enter, and the unheralded coming gives Sergeant Meryll an idea. "Give me the dispatch," he says . . . "lie hidden for a space." Leonard does so willingly, for Fairfax was once his great friend. A moment later Fairfax passes by, under guard, on his way to the Cold Harbour Tower to await his end in solitude. He sees and recognizes Sergeant Meryll and bids him cheer up; as a soldier, he says, he knows how to die. If life is a boon *(C 17-5),* he says, death must inevitably come too soon. Phoebe and her father are overcome with emotion and leave him. Fairfax asks the Lieutenant of the Tower to grant him a favor. He is, he says, imprisoned as a result of the machinations of his cousin, Sir Clarence Plotwhistle—a greedy fellow to whom the Fairfax estates must naturally fall if Colonel Fairfax should die unmarried. Fairfax's request is therefore that the Lieutenant shall find him a woman willing to go through a form of marriage with him: her dower shall be Fairfax's name and a hundred crowns. Since he is to be executed in an hour's time it should be easy enough to find someone. As Fairfax moves on his way there is laughing and shouting, and a roistering throng of men and women, pursuing a wandering jester and a merrymaid, appear *(C 17-6).* The jester, Jack Point, and the girl, Elsie Maynard, are both more than a little terrified, for the crowd, in demanding entertainment, threaten to throw them into the river if they do not come up to expectations. They sing them the "singing farce of the Merryman and his maid," and are about to be mobbed by the less appreciative members of the audience when the Lieutenant reappears from the Cold Harbour Tower. The crowd is dispersed and the Lieutenant, learning all about Elsie and Jack Point, suggests to Elsie that she be Fairfax's bride for the short hour he has to live *(C 17-7).* The hundred crowns which she is to receive tempt and persuade her. She is led blindfold to the cell where Fairfax and his confessor await her. While she is gone Point (in the song "I've jibe and joke" *C 17-7*) explains his calling of a jester and is engaged by the Lieutenant as his jester. Then Phoebe reflects on her state *(C 17-8)*, and finally finds Wilfred alone. She determines to get the keys of Fairfax's cell from him. Exerting all her charms and flattering Wilfred, she compliments him on his jollity and wit, though he is in truth the heaviest-minded dolt. Slyly she takes the keys from his belt and hands them to her father, who disappears immediately. Whilst her father is away she sings *(C 17-9)* a tempting little ditty "Were I thy bride." As she begins the last verse the keys are pushed back into her hand and she cleverly puts them back on Wilfred's belt. She runs off and Wilfred wanders away bewildered and happy. No sooner has he gone than Sergeant Meryll and Fairfax appear from the Tower. Fairfax has shaved off his beard and has put on the dress of a Yeoman of the Guard. He is to pose as the Sergeant's son Leonard. Sergeant Meryll presents his "son" to the assembled yeomen, who cheer him *(C 17-10)* to the echo. Phoebe, too, welcomes this "brother" far more lingeringly and ecstatically than might be considered perfectly natural *(C 17-11)*. Then while "brother and sister" are greeting one another the clock of St. Peter's begins to toll *(C 17-12)* and crowds surge around to witness the execution of Fairfax. Fairfax (alias Leonard) and two other Yeomen are ordered to fetch the prisoner, but are back in a moment *(C 17-13)*: the prisoner has escaped!

ACT II

(Two Days Later)

De Bellis

MARJORIE EYRE OF THE D'OYLY
CARTE COMPANY AS PHOEBE

JACK POINT is now in a quandary. He has agreed to Elsie's marrying the imprisoned Fairfax because he was assured that Fairfax would die within the hour. Now that Fairfax has escaped *(C 17-14)* Elsie is still a married woman, and Jack Point cannot himself marry her. He conceives a plan, however. With the dazzling bribe of a free schooling in the trade of a jester *(C 17-15 and 16)* he persuades Wilfred to help him in his scheme. They move off mysteriously. Meanwhile Fairfax has learned of the identity of the woman whom he married and resolves to woo her and thus test her fidelity. A shot from the tower sets everyone agog and an excited crowd quickly gathers. Wilfred and Point both appear with an air of importance. Wilfred asserts that he has had a desperate struggle with Colonel Fairfax, whom he discovered in a

525

dark corner of the battlements. Fairfax *(C 17-17),* after a cunning twist, eluded Wilfred and dived into the river. Wilfred, however, was equal to the occasion and shot Fairfax with his arquebus *(C 17-18)* as he swam in the Thames. All this Jack Point endorses most heartily. Elsie admits to the supposed Leonard Meryll that she loves him, when there is an interruption. A pardon for Fairfax has arrived, and simultaneously comes news that Fairfax is returning to claim his bride. Poor Elsie is distracted: she must follow Fairfax, though her heart is elsewhere. There is much musical analysis of love *(C 17-19, 20 and 21).*

Fairfax comes. Elsie comes forward with bowed head, lamenting her cruel fate. She looks up and with a start she sees that the "Leonard" she loves is none other than this detested Fairfax. With a cry of joy she falls into his arms amid general rejoicing *(C 19-22).* Meanwhile Dame Carruthers has forced Sergeant Meryll into a proposal, and Phoebe Meryll is promised in marriage to the uncouth Wilfred.

The final scene is one of general gaiety—only Jack Point is left without a mate—and still singing the refrain "Heigh-dy, heigh-dy! Misery me, lack-a-day-dee! . . . all for the love of a ladye!" he falls insensible at the feet of the now happily united couple.

Gems *Light Opera Company* 36145-1.25

MUSIC IN WORDS

Just as the *Victor Book of the Opera* interprets the great music —rhythmical dramas of past and present . . . just as it helps you derive more pleasure from operatic masterpieces because it gives you greater insight into their meaning . . . so *The Victor Book of the Symphony*, by Charles O'Connell, can give you a new appreciation and a new love of the most distinguished orchestral works of all time.

A companion to the volume you are reading, *The Victor Book of the Symphony* "humanizes" and makes intelligible more than 240 symphonic selections. In addition, it summarizes the lives of their composers, explains the construction and function of every instrument in the modern orchestra . . . in short, tells you everything you want to know about symphonic music. The five hundred page volume is illustrated, and contains a vivid introduction by Leopold Stokowski. $3.50.

Here are several other Victor books that are *musts* for the music-lover's library:

What We Hear in Music—a newly revised, popular history that is the equivalent of a college course in music appreciation. Six hundred pages, profusely illustrated. $2.00.

Music and Romance—A fascinating book on music appreciation intended for readers of Junior High School age. 480 pages. 160 illustrations. $1.00.

Music Appreciation for Children —a complete study of music fundamentals for children in elementary grades. $1.75.

To order any or all of these volumes, see your nearest RCA Victor dealer—or, if he cannot supply you, write to RCA Victor, Camden, New Jersey.

KEY
to the World's
Greatest Storehouse of Music

If you are a student or lover of music—even though you do not own a modern phonograph with its inevitable complement of Victor Records—you will find Victor's Record Catalog of inestimable worth in guiding you toward greater musical enjoyment.

Primarily, of course, the Catalog is an index to Victor's imposing array of records. But since nearly all the world's great music is Victor-recorded, the Catalog is also a volume of panoramic scope . . . a 388-page encyclopaedia of musical facts gathered over a period of 30 years, indexed and cross-indexed to form one of the most valuable of all musical references.

Let us suppose that you know the aria "Vesti la Giubba," but cannot remember the opera or composer. The Victor Catalog will give it to you in an instant. Let us suppose that you are familiar with the opera "Carmen" by name, but would like to recall its leading arias. The Catalog will give you that too.

Can you name the major works of Beethoven, or of any other important composer? The Catalog contains *that* information also. Are you familiar with the titles of the really great symphonies? The Oratorios? Tone Poems? Chamber Music? And the names of the men who wrote them? The Catalog answers all these questions—and hundreds of others just like them. And, to top it all off, there is a special biographical section on your favorite musical artists!

Ask your RCA Victor dealer for your copy of the Catalog. If he cannot supply you, write to RCA Victor, Camden, N. J., enclosing 25 cents.